Everything that Linguists
have Always Wanted to Know
about Logic*

*but were ashamed to ask

James D. McCawley

Everything that Linguists have Always Wanted to Know about Logic*

*but were ashamed to ask

The University of Chicago Press

JAMES D. McCAWLEY is professor in the Department of Linguistics and in the Department of Far Eastern Languages and Civilizations at the University of Chicago. His other books include *Adverbs, Vowels, and Other Objects of Wonder*, published by the University of Chicago Press.

The University of Chicago Press, Chicago 60637
Basil Blackwell, Oxford

© 1981 by The University of Chicago
All rights reserved. Published 1981
Printed in the United States of America
84 83 82 81   5 4 3 2 1

Library of Congress Cataloging in Publication Data

McCawley, James D
    Everything that linguists have always wanted to
know about logic but were ashamed to ask.
    Bibliography: p.
    Includes index.
    1. Language and logic. I. Title.
P39.M3   401   80–345
ISBN 0–226–55617–4
ISBN 0–226–55618–2 pbk.

Contents

v

Contents

Preface

I didn't really want to write this book, but I decided in 1974 that it would be easier for me to write it than to not write it, assuming, that is, that I was going to continue teaching courses on logic for linguists regularly. While there are many admirable logic textbooks, several of which I had used to considerable advantage in my courses (those of Reichenbach, Strawson, Thomason, and Massey), none matched very well my conception of what a course of logic for linguists should provide: a survey of those areas of logic that are of real or potential use in the analysis of natural language (not just 'basic' areas of logic, but areas such as presuppositional logic and fuzzy logic that are usually ignored in elementary logic courses), rich in analyses of linguistically interesting natural language examples, doing justice both to the logician's concerns and to the linguist's in the analysis of those examples, and making clear to the linguist what the logician's concerns are, in particular, what reasons logicians have for doing many things that may strike a linguist as perverse. I was able to offer a course along these lines only by supplementing an assigned textbook with numerous extra readings and lectures aimed at filling in what from my point of view were major gaps in the textbook and correcting naive and superficial treatments of linguistic matters. I soon concluded that the only way I was likely to be able to offer a relatively exasperation-free course on logic for linguists would be to write a textbook that conformed to my list of desiderata.

I intend this book to be useful as a textbook in courses of logic that give heavy emphasis to considerations of the analysis of natural language, especially courses aimed at students in linguistics. I have used preliminary versions of it in a two-quarter sequence on linguistic logic at the University of Chicago in which I have generally covered chapters 1–6 and selected sections of chapters 7–10 in the first quarter and the bulk of the remainder in the second quarter. The students in these courses have typically been advanced undergraduate and first-year graduate linguistics majors, with a sprinkling of students from philosophy and psychology. The prerequisite for this sequence has been an introductory syntax course, and this book correspondingly presumes some familiarity on the reader's part with the kind of analysis and use of linguistic data that is familiar in transformational grammar, though not with arcane points of transformational syntactic theory. Where linguistic questions have raised their heads, I have cited literature that the reader can consult for further exposition. I anticipate that this book will also prove useful for individual study and reference, though its fetal forms have not been tested in that capacity.

What the student can hope to get out of this book, besides familiarity with a number of areas of logic and their relation to linguistic questions, includes: (i) training of his semantic perceptions through exposure to linguistic examples in which considerations of logic help bring out certain subtle details of meaning; (ii) awareness of the intimate relationship between many linguistic problems (such as that of accounting for the distribution of reflexive pronouns) and many philosophical problems, particularly those relating to reference; (iii) development of an awareness of the distinction between those details of standard formal logic that represent serious conclusions worth defending and those details that merely reflect arbitrary decisions on the part of earlier logicians, and concomitant realization that standard versions of logic need not be accepted as package deals (this sort of perspective is of course something that linguistics students should hope to get not only from logic courses but also from their linguistics courses: a course in transformational syntax does a great disservice to students if it merely teaches them to do transformational analyses like a native but gives them no appreciation that those analyses embody both serious claims for which there is substantial backing and uncritical repetitions of features of earlier analyses that no one has seen fit to either provide support for or challenge); (iv) a conception of logic as a resource to be exploited according to one's own aims rather than as a legal code to be obeyed, and of logicians as merchants and manufacturers of potentially useful products that one is free to buy or not, according to one's needs and resources, with no obligation to buy all the standard accessories. In one's consultations with logicians, as with any other experts, one should keep in mind the advice of Bakunin (1871; p. 32 of 1970 reprint of 1916 translation):

Does it follow that I reject all authority? Far from me such a thought. In the matter of boots, I refer to the authority of the bootmaker; concerning houses, canals, or railroads, I consult that of the architect or engineer. For such or such special knowledge I apply to such or such a *savant*. But I allow neither the bootmaker nor the architect nor the *savant* to impose his authority upon me. I listen to them freely and with all the respect merited by their intelligence, their character, their knowledge, reserving always my incontestable right of criticism and censure. I do not content myself with consulting a single authority in any special branch; I consult several; I compare their opinions, and choose that which seems to me the soundest. But I recognize no infallible authority, even in special questions; consequently, whatever respect I may have for the honesty and sincerity of such or such an individual, I have no absolute faith in any person. Such a faith would be fatal to my reason, to my liberty, and even to the success of my undertakings; it would immediately transform me into a stupid slave, an instrument of the will and interests of others.

Finally I hope that the student will develop an appreciation of the way that considerations of logic, especially of the supposedly more esoteric areas that this book deals with, can help one to gain insight into important problems outside of logic and mathematics. Besides the various problems in linguistics and in philosophy of language that are dealt with in this book, I can mention a number of other areas to which certain points taken up below are relevant. Anderson and Belnap's relevant entailment logic (10.4) allows one to reevaluate the role of contradiction in the philosophy of science developed by Sir Karl Popper and his students. Popper lays great emphasis on the fact that in standard logic a contradiction causes all hell to break loose: "For it can easily be shown that if one were to accept contradictions then one would have to give up any kind of scientific activity: it would mean a complete breakdown of science. This can be shown by proving that *if two contradictory statements are admitted, any statement whatever must be admitted*; for from a couple of contradictory statements any statement whatever can be validly inferred" (Popper 1962:317, original emphasis). But for Anderson and Belnap, a contradiction causes only *some* hell to break loose: a contradiction implies only propositions to which it is relevant, and not even all of those. Thus adoption of Anderson and Belnap's version of logic allows the philosopher of science to demote contradictions in science from the status of crises to that of problems, not necessarily greater in importance than other types of 'problem' with which a scientific community may be faced. (See Laudan 1976 for insightful discussion of the notion of 'problem' in the history and philosophy of science). The arguments given by such economists as Frederic Bastiat (1850) for a free market economy implicitly involve a possible worlds semantics in which individuals can be identified across worlds but individuals existing in one world need not exist in all other worlds. In saying "Let us accustom ourselves, then, not to judge things solely by *what is seen*, but rather by *what is not seen*" (Bastiat 1850:9), Bastiat was contrasting the events and objects in the real world (what is seen) with those that exist in alternative worlds in which different laws were enforced (what is not seen). For example, the prosperity of existing weavers in a state that imposes a high import tariff on textiles does not in itself justify the tariff: their actual prosperity must be weighed against the interests of other workers who would have access to currently nonexistent jobs that would exist if textiles could be imported without tariff, of the consumers who would have access to cheaper clothing, and of those dealing in goods that consumers might buy more of if clothing were cheaper. Finally, fuzzy logic (chapter 12) has a bearing on status of legal distinctions such as adult/minor, sane/insane, and human/ nonhuman. Legal codes are normally drawn up in such a way that they provide a simple two-way distinction, with fine details of the drawing of the distinction having profound effects on who will go to prison and who will go free, what rights different persons have, and even who will live and who will die. However each distinction is drawn, legal decisions relating to persons on one side of the dividing line have no bearing on persons on the other side; for example, rights that adults accused of crimes have been held to possess are not automatically extended to minors, with the result that minors are often at a serious legal disadvantage in comparison with adults, even though special provisions for minors have been legislated in most cases for the purpose of protecting minors. The anomaly could be alleviated if laws recognized fuzzy rather than sharp distinctions, for example, if laws providing for a different status for adults and minors admitted a broad range of 'borderline cases', within which the person in question could choose the status which he was to be treated as having.

This book is unconventional not only in its goals and the choice of topics but also in the attitudes that I take in it and some of the conclusions that I arrive at. For example:

(i) In keeping with Lakoff's (1972a) program of 'natural logic', I take the subject matter of logic to be open-ended: I hold that all elements of meaning can play a role in inference and in truth conditions and that it is only by historical accident that logicians have largely confined themselves to the study of the logical properties of comparatively few elements of meaning (those expressed by *and, or, not, if, all, some, may,* and *must*). I thus reject the distinction that is usually drawn between 'logical' and 'nonlogical' vocabulary. In the process of writing this book I have realized that my rejection of that distinction forces me to reject another standard distinction, namely, that between axioms and rules of inference on the one hand and meaning postulates on the other: meaning postulates, in the sense of Carnap (1947), are axioms and rules of inference for 'nonlogical vocabulary', and there is no more grounds for singling them out for special status than there is for distinguishing 'logical' from 'nonlogical' vocabulary.

(ii) I take the units that one does 'the logic of' to be the elements of meaning and thus to be in the province of linguistics as much as of logic. Logic is an empirical enterprise at least to the extent that investigation of natural language provides evidence about what elements of meaning there are and what their combinatoric possibilities are (see, e.g., 3.5 for arguments from natural language facts to the conclusion that the logical counterparts of *and* and *or* combine not with just two propositions at a tim , as is standardly assumed in logic, but with any number at a time).

(iii) I take as mentalistic a position with regard to logical units as I do with regard to linguistic units. In particular, I feel free to distinguish in logic between conceptually distinct entities regardless of whether they ever have distinct denotations. This policy is responsible for the terminological detail in this book that is likely to offend the greatest number of logicians: my use of 'proposition' to refer to a conceptual unit rather than to a function giving truth conditions. To most modern logicians, a proposition is simply a function associating a truth value to each state of affairs. Under that conception of 'proposition', any two self-contradictory sentences correspond to the same proposition: the function that associates the value 'false' to every state of affairs. As 'proposition' is used here, there are infinitely many different self-contradictory propositions, and any self-contradictory sentence can be said to express some particular self-contradictory proposition. (Note also that I use the term 'proposition' in such a way that it makes perfect sense to speak of a sentence as expressing a proposition, whereas the way that modern logicians usually use 'proposition', a sentence does not strictly speaking *express* but only *denotes* a proposition, the way that a proper name denotes the individual that it is used as a name of).

(iv) I disown the prescriptive attitude toward natural language that logicians commonly adopt (with notable exceptions, such as the authors alluded to at the beginning of this preface): the attitude that formal logic must remedy deficiencies in natural language that render natural language at best a clumsy and limited tool for reasoning. I hold rather that in instances where formal logic has allegedly improved on natural language, it has merely given prominence to features that natural language has had all along though they have been overlooked in superficial analyses of natural language; for example, I have argued (McCawley 1970, 1972) that the 'referential indices' of formal logic are linguistically real and play a role in such syntactic phenomena as the occurrence of reflexive pronouns and of understood subjects of infinitives. Apparent discrepancies between natural language and formal logic provide no evidence of any defect in natural language: they are rather evidence that our analysis of natural language is deficient, or our formalization of logic is deficient, or our understanding of the relationship between language and logic is deficient, or our data reflect the interaction of language and logic with some third factor that we have not yet properly accounted for. See 8.3 for discussion of one factor that is responsible for many of the apparent discrepancies between standard formal logic and natural language, namely, Grice's (1967) principles of cooperativity in language use. While Grice's approach allows one to explain away many of the better-known putative examples where formal logic conflicts with natural language, it does not serve to explain them all away: certain properties of conditional sentences and of sentences containing *all* or *every* diverge from those of their counterparts in standard formal logic in ways that are not attributable to Grice's cooperative principles. In those particular cases, I have accordingly concluded that standard formal logic misrepresents the elements of meaning that it purports to deal with, and I have indicated how the logic might be done differently so as to avoid those discrepancies.

(v) I have rejected (on the basis of several arguments given in chapter 4) one of the most universally accepted policies of modern formal logic, namely, that of 'unrestricted quantification'. I regard that policy as the most pernicious and perverted idea in the history of logic and hold it responsible for an immense volume of pseudo-problems (particularly the alleged difficulties raised by the recognition of 'nonexistent objects') that have consumed the energies of many otherwise productive philosophers.

(vi) I have adopted a highly idiosyncratic notational system from the outset, rather than indoctrinating the student first in more widely used notational systems. Since students in a course of logic for linguists can reasonably expect to derive from the course some facility in reading the logical formulas that appear in existing works by linguists and philosophers, I have provided exercises in which the student is required to translate from standard notations into the notation of this book. The student who faithfully does all the exercises in this book can thus expect to acquire a useful reading knowledge of standard notations but will probably never be able to pass for a native speaker of them. When he is laughed at for his foreign accent, he can take consolation in the fact that his vocabulary is probably much larger than that of his derogators.

I have learned more in the process of writing this book than in any other project that I have ever undertaken. In attempting to produce a book that I, at least, find satisfactory both as logic and as linguistics, I have had to grapple with countless important questions in both fields that I had never thought about before, not only questions relating to fairly esoteric areas, but quite fundamental questions, such as what a proposition is and what it is to call a proposition true or false. I do not mean to suggest that this educational experience is complete, and I will not be surprised if comments of readers cause me to change my thinking substantially on many of the points covered here.

In preparing this book, I have derived much benfit from the comments, questions, and suggestions of many persons, including Gilbert Harman, S.-Y. Kuroda, Larry Martin, Uwe Mönnich, Alan Reeves, Valerie Reyna, Ivan Sag, Takashi Sugimoto, Richmond Thomason, Bas van Fraassen, and the many students who have used preliminary versions of parts of this book in my courses at the University of Chicago and at the 1977 Linguistic Institute at the University of Hawaii. I am particularly grateful to Richmond Thomason for detailed criticisms of the final draft of this book, criticisms which have left me with a significantly sharpened understanding of many of the matters with which I deal; while I have not accepted all of his advice, I may eventually wish that I had. Finally, I wish to acknowledge the stimulation that I have received from several scholars whose influence on my thinking is in part responsible for the fact that this book takes the form that it does: Noam Chomsky, from whom I learned to turn my questions about language into questions about human beings and their minds; George Lakoff, who has nearly convinced me that I should do the same with my questions about logic; Peter Geach, who has provided logic with an ample supply of that most basic necessity for scientific endeavour, namely, problems; Paul Grice, for whom I have learned to look for the effects of context on linguistic examples, especially of that particularly potent context, the null context; and Paul Feyerabend, from whom I have learned that diversity is as essential to the quality of life in science as in any other human endeavor.

1. The Subject Matter of Logic

1.1. Logic and 'Logical Form'

Logic is concerned with TRUTH and INFERENCE; that is, with determining the conditions under which a proposition is true and the conditions under which one proposition may be inferred or deduced from other propositions. For example, an adequate system of logic must provide an account of the fact that the proposition expressed by example 1.1.1*a* is always true, that expressed by 1.1.1*b* can be true on some occasions and false on others, and that expressed by 1.1.1*c* is always false:

1.1.1   a. Either there are unicorns or there aren't any unicorns.
          b. The number of books in the Library of Congress is a multiple of 7.
          c. All linguists are insane, and some linguists are not insane.

It must provide an account of the fact that the conclusion in 1.1.2*a* follows from the premises but the conclusion in 1.1.2*b* does not:

1.1.2   a. All linguists are insane.
           Some linguists are musicians.
           Therefore, some musicians are insane.
          b. All linguists are insane.
           Most linguists are musicians.
           Therefore, most musicians are insane.

These two tasks are intimately related in that principles of inference can be regarded as acceptable only if they always yield true conclusions when applied to true premises; that is, if given principles of inference allow one to deduce a certain conclusion from given premises, then the conditions for truth of propositions must insure that conclusion is true in all cases in which the premises are all true.

Logic is of necessity also concerned with SEMANTIC ANALYSIS, that is, with determining what propositions are expressed by or involved in the sentences of natural languages such as English or Japanese or Wolof: since inferences framed in ordinary language form a major part of the 'data' that logicians must provide an account of, semantic analysis will be a major part of the practising logician's activity and of what must be learned in order to understand logic, regardless of whether one regards semantic analysis as a part of logic or as something outside of logic that is a prerequisite for the application of logic.

In this book I will give the analysis of natural language a much more central role than is generally assigned to it in logic textbooks. Specifically, I will adopt the following policies:

(i) I will assume that the linguist's semantic analysis and the logician's have the same subject matter and that the linguist's goals do not conflict with the logician's. Thus I will assume that it is possible to provide an analysis of 'content' that is appropriate both for the linguist's goal of specifying what sentences are possible in a given natural language and how they are related to their meanings and for the logician's goal of formulating truth conditions and rules of inference.

(ii) Accordingly, I will assume that linguistic facts are relevant to choosing among otherwise equivalent proposals for the 'logical form' of various propositions. For example, I will reject the traditional policy of logicians of taking *and* as basically conjoining propositions two at a time (and thus of analyzing all apparent conjunctions of three or more propositions as iterated two-term conjoining) and will treat it instead as conjoining arbitrarily many propositions at a time. Among my reasons for this is the fact (see 3.5 for details) that the syntactic rules of English and other languages respect the distinction among '(p and q) and r', 'p and (q and r)' and 'p and q and r'. A less trivial example of this policy in action is given by my treatment of the expression *only if*. Logicians (e.g., Quine 1962:41) have generally treated 'p only if q' as merely an alternative expression (an 'idiomatic variant', in Quine's words) of 'If p, then q' or 'q if p', and thus make *only if* appear to be merely an idiosyncratic way of expressing the converse of *if*. But note that *only* does not otherwise express the notion of 'converse', for example, *John only likes Mary* does not express the proposition that Mary likes John. However, the expression *only if* clearly is not just an idiom (like *kick the bucket* or *go for broke*), whose meaning is not predictable from the meanings of its constituents: an English speaker who knows the use of the words *only* and *if* can understand and use *only if* without having to learn anything extra about that combination of words. I thus will not be satisfied with an analysis of *only if* unless it treats *only if* as put together from *only* and *if* by ordinary syntactic rules and as having a meaning derived from the meanings of *only* and *if* in the same way that the meanings of syntactically similar expressions are derived from the meanings of their parts. But since the traditional renderings of *only* and *if* by logicians cannot be combined with each other in any coherent way, either *only* or *if* will have to be given a treatment different from the one logicians generally give it; see 2.6 and 11.1 for considerations suggesting that *if* is the one requiring a nonstandard analysis and for a sketch of an analysis of *if* that makes it syntactically and semantically compatible with *only*, *even*, and the other things that it combines with.

(iii) I will take the domain of logic as encompassing all elements of meaning; that is, I will not draw any distinction between 'logical' and 'nonlogical' elements of meaning. I thus take the logical properties of 'and', 'or', 'not', 'if', 'all', and 'some' as forming neither the whole of logic nor even the core of logic but as simply the part of logic which happens, in part through historical accident, to be the most thoroughly investigated and best understood.

1.2. On the Nature of Propositions

In the last section, I used the term 'proposition' repeatedly but did not define or explain it. Since propositions are whatever logic is done on if logic is to provide an account of truth and inference, propositions must be things that can be said to be true or false and must also be things that can serve as premises or conclusions of inferences.

It is clear then that a proposition cannot be simply a sentence of English (or Japanese or Wolof or...). For example, it makes no sense to speak of the English sentence 1.2.1 as being in itself true or false:

1.2.1   It was raining.

This is because different occurrences of 1.2.1 express different propositions, sometimes a true proposition (if it was in fact raining at the place the speaker was referring to at the time he was referring to) and sometimes a a false proposition (if it was not raining at that time and place). Thus, 1.2.1 can express any of an infinite number of propositions (one for each combination of time and place that might be the ones in question), but it is still the same sentence in each case. Accordingly, the closest thing to a sentence that one might be able to take as fulfilling the role of a proposition is a sentence supplemented by information about REFERENCE, in particular, the time and place that that particular occurrence of the sentence purports to refer to. The same conclusion follows from a consideration of 1.2.2:

1.2.2   John told Fred's father that he was expected to help him.

There are a great many possibilities for the reference of the *he* and the *him* of 1.2.2: either could refer to John or to Fred or to Fred's father or to some fourth person (and if *he* refers to some fourth person, *him* might refer to some fifth person). The reference of the various elements of the sentence (and of elements that are only understood, such as the place in 1.2.1) is also relevant to the question of whether inferences in which they appear are valid. Consider the inferences:

1.2.3   a. Bill knew that it was raining.
          Sam told Bill that it was raining.
          Therefore, Sam told Bill something that Bill knew.

          b. Bill knew that John had told Fred's father that he was expected to help him.
          Sam told Bill that John had told Fred's father that he was expected to help him.
          Therefore, Sam told Bill something that Bill knew.

Whether 1.2.3*a* is valid will depend on whether the two premises purport to refer to the meteorological conditions of the same place and the same time. If the first premise refers to Bill's knowledge about the weather at some time and place referred to earlier in the discourse (say, 1.2.3*a* comes in the middle of a report of a conversation about one of the Boston Strangler's crimes and the first premise refers to Bill's knowledge about what the weather was doing when that crime was committed) but the second premise refers to the weather at the time Sam uttered his statement to Bill, then the conclusion does not follow from the premises: in that case what Sam told Bill was not necessarily something that Bill knew. Similarly, 1.2.3*b* is not valid unless the two *he*'s have the same reference and the two *him*'s do: if the first premise relates to Fred's being expected to help John and the second premise to Bill's being expected to help Fred's father, then what Sam told Bill need not be something that Bill knew, and thus 1.2.3*b* is invalid. Thus, whatever rule of inference gets one from the premises to the conclusion in 1.2.3*a* and *b* must be sensitive to the purported reference of the various parts of the premises: if the references do not match, the rule of inference must not apply.

    However, it will not do just to take a sentence supplemented with referential information as filling the role of a 'proposition'. Consider the inference:

1.2.4   All experts think that Nixon likes Mao better than Brezhnev.
       Mike Royko is an expert.
       Therefore, Mike Royko thinks that Nixon likes Mao better than Brezhnev.

The first premise and the conclusion of 1.2.4 are ambiguous: *Nixon likes Mao better than Brezhnev* may mean either *Nixon likes Mao better than he likes Brezhnev* or *Nixon likes Mao better than Brezhnev likes Mao.* It only makes sense to speak of 1.2.4 as valid or invalid if one assigns a specific interpretation to each of the sentences in it. Thus, 1.2.4 strictly speaking is not AN inference but something ambiguous among four different inferences.[1] Two of those inferences are valid (namely, the two in which the premise and conclusion are given like interpretations), and the other two are invalid.

If the different meanings of a sentence must be kept separate in determining the validity or invalidity of an inference apparently involving that sentence, one must ask whether it is not in fact simply the meanings that function as the premises and conclusions of arguments. Since the validity of an argument clearly depends on the meanings of the sentences that are used to frame the argument but does not obviously depend in any way on the sentences themselves (that is, it does not obviously depend in any way on the choice of words used to express those meanings), I will assume provisionally that the things that constitute the premises and conclusions of inferences are simply meanings such as can be expressed by sentences, with the qualification that 'meaning' here must be taken as including reference, in accordance with the discussion of 1.2.1 above.

This provisional conclusion raises a huge number of questions, of which the most important are: (i) What is the structure of a meaning? That is, what are the bits and pieces of which a meaning consists, and how do they fit together? (ii) How does one identify the bits and pieces of the meaning (or rather, of each of the meanings) expressible by a given sentence? (iii) How does one individuate meanings? That is, how does one tell whether a particular sentence is really ambiguous, as opposed to just having a single meaning that happens to be applicable to a broad range of cases? These are not easy questions to answer, and it is easy to find disagreement as to their answers, even disagreement as to whether they have answers. In the course of this book, I will offer partial answers to each of these questions. However, the reader would do well to think critically about the answers offered, since he can rest assured that any position whatever regarding these questions will be controversial.

1.3. Ambiguity

In the chapters that follow, the question will often arise as to whether some class of sentence is ambiguous.[2] For example, consider the question of whether the logicians' standard account of *and* really accords with the use of *and* in ordinary English. The logicians' rendition of *and*, which I will henceforth symbolize with $\wedge$, is completely symmetric: $A \wedge B$ is true under the same circumstances as is $B \wedge A$, and anything that can be inferred from $A \wedge B$ can be inferred from $B \wedge A$. But there are instances in which ordinary English *and* appears to be asymmetric; for example, under the most obvious interpretation, 1.3.1*a* would be true under different circumstances from those under which 1.3.1*b* is true:

1.3.1   a. John got up and fell down.
             b. John fell down and got up.

These sentences are normally taken as referring to an order of events that matches the order of the conjuncts: in 1.3.1*a* the rising precedes the falling, and in 1.3.1*b* the falling precedes the rising. Logicians who have confronted sentences such as 1.3.1 have generally adopted the position that English *and* is ambiguous between (at least) two senses: a 'symmetric' sense which conforms to the logicians' $\wedge$, and a 'consecutive' sense in which the order of the conjuncts agrees with the purported temporal order of the events reported in the conjuncts (Massey 1970:5). This conclusion may very well be correct. However, logicians have been remiss in simply accepting it without even attempting to provide arguments that English *and* really is ambiguous. There are a number of possible alternatives to the position that *and* is ambiguous: (i) Perhaps there is only one *and*, it is basically asymmetric, and the logicians who have concerned themselves with a symmetric *and* have deluded themselves by restricting their attention to instances where the order of the conjuncts happened not to be of any particular significance. (ii) Perhaps there is only one *and*, it is basically symmetric, and the supposed asymmetry of *and* in 1.3.1 is really something else, namely, either (ii*a*) an ambiguity in some other element of the sentence (for example, in the past tense marker) or (ii*b*) the result of something outside of logic and grammar, for example, principles of sportsmanlike behavior that would dictate that one avoid misleading one's hearers; these principles might dictate that one provide an overt signal whenever one relates events in an order that is not (or is not known to be) the order in which they happened.

   In order to choose among these alternatives, it will be necessary to invoke an account of the notion of ambiguity which provides a basis for determining whether a sentence has some putative ambiguity or does not, and for identifying the exact nature of the ambiguity. To develop such an account, it will be worthwhile to start with some clear cases of ambiguity and clear cases of nonambiguity and determine what characteristics of the two classes of cases might be used as tests to settle the unclear cases. Let us start by seeing if we can come up with a principled basis for accepting the proposition that *bastard* is ambiguous between the senses 'person whose parents were not married' and 'nasty person', and for rejecting the proposition that *carp* is ambiguous between the senses 'male member of the species *Cyprinus carpio*' and 'female member of the species *Cyprinus carpio*'. There is, of course, an obvious definition, namely, 'member of the species *Cyprinus carpio*', that would cover the domains of applicability of both of the supposed senses of *carp*, whereas there does not appear to be any way of defining *bastard* so as to take in both illegitimate persons and nasty persons without at least in effect enumerating the two cases ('person who either is nasty or is the offspring of persons who were not married to each other'). While these observations lend plausibility to the claim that *bastard* has two separate senses but *carp* has a single general sense that covers the cases taken in by each of the putative senses, they do not settle the issue. For one thing, we have no basis for assuming that a single sense cannot involve a list of separate cases; thus, dictionaries might be correct when they give 'female ruler or wife of male ruler' as a definition of a supposed single sense of *queen*. For another, our failure to come up with a single definition that covers both 'illegitimate person' and 'nasty person' may be merely the result of insufficient ingenuity on our parts, and we have no justification for calling *bastard* ambiguous just on the basis of an argument from ignorance. In fact, the problematic sense of *queen* just noted can be defined, as Michael LaGaly has observed, as 'enthroned female'. Perhaps our perplexity about *bastard* may vanish when someone with LaGaly's ingenuity hits upon a nonenumerative definition that covers both 'nasty person' and 'illegitimate person'. Finally, the existence of a sense that covers the whole domain of applicability of a word does not imply that it does not have additional more restricted senses; for example, I will argue that *Yankee* is ambiguous among the three senses 'native of the U.S.A.', 'native of the north of the U.S.A.', and 'native of New England'.

A question of ambiguity can often be resolved by a consideration of grammatical phenomena that depend on whether the two items are identical. Consider, for example, deletion of repeated verb phrases or of repeated nouns:[3]

1.3.2   a. Marcella believes that the world will end soon, and Ben does too.
          b. Sam owns four sweaters, and Bill owns five.

I will assume that these sentences are derived from a more complete underlying structure by grammatical transformations that respectively delete a repeated VP and delete a repeated noun. Let us see whether these transformations respect the putative differences between *bastard* 'illegitimate person' and *bastard* 'nasty person' and between *carp* 'male *Cyprinus carpio*' and *carp* 'female *Cyprinus carpio*'. If there are two distinct items *bastard*$_1$ 'illegitimate person' and *bastard*$_2$ 'nasty person', then 1.3.3*a–b* involve two identical nouns and 1.3.3*c–d* involve two distinct nouns, and thus only 1.3.3*a–b* ought to give rise to 1.3.3*e* by deletion of a repeated noun:

1.3.3   a. Maxine married a bastard$_1$, and then Frieda married a bastard$_1$.
        b. Maxine married a bastard$_2$, and then Frieda married a bastard$_2$.
        c. Maxine married a bastard$_1$, and then Frieda married a bastard$_2$.
        d. Maxine married a bastard$_2$, and then Frieda married a bastard$_1$.
        e. Maxine married a bastard, and then Frieda married one.

This is in fact the case: 1.3.3*e* can be used with reference to Maxine and Frieda both marrying illegitimate sons or to their both marrying nasty persons but not with reference to one of them marrying an illegitimate but nice man and the other marrying a nasty man whose parents were married. By contrast, a putative difference between *carp* 'male *Cyprinus*' and *carp* 'female *Cyprinus*' is ignored when N-deletion applies—1.3.4 can be used just as well when Susan has caught a male carp and George a female one as when both have caught female carps:

1.3.4   Susan caught a carp, and then George caught one.

Examples involving VP-deletion work in exactly parallel fashion:

1.3.5   a. Maxine married a bastard, and then Frieda did.
        b. Susan caught a carp, and then George did.

Thus we have confirmation of our original judgment that *bastard* was ambiguous between 'illegitimate person' and 'nasty person', whereas *carp* was not ambiguous between 'male Cyprinus' and 'female Cyprinus'. Of course, this leaves open the question of whether *carp* might have some other ambiguity (for example, might it be ambiguous between '*Cyprinus carpio*' and 'male *Cyprinus carpio*', the same way that *dog* is often claimed to be ambiguous between '*canis*' and 'male *canis*'?).

Let us apply this test to a case where it is not so obvious whether the word is ambiguous. The word *uncle* is occasionally claimed to be ambiguous among the four senses 'brother of father', 'brother of mother', 'husband of sister of father', and 'husband of sister of mother'. To see whether it has these four senses or instead has a single sense that covers all four cases (or has two senses, each of which covers two of the cases, or...), let us consider:

1.3.6   Bill is Marty's uncle, and Tom is too.

Example 1.3.6 is applicable not only to the four cases in which Bill and Tom have the same genealogical relation to Marty (they are both brothers of Marty's father; they are both husbands of sisters of Marty's father;...) but also to the 12 cases in which they have different genealogical relations to Marty (e.g., Bill is Marty's father's brother, and Tom is the husband of Marty's mother's sister). Thus the difference between the putative four senses of *uncle* is not respected by VP-deletion, and there is thus a single sense of *uncle* that covers all four genealogical relationships. (Giving a nonenumerative definition that covers all four cases is another matter; it turns out not to be at all easy to do).

The test embodied in 1.3.3–6 gives fairly clear results when the putative senses are nonoverlapping (or where their overlap is only fortuitous, as in the case of *bastard*: some people are both illegitimate *and* nasty). It is important that we find a test that will be applicable even in the case where one of the putative senses is contained in another, since many plausible cases of ambiguity are of this type (for example, *Yankee* and *dog*). Consider questions and negative declaratives such as

1.3.7   a. Is Bill Marty's uncle?
         b. Is John a bastard?
         c. Is Barney a Yankee?
         d. Bill isn't Marty's uncle.
         e. John isn't a bastard.
         f. Barney isn't a Yankee.

If you know the exact genealogical relationship between Bill and Marty, you know the answer to 1.3.7a: if Bill is related to Marty in any of the four ways listed above, the answer is 'Yes', and otherwise the answer is 'No'. Suppose now that you have full information about whether John's parents were married and whether he is a nasty person. Are you in a position then to answer 1.3.7b? If John is nasty and illegitimate, the answer to 1.3.7b will be 'Yes', and if he is pleasant and legitimate, the answer will be 'No'. But what about the case where he is pleasant and illegitimate or where he is nasty and legitimate? If there were just a single sense 'illegitimate or nasty', then the answer ought to be 'Yes', since John in these cases does meet the condition 'illegitimate or nasty'. But in these cases, the answer is sometimes 'Yes' and sometimes 'No', depending on the intentions of the person who asked the question: either he was asking whether John is illegitimate or he was asking whether John is nasty, and to answer the question you have to know which question he was asking. Things are similar with 1.3.7c: if Barney comes from Birmingham, Alabama, then the right answer to 1.3.7c may be either 'Yes' (if it was a question about Barney's nationality) or 'No' (if it was a question about what part of the country Barney is from). The negative sentences 1.3.7*d–f* are exactly parallel to the questions 1.3.7*a–c*: while 1.3.7*d* is true if Bill holds none of the four relationships to Marty and false if he holds one of them, it does not make sense to speak of 1.3.7*e* as being true or as being false in the case where John is a nasty person whose parents were married. Example 1.3.7*e* has to be assigned two distinct senses. The one sense of 1.3.7*e* is true and the other one false in the case just mentioned, and it makes no more sense to ask whether 1.3.7*e* itself is true or false in this case than to ask whether Springfield (not specifically Springfield, Missouri, or Springfield, Illinois, or Springfield, Massachusetts, but just plain Springfield) is west of the Mississippi.

We are now in a position to obtain a partial answer to our questions about whether *and* is ambiguous between a symmetric sense and a consecutive sense. Consider the question

1.3.8   Did John get up and fall down?

If John got up and fell down, in that order, then the answer to 1.3.8 is clearly 'Yes'. What if he fell down and then got up without then falling down again? Are we then in a quandary about how to answer 1.3.8; that is, can 1.3.8 be taken either as asking whether he got up and then fell down (in which case the answer would be 'No') or as asking whether he both got up and fell down, irrespective of order (in which case the answer should be 'Yes')? The judgment is fairly subtle, but I believe that there in fact is such a quandary here (i.e., that either answer might be correct, depending on how the speaker intended the question, and that one cannot answer the question without deciding which way the speaker meant it). This supports, albeit weakly, the conclusion that there is both such a thing as a symmetric *and* and a temporally consecutive *and*[4] and shows that logicians have not been engaging in a total flight of fancy when they speak of such a thing as a symmetric SENSE of *and* (as opposed to merely cases where, perhaps fortuitously, the order of the conjuncts does not matter).

1.4. Logic and the Division of Labor

To a far greater extent than is generally recognized, logic is an empirical science. Putative rules of inference and truth conditions are not self-evident propositions that one is obliged to accept at all costs: they might turn out to be wrong, and facts about the use and interpretation of sentences of ordinary language are relevant to the confirmation or refutation of hypothesized principles of logic. However, logic is only one of several factors that may play a role in any fact about language. For example, several things interact in a person's judgment that there is something wrong with each of the following arguments:

1.4.1   If the door is unlocked, someone has entered the house. Someone has entered the house. Therefore, the door is unlocked.

1.4.2   Nothing is a square circle. Otto bought nothing. Therefore, Otto bought a square circle.

1.4.3   Chicago is in Illinois. Therefore, Chicago is in either Illinois or Uruguay.

To judge that any of these arguments is 'unacceptable', one makes use not only of one's knowledge of and abilities in logic but also of one's knowledge of the syntax and vocabulary of the English language, of the uses that such arguments play in exposition and discussion, and of how behavior (such as the uttering of the above sentences) relates to the context in which it takes place and to one's goals.

The source of the unacceptability might be purely a matter of logic: that there are no general principles guaranteeing that the conclusion is true whenever the premises are true. But the unacceptability might rest in part or in total on a faulty linguistic analysis, in which two expressions that make different contributions to the meanings of the sentences in which they occur are mistakenly treated alike. For example, one could reasonably maintain that 1.4.2 is faulty because it wrongly treats *nothing* and *is* as if they figured in 1.4.2 the same way that *a pen* and *is* figure in 1.4.2':

1.4.2'   A pen is a writing instrument. Otto bought a pen. Therefore, Otto bought a writing instrument.

Or the unacceptability of an argument might simply rest on its pointlessness. For example, one could reasonably hold that 1.4.3 sounds as odd as it does simply because no reasonable purpose would be served by drawing its conclusion from its premise, since its conclusion contains less information than does its premise, and one is normally expected to be informative. On this account, the unacceptability of 1.4.3 is like the unacceptability of opening a chess game by moving P-KB3: it is a legal move but a stupid one, since other moves (such as P-K4) put one in a better position to accomplish the presumed goal of winning the game (though it might be a clever move if the goal were different, say, if one were in a contest to see who could play the longest chess game). In 2.2 this account of 1.4.3 will be defended and it will be pointed out that arguments of the form of 1.4.3 are often perfectly acceptable provided that they are used as parts of larger arguments rather than being used by themselves.

Similarly, a sentence may in some sense conflict with the facts without necessarily expressing a false proposition: it might just be a pointless or stupid or misleading thing to say, given what the facts are. For example, Grice (1967) has argued that sentences such as the conclusion of 1.4.3 will convey that the speaker does not know which alternative is correct (in this case, that he does not know whether Chicago is in Illinois or in Uruguay) and will thus be misleading if he does know, since if he does know, he is in a position to utter the shorter and more informative sentence *Chicago is in Illinois* and is thus going out of his way to be uninformative if he utters instead the sentence *Chicago is in either Illinois or Uruguay*. Here what is in conflict with the facts is not the proposition expressed by the sentence but the speaker's behavior in choosing to utter that sentence rather than one of the alternatives available to him.

The fact that a given ordinary language argument is in some way acceptable is generally of some relevance to logic, but what exactly its relevance is cannot be determined without exploration of the linguistic, psychological, and sociological factors that might be involved in its unacceptability. The more thorough knowledge one has of those factors, the better prepared one is to identify whether the argument is wrong in any strictly logical way (i.e., is not merely 'unacceptable' but 'invalid'). Thus, to place claims about logic on a really firm footing, one must have a firm understanding of the linguistic structures, the meanings of the words, the principles of language use, and perhaps many other things that interact with logical principles in the construction and evaluation of arguments in natural language. A serious but not fully systematic attempt has been made in the following chapters to give due consideration to these factors.

1.5. Exercises

1. Give facts that are relevant to deciding which of the following is a real ambiguity:

   a. Two putative senses of *apple*, one referring to a fruit with red skin and one referring to a fruit with green or yellow skin.
   b. Two putative senses of *coffee*, one referring to the beans from which a certain beverage is made and the other referring to that beverage.
   c. Two putative interpretations of the sentence *Someone is renting a house*, one in which *someone* refers to the landlord (cf. *Someone rented me a house for $400 a month*) and one in which *someone* refers to the tenant (cf. *I rented a house from Schwartz for $400 a month*). NB: these two putative senses have exactly the same truth conditions.
   d. Two putative senses of *may*: 'permitted' and 'possible', as in the interpretation of *Shirley may dance* as 'Shirley is permitted to dance' or as 'It is possible that Shirley dances'.

2. Suppose that a Navaho linguist interested in the question of whether different languages can reflect different logical systems carries out fieldwork on the language of an exotic tribe, the Anglos. After several years of investigation he publishes an article in which he makes the following claims: (i) in the language of the Anglos, the negation of a declarative clause is formed by putting *not* or *n't* after the first auxiliary verb (and creating an auxiliary verb out of *do* and the tense marker if there was no auxiliary verb there to begin with); (ii) Anglos readily assent to many sentences of the form '*p* and negation-*p*', for example, *Some men are bald and some men aren't bald*; and (iii) therefore in the logic of the Anglos the familiar (to the Navahos) 'law of double negation', (according to which a proposition '*p* and negation-*p*' can never be true) is invalid. How could one argue against the Navaho linguist's claim that Anglo logic is different from Navaho logic? (Note: a large part of this problem revolves about the question of how one can tell whether one sentence 'is the negation of' another sentence). Don't expect to solve this problem, only to gain appreciation of the fact that it poses a serious problem.

2. Propositional Logic I: Syntax

2.1. Remarks on the Notion of 'System of Formal Logic'

Logicians have widely adopted the terms 'syntax' and 'semantics' to refer to certain portions of their endeavors. A logician is doing 'syntax' when he is constructing RULES OF INFERENCE, that is, general principles that specify what conclusions may be inferred from what premises, or is investigating the implications of particular rules of inference. He is also doing 'syntax' when he is constructing FORMATION RULES, that is, rules that specify the class of propositions he is dealing with. A logician is doing 'semantics' when he is setting up conditions on what the TRUTH VALUES of the various propositions under consideration can be.[1] For example, a logician dealing with an extremely restricted portion of logic might state the following 'logical principles':

2.1.1 Formation rules:
> *God is good* is a proposition.
> *Cincinnati is in Mongolia* is a proposition.
> *Bamboo shoot goes good with mushrooms* is a proposition.
> If *A* and *B* are propositions, then *A and B* is a proposition.

Rules of inference:
> From *A and B* you may infer *A*.
> From *A and B* you may infer *B*.
> From *A* and *B* you may infer *A and B*.

Truth conditions:
> Every proposition is either true or false (but not both).
> If *A* and *B* are both true, then *A and B* is true.
> Otherwise, *A and B* is false.

The formation rules, though only four in number, commit one to recognizing an infinite number of propositions: anything that one can get from the three given ATOMIC propositions by conjoining them to one's heart's content will be a proposition of this system. For example, the formation

14

rules of 2.1.1 imply that ((*God is good and Cincinnati is in Mongolia*) *and* ((((*God is good and bamboo shoot goes good with mushrooms*) *and* (*God is good and God is good*)) *and* (*Cincinnati is in Mongolia and bamboo shoot goes good with mushrooms*))) is a proposition.[2] The rules of inference sanction such reasonable (albeit trivial) inferences as 2.1.2:

2.1.2   God is good and bamboo shoot goes good with mushrooms. Therefore, God is good.

The truth conditions restrict the class of 'states of affairs' that can come into consideration. In a state of affairs in which *God is good* is true, *Cincinnati is in Mongolia* false, and *Bamboo shoot goes good with mushrooms* true, it will have to be the case that *God is good and bamboo shoot goes good with mushrooms* is true and *God is good and Cincinnati is in Mongolia* false if the 'truth conditions' given in 2.1.1 are to be satisfied. While these truth conditions have been given just by fiat in 2.1.1, they are eminently reasonable: one could not assign truth values in violation of 2.1.1 without being blatantly inconsistent. Note, though that 2.1.1 places no constraint on what truth values the atomic propositions have; 2.1.1 thus allows for states of affairs in which *Cincinnati is in Mongolia* is true and *God is good* false.

While 'rules of inference' and 'truth conditions' are separate parts of a 'logical system' such as the fragment of logic given in 2.1.1, they must fit together properly if the 'system' is to make any sense. When rules of inference are applied to true premises, true conclusions must result: a rule of inference is supposed to be a guarantee that the conclusion resulting from applying it to true premises will be true. The rule 2.1.1 meets this criterion of 'fit': the truth conditions have been set up in such a way that anything that the rules of inference of 2.1.1 allow you to infer from any given true premises will also be true. Example 2.1.1 in fact satisfies an even tighter criterion of 'fit': if the truth conditions in 2.1.1 guarantee that some proposition B will be true whenever some proposition A is true, then B is inferrable from A by the rules of inference of 2.1.1 (possibly in several steps, but inferrable all the same). This means that what is inferrable from a particular proposition A is PRECISELY the propositions that have to be true when A is true. The first criterion of 'fit' says that the rules of inference work; the second criterion says that they work as well as anyone could demand of them: that there is nothing that you ought to be able to infer (within the set of propositions under consideration) but can't.

In this text, I will often treat 'syntax' and 'semantics' separately, simply to impress on the reader the fact that they are separate and that making them 'fit together' is a nontrivial task. The remainder of this chapter will be concerned with the 'syntax' of the garden-variety uses of the words *and, or, if*, and *not*. That is, we will be concerned only with the syntax of complex propositions that can be assembled from simpler propositions by means of *and*, *or*, *if*, and *not*, and we will treat as ATOMIC (that is, ignore any details of internal structure) any propositions that are not decomposable into simpler propositions combined by *and*, *or*, *if*, and *not*. Thus, for the purposes of this realm of logic, which is called PROPOSITIONAL LOGIC (or PROPOSITIONAL CALCULUS), a proposition can be identified with an expression made up of atomic propositions and 'propositional connectives'. We will use lower-case letters such as p, q, r, s to stand for atomic propositions; capital letters such as A, B, C will be reserved for (not necessarily atomic) propositions. We will use the following symbols, all of which are in common use, for the propositional connectives:[3]

and	$\wedge$
or	$\vee$
not	$\sim$
if (. . . then)	$\supset$

Let p be any proposition. Then $\sim p$ is the negation of p; for example, if p is the proposition that Cincinnati is in Mongolia, then $\sim p$ is the proposition that Cincinnati isn't in Mongolia. *Not* (or its contracted form *n't*) generally expresses negation, for example, *Cincinnati isn't in Mongolia* expresses the negation of the proposition expressed by *Cincinnati is in Mongolia*. However, striking out *n't* doesn't always take you from one proposition to another of which it is the negation. For example, if you strike out the *n't* of 2.1.3*a*, you get something (2.1.3*b*) that isn't quite what 2.1.3*a* is the negation of, and if you strike out the *n't* of 2.1.3*c*, you get something (2.1.3*d*) of which 2.1.3*c* is clearly not the negation:

2.1.3   a. John doesn't love his wife.
             b. John does love his wife.
             c. Some people aren't afraid of dying.
             d. Some people are afraid of dying.

The fact that the proposition of which 2.1.3*a* expresses the negation is normally expressed by *John loves his wife* and not by the somewhat odd-sounding 2.1.3*b*[4] reflects a peculiarity of negative clauses in English: they require that *n't* and the tense marker (the *-s* of *loves*) be suffixed to an auxiliary verb, and if there isn't any auxiliary verb there, a *do* is supplied in lieu thereof. Example 2.1.3*c* does not assert the contrary of 2.1.3*d*. Indeed the propositions that they express clearly are both true. That fact doesn't mean that the *n't* of 2.1.3*c* doesn't express negation. It does express negation, though not negation of the whole proposition expressed by 2.1.3*d*. I will claim in chapter 4 that the meanings of sentences like 2.1.3*d* involve three constituents: a 'quantifier' (such as *some, all, most, few,...*), an expression giving the 'domain' under discussion (in this case, the set of people) and a 'propositional function' (in this case, '*x* is afraid of dying') whose applicability in that domain is at issue. In 2.1.3*c* it is not the whole of 2.1.3*d* that it negated but only the propositional function: 2.1.3*c* says that some members of the domain 'people' have the property '*x* isn't afraid of dying', that is, the property which is the negation of '*x* is afraid of dying'. Thus, a proposition expressed by a sentence containing *not* or *n't* need not fit the formula $\sim p$: it may CONTAIN a proposition (or propositional function) of the form $\sim p$ without itself BEING of that form.

Logic texts generally adopt the practise of writing formulas such as

2.1.4   a. $p \wedge q$
              b. $p \vee q$

for propositions in which *and* or *or* conjoins two propositions; for example, if *p* is the proposition expressed by *John loves his wife* and *q* the proposition expressed by *Bert loves his parakeet*, $p \wedge q$ would be the proposition expressed by *John loves his wife and Bert loves his parakeet*, I will deviate from this practise by writing the $\wedge$ or $\vee$ before the propositions that it conjoins,[5] for example,

2.1.5   a. $\wedge pq$ [alternatively: $\wedge (p, q)$]
              b. $\vee pq$ [alternatively: $\vee (p, q)$]

I adopt this policy because (i) *and* and *or* can conjoin any number of propositions at a time, not just two (see 3.5 for some justification of this claim); (ii) to write $p \wedge q \wedge r \wedge s$ for the *and*-conjunction of *p, q, r*, and *s*, as is often done, is misleading, since three $\wedge$'s appear in the formula, whereas the meaning involves only a single conjunction, and (iii) if there is to be a uniform notation for conjunctions of arbitrarily many propositions, the extreme beginning and the extreme end are the most innocuous places to write the $\wedge$ or $\vee$ (there are other possibilities, such as writing the $\wedge$ or $\vee$ after the first of the conjunct propositions, regardless of how many of them there are; however, such a notation is baroque to no apparent purpose).

And and *or* have an important characteristic which will recur throughout the examples to be given in this book and which it is worth devoting a little attention to right now, namely, that when they conjoin propositions that are the same but for one item, the conjoined proposition may be expressed in the form of a simple sentence with a conjoined part. For example, in the following pairs of examples, the first example expresses what could be given more explicit expression by the second example:

2.1.6   a. Fred and Myron are athletes.
              a'. Fred is an athlete, and Myron is an athlete (too).

    b. Brazil is both larger and more densely populated than Baffin Island.

    b′. Brazil is larger than Baffin Island, and it is more densely populated than Baffin Island.

    c. The poem was written by either Whitman or Tennyson or e. e. cummings.

    c′. Either this poem was written by Whitman or it was written by Tennyson or it was written by e. e. cummings.

    d. Jack both admires and respects von Ribbentrop.

    d′. Jack admires von Ribbentrop and he respects von Ribbentrop.

The relationship between these pairs of sentences corresponds to the grammatical transformation of CONJUNCTION REDUCTION,[6] whereby conjoined clauses that differ in only one item can be replaced by a simple clause that involves conjoining of that item. This is not to say that all sentences having conjoined parts are derived from conjoined sentences; indeed there are clear cases of conjoined elements that do not admit such a derivation:

2.1.7   a. The king and the queen are an amiable couple.

    a′. *The king is an amiable couple and the queen is an amiable couple.

    a″. The king is amiable and the queen is amiable.

    b. Alex became more and more ashamed of his past.

    b′. *Alex became more ashamed of his past and he became more ashamed of his past.

The supposed sources 2.1.7a′ and 2.1.7b′ for a derivation of 2.1.7a and 2.1.7b by conjunction reduction are incoherent. Moreover, 2.1.7a could not even be derived from 2.1.7a″, since 2.1.7a″ has a different meaning: note that the king and the queen can be amiable individually without their being an amiable couple—they might be two very amiable persons who turn into raving maniacs when they are in each other's presence.

    There are also sentences with conjoined pieces for which the most simple-minded way of 'undoing conjunction reduction' yields nonsense like 2.1.7a′ or 2.1.7b′, but which allow a less simple-minded analysis involving conjunction reduction. Consider the sentences 2.1.8a–d and the supposed results of undoing conjunction reduction:

2.1.8   a. John isn't an athlete or a musician.

    b. Richie wants to buy either a Mustang or a Chevy.

    c. Richie wants either a Mustang or a Chevy.

    d. Bill must be in either Amsterdam or Copenhagen right now.

    a'. Either John isn't an athlete or he isn't a musician.
    b'. Either Richie wants to buy a Mustang or he wants to buy a Chevy.
    c'. Either Richie wants a Mustang or he wants a Chevy.
    d'. Either Bill must be in Amsterdam right now or he must be in Copenhagen right now.

Example 2.1.8a says that John is neither athlete nor musician, whereas 2.1.8a' says only that he isn't both. However, 2.1.8a need not be analyzed as a conjunction of negative sentences—it can be interpreted as the negation of a conjoined sentence: $\sim \vee pq$, where p is 'John is an athlete' and q is 'John is a musician'. Sentences 2.1.8b and 2.1.8c are actually ambiguous: they can be interpreted either like 2.1.8b' and 2.1.8c', which suggest that the speaker doesn't know which of two things Richie wants, or in a way that involves not the speaker's uncertainty about Richie's wishes but a single wish on Richie's part that can be fulfilled in either of two ways; I will consider only the latter interpretation here. While standard English does not allow such sentences as *Richie wants that he'll buy a Mustang*, such a sentence would in fact represent more directly the content of a sentence such as *Richie wants to buy a Mustang*. The direct object of *want* is really a sentence describing the state of affairs that fulfills the want, though in standard English that sentence can only manifest itself in truncated form, as an infinitive expression (as in 2.1.8b) or as even less than that (as in 2.1.8c, which has the same meaning as *Richie wants to have either a Mustang or a Chevy*). I maintain that 2.1.8b and c demand analyses in which *want* has a conjoined sentence as its direct object: 'Richie will buy a Mustang or Richie will buy a Chevy' in the case of 2.1.8b and 'Richie will have a Mustang or Richie will have a Chevy' in the case of 2.1.8c. In either case conjunction reduction is applicable, yielding *Richie will buy/have a Mustang or a Chevy*; in both cases rules apply deleting the subject of the embedded sentence and putting the verb in the infinitive form, yielding *to buy/have a Mustang or a Chevy*, and *to have* is optionally deletable, yielding 2.1.8c.[7] Thus in both 2.1.8b and 2.1.8c the *or* conjoins sentences, but those sentences do not appear in full in the surface form of 2.1.8b and 2.1.8c. The *must* of 2.1.8d can be analyzed as a predicate (meaning something like 'certain') which is predicated of a proposition; thus 2.1.8d allows the paraphrase *It is certain that Bill is in either Amsterdam or Copenhagen right now*, and that paraphrase can be derived by conjunction reduction from a structure in which the *or* conjoins sentences: *It is certain that either Bill is in Amsterdam right now or he is in Copenhagen right now*. While these examples thus do in fact involve conjunction reduction, they should put you on your guard against a mistake that is easily made: the fact that a sentence contains *and* or *or* does not imply that it EXPRESSES a conjoined proposition—it may only express something that CONTAINS a conjoined proposition.

In conformity with my notation for the 'logical operators' mentioned so far, which I write to the left of the propositions that they are combined with, I will also write the symbol for 'if (...then)' before the propositions in question:

2.1.9 $\supset pq$ [alternatively: $\supset (p, q)$]

The standard notation is $p \supset q$. It must be kept in mind that while $\wedge$ and $\vee$ can combine with any number of propositions at a time, $\supset$ can only combine with two at a time; thus 2.1.10*a* makes sense but 2.1.10*b* does not:

2.1.10   a. $\wedge (p, q, r)$
                b. $\supset (p, q, r)$

The function of the parentheses in 2.1.5, 2.1.9, and 2.1.10 is to indicate how the elements of meaning are grouped together. That the grouping is significant can be seen by comparing the expressions

2.1.11   a. $\wedge (\vee (p, q, r), s)$
                b. $\wedge (\vee (p, q), r, s)$

These formulas correspond to clearly distinct meanings, for example,

2.1.12   a. Either Tom or Dick or Harry is sick, and George is sick (too).
                b. Either Tom or Dick is sick, and Harry is sick, and George is sick (too).

From 2.1.11*b* one can infer *r*, but from 2.1.11*a* one cannot.

I adopt the policy that it is not the parentheses themselves but the grouping indicated by them that is significant in logic. I thus relegate the differences among $\sim p$, $\sim (p)$, and $(\sim p)$ to the realm of typography: the differences can be ignored in the same way that we ignore the difference between 8-point and 10-point type or ignore spaces (i.e., '$p \wedge q$' and '$p \wedge q$' count as 'the same expression'). The grouping can be indicated more perspicuously (though more expensively for the publisher who is paying for the typesetting) in the form of tree diagrams:

2.1.13   a.   b.

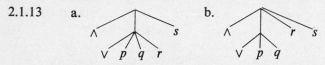

Each node in these diagrams corresponds to a part of the meaning, and the lines indicate how the various pieces of meaning group together into larger pieces.

The sort of structure that is represented by diagrams as in 2.1.13 is known as a LABELED TREE: something that is comprised of a set of items (called NODES), a relation of CONSTITUENCY specifying which smaller items each item consists of (the constituency relation is represented in the diagram by the lines), an ORDERING relation specifying the left-to-right arrangement of the nodes, and an assignment of LABELS to the nodes.[8] In the diagrams in 2.1.13, only the TERMINAL nodes (those which have no other items below them) have been explicitly supplied with labels. It will be useful to treat all nodes, nonterminal as well as terminal nodes, as having labels, with the labels on nonterminal nodes corresponding to syntactic categories. The nonterminal nodes here all belong to the same category, namely, 'proposition'; moreover, some of the terminal nodes (those labeled p, q, r, s) also correspond to instances of that category. Let us accordingly modify the diagrams of 2.1.13 slightly by supplying the label S (corresponding to 'proposition')[9] to the nonterminal nodes and by adding nonterminal nodes with that label above each of the 'atomic propositions':

2.1.14   a.   b.

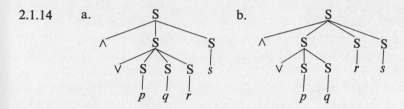

According to the policy adopted in this section, a proposition is a tree, and thus to specify what propositions figure in the fragment of logic presented in this section is to characterize a set of trees. Specifying the membership of that set of trees can be done in a simple fashion by giving rules that say what a node of a given label may have under it, for example, a rule saying that a node labeled S may have under it a node labeled $\supset$ followed by two nodes labeled S (i.e., a proposition may consist of 'if-then' and two propositions). The formulas in 2.1.15 can serve as a 'grammar' for the set of propositions, where the interpretation of each formula is: if a node has the label that precedes the colon, it may have under it nodes labeled as indicated after the colon.

2.1.15 $S: \vee S^n \ (n \geq 2)$ $S: p$
           $S: \wedge S^n \ (n \geq 2)$ $S: q$
           $S: {\sim}S$ $S: r$
           $S: {\supset}S\,S$ $S: s$

                    . . .

The 'grammar' 2.1.15 allows for an arbitrary number of 'atomic propositions', here designated p, q, r, ... Strictly speaking, there is no such thing as an 'atomic proposition': any actual proposition is decomposable into two or more elements of meaning. The 'atomic' propositions here are atomic only relative to the fragment of logic under consideration: they are propositions that are neither a conjunction of propositions nor the negation of a proposition nor a conditional proposition formed from two other propositions.

Rules like those in 2.1.15 are well-formedness conditions on trees. To check whether a given tree is well formed relative to such a 'grammar', one checks whether each nonterminal node has below it nodes that one of the formulas says it may have and whether each terminal node is labeled with a TERMINAL SYMBOL (that is, a symbol other than a category name; in 2.1.15 S is the only nonterminal symbol, and $\vee$, $\wedge$, $\sim$, $\supset$, p, q, r, s, ... are the terminal symbols). For example, in 2.1.14a the terminal nodes have the labels $\wedge$, $\vee$, p, q, r, s, all of which are terminal symbols; the topmost node is labeled S and has under it nodes labeled $\wedge$SS, in that order, and thus conforms to the second rule of 2.1.15, which allows a node labeled S to have under it a node labeled $\wedge$, followed by two or more nodes labeled S; the middle of the three nodes under the topmost node has under it nodes labeled $\vee$SSS, in that order, and thus conforms to the first rule of 2.1.15, which allows a node labeled S to have under it a node labeled $\vee$, followed by two or more nodes labeled S; the four remaining nonterminal nodes conform to other rules of 2.1.15; for example, the first of them conforms to the fifth rule of 2.1.15, since it is labeled S and has under it a node labeled p (and no other nodes). By contrast, the following trees are not well formed relative to the rules of 2.1.15:

2.1.16

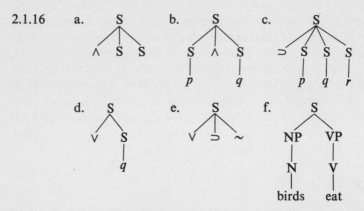

Example 2.1.16a is ill formed, since it has terminal nodes which are not labeled with terminal symbols; of course, addition of, say, a node labeled

p under one of the lower S-nodes and a node labeled *r* under the other one would convert 2.1.16*a* into a well-formed tree. Example 2.1.16*b* is ill formed since it has a ∧ between the two S's that the ∧ is combined with, whereas 2.1.15 only allows a ∧ to precede the S's that it is combined with; of course, had we chosen to write conjunctions between rather than before the conjuncts, we would have set up a different system of formation rules and, relative to *those* rules, 2.1.16*b* would have been well formed. Example 2.1.16*c* is ill formed because the ⊃ is combined with three S's, whereas 2.1.15 only allows it to be combined with two. Example 2.1.16*d* is ill formed because the ∨ is combined with only one S, whereas 2.1.15 only allows ∨ to be combined with two or more S's. Example 2.1.16*e* is ill formed because none of the three 'connectives' is combined with S's, as they are required to be by 2.1.15. Finally, 2.1.16*f* is ill formed relative to 2.1.15 since it involves node labels that do not appear in 2.1.15 (NP, VP, *birds*, *eat*). Of course, if we were to modify 2.1.15 so as to allow English (or Englishlike) expressions rather than *p*'s and *q*'s as the 'atomic propositions', 2.1.16*f* might very well be well formed relative to *those* rules.

Throughout most of the book I will use parenthesized formulas rather than tree diagrams to represent propositions. However, I will regard the parenthesized formulas as only an informal makeshift for representing information that appears more directly in tree diagrams. Actually, to a large extent, parentheses will be unnecessary; for example, the formulas in 2.1.17 can be given a coherent interpretation only if they are assigned the structures in 2.1.18:

2.1.17   a. ⊃ ∧ ~ ∨ *pqpr*
          b. ~ ∧ ⊃ *p* ~ ∨ *qrq*

2.1.18   a.   b.

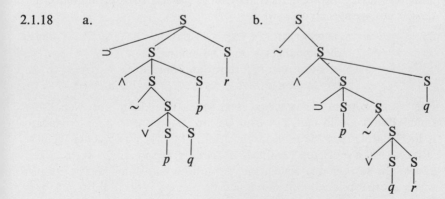

In fact, if conjoining (both *and*-conjoining and *or*-conjoining) were restricted to two conjuncts at a time, parentheses would be unnecessary when the 'connectives' are written before the propositions that they combine with, as they are here; a proof of this claim will be given in 5.4. However, if conjunctions of arbitrarily many conjuncts at a time are allowed, a formula without parentheses could be ambiguous with regard to constituent structure; for example, the formula $\wedge \vee pqrs$ would be ambiguous between the interpretation $\wedge(\vee pq, r, s)$ and the interpretation $\wedge(\vee(p, q, r), s)$, and that ambiguity would be pernicious, since those two interpretations have different truth conditions (for example, falsehood of r would suffice to make the first interpretations false but not the second one). While the possibility of a parenthesis-free notation is of some inherent interest (and such a notation has even been given a name: 'Polish notation' or 'Polish parenthesis-free notation'), the possibility of omitting parentheses is of no particular relevance to the issues treated in this book. Thus, having advised the reader that if conjunctions are restricted to two conjuncts at a time, the notational scheme adopted here is for all practical purposes identical to 'Polish parenthesis-free notation',[10] I will proceed to write parentheses anywhere that they lend clarity to the formulas in question, even when, strictly speaking, they are superfluous.

2.2. Rules of Inference

In the system of propositional logic to be presented in this chapter, there are two 'rules of inference' for each 'connective': one rule for introducing an occurrence of the connective into an inference and one for making use of an occurrence of it that appears in an earlier step of the inference.[11] A simplified version of the two rules for $\wedge$ was given in 2.1.1; the simplification consisted in the fact that the rules given there applied only to conjunctions having two conjuncts. The more general rules of inference that those rules are special cases of are:

2.2.1   a. $\wedge$ -EXPLOITATION. From a proposition $\wedge A_1 A_2 \ldots A_n$, any of the conjuncts A_i may be inferred.

          b. $\wedge$ -INTRODUCTION. From the propositions $A_1, A_2, \ldots, A_n$, the conjunction $\wedge A_1 A_2 \ldots A_n$ may be inferred.

For example, from 'Trivandrum is in India, Bhagdaon is in Nepal, and Luang Prabang is in Laos', $\wedge$ -exploitation allows one to infer 'Bhagdaon is in Nepal'. From the three propositions 'Mantle was a center-fielder', 'Rizzuto was a shortstop', and 'Mize was a first-baseman', $\wedge$ -introduction allows one to infer the conclusion 'Mantle was a center-fielder, Rizzuto was a shortstop, and Mize was a first-baseman'. When used alone, as in these examples, the rules of inference for $\wedge$ seem to be totally trivial, but they often play an important role as steps in more complicated inferences, as may become clear from examples later in this chapter.

The rule of ⊃-EXPLOITATION says that from ⊃AB and A you may infer B. For example, from 'If Socrates is a man, then he is mortal' and 'Socrates is a man', you may infer 'Socrates is mortal'. The rule of ⊃-exploitation is better known by the name of MODUS PONENS; however, I will use the name ⊃-exploitation in this book in order to make clearer the role that this rule of inference plays in the entire system of rules of inference. The rule of ⊃-INTRODUCTION is best introduced via an example:

2.2.2   Whoever committed the murder left by the window.
           Anyone who left by the window would have mud on his shoes.
           Suppose that the butler committed the murder. Then he left by
               the window. In that case, he has mud on his shoes.
           So if the butler committed the murder, he has mud on his
               shoes.

The conclusion of 2.2.2 is of the form ⊃pq (p is 'The butler committed the murder', q is 'The butler has mud on his shoes'). The way that the conclusion is proved is by setting up a subproof in which you suppose p and infer q from that supposition plus whatever propositions have been established up to that point. The structure of the argument 2.2.2 can be displayed in the diagram:

2.2.3   . . .
           . . .
              | p
              |———
              | . . .
              | q
           ⊃pq

The vertical line here marks off the 'subproof' from the whole inference of which it is part. The horizontal line separates the supposition p from the rest of the subproof. An entire inference (or 'proof') can be displayed in the form of such a diagram, and the rules of inference can be taken as giving the conditions under which such a diagram represents a valid inference. Consider, for example, the diagram:

2.2.4   1 ⊃pq
           2 ⊃qr
              ┌────
           3 │ p
              ├────
           4 │ q
           5 │ r
           6 │ ∧qr
           7 ⊃(p, ∧qr)

This would correspond to, say, inferring 'If Greece invades Portugal, then the yen will drop in value and American soybean production will decrease' from the premises 'If Greece invades Portugal, the yen will drop in value' and 'If the yen drops in value, American soybean production will decrease'. Lines 3–6 are the subproof which allows one to infer line 7 as the conclusion of the main proof. Line 4 follows from lines 1 and 3 by ⊃-exploitation. Line 5 follows from lines 2 and 4 by ⊃-exploitation. Line 6 follows from lines 4 and 5 by ∧-introduction. Lines 1 and 2 are suppositions ('premises') of the main proof, and line 3 is a supposition of the subproof.

There is no restriction on what can occur as suppositions of a proof. However, that lack of restriction does not mean that all hell breaks loose. You can make suppositions to your heart's content in subproofs, but all you can get out of them *as conclusions of the main proof* is propositions of the form ⊃AB, where A is the supposition; more generally, a subproof can only terminate via a step in which its supposition(s) is (are) 'discharged', and the rules of inference specify what is possible as such a step. If the supposition is something wild, the conclusion that you will be able to derive will not be particularly interesting (e.g., your conclusion might be 'If all popes have been Zoroastrians, then Pope Innocent II was a Zoroastrian', which isn't a proposition that would be of much use to anyone, despite its being true). Likewise, the freedom to make suppositions in the main proof is quite innocuous: while there is inherent interest in what can be inferred from Euclid's axioms for geometry, there is no particular interest in what can be inferred from the premises 'Bertrand Russell's native language was Kikuyu' and 'All cities of population over 2 million are located in Tierra del Fuego'. A pearl of wisdom from the domain of computer programming is worth quoting here: 'Garbage in, garbage out'.

Diagram 2.2.4 can be 'annotated' as follows to indicate each line's 'justification':

2.2.4′   1 ⊃*pq*   supp
           2 ⊃*qr*   supp

           3 | *p*   supp

           4 | *q*   1, 3, ⊃-expl
           5 | *r*   2, 4, ⊃-expl
           6 | ∧*qr*   4, 5, ∧-intro
           7 ⊃(*p*, ∧*qr*) 3–6, ⊃-intro

A proof may contain several subproofs and may contain subproofs within subproofs. For example, the following proof conforms to the rules of inference given so far:

2.2.5
$$
\begin{array}{lll}
1 & \supset(p, \supset qr) & \text{supp} \\
2 & \quad q & \text{supp} \\
3 & \quad\quad p & \text{supp} \\
4 & \quad\quad \supset qr & 1, 3, \supset\text{-expl} \\
5 & \quad\quad r & 2, 4, \supset\text{-expl} \\
6 & \quad \supset pr & 3\text{--}5, \supset\text{-intro} \\
7 & \supset(q, \supset pr) & 2\text{--}6, \supset\text{-intro}
\end{array}
$$

The rule of $\sim$-EXPLOITATION is simply a rule of cancelling out double negations: from 'it is not the case that not p', one can infer p. It should be emphasized that this rule refers to *double* negation, that is, to a negation of a negation, rather than to just anything that contains two negations. Thus, it doesn't justify your going from $\sim \supset(\sim p, q)$ to $\supset pq$, since $\supset(\sim p, q)$ is not the negation of $\supset pq$, and thus $\sim \supset(\sim p, q)$ is not a double negation.

The rule of $\sim$-INTRODUCTION involves a subproof: you prove $\sim A$ by supposing A and showing that a contradiction follows. For example:

2.2.6   The butler doesn't have mud on his shoes.
             If the butler is the murderer, he left by the window.
             If he left by the window, he has mud on his shoes.
             Suppose the butler is the murderer. Then he left by the window
                 and thus he had mud on his shoes. But he doesn't have mud
                 on his shoes.
             Therefore, the butler isn't the murderer.

The argument which 2.2.6 spells out in such laborious detail can be spelled out equally laboriously in the following graphic form:

2.2.7
$$
\begin{array}{lll}
1 & \sim r & \text{supp} \\
2 & \supset pq & \text{supp} \\
3 & \supset qr & \text{supp} \\
4 & \quad p & \text{supp} \\
5 & \quad q & 2, 4, \supset\text{-expl} \\
6 & \quad r & 3, 5, \supset\text{-expl} \\
7 & \quad \sim r & (= 1) \\
8 & \sim p & 4\text{--}7, \sim\text{-intro}
\end{array}
$$

Arguments in which the conclusion is established by $\sim$-introduction are generally referred to as arguments by REDUCTIO AD ABSURDUM. One step in 2.2.7 is worth mentioning, namely, step 7, in which one of the suppositions of the main proof is repeated. This step fits exactly one of the steps in 2.2.6 and seems reasonable here, since a contradiction involving suppositions of the main proof is just as much a ground for rejecting a proposition as a contradiction involving only matter in the subordinate proof. I will thus assume that there is a rule of inference, called REITERATION, which allows one to repeat any line of a proof as a line of a subproof that occurs later and 'subordinate to' the line in question.

The following are some examples of proofs that conform to the rules of inference given so far:

2.2.8 a. 1 $\supset pq$ supp

2    $\sim q$ supp

3   p supp

4   q 1, 3, $\supset$-expl

5     $\sim q$ 2, reit

6    $\sim p$ 3–5, $\sim$-intro

7 $\supset(\sim q, \sim p)$ 2–6, $\supset$-intro

b. 1 $\sim p$ supp

2    $\wedge pq$ supp

3   p 2, $\wedge$-expl

4    $\sim p$ 1, reit

5 $\sim \wedge pq$ 2–4, $\sim$-intro

c. 1 $\wedge(p, \sim q)$ supp

2    $\supset pq$ supp

3   p 1, $\wedge$-expl

4   q 2, 3, $\supset$-expl

5    $\sim q$ 1, $\wedge$-expl

6 $\sim \supset pq$ 2–5, $\sim$-intro

d. 1 $\sim \supset pq$ supp

2   q supp

3   p supp

4   q 2, reit

5    $\supset pq$ 3–4, $\supset$-intro

6    $\sim \supset pq$ 1, reit

```
 7  ~q                    2–6, ~-intro
 8  | ~p                  supp
 9  |  | p                supp
10  |  |  | ~q            supp
11  |  |  | p             9, reit
12  |  |  | ~p            8, reit
13  |  |  ~~q             10–12, ~-intro
14  |  | q                13, ~-expl
15  | ⊃pq                 9–14, ⊃-intro
16  | ~⊃pq                1, reit
17  ~~p                   8–16, ~-intro
18  p                     17, ~-expl
19  ∧(p, ~q)              7, 18, ∧-intro
```

```
e. 1  p                   supp
   2  ~p                  supp
   3  | ~q                supp
   4  | p                 1, reit
   5  | ~p                2, reit
   6  ~~q                 3–5, ~-intro
   7  q                   6, ~-expl
```

Proofs 2.2.8*a–c* are eminently reasonable results: from 'If *p*, then *q*' you can infer 'If not *q*, then not *p*'; from 'Not *p*' you can infer 'Not both *p* and *q*'; from '*p* and not *q*' you can infer 'It is not the case that if *p* then *q*'. The other two results are much less obviously reasonable. While they conform in all details to the rules of inference given so far, they contain steps that may feel somewhat fishy, and both results are matters of serious controversy in logic and philosophy. The result in 2.2.8*e* is particularly controversial: from contradictory premises you can infer any conclusion whatever. That result can be rationalized in a number of ways; for example, one might say that all a proof is supposed to do is show that in any state of affairs in which the premises are all true, the conclusion is also true, and since there is no state of affairs in which contradictory premises are all true, it is really not saying anything to say that *q* (or anything else you might pick) is true in any state of affairs in which *p* and ~*p* are both true. However, one should not be too hasty in accepting such rationalizations. There remains something quite odd about the conclusion that any contradiction causes *all* hell to break loose; can we not perhaps set things up differently, so that minor contradictions cause only a little bit of hell to break loose? Many attempts have been made in such a direction; the most elaborately worked out is the 'relevant entailment logic' of Anderson and Belnap 1975, sketched below in 10.4.

For the bulk of this book, I will stick to the 'classical' logic which accepts the proof 2.2.8*e* and the rationalizations that go with it. I will confine myself here to noting that the steps in 2.2.8*e* that one could reasonably have doubts about are steps 4–5, in which a higher line is reiterated, and step 6, in which $\sim$-introduction is applied to yield the conclusion. The fishy air that step 6 may give off is related to the fact that the contradiction (lines 4 and 5) has not been inferred FROM the supposition (line 3) that is being 'disproved' by reductio ad absurdum; in fact, line 3 played no role whatever in the derivation of lines 4 and 5. However, it is not at all obvious how one could restrict either reiteration or $\sim$-introduction so as to rule out such steps. Note that in the quite innocuous argument 2.2.7 (see also 2.2.6, of which 2.2.7 is a mechanical formalization), reiteration provided one half of the contradiction that was the basis for the application of $\sim$-introduction. Could one rule out 2.2.8*e* while still allowing 2.2.7 by requiring that at least one of the contradictory lines of a proof by $\sim$-introduction not be derived by reiteration? Such a requirement would in fact change nothing, since it is always possible to add spurious steps that evade the restriction; for example, one could replace lines 4–7 of 2.2.8*e* by the following and thus get an alternative proof in which neither of the contradictory lines was derived by reiteration:

2.2.9   . . .

4	p	1, reit
5	$\sim p$	2, reit
6	$\wedge(p, \sim p)$	4, 5, $\wedge$-intro
7	p	6, $\wedge$-expl
8	$\sim p$	6, $\wedge$-expl
9	$\sim \sim q$	3–8, $\sim$-intro
10	q	9, $\sim$-expl

The result of 2.2.8*d* is also controversial, because of its intimate relationship with another point of controversy, namely, the classical truth table for $\supset$ (to be discussed in detail in chap. 3). According to the classical truth table, $\supset$AB is false when A is true and B false and is true otherwise (i.e., is true when either A is false or B is true), and thus all of the following are true:

2.2.10   a. If Kathmandu is the capital of Nepal, then the Yankees
                won the 1938 World Series.
            b. If Kathmandu is the capital of Denmark, then the Yankees
                won the 1938 World Series.

      c. If Kathmandu is the capital of Denmark, then the
         Milwaukee Brewers won the 1938 World Series.

(I assume here the common knowledge that Kathmandu is the capital of
Nepal and that the Yankees won the 1938 World Series.) If a proposition
and its negation always have opposite truth values and if an *and*-conjunc-
tion is true if and only if all its conjuncts are true, then the result of 2.2.8*d*
forces upon one the controversial part of the truth table for $\supset$: it implies
that $\supset$AB is false *only* when A is true and B false, that is, that $\supset$AB is
true otherwise. A reasonable defence of the classical truth table can be
made by arguing that the sentences of 2.2.10 are misleading rather than
false, in that a person who was in a position to assert any of them would
normally be in a position to assert a more informative proposition (e.g., to
assert that Kathmandu is the capital of Nepal) and would be required to do
so by the rules of sportsmanlike behavior. See chapter 8 for an elaboration
of this argument. However, that ploy cannot so easily dispose of a related
problem raised by 2.2.8*d*, namely, that it commits one to accepting as valid
such bizarre arguments as

2.2.11   It is not the case that if God is dead, life is meaningless.
           Therefore, God is dead.

   One possible way out of the bind raised by 2.2.11 is to hold that *if* is
ambiguous and that the rules of inference given here apply only to one of
its senses, which is not entirely implausible in view of the fact that distinctions among conditional sentences have to be drawn anyway; for example,
one must distinguish the indicative conditional of the valid argument
2.2.12*a* from the counterfactual conditional of the otherwise parallel
invalid argument 2.2.12*b*:

2.2.12   a. If the butler is the murderer, he has blood on his hands.
          Therefore, if the butler doesn't have blood on his hands, he
          isn't the murderer.
      b. If Germany had invaded England, it would have won the
          war.
          ?Therefore, if Germany hadn't won the war, it wouldn't
          have invaded England.

Moreover, the *if* is not too implausible a place to localize the difference
among different kinds of conditional sentences.[12] However, there is no
immediately obvious way of getting that approach to work here, since
there is no apparent difference between the conditional clause of 2.2.11 and
that of 2.2.12*a* that can be held responsible for the oddity of 2.2.11 as an
argument.

Let us drop this matter for the present and return to the survey of rules of inference, though at least keeping in mind the possibility that the 'classical' rules of inference which we will assume may have to be revised in the direction of 'relevant entailment logic' in view of certain relatively bizarre conclusions that they lead to.

The rule of ∨-EXPLOITATION allows one to infer from an *or*-conjunction any proposition that can be inferred from all of the conjuncts. It is illustrated by inferences like the following:

2.2.13   Creepy Calabresi got off the plane in either Chicago, Kansas City, or Las Vegas.
          Suppose he got off in Chicago; then he would have called his brother; but his brother doesn't like Creepy and would have tipped off the Feds.
          Suppose Creepy got off the plane in Kansas City; then he would have called his girlfriend; but his girlfriend is working for the IRS, and she would have tipped off the Feds.
          Suppose Creepy got off the plane at Las Vegas; then he would have called the Fettucini Kid; but the Fettucini Kid has been arrested and the fuzz would have a stoolie taking the phone calls, and he would have tipped off the Feds.
          So someone has tipped off the Feds.

The first premise of this argument is of the form ∨ (p, q, r). There then follow subproofs, one with the supposition p, one with the supposition q, and one with the supposition r. In each case the subproof establishes: 'Someone has tipped off the Feds'. (Actually, the statement of each of the above subproofs stops just short of saying 'Someone has tipped off the Feds'; however, the purpose of each of the subproofs is in fact to establish that). The conclusion is the proposition that is the common conclusion of those subproofs: 'Someone has tipped off the Feds'.

The rule of ∨-INTRODUCTION allows one to infer from any proposition a conclusion which is an *or*-conjunction which has that proposition as one of its conjuncts. Any simple instance of ∨-introduction will sound quite fishy:

2.2.14   Kathmandu is the capital of Nepal.
          Therefore, either Jersey City or Kathmandu or Istanbul is the capital of Nepal.

This sounds fishy simply because the conclusion would be a misleading thing to assert if you already knew the premise: if you know what the capital of Nepal is, it is misleading to say something that suggests you have narrowed it down to three possibilities but (presumably) don't know which one of them is the capital. However, this fishiness vanishes when

$\vee$-introduction is embedded in a larger proof and the proposition to which it applies is not *being asserted*. For example:

2.2.15

1	$\wedge\,(\vee pq, r)$	supp
2	$\vee pq$	1, $\wedge$-expl
3	p	supp
4	r	1, $\wedge$-expl
5	$\wedge pr$	3, 4, $\wedge$-intro
6	$\vee\,(\wedge pr, \wedge qr)$	5. $\vee$-intro
7	q	supp
8	r	1, $\wedge$-expl
9	$\wedge qr$	7, 8, $\wedge$-intro
10	$\vee\,(\wedge pr, \wedge qr)$	9, $\vee$-intro
11	$\vee\,(\wedge pr, \wedge qr)$	2, 3–6, 7–10, $\vee$-expl

Here $\vee$-introduction is used in a quite reasonable inference; for example, the inference would take you from the premise 'He's in either Kansas City or Las Vegas, and he's been arrested' to the conclusion 'Either he's in Kansas City and he's been arrested, or he's in Las Vegas and he's been arrested'. The difference between the fishiness of 2.2.14 and the innocuousness of 2.2.15 can be attributed to the fact that in 2.2.14 $\vee$-introduction was applied to something that had been asserted, whereas in 2.2.15 it was applied (steps 6 and 10) to 'hypothetical' propositions: propositions that are only parts of subproofs and do not serve as lines of the 'main' proof. It thus appears as if $\vee$-introduction is a valid rule of inference (i.e., it does in fact lead to true conclusions when applied to true premises), and the apparent fishiness of certain arguments in which it is used merely reflects the fact that the conclusions that it leads to, while true, are less informative than the premises to which it was applied, and it is misleading to assert something which takes more words to say but is less informative than another thing that you were in a position to assert.

One qualification must be made, relating to a possible ambiguity in the word *or*. The English word *or* can be used both 'inclusively', as in *Shirley visited either Ayuddha or Lopburi last year*, which does not rule out the possibility that she visited both Ayuddha and Lopburi, and 'exclusively', as in *On the $1.25 lunch you can have either a soup or a dessert*, which grants you permission to take one or the other but does not grant you permission to take both a soup and a dessert for your $1.25. Assuming for the moment that it makes sense to distinguish between two 'connectives', an INCLUSIVE OR, which is true when at least one of the conjuncts is true and false otherwise, and an EXCLUSIVE OR, which is true when exactly one of the conjuncts is true and false otherwise, the rule of

∨-introduction given above clearly relates only to inclusive *or*: the truth of one conjunct is enough to insure that an inclusive *or* is true, but all the conjuncts would have to be examined to determine whether an exclusive *or* was true. There is actually some doubt about whether an 'exclusive *or*' has to be recognized; in 8.3, I will present considerations that suggest that English has only an inclusive *or*, and that supposed instances of exclusive *or* are really instances of inclusive *or* whose nature is masked by interactions with other factors. However, I will leave open the question of whether an 'exclusive *or*' must be recognized. In any case, the rule of ∨-introduction given above has to do only with inclusive *or*, not with exclusive *or*, if there is such a thing.

We have now gone through the complete system of rules of inference for propositional logic. The rules can be summarized in graphic form as follows:

2.2.16

∧-introduction
A_1
A_2
. . .
A_n
$\wedge(A_1, A_2, \ldots, A_n)$

∧-exploitation
$\wedge(A_1, A_2, \ldots, A_n)$
A_i $[1 \leq i \leq n]$

∨-introduction
A_i
$\vee(A_1, \ldots, A_n)$ $[1 \leq i \leq n]$

∨-exploitation
$\vee(A_1, A_2, \ldots, A_n)$
A_1
B
. . .
A_n
B
B

~-introduction
A
. . .
B
~B
~A

~-exploitation
~~A
A

⊃-introduction
A
. . .
B
⊃AB

⊃-exploitation
⊃AB
A
B

reiteration

In each of these diagrams, the bottom line indicates what may be inferred from the lines above. The lines prior to the last line need not be consecutive (i.e., other lines can intervene in any proof in which these rules are applied) and need not be in the order given here, though the arrangement into 'main' and 'subordinate' proofs must be as given here. Strictly speaking, the rule of reiteration displayed in 2.2.16 allows one to reiterate a line only into an *immediately* subordinate proof; however, by repeated application of the rule given in 2.2.16 one can duplicate the effect of the reiteration rule in its full glory and reiterate lines down into an arbitrary depth of subordination.

Let us now go through some examples of proofs illustrating the whole system of rules of inference and what can be done with them.

2.2.17   a.   1   ∼(∨ AB)   supp

          2   A   supp

          3   ∨ AB   2, ∨ -intro
          4   ∼ ∨ AB   1, reit
          5   ∼A   2–4, ∼-intro
          6   B   supp

          7   ∨ AB   6, ∨ -intro
          8   ∼ ∨ AB   1, reit
          9   ∼B   6–8, ∼-intro
       10   ∧(∼A, ∼B)   5, 9, ∧-intro

     b.   1   ∧(∼A, ∼B)   supp

          2   ∨ AB   supp

          3   A   supp

          4   ∼A   1, ∧-expl
          5   B   3, 4, 2.2.8*e*
          6   B   supp

          7   B   6, reit
          8   B   2, 3–5, 6–7, ∨ -expl
          9   ∼B   1, ∧-expl
       10   ∼ ∨ AB   2–9, ∼-intro

c. 1 ∨ AB   supp
    2 ~A   supp

    3 │ A   supp
    4 │ ~A   2, reit
    5 │ B   3, 4, 2.2.8e
    6 │ B   supp
    7 │ B   6, reit
    8 B   1, 3–5, 6–7, ∨-expl

The result proved in 2.2.17c is widely known as the DISJUNCTIVE SYLLOGISM and is often given as a rule of inference; while it is not, strictly speaking, a rule of inference of the system of logic adopted here, it is a DERIVED RULE OF INFERENCE, in the sense that it can be simulated by a combination of applications of rules of this system. The proofs given in 2.2.17b and 2.2.17c conform to our rules of inference only in an extended sense, since the justification given for step 5 is not one of the rules of inference; however, since the steps that were carried out in establishing 2.2.8e could have been repeated at the places where 2.2.8e is invoked in these proofs, 2.2.17b and 2.2.17c establish that there are proofs leading from the given premises to the conclusions, with every step conforming to one of the rules in 2.2.16. From here on I will feel free to give 'justifications' such as '2.2.8e' and not distinguish between proofs in which all the steps are spelled out in laborious detail and proofs in which the reader is referred to other proofs in the justification of some step.

2.2.18   a. 1 │ A   supp

            2 │ │ B   supp

            3 │ │ A   1, reit
            4 │ ⊃ BA   2–3, ⊃-intro
            5 ⊃(A, ⊃ BA)   1–4, ⊃-intro

         b. 1 │ ∧(A, ~A)   supp

            2 │ A   1, ∧-expl
            3 │ ~A   1, ∧-expl
            4 ~ ∧(A, ~A)   1–3, ~-intro

         c. 1 │ ~ ∨(A, ~A)   supp

            2 │ ∧(~A, ~~A)   1, 2.2.17a
            3 │ ~A   2, ∧-expl
            4 │ ~~A   2, ∧-expl
            5 ~~ ∨(A, ~A)   1–4, ~-intro
            6 ∨(A, ~A)   5, ~-expl

In 2.2.18 the main proofs have no premises (i.e., the only 'suppositions' are suppositions of subordinate proofs). Thus, the three conclusions have been established 'categorically', in contrast with the proofs in 2.2.17, where the conclusions were proven from the given premises. A conclusion that can be proven categorically in a given system is called a THEOREM of that system. The theorems proven in 2.2.18b and c are well known under the names of the LAW OF NONCONTRADICTION and the LAW OF THE EXCLUDED MIDDLE, respectively.[13]

Note the appropriateness of invoking 2.2.17a in step 2 of 2.2.18c; while 2.2.17a was presented in the form of a derivation of $\wedge(\sim A, \sim B)$ from $\sim \vee AB$, the exact same steps would be carried out even if something else were substituted for A and for B throughout 2.2.17a, in particular, if $\sim A$ were substituted for B, in which case the proof 2.2.17a would become a proof of line 2 of 2.2.18c from line 1.

2.2.19   a.   1 $\wedge(\supset AC, \supset BC)$ supp

2   $\vee AB$ supp

3   A   supp

4   $\supset AC$ 1, $\wedge$-expl

5   C   4, 3, $\supset$-expl

6   B   supp

7   $\supset BC$ 1, $\wedge$-expl

8   C   7, 6, $\supset$-expl

9   C   2, 3–5, 6–8, $\vee$-expl

10   $\supset(\vee AB, C)$ 2–9, $\supset$-intro

b.   1 $\wedge(A, \vee BC)$ supp

2   A   1, $\wedge$-expl

3   $\vee BC$ 1, $\wedge$-expl

4   B   supp

5   $\wedge AB$ 2, 4, $\wedge$-intro

6   $\vee(\wedge AB, \wedge AC)$ 5, $\vee$-intro

7   C   supp

8   $\wedge AC$ 2, 7, $\wedge$-intro

9   $\vee(\wedge AB, \wedge AC)$ 8, $\vee$-intro

10   $\vee(\wedge AB, \wedge AC)$ 3, 4–6, 7–9, $\vee$-expl

Both of the results in 2.2.19 can be turned around: not only can you infer $\supset(\vee AB, C)$ from $\wedge(\supset AC, \supset BC)$, but you can also infer $\wedge(\supset AC, \supset BC)$ from $\supset(\vee AB, C)$; not only can you infer $\vee(\wedge AB, \wedge AC)$ from $\wedge(A, \vee BC)$, but you can also infer $\wedge(A, \vee BC)$ from $\vee(\wedge AB, \wedge AC)$;

the proof of these claims is left to the reader as an exercise. When two expressions can each be inferred from the other, the two expressions are said to be DEDUCTIVELY EQUIVALENT, in view of the fact that if each can be inferred from the other, then anything inferrable from the one is inferrable from the other and anything that the one is inferrable from the other is inferrable from. The proofs in 2.2.17 established that $\sim(\vee AB)$ and $\wedge(\sim A, \sim B)$ are deductively equivalent. The following proofs establish another deductive equivalence that is similar to that proved in 2.2.17; the two deductive equivalences 2.2.17 and 2.2.20 are known together as DE MORGAN'S LAWS.

2.2.20   a.   1 $\sim \wedge AB$ supp

2   $\sim \vee (\sim A, \sim B)$ supp

3   $\wedge(\sim\sim A, \sim\sim B)$ 2, 2.2.17a

4   $\sim\sim A$ 3, $\wedge$-expl

5   $\sim\sim B$ 3, $\wedge$-expl

6   A   4, $\sim$-expl

7   B   5, $\sim$-expl

8   $\wedge AB$ 6, 7, $\wedge$-intro

9   $\sim \wedge AB$ 1, reit

10   $\sim\sim \vee (\sim A, \sim B)$ 2–9, $\sim$-intro

11   $\vee(\sim A, \sim B)$ 10, $\sim$-expl

b.   1 $\vee(\sim A, \sim B)$ supp

2   $\sim A$ supp

3   $\wedge AB$ supp

4   A   3, $\wedge$-expl

5   $\sim A$ 2, reit

6   $\sim \wedge AB$ 3–5, $\sim$-intro

7   $\sim B$ supp

8   $\wedge AB$ supp

9   B   8, $\wedge$-expl

10   $\sim B$ 7, reit

11   $\sim \wedge AB$ 8–10, $\sim$-intro

12   $\sim \wedge AB$ 1, 2–6, 7–11, $\vee$-expl

2.3. Language and Metalanguage

The symbols introduced so far have been the vocabulary of a system of formal logic; that is, the symbols represent various elements of meaning that are parts of the propositions that figure as premises and conclusions of inferences in that system of logic. In this section, I will introduce some symbols that are not part of the system of logic but are part of a METALAN-GUAGE in which one talks about that system of logic.

The first symbol that I will introduce here is ⊢ (read 'turnstile'), which is used in two ways. When ⊢ is put before a formula, what it expresses is that that formula can be proven (that is, that it is a theorem) in the given logical system. Thus, the results that we proved in 2.2.18 of the last section can be expressed as:

2.3.1   a. ⊢⊃(A, ⊃BA)
           b. ⊢∼∧(A, ∼A)
           c. ⊢∨(A, ∼A)

Note that while '∨(A, ∼A)' is a proposition *in* our system of propositional logic, '⊢∨(A, ∼A)' is a proposition *about* that system. The second way in which ⊢ is used is to indicate that a conclusion can be inferred from a given set of premises: to indicate that the conclusion B can be inferred from the premises $A_1, A_2, \ldots, A_n$, one writes $A_1, A_2, \ldots, A_n \vdash B$, or alternatively, $\{A_1, A_2, \ldots, A_n\} \vdash B$.[14] The result proved in 2.2.8e could thus be expressed in either of the forms in 2.3.2:

2.3.2   a. $p, \sim p \vdash q$
           b. $\{p, \sim p\} \vdash q$

It should be emphasized that we are speaking here of inferring the con-clusion from the premises jointly, not inferring it from each one indi-vidually; thus, while 2.3.2 expresses a correct result about our rules of inference, it is not the case that $p \vdash q$ or that $\sim p \vdash q$ in our system. The version of the notation in which the curly brackets are omitted from the list of premises is especially common in cases where there is only one premise. Thus, the de Morgan laws would commonly be expressed as in 2.3.3:

2.3.3   a. ∼∨AB ⊢ ∧(∼A, ∼B)
           b. ∧(∼A, ∼B) ⊢ ∼∨AB
           c. ∼∧AB ⊢ ∨(∼A, ∼B)
           d. ∨(∼A, ∼B) ⊢ ∼∧AB

In view of the rules of ⊃-introduction and ⊃-elimination, the de Morgan laws could be given the following alternative formulation:

2.3.4   a. ⊢⊃(∼∨AB, ∧(∼A, ∼B))
           b. ⊢⊃(∧(∼A, ∼B), ∼∨AB)
           c. ⊢⊃(∼∧AB, ∨(∼A, ∼B))
           d. ⊢⊃(∨(∼A, ∼B), ∼∧AB)

While the results expressed in 2.3.3 and in 2.3.4 are equivalent, one must not confuse ⊢ with ⊃. The sign ⊢ is a symbol of our metalanguage, that is, the language in which we talk about the language that the formation rules and rules of inference have to do with. It makes sense to speak of a formula ⊃AB as being true in a particular state of affairs or as being false in a particular state of affairs. However, it makes no sense to speak of A⊢B as being true *in such-and-such state of affairs*: the truth of A⊢B has nothing to do with states of affairs but with whether the rules of inference of the system of logic in which one is operating allow one to infer B from A. The only direct relationship between ⊢ and ⊃ is the following:

2.3.5   A⊢B if and only if ⊢⊃AB.

The correctness of 2.3.5 follows from the two rules of inference for ⊃: ⊃-introduction in fact says that a proof of B from A constitutes a proof of ⊃AB (thus, if A⊢B, then ⊢⊃AB), and from ⊃-exploitation it follows that if there is a proof of ⊃AB, it can be converted into a proof of B from A as follows:

2.3.6   1   A
                        ─────────
                        . . .
                        . . .   the given proof of ⊃AB
                  n   ⊃AB
                  n+1   B   n, 1, ⊃-expl

and thus, if ⊢⊃AB, then A⊢B.

It should be emphasized that ⊢ refers to provability in the particular logical system under discussion, and a formula can be a theorem relative to one particular system of logic without being a theorem relative to some other system. For example, while ⊃(∧(A, ∼A), B) is a theorem in the 'classical' logic under discussion here, it is not a theorem of the 'relevant entailment logic' that was alluded to briefly in the last section. When there is need to make explicit the system of logic being referred to, this can be done with a subscript on the turnstile. Thus, if C denotes classical propositional logic and E denotes relevant entailment propositional logic, 2.3.7*a* is correct but 2.3.7*b* is incorrect:

2.3.7   a. ⊢$_C$ ⊃(∧(A, ∼A), B)
             b. ⊢$_E$ ⊃(∧(A, ∼A), B)

Two important metatheoretic notions based on the notion of a proposition being proven from a given set of premises are the notions of CONSISTENCY and of INCONSISTENCY. A set of propositions is inconsistent if contradictory propositions can be inferred from it, that is, $\{A_1, A_2, \ldots, A_n\}$ is inconsistent if and only if there is a proposition B such that

$A_1, A_2, \ldots, A_n \vdash B$ and $A_1, A_2, \ldots, A_n \vdash \sim B$. A set of propositions is consistent if and only if it is not inconsistent, that is to say that $\{A_1, A_2, \ldots, A_n\}$ is consistent is to say that for any B for which $A_1, A_2, \ldots, A_n \vdash B$, it is not the case that $A_1, A_2, \ldots, A_n \vdash \sim B$. It should be emphasized that the notion of consistency is relative to a given system of rules of inference. Thus, a set of propositions that is inconsistent with respect to one system of rules of inference could very well be consistent with respect to a 'weaker' system. Since the rules of inference with which we are operating here allow any conclusion whatever to be inferred from contradictory premises (this was proved in 2.2.8e), a set of propositions is inconsistent relative to these rules of inference only if *all* propositions can be inferred from it, that is, a set of propositions is consistent if any only if some propositions cannot be inferred from it.

The symbol $\dashv\vdash$ is a natural choice (though for some reason not widely used) to represent the relation of deductive equivalence, that is, to indicate that the formulas written on either side of it are inferrable from each other. Thus some of the results proven in the last section can be expressed as follows:

2.3.8   a. $\sim(\vee AB) \dashv\vdash \wedge(\sim A, \sim B)$
          b. $\sim(\wedge AB) \dashv\vdash \vee(\sim A, \sim B)$
          c. $\wedge(\supset AC, \supset BC) \dashv\vdash \supset(\vee AB, C)$

Just as a result of the form $A \vdash B$ is equivalent to $\vdash \supset AB$, a result of the form $A \dashv\vdash B$ is equivalent to something in which no premises appear before the $\vdash$, namely, to $\vdash \equiv AB$. This latter formula involves a connective that hitherto has not appeared in this book, the so-called 'biconditional'. $\equiv AB$, traditionally read 'A if and only if B', is definable as $\wedge(\supset AB, \supset BA)$, from which it follows that $A \dashv\vdash B$ if and only if $\vdash \equiv AB$. I have avoided using $\equiv$ since I hold that it does not really match any device of natural language, not even *if and only if*; see 2.6 for further discussion.

A number of additional deductive equivalences can easily be established.

2.3.9a.
$A \dashv\vdash \sim\sim A$

Proof that $A \vdash \sim\sim A$

1	A		supp
2		$\sim A$	supp
3		A	1, reit
4		$\sim A$	2, reit
5	$\sim\sim A$		2–4, $\sim$-intro

Proof that $\sim\sim A \vdash A$

| 1 | $\sim\sim A$ | supp |
| 2 | A | 1, $\sim$-expl |

b.

$\supset AB \dashv\vdash \supset (\sim B, \sim A)$

Proof that $\supset AB \vdash \supset (\sim B, \sim A)$

(see 2.2.8a)

Proof that

$\supset (\sim B, \sim A) \vdash \supset AB$

Left to the reader as an exercise

c.

$\vee AB \dashv\vdash \vee (A, \wedge (\sim A, B))$

Proof that $\vee AB \vdash \vee (A, \wedge (\sim A, B))$

1	$\vee AB$	supp
2	$\vee (A, \sim A)$	2.2.8c
3	$\quad$ A	supp
4	$\quad \vee (A, \wedge (\sim A, B))$	3, $\vee$-intro
5	$\quad \sim A$	supp
6	$\quad\quad$ A	supp
7	$\quad\quad \sim A$	5, reit
8	$\quad\quad \vee (A, \wedge (\sim A, B))$	6, 7, 2.2.8c
9	$\quad\quad$ B	supp
10	$\quad\quad \wedge (\sim A, B)$	5, 9, $\wedge$-intro
11	$\quad\quad \vee (A, \wedge (\sim A, B))$	10, $\vee$-intro
12	$\quad \vee (A, \wedge (\sim A, B))$	1, 6–8, 9–11, $\vee$-expl
13	$\vee (A, \wedge (\sim A, B))$	2, 3–4, 5–12, $\vee$-expl

Proof that

$\vee (A, \wedge (\sim A, B)) \vdash \vee AB$

Left to the reader as an exercise

The notion of deductive equivalence is involved in a principle that often allows one to simplify proofs that would otherwise be very elaborate, namely, the principle that if two formulas are deductively equivalent, either may be substituted for any occurrence of the other. This principle allows one, for example, to cancel out double negations that are deeply embedded in a complex formula, as in the step from 2.3.10a to 2.3.10b:

2.3.10   a. $\supset (\wedge (A, \sim \sim B), C)$
            b. $\supset (\wedge AB, C)$

Since there is another quite distinct substitution principle that has raised its head already, it would be worthwhile to contrast the two principles here before any further proofs appear in which a 'substitution' plays a role.

In line 3 of 2.2.20*a*, we invoked the result 2.3.11*a* to justify the step from
2 to 3 in 2.3.11*b*:

2.3.11   a. $\sim \vee AB \vdash \wedge (\sim A, \sim B)$
            b. 2 $\sim \vee (\sim A, \sim B)$
                3   $\wedge (\sim \sim A, \sim \sim B)$

Line 2 is what you would get from the left half of 2.3.11*a* by substituting
$\sim A$ for A and $\sim B$ for B; line 3 is what you would get by making the same
substitution in the right half of 2.3.11*a*. Example 2.3.11*a* provides justification for the step from line 2 to line 3, since the steps involved in the proof
of 2.3.11*a* are equally valid if some complex proposition stands in place of
A (or of B), just as long as the same expression stands in place of A (or of
B) in the conclusion. This follows from the fact that the rules of inference
are sensitive to what the *immediate* constituents of a formula are (e.g., to
whether the formula is of the form $\supset AB$) but not to what its *ultimate*
constituents are. This principle is not restricted to the replacement of (all
occurrences of) *one* symbol by a given formula: two or more substitutions
can be performed simultaneously (as in the proof under discussion), just as
long as each occurrence of any proposition letter is replaced by the same
formula (e.g., each occurrence of A is replaced by $\sim A$ and each occurrence
of B is replaced by $\sim B$). Note that it is a mistake to speak of 'setting A
equal to $\sim A$' here. Of course, A could not possibly be 'equal to $\sim A$'.
Rather than taking the original letter to be 'equal to' the substituted
formula in any sense, one is merely recognizing that if the substituted
formula had stood in place of that letter in the original proof, the proof
would still have gone through. Let us refer to this substitution principle as
SUBSTITUTION FOR PROPOSITIONAL VARIABLES (SPV).

SPV works quite differently from the principle of SUBSTITUTION OF
DEDUCTIVE EQUIVALENTS (SDE), which, unlike SPV, does involve a kind of
'equality', namely, deductive equivalence. According to SDE, for any two
formulas φ and ψ of arbitrary complexity, if $\varphi \dashv\vdash \psi$, then from any formula
containing an occurrence of φ one may infer the formula obtained by
substituting ψ for that occurrence of φ, as in 2.3.10, where ψ is $\sim \sim B$ and φ
is B. Similarly, SDE allows one to infer 2.3.12*a* from 2.3.12*b*, or vice versa,
on the basis of 2.3.9*b*:

2.3.12   a. $\supset (\supset AB, C)$
            b. $\supset (\supset (\sim B, \sim A), C)$

Let us list the differences between SPV and SDE. (i) In SPV, an atomic
proposition symbol is replaced, whereas in SDE, any constituent may be
replaced, irrespective of its complexity. (ii) In SPV, all occurrences of the
atomic proposition symbol must be replaced, whereas in SDE, different

occurrences of the formula in question can be substituted for or left alone, as one pleases. For example, 2.3.13*b–d* can all be obtained from 2.3.13*a* by SDE:

2.3.13   a. $\supset(\supset AB, \supset(\sim B, \sim A))$
           b. $\supset(\supset(\sim\sim A, B), \supset(\sim B, \sim A))$
           c. $\supset(\supset(\sim\sim A, B), \supset(\sim B, \sim\sim\sim A))$
           d. $\supset(\supset AB, \supset(\sim B, \sim\sim\sim A))$

(iii) In SPV, any formula at all can replace the atomic proposition symbol, whereas in SDE, only a formula deductively equivalent to the given formula may replace it. (iv) SPV is applicable only to the proposition symbols appearing in a theorem $\vdash A$ or in a proven inference $\{B_1, \ldots, B_n\} \vdash A$, whereas SDE is applicable to constituents of any line of a proof. These four remarks have had to do with the applicability of the two principles. To this, let us add a couple of remarks about what it takes to establish the validity of the two principles. First, it is quite easy to show that SPV follows from the given rules of inference, but relatively difficult to show that SDE follows from them. Second, the validity of both principles depends on details of the logical system to which they refer, and thus one cannot blithely assume that they will be valid in all other logical systems. One could not expect, for example, that SDE would be valid in a system of logic that covered not only negation, *if-then*, etc., but also such notions as belief. Note that, given that S_1 is deductively equivalent to S_2 and that Larry believes that S_1, one cannot conclude that Larry believes that S_2: one can hold a belief without recognizing what all its logical consequences are.

2.4. Axiom Versus Rule of Inference Versus Meaning Postulate

In addition to formation rules, rules of inference, and truth conditions, formal treatments of logic often involve what appears to be yet another type of formal apparatus, namely, AXIOMS. For example, the system presented in chapter 5 of Thomason 1970 does without the rules of $\supset$-introduction, $\sim$-introduction, and $\sim$-exploitation but has instead the axioms:[15]

2.4.1   a. $\supset(A, \supset BA)$
           b. $\supset(\supset(A, \supset BC), \supset(\supset AB, \supset AC))$
           c. $\supset(\supset(\sim B, \sim A), \supset AB)$

The role of the axioms in proofs is that any axiom (or rather, any SUBSTITUTION INSTANCE of an axiom, that is, any formula obtainable from an axiom by substituting some formula for all occurrences of A, some formula for all occurrences of B, and some formula for all occurrences of C) may appear at any point in a proof.

There is a large amount of trade-off between axioms and rules of inference. For example, the three formulas 2.4.1a–c are all theorems relative to the rules of inference given earlier in this chapter (we have already given proofs of two of them), which means that if those rules of inference are accepted, there is no need to assume any of the axioms 2.4.1a–c. Conversely, any theorem that can be proven by means of $\supset$-exploitation, $\supset$-introduction, $\sim$-exploitation, and $\sim$-introduction can also be proven by means of $\supset$-exploitation and the axioms 2.4.1a–c (this is in effect proven in Thomason 1970, chapter 5), and thus one could do without three of the rules of inference if one accepts instead the axioms 2.4.1a–c.

I maintain that the difference between 'axiom' and 'rule of inference' is best regarded as one of detail rather than one of general nature: axioms are merely rules of inference that involve no premises. Note that we have seen above both rules of inference that involve one premise ($\vee$-introduction, $\wedge$-exploitation, $\sim$-exploitation) and rules of inference that involve two premises ($\supset$-exploitation, $\wedge$-introduction). The difference between axioms and one-premise rules of inference is comparable to that between one-premise rules of inference and two-premise rules of inference: they differ in regard to how much of the earlier part of the proof plays a role in justifying the line of the proof that is at issue. For a system of rules of inference (including axioms, if any) to be of interest, it will have to include rules that have premises, since otherwise all that could be derived would be substitution instances of axioms, which would not be a very interesting system of inference; indeed, it will have to include at least one rule of inference that has more than one premise, since if there were only zero-premise and one-premise rules of inference, the kinds of interactions between premises that provide both the fun and the glory of logic would not be possible. However, given that there are rules of inference with more than one premise, there is a great deal of freedom in how much of the inferential apparatus of the system one chooses to embody in the form of zero-premise rules (= axioms) and how much in the form of rules that refer to premises. For example, it will not particularly matter whether we have the rule of $\sim$-exploitation or the axiom $\supset(\sim\sim A, A)$, provided that we have the rules of $\supset$-introduction and $\supset$-exploitation available.

Different sets of rules of inference (including axioms, if any) thus may perfectly well sanction exactly the same inferences. In that event the rules of either system will be DERIVATIVE rules of the other system; that is, the effect of any rule of the one system can be replicated by a series of applications of the rules of the other system, and any proof in the one system can be converted into a proof of the other system by replacing each step by the corresponding sequence of applications of the rules of the other system. The difference between 'basic' and 'derivative' rules of inference is thus somewhat arbitrary. The only real advantage of the choice I have made about what rules of inference to take as basic is the relatively systematic structure of the set of rules presented here: aside from the rule of reiteration what we have is for each connective a rule saying how to use premises that contain it and a rule saying how to derive conclusions that contain it. By contrast, the three axioms 2.4.1a–c simply appear to give fairly esoteric properties of $\supset$ and $\sim$ which are not correlated with obvious functions in constructing inferences, although in reality 2.4.1 plus $\supset$-elimination justifies exactly the same inferences as do the rules for introduction and elimination of $\supset$ and $\sim$ given earlier in this chapter.

The term MEANING POSTULATE also occasionally occurs in expositions of the details of a logical system (e.g., Carnap 1956:222–29). The term has generally been used in connection with 'nonlogical elements' that might play a role in a formal analysis. For example, one might encounter the 'meaning postulate' 2.4.2 in an analysis in which propositions of the form 'x knows A' play a role:

2.4.2 $\supset$(Know x A, A).

Meaning postulates are supposed to supply steps in inferences that follow from the meaning of the 'nonlogical element' in question (here, the fact that you can only know a proposition which is true, as contrasted with the fact that you can believe false propositions as well as true ones). The distinction between meaning postulate and rule of inference is only as good as the difference between 'nonlogical element' and 'logical element', which is to say that it is far from clear that the difference has any substance. Rules of inference can be thought of as meaning postulates for the 'logical elements'; that is, they distinguish among the various 'logical elements' on the basis of characteristics of their roles in inference that are associated with their meanings. I will avoid the term 'meaning postulate' on the grounds that it is superfluous and creates pseudoproblems regarding the application of the term 'meaning'. 'Meaning postulates' are not strictly speaking parts of the meanings of the elements involved. Any logical system will provide a set of 'primitive' elements which figure in its logical structures, and those elements are the 'elements of meaning'. The 'meaning postulates' can distinguish among those elements of meaning, much as facts about the location and population of cities can distinguish among the meanings of the words *Vienna*, *Brussels*, and *Istanbul*, although the fact that Vienna is on the Danube is not part of the meaning of the word *Vienna*.

2.5. On the Structure of Proofs

Consider the following illegitimate variant of the proof given in 2.2.15:

2.5.1

1	$\wedge(\vee pq, r)$	supp
2	$\vee pq$	1, $\wedge$-expl
3	p	supp
4	r	1, $\wedge$-expl
5	$\wedge pr$	3, 4, $\wedge$-intro
6	$\vee(\wedge pr, \wedge qr)$	5, $\vee$-intro
7	q	supp
8	p	5, $\wedge$-expl
9	$\dots$	

Where the proof goes from that point on doesn't particularly matter. What I wish to call attention to is the illegitimacy of step 8: it makes reference to a part of the proof that has nothing to do with the subproof to which step 8 belongs. Line 8 belongs to a subproof with the supposition q; line 5 belongs to a subproof with the supposition p and that subproof does not contain the one in which line 8 occurs. The same illegitimacy is found in the following argument:

2.5.2   Creepy Calabresi got off the plane either in Las Vegas or in LA.
          Suppose he got off in Las Vegas; then he called the Fettucini
          Kid and the Fettucini Kid tipped off the feds.
          Suppose he got off in LA; since the Fettucini Kid tipped off the
          Feds, they must have been waiting for him at the airport.

In a legitimate proof based on $\vee$-exploitation, you are considering two or more alternatives separately, and what happens in one of those alternative states of affairs need not be the case in other alternatives; for example, what happens if Creepy Calabresi gets off the plane in Las Vegas need not be the same as what happens if he gets off in LA.

The statements of the various rules of inference in this chapter have been deficient in that they have not been explicit about the structure of the proofs in which the rules apply. A proof has a structure, and the rules of inference must respect that structure. It will be useful to have a term for the structural relation that rules of inference are sensitive to, and there is in fact a term current among linguists that can without much stretching be made to cover the relation in question: COMMAND.[16] Let us revise the syntactician's notion of command, which relates to a structure of sentences embedded in larger sentences, so that it will instead relate to a structure of proofs embedded in larger proofs: we will say that one line x of a proof commands another line y if the (sub)proof of which x is an IMMEDIATE CONSTITUENT[17] contains y. For example, in 2.5.3 (which was given as 2.2.19a), line 2 commands lines 2 through 9, line 3 commands lines 3 through 5, line 8 commands lines 6 through 8, and line 1 commands all the lines of the proof.

2.5.3

1	$\wedge(\supset AC, \supset BC)$		supp
2		$\vee AB$	supp
3		A	supp
4		$\supset AC$	1, $\wedge$-expl
5		C	4, 3, $\supset$-expl
6		B	supp
7		$\supset BC$	1, $\wedge$-expl
8		C	7, 6, $\supset$-expl
9		C	2, 3–5, 6–8, $\vee$-expl
10	$\supset(\vee AB, C)$		2–9, $\supset$-intro

Since the various rules of inference refer not only to earlier lines but also to earlier subproofs, it will be necessary to generalize the notion of command so that one can also speak of a subproof commanding a line, or a line commanding a subproof, or a subproof commanding a subproof. Specifically: a line or subproof commands all lines or subproofs which are contained in the (sub)proof that that line or subproof is an immediate constituent of.[18] To rule out absurd 'proofs' like 2.5.1 and 2.5.2, one must impose the following condition:

2.5.4   The 'justification' of any line in a proof can make reference only to lines and subproofs that both precede and command it.

Of the lines and subproofs that precede a given line, those that do not command it are those that are irrelevant to it by virtue of belonging to a subproof to which the given line does not belong. The formal structure of a proof can be displayed in a tree diagram, as in the following representation of the structure of 2.5.3:

2.5.5

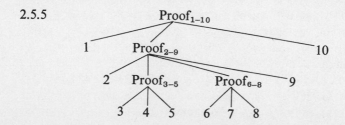

The lines and subproofs that a particular line or subproof commands are those that can be reached from it by tracing up until one hits a node labeled 'Proof' and then downward by any amount; for example, line 2 commands all those lines and proofs that one can reach by tracing downward from 'Proof$_{2-9}$': Proof$_{3-5}$, Proof$_{6-8}$, and lines 2–9.[19]

2.6. More on *If*

Elementary logic texts commonly contain statements to the effect that 'If A, then B' can be paraphrased by 'A only if B', as when Quine (1962:41) says, 'But whereas "if" is thus ordinarily a sign of the antecedent, the attachment of "only" reverses it; "only if" is a sign of the consequent'. Thus the student is generally directed to assign the same logical form to pairs of sentences such as:

2.6.1   a.   If all men are mortal, then Aristotle is mortal.
           a'. All men are mortal only if Aristotle is mortal.

           b.   If a set has only finitely many subsets, it is finite.
           b'. A set has only finitely many subsets only if it is finite.

While it is reasonable to regard 2.6.1*a* and 2.6.1*a'*, or 2.6.1*b* and 2.6.1*b'*, as merely variant ways of expressing the same idea, it is in fact not at all easy to find pairs of sentences like 2.6.1*a* and *b*, where a sentence 'If A, then B' and a sentence 'A only if B' sound equally normal and appear to express the same thing. Consider the following sample pairs of sentences in which 'If A, then B', and 'A only if B' are not interchangeable:

2.6.2   a.   If you're boiled in oil, you'll die.
           a'. You'll be boiled in oil only if you die.[20]

           b.   If Mike straightens his tie once more, I'll kill him.
           b'. Mike will straighten his tie once more only if I kill him.

           c.   If butter is heated, it melts.
           c'. Butter is heated only if it melts.

           d.   If Pittsburgh won the 1971 World Series, I've lost my bet.
           d'. ?Pittsburgh won the 1971 World Series only if I've lost my
                bet.

           e.   If we're having fish, we should order white wine.
           e'. ?We're having fish only if we should order white wine.

           f.   If you're insured, you have nothing to worry about.
           f'. ?You're insured only if you have nothing to worry about.

2.6.3   a. I'll leave only if you have somebody to take my place.
           a'. If I leave, you('ll) have somebody to take my place.

           b. My pulse goes above 100 only if I do heavy exercise.
           b'. If my pulse goes above 100, I do heavy exercise.

           c. You're in danger only if the police start tapping your
              phone.
           c'. If you're in danger, the police (will) start tapping your
              phone.

In 2.6.2, a perfectly normal sentence 'If A, then B' is paralleled by a
(grammatically or factually) bizarre sentence 'A only if B'. Note that in
many cases the sentence with *only if* reverses the temporal or causal
relations expressed by the sentence with *if*. For example, 2.6.2a refers to
death that results from one's being boiled in oil, whereas 2.6.2a' refers to
boiling in oil taking place after one's death. In 2.6.3 it is the sentence with
only if that is normal and the sentence with *if* that is bizarre.

While 'If A, then B' is thus often a poor paraphrase of 'A only if B',
'If not B, then not A' is generally a rather good paraphrase of it; compare
2.6.3a, b, and c with:

2.6.4   a. If you don't have somebody to take my place, I won't leave.
           b. If I don't do heavy exercise, my pulse doesn't go above 100.
           c. If the police don't start tapping your phone, you're not in
              danger.

The fact that *If not B, then not A* is so much better a paraphrase than is
If A, then B is a bit surprising since the logical formulas that those two
sentence forms correspond most directly to are deductively equivalent
according to the rules of inference of this chapter:

2.6.5 $\supset AB \dashv\vdash \supset (\sim B, \sim A)$

However, in the cases given in 2.6.3, the law of 'contraposition' 2.6.5
appears to fail (e.g., 2.6.4a ≠ 2.6.4a'), and this fact suggests that either the
logical system should be revised so that 2.6.5 does not hold (or holds only
in a restricted class of cases) or ordinary *if* should not be identified with $\supset$.

In view of the fact that *only* behaves syntactically like a negative (2.6.6a,
b) by virtue of serving as the 'trigger' for 'negative polarity items' such as
any and *give a hoot* and in view of the fact that *only* can be paraphrased by
expressions involving two negatives in combinations such as *No X other
than Y* (see 2.6.7), the fact that *Not A if not B* is so much better a paraphrase
of *A only if B* than is *If A, then B* (or *B if A*) suggests that one should search
for an analysis of *A only if B* in which the *only* is identified with the ordinary *only* of sentences such as 2.6.7a and b, with the *only* in turn being

analyzed in terms of a structure involving two negatives that can be combined with *if B* as well as with NP's:

2.6.6   a. Only John said anything.
           a'. *John said anything.

           b. Only your wife gives a hoot about what happens to you.
           b'. *Your wife gives a hoot about what happens to you.

2.6.7   a. John read only the first chapter.
           a'. John read nothing other than the first chapter.

           b. Only Susan has a key to this room.
           b'. No one other than Susan has a key to this room.

Since expressions such as *only if, even if, except if,* and *especially if* appear to be immediately intelligible to anyone who knows the words of which they are composed (i.e., they are in no sense idioms), an analysis in which *only if* is treated as ordinary *only* plus ordinary *if* seems to be inescapable. Note that the logicians' standard analysis, in which *only if* is regarded as simply the converse of *if*, involves treating *only if* as an idiom, since *only* does not otherwise mean 'converse'; for example 2.6.8*a* cannot be paraphrased as 2.6.8*b*:

2.6.8   a. Bill only kissed Betty.
           b. Betty kissed Bill.

However, if *if* is treated as simply a sentential connective, on a par with *and* and *or*, the relationship of the *only* to the *if* cannot be exactly parallel to the relationship of the *only* to the NP in 2.6.7*a* and *b*, since while 2.6.7*b* (= 2.6.9*a*) implies 2.6.9*a'*, 2.6.9*b* does not imply 2.6.9*b'* or 2.6.9*b"*:

2.6.9   a. Only Susan has a key to this room.
           a'. It is not the case that Tom has a key to this room.

           b. I'll leave only if you ask me to.
           b'. It is not the case that I'll leave and you'll ask me to.
           b". It is not the case that I'll leave or you'll ask me to.

This is obvious, since 2.6.9*b* clearly allows for the possibility that you will ask me to leave and I will leave, whereas 2.6.9*b'–b"* do not.

In 9.3, I will explore briefly an analysis of *if* that appears to allow *if* to combine in the appropriate way with *only*, etc. In that analysis, which was proposed by Geis (1973), who also notes that it provides the solution to the problem of accounting for *only if*, etc., *if* is analyzed as 'in cases in which' (e.g., *If Bill comes tomorrow, I'll give him the books* would be analyzed as 'In (all) cases in which Bill comes tomorrow, I'll give him the books'), which allows *only if* to be analyzed as 'only in cases in which' (here, *I'll give Bill the books only if he comes tomorrow* = 'I'll give Bill the books only in cases in which he comes tomorrow' = 'I won't give Bill the books in cases other than those in which he comes tomorrow'). The notion of 'case' that figures in these paraphrases is heavily context-dependent: the 'cases' over which the quantifier ranges are those states of affairs that are relevant in the appropriate way to the given utterance. The logician's ⊃ can be interpreted as involving a degenerate notion of 'case': that in which the only 'case' considered is the actual state of affairs. (While I support Geis's analysis of conditionals as more realistic than the analysis given in standard logic, I will nonetheless operate in terms of the ⊃ of standard logic throughout most of this book).

Some experimental data summarized in Braine 1978 support the claim that *A only if B* should be identified with *Not A if not B* (or *If not B, then not A*) rather than with *If A, then B*. Wason and Johnson-Laird (1972) have demonstrated sharp differences between subjects' abilities to evaluate 'modus ponens' arguments 2.6.10*a* and 'modus tollens' arguments 2.6.10*b*:

2.6.10   a. If A, (then) B   b. If A, (then) B
              A   Not B
              Therefore, B   Therefore, not A.

Specifically, when asked to judge arguments for validity, subjects usually make few errors and give rapid responses for modus ponens arguments but make many errors and give slower responses for modus tollens arguments. Braine replicated Wason and Johnson-Laird's experiments but included not only stimuli of the form 2.6.10 but also stimuli in which the first premise takes the form *A only if B*. He reports that with the latter stimuli, the difference between modus ponens and modus tollens is eliminated or reversed. But note that what Braine here calls modus ponens is an instance of modus tollens under the analysis of *only if* sketched above, and what he calls modus tollens is an instance of modus ponens:

2.6.11   a. A only if B (= Not A if not B)
              A
              Therefore, B.
           b. A only if B (= Not A if not B)
              Not B
              Therefore, not A.

Thus, if one of the two should yield faster and more accurate responses, it should be 2.6.11*b*, though the difference should be less sharp because of the less transparent relationship between the sentences and their logical forms.

The differences noted above between *If A, then B* and *If not B, then not A* also manifest themselves when one considers sentences involving the expression *if and only if*. I maintain that *A if and only if B* is exactly what the words suggest it is: the conjunction of *A if B* and *A only if B*. In view of what I argued above, 2.6.12*a* ought to be better paraphrased by 2.6.12*c–c'* than by 2.6.12*b*:

2.6.12   a. A if and only if B.
              b. If A, then B, and if B, then A.
              c. If not B, then not A, and if B, then A.
              c'. If B, then A, and if not B, then not A.

This prediction is borne out by examples formed on the analogy of 2.6.2 and 2.6.3:

2.6.13   a. I'll leave if and only if you have someone to take my place.
              a'. If I leave, you'll have someone to take my place, and if you have someone to take my place, I'll leave.
              a". If you have someone to take my place, I'll leave, and if you don't have anyone to take my place, I won't leave.

              b. My pulse goes above 100 if and only if I do heavy exercise.
              b'. If my pulse goes above 100, I do heavy exercise, and if I do heavy exercise, my pulse goes above 100.
              b". If I do heavy exercise, my pulse goes above 100, and if I don't do heavy exercise, my pulse doesn't go above 100.

              c. Butter melts if and only if it is heated.
              c'. If butter melts, it is heated, and if butter is heated, it melts.
              c". If butter is heated, it melts, and if butter is not heated, it doesn't melt.

The third sentence of each group is in each instance an excellent paraphrase of the first sentence. The second sentence of each group is at best a paraphrase of an extra interpretation that the first sentence allows, over and above its most obvious interpretation.

It follows from these observations that the expression *if and only if* is ASYMMETRIC, that is, that *A if and only if B* is not interchangeable with *B if and only if A*: while 2.6.12*b* is symmetric with respect to A and B (i.e., if you interchange A and B, the result is essentially the same as what you started with), 2.6.12*c* is not. This conclusion is likewise borne out by the facts. Note the result of interchanging A and B in 2.6.13*a*, *b*, and *c*:

2.6.14   a. You'll have someone to take my place if and only if I leave.
            b. I do heavy exercise if and only if my pulse goes above 100.
            c. Butter is heated if and only if it melts.

In each case the temporal and/or causal relations between the two clauses are the reverse of what they were in 2.6.13*a*, *b*, and *c*. For example, 2.6.13*b* treats the exercise as the cause of the rise in your pulse, whereas 2.6.14*b* makes it sound as if a prior change in your pulse is the reason for which you do heavy exercise (perhaps because of the mistaken belief that doing heavy exercise will lower your pulse).

I thus take it as unfortunate that logicians have generally identified the expression *if and only if* with a putative logical connective (most frequently written with the symbol $\equiv$) which is symmetric both syntactically (i.e., $\equiv$AB $\dashv\vdash \equiv$BA) semantically (i.e., the truth conditions are symmetric: $\equiv$AB is true if A and B have the same truth value and is false if they have different truth values). While these properties are in fact possessed by the formula that is most often offered as a 'definition' of $\equiv$AB, namely, $\wedge(\supset$AB, $\supset$BA), it is highly questionable that those properties carry over to the English expression *if and only if* (or its counterparts in other languages, e.g., German *wenn und nur wenn*), with which it is generally equated.

2.7. Exercises

1. Represent the meanings of the following sentences in the notational scheme used in this chapter, indicating what you take $p, q, \ldots$ to stand for in each case.

   a. They won't catch me if I keep quiet.
   b. If you quit, then I'll quit if they don't hire someone else.
   c. Tom will quit if they don't promote him, and if Tom doesn't quit, Bert will ask for a transfer.

2. For each of the following arguments, (i) translate the premises and conclusion into the notational system used in this chapter, to the extent that that is possible, (ii) state whether the conclusion follows from the premises or not, according to the rules of inference given here, and (iii) if the conclusion does in fact follow from the premises, spell out in detail how it can be derived from the premises by means of the rules of inference of this chapter.

   a. If Sam lives in Manhattan, he doesn't have a car. Sam has a car. Therefore, Sam doesn't live in Manhattan.

b. Today is either Saturday or Sunday. If today is Sunday, there isn't any mail delivery today. So if there's a mail delivery today, it's Saturday.
c. If the attorney general is a burglar, then if the postmaster general is an embezzler, the president is a dolt. Therefore, if the postmaster general is an embezzler and the president isn't a dolt, the attorney general isn't a burglar.
d. All men are mortal. Socrates is a man. Therefore, Socrates is mortal.
e. If federal spending increases and taxes don't go up, there will be inflation. If there is inflation, a lot of congressmen will be defeated in the next election. Therefore, if taxes go up, not many congressmen will be defeated in the next election.

3. In the notational schemes used in most publications on logic, $\vee$, $\wedge$, and $\supset$ are written between rather than before the items that they combine with. Convert the following formulas in the most direct way possible from that notational scheme into the one used here.

a. $(A \wedge B) \supset (\sim C \vee \sim D)$
b. $A \vee (B \vee (C \vee D))$
c. $(A \wedge (C \supset \sim B)) \supset (\sim B \supset (\sim A \vee C))$

4. Supply details of proofs showing that

a. $\vee AA \vdash A$
b. $\supset (\sim B, \sim A) \vdash \supset AB$
c. $\vee (A, \wedge (\sim A, B)) \vdash \vee AB$
d. $\vee AB \vdash \vee (A, \wedge (\sim A, B))$
e. $\supset (A, \supset BC) \vdash \supset (\supset AB, \supset AC)$
f. $\sim A \vdash \sim (\wedge AB)$
g. $\supset AB \vdash \supset (\wedge AC, \wedge BC)$

5. For each of the following sentences, either sketch how the conjoined constituents might plausibly be derived from conjoined clauses by conjunction reduction, or provide reasons for maintaining that they cannot plausibly be derived from conjoined clauses.

a. He wept and wept.
b. John invited Bill and either Maureen or Sheila.
c. All work and no play makes Jack a dull boy.
d. Tom promised Cheryl a fur coat and a diamond ring.
e. How much is five and three?

6. Suppose that the rule of ∼-introduction given in this chapter were replaced by the following rule of inference:

(i.e., you may infer ∼A if the supposition A leads to a conclusion that contradicts something you have already established). Find a proof in chapter 2 that would be invalid under this version of. ∼-introduction, and say explicitly why the proof would fail.

Show that A ⊢∼ ∼A even with this weakened version of ∼-introduction.

3. Propositional Logic II: Semantics

3.1. Truth Tables

Logicians have generally held $\wedge$, $\vee$, $\sim$, and $\supset$ to be TRUTH-FUNCTIONAL; that is, they have held that to tell whether $\wedge$AB (likewise, $\vee$AB, $\sim$A, $\supset$AB) is true, all one needs to know is whether A is true and whether B is true. Specifically, they have held that the relationship between the truth-value of a complex proposition and the truth-values of its constituents is given by the following TRUTH TABLES:

3.1.1

A	~A
T	F
F	T

A	B	$\wedge$AB	$\vee$AB	$\supset$AB
T	T	T	T	T
T	F	F	T	F
F	T	F	T	T
F	F	F	F	T

We assume here that every proposition is either true or false (in chapter 9 we will consider a way in which this assumption might be relaxed and propositions allowed sometimes to be neither true nor false). Each line of the truth table corresponds to a possible combination of truth values for the constituent propositions. Except for the column corresponding to $\supset$, these truth tables are not particularly controversial. They say that (i) a proposition and its negation have opposite truth-values, (ii) an *and*-conjunction is true when both (more generally, all) of its conjuncts are true, and false when at least one of its conjuncts is false, (iii) an *or*-conjunction is true when at least one of its conjuncts is true, and false when both (more generally, all) of them are false, and (iv) an *if-then* proposition is false when the antecedent is true and the consequent false, and is true otherwise.

The claim iv is a bit hard to swallow: it means that not only do the sentences in 3.1.2 count as true, which is reasonable, but so do those of

57

3.1.3, which isn't so reasonable:

3.1.2   a. If 6 is an even number, then 7 is an odd number.
             b. If 3 is an even number, then 6 is an even number.
             c. If 3 is an even number, then 4 is an odd number.

3.1.3   a. If 6 is an even number, then Kathmandu is in Nepal.
             b. If 6 is an odd number, then Kathmandu is in Nepal.
             c. If Kathmandu is in Denmark, then Lima, Peru, is farther
                 west than Miami.[1]

The following alternatives are open to one: either deny that $\supset$ is truth-functional and allow some instances of $\supset$AB to be true and others false in the cases where the truth table has T (e.g., treat 3.1.2*a* as true and 3.1.3*a* as false, even though in both cases the antecedent is true and the consequent true), or accept the standard truth table and attribute the oddity of such sentences as 3.1.3 to something other than falsehood. For example, Grice has argued that sentences like those in 3.1.3 are really true, but that it would not be normal behavior for a person to assert them, since if one had the knowledge necessary to know that they were true, one could say something more informative without exerting oneself to any greater extent (e.g., if you know that 6 is an even number and that Kathmandu is in Nepal, you could be more informative to your hearers by asserting either of those propositions separately than by asserting 3.1.3*a*). A third alternative, namely, that $\supset$ is truth-functional but has a different truth table from the standard one, can be rejected outright. The second line has to be F, since if $\supset$AB were true in that case, it would be possible to infer a false conclusion (B) from true premises ($\supset$AB and A) by $\supset$-exploitation (and if there is any rule of inference that we must retain at all costs, it is $\supset$-exploitation). If $\supset$ is to be truth-functional and to be in reasonable accord with ordinary language, the first and last lines had better well both be T, since ordinary language abounds in cases in which A and B are both true and in cases in which A and B are both false (e.g., 'If the butler is the murderer, he left before 10:00. But he didn't leave until 10:45, so . . .'), where 'If A, then B' is accepted as true. Thus, if $\supset$ is to be truth-functional, the only place where it could conceivably diverge from the standard table is the case where A is false and B true. However, if $\supset$AB were uniformly false in that case, then $\supset$AB and $\supset$BA would be true under exactly the same circumstances, namely, when A and B agreed in truth value. There would then be a serious mismatch between rules of inference and truth conditions: with regard to truth conditions, $\supset$ would be symmetric (i.e., you could always interchange antecedent and consequent without changing the truth value of the whole proposition), whereas with regard to inference, $\supset$ is asymmetric, that is, you can infer different things from $\supset$ AB than you can infer from $\supset$ BA.[2] (For example, from 'If Joe is married, he's over 21' and 'Joe is married', you can infer 'Joe is over 21'; however, from 'If Joe is over 21, then he's married' and 'Joe is married', you can't infer 'Joe is over 21').

The following argument provides further reason for saying that if $\supset$ is truth-functional, its truth conditions must conform to the standard truth table. The following three assumptions are reasonably noncontroversial: (i) from a 'universal' proposition one can infer all of the 'special cases' of that proposition (e.g., from 'All men are mortal' one can infer 'Frank Sinatra is mortal', 'Gordon Liddy is mortal', 'Evel Knievel is mortal', etc.); (ii) 3.1.4 is true:

3.1.4   If a person is over 6′8″ tall, he has trouble buying clothes.

(iii) Example 3.1.4 is a 'universal' proposition in which 'If x is over 6′8″ tall, then x has trouble buying clothes' is applied to all persons. Under these assumptions, the following conclusions can be inferred from 3.1.4 and are thus true:

3.1.5   a. If Wilt Chamberlain is over 6′8″ tall, he has trouble buying clothes.
          b. If Max Abramowitz is over 6′8″ tall, he has trouble buying clothes.
          c. If Angel Gonzales is over 6′8″ tall, he has trouble buying clothes.

Wilt Chamberlain is about 7 feet tall and has trouble buying clothes; thus 3.1.5a is a true conditional in which both antecedent and consequent are true. Max Abramowitz is 5′3″ tall, weighs 380 pounds, and has arms that reach down to his knees, and accordingly he has trouble buying clothes; thus 3.1.5b is a true conditional in which the antecedent is false and the consequent true. Finally, Angel Gonzales is 5′6″ tall, weighs 130 pounds, and has no trouble whatever in buying clothes; thus 3.1.5c is a true conditional in which both antecedent and consequent are false. Moreover, the facts that I have just cited about Wilt Chamberlain, Max Abramowitz, and Angel Gonzales are clearly consistent with 3.1.4. But then for every line where the standard truth table for $\supset$ has T, there are conditionals that conform to that line of the table (and must conform to it if assumptions i–iii are to be maintained), and consequently, if $\supset$ is truth-functional, its truth table must be the standard one.

In 3.2 and in 9.3 and 10.4, I will discuss in some detail the possibility that $\supset$ is not truth-functional. For the time being, however, let's assume that it is truth-functional and, since any other truth table would entail even stranger conclusions than does the standard one, that its truth table is the standard one. We have already accepted the idea that the other three connectives of propositional logic are truth-functional. There is then a mechanical procedure whereby one can determine the truth value of any complex proposition of propositional logic, given the truth values of the atomic propositions. For example, suppose that p is true, q false, r true, and s false. Consider the proposition

3.1.6

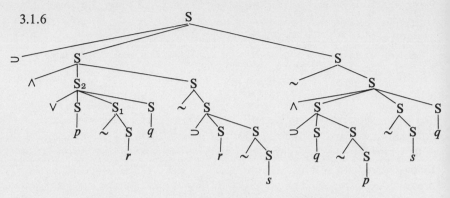

The truth value of 3.1.6 can be determined by starting from the bottom of the tree and working one's way up, attaching a truth value to each S-node on the basis of the truth values associated with the nodes that it directly dominates. For example, since r is T, the truth value associated with S_1 in 3.1.6 would be F, and since S_2 is then an *or*-conjunction of propositions that are T, F, and F, respectively, S_2 would be T. The computation may be facilitated by writing the T's and F's on the diagram as one does the computation:

3.1.7

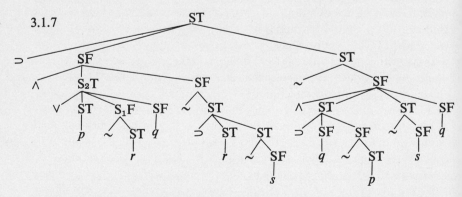

The same steps can be carried out using a linear representation instead of a tree diagram, by writing a truth value under each connective to indicate

the truth value of the constituent composed of that connective and whatever it is combined with:

3.1.8 $\supset(\sim p, \wedge(q, \sim \supset pq))$
           T FT F F T F TF

The order of the steps in this computation is as indicated in 3.1.9:

3.1.9 $\supset(\sim p, \wedge(q, \sim \supset pq))$
       0   T   F   TF
       1   F   F
       2   T
       3   F
       4 T

3.2. How do the Rules of Inference Constrain Truth Values?

Rules of inference are supposed to lead to true conclusions when applied to true premises. Let us assume that the rules of inference that were presented in chapter 2 do what they are supposed to do. Then some sharp constraints are imposed on the relationship between the truth value of a complex proposition and the truth values of its constituents. For example, $\wedge$ must conform to the standard truth table if $\wedge$-introduction and $\wedge$-exploitation are to lead from true premises to true conclusions. When A and B are both true, $\wedge$AB must also be true, since it is inferrable from them (by $\wedge$-introduction) and since, by assumption, the given rules of inference yield true conclusions when applied to true premises. If either or both of A and B is false, then $\wedge$AB must be false, since if it were true one could infer a false conclusion (A or B, as the case may be) from a true premise ($\wedge$AB) by $\wedge$-exploitation. Thus, if the given rules of inference lead to true conclusions when applied to true premises, $\wedge$ must be truth-functional and indeed conform to the standard truth table. (It is easy to generalize this argument so that it covers $\wedge$-conjunctions of arbitrarily many conjuncts: if the given rules of inference always yield true conclusions when applied to true premises, then an *and*-conjunction must be true when all of the conjuncts are true and must be false when one or more of the conjuncts are false).

The fact that the rules of inference force $\wedge$ to be truth-functional is of considerable interest, since there is no reason to assume that an understanding of how a particular connective functions in inferences will carry with it a means for assigning truth values in all cases, nor that the truth values will depend only on the truth values (rather than on the content) of the constituent propositions. It is quite easy to come up with connectives that are non-truth-functional. For example, the connective 'logically implies' is not truth-functional, where one proposition is said to 'logically imply' another if the second proposition can be deduced from the first by the rules of inference of the logical system under discussion. 'Aristotle taught Alexander, and Haydn taught Beethoven' logically implies 'Aristotle taught Alexander', but 'Aristotle taught Alexander' does not logically imply 'Ankara is the capital of Turkey'. In both cases the various propositions are true, but only in the first case does the first proposition logically imply the second. Thus, the fact that A is true and the fact that B is true do not provide enough information to determine whether 'A logically implies B' is true, and thus 'logically implies' is not truth-functional.

What about the other three connectives? Do they have to be truth-functional if the given rules of inference are to lead to true conclusions when applied to true premises? Negation looks like a prime candidate for truth-functionality, and surely ought to conform to the standard table

3.2.1 | A | $\sim$A |
           |---|---|
           | T | F |
           | F | T |

Let us see whether the given rules of inference force 3.2.1 on us, under the assumption that they lead to true conclusions when applied to true premises. Given just that one assumption, they in fact do not force 3.2.1 on us. For example, nothing in the rules of inference conflicts with the absurd possibility that all propositions might be true, since if all propositions are true, then no matter what the rules of inference are, they yield true conclusions when applied to true premises. And obviously, if there is a 'state of affairs' in which all propositions are true, then negation does not conform to 3.2.1, since in that state of affairs there would be true propositions whose negations were true, contrary to the demand of 3.2.1 that their negations be false.

Clearly we ought to impose some restriction which would exclude something as outlandish as a 'state of affairs' in which all propositions are true. However, before making any specific proposals for such a restriction, let's get clear what we're talking about. Propositional logic is generally discussed at an extremely high level of generality and abstraction. When a logician is doing propositional logic, he cares whether a proposition is the *and*-conjunction of two other propositions, but he doesn't care whether the first of the conjuncts is 'The moon is made of styrofoam' or 'Sea cucumbers expel their intestines when frightened'. In propositional logic, the ultimate units into which complex propositions are analyzed are 'connectives' and 'atomic propositions', and all that matters about the individual atomic propositions is (i) that one can tell whether two atomic propositions are the same or different, and (ii) what the truth value of each proposition (atomic or not) is in each 'state of affairs' that comes into consideration. For the purposes of propositional logic, a 'state of affairs' can thus be identified with an assignment of truth values: the only difference between 'states of affairs' that ever plays a role in propositional logic is a difference with regard to which propositions are true and which ones false.

The kind of restriction on the use of the term 'true' called for in propositional logic is not a condition on how one ought to apply the term 'true' to concrete propositions (e.g., a condition that would force one to say that 'The moon is made of styrofoam' is false and that 'Sea cucumbers expel their intestines when frightened' is true) but rather a FORMAL condition (i.e., a condition that does not make reference to the content of individual propositions) on the assignment of truth values to propositions that will rule out assignments of truth values that are not internally coherent. One possible condition of this type would be the condition that a proposition and its negation must have opposite truth values in any state of affairs. That condition is of course equivalent to the truth table 3.2.1. Let's see, however, if 3.2.1 follows from some less stringent condition. Suppose, as a first try, that we impose the minimum condition that would exclude the absurd 'state of affairs' in which all propositions are true, namely, the condition that we will only admit states of affairs in which at least one proposition (N.B.: not necessarily an atomic proposition) is false. That condition in fact forces on us the first line of 3.2.1; that is, it implies that if our rules of inference yield true conclusions when applied to true premises, then in any admissible state of affairs, the negation of every true proposition must be false. Recall that we have shown (2.2.8e) that from a contradiction anything whatever can be inferred. Suppose that in some state of affairs there were a proposition A such that both A and $\sim$A were true. Since we are assuming that in every state of affairs there are false propositions, there is some proposition B which is false in this state of affairs. But then we can derive a false conclusion (B) from true premises (A and $\sim$A) by our rules of inference. Thus, if our rules of inference are to lead from true premises to true conclusions and if we only allow states of affairs in which there are at least some false propositions, then we can only admit states of affairs in which the negation of any true proposition is false.

Okay—from a nice innocuous assumption we've been able to get the first line of 3.2.1; can we get the second line too? I will argue shortly that we can't, that nothing said so far rules out states of affairs in which there are false propositions whose negations are also false. For the time being, let's just observe that the rules of inference for negation don't appear to rule out the possibility of a proposition and its negation both being false. For example, ~-exploitation only shows that if A and ~A are both false, then ~~A must also be false (since if it were true, you could derive the false conclusion A from the true premise ~~A). The rule of ~-introduction won't help either. If A and ~A were both false, then deriving something false from them by ~-introduction would not show any breakdown of the system (since only inferences from *true* premises provide a test for the system), and deriving the contradictory false propositions A and ~A in the course of an argument that used ~-introduction would indicate no more of a breakdown than would deriving either of them alone.

Let's then turn to (inclusive) ∨ and see how much of its truth table is forced on us by our assumptions. The standard truth table for ∨ is

3.2.2

A	B	∨ AB
T	T	T
T	F	T
F	T	T
F	F	F

The first three lines of 3.2.2 are forced on us by ∨-introduction. From A you can infer ∨ AB, so when A is true (the first two lines), ∨ AB must also be true, since otherwise you could infer a false conclusion (∨ AB) from a true premise (A). Similarly, the third line must also have T as the value for ∨ AB: if it were F, then you could derive a false conclusion (∨ AB) from a true premise (B). This leaves the last line, which ought to be a snap—surely we can show that when A and B are both false, ∨ AB must also be false. So let's see if we can figure out how to show that. The obvious rule of inference to try to put to work is ∨-exploitation, which says that if you can infer something from each conjunct of an ∨-conjunction, you can infer it from the whole ∨-conjunction. Our job will be over if, given false A and false B, we can always come up with a proposition C such that (i) we can show that C has to be false, (ii) C can be inferred from A, (iii) C can be inferred from B. If we have such a proposition, then ∨ AB would have to be false: if ∨ AB were true, then we would be able to infer a false conclusion (C) from a true premise (∨ AB). As an exercise, you should spend a few minutes trying to construct such a C; I guarantee that you won't find one.

If that doesn't work, maybe we can employ some of the many theorems about ∨ to justify the fourth line of 3.2.2. For example, we have the de Morgan laws. So let's assume that A and B are both false and see what we can conclude from the deductive equivalence of $\sim \vee AB$ and $\wedge (\sim A, \sim B)$. Suppose that $\vee AB$ were true. Then $\sim \vee AB$ would be false (since the assumptions in force here allow only states of affairs in which the negation of every true proposition is false). Thus $\wedge (\sim A, \sim B)$ is also false: deductive equivalents must have the same truth value, since if they didn't you would be able to deduce the false one from the true one and the system would break down. Since we have established that $\wedge$ must conform to the standard table, that means that either $\sim A$ or $\sim B$ must be false. If we knew that negation was truth-functional, we would be home: saying that either $\sim A$ or $\sim B$ is false would be equivalent to saying that either A or B is true, which would conflict with the assumption that A and B were both false. But for the moment the truth-functionality of negation is up in the air: we haven't conclusively ruled out the possibility of a proposition and its negation both being false, and if A and B were such that they and their negations were all false, we might for all we know be in a situation in which A and B were both false but $\vee AB$ was true.

It's beginning to look as if whether $\vee$ is truth-functional hinges on whether $\sim$ is truth-functional. In fact it does, as does the truth-functionality of $\supset$. I will prove shortly that negation is truth-functional if and only if *or*-conjunction is truth-functional and that negation is truth-functional if and only if $\supset$ is truth-functional. Before giving that proof, however, it would be worthwhile to digress for a minute and show that the idea of a proposition and its negation being simultaneously false isn't as outlandish as it at first might seem.

Consider the sentence

3.2.3   Queen Elizabeth regrets that she had an affair with George Jessel.

Given the factual assumption that Queen Elizabeth has never had an affair with George Jessel, no one would want to call the proposition expressed by 3.2.3 true. However, few would want to call the proposition expressed by its negation true either:

3.2.4   Queen Elizabeth doesn't regret that she had an affair with George Jessel.

The following choices are available: (i) say that the falsehood of the 'presupposition' embodied in 3.2.3 and 3.2.4 (namely, the presupposition that Queen Elizabeth had an affair with George Jessel) causes them to have no truth value at all, that is, to be neither true nor false; (ii) say that 3.2.3 is false and 3.2.4 true and forget about the uneasiness that one might feel at calling 3.2.4 true; or (iii) say that 3.2.3 and 3.2.4 are both false.[3] Choices i and iii are actually not all that different from each other. Indeed, they differ only in how broadly one interprets the word 'false': it is given a narrow interpretation in i but a broad interpretation in iii. Both in i and in iii one allows for the possibility of a proposition such that neither it nor its negation is true, and the only apparent difference between i and iii is whether one takes such a proposition to count as 'false'. I will not attempt to choose among i, ii, and iii here; it will suffice to point out that iii is not any less plausible than the available alternatives, and thus the possibility of a proposition and its negation being simultaneously false cannot be dismissed out of hand. While 'classical' logic in fact rules out that possibility, and while a large part of this book is concerned with 'classical' logic, it is worth giving serious consideration here to what classical logic rules out in this case.

Given the rules of inference of chapter 2 plus the assumptions that those rules lead to true conclusions when applied to true premises and that only states of affairs in which at least one proposition is false come into consideration, two alternatives are open to us: either negation is truth-functional, in which case all of the other connectives are truth-functional and have their standard truth tables, or negation is not truth-functional, in which case $\vee$ and $\supset$ are not truth functional either, though their deviation from truth-functionality is limited to the cells marked T/F in 3.2.5:

3.2.5   a. If negation is truth-functional:

A	$\sim$A		A	B	$\sim$AB	$\vee$AB	$\supset$AB
T	F		T	T	T	T	T
F	T		T	F	F	T	F
			F	T	F	T	T
			F	F	F	F	T

b. If negation is not truth-functional:

A	$\sim$A		A	B	$\sim$AB	$\vee$AB	$\supset$AB
T	F		T	T	T	T	T
F	T/F		F	F	F	T	F
			F	T	F	T	T
			F	F	F	T/F	T/F

To show that these are the alternatives, what I still have to show is the following: (i) if negation is truth-functional, then $\supset$ is truth-functional and conforms to the standard table; (ii) even if negation is not truth-functional, the rules of inference demand that $\supset$AB be true whenever B is true; (iii) it is possible to assign truth values consistently in such a way that negation is not truth-functional; and (iv) under such an assignment of truth values, there are choices of false A and false B which make ∨AB true and other choices which make ∨AB false, and there are choices of false A and false B which make ⊃AB true and others which make it false. Let's take up i–iv in turn:

(i) Suppose that negation is truth-functional in some state of affairs. It was proven in chapter 2 that ⊃AB and ∨(∼A, B) are deductively equivalent; thus they always have the same truth value. It was proven earlier in this chapter that if ∼ is truth-functional, then ∨ conforms to the standard truth table. Thus, if ∼ is truth-functional, then the truth value of ⊃AB is what results by computing the truth value of ∨(∼A, B) according to the standard tables, which in fact is the truth value of ⊃AB according to the standard tables.

(ii) From B, we can deduce ⊃AB:

3.2.6   1 B

2 | A   supp

3 | B   1, reit

4 ⊃AB   2, 3, ⊃-intro

Thus, if the rules of inference are to lead from true premises to true conclusions, ⊃AB must be true whenever B is true.

(iii) Suppose you were to demand the highest possible standard of truth: you accept as true only what can be proven true (on the basis of the rules of inference adopted here) and call everything else false.[4] This assignment of truth values is consistent with the rules of inference assumed here; when you apply the rules of inference to true premises, you get a true conclusion: since the premises are provable (that's the only way they can be true, according to this standard of truth), you can put together the proofs of the premises and the step that leads you from the premises to the conclusion, which will add up to a proof of the conclusion, and thus the conclusion will be true. Under this assignment of truth values, negation is not truth-functional. For example, any atomic proposition will be a false proposition whose negation is false: under this assignment of truth values, any atomic proposition has to be false, since you cannot prove an atomic proposition (think what hell would break loose if you could!), and the same is true of the negation of any atomic proposition. There would also be false propositions whose negations were true. For example, ∧(p, ∼p) would be a false proposition whose negation was true, since its negation is a theorem.

This is not the only way that you could assign truth values so as to allow cases where a proposition and its negation were both false. For example, if you were to admit as true not just propositions that can be proven categorically but also those which are provable from some given consistent set $\{A_1, A_2, \ldots, A_n\}$ of premises, with all other propositions assigned the value F, the assignment of truth values would still allow for a proposition and its negation being simultaneously false unless the set of premises were so big as to allow you to prove or disprove all propositions expressible in the language of the given system.

(iv) Suppose that we have assigned truth values in a way that conforms to the rules of inference but leaves negation not truth-functional. We can then find both false propositions whose ∨-conjunction is false and false propositions whose ∨-conjunction is true. Since negation is not truth-functional in the given assignment of truth values, there is some proposition A such that both A and ∼A are false. The proposition ∨(A, ∼A) is provable categorically and is thus provable from any set of premises; thus if there are any true propositions in the given assignment of truth values, ∨(A, ∼A) will have to be true. Strictly speaking, nothing we have said so far rules out the absurd state of affairs in which all propositions are false, and in that state of affairs it would be 'vacuously true' that any rules of inference lead to true conclusions when applied to true premises. Let us supplement our earlier stipulation to admit only states of affairs in which at least some propositions are false with the further stipulation that we will consider only states of affairs in which at least some propositions are true. Then, in any state of affairs remaining in consideration, if A and ∼A are both false, then ∨(A, ∼A) is a true ∨-conjunction of false conjuncts. To find an example of a false ∨-conjunction of false conjuncts, take any contradictory proposition, say ∧(p, ∼p), and *or*-conjoin it with a copy of itself:

3.2.7   ∨(∧(p, ∼p), ∧(p, ∼p)).

Since ∨AA is deductively equivalent to A, 3.2.7 will have to have the same truth value as ∧(p, ∼p), and is thus false, since the negation of ∧(p, ∼p) is a theorem and is thus true under any admissible assignment of truth values. This establishes that if negation is not truth-functional, then just from the fact that C and D are both false you can't tell whether ∨CD is true or false.

The same is true of ⊃. Suppose that ∼ is not truth-functional. Then there is a proposition A such that A and ∼A are both false. Then ⊃(A, ∼A) will be false, since it is deductively equivalent to ∨(∼A, ∼A), which is in turn deductively equivalent to ∼A, which is by assumption false. But there are also cases where two propositions are false but the result of combining them with ⊃ is true. A trivial example of that is ⊃BB, where B is any false proposition: ⊃BB is provable and hence true. Thus, if negation is not truth-functional, then just from the fact that C and D are both false, you can't tell whether $\supset$ CD is false or true.

The truth table 3.2.5*b*, corresponding to states of affairs in which negation is not truth-functional, can be sharpened if one notes that in the cells where T/F appears, one of the two values will be attested in every state of affairs (e.g., in any admissible assignment of truth values, there will be false propositions whose negations are true) but the other one will not occur in every state of affairs (e.g., there are admissible assignments of truth values in which the negation of every false proposition is true). Using parentheses to indicate those truth values which do not figure in every state of affairs, 3.2.5*b* can be revised to

3.2.8

A	~A
T	F
F	T/(F)

A	B	$\wedge$ AB	$\vee$ AB	$\supset$ AB
T	T	T	T	T
T	F	F	T	F
F	T	F	T	T
F	F	F	F/(T)	T/(F)

In every state of affairs there are false propositions whose negations are true: $\supset$ AA is a theorem and thus true in every state of affairs, and $\sim \supset$ AA is thus false; thus $\sim \supset$ AA is a false proposition whose negation ($\sim \sim \supset$ AA, which is of course deductively equivalent to $\supset$ AA) is true, since it is a theorem. In every state of affairs, there will be false propositions whose *or*-conjunction is false: $\vee (\sim \supset$ AA, $\sim \supset$ AA) will be an *or*-conjunction of false propositions which is false, since its negation, being deductively equivalent to the theorem $\supset$ AA, will be true. And in every state of affairs, there will be true conditional propositions with false antecedent and false consequent, since $\supset (\sim \supset$ AA, $\sim \supset$ AA) is a theorem and hence true but has as antecedent and consequent propositions which are the negations of theorems and are thus false. If a state of affairs includes an instance of any of the three parenthesized values in 3.2.8, it will include instances of the other two; this has in effect already been proven.

3.3. Validity and Satisfiability

For the purposes of this section, let us assume that negation is truth-functional and thus that the connectives all have their standard truth tables. Certain complex propositions are true in all states of affairs; others are false in all states of affairs; others are true in some states of affairs but false in others. For example, $\supset (\supset$ AB, $\supset (\sim$ B, $\sim$ A)) is true in all states of affairs (or at least, in all states of affairs such as we are admitting into consideration), as can be shown simply by computing its truth value for each combination of truth values for A and B:

3.3.1

A	B	⊃(⊃	AB,	⊃(~	B,	~	A))
T	T	T	T		T	F	F
T	F	T	F		F	T	F
F	T	T	T		T	F	T
F	F	T	T		T	T	T

The proposition ⊃(⊃AB, ⊃(~A, ~B)) is true in some states of affairs and false in others; specifically, it is false when A is false and B true, and it is true otherwise:

3.3.2

A	B	⊃(⊃	AB,	⊃(~	A,	~	B))
T	T	T	T		T	F	F
T	F	T	F		T	F	T
F	T	F	T		F	T	F
F	F	T	T		T	T	T

The proposition ∧(A, ⊃(A, ~A)) is false in all states of affairs:

3.3.3

A	∧(A,	⊃(A,	~	A))
T	F	T	F	T F
F	F	F	T	F T

A proposition which is true in at least one state of affairs is said to be SATISFIABLE. A proposition which is true in all states of affairs is said to be VALID. This terminology is unfortunate, since 'valid' is used in a different sense with regard to inferences: an inference is said to be valid if its conclusion follows from its premises. However, the use of 'valid' in the sense of 'true in all states of affairs' is sufficiently standard in logic that there is little point in avoiding the term. Valid propositions are also called TAUTOLOGIES.

Note that proving a proposition isn't the same thing as proving that it is valid: proving the proposition means showing that it follows from the rules of inference, whereas proving that it is valid means showing that its truth value is 'T' regardless of what the truth values of the atomic propositions in it are. Nonetheless, if everything works right, the propositions that you can prove ought to be precisely the ones that are valid, that is, the logical system ought to be SEMANTICALLY COMPLETE.

The logical system that we are talking about, that is, the logical system whose rules of inference are the nine that were given in the last chapter and whose truth conditions are given by the 'standard' truth tables, can in fact be proved to be semantically complete. Half of this result is fairly easy to prove, namely, the half that says that if a proposition is provable, then it is valid, though making the proof explicit is a little tricky, as a result of the complete freedom that we have to make 'suppositions' in subordinate proofs and the freedom we have to reiterate any line of a superordinate proof. Note in particular that the suppositions of the subordinate proofs are not required to be true; indeed, it is essential that they not be required to be true, since the results proved have to be true regardless of whether the suppositions are true; for example, if you prove ⊃AB by ⊃-introduction, you make the supposition A in a subordinate proof, but your result has to be true regardless of whether A is true. Note also that suppositions are the only way that the various proposition symbols get into the proof; that is, without suppositions you can't prove anything categorically.[5]

As an illustration of what has to be done to show that anything provable in the given system is true in all states of affairs, consider ∨-exploitation:

3.3.4   ∨AB
             │ A
             ├───
             │ . . .
             │ C
             │ B
             ├───
             │ . . .
             │ C
          C

An application of this rule might occur deeply embedded within a larger proof: ∨AB might be a supposition of a subproof, or it might be something that had been inferred from higher lines of the proof. The proof of C from A and the proof of C from B can involve any of the apparatus of the logical system: any number of lines and any number of applications of the nine rules of inference might intervene between the supposition and the conclusion in these subproofs, and the intermediate lines can involve reiteration of lines of a superordinate proof. Suppose that we have established that the steps involved in getting from A to C and the steps involved in getting from B to C yield true conclusions when applied to true premises (NB: the 'premises' here are not just A in the one case and B in the other, but A or B as the case may be, plus whatever 'higher' suppositions play a role in the proof). Then the proof of C from ∨AB also yields a true conclusion when applied to true premises: if ∨AB is true and all the suppositions that 'command' the two subproofs are true, then at least one of A and B is true (since, according to the truth table for ∨, ∨AB can be true only if at least one of A and B is true), and by assumption, the proof of C from that premise (A or B as the case may be) plus the relevant super-ordinate premises yields a true conclusion when the premises are true.

It is much easier to show that those rules of inference that do not involve subordinate proofs lead to true conclusions when applied to true premises: all that need be done is to check them against the truth tables (for example, $\supset$-exploitation yields a true conclusion when applied to true premises, since the only way that its premises, A and $\supset$ AB, could both be true is for A and B both to be true). In the case of rules of inference that involve subproofs, the same kind of result can be proven as just was proven for $\lor$-exploitation: any occurrence of the rule will lead from true premises (including all 'higher' suppositions) to true conclusions provided that the same is true of the subproofs. This means that the 'goodness' of the whole proof hinges on the 'goodness' of the subordinate proofs, which will in turn hinge on the 'goodness' of any proofs that are subordinate to them, etc. However, as you burrow into the depths of a proof, you will eventually hit bedrock, which in this case means proofs to which nothing is sub-ordinate. But the 'goodness' of the bedrock proofs has been established (or at least, it has if you've checked the truth tables to verify the claim that I made at the beginning of this paragraph: that the rules of inference that do not involve subordinate proofs all lead to true conclusions when applied to true premises). Putting these results together, we obtain the conclusion that for any argument that conforms to the given rules of inference, its conclusion is true in any state of affairs in which the suppositions of the whole argument (i.e., the 'premises') are true. But note that this is the case even if there aren't any premises (i.e., if the only 'suppositions' are those of subordinate proofs, not of the main proof). With a bit of meditation, you should be able to convince yourself that that means that if the argument has no 'premises', its conclusion is true under any state of affairs whatever. But that is precisely what we are trying to prove.

Or at least, it's the easier half of what we want to prove. We have sketched a proof that every provable formula is 'valid'; that is, if a formula can be proven by means of the given rules of inference, it is true in all states of affairs. We have yet to prove the converse: that every valid formula is provable. Proving that result is quite involved; accordingly, I have banished a sketch of the proof to an appendix (3.7), so that anyone who does not feel up to going through it can skip it easily. However, you should at least think about the result long enough to appreciate why it would be difficult to prove it: one is required not just to come up with a proof of some formula but to show that for any formula, no matter how complicated, if it is true in all states of affairs, then there is a way of proving it by means of the given rules of inference. The task of establishing this theorem is made easier if we concentrate our energies on establishing an equivalent result: any formula that is not provable is not valid, that is, if a formula is not provable from the given rules of inference, then there is a state of affairs in which it is false. Note that to establish this result one must make use of fine details of the rules of inference: the result shows that the rules of inference allow you to prove the maximum that you could hope to prove, and you can thus expect that if you were to drop or weaken one of the rules the result need not remain true.[6]

The semantic completeness theorem provides us with a DECISION PROCEDURE for the deductive system of chapter 2: given any formula of propositional logic, one can determine whether it is provable by the given rules of inference by determining whether it is valid according to the classical truth tables, which one can do simply by computing its truth value for each possible combination of truth values of the atomic propositions contained in it. If there are n different atomic propositions in a given complex proposition A, one can determine the truth value for each of the 2^n combinations of truth values for those atomic propositions; if the value in each case is T, then the complex proposition can be proven by the rules of inference of chapter 2, and if the value in any of the 2^n cases is F, it cannot be proven. The classical truth tables are thus valuable tools even if one does not think they give an accurate account of truth values; one can accept the less constrained account of truth values given in 3.2 but still use the classical truth tables as a device for determining whether a given proposition is provable by the rules of inference of chapter 2.

The symbol $\Vdash$ is commonly used to indicate 'true in all states of affairs', that is, '$\Vdash$A' means 'A is true in all states of affairs', that is, 'A is valid'. Just as $\vdash$ is used not only to indicate that a proposition is provable categorically but also to indicate that it is provable from given premises, $\Vdash$ is used not only to indicate that a proposition is valid but also to indicate that it is true whenever given propositions are true, that is,'$B_1, B_2, \ldots, B_n$ $\Vdash$ A' means 'in all states of affairs in which $B_1, B_2, \ldots, B_n$ are true, A is also true'. The term ENTAILMENT (or SEMANTIC ENTAILMENT) is commonly used for this relationship, that is, we say that the set of propositions $\{B_1, B_2, \ldots, B_n\}$ (semantically) entails A if $B_1, B_2, \ldots, B_n$ $\Vdash$ A. As in the case of $\vdash$, $\Vdash$ is used relative to a particular system of logic. The intended system of logic can be made explicit by a subscript whenever the occasion arises (say, whenever one is comparing two or more different systems), for example, if c is the system of 'classical propositional logic' having the formation rules and rules of inference of chapter 2 and the truth conditions embodied in the truth tables of 3.1, one can write $\Vdash_c$A to mean that A is true in all states of affairs that conform to the classical truth tables, just as one writes $\vdash_c$A to indicate that A is provable according to the classical rules of inference. The semantic completeness theorem referred to in this section can be restated as: For any proposition A of propositional logic, $\vdash_c A$ if and only if $\Vdash_c A$.

3.4. Different Kinds of 'Completeness'

The term 'completeness' is used to cover a number of quite distinct properties of logical systems; the only thing that these properties have in common is that each is some kind of maximum demand that one could reasonably impose on a system. This section, which is a brief summary of three notions referred to by the word 'completeness', is inserted solely for clarity's sake, for example, so as to decrease the likelihood that the reader will assume that 'Gödel's incompleteness theorem' has something to do with 'semantic completeness'.

A logical system is said to be SEMANTICALLY COMPLETE if its rules of inference allow you to prove all the propositions that could stand a chance of being proved, that is, all propositions that are true in all states of affairs. (If the system is consistent, then the fact that a given proposition is false in some state of affairs guarantees that that proposition cannot be proven in the system).

A second kind of 'completeness' that is often mentioned in logic texts is EXPRESSIVE COMPLETENESS. A system is 'expressively complete' if the formulas that it provides are sufficient to draw all possible distinctions among states of affairs. A 'state of affairs' in this case is taken to be a set of truth values for the atomic propositions of the system, that is, a 'state of affairs' amounts to a line of a truth table.[7] To say that the system is 'expressively complete' is to say that for any set of states of affairs, there is a formula of the system which is true in those states of affairs and false in all other states of affairs. It is obvious that the system of propositional logic that we have been discussing here is expressively complete. For any one state of affairs there is a formula that is true only in that state of affairs (e.g., suppose the given state of affairs is 'p true, q true, and r false'; then $\wedge(p, q, \sim r)$ is true precisely in that 'state of affairs'). So for any finite set of states of affairs, we can get a formula which is true in those states of affairs and false otherwise: for each state of affairs, construct a proposition that is true in that state of affairs and false in any other state of affairs, and form the $\vee$-conjunction of those propositions. For example, given the three states of affairs 'p true, q true, r false', 'p true, q false, r false', and 'p false, q false, r true', the following formula would be true in those states of affairs and false otherwise:

3.4.1 $\vee(\wedge(p, q, \sim r), \wedge(p, \sim q, \sim r), \wedge(\sim p, \sim q, r))$.

It is interesting to note that expressive completeness can be attained without some of the connectives of the given system. For example, observe that the procedure just given for finding a formula true only in given states of affairs utilizes only three of the four connectives: no use is made of $\supset$. In fact, you could get along with two, since $\vee(p_1, \ldots, p_n)$ has the same truth value as $\sim \wedge(\sim p_1, \ldots, \sim p_n)$ and thus you could eliminate the $\vee$'s in favor of combinations of $\sim$'s and $\wedge$'s without changing the set of states of affairs in which the formula is true. Likewise, since $\wedge(p_1, \ldots, p_n)$ has the same truth value as $\sim \vee(\sim p_1, \ldots, \sim p_n)$, you could replace all the $\wedge$'s by combinations of $\sim$'s and $\vee$'s without changing the set of states of affairs in which the formula is true. Thus, just $\sim$ and $\vee$ (or just $\sim$ and $\wedge$ or just $\sim$ and $\supset$) would be sufficient in order for the system to be 'expressively complete'. What this means is that if all you care about is the conditions under which formulas are true, you can define two of the connectives away: for any formula of the given system, you can find another that involves only $\sim$ and $\vee$ and which is true under exactly the same conditions as is the given formula.

You can't get expressive completeness with just one of the given connectives, as you should be able to convince yourself by thinking about the truth tables (for example, why can't you get a formula containing only $\wedge$'s which is true when p is false and is false otherwise?). However, it is possible to have expressive completeness in a system with just one connective, provided you allow that connective to be something 'nonstandard'. Specifically, suppose that there is a two-place connective | (read 'stroke') which has the following truth table (and thus corresponds to English *neither . . . nor*):

3.4.2

A	B	A|B
T	T	F
T	F	F
F	T	F
F	F	T

It is then possible to construct formulas involving no connective other than | which have the same truth conditions as $\sim p$, $\vee pq$, $\wedge pq$, and $\supset pq$:

3.4.3
$$\begin{array}{ll} \sim p & p|p \\ \wedge pq & (p|p)|(q|q) \\ \vee pq & (p|q)|(p|q) \\ \supset pq & ((p|p)|q)|((p|p)|q) \end{array}$$

There is no loss of expressive completeness if $\vee$ and $\wedge$ are restricted to two conjuncts at a time. This follows from the fact that an n-term $\vee$-conjunction or $\wedge$-conjunction has the same truth conditions as a repeated two-term conjunction. For example, each of the formulas in 3.4.4 is true if at least one out of A, B, C, D, E is true and is false otherwise, and each of the formulas in 3.4.5 is true if all of A, B, C, D are true and is false otherwise:

3.4.4   a. ∨ (A, B, C, D, E)

          b. ∨ (A, ∨ (B, ∨ (C, ∨ DE)))

          c. ∨ (∨ (∨ (∨ AB, C), D), E)

          d. ∨ (∨ (∨ AB, C), ∨ DE)

3.4.5   a. ∧ (A, B, C, D)

          b. ∧ (A, ∧ (B, ∧ CD))

          c. ∧ (∧ AB, ∧ CD)

It is this fact which has led logicians generally to operate only in terms of two-term conjoining: if all you are interested in is truth conditions, you can define away conjunctions of 3 or more conjuncts (e.g., 'define' 3.4.4*a* as 'meaning' 3.4.4*b* or 3.4.4*c*; it is of course arbitrary which of the rested two-term conjunctions one would take as the definiens). In the next section it will be argued that conjunctions must nonetheless be taken as allowing any number of conjuncts if there is to be a close fit between formal logic and the grammar of natural languages.

A third kind of 'completeness' is DEDUCTIVE COMPLETENESS: a system is deductively complete if for every proposition A of the system, either A or ∼A is a theorem of the system. A system is 'deductively complete' if it imposes the most stringent possible restriction on states of affairs: that there is only one state of affairs in which the rules of the system lead only to true conclusions when applied to true premises. The question of 'deductive completeness' arises not in connection with systems that would normally be spoken of as systems *of* logic, but rather in connection with systems that include axioms for a particular subject matter, for example, a formal system that is intended as an axiomatization of the arithmetic of positive integers. The most celebrated result regarding deductive completeness is Gödel's incompleteness theorem, which shows that any axiomatization of the arithmetic of positive integers either is deductively incomplete or is inconsistent; that is, if your supposed axioms for arithmetic are consistent (that is, they don't allow you to deduce any contradictions), then there are propositions of arithmetic that are 'undecidable' relative to those axioms: propositions A such that neither A nor ∼A can be proven from those axioms.

3.5. More on Conjunction

I have given short shrift to 'exclusive *or*': except for the place where I simply drew the distinction between 'inclusive *or*' and 'exclusive *or*', we have been concerned only with the former. In this section, let us suppose that there are in fact two distinct *or*'s and that both deserve to be recognized as elements of logical structure.[8]

The generally accepted truth table for exclusive *or*, when there are two conjuncts, is

3.5.1

A	B	$\vee_e AB$
T	T	F
T	F	T
F	T	T
F	F	F

In fact, if exclusive *or* is to be truth-functional and to be distinct from inclusive *or*, the only conceivable truth table is 3.5.1, since the only state of affairs in which its truth value might differ from that of inclusive *or* is that in which both conjuncts are true. If we embed an $\vee_e$-conjunction in an $\vee_e$-conjunction and compute the truth conditions according to 3.5.1, it becomes clear that it is not so easy to 'define away' multiterm $\vee_e$-conjunction in terms of iterated two-term conjunction, the way that logicians have 'defined away' multiterm $\vee$-conjunctions and $\wedge$-conjunctions.

3.5.2

A	B	C	$\vee_e(A,$	$\vee_e BC)$	
T	T	T	T	T	F
T	T	F	F	T	T
T	F	T	F	T	T
T	F	F	T	T	F
F	T	T	F	F	F
F	T	F	T	F	T
F	F	T	T	F	T
F	F	F	F	F	F

The iterated two-term conjunction is true when one of the three ultimate conjuncts is true or when all three of them are true, and is false when none of them is true or when two of them are. More generally, any iterated two-term $\vee_e$-conjunction of any number of items will be true if an odd number of those items are true and false if an even number of them are true. For example, the following expression will be true if one, three, or five of A, B, C, D, E, F are true and will be false if none, two, four, or six of them are true:

3.5.3

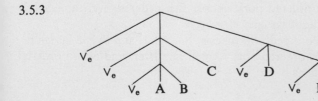

However, the truth conditions of English sentences in which *or* could be held to be used in an exclusive sense with more than two conjuncts do not conform to this pattern. For example, *On the $1.25 lunch you can have french fries, boiled potato, or mashed potato* does not invite you to take one or three but not two of the alternatives: it simply invites you to take one. Likewise, the question *Did Larry study physics, chemistry, or geology?* (pronounced with falling intonation on *geology*) presupposes that Larry studied one of the three subjects, not that he studied an odd number of them. Thus, the natural generalization of the truth table 3.5.1 to an $\vee_e$-conjunction of arbitrarily many conjuncts is that $\vee_e(A_1, \ldots, A_n)$ is true when exactly one of the conjuncts is true and is false when either none of them or more than one of them is true. The most natural truth table for n-term $\vee_e$-conjunctions is thus distinct from that for an iterated two-term $\vee_e$-conjunction: when the number of true conjuncts is odd and greater than one, the former is false but the latter true.[9]

Thus, if $\vee_e$ is to be one of the connectives of a logical system and if its logical properties are to match those of apparent 'exclusive' uses of *or* in English, it cannot be a two-term conjunction: it will have to be allowed to conjoin any number of propositions at a time, from two on up. It can then be argued that (inclusive) $\vee$ and $\wedge$ must also be allowed to conjoin any number of propositions at a time: there is no syntactic difference between, on the one hand, $\vee_e$, and on the other hand, $\vee$ and $\wedge$; any number of conjuncts have to be allowed with $\vee_e$, since otherwise the truth conditions come out wrong; but then $\vee$ and $\wedge$ must also be allowed to take any number of conjuncts, since otherwise a spurious syntactic difference among the three conjunctions would be created.

This argument for allowing arbitrarily long $\vee$-conjunctions and $\wedge$-conjunctions is weak because there is some doubt that such a connective as $\vee_e$ has to be admitted in semantic structures corresponding to sentences of natural languages. However, there are many linguistic reasons for allowing *and* and *or* (and their analogues in other languages) to conjoin any number of items at a time. Most importantly, there are grammatical processes that affect all conjuncts or all but the first conjunct of a conjoined structure. For example, GAPPING deletes repeated material from all conjuncts after the first when conjoined clauses are identical except for one item before the verb and one after the verb in each conjunct:

3.5.4   a. Alice ordered pork chops, Ben ordered liver, and Sylvia ordered lasagna.
         b. Alice ordered pork chops, Ben liver, and Sylvia lasagna.
         b'. ?Alice ordered pork chops, Ben liver, and Sylvia ordered lasagna.

b″. ?Alice ordered pork chops, Ben ordered liver, and Sylvia
     lasagna.

There is no obvious way of describing this 'across the boards' deletion
other than in terms of a single coordinate structure with multiple conjuncts
of the same shape. To formulate a transformation of gapping so that it
applied to a nested structure of two-term conjunctions, one would have to
make it delete material one conjunct at a time; for example, if it were to
apply to a structure $(A_1$ and $(A_2$ and ... and $(A_{n-1}$ and $A_n)$ ... $))$, its
formulation would have to call for a structure of the form A and [B (and
X)], where A and B had the necessary parallelism, so that it would first
delete material in A_n on the basis of parallelism to A_{n-1}, then delete
material in A_{n-1} on the basis of parallelism to A_{n-2}, and so on. But there
are three major obstacles to such a formulation of gapping. First, since
gapping is optional, if it applied first to A_2 and A_3 and then to A_1 and
$(A_2$ and $A_3)$, it ought to be possible to derive sentences like 3.5.4b' and b″
by exercising the option on one domain of application and not exercising
it on the other. Second, under the suggested reformulation of gapping, it
should be possible to apply it whenever there are parallel consecutive
conjuncts even if the parallelism does not extend to the whole coordinate
structure, whereas gapping is in fact not possible in such cases:

3.5.5   a. *Alice ate a hamburger, Ben drank some beer, and Sylvia a
               Coke.
           b. *Alice ate a hamburger, Ben a hot dog, and Sylvia drank a
               Coke.

Third, conjuncts can sometimes be factored into shared and contrasting
parts in more than one way. For example, 3.5.6a can be taken either as
involving three instances of the 'frame' _____ wrote _____ (in which case
about quasars is contrasted with about black holes and about supernovas) or
three instances of the frame _____ wrote about _____ (in which case
quasars is contrasted with black holes and supernovas). Gapping requires
that a uniform factoring of all the conjuncts be used:

3.5.6   a. Alice wrote about quasars, Ted wrote about black holes,
               and Oscar wrote about supernovas.
           b. Alice wrote about quasars, Tom black holes, and Oscar
               supernovas.
           b'. Alice wrote about quasars, Tom about black holes, and
               Oscar about supernovas.
           c. *Alice wrote about quasars, Tom black holes, and Oscar
               about supernovas.
           c'. *Alice wrote about quasars, Tom about black holes, and
               Oscar supernovas.

If gapping applied separately to the third conjunct and to the second conjunct, there would be nothing to prevent A_1 and A_2 from being factored differently than A_2 and A_3 were, and thus nothing to exclude a derivation of 3.5.6c and c'.

Conjoining is normal only when the conjuncts are instances of the same general proposition, and conjunction reduction is sensitive to the understood general proposition. Thus, while 3.5.7a is somewhat odd in view of the difficulty of finding a general proposition that might subsume the two conjuncts (perhaps 'Two conditions characterized Western European intellectual life in the early sevententh century' would fill that bill),[10] Conjunction reduction renders it totally bizarre (3.5.7b), since *Galileo* and *adolescents* cannot match the same part of such a general proposition:

3.5.7   a. ?Galileo scanned the skies and adolescents scorned the schools.

b. *Galileo and adolescents scanned the skies and scorned the schools, respectively.

By contrast, conjunction reduction is normal in 3.5.8, since each of the conjuncts in 3.5.8a can be regarded as an instance of 'Some boys gave their girlfriends presents', with each of the derived coordinate structures in 3.5.8b corresponding to a constituent of that general proposition:

3.5.8   a. Tom gave Susie candy, Bill gave Janet flowers, and Mike gave Debbie perfume.

b. Tom, Bill, and Mike gave Susie, Janet, and Debbie, respectively, candy, flowers, and perfume, respectively.

The oddity of examples like 3.5.7b cannot be attributed to any inherent inability of the constituents to conjoin with each other, in view of the possibility of conjoining the same constituents acceptably in other contexts:

3.5.9   a. The score was tied and Yastrzemski was at bat.

a'. *The score and Yastrzemski were tied and at bat, respectively.

b. The score and Yastrzemski worried the manager and the pitcher, respectively.

The following three sentences involve the same three ultimate conjuncts but differ as regards the 'common assertion'.

3.5.10   a. Bill is overweight, Myra is overweight, and Myra is cross-eyed.

b. Bill is overweight, and Myra is overweight and cross-eyed.

c. Bill and Myra are overweight, and Myra is cross-eyed.

Example 3.5.10*b* would be appropriate to convey the idea that both of your friends are unattractive (the first conjunct tells you the respect in which Bill is unattractive, the second the respects in which Myra is unattractive). Example 3.5.10*a* is not appropriate when that is what you want to convey, though it would be appropriate in conveying other things; for example, it could be used in listing reasons why Bill and his wife Myra should not be named 'Mr. and Mrs. Jet Set': each conjunct gives an independent reason for that conclusion. Example 3.5.10*c* would be appropriate for quite different purposes, for example, to convey that there are cosmetic disabilities even among close friends of yours; with 3.5.10*b* you say what is wrong with each of your friends, whereas with 3.5.10*c* you say who suffers from each kind of unattractiveness. This means that English (and presumably, natural languages in general) distinguishes among the three structures

3.5.11   a.   b.

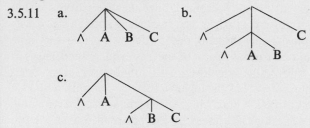

The logician's standard policy of 'defining away' many-termed conjunction obliterates this distinction, since it forces 3.5.11*a* to be identified with 3.5.11*b* or 3.5.11*c* or both. Wundt (1900:310) made the same point with regard to the German equivalents of

3.5.12   a. Caesar and Alexander were both great generals and ex-
               cellent statesmen.
           b. Caesar was a great general, Caesar was an excellent states-
               man, Alexander was a great general, and Alexander was
               an excellent statesman.

Example 3.5.12*a* conveys something that is not conveyed by 3.5.12*b*, namely, that Caesar and Alexander had something in common: the property of being both a great general and an excellent statesman. By contrast, 3.5.12*b* would be a more appropriate answer than 3.5.12*a* to a request 'Tell me something about some famous figures of antiquity'.

3.6. More on Metalanguage

It is important to distinguish between proving results *about* a logical system and proving results *in* that system. In the course of this chapter, we have proven many things *about* the system of propositional logic that was given in chapter 2 and about the notion of truth for that system. These proofs have often involved elements of meaning and principles of logic that are not part of propositional logic, for example, logical principles governing the notion of 'all', and the so-called principle of induction, which allows one to prove a result about complex propositions by showing that the result holds for simple propositions and that it is preserved as one builds up complex propositions from simple pieces. Indeed to prove results *about* propositional logic that are of any interest, it will be necessary to use much richer logical principles and a much richer analysis of logical structure than is available in propositional logic.

We have accordingly been making informal use of powerful logical tools in proving results about the formal proofs of a very rudimentary system. One may find this situation disturbing; isn't it rather like using a filthy scalpel and rusty clamps in applying a well-sterilized bandaid to someone's aorta? It can be made a little less disturbing if one takes the attitude that in making informal use of powerful logic in proving results about a rigorously formalized but elementary logical system, one is offering a promissory note that is payable by eventual formalization of the powerful system that is at present being used informally. However, this attempt to allay one's worries raises a separate worry: has the logician thereby committed himself to a policy of perpetual deficit financing, in which he is at every step proving results about one logical system by the informal use of a more powerful logical system whose formalization he must put on the agenda for subsequent years? Or will one eventually reach an all-encompassing logical system which will contain all the logical apparatus that one needs to prove all conceivable results about that very system?

Whatever the answer to these mind-boggling questions, you will have to resign yourself at least temporarily to some deficit financing. In particular, you should recognize that until we have arrived at the promised land of the all-encompassing logical system, it will not be possible to force proofs *about* a system into the format adopted for proofs *in* the system. Indeed, it would be quite misguided to try to force into the format for proofs in propositional logic such 'metaproofs' as the proof that every formula that is provable in propositional logic is true in all states of affairs. When you prove something about proofs in propositional logic, you have to keep the proofs that you're talking about separate from the proof that you're doing (the 'metaproof'). You in fact would still have to keep them separate in the promised land of the all-encompassing logic, since what you're doing and what you're talking about are in any event distinct; but it is even more essential to keep them apart when (as is the case here) the metaproofs involve the logical apparatus of a much richer system than the one about which something is being proved in the metaproof.

The distinction between language and metalanguage must also be maintained. The 'language' of propositional logic is quite rudimentary: propositions are built up from atomic propositions by means of just four connectives, and propositions are arranged into proofs having the structures given by the nine rules of inference. Call the language of the system you are discussing the OBJECT LANGUAGE and a language with which you discuss that system a METALANGUAGE.[11] Distinguishing between object language and metalanguage is essential if you are to avoid getting tangled up in your own feet. For example, it is essential to be clear than when one speaks of a formula having the form ∨AB, the symbols A and B belong to the metalanguage rather than to the object language: the ultimate constituents of the formulas of propositional logic are atomic propositions (for which $p, q, r, \ldots$ have been used here as symbols), and the A's and B's that have appeared in the statements of the rules of inference and the various metaproofs have been symbols of the metalanguage and have *stood for* formulas of arbitrary complexity (i.e., not necessarily atomic formulas) of the object language. This distinction is essential, for example, to an understanding of the proof that negation need not be truth-functional for the rules of inference to 'work'; thus, I was able to speak of assigning truth values so that 'A is true only if A is provable' but was still able to say that no atomic proposition is provable and thus that all atomic propositions are false under that assignment of truth values.

3.7. Appendix: Sketch of a Proof of Semantic Completeness

I will sketch here how semantic completeness can be proven for the system of propositional logic developed here and in chapter 2. This is but a rough sketch, given only to show the reader how such a proof can be constructed (for a more detailed treatment relating to a different version of propositional logic, but easily modified to fit the present system, see chap. 7 of Thomason 1970).

I have already sketched a proof of the easy half of the completeness theorem: if a formula is provable by the rules of inference of chapter 2, then it is true according to every assignment of truth values that conforms to the truth tables 3.1.1. What we must now prove is that if a formula is true according to every such assignment of truth values, then it is provable by the given rules of inference, or equivalently, if a formula is not provable by the given rules of inference, then it is false in at least one such assignment of truth values.

The proof, which was originally worked out by Leon Henkin (1950), will make use of the notion of a SATURATED set of formulas. A set of formulas is saturated (with respect to a given inventory of atomic propositions) if (i) it is consistent and (ii) for every formula built up from the given atomic propositions and the propositional connectives, either it or its negation belongs to the set. A saturated set of formulas is thus a maximal consistent set of formulas: it is consistent, and it could not be made any larger without becoming inconsistent. It can be proven that every consistent set of formulas can be expanded into a saturated set. Specifically, let M be a consistent set of formulas, and let $A_1, A_2, A_3, \ldots$ be a complete enumeration of the formulas of propositional logic that can be built up from the given inventory of atomic propositions.[12] Define a sequence of increasingly large consistent sets as follows: $M_0 = M$, and for each $i \geq 1$, let $M_i = M_{i-1} \cup \{A_i\}$ if $M_{i-1} \cup \{A_i\}$ is consistent, and let $M_i = M_{i-1} \cup \{\sim A_i\}$ otherwise. It can be shown that the union of all the M_i is a saturated set, and since it contains M, that shows that M is contained in a saturated set. It can also be proven that every saturated set of formulas is closed under the given rules of inference, that is, if M is a saturated set of formulas and $M \vdash A$, then $A \in M$.

For any saturated set M of formulas, we can define an assignment of truth values V_M as follows: if p is an atomic formula, then $V_M(p) = T$ if $p \in M$, and $V_M(p) = F$ is $p \notin M$; if A is not atomic, then $V_M(A)$ is what is computed from the values under V_M of the atomic constituents of A according to the truth tables 3.1.1. It can be proven that $V_M(A) = T$ if and only if $A \in M$. The proof of this latter result relies heavily on the details of the rules of inference. It is an inductive proof, constructed by supposing that the result holds for all formulas whose 'degree of complexity' (measured, say, by the depth to which the most deeply embedded atomic constituent is embedded in the formula) is less than an amount n and showing that it must then also hold for formulas of complexity n. Let A be any formula of complexity n. To show that $V_M(A) = T$ if and only if $A \in M$, it is necessary to go one by one through all the possibilities for the gross form of A. For example, suppose that for all formulas C of complexity less than n, $V_M(C) = T$ if and only if $C \in M$, and suppose that A is an or-conjunction, that is, $A = \vee(B_1, \ldots, B_m)$. Suppose $V_M(A) = T$; then for some i, $V(B_i) = T$ (since V_M satisfies the truth table for $\vee$); then (by the inductive hypothesis) $B_i \in M$ and thus (since A can be deduced from B_i by $\vee$-introduction and saturated sets are closed under the rules of inference) $A \in M$. Suppose that $V_M(A) = F$; then $V_M(B_1) = \ldots = V_M(B_m) = F$ (since V_M conforms to the truth table for $\vee$); according to the inductive hypothesis, this means that each $B_i \notin M$ and thus each $\sim B_i \in M$ (since M is saturated), whence $\wedge(\sim B_1, \sim B_2, \ldots, \sim B_m) \in M$ (since M is closed under a set of rules of inference that includes $\wedge$-introduction), thus $\sim \vee(B_1, B_2, \ldots, B_m) \in M$, that is, $\sim A \in M$, and thus $A \notin M$, since M is saturated. Similar proofs can be given for all the other possibilities for the form of A. Thus, $A \in M$ if and only if $V_M(A) = T$, and the principle of induction allows us to conclude that that is the case for all formulas A.

We are now in a position to prove the theorem. Suppose we have a formula A that cannot be proven by the given rules of inference. Since A cannot be proven, $\{\sim A\}$ is a consistent set, and by the result proven earlier, that set can be extended to a saturated set. Let M be a saturated set of formulas that contains $\sim A$. $V_M(\sim A)$ then is T (since V_M makes a formula true if and only if that formula belongs to M) and thus $V_M(A) = F$. This establishes that if A cannot be proven by the given rules of inference, then it is false in at least one assignment of truth values that conforms to the given truth tables.

3.8. Exercises

1. Suppose that in a given state of affairs, p is T, q F, r T, and s F. For each of the following formulas, (i) convert it into the tree format of chapter 2, and (ii) determine its truth value in the given state of affairs, according to the standard truth tables.

a. $\supset(\sim \supset(\wedge pq, \vee qr), \supset rp)$
b. $\wedge(\supset(p, \sim q), \supset rs)$
c. $\sim \vee(p, \wedge(\supset qr, \supset(r, \sim p)), \supset(\sim p, \wedge qr))$
d. $\supset(\vee(\wedge pr, \wedge qs), \sim \vee(\wedge ps, \wedge qr))$

2. Suppose that instead of 'truth values' you work with the following set of 'information values' (Belnap 1977):

t: 'I've been given information implying that the proposition is true and haven't been given information implying that it is false'
f: 'I've been given information implying that the proposition is false and haven't been given information implying that it is true'
b: 'I've been given both information implying that the proposition is true and information implying that it is false'
o: 'I've been given neither information implying that the proposition is true nor information implying that it is false'

i. Work out the 'information table' for $\sim$, that is, for each 'information value' that A could have, determine the corresponding information value for $\sim A$.

ii. Work out the following entries in the 'information table' for $\wedge$; keep in mind that a given combination of information values for A and B need not uniquely determine the information value for $\wedge AB$.

a. The case where A is t and B is b.
b. The case where A is t and B is o.

c. The case where A is b and B is o.

d. The case where A is f and B is b.

3. Show that the fragment of propositional logic having only the connectives ∧, ∨, and ⊃ is not expressively complete with regard to the class of states of affairs defined by the standard truth tables.

4. Show that propositional logic is not expressively complete with regard to the broader class of states of affairs that is developed in 3.2. Suggest an addition to the object language that would make propositional logic expressively complete with respect to that class of states of affairs (i.e., for expressive completeness, what else would you have to be able to say besides what standard propositional logic lets you say?).

4. Predicate Logic I: Syntax

4.1. Quantifiers, Predicates, and Variables

Propositional logic does not provide any justification for such obviously valid arguments as:

4.1.1   a. All men are mortal.
           Socrates is a man.
           Therefore, Socrates is mortal.

         b. All philosophers are eccentric.
            Some wife-beaters are philosophers.
            Therefore, some wife-beaters are eccentric.

To formulate logical principles that will say why these arguments are valid, it will be necessary to analyze propositions more finely than is done in propositional logic. For example, it will be necessary to recognize that *All men are mortal* is a combination of the QUANTIFIER *all* with the notion of 'being a man' and the notion of 'being a mortal' and to recognize that the latter notions recur in *Socrates is a man* and *Socrates is mortal*, respectively.

Such notions as 'being a man' are generally dealt with in logic in the form of PROPOSITIONAL FUNCTIONS such as '*x* is a man'. A simple Propositional function consists of one or more VARIABLES (here, the *x*) and a PREDICATE (here, *man*). Let us assume that the *is* and the *a* of '*x* is a man' are simply meaningless syllables that are forced on us by quirks of English grammar and accordingly shift to a notation in which only the predicate and the variables appear: 'man *x*'. A propositional function is something that yields a proposition when specific entities are substituted for the variables. For example, if you substitute *Socrates* for *x* in 'man *x*', you get 'man Socrates', which expresses the proposition that Socrates is a man. A propositional function with two variables is involved in the meaning of

Some men love all women, namely 'love *x y*'. Complex propositional functions can be formed from simple propositional functions by combining them with connectives and quantifiers, as in *Some persons love all dogs and hate most cats*, which contains the propositional function '*x* loves all dogs and *x* hates most cats', which is constructed from the simple propositional functions 'love *x y*', 'hate *x y*', 'dog *x*', and 'cat *x*', plus some quantifiers and the connective *and*.

The roles of the two propositional functions 'man *x*' and 'mortal *x*' in *All men are mortal* are different: 'man *x*' indicates what kind of objects you are allowing to be substituted for *x*, and 'mortal *x*' is the thing into which that substitution is made. As a makeshift, let us indicate this difference in roles by grouping the former propositional function together with the quantifier. We will thus write formulas such as 4.1.2*a* and draw trees such as 4.1.2*b*:

4.1.2   a. (all: man *x*)(mortal *x*)   b.

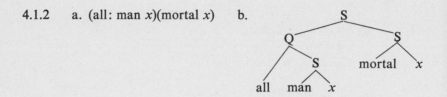

For the moment, the labeling of the nonterminal nodes is not to be taken seriously; later I will argue that I am justified in one aspect of it, namely, treating 'proposition' and 'propositional function' as belonging to the same category (here called 'S').

A propositional function with two variables can be combined wth a quantifier to yield a propositional function that has only one variable. For example, the propositional function '*x* loves all women' is what you get by combining the propositional function 'love *x y*' with 'all: woman *y*':

4.1.3   a. (all: woman *y*)(love *x y*)   b.

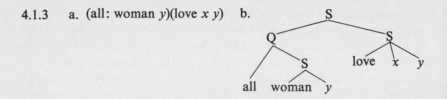

The resulting propositional function can in turn be combined with a quantifier to yield a proposition; for example, by combining '*x* loves all women' with 'some: man *x*', you get the proposition that some men love all women:

4.1.4   a. (some: man x)[(all: woman y)(love x y)]

b.

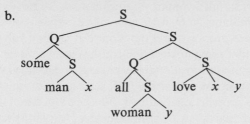

Actually, to many speakers of English, the sentence *Some men love all women* is ambiguous: it may have either the meaning that we have just been talking about (that is, that there are men who love all women) or the meaning that every woman has the property that some men love her. The latter meaning would be expressible as follows:

4.1.5   a. (all: woman y)[(some: man x)(love x y)]

b.

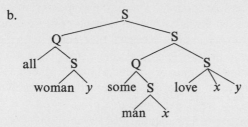

This type of ambiguity is manifested even more clearly in the sentence *You can fool some of the people all of the time*: it can mean either 'There are people whom you can fool all of the time' (which is the way that Lincoln evidently intended it) or 'At any time there are people whom you can fool'. According to the former meaning, there are people who are suckers all their lives; according to the latter, there are always suckers, though it need not be the case that anyone remains a sucker for very long.

The constituent labeled 'Q' in the above diagrams combines with an n-place propositional function (that is, a propositional function of n variables) to yield an $(n - 1)$-place propositional function. The Q is said to BIND the variable with which it is associated; that variable is referred to as a BOUND VARIABLE. Variables which are not bound by anything in a given formula are called FREE VARIABLES (or better, they are said to be free in that formula). For example, in 4.1.3, y is a bound variable and x a free variable. A propositional function is a function of its free variables, not of its bound variables; that is, it makes sense to speak of substituting *Dean Martin* for x in 4.1.3, but not of substituting *Sophia Loren* for y in 4.1.3. It makes sense to speak of substituting *Sophia Loren* for y in 'love x y', which is a constituent of

4.1.3, but the result of that substitution is not something that can coherently be combined with (all: woman y), since it contains no y.

The fact that combining a Q with an n-place propositional function yields an $(n - 1)$-place propositional function (if it yields a coherent combination at all) provides some justification for the use of a single label ('S') for both proposition and propositional function. A Q combined with a one-place propositional function should yield a 0-place propositional function. But what it yields is a proposition, and so if '0-place propositional function' is to have a meaning that fits with the meaning of 'n-place propositional function' ($n \geq 1$), it must mean 'proposition'. Thus there is reason to take 'proposition' to be a special case of 'propositional function', namely, the case in which there are no free variables. The word 'sentence' is in fact commonly used by logicians to take in both what they call OPEN SENTENCES (corresponding to' propositional functions') and CLOSED SENTENCES (corresponding to 'propositions').

We are now almost ready to take a first crack at writing a 'grammar' that will specify the possible combinations of the elements that have figured in 4.1.2–5. First, however, I must draw an important distinction that was obscured in the above discussion, namely, that between PROPER NAMES (such as *Dean Martin* or *Cincinnati*) and CONSTANTS that correspond directly to the purported referents of proper names or other noun phrases, and which serve as the meanings of personal pronouns in many instances; for example, *He loves her* will correspond to a proposition love (x_{173}, x_{81}), with the two positions of the predicate filled by constants corresponding to the purported referents of the pronouns. In the bulk of the cases to be discussed below, it will be constants or variables and not proper names that are directly combined with the given predicates. Proper names figure as parts of the meanings of such sentences as *That man is called Fred*, in which *is called* expresses a relationship between a person and a name. In Quine's celebrated example (1953:139–41) *Giorgione is so-called because of his size*, the person Giorgione and the name *Giorgione* are both referred to: *so* refers to the name and *his* refers to the person. Since the person is also called Barbarelli, the meaning of Quine's example could also be expressed by the sentence *Barbarelli is called Giorgione because of his size*. The position adopted here on the function of proper names in ordinary contexts such as *Brutus killed Caesar* is that they are not strictly speaking parts of the meanings of sentences but are aids to the hearer or reader in identifying the constants that really are parts of the meaning. The term REFERENTIAL INDEX will occasionally be used below as a cover term taking in both constants and variables.

Now let us attempt to give a grammar for the formulas of predicate logic with which we are dealing in this chapter. Since propositional functions and complex propositions can be negated, conjoined, and made into conditional structures, part of the grammar for propositional logic will have to be repeated (4.1.6*a*). There will also have to be a rule allowing a sentence (open or closed) to consist of a Q and a sentence (4.1.6*b*), and rules allowing the Q to consist of a quantifier (*all, some, most, many,* ...) plus an S (4.1.6*c*). In addition, we will have to let a sentence consist of a predicate followed by the appropriate number of items. Let us here introduce the term that is most commonly used for the items of which a predicate is predicated: ARGUMENTS.[1] Each predicate will be combinable with a specific number of arguments; for example, 'mortal x' and 'love x y' are well formed, but 'mortal x y', 'love x', and 'love x y z' are not. We will incorporate the restriction that each predicate imposes on the number of arguments with which it may be combined by having a rule saying that a sentence may consist of a predicate followed by any number of arguments (4.1.6*d*) plus for each predicate a 'context-sensitive' rule allowing it to be used in a predicate position that has the appropriate number of arguments (4.1.6*e*); for example, a predicate may be 'man' if it is followed by one argument, 'love' if it is followed by two arguments, and 'between' if it is followed by three arguments (as in *Syracuse is between Buffalo and Albany*). There are also rules (4.1.6*f*) allowing an argument to be a variable ($x, y, z, \ldots$) or a constant ($x_1, x_2, \ldots, y_1, y_2, \ldots$).

4.1.6   a. S: ~S
               S: ∨ S^n (n ≥ 2)
               S: ∧ S^n (n ≥ 2)
               S: ⊃SS
         b. S: QS
         c. Q: all S
               Q: some S
               Q: most S
               Q: many S
               . . .
         d. S: Pred Arg^n ($n \geq 1$)
         e. Pred: man / _____ Arg (the '/' may be read 'in environment')
               Pred: love / _____ Arg Arg
               Pred: between / _____ Arg Arg Arg
               . . .
         f. Arg: x Arg: x_1 Arg: y_1
               Arg: y Arg: x_2 Arg: y_2
               Arg: z . . .   . . .
               . . .

While these rules cover all of the structures presented so far, which made sense as analyses of ordinary sentences, they have the defect of also covering many other structures which correspond to no English sentences and in which the variables and quantifiers are combined in an incoherent fashion. For example:

4.1.7   a. (all: man x)(love x_1 y_1)

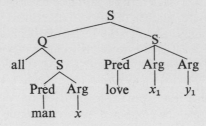

b. (all: man x_1)(love x y_1)

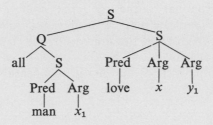

c. (all: man x)(all: woman x)(love x x)

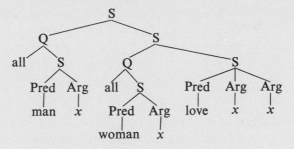

d. $\wedge$(mortal x, (all: man x)(love x y_1))

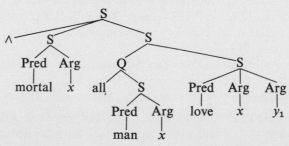

Example 4.1.7*a* is incoherent because the bound variable *x* doesn't appear in the sentence in which it it to be substituted: It makes no sense to ask for which values of *x* Dean Martin loves Sophia Loren. Example 4.1.7*b* is incoherent because the Q does not contain any variable. In the cases discussed prior to now, the Q has always contained exactly one variable, and that variable was the one that the quantifier bound. We cannot in general demand that each Q contain exactly one variable, since (as we will soon see) there are perfectly coherent structures in which the Q contains more than one variable. However, it is necessary that the structure make clear what variable the quantifier binds and that the S of the Q specify what values of that variable are relevant, and in 4.1.7*b* the S of the Q does not give any such condition (i.e., saying that Dean Martin is a man doesn't tell you what the possible values of *x* are). Example 4.1.7*c* is incoherent because it does not make clear which occurrences of *x* are bound by which quantifier. There are two quantifiers, both of which lay claim to the variable *x*, and there is no possibility for both of them to have their way. Finally, 4.1.7*d* is incoherent because one of the occurrences of *x* (namely, the one of which *mortal* is predicated) is not in the part of the structure that the quantifier which binds *x* governs, or, as we will henceforth say, it is not in the SCOPE of the quantifier which binds *x*. The formula '(all: man *x*)(love *x* y_1)' says that no matter what man you substitute for *x* in 'love *x* y_1', the resulting proposition is true. In 4.1.7*d*, 'mortal *x*' is outside the part of the tree for which substitutions for *x* are considered. Note that there is nothing incoherent about

4.1.8   (all: man *x*) ∧ (mortal *x*, love *x* y_1)

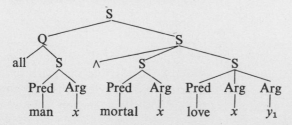

It would in fact be the logical structure of *All men are mortal and love Sophia Loren*. However, 4.1.8 and 4.1.7*d* are distinct structures, and only 4.1.8 is a coherent combination of the elements of content that figure in the two structures.

In the examples considered so far, each Q has contained exactly one variable, and so that variable must be the one that the Q binds. An example will be given in a minute of an obviously coherent combination in which a Q contains more than one variable. It is not immediately obvious whether coherent structures can differ distinctively as regards which Q binds which variable (i.e., it is not immediately obvious whether two coherent structures could be identical save for the fact that in one of them a certain Q binds x and another Q binds y, whereas in the other structure the former Q binds y and the latter one x). In order to facilitate discussion of that question and increase intelligibility of complicated structures, I will adopt the practise of writing subscripts on a Q to indicate what variable it binds, as in 4.1.9, leaving open for the time being the question of whether the subscripts are predictable from the rest of the structure; in the event that they are not predictable, a revision of the formation rules in 4.1.6 will be called for to provide for the subscripts, though I will not present the revised rules here.

4.1.9 (some: man x)$_x$($\wedge$ [happy x, (all: $\wedge$ (woman y, hate y x))$_y$(love x y)])

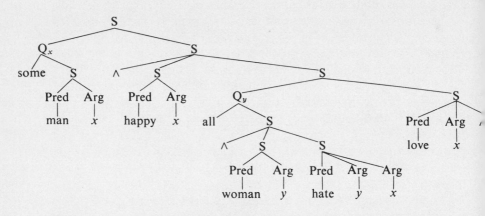

Example 4.1.9 would represent the content of the sentence *Some men are happy and love all women who hate them*.[2] Note that with the second Q interpreted as binding y, the structure makes perfect sense: the combination of that Q with 'love x y' is the propositional function 'x loves all women that hate x'; 4.1.9 is thus a coherent structure in which a single Q contains more than one variable.

Now to the task of formulating precise conditions on when quantifiers and variables are combined coherently.[3] As a first attempt, suppose that we were to impose the condition that every Q must command all occurrences of the variable with which it is subscripted. Example 4.1.9 conforms to that condition: the Q$_x$ commands all occurrences of x (since it indeed commands the entire tree), and the Q$_y$ commands all occurrences of y. This condition would serve to exclude 4.1.7c–d, on the assumption that each of the Q's is supposed to bind x: it excludes 4.1.7d since 'mortal x' is not commanded by the Q that binds x, and it excludes 4.1.7c since 'man x' is not commanded by the second Q, but that Q is required to command all occurrences of the variable that it binds, that is, x. The condition does not suffice to rule out 4.1.7a and 4.1.7b, since the problem with them is not that they have variables in places where they don't fit but that they do not have variables in places where variables are needed. Thus apparently an additional condition is needed: that in any 'QS' combination, both the Q and the S must contain occurrences of the variable with which the Q is subscripted. In 4.1.7a, the S does not contain the variable that the Q binds, and in 4.1.7b, the Q does not contain the variable that it binds.

The first condition is slightly too stringent, since it would exclude such perfectly coherent structures as 4.1.10.

4.1.10 $\wedge$ ((all: man x)$_x$(mortal x), (all: man x)$_x$(happy x))

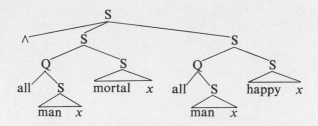

Example 4.1.10 is an obvious way to represent the content of the sentence *All men are mortal and all men are happy*. The reason that 4.1.10 is not incoherent is that the scopes of the two quantifiers are 'disjoint': the one quantifier lays claim to x's in one part of the structure and the other to x's in another part of the structure, and the two parts do not overlap. How then can we revise the condition so that it will not exclude 4.1.10? Should we perhaps make the condition just that every occurrence of variable must be COMMANDED by a quantifier that binds that variable? That would let 4.1.10 pass, since each x in 4.1.10 is commanded by exactly one of the quantifiers, and thus no jurisdictional dispute between quantifiers can arise, as happened in 4.1.7c. It would also exclude all open sentences: 'man x' would be excluded, since its variable is not commanded by any quantifier. I will sidestep the last problem by giving coherence conditions only for closed sentences. Certain open sentences will then be excluded indirectly in that there will be no way of embedding them in coherent closed sentences; for example, if 4.1.7d were combined with material containing a quantifier that bound the free occurrence of x, the resulting structure would be incoherent since the x of 'man x' and 'love $x\,y$' would then be commanded by

two occurrences of Q_x. As the coherence conditions on closed sentences, I propose:

4.1.11 the variables in a closed sentence are combined coherently if
    a. every occurrence of a variable is commanded by exactly one Q that has that variable as a subscript; and
    b. in every Q S combination, both the Q and the S contain occurrences of the variable with which the Q is subscripted.

It is rather hard to devise structures which conform to 4.1.11 but in which the subscripts on the Q's are not predictable from the rest of the structure. In 4.1.9, for example, the subscript on the first Q would have to be x, since x is the only variable in the S that the Q contains (thus, unless that Q had x as its subscript, 4.1.11b would be violated) and the subscript on the other Q would have to be y, since, while both the S that it contains and the S that is combined with contain occurrences both of x and of y, it is commanded by a quantifier that lays claim to the x and it thus could not lay claim itself to x without violating 4.1.11a. The simplest structure that I have been able to devise in which the subscripts are not completely predictable from the coherency conditions (that is, the simplest structure for which there is more than one way of assigning subscripts to Q's without violating the conditions 4.1.11) is 4.1.12:

4.1.12

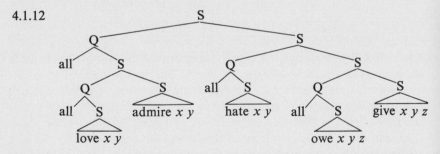

Example 4.1.12 is ambiguous between the following two interpretations:

4.1.13   a.   b.

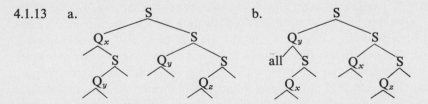

Using numerical subscripts to indicate the antecedents of the pronouns, one can paraphrase interpretation 4.1.13a roughly as 'All people$_1$ who admire all people that they$_1$ love give all people$_2$ that they$_1$ hate all things that they$_1$ owe them$_2$'. Interpretation 4.1.13b can be paraphrased roughly as 'All people$_1$ who are admired by all people that love them$_1$ are given by all people$_2$ that hate them$_1$ all things that they$_2$ owe them$_1$'. These two interpretations are thus quite different meanings (though you should think for a minute about the paraphrases that I have just given before taking my word that they are different). and they could very well differ in truth value. The paraphrases are rough in that 4.1.12 contains nothing corresponding to the nouns *people* and *things* that appear in the paraphrases. If predicates corresponding to those nouns were incorporated into 4.1.12 in the obvious way (e.g., instead of 'love $x\,y$' we would have ' $\wedge$ (person y, love $x\,y$)', the structures would then be unambiguous about which Q binds which variable: depending on whether you have 'person x' or 'person y' combined with the first *all*, the first Q would have to bind x or y respectively. Thus, while 4.1.11 does not enable one to predict the subscripts in 4.1.12 from the rest of the structure, it is conceivable that the structures in which the subscripts are not predictable might all violate some defensible requirement that there be 'sufficiently many nouns' in logical structures. Since for the time being, however, I am not in a position to formulate such a condition, I will thus henceforth assume that the Q's are subscripted with the variables that they bind, though I will often omit the subscripts in cases where they are predictable through the coherency conditions.

The coherence conditions 4.1.11 are not expressible in the form of 'constituent structure rules' such as have figured in the 'grammars' given above: a constituent structure rule gives only a 'local' condition on what a structure may contain (i.e., it tells what may be directly under a given node, possibly subject to a restriction on what is adjacent to that node), whereas the coherence conditions are 'overall' conditions. To determine whether a particular Q is used coherently, it is necessay to examine not only the nodes

4.1.14

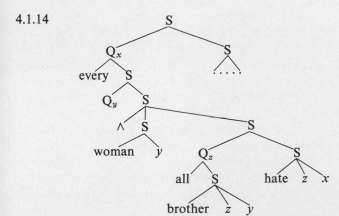

that are immediately below or adjacent to the Q-node, but also nodes that are an arbitrary distance down the tree from it. For example, in the structure in 4.1.14, the only occurrence of x under the Q that binds it is 5 steps down the tree from it, and by appropriate combination of the available logical elements, one could easily construct structures in which a Q_x was 10 or 100 steps above the closest occurrence of x.

Thus the 'grammars' of logical systems must be allowed to contain at least two distinct kinds of rules: 'constituent structure rules' and 'overall conditions'. In this respect, logical structure is like ordinary syntactic structure: syntax involves not only rules specifying what a noun phrase or the like may consist of, but also overall structural conditions on the location of a pronoun relative to its antecedent or of a negative polarity item (such as *a red cent*, as in *Phil won't give Lucy a red cent*; see 4.7 for some discussion of negative polarity items) in relation to the negation on which it depends.

4.2. The Logicians' Favorite Quantifiers

Most modern works on logic operate in terms of just two quantifiers: the UNIVERSAL QUANTIFIER and EXISTENTIAL QUANTIFIER. The so-called universal quantifier corresponds to several different English words: *all, every, any, each*; the existential quantifier corresponds to certain uses of the words *some* and *a/an*. Thus, most logicians would assign (or at least, would expect their pupils to assign) the same logical formula to the sentences

4.2.1   a. All doctors will tell you that Stopsneeze helps.
    b. Every doctor will tell you that Stopsneeze helps.
    c. Any doctor will tell you that Stopsneeze helps.
    d. Each doctor will tell you that Stopsneeze helps.

These sentences in fact are not interchangeable, as was noted in an insightful discussion of the differences in the conditions of use of the four 'universal quantifier words' by Vendler (1967*b*). For example, 4.2.1*c* refers to a hypothetical situation (if you solicit any doctor's opinion about Stopsneeze, he will tell you that it helps) and can be true even if many doctors never express an opinion about Stopsneeze; however, the other sentences will not be true unless every doctor expresses a favourable opinion about Stopsneeze.

Example 4.2.1*d* refers to a sequence of events (i.e., it suggests that you will consult the doctors one by one), whereas the other sentences leave open the possibility that you will get all the opinions simultaneously. More generally, *each* requires a 'matching' between the domain of the quantifier and the objects or events referred to in a way that *every, any*, and *all* do not. For example, the difference in normalness between 4.2.2*a* and 4.2.2*b* correlates with the fact that in our society a woman has her husbands in succession but has her uncles at the same time:

4.2.2   a. Marge admired each of her husbands.
          b. ?Marge admired each of her uncles.
          b'. Marge admired each of her uncles in a different way.

In 4.2.2*a* the *each* matches the various periods when Marge was married with the proposition that at the time she loved her current husband. The addition of *in a different way* to 4.2.2*b* yields the requisite matching: each uncle is matched with a way of admiring someone.

All differs from *each*, *any*, and *ever*, in that it need not express a quantifier but can be used simply to designate a 'group', as in 4.2.3*a* and in one interpretation of 4.2.3*b*:

4.2.3   a. Köchel compiled a catalog of all of Mozart's works.
          b. All of the boys carried the piano upstairs.

In one interpretation, 4.2.3*b* refers to several events of carrying the piano, one involving each boy (indeed, in that interpretation, it can be paraphrased *Each of the boys carried the piano upstairs*); in the other interpretation, the 'group' interpretation, it refers to an event (or perhaps several events) in which all the boys participated. Since a catalog must be of a set of things and not of a single thing (e.g., one could not speak of 'A catalog of the C minor mass', except perhaps in the extended sense of a catalog of the editions, performances, and/or recordings of the C minor mass), 4.2.3*a* has only a reading of the former type.

This last point illustrates an important respect in which *all* differs from the universal quantifier of standard logic: while universal propositions allow one to infer particular cases, as in 4.2.4*a–d*, the 'group' use of *all* does not:

4.2.4   a. Every one of Mozart's works is a masterpiece.
             The quintet for horn and strings is one of Mozart's works.
             Therefore, the quintet for horn and strings is a masterpiece.

          b. Each speaker answered questions.
             Schwartz was a speaker.
             Therefore, Schwartz answered questions.

          c. Any doctor will tell you that Stopsneeze helps.
             Dr. Krankheit is a doctor.
             Therefore, Dr. Krankheit will tell you that Stopsneeze helps
                (if you ask him).

      d. All men are mortal.
         Socrates is a man.
         Therefore, Socrates is mortal.

      e. Köchel compiled a catalog of all of Mozart's works.
         The C minor mass is one of Mozart's works.
         *Therefore, Köchel compiled a catalog of the C minor mass.

Actually, even the group use of *all* can be analyzed as allowing the inference to special cases, provided we take an appropriate view of what a 'special case' of a proposition with 'group' *all* is. Note that group *all* is not equivalent to a simple plural NP denoting the group, since group *all* implies that every member was involved in the event or state in question (thus, 4.2.5*b* is valid), whereas the simple plural does not (4.2.5*a* is invalid):

4.2.5   a. The boys carried the piano upstairs.
            Billy is one of the boys.
            *Therefore, Billy was involved in carrying the piano upstairs.

           b. All of the boys carried the piano upstairs. (group interpretation)
            Billy is one of the boys.
            Therefore, Billy was involved in carrying the piano upstairs.

The fact that even 'group' *all* can be interpreted as allowing this rule of inference suggests that logicians have not been unreasonable in factoring out a single 'universal quantifier' from *each*, *every*, *any*, and *all* and giving rules of inference for that single quantifier (here symbolized by ∀) rather than for *each*, *every*, *any*, and *all*. The sketch given above of the differences among those four words suggests that it may in fact be possible to analyze them all as involving ∀: either consisting of ∀ plus something else or consisting of ∀ in some particular environment.

One particular proposal in which a word is analyzed as a conditioned variant of ∀ is worth some discussion here, namely, the proposal by Quine (1960:138–41) that *any* is a universal quantifier with 'wide scope', whereas *every* and *all* have 'narrow scope'. Specifically, Quine proposed analyzing 4.2.6*a*–*d* as follows[4]

4.2.6   a. If you ask any doctor, you'll be arrested.
            $(\forall: \text{doctor } x)_x \supset (\text{you ask } x, \text{you be arrested})$
          b. If you ask every doctor, you'll be arrested.
            $\supset ((\forall: \text{doctor } x)_x (\text{you ask } x), \text{you be arrested})$
          c. John didn't talk to anyone. $(\forall x) \sim (\text{John talk to } x)$
          d. John didn't talk to everyone. $\sim (\forall x)(\text{John talk to } x)$

That is, he took *any* to be the form that a universal quantifier assumes when certain logical elements (such as the $\supset$ in 4.2.6*a* and the $\sim$ in 4.2.6*c*) intervene between it and the clause containing the variable that it binds. For Quine, thus, the difference in meaning between 4.2.6*a* and 4.2.6*b* or between 4.2.6*c* and 4.2.6*d* corresponded not to a difference in meaning between *any* and *every* but to a difference in scope that is signaled by the superficial difference between *any* and *every*. Certain other instances where *any* and *every* appear to contrast in meaning can be analyzed in accordance with Quine's proposal, provided the language in which the analysis is carried out is richer than that of ordinary predicate logic. For example, 4.2.7*a* and *b* (taken from Geach 1972:7) can be analyzed as 4.2.7*a'* and *b'* provided one admits *may* as combining with sentences:

4.2.7   a. You may marry anyone you want to.
            a'. ($\forall$: you want (you marry x))$_x$ may(you marry x)
            b. You may marry everyone you want to.
            b'. may ($\forall$: you want (you marry x))$_x$(you marry x)

It is far from clear, however, that all instances of *any* can be analyzed as $\forall$ with wide scope. For example, if *any* were just a universal quantifier with wide scope, there would be no reason why it should not combine with *almost* the way that *all* and *every* do (*Almost all of the glasses are cracked*; *Almost every student found problem 3 difficult*); yet the *any* of 4.2.6*c* does not allow *almost*: **John didn't talk to almost anyone*.[5] Moreover, there is no obvious way of providing a 'wide scope' analysis for such sentences as *Hardly any Americans enjoy opera*. It is also not clear that a distinction between 'wide scope' and 'narrow scope' can be drawn in such a way as to accord with the use of *any* versus *every*. The instances of 'wide scope' discussed above all involve a universal quantifier commanding a $\sim$ or $\supset$ or *may* that commands the variable which the quantifier binds. But what happens when the intervening 'operator' is a conjunction or a quantifier, or if more than one operator intervenes—can the universal quantifier then be realized as *any*? Or as *every*? Or can it be rendered into normal English at all? Exploration of this series of questions is left to the reader as an exercise.[6]

For the purposes of this book, I will adopt the position that $\forall$ should be part of the vocabulary available for representing meanings, that it is all or part of the meanings of *all*, *every*, *each*, and *any* (or at least, the use of *any* found in 4.2.1*c*), and that the differences in meaning among those four words correspond to extra material that in some cases may legitimately be ignored.

The EXISTENTIAL QUANTIFIER, henceforth represented by the symbol $\exists$, is also the common element in a number of things that natural languages often distinguish, for example, various uses of *a/an* and *some* in English.[7] The formula (∃: man x)$_x$(admire x Hitler) is supposed to be true if at least one man admires Hitler and false if no man admires Hitler. It is noncommittal on whether exactly one man or more than one admires Hitler. However, English sentences must draw the distinction between one and more than one:

4.2.8   a. Some man admires Hitler.
             b. Some men admire Hitler.

The singular/plural distinction is an extremely pervasive characteristic of English grammar: when you use a noun, you are generally required by the language to commit yourself on whether you are referring to one or more than one object, regardless of whether you have any interest in conveying that information. For example, if you have one nephew and three nieces, you have to use the singular form *nephew* and the plural form *nieces* in the sentence *I'm shopping for Christmas presents for my nephew and nieces* even if all that you want to convey is that the presents are for the children of whom you are an uncle or aunt, and you have no particular reason to inform your hearers about how many of the children are of each sex.

The information conveyed by the singular/plural distinction sometimes is part of the information that one wishes to convey in what one says, and sometimes it is not, and if a system of logic is to deal with the propositions that are intended in the various sentences that are used in stating arguments, rather than the propositions that happen to be conveyed as a result of quirks of a particular language, it will be necessary to allow logical formulas to contain elements that are unspecified with regard to the singular/plural distinction but which may be combined, when appropriate, with elements that specify whether one object or more than one is being referred to.

All natural languages contain words that appear in the same positions as do *all* and *some* (or their equivalents in the language in question) but which are not identifiable with ∀ or ∃. For example, there are such words as *most*, *many*, *few*, *no*, *several*, and the numerals (*one, two, three, . . .*), as well as such compound expressions as *almost all*, *all but one*, *hardly any*, *at least five*. In some cases an analysis of the word as a combination of ∀ or ∃ with other material is possible. For example, it is reasonable to propose that *no* means '∼∃', for example,

4.2.9   No Republican admires Truman
             ∼ (∃: Republican x)$_x$(admire x Truman)

However, the 'other material' may have to be something other than just propositional connectives. For example, one might propose to analyze

Many Americans enjoy sports as involving an existential quantifier ('There is a set of Americans such that. . .'), a universal quantifier ('All the individuals in that set enjoy sports'), and a size specification ('That set is large'). That analysis involves the conceptual apparatus of set theory (the notion of a set, the notion of being a member of a set), as well as the conceptual apparatus involved in notions of size; and an adequate treatment of notions of size may be fairly involved, since it is necessary to refer to relative sizes rather than just to absolute sizes and since such notions as 'normal' or 'expected' may be involved in determining how many shall count as 'many' or as 'few' (for example, one might say *Very few people went to the football game* when there were 5000 in attendance, yet *Lots of people came to Fred's party* when 50 people came). For the present, I will leave open the question of whether it is reasonable to analyze all other quantifiers into combinations of ∀ and/or ∃ with other material. The discussion in the rest of this chapter and in chapter 6 will in fact concentrate on ∀ and ∃, though occassional references will be made to other quantifiers. I will make a point, however, of avoiding an error that it is easy to fall into: the error of taking properties that ∀ and ∃ share to be properties of quantifiers in general. For example, by interchanging consecutive Q's that both have ∀ or both have ∃ as the quantifier, one obtains a result that is deductively equivalent to the original formula.[8]

4.2.10   a. $(\forall: Fx)_x(\forall: Gy)_y Hxy \dashv\vdash (\forall: Gy)_y(\forall: Fx)_x Hxy$
           b. $(\exists: Fx)_x(\exists: Gy)_y Hxy \dashv\vdash (\exists: Gy)_y(\exists: Fx)_x Hxy$

However, this fact must not lead one to conclude that the result of interchanging consecutive occurrences of the same quantifier always produces a result deductively equivalent to the original. For example, the result of interchanging consecutive occurrences of *most* can differ in truth value from the original formula. Suppose that $(\text{Most}: Fx)_x Gx$ is true if more than half of the things that have the property of F also have the property G and is false otherwise.[9] Example 4.2.11*a* is three-ways ambiguous, having the interpretations 4.2.11*b–d*, where Bx stands for 'is one of the boys', Gy for 'is one of the girls', and Dxy for 'danced with':

4.2.11   a. Most of the boys danced with most of the girls.
           b. $(\text{Most}: Bx)[(\text{Most}: Gy)Dxy]$
           c. $(\text{Most}: Gy)[(\text{Most}: Bx)Dxy]$
           d. The dancing involved most of the boys and most of the girls.

I will ignore 4.2.11*d*, which is listed here only for completeness' sake; in fact it does not fit neatly into the notational scheme being developed here. By setting up a possible state of affairs, it is easy to see that 4.2.11*b* and

4.2.11*c* need not have the same truth value. Let lines indicate who danced with whom, as in 4.2.12:

4.2.12

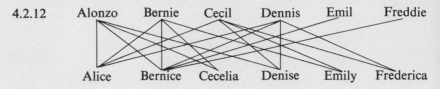

Alonzo danced with most of the girls (namely, with four of them); so also did Bernie, Cecil, and Dennis. Thus there are four boys who danced with most of the girls, and since four is most of the boys, 4.2.11*b* is true. Yet there are only two of the girls that most of the boys danced with: four boys danced with Alice and five with Bernice, but at most three boys danced with any of the other girls. Thus '(Most: B*x*)D*xy*' is true of only two of the girls and is thus not true of most of the girls, which means that 4.2.11*c* is false. Thus, interchanging (Most: B*x*) with (Most: G*y*) may change the truth value. The same is true of interchanging occurrences of *many* or of *almost all* or of *all but one*, as can be seen by constructing an appropriate state of affairs. Thus, the property of ∀ and ∃ given in 4.2.10, far from being a general property of quantifiers, appears to be shared by no other quantifiers.[10]

4.3. Rules of Inference

As in the case of the propositional connectives, there will be two rules of inference for each of the two quantifiers considered here: one rule introducing it into inferences, the other exploiting occurrences of it.

The rule of ∀-exploitation is the rule that allows one to infer from a general proposition to a special case, for example,

4.3.1   All men are mortal.
             Socrates is a man.
             Therefore, Socrates is a mortal.

Expressed in the notation used in this chapter, the general pattern of inference is the following:

4.3.2 $(\forall: Fx)_x\ Gx$
             Fa
             Ga

The rule of ∀-introduction is best introduced through an example of how one can argue for a universal proposition. Suppose that you want to show that the square of every odd number is odd. To do that, take an arbitrary odd number n. An odd number is one more than an even number, so n will be equal to $2m + 1$ for some whole number m (an even number is twice a whole number). Since $n^2 = (2m + 1)^2 = 4m^2 + 4m + 1 = 2(2m^2 + 2m) + 1$, n^2 is one more than twice a whole number and is thus odd. This will be the case no matter what odd number we picked, and so every odd number will have an odd number for its square.

The important feature of this argument is the subproof in which one 'picks an arbitrary element' and shows, on the basis of what has already been established, that that element, no matter what it is, will have the characteristic in question. The words 'pick an arbitrary element' are misleading, since there isn't any 'picking' involved (you don't, for example, say 'Let's pick 37, since that's as arbitrary an odd number as you're likely to find'). What is going on, rather, is that a subproof is set up in which a supposition is made involving a variable that has not hitherto appeared in the proof. The only 'information' in which that variable appears is the supposition (e.g., the only thing you know about n is that it is an odd number). The scheme of inference can be displayed as follows:

4.3.3
$$
\begin{array}{|l}
\text{F}n \\\hline
\quad \ldots \\
\text{G}n
\end{array}
$$
$(\forall : \text{F}x)_x \text{G}x$

In the given case, 'Fn' is 'n is an odd number' and 'Gn' is 'n^2 is an odd number'.

The rules of $\forall$-exploitation and $\forall$-introduction are both involved in the following inference, in which from 'All men are mortal and imperfect' one deduces 'All men are mortal':

4.3.4

1	$(\forall x: \text{man } x) \land (\text{mortal } x, \text{imperfect } x)$	supp
2	man u	supp
3	$\land$ (mortal u, imperfect u)	1, 2, $\forall$-expl
4	mortal u	3, $\land$-expl
5	$(\forall x: \text{man } x)(\text{mortal } x)$	2-4, $\forall$-intro

Note the propriety of step 3, where in applying $\forall$-elimination we have substituted not a real constant (such as 'Evel Knievel') for the bound variable, but rather the 'arbitrary element' that figures in the application of $\forall$-introduction. Since line 1 asserts that any man whatever has the property 'x is mortal and x is imperfect' and the supposition of the subproof is that 'u is a man', with no further assumptions made about 'what u is', it is correct to infer 'u is mortal and u is imperfect' as a step of the subproof.

The rule of ∃-introduction allows one to infer from a particular instance of something to an existential proposition, for example, to go from the premises 'Aristotle is a man' and 'Aristotle is bald' to the conclusion 'Some man is bald' or 'There is a man who is bald'. The general scheme is

4.3.5 Fa
             Ga
             $(\exists: Fx)Gx$

The rule of ∃-exploitation is somewhat more complicated and is best introduced through an example. From the premise 'Every person has a father' you can deduce the conclusion 'Every person has a grandfather'. Take an arbitrary person. Then there will be a second person who is the father of the first person. But the second person also has a father (since every person has a father), and so there is a third person who is the father of the second person. The father of the father of a person is that person's grandfather; thus, the third person is the first person's grandfather. Thus, the first person has a grandfather, and since the first person could be anyone at all, that means that every person has a grandfather. This argument can be formalized as follows:

4.3.6   1 $(\forall: \text{person } x)(\exists: \text{person } y)(\text{father } y\, x)$ supp
        2 | person u supp
        3 | $(\exists: \text{person } y)(\text{father } y\, u)$ 1, 2, ∀-expl
        4 | | person v supp
        5 | | father $v\, u$ supp
        6 | | $(\exists: \text{person } y)(\text{father } y\, v)$ 1, 4, ∀-expl
        7 | | | person w supp
        8 | | | father $w\, v$ supp
        9 | | | $\land (\text{father } w\, v, \text{father } v\, u)$ 5, 8, ∧ intro-
       10 | | | grandfather $w\, u$ 9, definition of 'grandfather'
       11 | | | $(\exists: \text{person } y)(\text{grandfather } y\, u)$ 7, 10, ∃-intro
       12 | | $(\exists: \text{person } y)(\text{grandfather } y\, u)$ 6, 7–11, ∃-expl
       13 | $(\exists: \text{person } y)(\text{grandfather } y\, u)$ 3, 4–12, ∃-expl
       14 $(\forall: \text{person } x)(\exists: \text{person } y)(\text{grandfather } y\, x)$ 2, 3–13, ∀-intro

The steps that don't obviously match the informal argument given above are 12 and 13. Let's concentrate on them, since they are in fact where the work of ∃-exploitation is done. Note that lines 11, 12, and 13 are identical except for their place in the hierarchy of the proof: line 13 is in the first subproof, line 12 in the second subproof, and line 11 in the third subproof. The third subproof is immediately preceded by line 6, which says that v has a father. In the third subproof, you start by saying in effect 'let w stand for an individual such as line 6 says exists'. Lines 7 and 8 give the properties which line 6 says that that individual has. While w appears in lines 7–10, it does not appear in line 11: the application of ∃-introduction has eliminated w, giving the conclusion 'u has a grandfather'. Thus what ∃-exploitation allows you to do is to set up a subproof in which you act as if you have a specific element such as your premises say exists, and, if you are able to infer a conclusion in which no reference to that element appears, 'export' that conclusion to the main proof. The scheme for ∃-exploitation then is

4.3.7

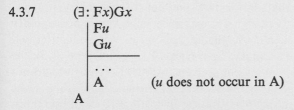

$(\exists: Fx)Gx$
| Fu
| Gu
|————
| . . .
| A   (u does not occur in A)
A

One qualification must be added to the statement of ∀-introduction and ∃-introduction given above. In both of these rules a bound variable is introduced, together with a quantifier that binds it. The absolute identities of bound variables are of no significance; that is, the following all represent exactly the same proposition:

4.3.8   a. $(\forall: \text{man } x)_x(\text{mortal } x)$
             b. $(\forall: \text{man } y)_y(\text{mortal } y)$
             c. $(\forall: \text{man } z)_z(\text{mortal } z)$

However, it does matter whether the variables occurring in two positions are the same or different. Thus, while 4.3.9a and 4.3.9b represent the same proposition, 4.3.9c is incoherent and represents no proposition at all:

4.3.9   a. $(\forall: \text{man } x)_x(\exists: \text{woman } y)_y(\text{love } x\ y)$
             b. $(\forall: \text{man } y)_y(\exists: \text{woman } x)_x(\text{love } y\ x)$
             c. $(\forall: \text{man } x)_x(\exists: \text{woman } x)_x(\text{love } x\ x)$

In applying ∀-introduction and ∃-introduction, the new bound variable must be chosen in such a way that the resulting combination is coherent. For all practical purposes, what this will mean is that the new bound variable must not appear in the lines of the proof from which the conclusion is inferred by ∀-introduction or ∃-introduction. I will assume henceforth that statements of rules of inference apply only to 'coherent' formulas; that is, the incoherence of a line of a proof is sufficient to exclude the proof, regardless of whether the proof conforms in all other details to the rules of inference. Thus, a proof containing the following would be excluded, though conforming to the rules of inference, since it contains an incoherent line:

4.3.10   . . .

> man w
> _____
>
> . . .
> ($\exists$: woman $x)_x$(love w x)
>
> ($\forall$: man $x)_x$($\exists$: woman $x)_x$(love x x)

If the policy of excluding things such as the last line of 4.3.10 as incoherent were not adopted, and instead a policy was adopted of imposing an interpretation on everything that conforms to the 'constituent structure rules' (as is done in most textbooks, e.g., Thomason 1970), it would be necessary to place additional restrictions on the application of $\forall$-introduction and $\exists$-introduction, since the formulas here rejected as incoherent would be interpreted as having meanings, but meanings which generally would not follow from the earlier steps of the proof. For example, according to the policy adopted in Thomason 1970, the last line of 4.3.10 would be interpreted as meaning 'There is a woman who loves herself' (since Thomason takes each occurence of a variable to be bound by the *lowest* quantifier that lays claim to it, and takes a quantifier as semantically empty when there are no occurrences of its variable left for it to bind). However, obviously you cannot conclude that there is a woman who loves herself just because you can show that for an arbitrarily selected man there is a woman that he loves. If formulas in which two quantifiers lay claim to a single occurrence of a variable are excluded as incoherent, the rules of inference can be stated in their pristine form, without extra clauses to rule out spurious applications of them.

I will conclude this section by presenting some important results that can be proved via the rules of inference of this section, together with their proofs.

4.3.11   Theorem: $(\forall: fx)(\forall: gy)hxy \dashv\vdash (\forall: gy)(\forall: fx)hxy$
Proof that the first formula $\vdash$ the second formula:

1	$(\forall: fx)(\forall: gy)hxy$	supp
2	gu	supp
3	fv	supp
4	$(\forall: gy)hvy$	1, 3, $\forall$-expl
5	hvu	2, 4, $\forall$-expl
6	$(\forall: fx)hxu$	3–5, $\forall$-intro
7	$(\forall: gy)(\forall: fx)hxy$	2–6, $\forall$-intro

Proof that the second formula $\vdash$ the first formula:
essentially identical to the proof just given.

4.3.12 $(\exists: fx)(\exists: gx)hxy \dashv\vdash (\exists: gy)(\exists: fx)hxy$
Proof that the first formula ⊢ the second:

1	$(\exists: fx)(\exists: gy)hxy$	supp
2	fu	supp
3	$(\exists: gy)huy$	supp
4	gv	supp
5	huv	supp
6	fu	2, reit
7	$(\exists: fx)hxv$	6, 5, ∃-intro
8	$(\exists: gy)(\exists: fx)hxy$	4, 7, ∃-intro
9	$(\exists: gy)(\exists: fx)hxy$	3, 4–8, ∃-expl
10	$(\exists: gy)(\exists: fx)hxy$	1, 2–9, ∃-expl

Proof that the second formula ⊢ the first: essentially identical to the above proof.

4.3.13 $(\exists: fx)(\forall: gy)hxy \vdash (\forall: gy)(\exists: fx)hxy$
Proof:

1	$(\exists: fx)(\forall: gy)hxy$	supp
2	fv	supp
3	$(\forall: gy)hvy$	supp
4	gu	supp
5	hvu	3, 4, ∀-expl
6	$(\exists: fx)hxu$	2, 5, ∃-intro
7	$(\forall: gy)(\exists: fx)hxy$	4–6, ∀-intro
8	$(\forall: gy)(\exists: fx)hxy$	1, 2–7, ∃-expl

You should be able to identify why the converse of 4.3.13 is *not* provable.

4.3.14 $(\forall: fx) \supset (gx, A) \dashv\vdash \supset ((\exists: fx)gx, A)$, where A does not involve x.
Proof that the first formula ⊢ the second:

1	$(\forall: fx) \supset (gx, A)$	supp
2	$(\exists: fx)gx$	supp
3	fu	supp
4	gu	supp
5	$\supset (gu, A)$	1, 3, ∀-expl
6	A	5, 4, ⊃-expl
7	A	2, 3–6, ∃-expl
8	$\supset ((\exists: fx)gx, A)$	2–7, ∼-intro

Proof that the second formula ⊢ the first: left to the reader as an exercise.

The assumption that A does not involve x has been incorporated tacitly into the proof by virtue of the fact that the A's that appear in lines 1, 5, 6, and 7 are treated as identical: only if A does not involve x does the substitution of u for x in line 5 leave A unchanged.

The following results are quantificational analogues to de Morgan's laws. One of the four results, namely, 4.3.15c is somewhat remarkable in that it purports to establish an existence proposition from a premise that does not apparently say anything about existence. See 4.4 for discussion of whether the proof of 4.3.15c should be admitted and identification of a questionable step in it.

4.3.15   a. $(\exists : fx) \sim gx \vdash \sim (\forall : fx)gx$

Proof:

1	$(\exists : fx) \sim gx$	supp
2	fu	supp
3	$\sim gu$	supp
4	$(\forall : fx)gx$	supp
5	gu	4, 2, $\forall$-expl
6	$\sim gu$	3, reit
7	$\sim (\forall : fx)gx$	4–6, $\sim$-intro
8	$\sim (\forall : fx)gx$	1, 2–7, $\exists$-expl

b. $(\forall : fx) \sim gx \vdash \sim (\exists : fx)gx$

Proof:

1	$(\forall : fx) \sim gx$	supp
2	$(\exists : fx)gx$	supp
3	fu	supp
4	gu	supp
5	$\sim gu$	1, 3, $\forall$-expl
6	$\wedge (A, \sim A)$	4, 5, 2.2.8e (A here may be any sentence not involving u)
7	$\wedge (A, \sim A)$	2, 3–6, $\exists$-expl
8	A	7, $\wedge$-expl
9	$\sim A$	7, $\wedge$-expl
10	$\sim (\exists : fx)gx$	2–9, $\sim$-intro

c. $\sim(\forall:fx)gx \vdash (\exists:fx)\sim gx$

Proof:

1	$\sim(\forall:fx)gx$					supp
2		$\sim(\exists:fx)\sim gx$				supp
3			fu			supp
4				$\sim gu$		supp
5				fu		3, reit
6				$(\exists:fx)\sim gx$		5, 4, $\exists$-intro
7				$\sim(\exists:fx)\sim gx$		2, reit
8			gu			4–7, $\sim$-intro
9		$(\forall:fx)gx$				3–8, $\forall$-intro
10		$\sim(\forall:fx)gx$				1, reit
11	$\sim\sim(\exists:fx)\sim gx$					2–10, $\sim$-intro
12	$(\exists:fx)\sim gx$					11, $\sim$-expl

d. $\sim(\exists:fx)gx \vdash (\forall:fx)\sim gx$

Proof:

1	$\sim(\exists:fx)gx$			supp
2		fu		supp
3			gu	supp
4			$(\exists:fx)gx$	2, 3, $\exists$-intro
5			$\sim(\exists:fx)gx$	1, reit
6		$\sim gu$		3–5, $\sim$-intro
7	$(\forall:fx)\sim gx$			2–6, $\forall$-intro

4.4. Possible Objections to the Rules of Inference

DOES 'SOME' IMPLY 'NOT ALL'? From 'Socrates is a man' and 'Socrates is mortal', by $\exists$-introduction you can infer 'Some man is mortal' or perhaps 'Some men are mortal' (the conclusion should be noncommittal regarding grammatical number, though the English language forces the noun to be either singular or plural). *Some man is mortal* or *Some men are mortal* isn't a normal thing to say if one knows that all men are mortal: it suggests that *only* some men are mortal, that is, that some men aren't mortal. Yet from 'All men are mortal' plus any extra premise that establishes that there are men, the rules given above allow one to infer 'Some men are mortal':

4.4.1   1 (∀: man x)(mortal x)   supp
             2 man Socrates   supp
             _____
             3 mortal Socrates   1, 2, ∀-expl
             4 (∃: man x)(mortal x)   3, 2, ∃-intro

To avoid inconsistency, it will be necessary to do one of the following: (i) change the rules of inference, (ii) change our conclusions about what English sentences correspond to the various logical formulas, or (iii) take the relationship between 'Some men are mortal' and 'Not all men are mortal' to be not that of entailment but rather that of 'conversational implicature', that is, to take 'Some men are mortal' to be true even if there are no men who are not mortal, though recognizing that it might be misleading to say *Some men are mortal*, since if you know that all men are mortal you could be more informative at no extra linguistic cost by saying *All men are mortal*, and if you didn't know whether all men were mortal, it would be more sportsmanlike of you to indicate the incompleteness of your knowledge by saying *At least some men are mortal*. For the present, I will simply rule by fiat that (iii) is the right one of these alternatives. In 8.3 I will present some argument in favor of iii, though far from a conclusive case.

SHOULD THE RULES FOR ∀ ACCOMMODATE EXISTENTIAL COMMITMENT? Sentences with *any* do not commit the speaker to the proposition that the domain of the quantifier is not empty, whereas sentences with *every* and *all* do:

4.4.2   a. Any philosopher who accepts Meinong's theory of reference is insane.
             b. Every philosopher who accepts Meinong's theory of reference is insane.
             c. All philosophers who accept Meinong's theory of reference are insane.

Examples 4.4.2*b* and 4.4.2*c* commit the speaker to the proposition that there are philosophers who accept Meinong's theory of reference, but 4.4.2*a* does not. The rules of inference given in 4.3 do not attach any existential commitment to ∀. Consider, for example, the fact that they allow the following proof:

4.4.3

1	$(\forall: fx)gx$	supp
2	$\sim gu$	supp
3	fu	supp
4	gu	1, 3, $\forall$-expl
5	$\sim gu$	2, reit
6	$\sim fu$	3–5, $\sim$-intro
7	$(\forall: \sim gx) \sim fx$	2–6, $\forall$-intro

This proof can be accepted only if $\forall$ is interpreted as not carrying existential commitment with it, since otherwise the conclusion would commit one to the proposition that there are non-g's, whereas the premise would not commit one to that, for example, if $\forall$ were identified with a quantifier that carries existential commitment, then 4.4.3 would allow one to go from the premise that all dogs bite postmen (a premise that commits one to the proposition that there are dogs but is neutral regarding whether there are nonbiters of postmen) to the conclusion that all nonbiters of postmen are nondogs (a conclusion that commits one to the proposition that there are nonbiters of postmen).

There are basically two ways that one can cope with this difference among universal quantifier words: either one gives rules of inference that directly match one of the quantifier words and analyzes the other quantifier words in terms of it (say, analyses *every* and *all* as *any* plus a conjoined existential clause) or one does one's logic in terms of two or more distinct universal quantifier words and gives rules of inference for each. I will sketch briefly here how the latter alternative might be carried out. Let us assume that we have a system of predicate logic involving two universal quantifiers, $\forall$ and $\forall'$, where $\forall$ does not carry an existential commitment but $\forall'$ does. The rules of inference given in the last section will cover $\forall$. The rules of inference for $\forall'$ will have to be similar to those for $\forall$ but will have to build in the existence commitment somehow. The most obvious rule of $\forall'$-introduction is one in which the premise that there are f's is simply grafted onto our present rule of $\forall$-introduction. The only problem in formulating this rule is in expressing this extra premise. Note that the means of expression that our version of predicate logic provides us do not yield a natural way of expressing, say, the proposition that there are gorillas. The existential quantifier demands two propositional functions, and this demand could be met in a purported translation of *There are gorillas* only through either duplication or irrelevancy, that is, the only available candidates would be formulas like $(\exists: \text{gorilla } x)_x(\text{gorilla } x)$ or $(\exists: \vee (px, \sim px))_x(\text{gorilla } x)$, which would correspond directly to such outlandish sentences as *Some gorillas are gorillas* or *Some unicorns or nonunicorns are gorillas*. Rather than employ such bizarre expressions, I will simply supplement the expressive devices of the predicate logic with a 'absolute' existential quantifier, here written E, which will combine with a single propositional function at a time instead of the usual two, giving representations of the content of such sentences as *There are gorillas*. The rule of ∀'-introduction will then be

4.4.4 $(Ex)fx$
        $\begin{array}{|l} fu \\ \hline \\ ... \\ gu \end{array}$
        $(\forall' : fx)_x gx$

Since what can be inferred from a ∀'-proposition appears to be precisely what can be inferred from the corresponding ∀-proposition plus the proposition that there are f's, the most obvious proposal for ∀'-exploitation is simply to have the following two rules:

4.4.5   ∀'-exploitation 1   ∀'-exploitation 2
        $(\forall' : fx)_x gx$ $(\forall' : fx)_x gx$
        $(\forall : fx)_x gx$ $(Ex)fx$

The fact that there are two 'exploitation' rules rather than one is no cause for alarm: it may very well be mere accident that for the connectives discussed so far one rule was enough to characterize how premises involving the connective could be used in inferences. Note that ∀'-exploitation 2 would be needed not only in deriving existential commitments but also in proving results such as the following:

4.4.6 $(\forall' : fx)_x (\forall' : gy)_y hxy \dashv\vdash (\forall' : gy)_y (\forall' : fx)_x hxy$

The proof of this result would be similar to the proof of its analogue that was given in the last section (4.3.11); however, extra steps would have to be interpolated in that proof if 4.4.6 is to be derived; for example, step 6 would have to be preceded by a demonstration that there are f's and step 7 would have to be preceded by a demonstration that there are g's, and ∀'-exploitation 2 would be needed to establish those propositions.

Isn't ∃-introduction too symmetric? The rule of ∃-introduction is suspect in that it does not differentiate between the roles of the two propositional functions: it sanctions the derivation of $(\exists : Gx)Fx$ as well as of $(\exists : Fx)Gx$ from the given premises. However, the sentences corresponding to those two formulas are by no means interchangeable, as witness such pairs as

4.4.7   a.   Some persons are left-handers.
        a'. Some left-handers are persons.

>   b. Some Freemasons have been U.S. Presidents.
>   b′. Some U.S. Presidents have been Freemasons.

I maintain that the difference between 4.4.7*a* and 4.4.7*a*′ or between 4.4.7*b* and 4.4.7*b*′ is (perhaps among other things) one of pragmatic presupposition (see 9.4): what must be taken for granted by the parties to the discourse for the use of the sentence to be normal. Example 4.4.7*a* takes for granted that there are persons, 4.4.7*a*′ that there are left-handers. What makes 4.4.7*a*′ so bizarre is that what is taken for granted implies what is asserted, and thus the conditions for its appropriateness could only be met in contexts in which it would be pointless. What I spoke of as an 'existential commitment' in the discussion of *every* and *all* earlier in this section may also really be a pragmatic presupposition.

It should also be noted that if one (i) accepts the classical truth table for $\sim$, (ii) demands that the rules of inference yield true conclusions when applied to true premises, (iii) requires that an existentially quantified proposition be false when the domain of the existentially quantified variable is empty (i.e., that $(\exists: fx)gx$ be false in any state of affairs in which fx is false of all things), and (iv) accepts the rules of inference of 4.3, then a universally quantified proposition must be true in any state of affairs where the domain of the universally quantified variable is empty. The results of 4.3.15 establish that

4.4.8 $(\forall: fx)gx \dashv\vdash \sim (\exists: fx) \sim gx$

Suppose that in a given state of affairs fx is false of all things. Then by iii $(\exists: fx) \sim gx$ is false, by i $\sim (\exists: fx) \sim gx$ is true, and by ii (which implies that deductively equivalent formulas always agree in truth value), $(\forall: fx)gx$ is true, Thus, under assumptions i–iii, the rules of inference of 4.3 require a universal proposition to be true whenever the domain of the universally quantified variable is empty, that is, no existential commitment is reflected in the truth values.

By giving up assumption i, one could admit truth value assignments that reflected an existential commitment, that is, if one allows the possibility of false propositions whose negations are false, one could conceivably have the right half of 4.4.8 false and thus the left half false also. In that case, not only the left half of 4.4.8 but also its negation would be false, in view of 4.4.9:

4.4.9 $\sim (\forall: fx)gx \dashv\vdash (\exists: fx) \sim gx$

The right half of 4.4.9 would be false by iii and thus (by ii) so would the left half. It is in fact possible to assign truth values consistently with the rules of inference in such a way that for some choices of f and g, both $(\forall: fx)gx$ and its negation would generally be false in a state of affairs in which there are no f's. If $fx \vdash gx$ (thus, in particular, if fx is contradictory), then the universal proposition will have to be true, since it is provable by an application of $\forall$-introduction. The truth value assignment in which $(\forall: fx)gx$ is true if $fx \vdash gx$ and is false otherwise is consistent with the given rules of inference. Thus, if one gives up strict adherence to the classical truth tables and accepts instead the more general range of truth value assignments discussed in 3.2, one can have truth value assignments that reflect an existential commitment in $\forall$.

SHOULD ∃-INTRODUCTION BE RESTRICTED TO OBJECTS THAT EXIST? In the last section, some doubt was raised about one of the results proved, namely, the derivation of $(\exists: fx)\sim gx$ from $\sim(\forall: fx)gx$, in which an existential proposition was proved from a premise that does not obviously imply anything existential. One step in that proof (4.3.15c) deserves to be singled out as suspicious, namely, step 6, in which $(\exists: fx)\sim gx$ is derived from fu and $\sim gu$ by ∃-introduction. What makes this step suspicious is that u got into the derivation only via a supposition (for the subproof 3–8, in which $(\forall: fx)gx$ was established by supposing fu and showing that gu could be derived from it). Note that you don't have to establish that anything has the property f in order to be able to suppose fu (recall that the rules of inference for $\forall$ do not provide for any existential commitment), and thus fu in 4.3.15c is a dubious premise on which to justify the derivation of an existence proposition. A second type of case in which an application of ∃-introduction would be highly suspicious relates to an issue that we have hitherto taken no position on, namely, whether individual constants always have a denotation. Suppose that we were to allow a constant s standing for 'Santa Claus' and allow states of affairs to differ with regard to whether s had a denotation (i.e., in some states of affairs there is a Santa Claus and in others there isn't). Suppose, further, that we allow propositions about Santa Claus to be true even in states of affairs in which there is no Santa Claus (e.g., you might want to take 'Santa Claus wears a red suit' and 'Santa Claus lives at the North Pole' to be true even in states of affairs in which there is no Santa Claus). This treatment of constants like s is innocuous just as long as we don't permit ∃-introduction to apply to fs and gs, yielding $(\exists: fx)gx$; for example, we mustn't allow ∃-introduction to let us infer 'Someone who wears a red suit lives at the North Pole' from 'Santa Claus wears a red suit' and 'Santa Claus lives at the North Pole'.

A possible way of tightening the rule of ∃-introduction to render it inapplicable in these two cases would be to demand that the a that figures in the formulation of the rule 'exist'. Thus, if we were to add to our language a one-place predicate 'exist', set up in such a way that 'exist a' is true when a has a denotation in the given state of affairs and false when it does not, then ∃-introduction might be reformulated as

4.4.10   exist a
fa
ga
$(\exists: fx)_x gx$

This reformation of ∃-introduction fits the Santa Claus case fine, but it is not clear that it will solve the problem of the variables in suppositions. For example, nothing so far rules out the possibility of a supposition like $\wedge$ (exist u, fu), which could then give rise (via an application of $\wedge$-elimination) to a proof in which the conditions for the revised ∃-introduction were met, even though the u still gets into the proof through the same kind of supposition as in the objectionable case. Note that the following exact analogue to the objectionable proof can be constructed:

4.4.11

1	$\sim(\forall: \wedge$ (exist $x, fx))gx$			supp
2		$\sim(\exists: fx)gx$		supp
3			$\wedge$ (exist u, fu)	supp
4				$\sim gu$
				supp
5			exist u	3, $\wedge$-expl
6			fu	3, $\wedge$-expl
7			$(\exists: fx)\sim gx$	5, 6, 4, revised ∃-intro
8			$\sim(\exists: fx)\sim gx$	2, reit
9		gu		4–8, $\sim$-intro plus $\sim$-expl
10		$(\forall: \wedge$ (exist $x, fx))gx$		3–10, $\forall$-intro
11		$\sim(\forall: \wedge$ (exist $x, fx))gx$		1, reit
12	$(\exists: fx)\sim gx$			2–11, $\sim$-intro plus $\sim$-expl

But this result is just as questionable as the one that precipitated this digression: the premise in 4.4.11 is, if anything, weaker than that of the earlier proof, but the same conclusion has been derived from it, and the application of ∃-introduction in step 7 involves the same dubious derivation of an existential proposition from premises that at most suppose rather than demonstrating existence. Thus, if proofs like 4.3.15c of the last section are to be excluded, more will have to be done than just revise ∃-introduction as in 4.4.10, such as excluding suppositions that involve 'exist' and thus preventing the crucial step 3 in 4.4.11. However, I have no clear idea of whether that revision is desirable.

One important school of mathematics and logic, INTUITIONISM, rejects a different detail of 4.3.15c, namely, the final step, in which an existential proposition is established by reductio ad absurdum. For intuitionists,

∃-introduction is the only rule by which an existential proposition can be derived.

Whether 4.3.15c should be excluded depends on whether one takes to be 'vacuously true' propositions $(\forall: fx)gx$ in which the f is false for all x. Note that it is only in that case that the possibility of the conclusion of 4.3.15c being false and the premise true arises: if there are individuals having the property f, then the only way the premise of 4.3.15c could be true would be for there to be an individual having the property f but not the property g, and the existence of such an individual is sufficient to make the conclusion of 4.3.15c true. The proposition $(\forall: fx)gx$ is in fact standardly taken to be true when nothing has the property f, and under that policy, 4.3.15c is not objectionable.

4.5. Restricted and Unrestricted Quantifiers

The quantifiers that have figured in the formulas given so far are RESTRICTED QUANTIFIERS: each quantifier comes with a propositional function that specifies what the DOMAIN of its variable is, as in $(\forall: \text{man } x)$ (mortal x), where 'man x' specifies that the relevant objects are those which possess the property of being a man. Modern logicians have generally operated instead in terms of UNRESTRICTED QUANTIFIERS, that is, they have taken all variables to have the same domain and have thus taken quantifiers as not requiring a special propositional function to indicate the domain of the variable in question.[11] How then do they distinguish between, say, *All pianists admire Beethoven* and *All violinists admire Beethoven*? This has been accomplished by incorporating *pianist* and *violinist* into the propositional function that the quantifier applies to (4.5.1a and b), or to use what is in fact a more common notation for quantifiers, 4.5.1a' and b':[12]

4.5.1   a. $(\forall)_x \supset (\text{pianist } x, \text{admire } x \text{ Beethoven})$
b. $(\forall)_x \supset (\text{violinist } x, \text{admire } x \text{ Beethoven})$
a'. $(\forall x) \supset (\text{pianist } x, \text{admire } x \text{ Beethoven})$
b'. $(\forall x) \supset (\text{violinist } x, \text{admire } x \text{ Beethoven})$

In predicate logic with restricted quantifiers, the quantifier is combined with two propositional functions: one specifying the domain of the variable bound by the quantifier, and one whose truth in that domain is at issue. In predicate logic with unrestricted quantifiers, the quantifier is combined with only one propositional function, generally a complex propositional function chosen to get the effect of a restriction on the domain of the variable.

A proposition with an unrestricted universal quantifier, $(\forall x)Px$, is supposed to be true if Px is true of every value of x. That means that $(\forall x) \supset (Fx,$

G*x*) will be true if ⊃(F*x*, G*x*) is true of every value of *x*. Since an if-then proposition is true when either the antecedent is false or the consequent is true, (∀*x*)⊃(F*x*, G*x*) will be true if for every value of *x* either F*x* is false or G*x* is true. But that condition is equivalent to the condition that for those values of *x* for which F*x* is true, G*x* is also true: whenever F*x* is false, ⊃(F*x*, G*x*) is true, and so it is precisely for the *x*'s for which F*x* is true that G*x* need be true. That means that the truth condition for (∀*x*)⊃(F*x*, G*x*) coincides with what we have tacitly been taking as the truth condition for (∀: F*x*)$_x$G*x*: only the *x*'s for which F*x* is true are relevant, and if for all of those, G*x* is true, then the whole proposition is true; and if G*x* is false for any of the *x*'s for which F*x* is true, then the whole proposition is false.

In the case of existential propositions, a theory of unrestricted quantification likewise combines the quantifier with a single propositional function, though in this case the way that the quantifier is in effect restricted to a specific domain is by applying the quantifier to an *and*-conjoined propositional function, as in the analysis of *Some men are bald* as

4.5.2   (∃*x*) ∧ (man *x*, bald *x*).

It is important to note that in a theory of unrestricted quantification, universal and existential quantifiers have to be treated differently: it takes an *if*-clause to (in effect) restrict the variable of a universal quantifier to a specific domain, but it takes an *and*-conjunct to (in effect) restrict the variable of an existential quantifier to a specific domain. An *if*-clause won't do the trick for an existential quantifier, since 4.5.3 is true just by virtue of the fact that there are objects that are not men.

4.5.3   (∃*x*)⊃(man *x*, bald *x*)

For example, ⊃(man Lake Baikal, bald Lake Baikal) is true since 'man Lake Baikal' is false; thus there are values of *x* for which ⊃(man *x*, bald *x*) is true, independent of whether any men are bald. However, the fact that Lake Baikal is not a man does not suffice to make 'Some men are bald' true. Thus, you can't extend the ⊃ of the universal cases to the existential cases. But you can't use an ∧ to fit the domain restriction into a universally quantified proposition either, since 4.5.4 is false just by virtue of the fact that there are objects that are not politicians:

4.5.4   (∀*x*) ∧ (politician *x*, crooked *x*).

For example, ∧(politician Ringo Starr, crooked Ringo Starr) is false, since Ringo Starr is not a politician (or at least, he is not one at the moment that I write this), and thus there are values of *x* for which ∧(politician *x*, crooked *x*) is false, independent of whether all politicians are crooked. However, the fact that Ringo Starr is not a politician ought not to be sufficient to make 'All politicians are crooked' false. Thus, you can't extend the ∧ of the existential cases to the universal cases.

This means that in a system of predicate logic with unrestricted quantification, the two sentences

4.5.5   a. Some politicians are crooked.
             b. All politicians are crooked.

differ in more than the quantifier: the logical structure of the one contains an ∧ where the logical structure of the other contains a ⊃. By contrast, in a system of predicate logic with restricted quantifiers, the quantifier is the only difference in their logical structures: in both cases the quantifier (∀ or ∃, as the case may be) is combined with the propositional function 'politician x', which gives the domain of the variable, and the combination of quantifier and domain restriction is combined with the propositional function 'crooked x'. The following sentences provide at least a weak basis for holding that *some* and *all* fit into identical logical contexts, as in the 'restricted' version of quantification:

4.5.6   a. Some politicians are crooked, but not all politicians are
                 crooked.
             a′. Some, but not all politicians are crooked.
             b. Those politicians are crooked, but not all politicians are
                 crooked.
             b′. *Those, but not all politicians are crooked.
             c. Only politicians are crooked, but not all politicians are
                 crooked.
             c′. *Only but not all politicians are crooked.

Example 4.5.6*a′* is evidently a variant of 4.5.6*a*, derived by an application of conjunction reduction that gives rise to a conjoined 'determiner'. However, as 4.5.6*b*–*b′* show, conjunction reduction is not applicable unless the 'determiner' is the right type of thing. Since *those* and *all* occupy the same surface syntactic role, it must be something other than surface syntactic structure that is responsible for the difference. Logical structure is a reasonable place to look for differences to which the difference in applicability of conjunction reduction can be ascribed, and under a scheme of 'restricted quantification', *some* and *all* are in corresponding places in otherwise identical logical structures in 4.5.6*a*, whereas *those* would have a different logical role from *some* in 4.5.6*b*. However, under the scheme of 'unrestricted quantification', *some* and *all* would not appear in corresponding places in otherwise identical logical structures. Moreover, the difference between 4.5.6*a′* and 4.5.6*b′* cannot be ascribed to the fact that *those* has a 'constant' reference whereas *some* is combined with a variable, since the *only* of

4.5.6*c* also binds a variable; as we will see in 7.1, *only* is a combination of several logical elements, and the logical structure of *Only politicians are crooked* differs markedly from that of *Some politicians are crooked*.

In a system with unrestricted quantifiers, the closest analogue to the rules of inference given above for restricted quantifiers are as follows:

4.5.7

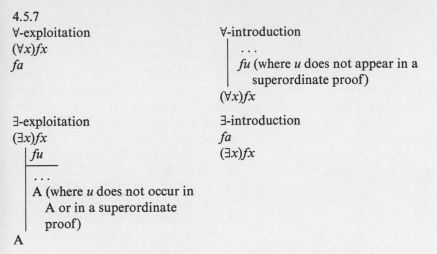

∀-exploitation

$(\forall x)fx$

fa

∀-introduction

    . . .

fu (where u does not appear in a superordinate proof)

$(\forall x)fx$

∃-exploitation

$(\exists x)fx$

    fu

    . . .

    A (where u does not occur in A or in a superordinate proof)

A

∃-introduction

fa

$(\exists x)fx$

The parallelism between the proofs allowed in the two systems is illustrated by the following derivations of parallel conclusions from parallel premises:

4.5.8

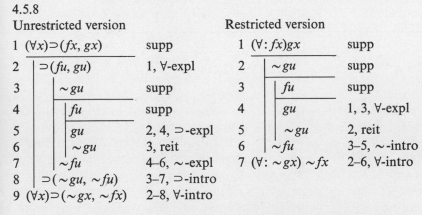

Unrestricted version

1	$(\forall x)\supset(fx, gx)$			supp
2		$\supset(fu, gu)$		1, ∀-expl
3			$\sim gu$	supp
4			fu	supp
5			gu	2, 4, ⊃-expl
6			$\sim gu$	3, reit
7			$\sim fu$	4–6, ∼-expl
8		$\supset(\sim gu, \sim fu)$		3–7, ⊃-intro
9	$(\forall x)\supset(\sim gx, \sim fx)$			2–8, ∀-intro

Restricted version

1	$(\forall : fx)gx$		supp
2		$\sim gu$	supp
3		fu	supp
4		gu	1, 3, ∀-expl
5		$\sim gu$	2, reit
6		$\sim fu$	3–5, ∼-intro
7	$(\forall : \sim gx)\sim fx$		2–6, ∀-intro

Note that with the unrestricted quantifier version of ∀-exploitation, the subordinate proof has no supposition: you simply derive conclusions 'about u' without assuming anything 'about u'.

If *many*, *most*, *almost all* and *all but one* are treated as quantifiers themselves (rather than being decomposed into more primitive elements, as in the proposal which would analyze *Most politicians are crooks* as 'There is a set M such that M consists of more than half of all politicians, and all members of M are crooks'), they will have to be restricted quantifiers. *Most Americans are right-handed* cannot be treated as a combination of a quantifier and the propositional function 'x is an American and x is right-handed'; the meaning of the sentence is not that that propositional function is 'true of most x', since that propositional function obviously is not 'true of most x': there are 800 million Chinese (to say nothing of trillions of bacteria and hydrogen atoms) of whom 'x is an American and x is right-handed' is false, and they far outnumber the 170 million or so right-handed Americans of whom it is true. The sentence likewise could not be interpreted as a combination of *most* with the propositional function 'if x is an American, then x is right-handed', since that propositional function is 'true of most x' for reasons that have no bearing on whether most Americans are right-handed (i.e., it is true of all Chinese and all bacteria and all hydrogen atoms). *Most* doesn't mean 'over 50 percent of all things': it means 'over 50 percent of the kind of things being referred to'.[13] Restricted quantifiers provide a natural basis for coping with *most* and other quantifiers of 'relative magnitude': they provide a characteristic that defines the domain of relevant items, and the sentence is true if the other propositional function is true in an appropriate-sized subset of that domain (e.g., if 'x is right-handed' is true of more than half of the x's that meet the condition 'x is an American'; similarly, *Many Americans are atheists* is true if, among the x's such that 'x is an American', the fraction who meet the condition 'x is an atheist' is large). Likewise, the following two sentences have different truth conditions:

4.5.9   a. Most politicians are crooks.
          b. Most crooks are politicians.

If there are one million crooks who are not politicians, 100,000 crooks who are politicians, and 50,000 politicians who are not crooks, then 4.5.9*a* is true (since 2/3 of all politicians are crooks) but 4.5.9*b* is false (since only 1/11 of all crooks are politicians). But then the truth of *Most A's are B's* could not just be a matter of counting the x's that meet the condition 'x is an A and x is a B', since 'x is a crook and x is a politician' is true of exactly the same x's as is 'x is a politician and x is a crook'. It likewise could not just be a matter of counting the x's that meet the condition 'if x is an A, then x is a B', since those are the same individuals as the x's that meet the condition 'if x is not a B, then x is not an A', and *Most nonpoliticians are noncrooks* obviously can differ in truth value from 4.5.9*b*. (If we restrict our attention to Americans and accept the above figures, then there are more than 200 million individuals who are neither crooks nor politicians, which means that *Most nonpoliticians are noncrooks* would be true though *Most crooks are politicians* is false).

For those quantifiers that carry an existential commitment (or, accepting the suggestion made in the last section, those quantifiers that carry a pragmatic presupposition that the domain over which the variable ranges is nonempty), one can argue that they must be treated as restricted quantifiers, since a treatment in terms of unrestricted quantification would provide no way of identifying the predicate involved in the pragmatic presupposition. In particular, treating existential quantifiers as restricted quantifiers makes the two propositional functions have different roles and thus provides a basis for identifying the difference between

4.5.10   a. Some Buddhists are vegetarians.
             b. Some vegetarians are Buddhists.

To make a real argument out of this suggestion, it is necessary to demonstrate that the existential commitment or pragmatic presupposition is not merely a conversational implicature (i.e., something that one would convey by uttering the sentence by virtue of considerations of cooperativity). Let us contrast the existential commitment of *all* with a clear case of conversational implicature: the fact that *some* usually conveys *not all*. Yes-no questions provide a good test for conversational implicature: the question calls for a *Yes* answer even in cases where the speaker does not accept the conversationally implicated proposition, for example,

4.5.11   Q. Are some politicians crooks?
             A. Yes, indeed, all of them are.
                *No, (but) all of them are.

If the existential commitment of *all* were a conversational implicature, the question in 4.5.12 should demand a positive answer:

4.5.12   Q. Do all unicorns eat clover?
             A. *Yes, but there are no unicorns.
                * ?No, indeed there are no unicorns.
                **Yes, indeed there are no unicorns.
                * ?Yes, but of course there are no unicorns.

Note that the least normal answer is the one that ought to be best if universal propositions whose variable ranges over an empty domain were vacuously true and the proposition that the domain was nonempty were only a conversational implicature.

4.6. Predicate Logic with Identity

So far I have left completely open the question of what predicates appear in any particular system of predicate logic. I will henceforth change this policy to the extent of assuming that a predicate of IDENTITY (written =) will always be included in the inventory of predicates. In view of my policy of writing predicates before their arguments, I will thus write '$=xy$' rather than the more common '$x = y$'. While identity is such a special notion that doubts might be raised about whether it is appropriate to treat it as a predicate, on a par with such other two-place predicates as 'is an uncle of' or 'is a divisor of', it is at least clear that it behaves syntactically just like any two-place predicate; that is, anywhere that a coherent formula contains 'pxy', it could just as well contain '$=xy$' and be just as well formed a formula of predicate logic.

Following Thomason 1970, I will assume that there are two rules of inference relating to identity: a rule of =-introduction and a rule of =-exploitation. The rule of =-introduction allows a step $=aa$ to appear at any point in a proof, where a can be any (constant or variable) element symbol. Thus, if the system involves an individual constant symbol c, one can construct the following trivial proofs:

4.6.1   a. 1 $=cc$ =-intro   b. 1 $=cc$ =-intro
                  2 $(\exists x)=xc$ ∃-intro   2 $(\exists x)=xx$ ∃-intro

The rule of =-exploitation allows one to substitute one side of an equation for the other. More specifically, =-exploitation allows inferences of the form

4.6.2 $=xy$
             A
             B

where B is a formula obtained from A either by substituting x for one or more occurrences of y or by substituting y for one or more occurrences of x. Note that it is not necessary to replace *all* occurrences of the one symbol by the other: from $=xy$ and Fxx you can infer Fyx, Fxy, or Fyy.

These two rules of inference insure that identity will have the familiar properties of being REFLEXIVE, SYMMETRIC, and TRANSITIVE:

4.6.3

a. (reflexive law)   b. (symmetric law)

   1 $=uu$ =-intro   1 | $=uv$ supp
                             2 | $=uu$ =-intro
                             3 | $=vu$ 1, 2, =-expl
                             4 $\supset(=uv, =vu)$ 1–3, $\supset$-intro

c. (transitive law)

1	$\wedge(=uv, =vw)$	supp
2	$=uv$	1, $\wedge$-expl
3	$=vw$	1, $\wedge$-expl
4	$=uw$	3, 2, $=$-expl
5	$\supset(\wedge(=uv, =vw), =uw)$	1–4, $\supset$-intro

Identity plays a role in the analysis of many semantically complex words. For example, *other* and *else* can be treated as minifestations of clauses containing $\sim$ and $=$:

4.6.4   a. Someone other than John got the job.
$(\exists x: \sim =xj)(x$ got the job)
b. (John was sure he'd be hired, but) someone else got the job.
(same analysis as in 4.6.4*a*)

Note that *else* incorporates not only $\sim$ and $=$ but also a referential index: *else* can be paraphrased as *other than him/her/it/them/* ....

4.7. Linguistic Justification for S: Q S

The logical forms that have been proposed in this chapter differ in an important respect from the surface of the corresponding English sentences, namely, that the quantifier and the noun that it goes with are outside of the clauses which, in the surface form of the sentence, they are inside of. This aspect of the proposed logical forms can be justified by demonstrating that there are linguistic phenomena which can be given a satisfying description only by making reference to the propositional function that figures in the logical form. If these grammatical phenomena are to be described in terms of grammatical transformations, those transformations will have to apply to a structure in which that propositional function is separate from the quantifier and the noun, as in logical structure, rather than containing them, as in surface structure.

Consider the conditions under which reflexive pronouns may be used. Reflexive pronouns are quite restricted in distribution: they must refer to an antecedent that occurs earlier in the same clause, and the antecedent may not be part of a larger noun phrase (though the reflexive may be)[14]

4.7.1   a. John admires himself.
b. *John$_i$ thinks that most people admire himself$_i$.

c. John asked Shirley$_i$ about herself$_i$.
d. John$_i$ asked Shirley about himself$_i$.
e. John gave Shirley$_i$ a picture of herself$_i$.
f. *A picture of John$_i$ rarely resembles himself$_i$.
g. *John$_i$'s mother loves himself$_i$.

In many works by transformational grammarians, an analysis has been proposed whereby this defective distribution is attributed to a transformation which creates reflexives out of something nonreflexive (generally it has been proposed that they are derived from duplicates of the antecedent). Such a transformation would of course have to be sensitive to coreference: 4.7.1a is possible only if *himself* is supposed to refer to the same *John* that the subject NP refers to, rather than to a different person who is also called *John*. A transformation which applies to a structure containing two identical NP's (identical even to the point of having the same purported reference) and turns the second one into a reflexive if it is in the same clause as the first and if the first is not a part of a larger NP works out all right in connection with structures in which the NP's are not quantified. However, it does not appear to provide a derivation for a sentence like

4.7.2   Every American admires himself.

The *himself* in 4.7.2 could not very well be derived from a second occurrence of *every American*, since it is not clear that it makes sense to speak of two occurrences of *every American* as being coreferential (or even to speak of *every American* as having reference at all, any more than it makes sense to speak of *only John* or *Tom or Dick* as having reference). Moreover, 4.7.3 involves occurrences of *every American* which have the same reference, to the extent that they can be said to have reference at all, yet the idea expressed by 4.7.3 cannot be expressed with *himself* in place of the second occurrence of *every American*.

4.7.3.   Every American admires every American.

Note also the difference in meaning between 4.7.2 and 4.7.3: every American can admire himself without admiring any other Americans, let alone admire every American.

Suppose that the SYNTACTIC DERIVATION, in whose course reflexivization and the other transformations apply, starts from a logical structure such as those that have been proposed in this chapter, rather than from structures in which *every American* appears as a syntactic unit and in a NP position. Suppose further that, as is generally accepted by transformational grammarians, transformations apply according to the principle of the CYCLE, that is, the transformations have their chance to apply to 'lower' S's in a structure before they apply to higher S's. Under these assumptions, there will then have to be a transformation (called QUANTIFIER-LOWERING) which moves a Q to where there is an occurrence of the variable that it binds.[15] The presumable logical structures of 4.7.2 and 4.7.3 are

4.7.4   a. (every: American x)(admire x x)[$= 4.7.2$]
             b. (every: American x)(every: American y)(admire x y)
                [$= 4.7.3$]

The derivation of 4.7.2 will then be as in 4.7.5:[16]

4.7.5

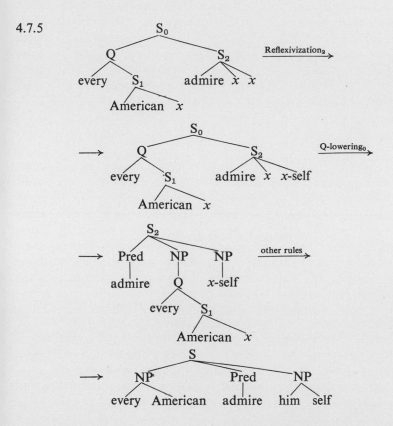

That is, reflexivization has a chance to apply to S_2 when *every American* is still external to S_2 and thus S_2 still contains two identical NP's; only after the second of those NP's has been made reflexive is *every American* moved

into S_2. By contrast, in the derivation of 4.7.3, the conditions for reflexivization are never met:

4.7.6

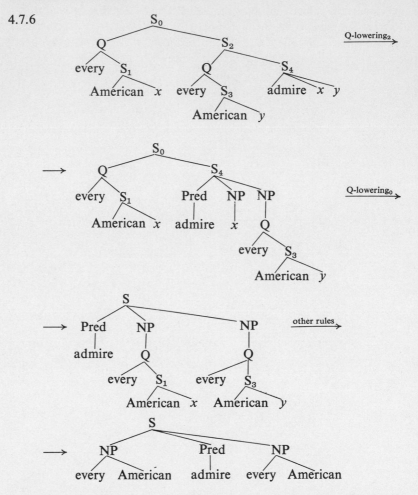

S_4 does not contain two identical NP's to begin with,[17] and nowhere in the subsequent course of the derivation does it ever contain two identical NP's, since (every: American x) is not identical to (every: American y).

The proposed underlying structures provide a similar solution to a similar problem involving EQUI-NP-DELETION, the transformation which under certain conditions deletes the subject of a subordinate clause if it is identical with a certain NP of the main clause, as in the following examples:

4.7.7   a. John wants to spend the summer in Mauritius.
          [< John wants (John spend the summer in Mauritius)]

   b. The court forced Nixon to hand over the tapes.
     [< The court forced Nixon (Nixon hand over the tapes)]

   c. Bill promised Marge to wash the dishes.
     [< Bill promised Marge (Bill wash the dishes)]

Some such transformation is needed to represent the relationship between sentences with and sentences without an overt subject of the infinitive (compare 4.7.7*a* with *John wants his wife to spend the summer in Mauritius*, which in this analysis differs from 4.7.7*a* only with regard to what the subject of the embedded clause is) and between sentences with a *that*-clause and sentences with a subjectless infinitive (compare 4.7.7*c* with *Bill promised Marge that he would wash the dishes*).[18]

Consider now the two sentences

4.7.8   a. Every American wants to get rich.
       b. Every American wants every American to get rich.

The two differ sharply in meaning; note that if every American desires wealth for himself and poverty for everyone else, 4.7.8*a* will be true and 4.7.8*b* false. Example 4.7.8*a* cannot plausibly be derived by deletion of a repetition of *Every American*, since coreferentiality is as much a condition for EQUI-NP-DELETION as it is for reflexivization (note, e.g., that 4.7.7.*a* refers to a trip to Mauritius by the same John that the subject of *want* refers to) and since, even if it made sense to speak of two instances of *every American* as being coreferential, that condition ought to be met in 4.7.8*b* and the structure underlying 4.7.8*b* ought to yield 4.7.8*a* instead.

The problem of providing syntactic derivations of 4.7.8a and 4.7.8b such that equi-NP-deletion applies only in the former derivation evaporates if the deepest stage of the derivations is logical structures of the sort that conform to the proposals of this chapter:

4.7.9   a. (every: American x)(x want (x get rich))
       b. (every: American x)(x want ((every: American y)(y get rich)))

In the derivation of 4.7.8*a*, equi-NP-deletion would apply to 'x want (x get rich)', and then quantifier-lowering would replace the remaining x by (every: American x). In the derivation of 4.7.8*b*, equi-NP-deletion would never be applicable, since at no stage of the derivation would there ever be two identical NP's.[19]

As a further illustration of a problem in associating logical structures with surface structures which is in part solved by the logical structures proposed in this chapter, provided that the usual transformations and quantifier-lowering apply according to the principle of the cycle, consider the following sentences, taken from Partee 1970:

4.7.10   a. Few rules are both correct and easy to read.
          b. Few rules are correct, and few rules are easy to read.

Example 4.7.10a and 4.7.10b obviously can differ in truth value: if many rules are correct but few of the correct ones are easy to read, then 4.7.10a is true and 4.7.10b false. They correspond to the following logical structures, under the assumption that 'x is easy to read' is derived from '(one read x) is easy' by the transformation that is generally referred to as TOUGH MOVEMENT:

4.7.11   a. (few: rule x) ∧ (correct x, easy (one read x))
          b. ∧ ((few: rule x)(correct x), (few: rule y)(easy (one read y)))

In the derivation of 4.7.10a tough-movement converts 'easy (one read x)' into '(easy to read) x', then conjunction reduction converts ∧ (correct x, (easy to read) x) into [∧ (correct, easy to read)]x, and finally quantifier-lowering puts the (few: rule x) in place of the x of the last formula, yielding ultimately 4.7.10a.

Since there obviously is a derivation leading from 4.7.11b to 4.7.10b, the only remaining problem is to show that a derivation starting with 4.7.11b cannot involve conjunction reduction and thus spuriously yield 4.7.10a. This will not be as easy as it was to show why reflexivization and equi-NP-deletion were inapplicable in the derivations of 4.7.3 and 4.7.8b; note that the treatment of those sentences rested on the fact that the logical structure had to involve two distinct variables and the assumption that the distinction between two variables x and y was sufficient to cause the identity condition in reflexivization and equi-NP- deletion not to be met and thus to prevent those transformations from applying. However, in 4.7.11b there is nothing to prevent both variables from being called x (i.e., it is only by whim that I happen to have given them different names): since the part of the structure that the first Q commands and the part that the second Q commands are disjoint from each other, no incoherence would result if the same letter were used for both variables. Thus, while we can say that the difference between x and y prevents conjunction reduction from applying in any derivation that starts from 4.7.11b, there is nothing so far to prevent it from applying in a derivation starting from the equivalent logical structure in which both variables are called x. We could, of course, rule out the latter derivation by ruling by fiat that different variables must have different names; however, that fiat would create a new problem, namely, it would prevent conjunction reduction from applying in some cases where it ought to apply, 4.7.12a ought to have the same logical structure as 4.7.12b and their derivations ought to differ only to the extent that conjunction reduction applies in the derivation of the former but not of the latter:

4.7.11   a. Both Tom and Dick admire few authors.
          b. Tom admires few authors, and Dick admires few authors.

But if we are required to call the two variables in 4.7.12*b* by different names, then conjunction reduction ought to be inapplicable, since the two occurrences of *few authors* will then count as nonidentical.

A way out of the dilema posed by 4.7.10 and 4.7.12 might be sought in terms of what has come to be known as the SLOPPY IDENTITY principle, that is, the principle that allows the difference in reference of the two pronouns in 4.7.13*a* to be ignored and thus allows 4.7.13*b* to be derived from a structure that also underlies 4.7.13*a*:[20]

4.7.13   a. John$_i$ loves his$_i$ wife, and Bill$_j$ loves his$_j$ wife too.
          b. John$_i$ loves his$_i$ wife, and Bill does too.

If the sloppy identity principle can be formulated in such a way that one can ignore the difference between the two variables in 4.7.12*a* but not between the two variables in 4.7.10*b*, then we could in fact impose the fiat restriction that variables bound by different Q's must have different names. See 13.1 for a specific proposal that in fact provides the basis for a sloppy identity principle that will allow one to ignore the difference between the variables in 4.7.12*a* but not in 4.7.10*b*.

The propositional functions that are set up in the analysis of quantified sentences can sometimes serve as the antecedents of pronouns. Consider, for example, the sentences

4.7.14   a. Most linguists admire most philosophers; that's true even of
             Hockett.
          b. Most linguists admire most philosophers; that's true even of
             Sartre.

These have the respective paraphrases

4.7.15   a. The linguists who admire most philosophers are a majority
             of linguists; even Hockett admires most philosophers.
          b. The philosophers who most linguists admire are a majority
             of philosophers; even Sartre is admired by most linguists.

In 4.7.14*a* the interpretation involves the propositional function '*x* admires most philosophers', and *that* refers to that propositional function: the second clause means that even Hockett possesses the property '*x* admires most philosophers'. In 4.7.14*b* the interpretation involves the propositional function 'most linguists admire *y*', and *that* refers to that propositional function: the second clause means that even Sartre has the property 'most linguists admire *y*'. Moreover, if one pronoun refers to the one propositional function, it is not possible for another pronoun to refer to other propositional function:

4.7.16   Most linguists admire most philosophers; that's true even of Hockett, though that isn't true of Halliday/*Sartre.

In the first version of 4.7.16, both *that*'s refer to '*x* admires most philosophers' and the sentence is normal (meaning '...though Halliday doesn't admire most philosophers'); however, the second version, in which one *that* is supposed to refer to '*x* admires most philosophers' and the other one to 'most linguists admire *y*', is decidedly abnormal. This observation provides syntactic confirmation for an analysis in which *Most linguists admire most philosophers* has two distinct underlying structures, one in which *most linguists* is combined with '*x* admires most philosophers', and one in which *most philosophers* is combined with 'most linguists admire *y*'. The availability of the one propositional function to serve as antecedent for a pronoun implies the nonavailability of the other, as would be predicted by an analysis in which two distinct structures underlie the sentence, one containing the one propositional function and the other containing the other one. It is interesting to note that everything that I have said in this paragraph about sentences with two *most*'s applies equally to parallel sentences with two *all*'s or two *every*'s. Thus facts about the interpretation of *that* also provide reason for distinguishing between (all: *fx*)(all: *gy*)*hxy* and (all: *gy*)(all: *fx*)*hxy*, notwithstanding their deductive equivalence. It follows from this observation that there are deductively equivalent structures that must be treated as distinct.

Interactions between quantifiers and the transformation of NEGATIVE TRANSPORTATION, which has been proposed in connection with sentences such as those in 4.7.17, provide the basis for a further argument (Carden 1973) for underlying structures in which quantifiers are external to their clauses.

4.7.17   a. Bill doesn't want Sam to finish the report until Friday.
            b. Lucy doesn't think that Phil will give her a red cent.

The negations in 4.1.17 appear to have the complement clauses as scope, that is, in 4.7.17*a*, Bill's desire is that Sam does not finish the report until Friday, and in 4.7.17*b*, Lucy's belief is that Phil will not give her a red cent, even though the *n't* appears in the main clause rather than the subordinate clause. The judgment that the scope of the negative is the subordinate clause is strengthened by the fact that here the subordinate clause contains a 'negative polarity item', which can only occur in the scope of a negation:[21]

4.7.18   a. *Sam finished the report until Friday.
          b. *Phil will give Lucy a red cent.

Negative transportation moves a negation out of the complement of an appropriate verb or adjective (e.g., *want*, *expect*, *think*, *believe*, *likely*) and into the clause containing that verb or adjective.

Consider now the interpretation of the sentences 4.7.19:

4.7.19   a. Victor doesn't want many people to know about his past.
          a'. Victor wants many people not to know about his past.
          b. Tim doesn't expect practically everyone to vote for him.

Example 4.7.19a allows the interpretation in which what Victor wants is that not many people know about his past, but not the interpretation that what he wants is that many people not know about his past. In 4.7.19a', however, the situation is exactly the reverse. In 4.7.19a the negation is in the main clause in surface structure, whereas in 4.7.19a' it is in the complement, as is clear from the corresponding 'tag questions':

4.7.20   a. Victor doesn't want many people to know about his past,
              does/*doesn't he?
          a'. Victor wants many people not to know about his past,
              doesn't he?

Thus negative transportation has applied in 4.7.19a but not 4.7.19a'. This means that the relative scopes of the *n't* and the *many* determine whether negative transportation can apply: in 4.7.19a, where the negative is 'higher than' the quantifier, negative transportation can apply, but in 4.17.19a', where the negative is 'lower than' the quantifier, negative transportation cannot apply. Example 4.7.19b does not allow an interpretation 'Tim expects that practically everyone won't vote for him': it can only be interpreted as 'Tim expects that it is not the case that practically everyone will vote for him' or as 'It is not the case that Tim expects that practically everyone will vote for him'. Again, what determines whether negative transportation can apply is the logical form of the complement (i.e., whether it is logically of the form $\sim S$) rather than the syntactic form that it would have if negative transportation did not apply.

Certain facts about the acceptability and interpretation of quantifiers in complex sentences can be explained if quantifiers in underlying syntactic structure are outside of their clauses and the transformation of QUANTIFIER-LOWERING, which moves them into their clauses, is subject to the same constraints that other movement transformations are subject to. Consider the sentences

4.7.21   a. John had a fight with Bill.
           b. John had a fight with each of my teachers.
           c. John and Bill had a fight.
           d. ??John and each of my teachers had a fight.

4.7.22   a. John and Bill despise each other.
           b. John despises many of my friends, and many of my friends despise John.
           c. *John and many of my friends despise each other.

The oddity of 4.7.21*d* and 4.7.22*c* can be attributed to violations of the COORDINATE STRUCTURE CONSTRAINT (Ross 1967), which rules out derivations in which material is moved out of or into a coordinate structure, as in

4.7.23   a. *Who did you invite John and?
           b. *The only substance which I mixed water and was sodium.

The coordinate structure constraint rules out the step in which the interrogative pronoun is moved to the beginning in 4.7.23*a* (and is thus moved out of the coordinate NP *John and who(m)*) and the step in which the relative pronoun is moved to the beginning of the relative clause in 4.7.23*b* (and is thus moved out of the coordinate NP *water and which*). Ross in fact only stated his constraint in terms of moving things OUT OF coordinate constructions and did not take up the question of whether the same restriction applies to movement INTO a coordinate structure. There in fact are not many transformations for which the possibility of something being moved into a coordinate structure arises, but one such transformation is conjunction reduction, since the conjunction ends up lower in the structure than the position in which it originated. Conjunction reduction in fact appears to be subject to the coordinate structure constraint:

4.7.24   Quine denounced either Chomsky or Davidson, and Hockett denounced either Chomsky or Postal ⫫ *Quine and Hockett denounced either Chomsky or Davidson and Postal, respectively.

The oddity of 4.7.21*d* and 4.7.22*c* can then be attributed to the violation of the coordinate structure constraint which takes place when the quantifier is moved into 'John and *x* had a fight' or 'John and *x* despise each other'.

In conjunction with the analysis of restrictive relative clauses adopted in this chapter, the positing of structures in which the material of the quanti-

fied NP is outside its surface clause allow an explanation of the fact noted
by Bouton 1970 (discussed further in Grinder 1976) that certain anaphoric
devices can occur contained in their antecedents:

4.7.25   Tom kissed a woman who had ordered him to.

According to the assumptions most commonly made by transformational
grammarians about the syntactic phenomena involved in 4.7.25, it should
not be possible to form such sentences as 4.7.25. Specifically, restrictive
relative clauses are usually assumed to appear as constituents of underlying NP's that have the same constituent structure as the corresponding
surface NP's, and the zero VP is assumed to be derived from a structure
containing two identical VP's by a transformation that deletes one of them.
Under those assumptions, the zero VP in 4.7.25 would have to be derived
by deletion of an occurrence of *kiss a woman who had ordered him to* or of
ordered him to, since those are the only VP's in the structure provided by
the standard assumptions. But neither of those two possibilities would
work, since a structure with either of those expressions in place of the zero
VP would still not contain two identical VP's but only a nest of VP's,
each contained within a larger one; moreover, the latter structure would
not mean the same as 4.7.25: the order in 4.7.25 can be complied with only
by kissing the woman who gave the order, whereas the 'restored' version
of 4.7.25 would refer to an order that could be complied with by kissing
another woman who had given him such an order or by giving himself an
order. In any case, the underlying structure thus obtained would still contain a zero VP that would have to be derived from another VP, yielding an
infinite regress. These problems can be avoided if 4.7.25 is derived from an
underlying structure of the form that the proposals of this chapter provide
as its logical structure, with the restrictive relative clause derived from a
coordinate structure in which what is to be the head noun is a predicate
noun in one of the conjuncts:

4.7.26   ($\exists$: $\wedge$ (woman x, x ordered Tom (Tom kiss x)))(Tom kiss x)

This contains two occurrences of *kiss x*, and as long as VP deletion applies
to this structure before quantifier-lowering, it can delete one occurrence of
kiss x (the first one, necessarily, since otherwise the derivation could not
be continued to completion for want of an index for quantifier-lowering to
substitute the quantifier expression for), whereupon quantifier-lowering
substitutes the quantifier expression for the x of the main clause, thus
giving rise to the peculiar structure noted by Bouton, in which an anaphoric
device is contained in its antecedent. That sort of structure is possible only
when the anaphoric device is of a type that must normally be derived from

a copy of its antecedent (*one, so,* zero VP, but not ordinary personal pronouns), and only when the anaphoric device is inside a relative clause that is contained in the antecedent. The analysis proposed here provides an explanation of why Bouton's phenomenon should be restricted to such cases.

4.8. Exercises

1. Give formulas that represent the logical structures of the following sentences:

    a. Some students admire all teachers and respect most authors.
    b. Many students and most teachers admire all authors.
    c. Many persons love all their relatives.
    d. Few students who admire all authors love most teachers who hate many authors.
    e. All students who admire all teachers and respect most authors love all of their relatives.

Treat *some, many, most, few,* and *all* as unanalyzable quantifiers (i.e., don't try to analyze any of them into more primitive notions) and analyze restrictive relative clauses in terms of coordination: '*x* is a student who admires Freud' $= \wedge$ (stud *x*, adm *x* Freud). Use the following predicates in your formulas:

stud x = '*x* is a student'
tea x = '*x* is a teacher'
per x = '*x* is a person'
auth x = '*x* is an author'
adm $x\ y$ = '*x* admires *y*'
resp $x\ y$ = '*x* respects *y*'
rel $x\ y$ = '*x* is a relative of *y*'

2. For each of the following formulas, construct an English sentence having that formula as its logical structure:

    a. $(\forall : fx)_x \supset ((\exists : gy)_y hyx, (\forall : kz)_z dxz)$
    b. $(\forall : fx)_x (\forall : \wedge (fy, \sim = yx))_y gxy$
    c. $\supset ((\exists : fx)_x (\forall : gy)_y hxy, (\forall : gz)_z (\exists : fx)_x hxz)$

3. Two treatments of the *any* of

John didn't talk to anyone.
If anyone catches me, I'll give up.

have been widely advocated. In the treatment by Quine, *any* is a universal quantifier with 'wide scope' and the sentences are analyzed as

$(\forall: \text{person } x)_x \sim (\text{John talked to } x)$
$(\forall: \text{person } x)_x \supset (x \text{ catches me, I give up})$

In the treatment by Klima 1964 and Horn 1972, *any* is an existential quantifier that is in the scope of an element such as $\sim$ or $\supset$ that triggers a process of *some-any* conversion: Klima and Horn would thus analyze the sentences as

$\sim (\exists: \text{person } x)_x(\text{John talked to } x)$
$\supset ((\exists: \text{person } x)_x(x \text{ catches me}), I \text{ give up})$

Say what problem the following sentence presents for either or both of these proposals:

If anyone asks me, I'll tell him [= the one who asks] the answer.

Say what it is about the sentence

Every man who owns a donkey beats it [= that donkey].

that makes it difficult to represent its meaning within the system developed in this chapter.

4. According to Quine's analysis (see preceding problem), formulas of the form

$(\forall: fx)_x \supset (A, gx),$

where the A does not involve x, ought to have English renditions in which *any* represents the $\forall$. Do they?

5. Construct an analysis of *all but one* in terms of $\forall, \exists, =,$ and propositional connectives, and show how

All but one poet hated himself.

would be analyzed under that proposal.

6. For each of the formulas in problem 2, give its CLOSEST analogue in a system with unrestricted quantification.

7. For each of the following sentences, construct a formula of predicate logic with identity that represents its meaning.

a. Any person who admires another person is sane.
b. Every philosopher hates all of every other philosopher's relatives.
c. Every donkey is owned by a man who beats no donkey but it.

8. Translate the following arguments into formulas of predicate logic with identity and determine for each whether the conclusion follows from the premise(s):

a. Every linguist who admires every other linguist is insane.
   Therefore, every linguist who is sane admires no linguist other than himself.
b. Every linguist admires any philosopher who is a relative of his.
   Any relative of a linguist is insane.
   Therefore, every linguist admires some insane philosopher.

5. A Digression into Set Theory

5.1. The Notion of 'Set'

Under what circumstances is the sentence 5.1.1 true?

5.1.1   Most linguists like Chinese food.

Assuming that *most* means 'more than half', 5.1.1 should be true provided that more than half of all linguists like Chinese food. This statement of the conditions under which 5.1.1 is true makes covert reference to two SETS: the set of all linguists, and the set of all linguists who like Chinese food; it reduces the question of whether 5.1.1 is true to a comparison of the size of these two sets.

To discuss truth conditions for sentences involving quantifiers, it will be necessary to make constant reference to sets. In addition, sets often figure not only in one's metalanguage for talking about propositions and their truth conditions but as elements of content in the propositions themselves. For example, in the sentence *All of them subscribe to the Saturday Review*, the word *them* refers to a set of persons, and the content of the sentence can only be analyzed by making reference to that set.

It will thus be appropriate if at this point we digress into the notion of set and clarify it and some related notions. The content of this chapter will be more mathematical than linguistic, but much of it will play a role in later chapters.

'Set' is one of those words for which it is impossible to give a real definition. Attempts at defining it generally consist in giving a list of synonyms, none of which is really any clearer than the word 'set': class, aggregate, collection, and the like. The clearest explanation of what a set is is probably an explanation in terms of the kinds of relationships that sets can stand in toward each other and toward other things. A set consists of elements, for example, the set of all U.S. presidents in the nineteenth century consists of Jefferson, Madison, Monroe, ..., and McKinley. The mathematical notion of set makes the identity of a set purely a matter of what members it has. Thus, the set of all British naval personnel on 1 January 1965 and the set of all British naval personnel on 1 January 1975 are two different sets, even though the British navy on 1 January 1965 is in some sense the same entity as the British navy on 1 January 1975 (or at least, they are the same entity in the sense in which I am the same person that I was ten years ago: I may have grown a mustache, lost a tooth, gained some fat, and changed many of my beliefs, just as the British navy has acquired and lost personnel, closed some bases, and scrapped some ships). It is thus a mistake to think of sets as typified by such 'corporate bodies' as the British navy, the Chicago city council, or the Juilliard String Quartet. Such bodies may 'consist of' persons, but the body remains the same body even when the set of persons of which it consists changes; it is reasonable to speak of the Juilliard Quartet changing its membership by getting a new second violinist, but it is absurd to speak of the set {Robert Mann, Earl Carlyss, Samuel Rhodes, Claus Adam} changing its membership: to describe that set as changing its membership when the quartet gets a new second violinist would be to make the same sort of error that one would commit if one described a rise in temperature from 30° to 35° as a change of the number 30 into the number 35.

There is no restriction on what kinds of elements can be members of a set: you can talk of a set of numbers, a set of persons, a set of formulas of predicate logic, a set of sentences of Amoy Chinese, even a set of sets. A set need not be the membership of any corporate body. Indeed, its members need not even have anything in common: you can talk of such sets of highly hetrogeneous elements as a set consisting of the number 38, Chester Alan Arthur, Mozart's nineteenth symphony, and the formula $\vee (p, \sim p)$. In actual fact, people do not normally refer to sets as outlandish as the one just described: you normally don't have occasion to refer to things together unless they have something significant in common. However, I will follow the standard practise of logicians and mathematicians and accept the broad conception of set that includes even such outlandish collections of heterogeneous objects.

The elements of which a set consists are called its MEMBERS, and they are said to BELONG TO the set. The symbol $\in$ is used to represent the relation of 'belonging to' a set; thus, if E is used to represent the set of all even numbers, we can write $2 \in E$ to express the proposition that 2 belongs to that set, that is, that 2 is an even number. The symbol $\notin$ is used to represent the negation of $\in$, for example, $3 \notin E$ means '3 is not a member of E', that is, '3 is not an even number'. To say that two sets are identical is to say that they have the same members; for example, to say that the set of all precincts in Chicago with 100 percent voter turnout is identical to the set of all precincts in Chicago that contain cemeteries is to say that every precinct in Chicago that has 100 percent voter turnout contains a cemetery and that every precinct in Chicago that contains a cemetery has 100 percent voter turnout.

The notion of an element belonging to a set must not be confused with the relationship of a set being a SUBSET of a set. If M and N are two sets and every element that is a member of M is also a member of N, then M is said to be a subset of N. The symbol ⊆ is used to indicate the subset relation: M ⊆ N means 'M is a subset of N'. A set can be a member of another set without being a subset of it and can be a subset of another set without being a member of it. To see this, let us accept the traditional concept of a line as a certain set of points; then saying that a point lies on a certain line or that the line passes through the point amounts to saying that the point is a member of the line. Take any point P and consider the set M consisting of all lines that pass through P; finally, let L be one of the lines that belong to M:

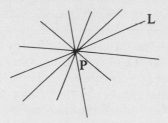

P ∈ L, L ∈ M, but P ∉ M: The members of M are lines, not points, and P is a point, not a line.

By contrast, the subset relationship [is TRANSITIVE, that is, if A ⊆ B and B ⊆ C, then A ⊆ C. Suppose that A ⊆ B and B ⊆ C; every member of B is a member of C, which means that every member of A, since they are all members of B, will be a member of C, and hence A ⊆ C.

According to the definition of 'subset' given above, every set is a subset of itself: this follows from the trivial fact that 'if $x \in A$, then $x \in A$' is always true.[1] However, the idea that a set might be a *member* of itself is fraught with paradox. To come up with a plausible example of a set that might be a member of itself, one has to get into the realm of misty abstractions such as 'the set of all sets', and one can rightly question whether it makes sense to speak of such a thing as a 'set of all sets', since if one allows the same freedom of expression that is innocuous in the case of less all-encompassing sets, one can describe subsets of that supposed 'set' that lead to contradictions under all circumstances. For example, if one denotes by S the 'set of all sets' and defines S′ as the subset of S consisting of all x

for which $x \notin x$, then both the proposition $S' \in S'$ and the proposition $S' \notin S'$ lead to contradictions (think about each of them for a minute, and you should be able to see why).[2] We thus have further reason to be sure to distinguish sharply between $\subseteq$ and $\in$: $M \subseteq M$ is as innocuous and trivial a formula as one could hope to find, obviously true of any set whatever, whereas $M \in M$ is a formula that could be true only of a rather outlandish set, and it is not even clear that the notion of set should be interpreted so broadly as to allow for such sets.

There are a number of ways in which one can specify what set one is referring to. One way is simply to enumerate the members of the set. For example, I can describe a certain set by saying that it consists of the numbers 37, 24893, and 701 and nothing else. Curly brackets and commas are standardly used in forming expressions such as {37, 24893, 701}, which denotes the set whose members are the elements listed inside the brackets. Note that the order of the elements in the enumeration is immaterial: {37, 24893, 701} denotes exactly the same set as does {701, 37, 24893}, since in both cases the set defined by the expression has exactly the same members. Defining a set by ENUMERATION is possible only when the set is FINITE: if a set has infinitely many members, then it has more members than you could possibly put into a list. A second way of specifying a set is to give a criterion for membership in the set. This is in fact what was done in defining most of the sets that have been referred to so far in this chapter; for example, the set of M of lines that we spoke of a few paragraphs earlier is defined by the condition: $x \in M$ if and only if x is a line and $P \in x$. Curly brackets and either a colon or a vertical stroke are standardly used in forming expressions that correspond to this kind of definition:

$$\{x: x \text{ is a line and } P \in x\} \quad \text{or} \quad \{x|x \text{ is a line and } P \in x\}$$

What appears to the left of the colon or stroke is a general formula for members of the set being defined. What appears to the right is the conditions that must be met for something of that general form to belong to the set. The 'general formula' in the example just given is quite trivial; a less trivial example would be an expression such as

$$\{x^2: x \text{ is an even number}\}$$

which would define the set of all squares of even numbers. It is of course possible to do without complex expressions before the colon by employing quantifiers after the colon; for example, the following expression also serves to define the set of all squares of even numbers:

$$\{y: (\exists: x \text{ is an even number})_x(y = x^2)\}$$

That is, y belongs to the set in question if and only if there is an even number such that y is the square of that number. Nonetheless, I will retain the more general version of 'definition by criterion' and allow complicated expressions to appear to the left of the colon.

There are other, less straightforward ways of specifying a set. For example, a certain set might be specified as 'the smallest set which contains the numbers $1/23$ and $\sqrt{7}$ and which contains both the sum and the difference of any two of its members'. However, there is not much point in going into the details of such types of definitions here. One thing that must be emphasized, though, is that there is nothing a priori that requires that every set be describable. Indeed, it is easy to show that there are more sets of numbers than there are possible descriptions of sets of numbers, and hence there must be sets of numbers which cannot be given a description that singles out that particular set unambiguously. Thus, 'the set of all sets of whole numbers' has as members not only sets with such nice straightforward definitions as $\{1, 5, 94\}$ or $\{x: x^3 - 43x \text{ is a prime number}\}$, but also sets (necessarily, infinite sets) whose members cannot be characterized by any formula built up from the basic concepts of arithmetic. This fact is no cause for alarm: it merely reflects the fact that the ways in which sets can differ from each other greatly exceed the ways in which descriptions of sets can differ from each other. Each of the infinitely many whole numbers constitutes an independent dimension on which two sets of whole numbers can differ from each other: a set can either contain a given number or fail to contain it, independent of what other numbers it contains or fails to contain; however, the great freedom that one has in constructing formulas is limited by the fact that every formula has to be of finite length. If formulas are represented as strings of symbols, including a 'period' which marks the end of the formula (and has no other typographical function), then every formula must contain a period, and there is absolutely no freedom in what can follow a period: only blank spaces can follow. The sets that cannot be described are necessarily things even more outlandish than a set consisting of a dozen randomly selected numbers. Their existence will be of importance only in connection with questions of generality: whether something can be allowed to be any set at all or must be restricted to the realm of the describable.

5.2. Operations on Sets

The operations of UNION, INTERSECTION, and DIFFERENCE (or (RELATIVE) COMPLEMENT) are defined as follows:

$A \cup B$ (the union of A and B) is $\{x: \vee (x \in A, x \in B)\}$
$A \cap B$ (the intersection of A and B) is $\{x: \wedge (x \in A, x \in B)\}$
$A - B$ (called the complement of B with repect to A)
is $\{x: \wedge (x \in A, x \notin B)\}$.

Thus the union of two sets consists of everything that belongs to either or both of them, the intersection of two sets consists of those elements that are common to the two sets, and the complement of one set with respect to another consists of those elements of the latter that do not belong to the former. If sets are represented by regions in a plane, the shaded areas in the following diagrams will illustrate the results of performing these three operations:

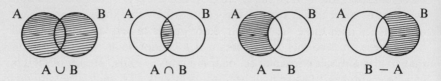

In addition, a notion of (ABSOLUTE) COMPLEMENT is sometimes recognized: the absolute complement $\overline{A}$ of a set A is defined as $\{x: x \notin A\}$. The notion of absolute complement is problematic, since it commits one to belief in a 'set of all objects', in that $A \cup \overline{A}$ would be such a set. If 'all objects' is interpreted in the fullest generality, thus as including all sets, acceptance of a set of all objects leads one into Russell's paradox (see note 2). In actual practise, most apparent references to absolute complements really relate to relative complements: the author is referring to complements relative to some fixed 'universe of discourse' U, and $\overline{A}$ is used as an abbreviation for $U - A$.

With a little meditation, you should be able to see that the following equalities are true

$$\{1, 2, 3, 4, 5\} \cup \{3, 4, 5, 6, 7\} = \{1, 2, 3, 4, 5, 6, 7\}$$
$$\{1, 2, 3, 4, 5\} \cap \{3, 4, 5, 6, 7\} = \{3, 4, 5\}$$
$$\{1, 2, 3, 4, 5\} - \{3, 4, 5, 6, 7\} = \{1, 2\}$$

If M consists of those whole numbers that are multiples of 3 and N consists of the even numbers, then $M \cap N$ = the multiples of 6, and $M - N$ = the odd multiples of 3.

A consideration of how intersection and difference work forces us to be more explicit than we have been with regard to how small a set can be. Suppose that M is the set of all persons who served as president of the U.S.A. in the nineteenth century and N is the set of all persons who have served as president of the U.S.A. in the twentieth century. Then what is $M \cap N$? The intersection is supposed to be the set consisting of all elements that belong to both of the sets. In this case, there is exactly one element common to both sets: William McKinley. If $M \cap N$ is to denote anything here, it will have to be a set that has William McKinley as its sole member.

There is in fact no obstacle to allowing sets that have a single element. Note, though, that it will be necessary to distinguish between a single-element set and that single element: William McKinley is not a set whose sole member is William McKinley. The notation involving curly brackets and commas for specifying a set by enumeration is equally applicable in the case of a one-element set as in the case of a larger set (though, of course, commas will be unnecessary if the list of elements has only one entry); thus we can write

$$M \cap N = \{\text{William McKinley}\}$$

Suppose now that M is the set of all persons who were elected president as candidates of the Whig party and N is (as before) the set of all persons who have served as president during the twentieth century. What is $M \cap N$? In this case the sets have no element in common: the last Whig elected president was Zachary Taylor, who died in office in 1850. Thus, if $M \cap N$ is to denote anything here, it will have to be a set that has no members. There is in fact no obstacle to admitting an EMPTY SET, which has no members. Using the symbol $\varnothing$ to represent this set, we can write $M \cap N = \varnothing$. Note that there can be only one empty set: two sets differ only if one has a member that the other does not, and since an empty set has no members, an empty set can be distinct only from a nonempty set; thus, the set of all Trappist monks who are members of the Interstate Commerce Commission = the set of all operas composed by Johannes Brahms. A set which has members is said to be NONEMPTY. To say that $M \cap N = \varnothing$ is to say that M and N are DISJOINT, that is, that they have no elements in common. To say that $M - N = \varnothing$ is to say that M is a subset of N. Note that the only way that $M \cup N$ could be $\varnothing$ is for both M and N to be $\varnothing$.

5.3. Finite and Infinite Sets

In the last section we had occasion to refer to many sets that had infinitely many members. For example, we referred to the set of all even numbers, and there are infinitely many even numbers; we referred to the set of all lines that pass through a given point, and there are infinitely many such lines.

The expression 'infinitely many' should not mislead one into assuming that there is exactly one infinite number and that all sets are not finite have that many members. It turns out that infinite sets can differ in size and that it makes perfect sense to speak of distinct infinite numbers, and of one infinite number being smaller than another one. However, to show that that is the case it will be necessary first to show how the notion of the 'size' of a set can be generalized so as to be applicable to infinite sets.

'Size' in the case of finite sets refers to number of elements. The set of all states that belonged to the U.S.A. in 1945 has the same size as the set of all preludes in Bach's Well-tempered Clavier: both sets have 48 members. To say that two finite sets have the same size is to say that if you count off the elements of the first set (i.e., point to one element and say 'one', point to another element and say 'two', point to yet another element and say 'three', etc., until you have exhausted the set) and separately count off the elements of the second set, you will end up with the same number. However, the role of numbers in this procedure is dispensable: instead of matching elements of the two sets to numbers, you could have just as easily matched elements in the one set to elements in the other set, and the two sets would have the same number of elements provided you can match each element of the one set to a different element of the other set (in perhaps a totally arbitrary way) and have no elements of either set left over. Thus, you could establish that there were as many states in the U.S.A. in 1945 as there are preludes in the Well-tempered Clavier by matching them up in, say, the following way:

Alabama	Arizona
C major, book 1	C minor, book 1
Arkansas	... Wyoming
C# major, book 1	... B minor, book 2

The 'alphabetical order' in which the states and the preludes are listed here is in fact of no theoretical significance (though it might be of practical help in making sure that you hadn't left anything out); a totally random pairing such as the following would equally well show that there were as many states in 1945 as there are preludes in the Well-tempered Clavier:

Montana	Ohio
A minor, book 1	C minor, book 2
New Mexico	... Indiana
E major, book 1	... F# minor, book 2

This notion of 'same size' is applicable regardless of whether the sets are finite or infinite. For example, you can justify the claim that there are as many positive even numbers as there are positive odd numbers by showing that there is a one-to-one correspondence between the two sets, for example, the correspondence in which every positive odd number corresponds to the even number that is one greater than it:

1	3	5	7	9	11	13	...	847	849	...	17,891	17,893 ...
2	4	6	8	10	12	14	...	848	850	...	17,892	17,894 ...

The only qualification that needs to be imposed in applying this notion of 'same size' to infinite sets is that while for finite sets it made no difference *how* you matched up the elements of the two sets (i.e., how you arrange the members of the two sets will have no bearing on whether any elements are left over), it can make a difference in the case of infinite sets, and thus it is somewhat harder to prove that two infinite sets DIFFER in size than it is to prove that two finite sets differ in size. For example, from the fact that you can match each positive even number to a positive whole number (namely, itself) and still have positive whole numbers left over (see *a* below), it does not follow that there are more positive whole numbers than there are even numbers; it is in fact possible to match the two sets in such a way that nothing is left over, namely, by matching every positive whole number with the even number that is twice that whole number (*b*):

$$\begin{array}{llllllllll}
a. & 1 & 2 & 3 & 4 & 5 & 6 & 7 & 8 & 9 & \ldots \\
 & - & 2 & - & 4 & - & 6 & - & 8 & - & \ldots \\
b. & 1 & 2 & 3 & 4 & 5 & 6 & 7 & 8 & 9 & \ldots \\
 & 2 & 4 & 6 & 8 & 10 & 12 & 14 & 16 & 18 & \ldots
\end{array}$$

In fact, it is easy to show that a set is infinite if and only if it can be matched up one-to-one with a proper subset of itself.

The positive whole numbers are the smallest infinite set. Smallest, that is, with respect to the notion of 'size' that was just introduced. There are, of course, infinite sets which are 'smaller than' the positive whole numbers in the sense of being proper subsets of that set; however, those sets have the same 'size' as the positive whole numbers: they can be put into a one-to-one correspondence with the positive whole numbers, with no element of either set left over. To see why the positive whole numbers should be the smallest infinite set, suppose you are given an infinite set. Pick any member of that set and call it x_1. There will be other elements of the set, since if x_1 were its only member it would not be infinite. So pick another element of the set and call it x_2. There will still be elements left in the set, since if x_1 and x_2 were all the elements it had, it would not be infinite; thus you can pick another element of the set and call it x_3. This can continue without limit. But this procedure gives you a one-to-one corresponence between the positive whole numbers and a subset (not necessarily a proper subset) of the given set:

$$\begin{array}{lllll}
1 & 2 & 3 & 4 & 5 & \ldots \\
x_1 & x_2 & x_3 & x_4 & x_5 & \ldots
\end{array}$$

There may be some elements of the given set that aren't included in the second line, but all of the positive integers will appear in the first line. Thus the positive integers are the smallest infinite set: it can be put into a one-to-one correspondence with a subset of any other infinite set.[3]

If every 'size' is to be represented by a number, there must be a number corresponding to the 'size' of the set of all positive integers, and that number will be the smallest infinite number. The symbol $\aleph_0$ is standardly used to denote that number (the Hebrew letter used here is 'aleph'; the whole symbol is read 'aleph sub zero', 'aleph zero', 'aleph naught'). The question must now be raised: are there any infinite numbers that are larger than $\aleph_0$, or is $\aleph_0$ the only infinite number? If a set is to have more than $\aleph_0$ members, it will have to be larger than the set of all positive whole numbers, indeed a lot larger than it: note, for example, that the set of all whole numbers (positive, zero, and negative) won't be big enough to have more than $\aleph_0$ members, since the same kind of one-to-one correspondence can be set up between all whole numbers and the positive ones as was set up between all positive whole numbers and the positive even numbers:

$$\ldots \quad -4 \quad -3 \quad -2 \quad -1 \quad 0 \quad 1 \quad 2 \quad 3 \quad 4 \quad 5 \quad \ldots$$
$$\ldots \quad \;\;8 \quad \;\;6 \quad \;\;4 \quad \;\;2 \quad 1 \quad 3 \quad 5 \quad 7 \quad 9 \quad 11 \quad \ldots$$

That is, the odd numbers are matched with zero and the positive whole numbers, and the even numbers are matched with the negative whole numbers, and nothing is left over. What about the rational numbers, then—all numbers that can be expressed as fractions with whole numbers for numerator and denominator? It turns out that despite the fact that between any two whole numbers there are infinitely many rational numbers, there are still the same number of rational numbers as there are positive whole numbers. To show this, it suffices to show that the rational numbers (let's only talk about the positive rational numbers here—bringing in the negative ones wouldn't change anything, though it would make the discussion slightly more complicated) can be arranged into a sequence r_1, r_2, r_3, ... which is exhaustive, that is, every rational number turns up somewhere or other in the sequence. To construct such a sequence, arrange all fractions in order of the sum of numerator and denominator: first the fractions whose numerator and denominator add up to 2 (since only positive rational numbers are under consideration here, they couldn't add up to less than 2), then those for which the sum of the numerator and and denominator is 3, then those for which it is 4, and so on:

1/1	2/1	1/2	3/1	2/2	1/3	4/1	3/2
2/3	1/4	5/1	4/2	3/3	2/4	1/5	...

There are duplications in this list; for example, 4/2 represents the same number as does 2/1. The desired sequence can be obtained by correcting that deficiency: delete all entries in the above sequence which duplicate earlier entries:

1/1	2/1	1/2	3/1	1/3	4/1	3/2	2/3
1/4	5/1	1/5	6/1	5/2	...		

Every rational number will occur somewhere or other in this sequence, since every rational number can be represented as a fraction a/b and there will be only finitely many rational numbers whose numerator and denominator add up to $a + b$ or less.

If we go significantly beyond the set of all rational numbers and consider the set of all real numbers, we finally get a set that demonstrably has more than $\aleph_0$ members. The real numbers include not only the rational numbers but also 'irrational numbers' such as π and $\sqrt{2}$, which do not correspond exactly to any ratio of whole numbers. Every real number can be represented in 'decimal form', for example, $\pi = 3.14159\ldots$, $\sqrt{2} = 1.414\ldots$. In the case of a rational number, the decimal form either terminates ($1/4 = 0.25$) or repeats ($1/11 = 0.090909\ldots$); in the case of an irrational number, the decimal form continues for infinitely many places, with no group of figures repeated more than a finite number of times in succession. If we treat terminating decimals as having repeated zero at the end ($1/4 = 0.250000\ldots$), all real numbers can be represented as nonterminating decimal forms. We have to show that there is no way to arrange all real numbers into an exhaustive sequence. Let's concentrate on the real numbers between 0 and 1; it is easy to show that there are as many of them as there are real numbers altogether, and it will simplify things if we can forget about what comes before the decimal point. Suppose that the real numbers between 0 and 1 could be arranged into an exhaustive sequence:

$$a^1 = .a^1{}_1 a^1{}_2 a^1{}_3 a^1{}_4 \ldots$$
$$a^2 = .a^2{}_1 a^2{}_2 a^2{}_3 a^2{}_4 \ldots$$
$$a^3 = .a^3{}_1 a^3{}_2 a^3{}_3 a^3{}_4 \ldots$$
$$a^4 = .a^4{}_1 a^4{}_2 a^4{}_3 a^4{}_4 \ldots$$

If I can show that a contradiction follows, I will have shown that the real numbers between 0 and 1 cannot be arranged into an exhaustive sequence, and that will establish that the real numbers between 0 and 1 (and thus the real numbers altogether) form a set with more than $\aleph_0$ members. I will show that there is a contradiction by showing that, regardless of what numbers appear in the various places in that sequence, it is possible to construct another real number between 0 and 1 that does not appear in the sequence, which will contradict the assumption that the sequence was exhaustive. I will construct such a number by giving a procedure for constructing each of the digits in its decimal form. If $a^1{}_1 = 5$, let $x_1 = 4$, and if $a^1{}_1 \neq 5$, let $x_1 = 5$. If $a^2{}_2 = 5$, let $x_2 = 4$, and if $a^2{}_2 \neq 5$, let $x_2 = 5$. If

$a^3{}_3 = 5$, let $x_3 = 4$, and if $a^3{}_3 \neq 5$, let $x_3 = 5$. In general, if $a^i{}_i = 5$, let $x_i = 4$, and if $a^i{}_i \neq 5$, let $x_i = 5$. This procedure defines a real number between 0 and 1 whose decimal form is $.x_1 x_2 x_3 x_4 \ldots$. This number, call it x, is different from all the numbers a^i: its first digit was picked so as to insure that $x \neq a^1$, its second digit was picked in such a way as to insure that $x \neq a^2$, its third digit was picked in such a way as to insure that $x \neq a^3$, and in general, its ith digit was picked in such a way as to insure that x was different from a^i. But this means that no matter how a sequence of real numbers between 0 and 1 was arranged, it could not contain all of them: it is always possible to construct a number that does not appear in the sequence. But that means that there is no one-to-one correspondence between the positive whole numbers and the real numbers between 0 and 1.

A set which has $\aleph_0$ elements is called COUNTABLE or DENUMERABLE.[4] An infinite set which has more than $\aleph_0$ elements is called UNCOUNTABLE or NONDENUMERABLE. The set of all real numbers is thus an uncountable set. Note that if M is any finite set of symbols and M* is the set of all *finite* sequences of symbols of M, then M* is countable. (This can be shown the same way that we showed that the set of all rational numbers was countable: you can arrange them into a sequence by listing first the sequences of length 1, then those of length 2, then those of length 3, etc.) Let us assume that all descriptions of sets of whole numbers can be expressed as formulas in some finite alphabet (for example, the alphabet might consist of curly brackets, commas, quantifiers, logical connectives, digits with which to write specific numbers, etc.). Then there are only countably many descriptions of sets of whole numbers. If I can establish that there are uncountably many sets of whole numbers, I will have established a point stated in the last section: that there are more sets of whole numbers than there are descriptions of sets of whole numbers, and thus that there are sets of whole numbers that literally cannot be singled out by any description.

For any set M, let P(M) denote the set of all subsets of M. We will now prove that P(M) has more members than M, not only in the special case where M is the set of all positive whole numbers, but indeed no matter what set M is. Proving that P(M) has more members than M amounts to showing that there is a one-to-one correspondence between M and a subset of P(M) but there is no one-to-one correspondence between M and the whole of P(M). The first part of this result is trivial: the correspondence which matches each element a of M to the set $\{a\}$ (i.e., the set whose only member is a) is a one-to-one correspondence between M and a subset of P(M). Thus, all we have to prove is:

Theorem. For any set M, there is no one-to-one correspondence between M and P(M).

Proof. The proof of this theorem is very similar to the proof that there is no one-to-one correspondence between the positive integers and the real numbers between zero and 1: any correspondence between M and P(M) will fail to exhaust P(M), since no matter what the correspondence is, it will always be possible to construct a member of P(M) which is not included in the correspondence. Suppose that we have a set M and a function f which associates to each element x of M an element $f(x)$ of P(M). Since the elements of P(M) are the subsets of M, $f(x)$ will be a subset of M. For each element x one can then raise the question of whether x is a member of $f(x)$ and define a set N as consisting of those x's for which the answer is negative, that is, $N = \{x: x \notin f(x)\}$. Then the function f does not associate N to any element of M. For suppose that it did, that is, suppose that there is some element a of M such that $f(a) = N$. There are two possibilities: either a belongs to N or it does not. Suppose $a \in N$; then $a \notin f(a)$ (since that is the criterion for membership in N); but since $f(a) = N$, that means $a \notin N$, which contradicts the supposition. Now suppose that $a \notin N$; since $N = f(a)$, that means that $a \notin f(a)$, which means that a meets the criterion for membership in N, and thus $a \in N$, which contradicts the supposition. Thus f cannot exhaust M, since the assumption that it does implies a contradiction ($a \in N$ and $a \notin N$). Thus there can be no one-to-one correspondence between M and P(M), no matter what set M is.

This shows that there are more infinite numbers than you can shake a stick at. The set of all sets of real numbers has more members than does the set of all real numbers; the set of all sets of sets of real numbers has more members than does the set of all sets of real numbers; and so on. The theorem also establishes that there is no largest infinite number.

5.4. Proof by Induction

There is an important principle, ostensibly a principle of arithmetic, but in fact of much greater applicability, which will figure in some proofs to be given in later chapters. Since this principle is commonly formulated in terms of sets of numbers, this chapter is as good a place as any to include a brief discussion of it.

The PRINCIPLE OF MATHEMATICAL INDUCTION is one of the axioms that Peano formulated in his attempt to derive all of arithmetic from a conceptual minimum. Peano's axioms involve two primitive notions: '1' and 'successor'. The 'successor' of a particular positive whole number (or NATURAL NUMBER, to use the terminology generally employed in this context) is the next higher natural number, for example, the successor of 3 is 4, and the successor of 794 is 795. Using 'S' to stand for 'successor', natural numbers greater than 1 can be given definitions such as '2 = S1', '3 = SS1' (i.e. S(S(1))), and so on. Among Peano's axioms was one which asserted that the natural numbers were precisely those things that could be constructed from '1' by iteration of 'S': if a set contains 1, and if for every element n that it contains, it also contains Sn, then it contains all of the natural numbers. This formulation is equivalent to the following, perhaps more familiar, formulation of the principle of mathematical induction:

> For any property $f(x)$, if $f(1)$ is true and if whenever $f(n)$ is true, $f(n + 1)$ is also true, then $f(x)$ is true of all natural numbers.

The latter formulation follows from Peano's since it is what you get when you apply Peano's formulation to the set $\{x: f(x)\}$; for example, to say that $f(1)$ is true is simply to say that 1 belongs to $\{x: f(x)\}$.

The following proof illustrates the way in which the principle of induction can be used in proving theorems of arithmetic:

Theorem. For any natural number n,

$$1 + 2 + \ldots + n = \frac{n(n + 1)}{2}.$$

Proof. Let $f(x)$ be the proposition that the sum of the first x natural numbers is $x(x + 1)/2$. Since the sum of the first 1 natural numbers is 1, and $1(1 + 1)/2 = 1$, $f(1)$ is true. Suppose that $f(n)$ is true for some natural number n, that is, that for that particular number, $1 + 2 + \ldots + n = n(n + 1)/2$. We can then find the sum of the first $n + 1$ natural numbers by adding $n + 1$ to both sides of this equation:

$$1 + 2 + \ldots + n + (n + 1) = \frac{n(n + 1)}{2} + (n + 1)$$

$$= \left(\frac{n}{2} + 1\right)(n + 1)$$

$$= \frac{n + 2}{2}(n + 1)$$

$$= \frac{(n + 1)[(n + 1) + 1]}{2}$$

But this shows that when $f(n)$ is true, $f(n + 1)$ is also true. Consequently, by the induction principle, $f(x)$ is true for all natural numbers x.

The following alternative formulation of the induction principle is equivalent to the two already given:

> If $f(1)$ is true, and for every natural number n, if all natural numbers less than n have the property, n has it also, then $f(x)$ is true of all natural numbers.[5]

This version of the induction principle can be illustrated by the following proof.

Theorem. Every natural number is a product of prime numbers.
'Product of prime numbers' is here taken in the broad sense which allows the degenerate case in which there are no factors (i.e., $1 = 2^0$) and that in which there is only one factor (e.g., $3 = 3^1$). Suppose that every natural number less than n is a product of prime numbers. Three cases must be distinguished: (i) $n = 1$; in this case, n is a (degenerate) product of primes: $n = 2^0$; (ii) n is a prime number; in this case, n is also a (degenerate) product of primes: $n = n^1$; and (iii) n is a composite number; that is, $n = ab$, where a and b are natural numbers less than n. By the inductive hypothesis, both a and b are products of prime numbers: $a = p_1 p_2 \ldots p_i$, $b = p'_1 p'_2 \ldots p'_j$. Then n is also a product of primes: $n = ab = p_1 p_2 \ldots p_i \, p'_1 p'_2 \ldots p'_j$. Thus, by the induction principle, every natural number is a product of primes.[6]

The reason that the induction principle can play a role outside of arithmetic is that nonarithmetic objects (e.g., formulas of predicate logic) allow numerical measures of 'size' or 'complexity': you can compare formulas as regards how many symbols long they are, or compare trees as regards how 'deep' they go (where the 'depth' of a node might be taken to be the number of S-nodes that one encounters in tracing from that node up to the top of the tree). It is then possible to reinterpret a statement 'all formulas of predicate logic are such that ...' as 'for every natural number n, all formulas of predicate logic which are of length n are such that ...' or 'for every natural number n, all formulas of predicate logic in which S's are embedded to at most a depth of n are such that ...'. The reinterpreted statement will be amendable to an inductive proof if it is possible to 'reduce' the behaviour of complex formulas to that of simpler formulas, for example, to show that if the immediate constituents of a formula have a certain property, then the whole formula will have it also.

Let us illustrate this by making explicit a proof that was sketched informally in chapter 4: the proof that a formula constructed by $\vee_e$-conjoining propositions two at a time is true if an odd number of the ultimate conjuncts are true and is false if an even number of them are true. If $f(n)$ is the proposition that all $\vee_e$-conjunctions of n ultimate conjuncts have that property, then $f(1)$ is true in the sense that 'the $\vee_e$-conjunction of one proposition' can be interpreted as that proposition, and a proposition A is true if and only if an odd number of members of the set {A} are true. Suppose that for some number n, every iterated two-term $\vee_e$-conjunction with less than n ultimate conjuncts is true if and only if an odd number of its ultimate conjuncts are true. Take any iterated two-term $\vee_e$-conjunction $\vee_e AB$ which has n ultimate conjuncts. Call m the number of ultimate conjuncts in A, in which case $n - m$ will be the number of ultimate conjuncts in B. Both m and $n - m$ are less than n. Thus, by the inductive hypothesis, A is true if and only if an odd number of its ultimate conjuncts are true, and B is true if and only if an odd number of *its* ultimate conjuncts are true. From the truth table for $\vee_e$, we know that $\vee_e AB$ is true if A is true and B false, or if A is false and B true, and is false otherwise. The sum of two natural numbers is odd if and only if one of them is odd and the other is even. Thus the number of true ultimate conjuncts in $\vee_e AB$ will be odd if and only if either the number of true ultimate conjuncts in A is odd and the number in B is even, or the number in A is even and the number in B is odd. By the inductive hypothesis, this will be the case if and only if either A is true and B false or A is false and B true. But we know that that will be the case if and only if $\vee_e AB$ is true. Thus $\vee_e AB$ is true if and only if an odd number of its ultimate conjuncts are true. The induction principle thus allows us to conclude that *any* iterated two-term $\vee_e$-conjunction will be true if and only if an odd number of its ultimate conjuncts are true.

For a final illustration of the principle of induction, let us prove the claim made in 2.1 that parentheses are in fact superfluous in so-called Polish parenthesis-free notation, that is, if $\wedge$ and $\vee$ are only allowed to conjoin things two at a time and all connectives are written before the items that they combine with, then the sequence of terminal symbols in a formula uniquely determines the constituent structure of the formula. Let us use the term 'Polish formula' for any sequence of connectives and atomic proposition symbols without parentheses that corresponds to a logical structure conforming to rules 2.1.15 in which each occurrence of $\wedge$ or $\vee$ has exactly two conjuncts. We need to show that for every positive integer n, every Polish formula of length n has only one syntactic analysis that conforms to the rules 2.1.15. That is trivially the case for Polish formulas of length 1: a Polish formula of length 1 can only be an atomic proposition symbol, and the formula can only be analyzed as a S consisting of that one symbol. Suppose that Polish formulas of length less than n never have more than one syntactic analysis. A Polish formula of length > 1 must contain a subformula of the form $\wedge pq$, $\vee pq$, $\supset pq$, or $\sim p$, with p and q atomic, since otherwise it would never come to an end. Let φ be a

Polish formula of length $n > 1$, and let φ' be the formula obtained from φ by replacing a subformula of the form $\wedge pq$, $\vee pq$, $\supset pq$, or $\sim p$ by an atomic proposition r. Then φ' is of length $n - 1$ or $n - 2$ (depending on whether r, which is of length 1, replaces something of length 2 or of length 3) and thus, by the inductive hypothesis, φ' has only one syntactic analysis, and φ has only the analysis that one obtains by replacing r by (as appropriate) $\wedge pq$, $\vee pq$, $\supset pq$, or $\sim p$ in the unique analysis of φ': it can have no other syntactic analysis, since the subformula that r replaces would have to be a constituent in any syntactic analysis of φ (note that this is where the assumption that connectives precede what they are combined with is used: in a Polish formula $\ldots \vee pq \ldots$, p and q would have to be the conjuncts that the $\vee$ is combined with, whereas in an 'Italian' formula $\ldots p \vee q \ldots$, either the p or the q could be part of a larger expression that was combined with the $\vee$) and since, by the inductive hypothesis, there can be only one syntactic analyis for the formula in which that subformula is embedded. Thus, by the principle of induction, for every positive integer n, every Polish formula of length n has only one syntactic analysis, that is, every Polish formula (of whatever length) has only one syntactic analysis.

5.5. Relations and Functions

Consider an expression such as 'is taller than' or 'went to the same school as' which expresses a relationship. For any given pair of objects, one can ask whether that pair of objects stands in the given relation, for example, whether the pair (Wilt Chamberlain, Dick Cavett) stands (stand?) in the relationship 'is taller than' (i.e., whether Wilt Chamberlain is taller than Dick Cavett) or whether the pair (Chomsky, Kissinger) stand/stands in the relationship 'went to the same school as' (i.e., whether Chomsky went to the same school as did Kissinger). Ordinary English would dictate the use of the form *stand* rather than *stands* in the last sentence, that is, the verb is chosen to fit the plural *Wilt Chamberlain and Dick Cavett* rather than to fit the singular *the pair*. However, it has become common among logicians and mathematicians to conceive of things in a way which would make the singular form more appropriate, that is, to think of a (two-place) relationship as identical with the set of pairs of objects that stand in that relationship, with the members of that set thus being (ordered) pairs such as (Chomsky, Kissinger) rather than individuals such as Chomsky and Kissinger.

Identifying a two-place relation with the set of pairs that it is true of is essentially the same thing as identifying a one-place predicate with the set of individuals that it is true of. In either case,[7] an element of meaning is being identified with the set of things that it is true of, its EXTENSION, to use widely accepted term. I will not adopt here the position that a predicate can be identified with its extension. However, whether that position is correct or not, the extension of a predicate will be of central importance in discussing truth conditions for complex propositions.

The notions of 'operation' and 'function' can to a large extent be explained away in terms of the notion of 'relation'. For example, the operation of addition of real numbers can be eliminated from an account of arithmetic if one instead talks in terms of the three-place relation 'the sum of a and b is c' (or 'a and b add up to c'). Using s to stand for that relation, '$a + b = c$' can be replaced by '$s(a, b, c)$'. The only respect in which that translation is questionable is that '$a + b$' occurs in other contexts than as the left half of an equation. For example, it occurs in such formulas as

5.5.1 $a + (b + c) = (a + b) + c$
$a + (b + c) > (a + b) + d$

It takes a bit of circumlocution to eliminate the $+$'s from 5.5.1 in favor of s's; specifically, it is necessary to bring in quantifiers, as in

5.5.2 $(\exists : s(b, c, x))_x(\exists : s(a, x, y))_y(\exists : s(a, b, z))_z(\exists : s(z, c, w))_w = yw$
$(\exists : s(b, c, x))_x(\exists : s(a, x, y))_y(\exists : s(a, b, z))_z(\exists : s(z, d, w))_w > yw$

While the formulas in 5.5.2 are in fact true under the same conditions as the corresponding formulas of 5.5.1, they have little more than that in common with 5.5.1. In fact, formulas like 5.5.1 illustrate a respect in which the intuitive notion of an 'operation' as something that is 'performed on' *operands* and yields a *result* makes sense: 'operations' can be iterated and complex formulas built up in which each of the constituents is not a proposition but an expression denoting an 'object'.

In any event, though, the extension of a two-place operation is the extension of the corresponding three-place relation, for example, the extension of the operation of multiplication is a complete multiplication table. There is no sharp distinction between the notions of 'operation' and 'function'. 'Function' is sometimes used as a more general term than 'operation': an n-place function is anything which associates to a sequence of n 'operands' a single 'value', that is, anything whose extension is a set of $(n + 1)$-tuples $(a_1, a_2, \ldots, a_n, b)$ such that for any choice of $(a_1, \ldots, a_n)$ there is exactly one b such that $(a_1, \ldots, a_n, b)$ is in the set. One particularly well-known kind of function is that which provides a way of getting from the operands to the value by performing specific operations, for example, the function f defined by $f(x, y, z) = x^2 + 2y^3 + 3z^4$ associates to any triple of numbers (x, y, z) the value obtained by squaring the first, cubing the second and multiplying the result by 2, and so on. The term 'operation' is most commonly used for the functions corresponding to the elementary steps in such a computation: one speaks of an operation of addition and an operation of multiplication, though not of an operation of dividing the square of one number by the cube of a second number. To a certain extent, however, it is arbitrary what computational steps one takes as basic (as one can easily convince oneself by comparing some of the popular computer programming languages with each other), and it is to an equal extent arbitrary how one would distinguish 'operations' from 'functions' in general.

The 'operands' and 'result' of a function need not be numbers. For example, one can speak of a function 'PB(x)' for which the operand is a person and the value is that person's place of birth, that is, the function which associates to each person his place of birth. A propositional function is also a function, for example, the propositional function ($\exists z$) $\wedge$ (parent x z, parent z y) is a function which associates to each pair of objects the proposition that the one is a parent of a parent of the other, that is, is a grandparent of the other. A function thus need not be expressible as a sequence of arithmetic operations. Indeed, a function can be a completely arbitrary association of members of one set to members of the same or another set, as in the functions discussed in 5.2, which associated to each state that belonged to the U.S.A. in 1945 one of the preludes of Bach's Well-tempered Clavier. There are in fact $48 \times 47 \times 46 \times \ldots \times 2 \times 1$ different functions which associate to each state a different prelude (i.e., functions which establish that there are as many states as there are preludes) and 48^{48} different functions which associate to each state a prelude, with no restriction against the same prelude being associated to different states; among those 48^{48} functions there is for example a function which associates to Kentucky the C$\#$ minor prelude of book two and to all other states the D major prelude of book one.

5.6. Valuations

In our informal discussion of 'states of affairs' above, I took the significant differences among states of affairs to be differences in what propositions were true in each state of affairs. The state of affairs can then for all practical purposes be identified with a specification of what propositions are true and what ones false in that state of affairs. We can thus identify a state of affairs with a function that associates to each proposition a truth value. The term VALUATION is commonly used for such a function: given a 'formal language' L, a valuation on L is a function which associates to each proposition of L a value T or F. The discussion in 3.2 made clear that not all valuations are equally worthy of consideration. If one is to develop a coherent notion of 'state of affairs', it will be necessary to exclude such absurd assignments of truth values as the one in which all propositions are assigned the value 'true', or the one in which 'God is dead and Cincinnati is in Mongolia' is assigned the value T and all other propositions (including the proposition that God is dead) the value F.

The most widely discussed restricted class of valuations is the CLASSICAL valuations: those valuations which assign to complex propositions values that are predictable by the classical truth tables from the values that they assign to the constituents of those propositions (e.g., if v is a classical valuation and $v(p) = $ F, then $v(\sim p)$ must be T). In 3.2 we considered a somewhat broader set of valuations than the classical valuations, namely, the valuations that 'conformed to' the rules of inference of chapter 2, in the sense that if a set of propositions are true according to the given valuation, then anything deducible from them by the given rules of inference will also be assigned the value T by the given valuation.

This notion of valuations conforming to a system of rules of inference can be generalized so as to be applicable with regard to any system of rules of inference. Specifically, suppose that for any formal language L and any system R of rules of inference, we define V(L, R) as consisting of those valuations f with respect to which R leads from true premises to true conclusions, that is, $f \in $ V(L, R) if and only if for all $A_1, \ldots, A_n, B \in $ L, if $f(A_1) = \ldots = f(A_n) = $ T and B is provable from $A_1, \ldots, A_n$ by the rules of R, then $f(B) = $ T. In 3.2 we proved that if L is a language of propositional logic and R is the rules of inference of chapter 2, then the set of all classical valuations on L is a proper subset of V(L, R): V(L, R) contains all classical valuations, but it also contains nonclassical valuations, in which there are cases where a proposition and its negation are both assigned the value F.

By referring to V(L, R), we can make sense out of a perplexing problem posed by Prior (1960). Prior, objecting to the common practise of speaking of the logical connectives as being 'defined by' their values of inference, pointed out that if we allow connectives to be defined by any imaginable rules of inference, there is nothing to prevent us from defining a connective *tonk* as that connective which obeys the rules

Tonk-introduction: A
                     A *tonk* B

Tonk-exploitation: A *tonk* B
                     B

Of course, these rules would allow any proposition to be inferred from any proposition at all; for arbitrary propositions A and B, the proof would be:

1   A   supp
2   A *tonk* B   1, *tonk*-intro
3   B   2, *tonk*-expl

Consider, now, V(L, R), where R includes the two rules for *tonk*. V(L, R) would contian at most two valuations: that which assigns to every proposition the value T and that which assigns to every proposition the value F. (Proof: suppose a valuation f does not assign all propositions the same value, say, $f(A) = T$, $f(B) = F$; B is inferrable from A by R; therefore $f \notin$ V(L, R), since f does not assign T to all propositions that are inferrable from propositions to which it assigns T). While there is nothing to prevent one from defining *tonk* as above, a system of rules of inference that contained the rules for *tonk* would allow only an extremely narrow and uninteresting set of valuations. Therefore, incluing *tonk* in a formal language and rules of inference would defeat the logician's purposes.

5.7. Exercises

1. Let A be the set of all nouns listed in *Webster's Third International*, let B be the set of all three-syllable words that it lists, and let C be the set of all Greek-derived words that it lists.

   a. Is *oligarchy* a member of $A \cap B$? $A \cap C$? $C - B$?
   b. Is *persecute* a member of $B - A$? $B \cap C$? $B - (A \cup C)$?

2. Use the principle of mathematical induction to prove that in any language in which every clause contains a non-zero subject and a non-zero verb and every subordinate clause is introduced by a one-word complementizer, a sentence in which subordinate clauses are embedded to a depth of n (i.e., a structure like that given below) must contain at least $2n + 3$ words.

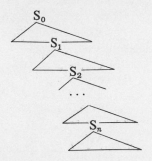

3. Suppose that v and w are classical valuations. For each of the following functions, determine whether it will necessarily also be a classical valuation.

a. The function f such that $f(A) = T$ if $v(A) = F$.
$$f(A) = F \text{ if } v(A) = T.$$

b. The function f such that $f(A) = T$ if either $v(A) = T$ or $w(A) = T$.
$$f(A) = F \text{ otherwise}$$

c. The function f such that $f(\vee A_1 \ldots A_n) = v(A_1)$
$$f(\wedge A_1 \ldots A_n) = w(A_n)$$
$$f(A) = F \text{ if A is not an } \vee\text{-conjunction or}$$
$$\text{an } \wedge\text{-conjunction.}$$

6. Predicate Logic II: Semantics

6.1. Truth in Predicate Logic

In propositional logic it was possible to get by with a very rudimentary notion of 'state of affairs': 'state of affairs' could be taken to be just an assignment of truth values to the propositions expressible in the given system, subject to the restrictions imposed by the system of rules of inference (e.g., if A and B are T, then $\wedge$ AB must be T also, since otherwise the rules of inference could draw a false conclusion from true premises). If the assumption is made that the connectives are truth-functional, then an even more rudimentary notion of state of affairs is possible: a state of affairs is any assignment of truth values to the *atomic* propositions of the system, with the truth values of the nonatomic propositions being predictable from those of the atomic propositions in accordance with the standard truth tables.

In predicate logic, it will be necessary to use a more involved notion of state of affairs. States of affairs can differ not only with regard to what propositions are true but also with regard to what objects exist. For example, the truth of the proposition that some Italians are bald will depend on whether there are bald Italians, and states of affairs can differ with regard to what individuals exist and what their properties are.

Let us assume that $\forall$ and $\exists$ are truth-functional, in the sense that the truth values of $(\forall: fx)gx$ and of $(\exists: fx)gx$ are predictable from information as to what objects fx and gx are true of, and also that the propositional connectives are truth-functional, and consider the question of what the closest analogue in predicate logic is to the rudimentary notion of state of affairs in propositional logic that we considered above. In any state of affairs, the atomic propositions will be the propositions consisting of predicates predicated of specific things. But what specific things? To even say what atomic propositions can play a role in a given state of affairs, it is necessary to know the set of things of which the predicates can be predicated in that state of affairs. Thus, one basic part of a state of affairs will

161

be a DOMAIN: the set D of objects which play a role in that state of affairs. The domain will be a set, possibly finite, possibly infinite. If the given logical has any individual constant symbols, they will generally denote elements of the domain, though it is useful to allow for the possibility of constants that in certain states of affairs lack denotations, for example, a constant for 'Santa Claus' would have a denotation in those states of affairs in which there is a Santa Claus but not in those in which there is no Santa Claus. More importantly, the domain will generally contain elements that correspond to no constant of the logical system, that is, it will generally contain objects that from the point of view of the given logical system 'have no names'. Whether or not an object has a name, it still has properties expressible in terms of the predicates of the given logical system. I have adopted a policy of interpreting the term 'proposition' so broadly as to encompass propositions that, strictly speaking, are not expressible in the given logical system, namely, propositions whose content is that a given object has a given property, where the property is expressible as a propositional function of the given system but the object need not have any name in the given system.[1] Note that this is a natural extension of the notion 'proposition' as used in chapters 2–4, since propositions have been the objects to which truth values are assigned, and the entities to which the term proposition is now to be applied are still things that are to have truth values, with the qualification that they may lack truth values in those states of affairs whose domains do not contain the objects of which the predicate is predicated. I will represent the proposition that the entity a has the property expressed by Fx by the expression Fa, that is, I will employ expressions in which a symbol for an object is used as if it were a constant of the given logical system; it should be kept in mind that 'Fa' is not an expression of the logical system but is the name of a proposition that is constructed from an expression of the logical system and an entity.

An object a SATISFIES a propositional function Fx if and only if Fa is true. The set of all objects in a given state of affairs α that satisfy a propositional function Fx is called the EXTENSION of F in α, abbreviated F$^\alpha$. For example, if a state of affairs α has a domain consisting just of the two objects a_1 and a_2, with F true of both of them and G true only of a_1, then F$^\alpha = \{a_1, a_2\}$ and G$^\alpha = \{a_1\}$.

Let us first attempt to state truth conditions for the simplest case of quantification, that in 6.1.1, where there is only one quantifier and one bound variable, and then attempt to extend it to the general case of arbitrary coherent combinations of quantifiers and variables.

6.1.1   a. $(\exists: Fx)Gx$
           b. $(\forall: Fx)Gx$

Fx and Gx can be taken to be any propositional functions of the single variable x built up from atomic propositional functions by means of the propositional connectives. Formula 6.1.1a should be true in the given state of affairs if and only if the domain D contains at least one element a_1 such that Fa_1 and Ga_1 are both true in that state of affairs and should be false in that state of affairs otherwise. I assume that a specification of the state of affairs includes a specification of what elements of its domain the various atomic propositional functions are true of, and thus, by virtue of the assumption that the propositional connectives are truth-functional, it determines truth values of Fa_1 and Ga_1 for any element a_1 of D. Alternatively, we can say that 6.1.1a is true in α if and only if $F^\alpha \cap G^\alpha \neq \varnothing$. Example 6.1.1$b$ should be true in α if and only if for every element a_1 of the domain of α for which Fa_1 is true in α, Ga_1 is also true in α; alternatively, 6.1.1b is true in α if and only if $F^\alpha \subseteq G^\alpha$.

The statement of the truth conditions on the universally quantified proposition 6.1.1b in terms of the extensions of its component propositional functions takes in an important special case that the informal statement did not so obviously take in, namely, the case where $F^\alpha = \varnothing$. Since the empty set is a subset of every set, the condition $F^\alpha \subseteq G^\alpha$ will be met if F is true of nothing in the state of affairs α, for example, in a state of affairs in which there are no unicorns, this version of the truth conditions for 6.1.1b will make $(\forall: \text{unicorn } x)(x \text{ drives a Cadillac})$ true. The standard policy of taking a universal proposition in this sort of case to be VACUOUSLY TRUE has some counterintuitive consequences but may be worth retaining nonetheless. Note that the standard policy allows the propositions expressed by the following sentences to differ in truth value:

6.1.2   a. Every person who loves all of his children is saintly.
         b. Every parent who loves all of his children is saintly.

A person who has no children would be a person who loves all of his children, according to the standard position; hence a person who has no children and is not saintly would be a counterexample to 6.1.2a, though he would not be a counterexample to 6.1.2b, since he is not a parent. Thus, in a state of affairs in which all persons who have children love all of them and are saintly but there is also a person who has no children and is not saintly, 6.1.2a would be false and 6.1.2b true. It is not completely clear that ANY uniform policy on the truth value of $(\forall: Fx)Gx$ in states of affairs in which Fx is true of nothing will yield acceptable results when $(\forall: Fx)Gx$ is used to specify the domain of another bound variable. For example, while 6.1.3a would normally be taken as including instances in which a member has not run up any bill, 6.1.3b would normally be taken as not including instances in which a senator received no campaign contributions at all:

6.1.3   a. Every member who has paid all his bills by the 15th of the month is entitled to a 10% discount on our publications.
         b. Every senator who got all his campaign contributions from the Teamsters' Union was defeated.

A policy always taking $(\forall: Fx)Gx$ to be true in states of affairs in which Fx is true of nothing would incorrectly make 6.1.3b cover those senators who received no campaign contributions, and a policy of always taking it to be false or to lack a truth value would incorrectly make 6.1.3a not cover those members who had incurred no bills.

The difference between 6.1.3a and 6.1.3b can probably be explained in terms of the purposes for which they would be uttered: in 6.1.3a, what is important is presumably whether a member has unpaid bills or not, and a member who has run up no bills at all is in conformity with the implied exhortation not to allow bills to accumulate; however, in 6.1.3b what is important is presumably whether a given senator owes fealty to the Teamsters' Union, and a senator who spends no money on campaigning would not owe any fealty to the union. While no uniform policy on the assignment of truth values to $(\forall: Fx)Gx$ in states of affairs where Fx is false of everything is sufficient to account for what is taken in by both sentences in 6.1.3, the standard policy of taking it to be vacuously true in such cases may be the optimal policy, for it allows the distinction between 6.1.3a and 6.1.3b to be drawn on the basis of an additional principle of language use that must anyway be invoked elsewhere, namely, that domains of bound variables are interpreted as restricted to those elements that are relvant to the given purposes. That principle also provides an explanation for the apparent synonymy of 6.1.2a and 6.1.2b: the additional persons covered by 6.1.2a, namely, persons who are not parents, would be irrelevant to the presumable purpose for uttering either of the sentences, namely, the expression of a connection between love of one's children and saintliness.

Let us now turn to the problem of specifying the truth conditions of propositions involving more than one bound variable, as in the following example, which could correspond to the sentence *Some Italian is fat and distrusts all Greeks* (px corresponding to 'x is an Italian', qx to 'x is fat', rx to 'x is a Greek', and sxy to 'x distrusts y'):

6.1.4 $(\exists: px) \wedge (qx, (\forall: ry)sxy)$

The problem in applying the above truth conditions here is in determining for which members of the domain the propositional function $\wedge (qx, (\forall: ry)sxy)$ is true, and more specifically, in determining for which elements its second conjunct $(\forall: ry)sxy$ is true. Note that we cannot just ask whether $r^\alpha \subseteq s^\alpha$, since that condition will fail to be met for a trivial and irrelevant reason, namely, that r^α is a set of objects but s^α is a set of pairs of objects. For each member a of the domain of α, we must ask whether r^α is contained in the set of all objects b for which $s(a, b)$ is true in α; the set of all such objects a will be the extension of $(\forall: ry)sxy$ in α. More generally, consider an expression (quantifier: $A(x, y, z, \ldots))_x$ $B(x, t, u, \ldots)$, where the lists $y, z, \ldots$ and $t, u, \ldots$ may overlap but need not. This expression should represent a propositional function of $y, z, \ldots$, $t, u, \ldots$, that is, of the variables other than the one that its quantifier binds, and the problem confronting us is that of specifying what that propositional function is.

It will be useful to introduce a notation that specifies which variables a given item is to serve as a value for; accordingly, let us use $(a/x, b/y, c/z, \ldots)$ to represent an assignment of a as a value for x, b as a value for y, c as a value for z, and so on (thus, the order of the terms in $(a/x, b/y, c/z, \ldots)$ is of no significance: all that is of significance is what element is associated with each variable). For each predicate, specification of a state of affairs includes a specification of what the predicate is true of, that is, for any predicate $f(x_1, \ldots, x_n)$, the specification of a state of affairs α indicates for which $(a_1/x_1, \ldots, a_n/x_n) f(x_1, \ldots, x_n)$ is true. I have assumed in saying this that $x_1, \ldots, x_n$ are the variables that actually occur in $f(x_1 \ldots, x_n)$. However, we can trivially also accommodate variables that do not occur in a propositional function: if $x_1, \ldots, x_n$ are involved in $f(x_1, \ldots, x_n)$ but $x_{n+1}, \ldots, x_m$ are not, we can take values for the supernumerary variables as not affecting whether the propositional function is satisfied; that is, we can take $(a_1/x_1, \ldots, a_n/x_n, a_{n+1}/x_{n+1}, \ldots, a_m/x_m)$ as satisfying $f(x_1, \ldots, x_n)$ if and only if $(a_1/x_1, \ldots, a_n/x_n)$ does; for example, if (Jimmy Carter/x) satisfies 'x eats peanut butter', then (Jimmy Carter/x, Yogi Berra/y) also satisfies it; if (Deng Xiaoping/x) does not satisfy 'x eats peanut butter', then neither does (Deng Xiaoping/x, Yogi Berra/y). The advantage of this apparently pointless introduction of irrelevancies is that it provides a simple way for us to talk about the satisfaction of formulas put together from constituents that do not involve the same variables. For example, we can say that the set of pairs of values for x and y that satisfy 'x is tall and y is fat' is the intersection of the set of pairs that satisfy 'x is tall' and the set of pairs that satisfy 'y is fat'; if a is Muhammad Ali and b is Robert Morley, then $(a/x, b/y)$ satisfies 'x is tall' because (a/x) does, $(a/x, b/y)$ satisfies 'y is fat' because (b/y) does, and thus $(a/x, b/y)$ satisfies 'x is tall and y is fat'.

The problem in giving truth conditions for 6.1.4 was that of specifying the extension of $(\forall: ry)sxy$, that is, specifying the set of values of x for which $(\forall: ry)sxy$ is true. We are now in a position to replace the absurd condition 'the extension of ry is contained in the extension of sxy' by something that makes sense and is relevant to the problem at hand. Specifically, we can compare the set of pairs of values for (x, y) that satisfy ry with the set of pairs that satisfy sxy and take a value a for x as satisfying $(\forall: ry)sxy$ if and only if every pair $(a/x, b/y)$ that satisfies ry also satisfies sxy, that is, (a/x) satisfies $(\forall: ry)sxy$ if and only if every pair $(a/x, b/y)$ that satisfies ry also satisfies sxy, which is to say that (a/x) satisfies $(\forall: ry)sxy$ if and only if there is no b such that $(a/x, b/y)$ satisfies ry but does not satisfy sxy. More generally, $(a_1/x_1, \ldots, a_n/x_n)$ satisfies $(\forall: F(x, x_1, \ldots, x_n))_x G(x, x_1, \ldots, x_n)$ (where any of $x_1, \ldots, x_n$ may fail to figure in F or in G—all that is required is that $x, x_1, \ldots, x_n$ include all variables that are free in the two expressions) if and only if there is no b such that $(b/x, a_1/x_1, \ldots, a_n/x_n)$ satisfies $F(x, x_1, \ldots, x_n)$ but does not satisfy $G(x, x_1, \ldots, x_n)$. Similarly, $(a_1/x_1, \ldots, a_n/x_n)$ satisfies $(\exists: F(x, x_1, \ldots, x_n))_x G(x, x_1, \ldots, x_n)$ if and only if there is a b such that $(b/x, a_1/x_1, \ldots, a_n/x_n)$ satisfies $F(x, x_1, \ldots, x_n)$ and also satisfies $G(x, x_1, \ldots, x_n)$.

Let us then take a specific state of affairs and determine the truth value of 6.1.4 in it. We start with a specification of what entities there are and what combinations of those entities the various predicates are true of (i.e., who is Italian, who is Greek, who is fat, and who distrusts whom). Such information can be tabulated as in 6.1.5:

6.1.5 $D = \{a_1, a_2, a_3, a_4, a_5\}$

	px	qx	rx		x $\backslash$	a_1	a_2	a_3	a_4	a_5
a_1	T	T	F		a_1	T	F	T	F	T
a_2	T	F	F		a_2	F	F	F	T	T
a_3	T	T	F		a_3	T	F	F	T	T
a_4	F	F	T		a_4	T	T	T	F	F
a_5	F	T	T		a_5	T	T	F	T	T

(above the second table: s $\diagdown$ y)

Here ry is true precisely of a_4 and a_5. Thus, 6.1.4 will be true precisely of those elements for which both sxa_4 and sxa_5 are true, that is, those elements whose rows in the s table have T in both the a_4 column and the a_5 column; thus 6.1.4 is true of a_2, a_3, and a_5. The next larger constituent, namely 6.1.6, will be true of a_3 and a_5 but false of all other elements:

6.1.6 $\wedge (qx, (\forall: ry)sxy)$

The elements for which its first conjunct is true are a_1, a_3, and a_5, and those those for which its second conjunct is true are a_2, a_3, and a_5, and thus a_3 and a_5 are the only elements for which both conjuncts of 6.1.1 are true and thus for which 6.1.6 is true. Formula 6.1.4 will be true if, among the elements for which px is true, that is, among a_1, a_2, and a_3, there is at least one for which 6.1.6 is true; since there is such an element, namely, a_3, 6.1.4 is true in the given state of affairs.

While the tables in 6.1.5 have a visual resemblance to truth tables, the whole of 6.1.5 is in fact more analogous to a line of a truth table. Each of the entries in 6.1.5 represents part of the same state of affairs. By contrast, each line of a truth table represents a different state of affairs. In 6.1.5 we have one line for each element of the domain, whereas in a truth table, each line corresponds to a different combination of truth values for the constituent propositions. The truth conditions for the logical elements peculiar to predicate logic, that is, the quantifiers, do not lend themselves to presentation in tabular form. One could, of course, make up such tables for special cases in which there are a fixed finite number of elements in the domain, for example,

6.1.7

Fa_1	Fa_2	Ga_1	Ga_2	$(\forall : Fx)Gx$	$(\exists : Fx)Gx$
T	T	T	T	T	T
T	T	T	F	F	T
T	T	F	T	F	T
T	T	F	F	F	F
F	T	T	T	T	T
F	T	T	F	F	F
F	T	F	T	T	T
F	T	F	F	F	F
T	F	T	T	T	T
T	F	T	F	T	T
T	F	F	T	F	F
T	F	F	F	F	F
F	F	T	T	?T	F
F	F	T	F	?T	F
F	F	F	T	?T	F
F	F	F	F	?T	F

The 16 lines of this truth table correspond to the possible combinations of truth values of two predicates in a two-element domain.

6.2. Satisfiability and Validity

The notions of 'satisfiable' (i.e., true in at least one state of affairs) and 'valid' (i.e., true in all states of affairs) that were introduced in chapter 3 for propositional logic carry over unchanged to predicate logic: for any formula of predicate logic, one can reasonably ask whether there are states of affairs in which it is true and whether there are states of affairs in which it is false. However, it is useful to factor out one basic feature of the state of affairs, namely, the domain, and speak of satisfiability and validity in a given domain. While some formulas are valid in any domain (i.e., valid, period), for example, 6.2.1a, there are also formulas such as 6.2.1b which are valid in some domains but not in others:

6.2.1   a. $\supset((\forall: Fx) \sim Gx, \sim(\exists: Fx)Gx)$
             b. $(\exists x)(\forall y) = xy$

Formula 6.2.1b is valid in any domain which contains exactly one element and is invalid in any domain with more than one element. This, of course, figures, since the content of 6.2.1b is that there is precisely one element. For any finite number n, it is quite easy to construct a formula which is valid in any domain which contains exactly n elements and is invalid in any domain containing fewer or more than n elements. For example, 6.2.2 is valid in domains containing 3 elements and is invalid in other domains:

6.2.2 $(\exists x)(\exists y)(\exists z) \wedge (\sim = xy, \sim = xz, \sim = yz, (\forall w) \vee (= wx, = wy, = wz))$

The content of 6.2.2, of course, is that there are three distinct elements such that every element is identical to one of those three.

Note the role that $=$ plays in 6.2.1b and 6.2.2. Without using $=$, one can construct formulas that impose a lower bound on the size of domains in which they are satisfiable, but not formulas that impose an upper bound. For example, the following formula is satisfiable in a domain having at least two elements, but not in a domain having only one element:

6.2.3 $(\exists x)(\exists y) \wedge (px, \sim py)$.

For 6.2.3 to be true in a given state of affairs, it is necessary and sufficient that there be at least two elements in that domain, one for which p is true and one for which p is false; however, what further elements there are is immaterial. More generally, if a given formula not involving $=$ is satisfied in a given state of affairs, one can construct an alternative state of affairs involving a larger domain, in which the formula is still satisfied: pick any element a of the domain, and add a 'Doppelgänger' of that element—an element a' such that the same predicates are true of a' (and combinations involving a') as of a. The addition of this extra element will not change the truth value of any of the constituents of the given formula, though it will change the size of the domain. (Note how the assumption that the given formula does not contain $=$ is tacitly utilized here: $=aa$ and $=a'a$ can not have the same truth value if a and a' are distinct elements, and thus if formulas involving $=$ are admitted, a new element can never be a complete Doppelgänger of a given element).

There are indeed formulas which are only satisfiable in infinite domains, for example, the following:

6.2.4 $\wedge\,((\forall x)(\exists y)\mathrm{R}xy,\ (\forall x)(\forall y)\supset(\mathrm{R}xy,\ \sim\mathrm{R}yx),$
$(\forall x)(\forall y)(\forall z)\supset(\,\wedge\,(\mathrm{R}xy,\ \mathrm{R}yz),\ \mathrm{R}xz))$

The content of 6.2.4 is that R is a partial ordering relation in which every element is 'followed by' another element: the first term says that every element stands in the R relation to something, the second says that R is an antisymmetric relation (if x has the relation R to y, then y does not have it to x), and the third says that R is a transitive relation. Example 6.2.4 can be satisfied only in an infinite domain. For, suppose that it were satisfied in a finite domain. No element stands in the R relation to itself (the second term of 6.2.4 insures that if $\mathrm{R}xx$ were ever true, $\sim\mathrm{R}xx$ would be also); but every element stands in the R relation to something; thus if you pick any element, then pick an element that that element is in the R relation to, then pick an element that the latter element is in the R relation to, and so on, you will eventually reach an element that previously appeared in the list (since the set is finite); thus there is a finite sequence of elements in the domain such that $\mathrm{R}x_1x_2,\ \mathrm{R}x_2x_3,\ldots,\ \mathrm{R}x_{n-1}x_n,\ \mathrm{R}x_nx_1$; but then by the third term of 6.2.4 we would have $\mathrm{R}x_1x_1$, which we have already established that we can't have. Thus the domain must be infinite.

There is, of course, a countable infinite domain in which 6.2.4 is satisfied: take the domain to be the natural numbers, and take $\mathrm{R}xy$ to be $x < y$. Are there formulas of predicate logic that are satisfiable only in uncountable domains? Surprisingly, the answer is negative: according to the Löwenheim-Skolem theorem, a formula of predicate logic which is satisfiable in an infinite domain is satisfiable in a countable infinite domain. This is a surprising result because it shows a sharp and not at all obvious limitation on the expressive power of predicate logic: predicate logic is not capable of expressing a property that is only possessed by domains having uncountably many elements. Thus, whatever property of the real numbers that one might formulate in predicate logic will not serve to characterize the real numbers: there will be a countable domain which possesses the same property.

There is one misleading thing in the last paragraph, namely, my use of the term 'predicate logic' to refer to the specific kind of predicate logic that was treated in chapter 4, which is more correctly called FIRST-ORDER PREDICATE LOGIC. 'First-order' here means that the bound variables are individual variables rather than set variables or predicate variables. A system of logic that allowed formulas such as

6.2.5 $(\exists f)(\forall x)(\forall y) \supset (fxy, fyx)$

would be of (at least) second order. A system allowing variable predicates of predicates or variable sets of sets would be third-order predicate logic (e.g., in third-order logic, you can formulate propositions such as 'for every set of sets of real numbers, there is a set of real numbers such that every member of the latter is a member of a member of the former'). The Löwenheim-Skolem theorem has to do only with first-order predicate logic.

A semantic completeness theorem for first-order predicate logic can be proven: a formula of first-order predicate logic is true in all states of affairs if and only if it is provable relative to the rules of inference of chapter 4. The proof of this theorem is a simple extension of the proof of the completeness theorem for propositional logic.

6.3. The Uniformity of the 'Domain'

We have so far taken a state of affairs to involve a single 'domain', with no restriction on the kinds of objects in the domain or on what kinds of things a predicate can be predicated of. The subsets of that domain which are defined by the various predicates provide the domains of quantifiers. For example, if we have a formal language that is to represent the content of sentences like *You can fool some of the people all of the time*, the language will have to involve predicates like 'is a person' and 'is a time', and we will be particularly interested in those states of affairs which have a domain D containing both times and persons. The more heterogeneous the predicates that the formal language contains, the more heterogeneous a set D will have to be allowed to be, and that may be pretty heterogeneous: in a short nontechnical text one could very well encounter references to persons, times, events, numbers, names, biological species, routes from Chicago to Houston, and Mozart symphonies.

In our description of what a 'state of affairs' is, we have said that it includes specifications of truth values for every predicate of the language combined with every possible value (in D) for its arguments. But that seems to be leading us to a rather disconcerting and bizarre prospect: for each state of affairs one now will apparently have to specify not only whether the number 11 is prime, whether Richard Nixon is Jewish, and whether the Battle of Hastings took place before the invention of the zipper, but also whether the invention of the zipper is prime, whether the Battle of Hastings is Jewish, and whether Richard Nixon took place before the number 11.

We ought thus to digress at this point to see how we can modify our assumptions so as to avoid being forced into a wild proliferation of 'possible states of affairs' in which we must distinguish states of affairs in which the Battle of Hastings is Jewish from states of affairs in which the Battle of Hastings is not Jewish.

If we wish to rule out the possiblity of states of affairs differing with regard to whether the Battle of Hastings is Jewish, there are basically two approaches that can be pursued: either try to set things up in such a way that the truth values of such propositions are always predictable (e.g., so that 'The Battle of Hastings is Jewish' and 'The invention of the zipper is prime' are false in every state of affairs) or try to set things up in such a way that such propositions are never assigned a truth value at all, that is, have a state of affairs contain not a *complete* table of truth values for each predicate but a table covering only those members of the domain for which the question of the truth of the predicate arises. Either way, for each predicate it will be necessary to draw a distinction between those members of D (or combinations of members of D) for which the predicate can differ in truth value from one state of affairs to another, and those members of D for which it cannot.

So far we have placed no restrictions on the propositional functions that appear in expressions like $(\forall : Fx)Gx$, beyond the conditions on coherent use of variables. Suppose that we adopt the first alternative of the last paragraph and try to set things up so that for any propositional functions F and G, Fx and Gx will have truth values no matter what member of the domain is substituted for x. There is then nothing to prevent us from constructing expressions in which the 'F' is somewhat more outlandish than what has appeared in the examples so far, for example,

6.3.1 $(\forall : \vee (\text{person } x, \text{time } x))(\text{mortal } x)$.

The truth value of 6.3.1 in any particular state of affairs will hinge upon what exactly we have chosen to impose as the truth value of 'mortal x' for the case in which x is a time rather than a person. If we have chosen to require 'mortal x' to be false in all such cases, then 6.3.1 comes out false, which is surely a more reasonable result than if it had come out true. Consider, however, the notions of 'rational' and 'irrational' as they figure in mathematics. It would be nice to be able to define 'rational' as 'is the ratio of two integers' and define 'irrational' as the negation of 'rational'. If we are then going to assign to 'x is rational' the value F when x is not a number (just as we assigned to 'x is mortal' the value F when x is a time, or perhaps, more generally, when x is not a living being) and if our truth value assignments are to conform to the classical truth tables (as we have been assuming throughout this chapter), then 'x is irrational' ought to get the value T whenever x is not a number, and thus 6.3.2 ought to be assigned the value T:

6.3.2   ($\forall$: $\lor$ (x is the square root of a prime number, x is a cigar box))(x is irrational)

Thus, if we are to maintain some fairly natural semantic analyses and retain the classical truth tables, while disallowing the bizarre profusion of 'possible states of affairs' that we are trying to avoid, we will be forced to assign the value T to some formulas and the value F to other formulas in which ($\forall$: $\lor$ ($F_1 x$, $F_2 x$)) is combined with a propositional function that 'makes sense' only for the values of x that have the property $F_1 x$.

One way that we might avoid the problem of assigning truth values to propositions in which quantifiers have domains with bizarre definitions would be to place heavy restrictions on what the F can be in formulas of the form (Quantifier: Fx)Gx. If we attempt to impose such a restriction, we should see whether in the process we can also make it necessary to assign truth values to *The Battle of Hastings is Jewish* and the like. This in fact ought to be possible, since in both cases the bizarre examples that we were forced to deal with were bizarre because they mixed entities of different sorts; thus the direction that seems most promising is to seek a restriction based on the notion of 'sort'.

Suppose that we single out a particular set of predicates as defining 'sorts'. Perhaps 'person x', 'time x', 'number x', and 'place x' would define sorts but 'redheaded x' and 'prime x' would not. Only some very specific types of atomic predicates need be taken as allowing arguments of all sorts, namely, sort predicates themselves (e.g., 'time x' will be true of any time and false of anything of any other sort) and 'metaphysical' predicates such as 'exists' or 'is identical to'. For other atomic predicates, each argument can be restricted to values of one particular sort (e.g., in 'x occurs at y', the values of x can be restricted to events and the values of y to times) and no truth value assigned to it for argument values that are not of the appropriate sorts.

Expressions like the $\lor$ (x is the square root of a prime number, x is a cigar box) of 6.3.2 are true of things of two different sorts (at least, under the normal assumption that $\lor$ AB is true if either A or B is true, even if the other conjunct has no truth value). Thus, if bound variables are to be restricted to ranging over values of a single sort, some restriction will have to be imposed to exclude such expressions as the domain expressions of quantifiers. One way of imposing such a restriction would be to require that the domain expression of a quantifier binding a variable x_i be an $\land$-conjunction that has a conjunct Fx_i, where F is a sort predicate. I will adopt a slightly different restriction so as to achieve conformity with the analysis of restrictive relative clauses for which I have argued elsewhere (McCawley 1978*a*, 1978*b*). Specifically, I will give a recursive definition of a notion 'extended sort predicate' and restrict domain expressions to being extended sort predicates predicated of the bound variable:

6.3.3   [First approximation, to be revised in 6.3.5]
  a. For any variable x_i, (i) if F is a sort predicate, then Fx_i is an extended sort predicate of x_i, and (ii) if F_1x_i is an extended sort predicate of x_i and $F_2(x_i, \ldots)$ is any propositional function of x_i (and perhaps other variables), $\land (F_1x_i, F_2(x_i, \ldots))$ is an extended sort predicate of x_i.
  b. In any constituent (Quantifier: $Fx_i)_{x_i}Gx_i$ of a logical structure, F must be an extended sort predicate of x_i.

The reason for adopting 6.3.3, which requires that the domain expression be an $\land$-conjunction that contains a sort predicate embedded in one of its conjuncts, though not necessarily *as* one of its conjuncts, is that, under the analysis in which restrictive relative clauses are derived by adjunction of one conjunct to a predicate noun in the other conjunct of an $\land$-conjunction, it automatically yields the right-branching structure that I have argued to be the surface constituent structure of 'stacked' relative clause constructions, as in 6.3.4:

6.3.4

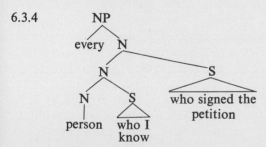

As it stands, 6.3.3 does not completely rule out mixed sorts, since it says nothing about the formula with which the given domain expression is combined and thus does not rule out expressions such as ($\forall$: person x) (prime x), in which a domain expression that restricts the variable to one sort is combined with an expression demanding values of a different sort for that variable. It likewise does not exclude domain expressions such as $\land$ (person x, prime x), in which the sort predicate is conjoined with an expression that requires values of another sort. The following revision of 6.3.3 will rule out mixed sorts:

6.3.5   a. For any variable x_i, (i) if $G(x_i, \ldots)$ is an atomic predicate for which x_i is restricted to values of sort F, then $G(x_i, \ldots)$

is of sort F for x_i; (ii) if $G_1(x_i, \ldots)$ and $G_2(x_i, \ldots)$ are of sort F for x_i, then so are $\sim G_1(x_i, \ldots)$, $\wedge (G_1(x_i, \ldots)$, $G_2(x_i, \ldots))$, $\vee (G_1(x_i, \ldots), G_2(x_i, \ldots))$ and $\supset (G_1(x_i, \ldots)$, $G_2(x_i, \ldots))$.

b. For any variable x_i, (i) if F is a sort predicate, then Fx_i is an extended sort predicate of x_i of sort F; (ii) if $G_1(x_i, \ldots)$ is an extended sort predicate of x_i of sort F and $G_2(x_i, \ldots)$ is of sort F for x_i, then $\wedge (G_1(x_i, \ldots)$, $G_2(x_i, \ldots))$ is an extended sort predicate of x_i of sort F.

c. For any expression (Quantifier: $G_1(x_i, \ldots))_{x_i} G_2(x_i, \ldots)$, there must be a sort F such that G_1 is an extended sort predicate of x_i of sort F and G_2 is of sort F for x_i.

'Sort predicates' are a very special type of 'essential properties': properties that an individual could not gain or lose without ceasing to exist or losing its identity. A person may become red-headed or become bald, but he cannot become a number or a battle or a route from Chicago to Houston. In comparing alternative states of affairs, we can identify a bank president in one state of affairs with a skid-row bum in another state of affairs (as we might need to in order to make sense out of sentences like *If Schwartz hadn't inherited his uncle's chicken ranch, he'd be a bum on skid row*), but we cannot identify a bank president in one state of affairs with the invention of the zipper, or with 21 March 1844, or with an 11th symphony of Beethoven in some other state of affairs (thus, we cannot make sense out of sentences like *If Schwartz hadn't inherited his uncle's chicken ranch, he'd be Beethoven's 11th Symphony*). Sort properties, however, are not the only essential propererties; for example, we could not identify the number 11 in one state of affairs with a number in another state of affairs that was divisible by 2, 7, and 31. Indeed, it is very odd even to raise the possibility of numbers differing from one state of affairs to another: we rather feel that the numbers are something outside of any state of affairs, albeit something that can be referred to in describing any state of affairs (e.g., part of a description of a state of affairs might be a specification of how many chickens each person owns).

Determining what 'sorts' there are is a philosophical activity that has a long tradition (in which the systems of categories of Aristotle, Kant, and Hegel are particularly noteworthy), though it has fallen into disrepute and been much neglected during the twentieth century. It is an activity which will have to be revived if a useful notion of 'state of affairs' is to be developed along the lines of the program suggested here.[2]

Let us see whether the acceptance of this program would require any modification in the system of rules of inference of 4.3. We would have to disallow the inference of 6.3.6*b* from 6.3.6*a*, since $\sim Gx$ is not a sort predicate or an $\wedge$-conjunction of a sort predicate with other conjuncts (though in special cases it might be deductively equivalent to such a conjunction):

6.3.6   a. $(\forall: Fx)Gx.$
           b. $(\forall: \sim Gx)\sim Fx.$

One way that we could disallow 6.3.6 is simply to impose the condition that conclusions must conform to 6.3.5. We could then maintain exactly the rules of inference given in chapter 4 and treat the inference from 6.3.6*a* to 6.3.6*b* (see 4.4.2 for details) as inadmissable by virtue of the ill-formedness of its conclusion. Note, however, that under this proposal, a close analog to 6.3.6, namely, the inference from 6.3.7*a* to 6.3.7*b*, would be permitted, where T*x* is a sort predicate:

6.3.7   a. $(\forall: \wedge(Tx, Fx))Gx$
           b. $(\forall: \wedge(Tx, \sim Gx))\sim Fx.$

This would correspond to an inference with premise *All animals which are dogs bite postmen* and conclusion *All animals which do not bite postmen are nondogs*. This inference shares a questionable feature with the inference from *All dogs bite postmen* to *All nonbiters of postmen are nondogs*, namely, that the conclusion appears to involve different existence presuppositions than does the premise. Thus, it may be necessary to adopt a restricted version of $\forall$-introduction even if steps in proofs are required to conform to 6.3.5.

6.4. Exercises

1. Consider the following state of affairs:

   Domain $= \{1, 2, 3, 4, 5\}$
   $f1$ and $f3$ are true, $f2, f4$, and $f5$ are false.
   $g11, g13, g25, g34$, and $g55$ are true, otherwise gxy is false.

Determine the truth value in this state of affairs of

   a. $(\forall x: fx)gxx$
   b. $(\forall x: (\exists y: gxy))fx$
   c. $(\forall x: (\exists y: fy)gyx) \vee (\sim fx, gxx)$

2. Assume that *No linguist admires no linguist* is ambiguous as to which *no* has higher scope (it's ambiguous for some people but not for others; act as if you're the former kind of person) and treat *no* as $\sim$ plus $\exists$. Show that the two interpretations can differ in truth value (i.e., show how it could happen that one interpretation was true while the other was false).

7. Applications and Extensions of Predicate Logic

7.1. Russell's Analysis of *The*

Bertrand Russell (1905) argued that an expression such as *the king of France* does not correspond to a constituent of logical structure: rather it represents a complex logical structure containing a predicate ('*x* is king of France') and various connectives and quantifiers, embodying the proposition that that predicate is true of one and only one element. Specifically, Russell proposed that the logical structure of 7.1.1*a* was 7.1.1*b*:

7.1.1   a. The king of France is bald.

    b. $(\exists x) \wedge (\text{KF}x, (\forall y) \supset (\sim \, = yx, \sim \text{KF}y), \text{B}x),$

where KFx stands for '*x* is king of France' and Bx for '*x* for '*x* is bald'. The content of 7.1.1*b* is that there is an individual such that he is king of France, no one but him is king of France, and he is bald. Russell's principal reason for proposing this analysis was to allow coherent discussion of sentences such as 7.1.1*a* even when there is no individual in existence who meets the description given (in this case, when there is no king of France). Thus, for Russell, 7.1.1*a* is true when there is one and only one king of France and that individual is bald; it is false in each of the three cases in which that fails to be so: when there is one and only one king of France and that individual is not bald, when there is no king of France, and when there is more than one king of France.

Discussion of Russell's analysis, both by Russell himself and by his critics and commentators, has been concerned almost exclusively with the second of these three cases. Thus, in the first serious attack on Russell's proposals, which had stood essentially unchallenged for forty-five years, Strawson (1950) devoted much space to arguing that 7.1.1*a* is not false when there is no king of France, that rather the question of truth or falsehood simply does not arise in that case; however, Strawson did not even mention the question of what should be said about 7.1.1*a* when there is more than one king of France. Odd as it is to say that 7.1.1*a* is false when

176

there is no king of France, it is far odder to say that 7.1.2 is false when there is more than one restaurant on Clark Street:

7.1.2   The restaurant on Clark Street is excellent.

Russell's analysis builds into the logical structure of the sentence two stringent criteria for the successful use of *the X*: that there is an X and that no more than one thing is an X, and it builds them in in exactly the same way, so that failure of either criterion results in the same thing, namely, falsehood of the proposition expressed by the sentence. Actual use of definite NP's in ordinary language is not constrained by quite so stringent criteria; for example, one can use 7.1.2, even knowing that there are easily one-hundred restaurants on Clark Street, provided that one restaurant on Clark Street is prominent relative to the linguistic or extra-linguistic context in which one utters 7.1.2 (e.g., you have just been talking about five Korean restaurants, exactly one of which is on Clark Street), and 7.1.2 will express the proposition that that restaurant is excellent.[2] See 9.6 for an alternative account of *the* in which this context-dependence plays a central role, and see 9.1–9.2 for discussion of the possibility that (as proposed by Strawson 1950), when there is no king of France, the proposition that 7.1.1*a* expresses is neither true nor false.

For the time being, however, let us stick within Russell's framework, which did not allow truth value gaps or interactions between logical form and context, and take 7.1.1*a* to have precisely the truth conditions that correspond to 7.1.1*b*. With regard to the first conjunct in 7.1.1*b*, this is not too unreasonable, in that while it may make one uncomfortable to call 7.1.1*a* false in a case where there is no king of France, it would be totally outrageous to call it true in that case; it is of course much harder to live with the second conjunct: the idea that the existence of more than one restaurant on Clark Street could make 7.1.2 express a false proposition is pretty hard to swallow, and no rationalization has yet been found to make it palatable.

What then about the apparent negation of 7.1.1*a*, namely, 7.1.3*a*? Russell held that 7.1.3*a* was ambiguous between an interpretation in which negation applied to an expression containing *the* (7.1.3*b*) and an interpretation in which *the* applied to an expression containing negation (7.1.3*c*):

7.1.3   a. The king of France is not bald.
$\quad\quad\quad$ b. $\sim(\exists x) \wedge (\mathrm{KF}x, (\forall y) \supset (\sim =yx, \sim \mathrm{KF}y), \mathrm{B}x)$
$\quad\quad\quad$ c. $(\exists x) \wedge (\mathrm{KF}x, (\forall y) \supset (\sim =yx, \sim \mathrm{KF}y), \sim \mathrm{B}x)$.

Example 7.1.3*b* denies that there is one and only one king of France and that individual is bald; 7.1.3*c* says that there is one and only one king of

France and that that individual is not bald. Thus, in the controversial cases, those in which there is no king of France and those in which there is more than one king of France, 7.1.3*b* is true and 7.1.3*c* is false. Example 7.1.3*a* is a simple (and not all that convincing) illustration of the point that a DEFINITE DESCRIPTION such as *the king of France* has a scope, just like a quantifier, and may be involved in scope ambiguities. Russell proposed a notation involving $(\iota x\colon \mathrm{KF}x)$ as an abbreviation of the combination of quantifiers and connectives into which he analyzed *the king of France*. We will adopt a variant of Russell's notation and represent the content of 7.1.1*a* and 7.1.3*a* as follows, thus displaying the scope of the definite description more transparently than in 7.1.3*b*–*c*:[3]

7.1.4   a. $(\iota x\colon \mathrm{KF}x)\mathrm{B}x$ $(= 7.1.1b)$
       b. $\sim(\iota x\colon \mathrm{KF}x)\mathrm{B}x$ $(= 7.1.3b)$
       c. $(\iota x\colon \mathrm{KF}x)\sim\mathrm{B}x$ $(= 7.1.3c)$

I will in fact employ this notation later in this book even in presenting analyses in which I do not presuppose Russell's analysis of definite descriptions: while Russell's specific analysis can be contested on quite serious grounds, his idea that definite NP's involve a quantifier that has a specific scope relative to other elements of logical structure has stood up well, and a notation that indicates the scope of definite descriptions is worth having.

Discussions of Russell's analysis have said nothing in particular about definite NP's in predicate position, for example,

7.1.5   a. Michael Moskowitz is the mayor of Heppleworth, Iowa.
      b. Sheila Ostrovsky is the student who wrote the best exam paper.

There are two ways in which one might fit such sentences into a Russellian analysis: either apply the Russellian analysis directly to them, taking them to involve constituents 'Michael Moskowitz is x' and 'Sheila Ostrovsky is x', with *is* meaning $=$, or give an analysis of predicate definite NP's that allows them to be identified with parts of formulas such as 7.1.1*b*. Under the former approach, 7.1.5*a* would be analyzed as in 7.1.6*a*, whereas the latter would lead one to an analysis such as 7.1.6*a'*, involving constituents similar to the first two conjuncts in 7.1.1*b*:

7.1.6   a. $(\iota x\colon \mathrm{mayor}(x, \mathrm{HI})) = (\mathrm{MM}, x)$, i.e., $(\exists x) \wedge (\mathrm{mayor}(x, \mathrm{HI}),$
          $(\forall y) \supset (\sim\, =yx, \sim\mathrm{mayor}(y, \mathrm{HI})), =(\mathrm{MM}, x))$
      a'. $\wedge (\mathrm{mayor}(\mathrm{MM}, \mathrm{HI}), (\forall y) \supset (\sim\, =(y, \mathrm{MM}), \sim\mathrm{mayor}(y, \mathrm{HI})))$

These two analyses have different implications for the possible interpretations of sentences involving predicate definite NP's: under the analysis in 7.1.6*a*, such sentences should potentially be ambiguous with regard to the scope of the definite description, whereas under the analysis in 7.1.6*a'* there should be no possibility of a scope ambiguity, since the only quantifier in 7.1.6*a'* has to have the second conjunct as its scope. We are thus led to compare the possible interpretations of sentences in which a predicate definite NP is embedded in a larger structure and of otherwise parallel sentences in which the definite NP is not in predicate position, for example,

7.1.7   a. Michael Moskowitz wants to be the mayor of Heppleworth, Iowa.
          b. Michael Moskowitz wants to meet the mayor of Heppleworth, Iowa.

There is a clear scope ambiguity in 7.1.7*b*: it can be interpreted either with the whole sentence as the scope of the definite description (this is the *de re* interpretation, which picks out a certain person as the mayor of Heppleworth, Iowa, and says that Moskowitz wants to meet that person, with the fact that that person is the mayor of Heppleworth not being a condition on the fulfillment of the wish—he could be thrown out of office and Moskowitz would still want to meet him), or with the definite description having only the embedded 'Michael Moskowitz meets x' as its scope (this is the *de dicto* interpretation, in which Moskowitz's wish is fulfilled if he meets whoever is mayor of Heppleworth, regardless of who that happens to be). The most obvious interpretation of 7.1.7*a* is a *de dicto* one in which Moskowitz's wish is fulfilled if he holds the office of mayor of Heppleworth. With a little strain one can find an extra interpretation of 7.1.7*a*, indeed, two extra interpretations. Both refer to Moskowitz changing his identity rather than his occupation. One is *de re*: there is a certain person who is the mayor of Heppleworth, Iowa, and Moskowitz wants to be him; the other is *de dicto*: Moskowitz desires that, regardless of who is mayor of Heppleworth, Iowa, he should become that person. The only way that I can see to accommodate the three-way ambiguity of 7.1.7*a* in an essentially Russellian analysis is to adopt BOTH 7.1.6*a* AND 7.1.6*a'* in analyses of 7.1.7*a* and represent its three senses as

7.1.8 a_1. $(\iota x: \text{mayor}(x, \text{HI})) \text{want}(\text{MM}, =(\text{MM}, x))$
          a_2. $\text{want}(\text{MM}, (\iota x: \text{mayor}(x, \text{HI})) = (\text{MM}, x))$
          a'. $\text{want}(\text{MM}, \wedge (\text{mayor}(\text{MM}, \text{HI}), (\forall y) \supset (\sim =(y, \text{MM}), \sim \text{mayor}(y, \text{HI}))))$

This discussion suggests that one must distinguish between a *be* of identity and a copula *be*, with a definite NP after the *be* of identity analyzed as in 7.1.6*a* and a definite NP after a copula *be* as in 7.1.6*a'*. Of course, only in the latter case is the NP strictly speaking a predicate NP. Since we thus have reason to analyze predicate definite NP's as in 7.1.6*a'*, we have reason to divide Russell's analysis of nonpredicate definite NP's into two steps: 7.1.1a is analyzed as in 7.1.9a, which amounts to 7.1.9b in virtue of the analysis of predicate definite NP's:

7.1.9   a. $(\exists x) \wedge (x$ is the king of France, x is bald)
             b. $(\exists x) \wedge (\wedge (KF(x), (\forall y) \supset (\sim =yx, \sim KF(y)), B(x))$

In this modified Russellian analysis, it is the existential quantifier rather than the *the* that is responsible for the scope of the definite description, and 7.1.3b–c will be reanalyzed as

7.1.10   b. $\sim (\exists x) \wedge (x$ is the king of France, x is bald)
             c. $(\exists x) \wedge (x$ is the king of France, $\sim (x$ is bald))

  Closely related to Russell's analyses of *the* is the following widely accepted analysis of *only*:

7.1.11   a. Only Bert got caught.
             b. $\wedge (caught\ B, (\forall x) \supset (\sim =xB, \sim caught\ x))$

Example 7.1.11a is analyzed as 'Bert got caught and no one other than Bert got caught'. In fact 7.1.11a matches point for point the analysis proposed in 7.1.6a' for predicate definite NP's, and thus if the analysis of *only* in 7.1.11 is accepted, Russell's analysis of 7.1.1a could be recast in the form 7.1.12 as well as 7.1.9a:

7.1.12 $(\exists x) \wedge (only\ x$ is king of France, x is bald)

  Example 7.1.11b provides an analysis for sentences in which *only* is combined with a singular noun with constant reference. Let us see whether the analysis of *only* embodied in 7.1.11b can be extended to cover such other cases as:

7.1.13   a. Only Bert and Jody got caught.
             b. Only these guys got caught.
             c. Only stupid people got caught.

The generalization of 7.1.11b to the case of 7.1.13a is obvious: the first conjunct should be replaced by 'Bert and Jody got caught' and the second by 'No one other than Bert and Jody got caught':

7.1.14 $\wedge (\wedge (caught\ B, caught\ J), (\forall x) \supset (\sim \vee (=xB, =xJ),$
             $\sim caught\ x))$

More generally, a sentence *Only A, B, ... and N got caught* would be analyzed as 7.1.15a, or perhaps as 7.1.15b:

7.1.15   a. $\wedge (\wedge (caught\ A, caught\ B, ..., caught\ N),$
             $(\forall x) \supset (\sim \vee (=xA, =xB, ... =xN), \sim caught\ x))$

b. $\wedge ((\forall: \in x\{A, B, \ldots, N\})(\text{caught } x),$
$(\forall: \sim \in x\{A, B, \ldots, N\})(\sim \text{caught } x)).$

The difference between 7.1.13*a* and 7.1.13*b* is that in 7.1.13*a* a set is given by enumeration whereas in 7.1.13*b* a set is merely referred to. Calling the set denoted by *these guys* 'M', the closest analogue to 7.1.11*b* and 7.1.15 that could serve as an analysis of 7.1.13*b* is

7.1.16 $\wedge ((\forall: \in x\text{M})(\text{caught } x), (\forall: \sim \in x\text{M})(\sim \text{caught } x))$

Formula 7.1.16 brings out the essence of this analysis of *only* better than do the earlier formulas: the expression to which *only* is attached gives a condition, and *only* is taken as saying that those individuals meeting the condition have the property in question (here, the property of having got caught) and that those individuals not meeting the condition do not have that property. Recasting 7.1.11*b* into the following form brings out the parallelism between the *only* of 7.1.11*a* and of 7.1.13*b*:

7.1.17 $\wedge ((\forall: = x\text{B})(\text{caught } x), (\forall: \sim = x\text{B})(\sim \text{caught } x))$

It thus appears that the analysis of 7.1.13*c* that would conform most closely to the analysis of the other examples is

7.1.18 $\wedge ((\forall: \text{stupid } x)(\text{caught } x), (\forall: \sim \text{stupid } x) \sim (\text{caught } x))$

The second conjunct of this formula is eminently reasonable: it says that no one who is not stupid got caught, and 7.1.13*c* clearly says that. But the first conjunct will not do at all; 7.1.13*c* does not involve such a strong claim as that all stupid persons got caught: while it would normally be taken as implying that some stupid people got caught, perhaps even that a lot of stupid people got caught, it is quite consistent with the proposition that some stupid people did not get caught. Compare 7.1.19, which clearly does not imply that ALL American citizens are employed by the FBI:

7.1.19   Only American citizens are employed by the FBI.

In 8.3, I will argue that only the second conjunct of these formulas is the meaning expressed by *only* and that 7.1.11*a* does not really assert that Bert got caught. This is quite plausible in view of the possibility of saying

7.1.20   a. Bert and only Bert got caught.
              b. Only Bert got caught, if even *he* did.

in which *only Bert* conveys only the proposition that no one else got caught, with the rest of the sentence supplying information about whether he did get caught or whether it is even known whether he got caught. Thus it appears that predicate *the* is not as similar to *only* as it appeared in the discussion of 7.1.11. A sentence involving *the X* in predicate position clearly does assert that the subject is X, as is shown by the oddity of analogues to 7.1.20 in which predicate *the* has the role of *only*:

7.1.21　　a. *Mike is a mayor and the mayor.
　　　　　b. *Mike is the mayor, if even *he* is a mayor.

7.2. The Bach-Peters Sentence

The following sentence, known as the Bach-Peters sentence, has been the subject of much controversy in generative grammar since it was first noticed in 1968 by Emmon Bach and Stanley Peters:[4]

7.2.1　　The pilot that shot at it hit the MIG that chased him.

The underscoring indicates the intended pronoun-antecedent relationships: the *him* is supposed to refer to *the pilot that shot at it* and the *it* to *the MIG that chased him*. The importance of this sentence was that it showed the untenability of the then popular analysis of personal pronouns as being derived from copies of their antecedent NP's: if each of the pronouns in 7.2.1 was derived from a copy of its antecedent, then the deep structure of 7.2.1 would have to contain infinitely much material (as can be seen if one tries to replace each pronoun by a copy of its antecedent and continue until no pronouns remain).

Lauri Karttunen (1971) discovered an important characteristic of 7.2.1 that had been missed in previous discussion of it, namely, that it is ambiguous. In one interpretation, 7.2.1 refers to the pilot that shot at the MIG that chased him and asserts that that pilot hit that MIG; in the other interpretation, 7.2.1 refers to the MIG that chased the pilot that shot at it and asserts that that pilot hit that MIG. Karttunen showed the two interpretations to be distinct on the grounds that (i) the conditions for the appropriateness of the one definite description can be met without the conditions for the appropriateness of the other one being met, and (ii) even in cases where the appropriateness conditions for both are met, the one may single out a different pilot-MIG pair than the other one does. The appropriateness conditions for the two definite descriptions are as follows:

7.2.2　　a. The pilot that shot at the MIG that chased him.
　　　　　　There is exactly one pilot x such that (x shot at the MIG that chased x).

b. The MIG that chased the pilot that shot at it.
There is exactly one MIG y such that (y chased the pilot
that shot at y).

Consider a restricted set of MIGs and pilots and let diagrams like those
given below indicate who shot at whom and who chased whom:

7.2.3

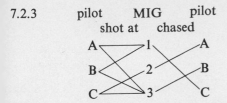

In the state of affairs represented by 7.2.3, the appropriateness conditions
for 7.2.2a are met: 1 is the MIG that chased C, 2 is the MIG that chased A,
3 is the MIG that chased B, and since B shot at 3 but C did not shoot at 1
and A did not shoot at 2, B is the only pilot having the property 'x shot at
the MIG that chased x'. However, the appropriateness conditions for
7.2.2b are not met: C is the pilot that shot at 2, but since two pilots shot at 1
and three pilots shot at 3, no one can be described as 'the pilot that shot at
1' or 'the pilot that shot at 3'; since 2 did not chase C, no MIG has the
property 'y chased the pilot that shot at y'. Thus, under the one interpretation, 7.2.1 asserts, relative to this state of affairs, that B hit 3 and
it will be true or false depending on whether B did in fact hit 3; however,
under the other interpretation, 7.2.1 is vacuously false regardless of who
hit whom: it is false in precisely the same way that *The king of France is
bald* is false. By interchanging the roles of the MIGs and the pilots in
7.2.3, one obtains a state of affairs in which the appropriateness condition
for 7.2.2b is met but not that for 7.2.1a:

7.2.4

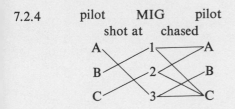

Relative to the state of affairs 7.2.4, there is exactly one MIG having the
property 'y chased the pilot that shot at y', namely, 2; however, there is no
pilot having the property 'x shot at the MIG that chased x'.
In the state of affairs 7.2.5, 2 is the MIG that chased A, 1 is the MIG

that chased B, but no MIG can be described as *the MIG that chased C*, since two MIGs chased C:

7.2.5   pilot   MIG   pilot
                     shot at   chased

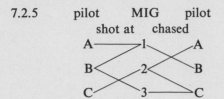

Since B shot at 1 but A did not shoot at 2, B is the only pilot having the property '*x* shot at the MIG that chased *x*', and in the 7.2.2*a* interpretation, 7.2.1 asserts that B hit 1. B is the pilot that shot at 3, C is the pilot that shot at 2, but, since two pilots shot at 1, no pilot can be described as 'the pilot that shot at 1'; since 2 chased C but 3 did not chase B, 2 is the only MIG having the property '*y* chased the pilot that shot at *y*', and thus in the 7.2.2*b* interpretation, 7.2.1 asserts that C hit 2. This means that in the state of affairs 7.2.5, the two interpretations of 7.2.5 assert different things: one of them asserts that B hit 1 and the other one asserts that C hit 2.

According to Karttunen's discussion of 7.2.1, its two interpretations should have logical structures involving stacked definite descriptions corresponding to 7.2.2*a* and 7.2.2*b*:

7.2.6   a. (ιx: $\wedge$ (pilot x, (ιy: $\wedge$ (MIG y, chase y x)) shoot x y))
                    b. (ιy: $\wedge$ (MIG y, (ιx: $\wedge$ (Pilot x, shoot x y)) chase y x))

But what exactly are 7.2.6*a* and 7.2.6*b* combined with? It won't do to say that they are combined with 'hit x y', since a combination of either of them with 'hit x y' would be incoherent: one of the two variables in 'hit x y' would be outside the scope of the definite description operator that binds that variable, for example,

7.2.7

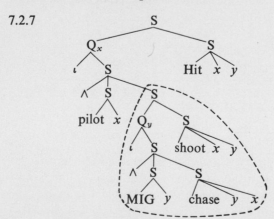

Only the part of the tree inside the dotted line is commanded by the quantifier that binds y.[5] The best that can be done using standard logical formulas is to analyze both interpretations of 7.2.1 as involving more definite description operators than are apparent in the surface, that is, take 7.2.6*a* as applying not to 'hit x y' but to 'x hit the MIG that chased x' and take 7.2.6*b* as applying not to 'hit x y' but to 'the pilot that shot at y hit y'. The resulting structure appears to have appropriate truth conditions and satisfies the coherence conditions, for example, the logical structure of the 7.2.2*a* interpretation of 7.2.1 would be given not by the incoherent 7.2.7 but by

7.2.8

An alternative approach will be discussed in 9.6. In that alternative, the coherence conditions are weakened in such a way as to allow expressions such as 7.2.7, and the truth conditions provided for such expressions in fact turn out to be appropriate for 7.2.1.

7.3. Comparatives

The meaning of a comparative construction, as in

7.3.1   a. Alaska is larger than Texas.
         b. Bob Hope has as much money as Nelson Rockefeller does.
         c. You're happier than I'll ever be.

involves not merely the individuals that are mentioned (Alaska, Texas, Bob Hope, Nelson Rockefeller, you, me) and the predicates represented by the verbs and adjectives (*large*, *have*, *money*, *happy*) but also 'quantities' and/or 'extents'. Example 7.3.1*a* says that the extent to which Alaska is large exceeds the extent to which Texas is large; 7.3.1*b* says that the quantity of money that Bob Hope has equals the quantity of money that Nelson

Rockefeller has; 7.3.1c says that the extent to which you are happy exceeds any extent to which I will ever be happy.

There are a variety of ways that the quantities and extents might be built into formulas that purport to represent the content of comparative sentences. Let us first consider the question of how the extents are related to the predicates. One might treat certain predicates as having an extra place, for example, treat *large* not as a one-place predicate ('x is large') but as a two-place predicate ('x is large to extent y'). Such a treatment is particularly attractive in the case of predicates which allow an explicit expression of measure, as in:

7.3.2   The table is 7 feet long.
               Susan is 14 years old.
               The wall is 6 inches thick.
               Sam weighs 210 pounds.[6]

If these predicates are basically two-place, then sentences where they appear to have only one place can be analyzed as covert comparative constructions, for example, *long* would be analyzed as 'more than c long', where c is some standard of length (which, of course, would vary depending on what you are talking about: a river that is ten miles long is short, but a table that is ten feet long is long). Under the proposal that *large* is two-place, the content of 7.3.1a would be represented by a formula along the lines of

7.3.3   (ιx: large(Alaska, x))(ιy: large(Texas, y))exceed x y.

This analysis requires quite different analyses to be given to paired opposites such as *long* and *short*. Note that only the positive member of such pairs allows a measure expression (except in comparative clauses, where the measure expression gives the DIFFERENCE between the things compared):

7.3.4   a. The rope is 5 feet long/*short.
               b. Billy is 12 years old/*young.
               c. This membrane is 5 microns thick/*thin.
               d. Billy is 3 years older/younger than his sister.

There is thus no 'two-place *short*' to define 'one-place *short*' in terms of; rather, *short* would have to be defined along the lines of 'less than d tall', where d is the dividing point between 'short' and 'not short'. This asymmetry is reasonable, since *long* and *short* (likewise, *old* and *young*, etc.) do not behave alike: the 'positive' adjective refers both to a 'scale' and to the upper part of that scale; the 'negative' adjective refers to the lower part of the 'scale' corresponding to the positive adjective.

Example 7.3.1*a* is generally interpreted as meaning that Alaska is larger in area than is Texas, that is, in 7.3.3 the x and the y would be the areas of Alaska and Texas, and 7.3.3 would assert that the area of Alaska exceeds that of Texas. The word *large* does not always refer to area; indeed, it is rather vague in its uses. Sometimes it refers to area and sometimes to volume. Sometimes it refers to internal dimensions and sometimes to external dimensions (e.g. *I need a larger saucepan* would normally be a request for a saucepan that holds more liquid, not for one that takes up more room). Sometimes it refers not to dimensions but to what the object can accommodate within it (e.g., when a teacher asks for a larger classroom, he generally means a room that will accommodate more students, regardless of whether it might in fact have a smaller floor area), or to what actually *is* accommodated in it (e.g., population). Nonetheless, in each case something of the form 7.3.3 makes sense: in each case to say that one thing is larger than another is to say that the 'size' of the one exceeds the 'size' of the other, for the appropriate notion of 'size'.

In many cases, the predicate does not correspond to a measure such as the areas, volumes, and seating capacities we have just been referring to:

7.3.5   a. Lenore is prettier than Pauline.
          b. Ford's speeches are more boring than Johnson's were.
          c. Acapulco Gold is more potent than Puebla Platinum.
          d. Albanian is a more euphonious language than Upper Chehalis.

No numerical measure of prettiness is likely ever to be constructed; and while it may be possible to find some chemical characteristic of marijuana samples that can serve as a measure of their potency, it is unlikely that someone who utters 7.3.5*c* would have that sort of measure in mind. Nonetheless, speakers who utter any of 7.3.5 have in mind some kind of ranking, albeit a subjective one, and can properly be accused of inconsistency if they say things such as 'Lenore is prettier than Pauline, and Pauline is prettier than Lenore', or 'Albanian is more euphonious than Upper Chehalis, Upper Chehalis is more euphonious than Achenese, and Achenese is more euphonious than Albanian'. Someone who utters any of 7.3.5 implicitly claims to have a subjective scale of prettiness, boringness, etc. and to have placed the things to which he refers on those scales, e.g. to have placed Lenore 'above' Pauline on the prettiness scale. The existence of a concrete numerical scale for a property is actually of no particular importance for the comparative construction, and an analysis of comparatives should not restrict itself to those properties for which such a scale is known. What is relevant is only that in each case there is a scale, with definite 'upper' and 'lower' ends, and comparative sentences report the relative positions of individuals on those scales. Formulas of the form 7.3.3 should then be applicable even in the case of sentences such as 7.3.5; the domains of the variables x and y are then not necessarily numbers but are points on the (subjective or objective) scale in question.

In many cases, points on different scales can be compared with each other:

7.3.6   a. This table is taller than it is wide.
             b. Bill is a better Catholic than Mike is a Jew.

Height and width are both measured in units of distance; indeed, both are measures of the distance from one plane to another.[7] The extent to which Bill is a good Catholic can be compared with the extent to which Mike is a good Jew, since both can be thought of as degrees of conformity to sets of religious tenets. When the points on the scales cannot reasonably be compared, bizarre sentences result.

7.3.7   a. This table is taller than it is heavy.
             b. Bill is a better Catholic than Mike is a bartender.
             c. Tom sings louder than Ed dances gracefully.

These sentences can only be given an interpretation like 'I am more willing to say that Bill is a good Catholic than that Mike is a good bartender'.

It should be remarked that 7.3.6b has to do with degrees of being a good Catholic and being a good Jew, not with degrees of being good. Indeed, in all comparatives involving 'Adj-er Noun', it is the scale defined by the Adj Noun combination that is at issue, not the scale defined by the adjective alone. This is illustrated by the following observations: (i) Unless a different noun appears in the than-clause (as in 7.3.6b), the noun must be taken as applying to both of the individuals compared, though that is not the case with 'Noun who/which is Adj-er than X':

7.3.8   a. Susan is a woman who is more brilliant than Einstein.
             b. *Susan is a more brilliant woman than Einstein.

In 7.3.8a, it is extents of being brilliant that are being compared, but in 7.3.8b it is extents of being a brilliant woman; 7.3.8b is odd because it makes no sense to speak of Einstein's being a brilliant woman to any extent. (ii) 'Adj-er N' is odd unless the scale defined by the Adj N combination is different from that defined by the adjective:

7.3.9   ??Sam is a taller pastry chef than George.
             Sam is a pastry chef who is taller than George.

Pastry chefs aren't different from other people as regards height. (iii)

Depending on the scale for the Adj N combination, the truth conditions for Adj-*er* N *than* may differ from those for N *who is* Adj-*er than*:

7.3.10   a. Larry is a midget who is shorter than Peter.
            b. Larry is a shorter midget than Peter.

Example 7.3.10*a* does not imply that either Larry or Peter is a short midget: only that Larry is a midget and is shorter than Peter. However, 7.3.10*b* implies that both are short midgets (i.e., short relative to the height standards of midgets) as well as that Larry is shorter than Peter. Thus, if Larry is 3′5″ tall (and an adult human being) and Peter is 4′9″, presumably 7.3.10*a* is true and 7.3.10*b* false.

An analysis of comparatives as involving definite descriptions implies that a sentence could be ambiguous with regard to the scope of a definite description that figures in the comparative construction. This prediction is borne out. Example 7.3.11*a* is ambiguous between a sense which attributes a contradictory belief to Bill (i.e., the belief 'I am taller than I am') and a sense which attributes a mistaken, though not contradictory belief to him. The two readings of 7.3.11*a* can be represented as in 7.3.11*b* and 7.3.11*c*, respectively:

7.3.11   a. Bill thinks he's taller than he is.
            b. Bill thinks $[(\iota x : \text{tall Bill } x)(\iota y : \text{tall Bill } y)(\text{exceed } y\ x)]$.
            c. $(\iota x : \text{tall Bill } x)$ Bill thinks $[(\iota y : \text{tall Bill } y)(\text{exceed } y\ x)]$.

The complement of *think* in 7.3.11*b* is contradictory (it is the proposition that Bill's height exceeds his height). In 7.3.11*c*, the complement of *think* is the (noncontradictory) proposition that Bill's height exceeds x, and 7.3.11*c* attributes a mistaken belief to Bill, since x is Bill's actual height. The following are further examples of this type, taken from Reinhart 1975:

7.3.12   a. The governor can spend less money than he does.
            b. Rosa didn't answer more questions than she did because she was drunk.

The 'reasonable' interpretations of these sentences can be represented as

7.3.13   a. $(\iota x :$ the governor spends x-much) can(the governor, $(\iota y :$ the governor spends y-much) less $y\ x)$)
            b. $(\iota x : r$ answered x-many questions) [because (r was drunk, $\sim (\iota y : r$ answered y-many questions)(exceed $y\ x$))]

It is also worth noting an alternative approach to comparatives that was proposed by Seuren (1973), elaborating on an earlier proposal by J. R. Ross. Seuren proposed analyzing comparatives in terms of a different notion of 'extent', in which 'x is tall to extent e' means not that x is exactly that tall but that he is at least that tall. With the notion of extent that we have been using so far, if 'x is tall to extent e_1' is true and $e_1 \neq e_2$, then 'x is tall to extent e_2' is false. With Seuren's notion of extent, if 'x is tall to extent e_1' is true and $e_1 > e_2$, then 'x is tall to extent e_2' is true. Seuren's proposal fits nicely with the fact that *John isn't as tall as Bill* is normally used to mean that John is less tall than Bill, not that John's height merely differs from Bill's (with perhaps John being the taller). If we interpret *John is as tall as Bill* to be literally 'John is tall to the extent that Bill is tall' and take '*the* extent to which Bill is tall' to be the most important of the many extents to which he is tall (i.e., take it to be his height rather than the various heights which he exceeds) then *John is as tall as Bill* would be true if John's height is either equal to or greater than Bill's, and false if John's height is less than Bill's, and thus *John isn't as tall as Bill* would be true if John's height is less than Bill's and false otherwise.

Seuren proposes analyzing *John is taller than Bill* as 'John is tall to an extent to which Bill is not', which, assuming Seuren's notion of extent, would have the correct truth conditions. Specifically, Seuren's analysis is $(\exists e) \wedge$ (John is tall to extent e, $\sim$(Bill is tall to extent e)). Both *John is taller than Bill* and *Bill isn't as tall as John* would be associated with this logical structure, the only difference being which conjunct of the coordinate structure is realized as the main clause and which as a relative clause (i.e., *John is tall to an extent to which Bill is not = John is taller than Bill; Bill is not (tall to an extent to which John is) = Bill is not as tall as John*). Seuren's proposal is attractive because the underlying negation which it posits in the *than*-clause can provide an explanation of some respects in which *than*-clauses 'behave negatively'. First of all, in many languages (e.g., French), *than*-clauses contain an overt negative marker (French *ne*: *Elle est plus intelligente qu'il ne pense* 'She is more intelligent than he thinks'). Second, as Seuren notes, 'negative polarity items' such as *all that* (*I wasn't/*was all that keen to lend him the money*) may occur in *than*-clauses, but 'positive polarity items' such as *pretty* (*He is/*isn't pretty smart*) are excluded from *than*-clauses:

7.3.14   a. He served me more food than I was *all that keen* to eat.
           b. He went further than I had *the slightest intention* of going.
           c. I'd rather lose my job than *budge* an inch.

7.3.15   a. I have read more novels than Sam is (*pretty*) familiar with.
           b. ?Bill is fatter than I *have a hunch* that his father is.

However, it is not clear that these last observations provide a real argument that there is an underlying negative in *than*-clauses, since (as Ross has observed) many negative polarity items are also possible in *as*-clauses, though under the Ross-Seuren analysis, *as*-clauses would not contain an underlying negative:

7.3.16   a. Two glasses was as much as I *cared to* drink,
              b. That was as much as he was willing to *lift a finger* to do.

7.4. Conjunctions as Quantifiers

In many respects $\forall$ is similar to $\wedge$ and $\exists$ is similar to $\vee$. Note, for example, the parallelism between the following pairs of theorems:

7.4.1   a. $\supset (\sim \wedge (A_1, \ldots, A_n), \vee (\sim A_1, \sim A_2, \ldots, \sim A_n))$
             a'. $\supset (\sim (\forall : fx)gx, (\exists : fx) \sim gx)$
             b. $\supset (\supset (\vee AB, C), \wedge (\supset AC, \supset BC))$
             b'. $\supset (\supset ((\exists : fx)gx, A), (\forall : fx) \supset (gx, A))$
             c. $\supset (\vee (\wedge AB, \wedge CD), \wedge (\vee AC, \vee BD))$
             c'. $\supset ((\exists : fx)(\forall : gy)hxy, (\forall : gy)(\exists : fx)hxy)$

Indeed, *any* theorem involving $\wedge$'s or $\vee$'s with arbitrarily many conjuncts corresponds to a theorem in which the corresponding quantifier appears in place of the conjunction (i.e., $\forall$ in place of $\wedge$, and $\exists$ in place of $\vee$) and a propositional function appears in place of the list of conjuncts. There is also an exact parallelism between the rules of inference for quantifiers and the rules of inference for conjunctions. For example, $\wedge$-elimination allows one to infer from $\wedge (A_1, A_2, \ldots, A_n)$ any particular conjunct A_i, and $\forall$-elimination allows one to infer from the general proposition $(\forall : fx)gx$ any of the propositions ga for which a meets the relevance condition f. In either case the rule of inference takes one from the 'general' proposition to any of the specific cases that that general proposition covers. Similarly, $\wedge$-introduction allows one to infer $\wedge (A_1, A_2, \ldots, A_n)$ from the individual conjuncts $A_1, A_2, \ldots, A_n$, and $\forall$-introduction allows one to infer $(\forall : fx)gx$ from a demonstration that anything having the property f has the property g. In either case one is allowed to infer the general proposition once one has established all of the cases that the general proposition covers.

The machinery developed in this chapter allow one to provide a solid basis for the observation that a universal quantifier is a 'big *and*' and an existential quantifier a 'big *or*'. Note first, though, that one cannot just analyze quantifiers as conjunctions, since one does not always have available an enumeration of the objects that are 'relevant' (the content of the sentence may indeed imply that it is not known exactly how many objects are relevant) and since the set of relevant objects may be infinite:

7.4.2   a. Everyone who has ever set foot in Saint Peter's Basilica has been astonished at its magnificence.
             b. Each of the approximately 100 persons interviewed expressed interest in emigrating to Fiji.
             c. Every number greater than 1 is less than its square.

Furthermore, even if one did have a complete list of those who have ever set foot in Saint Peter's, the content of 7.4.2a would not be represented accurately by the conjoined proposition 7.4.3:

7.4.3   Pope Pius IX was astonished at the magnificence of Saint Peter's, and Jacqueline Onassis was astonished at the magnificence of Saint Peter's, and Msgr. Umberto Quattrostagioni was astonished at the magnificence of Saint Peter's, and . . .

since 7.4.3 does not include the information that Pope Pius IX, Jacqueline Onassis, Msgr. Quattrostagioni, et al. are all the persons who have ever set foot in Saint Peter's. A person who has set foot in Saint Peter's and was not astonished at its magnificence would be a counterexample to 7.4.2a; however, he would not be a counterexample to 7.4.3 unless he happened to appear in the list. What it takes to falsify 7.4.3 is to show that one of the persons on the list was not astonished at the magnificence of Saint Peter's, irrespective of whether that person ever set foot in Saint Peter's; what it takes to falsify 7.4.2a is to show that someone who has set foot in Saint Peter's was not astonished at its magnificence, irrespective of whether that person is mentioned in 7.4.3.

The only way I know of to identify quantified propositions with conjoined propositions and get the details to work out correctly is to treat conjunctions and quantifiers as both applying to sets of propositions but differing in how the sets of propositions are specified, whether by enumeration or by description. Specifically, suppose that we introduce elements 'All' and 'Some', which combine with sets of propositions, and employ them as in the following translations:

7.4.4   a. Tom is Polish, Dick is Norwegian, and Harry is Portuguese.
                 All {Tom is Polish, Dick is Norwegian, Harry is Portuguese}
             b. All men are mortal.
                 All {mortal x: man x}

   c. Either Bill will help Mike or Mike will ask Karen for help
      Some {Bill will help Mike, Mike will ask Karen for help}
   d. Some linguists are insane.
      Some {insane x: linguist x}

In 7.4.4a and 7.4.4b, the content expressed is that all of the propositions in the set are true; in 7.4.4a the propositions in question are simply enumerated, whereas in 7.4.4b the set of propositions is described as consisting of those propositions 'x is mortal' for which x is a man. In 7.4.4c and 7.4.4d, the content expressed is that at least one of the propositions in the set is true; in 7.4.4c the propositions in question are simply enumerated, whereas in 7.4.4d the set of propositions is described as consisting of those propositions 'x is insane' for which x is a linguist.[8]

   The rules of inference for both quantifiers and conjunctions can now be stated in the form of rules that are applicable both to cases in which the set of propositions is specified by enumeration and cases in which it is specified by description:[9]

7.4.5

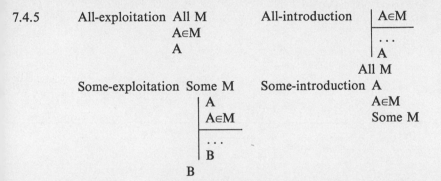

In cases where M is specified by enumeration, the premise A∈M will be trivial and thus need not be mentioned; for example, in the following inference, the parenthesized premise need not be mentioned, since it is guaranteed to be true in virtue of what curly brackets and ∈ mean:

7.4.6   All {Tom is Polish, Dick is Norwegian, Harry is Portuguese}
         (Dick is Norwegian ∈ {Tom is Polish, Dick is Norwegian, Harry is Portuguese})
         Dick is Norwegian

Inferences like 7.4.6 are what the rule of ∧-exploitation was for. The

'All-exploitation' rule of 7.4.5 does not only the work of ∧-exploitation but also that of ∀-exploitation, as becomes clear if one notes that when M is given in the form $\{gx: fx\}$, the proposition that $ga\in\{gx: fx\}$ is equivalent to the proposition fa, that is, a proposition belongs to $\{gx: fx\}$ if and only if it is of the form ga, where a has the property f. Thus, when the set of propositions is specified by description, the inference done by All-exploitation exactly matches an inference done by ∀-exploitation:

7.4.7   1 All {mortal x: man x}   1' (∀: man $x)_x$ (mortal x)
             2 (mortal Socrates) ∈   2' man Socrates
                {mortal x: man x}
             3 mortal Socrates   3' mortal Socrates

The rules given in 7.4.5 are in fact not enough to do all the work that was done by the rules for conjunctions and for quantifiers. To apply the rules in 7.4.5 to the concrete cases to which the rules of inference of chapters 2 and 4 applied, one must have rules of inference for the introduction and exploitation of the set-theoretic apparatus that appears in 7.4.4. The following rules of inference enable one to simulate the rules of inference for quantifiers and conjunctions with the rules 7.4.5:[10]

7.4.8   SF-intro₁ $a \in \{\ldots, a, \ldots\}$
             SF-intro₂ Fa

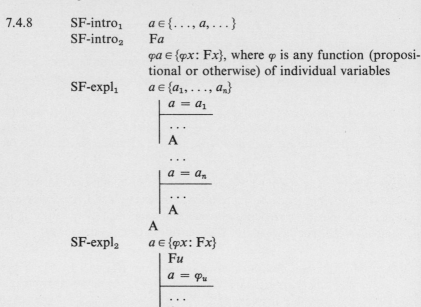

As the simulation of the old rules in terms of the new proceeds, it should become clear to the reader that much of the work of the old rules of inference is now built into the rules of inference for set formation 7.4.8. This should come as no shock: it will have to be up to the set formation rules to mediate between the highly general and abstract rules 7.4.5 and the much more specific types of expressions that figured in the earlier rules.

Let us first attempt to simulate $\wedge$-introduction in terms of the rules 7.4.5 (and 7.4.8). What we need is thus a way of getting from premises A and B (or rather, $A_1, A_2, \ldots,$ and A_n; for expository ease, I will discuss just the two-term case here) to the conclusion All $\{A, B\}$. Rules 7.4.5 and 7.4.8 in fact allow one to derive that conclusion, albeit by a somewhat devious path:

7.4.9

1	A	supp
2	B	supp
3	$C \in \{A, B\}$	supp
4	$C = A$	supp
5	A	1, reit
6	C	4, 5, =-expl
7	$C = B$	supp
8	B	2, reit
9	C	7, 8, =-expl
10	C	3, 4–6, 7–9, SF-expl$_1$
11	All $\{A, B\}$	3–10, All-intr

This derivation simulates the earlier rule of $\wedge$-intro, in that its premises and conclusion are the analogues in the notational system of this chapter to the premises and conclusion of the earlier rule. The simulation of $\wedge$-expl is far more straightforward:

7.4.10

1	All $\{A_1, \ldots, A_n\}$	supp
2	$A_i \in \{A_1, \ldots, A_n\}$	SF-intro$_1$
3	A_i	1, 2, All-expl

The rules for $\vee$ can be simulated as follows:

7.4.11   a. $\vee$-intro

1	A_i	supp
2	$A_i \in \{A_1, \ldots, A_n\}$	SF-intro$_1$
3	Some $\{A_1, \ldots, A_n\}$	1, 2, Some-intro

b. ∨-expl

1	Some $\{A_1, \ldots, A_n\}$	supp
2	A	supp
3	$A \in \{A_1, \ldots, A_n\}$	supp
4	$A = A_1$	supp
5	A	2, reit
6	A_1	4, 5, =-expl
7	...	various intermediate steps
8	B	(by the proof of B from A_1 in the proof being simulated)
	...	
9	$A = A_n$	supp
10	A	2, reit
11	A_n	9, 10, =-expl
12	...	various intermediate steps
13	B	(by steps in the proof being simulated)
14	B	3, 4–8, 9–13, SF-expl$_1$
15	B	1, 2–14, Some-expl

Note how steps 7–8 and 12–13 make reference to subproofs in the proof being replicated. It would actually take an argument by induction to demonstrate that those can always be simulated in the system of this section; I will omit details of such a proof.

The simulation of the quantifier rules is as follows:

7.4.12   a. ∀-intro

1	$A \in \{Gx: Fx\}$	supp
2	Fu	supp
3	$A = Gu$	supp
4	...	various intermediate steps
5	Gu	(by the proof of Gu from Fu in the proof being simulated)
6	A	5, 3, =-expl
7	A	2–6, SF-expl$_2$
8	All $\{Gx: Fx\}$	1–7, All-intro

b. ∀-expl

1	All $\{Gx: Fx\}$	supp
2	Fa	supp
3	$Ga \in \{Gx: Fx\}$	2, SF-intro$_2$
4	Ga	1, 3, All-expl

c. ∃-intro

1	Fa	supp
2	Ga	supp

| 3 | $Ga \in \{Gx: Fx\}$ | 1, SF-intro$_2$ |
| 4 | Some $\{Gx: Fx\}$ | 3, 2, Some-intro |

d. ∃-expl

1	Some $\{Gx: Fx\}$	supp
2	$A \in \{Gx: Fx\}$	supp
3	A	supp
4	Fu	supp
5	$A = Gu$	supp
6	Gu	5, 3, =-expl
7	. . .	various intermediate steps
8	B	(by the proof of B from Fu and Gu in the proof being simulated)
9	B	2, 4–8, SF-expl$_2$
10	B	1, 2–9, Some-expl

The proofs involving the rules 7.4.5 and 7.4.8 are of course significantly more involved than the proofs in the earlier system that they simulate. However, while it would rarely make sense to give a proof of a concrete result in terms of the rules of this section rather than in terms of rules specific to quantifiers and conjunctions, it is of considerable significance that alternative proofs are always available in which the difference between quantifiers and conjunctions is reduced to the difference between the two species of set formation.

Humberstone (1975) has pointed out a difficulty with the proposals of this section that is worth noting here. As conjoining has normally been understood in logic, there is no constraint requiring that conjuncts be mutually distinct.[11] Indeed, logic texts customarily give proofs of results involving repeated conjuncts, for example, $\wedge AA \dashv\vdash A$. Under the approach presented here, the latter result would follow from the identity of $\{A, A\}$ with $\{A\}$. But what about sentences in which exclusive *or* has two identical conjuncts? Humberstone notes that $\vee_e AA$ is always false (since it can never be the case that only one of its conjuncts is true), and hence $\vee_e AA$ can differ in truth value from A. If an $\vee_e$-conjunction is to be true when exactly one conjunct is true and false otherwise, then $\vee_e AAB$ and $\vee_e AB$ can differ in truth value: if A is T and B is F, then $\vee_e AAB$ is F but $\vee_e AB$ is T. However, $\{A, A, B\} = \{A, B\}$, and hence $\vee_e AAB$ ought to agree in truth value with $\vee_e AB$ if $\vee_e$ is predicated of a set of propositions.

Sentences that exemplify formulas such as $\vee_e AAB$ or $\vee_e ABA$ are sufficiently bizarre that it is unclear whether they should be held to have 7.4.13a or 7.4.13b as truth table:

7.4.13   a. Truth table if $\vee_e$ is   b. Truth table if $\vee_e(A_1, \ldots, A_n)$
              predicated of a set   is to be true when exactly one
              of propositions A_i is true

A	B	$\vee_e AAB$	A	B	$\vee_e AAB$
T	T	F	T	T	F
T	F	T	T	F	F
F	T	T	F	T	T
F	F	F	F	F	F

For example, can one comply with the request *Play Brahms ór Brahms ór Chopin*, where the request is interpreted as involving exclusive *or*, by playing Brahms, or can one comply only by playing Chopin? The former interpretation seems less outlandish than the latter, though that may be because the request would be even more bizarre if it were interpreted the latter way than the former way, since not just one but BOTH occurrences of *Brahms* would be superfluous (as would the *or*'s). I conclude tentatively that while Humberstone is correct that my position here forces $\vee_e$'s with duplicated conjuncts to be interpreted in a way that conflicts with what has usually been done in formal logic (which is not to imply that logicians have said much about exclusive *or*), it is not clear that the discrepancy constitutes a fault in this treatment.

7.5. Sets in the Object Language; Extended Predicate Logic

The 'grammar' for predicate logic that we constructed in 4.1 allowed as arguments only INDIVIDUAL constants and individual variables, that is, constants that denoted an object (rather than a set) and variables whose values were individual objects rather than sets. If our system of logical form is to be rich enough to accommodate sentences such as *One of them killed Lefty* or *He's one of them*, propositions of the form '$x \in M$' will have to be admitted into logical structure. $\in$ will fit into logical structure as a two-place predicate having an individual in its first place and a set in its second place. There are in fact many expressions of natural language which can reasonably be interpreted as predicates which have a set as argument:

7.5.1   a. The king and the queen are an amiable couple.
          b. Tom, Dick, and Harry conspired to assassinate the Postmaster General.

      c. Your friends are similar in that they are all canasta freaks.
      d. Bob and Carol met Ted and Alice at O'Rourke's Pub.
      e. The boys carried the piano up the stairs.
      f. Sammy, Mike, and Billy ganged up on George.

The analysis of these examples is controversial. First of all, it is not completely clear that it is the set of persons rather than some entity associated with that set that serves as argument. For example, one might hold that the 'couple' consisting of the king and the queen was not identical to the set consisting of the king and the queen but was rather some object of a different type (more like, say, a club or a partnership) though it also consists of members. Second, it has been suggested (e.g., Gleitman 1965) that sentences such as 7.5.1*b* and 7.5.1*c* have an understood reciprocal pronoun (cf. *Tom, Dick, and Harry conspired with each other to assassinate the Postmaster General*) and really involve individual variables or constants as the arguments of the predicates, just as in *Tom, Dick, and Harry hate each other*.

    The plausibility of the first objection to positing set arguments in 7.5.1 depends on the extent to which one is forced to distinguish among different 'associated objects'. Suppose that the king pitches and the queen catches on the palace softball team. Then the king and the queen form a battery and one could say 7.5.2*a*; however, the couple consisting of the king and the queen and the battery consisting of the king and the queen count as identical for the purposes of conjunction reduction, as in 7.5.2*b*:

7.5.2   a. The king and the queen are an excellent battery.
          b. The king and the queen are both an amiable couple and an
             excellent battery.

The existence of sentences such as 7.5.2*b* strongly suggests that 'amiable couple' and 'excellent battery' are being predicated of the same thing, which would presumably be the set consisting of the king and the queen.

    The correctness of the second objection can be evaluated only on the basis of facts about reciprocal pronouns and about the sentences in which a supposed understood reciprocal occurs. It should be noted at the outset that not all candidates for an analysis with set arguments are open to an analysis with individual arguments and an understood reciprocal; for example, 7.5.1*a* does not allow any paraphrases along the lines of

7.5.3   a. *The king and the queen are an amiable couple to each
             other.
          b. *The king is an amiable couple to the queen and the queen
             is an amiable couple to the king.

For the sentences for which an analysis involving an understood reciprocal is plausible, two questions must be raised: (i) do they mean the same as corresponding sentences containing reciprocals? And (ii) can the sentences with reciprocals be analyzed as having only individual arguments? The most obvious first approximation to an analysis of reciprocals is to say that a sentence with *each other* involves universal quantifiers that range over all pairs of distinct elements of the given set:[12]

7.5.4   They hate each other.

$(\forall: x \in M)(\forall: \wedge (y \in M, \sim = yx))$hate $x\, y$

This is only a first approximation and will not work as an analysis of some of the more interesting examples of reciprocals, such as

7.5.5   a. Linguists are always insulting each other.
             b. They spent the afternoon taking group photographs of each other.
             c. Those boys have a tendency to gang up on each other.

However, let's accept it for the time being and see how it would work as an analysis of reciprocal analogues of 7.5.1b–c:

7.5.6   a. Tom, Dick, and Harry conspired with each other to assassinate the Postmaster General.
             b. Your friends are similar to each other in that they are all canasta freaks.

Example 7.5.6a does in fact seem to be an accurate paraphrase of 7.5.1b, but it resists analysis along the lines of 7.5.4: it doesn't assert that each of the three men conspired with each of the others (i.e., that Tom conspired with Dick, Dick conspired with Harry, etc.) but rather that there was a single conspiracy in which all three participated (as opposed to, say, three different conspiracies, each involving two of them). The only obvious alternative to allowing a set as the first argument of *conspire* is to recognize a strange type of entity, called a 'conspiracy', and analyze 7.5.1b as asserting the existence of a conspiracy such that Tom, Dick, and Harry all participated in it and such that its goal was the assassination of the Postmaster General. Essentially the same alternatives are available in some examples (such as 7.5.1e) to which no reciprocal sentence corresponds: in the interpretation of 7.5.1e which refers to an event in which the boys jointly carry the piano (as opposed to the interpretation which is paraphraseable as *Each of the boys carried the piano up the stairs*), one must either allow a set as subject of *carry* or analyze the sentence in terms of auxiliary notions like 'an act' and 'participate': there was an act x such that each of the boys participated in x and x consisted in carrying the piano up the stairs. However, the latter analysis still has to contend with the problem of what the subject of *carry* is. Example 7.5.6*b* would fit into the mold of 7.5.4 if it weren't for the problem of how to fit in the *in that S*. You could of course construct the formula

7.5.7 $(\forall : x \in M)(\forall : \wedge (y \in M, \sim\; = yx))[x$ is similar to y in that (x is a canasta freak and y is a canasta freak)]

However, 7.5.7 does not accord with the *all* that occurs in the surface form of the *in that* clause. If *all of them are canasta freaks* is to be a logical constituent of 7.5.1*c*, as it presumably has to, 7.5.7 will have to be rejected, and the remaining alternatives are as before: either *similar* has a set subject or the analysis makes reference to 'a similarity' which all the individuals participate in.

The proposal that the predicates involved in 7.5.1 have set arguments thus withstands the more obvious objections to it and deserves to be treated seriously. Let us then see what revisions have to be made in the grammar of 4.1 in order to accommodate set arguments. It will be necessary to draw a distinction between set-type and individual-type constants and variables. It will not do just to use the brute force ploy of different typography (using capital letters for set indices and small letters for individual indices), since the rules giving the contexts in which each predicate may be used will have to distinguish between the two types. For the moment, let me use close to brute force and take the grammar to have a rule which adds to each argument (Arg) node a feature specification '+ Set' or '− Set' and have those feature specifications play a rule in the remainder of the grammar. These feature specifications correspond not to extra nodes dominated by the Arg nodes but to extra labels ON the Arg nodes:

7.5.8   Arg is + Set or − Set
          Arg + Set: M   Arg + Set: M_1 ...   Arg − Set: x Arg − Set: x_1
          Arg + Set: N   Arg + Set: M_2 Arg − Set: y Arg − Set: x_2
          . . .   .
          Pred: love / _____ Arg − Set   Arg
          Pred: couple / _____ Arg + Set
          Pred: gang up / _____ Arg + Set   Arg

The rule for 'love' given here restricts the first argument to being an individual but imposes no restriction on whether the second argument is + Set or − Set. I have formulated it this way in accordance with my feeling that only an individual can love, though the objects of his love may be either individuals or sets of individuals, and loving a set is not the same thing as loving each of its members; for example, you can love the Marx brothers without it necessarily being the case that you love Groucho, love Chico, and love Harpo.

Since the sets that figure as the arguments of the predicates in 7.5.1 are described in natural language by expressions that correspond to specification by enumeration and specification by description (*Tom, Dick, and Harry carried the piano* vs. *The boys who live in the next apartment carried the piano*), the grammar ought to be further modified to allow Arg+Set to dominate other things besides set indices. If we just by brute force convert our formulas for enumeration and description into tree form, substituting a symbol like 'SET' for the operation that the brackets and commas and colon represent, we would get

7.5.9   a. Arg+Set:SET Arg S
             b. Arg+Set:SET Arg^n ($n \geq 1$)

Note, incidentally, that the 'set formation' operation in 7.5.9a binds a variable; thus the coherency conditions of 4.1 must be imposed here. Actually, the symbol 'SET' in 7.5.9 is redundant: since there is no other case where our grammar allows an Arg to consist of an Arg and a S or of a sequence of Arg's, 'SET' could just as well be omitted from 7.5.9:

7.5.9'   a. Arg+Set:Arg S
             b. Arg+Set:Arg^n ($n \geq 1$)

There is one minor terminological inconsistency in 7.5.9' (or 7.5.9), namely, that we now have 'Arg' appearing in positions other than 'argument positions'. For example, if *Tom, Dick, and Harry* is the subject of *conspire*, then neither *Tom* nor *Dick* nor *Harry* is an argument of *conspire*: *conspire* is predicated of the set, not of each of its members. Terminological purism would demand that we distinguish between the RELATIONAL notion of 'argument' (i.e., the notion of being an argument *of* something) and the CATEGORIAL notion that we have been calling 'Arg'. Since the linguist's category 'noun phrase' (NP) has been used in a way that corresponds closely to our 'Arg' (i.e., items of types that 'fill argument positions' are all labeled 'NP'), a terminological purist might prefer to write 'NP' where we have written 'Arg', for example,

7.5.10

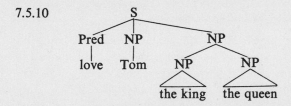

If our rules are to cover the logical forms of all of the examples discussed in this section, a further revision in the grammar will have to be made: we will have to allow some predicates to have propositions as arguments; for

example, *conspire* will have a set of persons as first argument and a proposition as second argument:

7.5.11   Arg:S   (alternatively, NP:S).

Let us adopt the term EXTENDED PREDICATE LOGIC for a system of logic involving set and proposition arguments as well as individual arguments. Note that in extended predicate logic the distinction between 'predicate' and 'operator' that we have hitherto been assuming becomes blurred. For example, there is no obvious reason why negation could not be taken as a one-place predicate with a sentential argument. Similarly, there is no reason why quantifiers, if they are analyzed as in 4.7, could not be taken to be one-place predicates whose argument was required to be both a set and sentential. Thus, in extended predicate logic it is possible to reduce the set of syntactic categories down to the bare minimum of S, Pred, and NP.[13] For example, the logical structure of *All men are mortal* could be displayed as

7.5.12

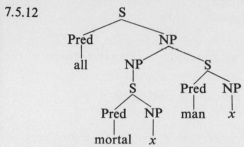

Note that while two S's are combined in the 'subject' of *all*, their roles are kept distinct by their relationship to the NP nodes.

7.6. Exercises

1. Suppose that time is treated as an extra argument of predicates to which time is relevant (e.g., there'll be a three-place predicate love $(x, y, t) = $ 'x loves y at time t'). Using predicate logic as developed in chapter 4, with the following predicates and constants:

$$\text{love}(x, y, t) = \text{'}x \text{ loves } y \text{ at } t\text{'} \qquad n = \text{'now'}$$
$$\text{time}(t) \quad\;\; = \text{'}t \text{ is a time'} \qquad\quad j = \text{'John'}$$
$$\text{prior}(t_1, t_2) = \text{'}t_1 \text{ is prior to } t_2\text{'} \qquad m = \text{'Mary'}$$

represent the meanings of the following sentences:

   a. John has never loved Mary.
   b. John will always love Mary.
   c. John has ceased to love Mary.

2. The sentence *John has always loved his wife* is at least two ways ambiguous. Using quantifiers (including ι) and the predicates and constants of the last problem, plus wife(x, y, t) = 'x is wife of y at t', give logical structures for each of its meanings.

3. The *always* of the sentence discussed in problem 2 is not normally interpreted as literally 'always'; describe how it is actually interpreted for each of the senses of that sentence, and form a generalization about what times *always* is normally taken to cover.

4. Using Pxy to stand for 'x pities y' and a to stand for Lucifer, give logical structures for the following sentences, using the analysis of *only* that is discussed in 7.1 or a defensible alternative:

a. Only Lucifer pities Lucifer.
b. Only Lucifer pities himself.
c. Only Lucifer pities only Lucifer.
d. Only Lucifer pities only himself.

5. Section 7.1 deals only with sentences like *John loves only Mary*, not with sentences in which there is an expression limiting the domain of the bound variable:

John is the only philosopher who admires Meinong.
Of his neighbors, Bill hates only Larry.

Construct logical structures for these sentences that are as close as possible to the analysis of *only* given in 7.1.

8. Speech Acts and Implicature

8.1. Speech Acts and Illocutionary Force

When people speak, they are not merely constructing a sequence of propositions but are performing actions of quite a wide variety of types: informing, reminding, requesting, challenging, offering, and so on. These acts generally INVOLVE propositions but must be kept distinct from the propositions that they involve; for example, the proposition that Lima is further east than Miami is distinct from an act of informing someone that Lima is further east than Miami or of reminding someone that Lima is further east than Miami.

The notions of truth and falsehood are strictly speaking applicable only to propositions, not to speech acts. In discussing the content of propositions, it is necessary to be able to refer both to propositions and to speech acts. Consider, for example, the following two dialogues:

8.1.1   A: The moon is owned by General Motors.
              B: That's false.

8.1.2   A: Your father is a retired pimp.
              B: That's pretty damn cheeky of you.

In 8.1.1, *that* refers to the proposition that *A* has just asserted. In 8.1.2, *that* refers to the act that *A* has just performed, that is, the act of telling *B* that *B*'s father is a retired pimp, and not to the proposition that *B*'s father is a retired pimp. The act of asserting that the moon is owned by General Motors cannot be said to be true or false any more than an act of buying a radio or of punching someone in the nose can be said to be true or false. A speech act can have any of a variety of things wrong with it, as is pointed out in the insightful discussion by Austin (1962, lectures II–III). For example, if a person who has no money and does not expect to come into a large sum of money were to promise to give you a million dollars next Thursday, you could object to his act of promising on the grounds that it was irresponsible (since he thereby made a commitment that he knew he could not fulfill) or that it was misleading (since it could lead you to believe the false proposition that he would have a million dollars next week) or that it was impudent (since he was acting as if you would believe an outrageous falsehood). While these objections involve certain propositions associated with the act, they also involve considerations of morality and of etiquette. A speech act (indeed, any kind of act) can be objectionable in one of these respects without being objectionable in others; for example, one can be irresponsible without being impudent or be impudent without being misleading. Of these dimensions of objectionability, the one most closely related to the notion of falsehood is that of misleadingness: an act is misleading if it leads one to believe a proposition which is in fact false (or at least, would so lead one if it were entirely successful). However, whether an act is misleading depends not only on the act but on the circumstances under which it is performed, and the false proposition which a misleading speech act leads one to believe may have no particular connection with the meaning of the sentence that the speaker utters. For example, if an orthodox jew who is eating a corned beef sandwich says *May I have a glass of milk?* he may be leading others to the false conclusion that he is not an orthodox jew; the same is true if he says *I'm flying to Toledo tonight* on a Friday evening. Of course, the proposition expressed by *I'm flying to Toledo tonight* is true or false independent of whether an act of uttering it misleads the hearers on the speaker's religion. Thus, the fact that it is misleading to utter a certain sentence does not imply that the proposition expressed by that sentence is false. This platitude will turn out to have considerable significance later in this chapter, where an attempt will be made to clear up a number of confusions that have resulted from making the mistake of calling a proposition false merely on the grounds that the act of asserting it is (generally) misleading or that a sentence expressing that proposition is 'a funny thing to say'.

In many cases, there is no chance of confusing a speech act with an associated proposition. For example, one could hardly confuse an act of saying *Shine my shoes* and thereby ordering someone to shine one's shoes with the proposition that that person will shine the speaker's shoes, nor could one confuse an act of thanking someone for a gift by saying *Thank you very much for your lovely gift* with the proposition that the speaker is grateful to that person for giving him that gift. The possibility of confusion arises principally in two classes of cases: (i) speech acts in which one asserts a proposition by uttering a sentence that expresses that proposition (as in 8.1.1, where A asserts that the moon is owned by General Motors by uttering the sentence *The moon is owned by General Motors*) and (ii) speech acts in which the speaker uses a verb PERFORMATIVELY, that is, makes explicit with it the type of act that he is performing (or at least, purports to be performing), as in

8.1.3   a. I order you to shine my shoes.
           b. I christen this ship the HMS Kreplach.
           c. I promise to return this money by next Thursday.
           d. I hereby inform you that we have no more money.

In uttering 8.1.3a, the speaker is ordering the addressee to shine the speaker's shoes; in uttering 8.1.3b, he is christening the ship; in uttering 8.1.3c, he is promising to return the money; in uttering 8.1.3d, he is informing the addressee that they have no more money. The danger of confusion in these two cases comes from two common tendencies: to identify a declarative sentence with the proposition that that sentence expresses, and to identify a declarative sentence with the act that one would (normally) perform by uttering that sentence. If one succumbs to both of these tendencies, he will identify the sentence *The moon is owned by General Motors* both with the proposition that the moon is owned by General Motors and with the act of asserting that the moon is owned by General Motors and will thus by implication identify that act and that proposition with each other.

So far in this section, I have been using an overly vague expression that had now better be replaced with more precise terminology. The objectionable expression is 'what the speaker is doing' when he says X. Suppose that one of the characters in a television program that you are watching says *I have more money than I know what to do with* and you are asked what that person has just done. Given certain assumptions about what has been going on, each of the following would be a correct answer:

8.1.4   a. He said, 'I have more money than I know what to do with'.
           b. He said something in a very affected English accent.
           c. He said that he had more money than he knew what to do
              with.
           d. He indicated that he was willing to pay off Oliver's mortgage.
           e. He offered to pay off Oliver's mortgage.
           f. He displayed contempt for Oliver.
           g. He embarrassed Oliver's wife.
           h. He woke up the baby.

Examples 8.1.4a and 8.1.4b make reference to his words and the way that he pronounced them, without regard for the meaning of the words, or the purpose for which they were uttered, or what resulted from his uttering them. Example 8.1.4c reports the meaning of what he said, though it is noncommittal about what words he used in saying it, and indicates that he asserted the proposition in question. Examples 8.1.4*d* and 8.1.4*e* bring in the purpose for which he made that assertion: by uttering the sentence that he uttered, he has offered to pay off Oliver's mortgage. Examples 8.1.4*f–h* refer to various results of his uttering that sentence, with 8.1.4*f* and 8.1.4*g* having to do with the meaning and function of the utterance, whereas 8.1.4*h* has to do only with its acoustic nature (i.e., he would have awakened the baby if he had said anything that loud, regardless of its meaning, whereas he would not have embarrassed Oliver's wife if he had uttered exactly the same words in another context where they would not have conveyed an offer to assume Oliver's debt).

The notion of 'what the speaker is doing' that appears in the above remarks on 8.1.4*e* (and, though less clearly, 8.1.4*c* and 8.1.4*d*) is the one that is relevant to the concerns of this section. Example 8.1.4*e* has to do with the ILLOCUTIONARY ACT that the speaker performed in saying what he did, that is, what he did IN saying it, as contrasted with what resulted from his saying it (as in the case of 8.1.4*g–h* and perhaps also 8.1.4*f*) or the verbal means by which he said it (i.e., the words or the pronunciation, as in 8.1.4*a–b*). The term 'illocutionary act' was coined by Austin, who also provided terms for the other types of acts that I have just contrasted it with: PERLOCUTIONARY ACT (i.e., act of accomplishing some effect by saying something) and LOCUTIONARY ACT (i.e., act of using language). The following are some important characteristics of illocutionary acts:

(i) To virtually every type of illocutionary act, there corresponds a PERFORMATIVE VERB, that is, a verb which can be used as an explicit indication that one is performing (or purports to be performing) an act of this type, as in 8.1.3 above. By contrast, verbs referring to perlocutionary and locutionary acts cannot be used in sentences like 8.1.3 as explicit indications of the acts being performed; for example while some of 8.1.5 have normal uses, the verbs do not really indicate what the speaker is doing in uttering the sentence, even if (coincidentally) the sentence does provide a correct description of something that he is doing:

8.1.5   a. I utter these words in an affected English accent.
          b. *I wake up the baby.
          c. I embarrass your wife.
          d. I insult you.
          e. *I force you to eat this cake.
          f. *I convince you that there is intelligent life on Uranus.

For example, you may embarrass someone's wife by telling him in her presence that you embarrass his wife; indeed, you probably *would* embarrass his wife by doing that. However, 8.1.5c can only be interpreted as a 'habitual present', that is, as a description not of the act that the speaker is at that moment performing but as a report of the usual state of affairs. Indeed, if you had hitherto never embarrassed that person's wife, you would be uttering a falsehood in saying 8.1.5c, even though you would thereby be embarrassing his wife (and the second time you uttered 8.1.5c you might very well be saying something true). Also, you could just as easily embarrass his wife by saying that you don't embarrass her as by saying that you do embarrass her; by contrast, you can't promise to return the money by saying *I don't promise to return the money soon*. If one utters 8.1.5a in an affected English accent, one is really performing two acts: the locutionary act of uttering those words in an affected English accent and the illocutionary act of telling your interlocutor that that is what you are doing. The latter act is the same sort of thing that one does when he gives a move-by-move account of a nonverbal act that he is carrying out (e.g., *I display the inside of the box. I roll up my sleeves to show that they are empty. I reach into the box with my right hand . . .*). Actually, the present progressive would be preferable to the simple present in 8.1.5a unless it were part of a narration such as the magician's patter just quoted:

8.1.6   I am uttering these words in an affected English accent.

Verbs cannot be used performatively except in the simple present tense. For example, in uttering any of the following, the speaker is not performing the act of christening, ordering, or sentencing:

8.1.7   a.   I am christening this ship the HMS Kreplach.
            a'. I have christened this ship the HMS Kreplach.
            b.   I am ordering you to shine my shoes.
            b'. I have ordered you to shine my shoes.
            c.   I am sentencing him to 20 years of hard labor.

Either the speaker is reporting an act that he has already performed (8.1.7a', 8.1.7b') or he is commenting on another act that he is in the process of performing (but interrupts in order to say 8.1.7a, b, c); for example, 8.1.7c might be a reply given by a very cooperative judge when he is interrupted by a television reporter just as he is about to pronounce the sentence and is asked what is going on, and 8.1.7b might be said by a colonel to an uncooperative private in order to make sure that the private has understood the order just issued.[1]

(ii) In uttering a sentence one sometimes performs more than one illocutionary act, with different parts of the sentence involved in each of the acts:

8.1.8   a. I order you to shine these shoes, and I warn you that if you don't obey that order immediately, you'll be court-martialed.

           b. Is Bill, who was standing here a minute ago, still in the building?

In 8.1.8*a*, the first conjunct corresponds to an act of ordering and the second to an act of warning. In saying 8.1.8*b* the speaker informs or reminds his interlocutor of Bill's recent whereabouts and asks him about Bill's present whereabouts. The nonrestrictive clause is not, strictly speaking, part of the speaker's question but corresponds to another act that he performs while in the process of asking his question.

(iii) Sentences having no overt performative verb are often ambiguous with regard to what illocutionary act they are used to perform. For example, 8.1.9*a* might be used to make either a promise or a prediction, and 8.1.9*b* might be used to inform, warn, or rebuke someone:

8.1.9   a. I'll be in my office until 5:30.

           b. You can get 10 years of hard labor for possession of pot in this state.

The term ILLOCUTIONARY FORCE provides an alternative way of speaking about illocutionary acts: the illocutionary force of an utterance is the type of illocutionary act that the speaker performs in uttering it; for example, some occurrences of 8.1.9*a* would have the illocutionary force of a promise and others would have the illocutionary force of a prediction. As noted above, an utterance may have two or more illocutionary forces, each associated with a different part of the sentence.

8.2. The Performative Analysis

An adequate account of the syntax of a natural language will have to distinguish somehow among different sentence types: declarative sentences, interrogatives, imperatives, exclamatory sentences, and the like. If one's scheme of linguistic description is that which I have assumed throughout this book, according to which a grammar of a language is a set of explicit rules that relate the sentences of that language to their meanings, it will be necessary to draw distinctions of meaning that correspond to the differences among the various sentence types. In this section, I will sketch one approach that has achieved a fair degree of popularity (though nothing approaching universal acceptance; see Anderson 1970, Fraser 1974*a*, and Gazdar 1979 for criticism of this approach), namely, that in which the illocutionary force of an utterance is treated as figuring in the meaning of the sentence in question as a performative verb, though that performative verb need not be manifested as such in the surface form of the sentence. For example, an imperative sentence such as 8.2.1*a* would be claimed to have the same meaning as sentence with an overt performative verb (8.2.1*b*), and the syntactic properties of imperative sentences would be formulated in terms of the (ultimately deleted) performative verb:

8.2.1   a. Open the door!
         b. I order/request you to open the door.

In the traditional classification of 'sentence types', 8.2.1*b* would generally be regarded as a declarative rather than an imperative sentence. The performative analysis thus involves deriving nondeclarative sentence types from the declarative type,[2] but with the important twist that the nondeclarative sentence appears as the complement of the underlying 'declarative' clause.

The term 'declarative' is somewhat confusing. It is not always clear whether it is being used as a grammatical term, denoting sentences of a particular form, or as a pragmatic or semantic term, denoting sentences of a particular type of meaning or of function. The stock examples of declarative sentences are those which are declarative in both senses:

8.2.2   a. Birds eat.
         b. The cat is on the mat.

Both examples are declarative in form and serve to assert a proposition expressed by the whole sentence. Such sentences were referred to in Austin 1963 and the first few lectures of Austin 1962 as CONSTATIVE sentences and were opposed to what Austin called 'performative sentences', which included sentences having an explicit performative verb, and perhaps other nonconstative sentences, though Austin was not completely clear about exactly what the term covered. In the latter part of Austin 1962 (see especially lecture XI), Austin, in accordance with his policy of 'playing Old Harry' with popular dichotomies, such as the fact/value dichotomy, adopted the position that there is not a great deal of difference between 'constative' sentences and 'performative' sentences in which the same proposition is asserted, for example,[3]

8.2.3   a. The cat is on the mat. (constative)
         b. I assert to you that the cat is on the mat. (performative)

The performative analysis is in the spirit of the later chapters of Austin 1962 in holding that 'constative' sentences do not have any privileged position and that whether the sentence involves an overt performative verb or not is a matter only of its superficial structure.

The presence or absence of an overt performative is not entirely a trivial matter for a number of reasons. First, there are grammatical phenomena which depend on whether a given clause is a main clause or is a subordinate clause IN SURFACE STRUCTURE and which thus give rise to differences between a sentence without an overt performative and a corresponding complement of an overt performative verb. For example, the movement of the auxiliary verb in a question to a position before the subject takes place only in surface main clauses and thus applies in 8.2.4a but not in 8.2.4b:

8.2.4   a. Where *were you* on the night of January 15th?
             b. I hereby ask you where *you were* on the night of January 15th.

Second, as pointed out by Davison (1973), while an overt performative clause can be the antecedent of a pronoun (such as the *so* of 8.2.5a), an understood performative verb generally cannot be:

8.2.5   a. I promise to never tell any more lies, and you should do so too.
             b. *I'll never tell any more lies, and you should do so too.

However, these facts present no obstacles to identifying the meanings of nonperformative sentences with those of corresponding sentences that have an overt performative verb: they simply show that some grammatical rules are sensitive to details of surface structure rather than, or in addition to, details of meaning.

In this section I will not devote a great deal of attention to the justification of the performative analysis; for detailed arguments in its favor, see Ross 1970 and Sadock 1974, and for important objections to some of those arguments, see Anderson 1970 and Fraser 1974a. I will limit myself to giving a couple of the more interesting arguments as illustrations of the way in which the performative analysis can interact with syntax. The first argument (from William Cantrall, cited in Lakoff 1972a), involves the phenomenon of SUPER-EQUI-NP-DELETION, which deletes the subject of a complement clause under identity not with a NP of the next higher clause (as with Equi-NP-deletion), but with a NP of a still higher clause:

8.2.6   a. [John wanted [John go home]] → John wanted to go home. (Equi)
             b. [John thought [[John buy a new hat] would be wise]] → John thought it would be wise to buy a new hat. (Super-equi)

Note that in 8.2.6*b* the NP that 'controls' the deletion is two clauses above the deleted NP. There is in principle no limit to how much higher in the structure than the deleted NP the controlling NP may be:

8.2.7   It appeared to John that it was unlikely that there would be any opportunity to buy himself a new hat.

Cantrall notes that first-person and second-person pronouns can be deleted even if there is no first-person or second-person pronoun elsewhere in the sentence to serve as antecedent, though a third-person NP cannot be deleted unless there is an antecedent in a higher clause:

8.2.8   It would be wise to buy myself/yourself/*himself a new hat.

(Examples with a reflexive pronoun as indirect object of *buy* are used here, since the deleted subject of *buy* is the only possible antecedent for the reflexive, and thus the reflexive indicates what the deleted subject is). Cantrall notes that the otherwise anomalous paradigm 8.2.8 is explained if the performative analysis is adopted: in that case the deletions in 8.2.8 are simply instances of Super-equi-NP-deletion operating under exactly the same conditions as in

8.2.9   a. I assert to you that it would be wise to buy myself/yourself/ *himself a new hat.
          b. Bill told Frieda that it would be wise to buy himself/her-self/?myself/?yourself a new hat.

The controller of the deletion of the subject of *buy* is either the subject or the indirect object of *assert* (in 8.2.9*a*) and *tell* (in 8.2.9*b*). Under the performative analysis, 8.2.9*b* would be analyzed as having an underlying performative clause such as 'I assert to you S', whose complement clause is *Bill told Frieda* .... The fact that the *I* and *you* of the understood performative clause in 8.2.9*b* are less acceptable as controllers of Super-equi-NP-deletion than are the *I* and *you* of the understood performative clause of 8.2.8 is a reflection of a general fact about Super-equi, namely, that only the lowest possible controller is actually allowed to control the deletion:

8.2.10   Frieda said that Bill had told me that it would be wise to buy himself/myself/?herself a new hat.

Just as the presence of *Bill* and *me* in the *tell*-clause of 8.2.10 prevents *Frieda* from controlling deletion in the *buy*-clause, the presence of *Bill* and *Frieda* in the *tell*-clause of 8.2.9*b* prevents the *I* and *you* of the understood performative clause from controlling deletion of the subject of the *buy*-clause.

This argument illustrates the most common form of argumentation for an understood higher clause: anomalous application (or nonapplication) of some rule is explained in terms of a proportion 'surface main clause is to hypothesized higher clause as complement clause is to clause of which it is complement'; for example, the deletion of *I* or *you* in 8.2.8 is to the hypothesized higher clause *I assert to you S* as the deletion of the *I* or *you* in 8.2.9*a* is to the overt higher clause *I assert to you S* or as the deletion of *he* or *she* in 8.2.9*b* is to the overt higher clause *Bill told Frieda S*.

The other common form of argumentation for an understood higher clause is that in which a higher clause is argued to be necessary in order to provide a 'resting place' for an element that otherwise does not have a structural role in the sentence. The two forms of argumentation can be combined when the element that is assigned a 'resting place' is one that otherwise has a syntactic function (such as modifier of some kind) and which can be treated as always having that function if there is an understood higher clause. For example, Rutherford (1970) and Davison (1973) have argued for the performative analysis on the basis of the adverbial clauses found in sentences such as

8.2.11   a. In case you haven't heard, Bob and Frieda have decided to get married.
           b. Since you're so smart, what's the capital of South Dakota?

These adverbial clauses function differently from similar clauses appearing in such examples as

8.2.12   a. In case you aren't home by 6:00, I'll start peeling the potatoes.
           b. Since you're so smart, you probably know what the capital of South Dakota is.

Example 8.2.12*a* gives a condition under which the speaker will start peeling the potatoes; however, 8.2.11*a* doesn't give a condition under which Bob and Frieda have decided to get married. The condition given in the adverbial clause in 8.2.11*a* is a condition under which the utterance of the sentence will accomplish what it purports to accomplish, namely, informing the addressee that Bob and Frieda have decided to get married. In 8.2.11*b*, the addressee's being so smart is the (ostensible) reason for the speaker's asking his question, not the reason why the capital of South Dakota is what it is; but if 8.2.12*b* is uttered without irony, the addressee's being so smart *is* (according to the speaker) the reason why that person will probably know what the capital of South Dakota is.

The various adverbial clauses in 8.2.11 can be interpreted as modifiers only if the sentences are analyzed as providing appropriate items for them to modify, and the performative analysis does precisely that: they would modify the understood performative clauses exactly as if the performative clauses were overtly present:

8.2.13   a. In case you haven't heard, I inform you that Bob and Frieda have decided to get married.
         b. Since you are so smart, I ask you to tell me what the capital of South Dakota is.

Sadock (1974:36–37) has given a similar argument based on the distribution of *in conclusion, once and for all,* and a number of such expressions. These items occur in two contexts: (i) where they modify a clause that describes one of the steps in a verbal presentation, and (ii) where they introduce a declarative sentence that is part of a verbal presentation:

8.2.14   a. Professor Smirk described in conclusion the mating habits of rotifers.
         a'. *Julia baked in conclusion a zucchini cobbler.
         b. In conclusion, the world is not ready for efficient postal delivery.
         b'. *In conclusion, shine my shoes!

Under the performative hypothesis, these expressions are always adverbs and always modify a clause that denotes one of the steps of a verbal presentation, whether an overtly occurring verb (as in 8.2.14*a*) or an understood performative (as in 8.2.14*b*).

8.3. Implicature: Grice Saves

The two questions 'What does the sentence X imply?' and 'What could you conclude if I uttered the sentence X?' are two quite different questions and have quite different answers. This point is made particularly clear by an example adapted from Grice 1975. Suppose that I am asked to write a letter of recommendation for a student of mine who is applying for a teaching position in linguistics and I write a letter which reads in its entirety: 'Mr. A was always on time for classes, and in his papers he always displayed excellent penmanship'. The reader of this letter could conclude that I regarded Mr. A as incompetent to teach linguistics. Nonetheless, one could hardly maintain that the proposition that Mr. A is incompetent is part of the meaning of the one sentence of which the letter consists, since if that sentence were part of a longer letter which extolled Mr. A for unusual knowledge, intelligence, and originality, the reader of the letter would not conclude that I regard Mr. A as incompetent (unless, say, the reader believed that I always extol my worst students for nonexistent virtues).

The conclusions that the hearer (or reader) draws from my uttering the sentence X depend not only on the content of X but also on (i) the fact that I uttered X, and (ii) the fact that I didn't utter any of the other sentences that I might have uttered instead. The letter is damning to Mr. A not because I extol his punctuality and penmanship but because I do not extol anything else. The conclusions that the hearer/reader draws reflect his conclusions about why I didn't say the other things that I could have said. The fact that I didn't say that Mr. A is a marimba virtuoso can be ascribed to the fact that, even if he is one, it is irrelevant to the purpose of the communication; thus the letter does not convey that Mr. A is not a marimba virtuoso. However, the fact that I did not say that he has an excellent understanding of linguistics cannot be ascribed to my believing it to be irrelevant to a testimonial to his qualifications to teach linguistics, particularly since it is clearly more relevant than the two things that I did mention in the letter. A more plausible reason for my failure to say it is that it is false. Thus, it is reasonable for the reader to conclude that I think Mr. A does not have an excellent understanding of linguistics.

The fact that I didn't mention that Mr. A has read Bloomfield's *Language* would have to be attributed to a different reason: while it is relevant to Mr. A's capacity to teach linguistics, there are sufficiently many more important questions to answer about Mr. A that I could easily tell the reader more than he wants to know about Mr. A without mentioning whether Mr. A has read Bloomfield. Indeed, if I had added to the one-sentence letter the second sentence 'He has read Bloomfield's *Language*', the reader would be justified in concluding that Mr. A has read little beyond Bloomfield's *Language*: if Mr. A knows the linguistic literature well, then there was more reason for me to say that than just to say that he has read Bloomfield, particularly since Bloomfield's *Language* is a standard reading assignment in elementary linguistics courses, and thus the fact that someone has read it is no reason to suppose that he has read other linguistic classics. By contrast, if I wrote in support of a candidate for a teaching position in Japanese that he has read the entire Genji Monogatari in the original Japanese, the reader would not be justified in concluding that the candidate has read little else: to read Genji Monogatari you need the kind of command of Japanese that you can only get by reading large quantities of less demanding stuff.

The conclusions that the hearer/reader draws from the fact that you said what you said (and didn't say what you didn't say) are based on the assumption that you are cooperating with him: that you are supplying him with information that is correct and is relevant to your/his purposes, that you are not withholding information that is important to him, and that you are not wasting his time by going into minor matters when there are more important things you could mention instead. (Or at least, this is what cooperation would consist in when you are responding to his request for information; given other purposes for the interchange, other things may constitute cooperation; for example, if a person is trying to solve a puzzle that you have posed to him, it is cooperative not to tell him the answer until he gives up).

Grice (1975) groups the principal dimensions of cooperation in communication under the following four headings, to which I have added capsule paraphrases of what he says about each. QUANTITY: you should assert neither more nor less than is appropriate for the purpose at hand. QUALITY: what you assert should be true, and you should have adequate grounds for holding it to be true. RELATION: what you mention should be relevant to the purpose at hand. MANNER: you should use linguistic means no more elaborate than what is needed to convey what you are asserting. Since cooperation plays a role not only in assertion but in all speech acts (indeed, in all acts that involve interaction between persons), these 'maxims of cooperation' should clearly be recast in a more general form which is not restricted to acts of assertion, and Grice (1975:47) indeed provides instances of them that do not even involve speech, let alone assertion.[4] However, for the time being, let us concentrate on assertion and the way that cooperation affects what one asserts and how one asserts it.

One aspect of cooperation that does not fit clearly under any of Grice's four maxims but perhaps can be subsumed under 'Manner' is that of 'effort': extra effort must be justified by extra cooperation, in the sense that one must only go to extra effort in saying something if one thereby makes what one says more informative or more relevant or more intelligible (or more desirable in some other way, e.g., more polite) than it would have been without the extra effort. The interaction of effort with cooperation can be seen by comparing 8.3.1a with 8.3.1b, assuming that the speaker in 8.3.1a and the answerer in 8.3.1b know that Truman was president in 1947:

8.3.1   a. In the middle of a lecture on the Cold War, the speaker says 'In 1947, the president of the United States was either Truman or Eisenhower'.
          b. When asked 'Was either Truman or Eisenhower the president of the United States in 1947?', a person answers
             i. 'Yes'.
             ii. 'Yes, either Truman or Eisenhower was president'.
             iii. 'Yes, as a matter of fact, Truman was president'.

In 8.3.1a, the speaker has been especially uncooperative, since he not only has been less informative than he could have been (i.e., it is more informative to say that Truman was president than to say that either Truman or

Eisenhower was) but he has gone out of his way to be uninformative: he could have been more informative by leaving out words (namely, the words *either* and *or Eisenhower*). In 8.3.1*b*, the first answerer is being somewhat uncooperative, though not nearly so uncooperative as was the speaker in 8.3.1*a*: to answer more cooperatively, he would have to add extra words, as in the third answer of 8.3.1*b*; he is being less informative than he could have been, but he is not going out of his way to be uninformative. The second answerer in 8.3.1*b* is being as uncooperative as was the speaker in 8.3.1*a*: he could have been more informative without greater effort by giving the third answer in 8.3.1*b* or the even shorter *Yes. Trúman was.*

A dimension of cooperation is EXPLOITED when the speaker chooses his words so that he will convey something other than (generally, more than) what he is, strictly speaking, asserting, as a result of the addressee's assuming that the speaker is being cooperative, as when a person conveys that he doesn't know (or doesn't remember) which of Truman and Eisenhower was president in 1947 by saying *Either Truman or Eisenhower was president in 1947*. While *or* usually conveys 'I don't know which', its dictionary entry need not, indeed, must not make that a component of its meaning: it conveys that only because cooperativity generally demands that the speaker say something else if he does not know which alternative is true. Similarly, Searle (1969:142–46) has argued that while (as noted by Austin 1957) adverbs such as *intentionally* and *voluntarily* usually convey that something is aberrant about the action described (e.g., *John intentionally brushed his teeth* suggests that, say, he was doing it to annoy me), that fact must not be entered in their dictionary entries: if the possibility of John's action being unintentional, involuntary, or the like is not under consideration, cooperativity demands that the speaker not go out of his way to mention something that would be taken for granted if they were not mentioned. When the intentionality of normally intentional actions is mentioned, the speaker conveys that their intentionality is deserving of mention, thus that normal conditions, in which it is not worthy of mention, do not prevail.

Grice gives the following example of exploitation of 'relevance':

8.3.2   A. I'm nearly out of gas.
             B: There's a filling station around the corner.

Here *B* conveys not merely the proposition that there is a filling station around the corner but also that it is likely to be open right now (note that *A* would be justified in being angry at *B* if it turned out that *B* knew that the filling station was closed). It conveys that because, if *B* did not think that the filling station was likely to be open, his utterance would be as irrelevant to *A*'s presumable concerns as if he had said *There's a grocery store on 14th Street*.[5] The relation between *B*'s utterance and the proposition that the filling station is probably open is not one of implication but one of what Grice calls CONVERSATIONAL IMPLICATURE: an utterance 'conversationally implicates' a proposition *p* when it conveys that *p* by virtue of the assumption that the speaker is being cooperative.[6]

The above discussion of 8.3.1 accomplishes part of a major goal that Grice undertook in his study of 'implicature': to show that the supposed discrepancies between natural language and standard formal logic are not real discrepancies but are instances of implicature, that is, the formula of logic and the corresponding sentence of a natural language really mean the same thing, but when one uses the sentence of natural language he will generally convey more than it means, as a result of the maxims of cooperation. Thus, the occasionally encountered claim that *or* is non-truth-functional, in that it implies that the speaker does not know which alternative is true, is a mistake according to Grice: 'A or B' is true whenever either or both of the conjuncts is true, though asserting that true proposition will generally be a misleading thing to do if one happens to know that A is true. Grice said the same thing of *if*: 'If A, then B' does not IMPLY that there is a connection between A and B, and the many strange-sounding sentences of the form 'If A, then B' which should be true according to the standard truth table, but in which there is no connection between A and B, really are true, though asserting them would generally be a misleading thing to do. Specifically, suppose one were to assert any of the following:

8.3.3   a. If Sapporo is the largest city on Hokkaido, then Beethoven lived in Vienna.
          b. If Philadelphia is in Burma, then Beethoven lived in Vienna.
          c. If Philadelphia is in Burma, then Beethoven lived in Istanbul.

Could a person assert any of these propositions (all of them true, according to the standard truth tables) and still be cooperative with regard to both quantity and quality? Consider first how quality could be satisfied, that is, how one could have a reasonable ground for believing the proposition expressed by one of these sentences. Either there is a connection between the antecedent and consequent that enables one to be sure that the antecedent can't be true and the consequent false simultaneously, or there is no such connection. In the latter case, one could have reasonable grounds for believing the proposition expressed by the conditional only by having reasonable grounds for believing the antecedent false or by having reasonable grounds for believing the consequent true. But if that is the nature of one's reasons for believing the conditional proposition to be true, then, with an important exception to be discussed momentarily, one could not assert the conditional without being uncooperative with regard to quantity: if you know that Beethoven lived in Vienna, it would be more informative for you to say that than to assert 8.3.3a or 8.3.3b, and if you know that Philadelphia is not in Burma, it would be more informative for you to say that than to assert 8.3.3c or 8.3.3b. Thus, argues Grice, a conditional usually conveys that the speaker sees a connection between the antecedent and consequent, since the speaker would have to base his belief in the conditional on such a connection if his act of asserting the conditional is to be a cooperative act.

The exception alluded to in the last paragraph is that in certain cases a conditional in which there is no connection between antecedent and consequent can be used as an assertion of the consequent or as a denial of the antecedent:

8.3.4   a. If $2 + 2 = 4$, my client is innocent. (Conveys: my client is innocent)
           b. If Nixon was innocent, then geraniums grow on the moon. (Conveys: Nixon wasn't innocent)

Note, however, that mere truth of the antecedent is not enough to allow a conditional to be used to assert the consequent, and mere falsehood of the consequent is not enough to allow a conditional to be used to deny the antecedent: it must be obvious truth in the one case and blatant falsehood in the other case, as is illustrated by comparing 8.3.4 with

8.3.5   a. If $847 \times 698 = 591,206$, then my client is innocent.
           b. If Nixon was innocent, then Seattle has more inhabitants than Columbus, Ohio.

Since the antecedent of 8.3.4a is obviously true, the only way that the hearer could conceive of 8.3.4a being true, connection or no connection, is for its consequent to be true; and since the consequent of 8.3.4b is blatantly false, the only way that the hearer could conceive of 8.3.4b being true, connection or no connection, is for the antecedent to be false. Note that 8.3.4 does not involve the violation of the quantity maxim that 8.3.3 exhibits: since the possibility of the antecedent of 8.3.4a being false is ruled out, it is just as informative to assert 8.3.4a as to assert its consequent, whereas in 8.3.3a, since the possibility of the falsehood of the antecedent is not ruled out by what people would normally take for granted, asserting 8.3.3a is significantly less informative than asserting its consequent; the comparison of 8.3.4b with 8.3.3c works similarly. If there is any lack of cooperation in the uttering of 8.3.4a or 8.3.4b, it is the minor one of taking more words than are needed to say what you want to say: using a long sentence rather than an equally informative short sentence. It could be argued indeed that in asserting 8.3.4*a* one is being more informative than if one asserted its consequent (and that in asserting 8.3.4*b* one is being more informative than if one denied its antecedent): the speaker is conveying not just that his client is innocent but that his client's innocence is as clear as the obvious fact that $2 + 2 = 4$. But saying that would involve changing ground: instead of talking about the information content of the proposition that you are asserting, we are talking about the information content of the proposition that you are conveying. But what then is to prevent one from saying that 8.3.3*a–c* are more informative than asserting the consequent (in 8.3.3*a–b*) or denying the antecedent (in 8.3.3*b–c*), in that they convey a highly informative (though quite bizarre) proposition such as that Sapporo's being the largest city on Hokkaido is a reason why Beethoven lived in Vienna? Presumably only the fact that in that case the conveyed proposition ('informative' as it is) is false. Exploitation of the cooperative maxims is itself cooperative: one takes the speaker to have conveyed something only if it is something that it would be reasonable to take him as having intended to convey.

One particularly appealing part of Grice's argument that a 'connection' between antecedent and consequent is not part of the meaning of *if* is his argument that paraphrases of conditionals in terms of *or* and *not* just as much commit one to a 'connection', despite the fact that *or* is not normally held to require a 'connection' between the things that it conjoins. Specifically, Grice notes that 8.3.6*b* is a good paraphrase of 8.3.6*a*:

8.3.6   a. If Labour doesn't win the next election, there'll be a depression.
           b. Either Labour will win the next election or there'll be a depression.

Both commit the speaker equally to the idea that there is a causal connection between Labour losing the election and a depression ensuing. Just as in the case of the conditional, knowledge of a connection between the two constituent propositions can be one's grounds for believing that some disjunctive proposition is true. My only qualm about this argument relates to the fact that conditionals do not always have an adequate paraphrase with *or*; for example, note how much less normal 8.3.7*b* and 8.3.8*b* are as paraphrases of 8.3.7*a* and 8.3.8*a* than 8.3.6*b* was as a paraphrase of 8.3.6*a*:

8.3.7   a. If Labour wins the next election, there'll be a depression.
           b. Either Labour won't win the next election or there'll be a depression.

8.3.8   a. If you come a step closer, I'll scream.
             b. Either you won't come a step closer or I'll scream.

On Grice's account of *if* and *or*, there is no obvious reason why 8.3.7*b* and 8.3.8*b* should be any less normal than 8.3.6*b*.

Grice's approach also explains away another well-known supposed discrepancy between formal logic and natural language: the fact that in English *some* is taken as implying *not all*, whereas $(\exists x)fx$ does not imply $\sim(\forall x)fx$. Grice argues that it is misleading to say 8.3.9*a* when you know that all men are mortal, since you could at no extra cost say the more informative 8.3.9*b*:

8.3.9   a. Some men are mortal.
             b. All men are mortal.

Thus, a person who utters 8.3.9*a* is taken as holding that not all men are mortal (or at least, that he does not know for sure that all men are mortal).

The use of *yes* and *no* in answers to questions provides confirmation of the position that *some* means $\exists$ and that it is only because of the principles of cooperation that a speaker who utters 8.3.9*a* is taken to mean that not all men are mortal. Recall that in the discussion of 8.3.1*b* I noted that the question 8.3.10*a* can be answered with 8.3.10*b*; but 8.3.10*b'* would be inappropriate as an answer:

8.3.10   a. Was either Truman or Eisenhower president in 1947?
             b. Yes, as a matter of fact, Truman was president.
             b'. *No, Truman was president.

The use of *yes* and *no* accords with the idea that *Either Truman or Eisenhower was president in 1947* is true even though the speaker could not utter that sentence without being misleading: he must use *yes*, the word that indicates truth of the proposition which the question asked about,[7] rather than *no*, the word which indicates the falsehood of that proposition. The same paradigm is exhibited by sentences involving *some*; note that 8.3.11*a* can be answered with 8.3.11*b* but not with 8.3.11*b'*:[8]

8.3.11   a. Are some men mortal?
             b. Yes, as a matter of fact, áll men are mortal.
             b'. *No, all men are mortal.

As was noted in chapter 4, one discrepancy between formal logic and natural language cannot be explained away by Grice's approach: the fact that while *All unicorns drive Chevrolets* commits the speaker to the existence of unicorns (and, in general, the use of *all* commits the speaker to the existence of elements in the domain over which its variable ranges),

$(\forall x) \supset (fx, gx)$ does not imply $(\exists x) \wedge (fx, gx)$. In this case, the use of *yes* and *no* in the answer to questions such as 8.3.12a does not accord with the claim that *All unicorns drive Chevrolets* is (vacuously) true:

8.3.12   a. Do all unicorns drive Chevrolets?
           b. *Yes, indeed, there are no unicorns.
           b'. ?No, there are no unicorns.
           b". *Yes, but there are no unicorns.

Grice's account of the alleged discrepancies between formal logic and natural logic has been challenged by L. J. Cohen (1972). Cohen argues that Grice's discussion is deficient because it covers only the cases where *If A, then B* (or *Either A or B* or *Some A's are B's*) is asserted and ignores the cases where it is a constituent of a larger logical structure or is involved in a speech act of another type. He holds that in many such cases a sentence of English does not mean what in Grice's account it ought to mean. For example, does 8.3.13 really attribute to Frank a belief of the form $\supset AB$, where $\supset$ is the standard truth-functional connective?

8.3.13   Frank believes that if God is dead, then everything is permitted.

Cohen argues that it does not, on the grounds that 8.3.13 attributes to Frank a belief about a connection between God being dead and everything being permitted and that, for example, 8.3.13 would be false if Frank did not believe in such a connection but merely believed that everything is permitted. One might report that in that case 8.3.13 would be a misleading thing to say: you could be more informative at less cost by saying that Frank believes that everything is permitted. However, that retort skirts the issue of whether 8.3.13 is TRUE in such a case. The use of *yes* and *no* does not accord with the position that 8.3.13 is true:

8.3.14   a. Does Frank believe that if God is dead, everything is
              permitted?
           b. ?Yes, indeed he believes that everything is permitted.
           b'. No, but he does believe that everything is permitted.
           b". Yes, and he also believes that everything is permitted.
           b'''. No, but he does believe that God is not dead.

If 8.3.13 attributed to Frank a belief $\supset AB$, then 8.3.14b' and 8.3.14b''' ought not to be possible answers: a belief that everything is permitted ought to be a special case of a belief that if God is dead, everything is permitted.

It might be objected that 8.3.13 and 8.3.14 are beside the point, since they involve 'belief contexts' and strange things happen in belief contexts.

Let us then take an example involving as innocuous a context as can be imagined, namely, mere negation:

8.3.15   It is not the case that if God is dead, everything is permitted.

According to classical logic, 8.3.15 implies that God is dead (i.e., from $\sim \supset AB$ you can infer both A and $\sim B$);[9] however, ordinary speakers do not accept arguments such as *It is not the case that if God is dead, everything is permitted; therefore, God is dead.* One could know the premise of that argument to be true either on the basis of knowledge of the truth values of the constituent propositions (i.e., knowing that God is dead and that not everything is permitted) or on the basis of some connection between those propositions. In the former case, one could hold that the argument was circular (i.e., its conclusion is something that you used in establishing its premise) and that that fact was responsible for the fact that people reject the argument. However, what basis could there be for rejecting the argument in the case where you know the premise on the basis of some connection between the proposition that God is dead and the proposition that everything is permitted? Doesn't the fact that it is odd in that case to say *Therefore, God is dead* (or *Therefore, not everything is permitted*) point to a real discrepancy between formal logic and natural language? The only apparent alternative to admitting a real discrepancy is to deny that the premise is really of the form $\sim \supset AB$, for example, to hold that there is a covert quantifier ('It is not the case that for every state of affairs, if God is dead in that state of affairs, then everything is permitted in that state of affairs'). However, that analysis is at least very close to the analysis that Cohen was arguing for: that *if* is not just the standard truth-functional connective but makes reference to a connection between the antecedent and consequent, for example, a connection such as could be formulated as 'In every state of affairs in which God is dead, everything is permitted'.

A further criticism of Grice by Cohen is worth mentioning here. Grice takes it to be an important characteristic of implicatures that they can be CANCELLED by putting the utterence in the appropriate context, for example, by adding an appropriate conjoined clause, as in 8.3.11*b*, where *as a matter of fact, all men are mortal* cancels the implicature that some men are not mortal, or in *Either Truman or Eisenhower was president in 1947, but I'm not going to tell you which*, where the *but*-clause cancels the implicature that the speaker does not know which of the two was president. Cohen argues that not only implicatures but also parts of meaning can be cancelled, as in the expressions *a fake diamond* and *plastic flowers*, where *fake* and *plastic* cancel out parts of the meanings of *diamond* and *flower*.[10] Cohen maintains that rather than holding, as Grice does, that *if* is basically truth-functional and that sentences where it appears not to be truth-functional have an implicature of a non-truth-functional connection between the constituent propositions, one could just as well take *if* to involve such a connection as part of its meaning and analyze the cases where *if* appears to be truth-functional as involving cancellation of that part of the meaning. This particular issue remains a standoff, pending further clarification of the notion of 'cancellation'. While Cohen is correct that other things than implicatures can be 'cancelled', he has left unanswered the general question of what the circumstances are that allow cancellation to take place; for example, why is it that *That is a plastic flower* is merely cancellation, but *All of my relatives are Catholics, but my uncle is a Buddhist* is a contradiction? (As contrasted with *All of my relatives are Catholics but for my uncle, who is a Buddhist*, which is not a contradiction.) I am confident that a fairly clear distinction between the two classes of cases can be drawn, but it is not clear how the distinction will apply to *if*-clauses.

I will now turn to brief sketches of a number of analyses in terms of implicature. Let us begin with the question of what the word *pink* means. A reasonable first approximation to the meaning of *pink* is 'pale red': pink differs from red in having relatively low 'saturation' (i.e., it is pale rather than deep), though its 'hue' is in the range covered by *red*. However, it is much harder to think of a normal use for the expression *pale red* than for such combinations as *pale blue/yellow/green*, which have obvious uses. Fred Householder (1971:75) has proposed an explanation of these facts in terms of a principle that when there is a single word equivalent of a multiword phrase, the single word must be used instead: *pale red* is odd because you have to say *pink* instead, whereas there is no alternative to saying *pale blue/yellow/green*.[11] However, the expression *pale red* in fact is occasionally encountered, not merely in a definition such as '*Pink*' means '*pale red*', but to indicate what color some object is, and moreover, it does not refer to the same range of color as *pink* does; specifically, *pale red* is used to refer to a color that is pale in comparison with true red, but not so pale as to be pink. Some sense can be made of these facts if the Householder and Gruber proposal is reinterpreted in terms of conversational implicature. When a person calls something *pale red*, he had the alternative of calling it *pink* but chose to call it *pale red* instead. His choice of words implies that the color is red in hue but is pale in comparison with true red, and his rejection of *pink* as the designation of the color would have to be because *pink* did not apply to it. Since the most obvious way that these conditions could be fulfilled is for the color to be somewhat pale but not very pale (i.e., not so pale as to be unqualifiedly pale), the use of *pale red* conveys that the color is deeper than pink but paler than red. Note that an analysis in terms of implicature thus allows one to define *pink* as 'pale red' but still admit cases where *pink* and *pale red* designate different colors.

Second, consider the difference between 8.3.16*a* and 8.3.16*b*:

8.3.16   a. Only Muriel, Lyndon, and Ed voted for Hubert.
              b. Only Southerners voted for Hubert.

While a person who utters 8.3.16*a* will be taken to hold that Muriel, Lyndon, and Ed all voted for Hubert, a person who utters 8.3.16*b* will not be taken as holding that all Southerners voted for Hubert (he will be taken as holding that at least some Southerners voted for Hubert, perhaps even that persons who voted for Hubert were widely distributed in the South, but not that ALL Southerners voted for Hubert). By the same token, *Only American citizens are employed by the FBI* does not imply that all American citizens are employed by the FBI.

If one of the persons enumerated in 8.3.16*a* is known by the speaker not to have voted for Hubert, then the speaker is being misleading: he could have been more informative by leaving that person out of the list. Thus, 8.3.16*a* could be uttered cooperatively only if for each of the three persons enumerated, either the speaker knows that that person voted for Hubert or he does not know whether that person voted for Hubert. But if he doesn't know, say, whether Ed voted for Hubert, cooperativeness would demand that he indicate that (say, by saying *Only Muriel, Lyndon, and perhaps Ed ...*), since it is so easy for him to indicate that his knowledge about Ed is incomplete, and since his addressee presumably cares who voted for Hubert (if he doesn't, then why utter the sentence at all?). Thus a speaker could utter 8.3.16*a* cooperatively only if he holds that Muriel, Lyndon, and Ed all voted for Hubert. However, since 8.3.16*b* does not involve an enumeration, it takes extra effort to exclude people rather than to include them (e.g. *Only Southerners other than Johnny Cash and George Wallace voted for Hubert*), and an expression indicating what Southerners were excluded would be misleading unless either it were complete (and thus incredibly long) or made explicit about the way in which it was incomplete (e.g., *Only Southerners other than Johnny Cash, George Wallace, and many others too numerous to mention ...*). Thus the reason why a person who utters 8.3.16*b* does not explicitly say that not all Southerners voted for Hubert need not be that that is false—it could as easily be that a non-misleading qualification would take more effort than it was worth. These considerations suggest that the analysis of *only* given in 7.1 (in which *Only Muriel voted for Hubert* was analyzed as 'Muriel voted for Hubert, and no one other than Muriel voted for Hubert') is incorrect: only the second conjunct is really part of the meaning of an *only*-sentence, with the first conjunct being conveyed by virtue of the assumption that the speaker is being cooperative. Of course, that implicature can be cancelled by adding the appropriate words:

8.3.17   Only Muriel voted for Hubert, if even she did.

The analysis of *only* in terms of implicature is important, since it makes it possible to associate *only* with the same logical analysis in 8.3.16*b* as in 8.3.16*a*, namely, to treat all instances of 'Only *f*'s are *g*'s' as $(\forall x: \sim fx) \sim gx$, where *fx* can be either an 'ordinary' propositional function such as '*x* is a Southerner' or a function such as '$x \in \{\text{Muriel, Ed, Lyndon}\}$'.[12]
    For a third example, consider 'reduced passives' such as

8.3.18   Bill was mugged.

These have generally been treated by transformational grammarians as having a deep structure with *someone* or *something* as subject; thus, 8.3.18 would have the same deep structure as

8.3.19   Someone mugged Bill.

The derivation of 8.3.18 would involve passivization followed by deletion of *by someone*. However, an indefinite pronoun is not indefinite enough to serve as the underlying subject. First of all, as has often been pointed out, reduced passives are possible even with verbs that demand a semantically plural subject and which thus do not admit *someone* (which can only be singular) as underlying subject:

8.3.20   a.   The fort was being surrounded.
              a'. *Someone was surrounding the fort.

              b.   A compromise was agreed on.
              b'. *Someone agreed on a compromise.

Second, consider what the following sentences imply about the authorship of *Syntactic Structures*:

8.3.21   a.   Chomsky's *Syntactic Structures* was written in 1955.
              a'. Someone wrote Chomsky's *Syntactic Structures* in 1955.

While 8.3.21*a* can be uttered by someone who believes Chomsky to be the author of *Syntactic Structures* (though it could also be uttered by someone who believes the author to be Bernard Bloch but who persists in calling it 'Chomsky's *Syntactic Structures*', just as many people persist in speaking of 'Purcell's Trumpet Voluntary' even though they know it is by Jeremiah Clarke), 8.3.21*a'* would only be appropriate if the speaker believes that the author was not Chomsky.
    Nevertheless, a reconsideration of these examples in terms of implicature provides a way of preserving the essence of the proposal to derive 8.3.18

and 8.3.19 from the same deep structure. I wish to propose that 8.3.21*a* and 8.3.21*a′* have the same logical form and that their difference in appropriateness conditions stems rather from the choice of words by which that common logical form is expressed. Note in particular that the *someone* of 8.3.21*a′* may serve as the antecedent of a pronoun, whereas the underlying subject of 8.3.21*a* may not:

8.3.22   a. *Chomsky's *Syntactic Structures* was written in 1955, but his identity has not been revealed. (* if *his* refers to the subject of *write*)

a′. Someone wrote Chomsky's *Syntactic Structures* in 1955, but his identity has not been revealed.

I will argue in 9.6 that existential quantifiers serve a dual function: they both quantify a bound variable and create a constant that can play a role in subsequent discourse (a constant corresponding to the individual that the quantified proposition says exists). Or at least, existential quantifiers that have overt linguistic manifestation have that dual function: as examples like 8.3.22*a* suggest, an existential quantifier (assuming that there is one in the logical structure of 8.3.22*a*) that does not appear overtly does not have the function of creating a constant.[13] However, in accordance with the maxim of quantity, constants are interpreted as distinct unless the speaker signals that they are or may be identical. Whether entities are the same or different will be relevant to virtually any discourse in which one refers to those entities, and since one can refer to identical entities by treating them as identical (that is, by using the same name for them, or by using anaphoric devices such as *he* or *that bastard*), one would be saying less than is relevant if one failed to advise the addressee that the constants were or might be identical. And since uncertainty about whether two entities are identical is far less common than certainty that they are distinct, it is the former and not the latter that requires comment. Yet 'reduced passives' like 8.3.21*a* allow one to remain noncommittal about whether the understood underlying subject is identical to some other individual that is referred to, since nothing corresponding to the understood subject is added to the 'cast of characters' that are available to the subsequent discourse.

For a final example, consider the use of transitive/intransitive pairs such as the uses of *open* in

8.3.23   a. I opened the door.
             b. The door opened.

The analysis of transitive *open* as a causative of intransitive *open* (e.g., analyzing 8.3.23*a* as 'I did something which caused the door to open') might be objected to on the grounds that there are cases where it is appropriate to say 8.3.23*a* but not appropriate to say 8.3.23*b*. In particular, it would be quite irresponsible for a person to say 8.3.23*b* in response to the question *How did the dog get out of the house?* when he had opened the door and thereby let the dog out. Note, though, that there are cases where 8.3.23*b* may be embedded in a larger context in which it is made clear that a particular agent is responsible for the door's opening:

8.3.24   I pulled and pulled at the door, and finally it opened.

Fillmore (1975) observes that 8.3.25*a* (which is the first sentence of Hemingway's "The Killers") differs from 8.3.25*b* not only in the location of the narrator (with *came*, the narrator views things from inside the lunchroom, and with *went*, he views things from outside), but also in who opens the door: 8.3.25*a* suggests that the two men opened the door, whereas 8.3.25*b* suggests that the door was opened from inside the lunchroom:

8.3.25   a. The door of Henry's lunchroom opened, and two men came in.
          b. The door of Henry's lunchroom opened, and two men went in.

As Fillmore notes, however, 8.3.25*a* is really noncommittal about who opened the door (you could use 8.3.25*a* even when a third person opened the door from outside for the two men, or when Henry pushed a button on some electronic door-opening device, thus causing the door to open), and the suggestions of both sentences would change radically if it had been established that Henry's lunchroom had an all-glass exterior, so that a person inside it could see what people outside it were doing, and vice versa. The generalization about when you can use intransitive *open* and when you must use transitive *open* appears to be: you may use intransitive *open* when there is no agent, or when you don't know who (if anyone) the agent is, or when you have expressly indicated who the agent is; otherwise you must use transitive *open*. But what this amounts to is that you have to indicate who the agent is, either by the use of the transitive verb or by some other means, when you know who the agent is. Witnessing an agent performing an act is the case par excellence of knowing who the agent is. If you are outside the lunchroom and see the two men open the door, or if you are inside looking through a glass door and see the two men open it, you have witnessed their act of opening the door; if you are inside the lunchroom and the doors and walls are opaque, or if you are looking in some other direction when the men open the door and you hear but do not see the men and the door, you have witnessed the event of the door opening, but not the men's act of opening the door, and you have only inferred, not witnessed, that such an act took place. This pattern reflects an interaction of the maxims of quantity, quality, and relevance: the existence of an act as the cause of a given event and the identity of the agent of that act will generally be relevant to a discourse in which that event is referred to, and it is misleading to leave out information about the existence of the act and identity of the agent, provided that one's information is of sufficient quality.[14] Thus, 'verbs of change' such as the intransitive *open* at most suggest, rather than imply, that no agent was involved. This should be contrasted with agentive verbs of change such as intransitive *dress*, which imply agency on the part of the subject. Transitive *dress* (similarly, *shave*, *wash*) cannot be a causative of intransitive *dress*, since it refers to only one agent, not two; for example, in *Wilbur dressed the baby*, the baby need not be an active participant in the dressing. Of course, an alternative analysis of the relationship between transitive and intransitive *dress* is available: treat the transitive as basic, and the intransitive as having an understood reflexive object.

For a final example of an analysis based on conversational implicature, let us turn to the supposed 'exclusive' sense of *or*. Pelletier (1977) challenges the popular view that there are two *or*'s, an inclusive *or* that combines propositions into a complex proposition that is true if and only if at least one of the conjuncts is true, and an exclusive *or* that combines propositions into a complex proposition that is true if and only if exactly one of the conjuncts is true. Pelletier notes that many of the supposed examples of exclusive *or* are merely examples in which, for reasons having nothing to do with *or*, it is impossible for more than one of the conjuncts to be true:

8.3.26   a. Today is either Monday or Tuesday.
           b. Either there is a God or there isn't.

Such examples are irrelevant to the question of whether there is a distinction between exclusive and inclusive *or*, since the case in which the two *or*'s are supposed to differ does not arise in these examples. Of considerably more interest are such examples as[15]

8.3.27   a. On the $1.50 lunch you get either a soup or a dessert.
           b. You can use either the hall closet or the attic to store your books.

While there is no logical impossibility about a state of affairs in which you get both a soup and a dessert for your $1.50 or in which you store books in both the hall closet and the attic, nonetheless these sentences at least suggest that you don't get both the soup and the dessert and that you aren't entitled to store books in both places. This does not mean, however, that an exclusive *or* is involved in the permissions that the sentences in 8.3.27 report, any more than the fact that 8.3.28 leaves one free to take only soup or only dessert or neither means that 8.3.28 involves a constituent 'You get a soup % you get a dessert', where % is a connective such that $p\%q$ is true regardless of the truth values of p and q:

8.3.28   On the $1.50 dinner you get a soup and a dessert.

Similarly, the fact that 8.3.29 leaves one free to take only one vegetable does not mean that 8.3.29 involves a special sense of *two* that includes *one* as a special case, distinct from the ordinary sense of *two* found in *John and Mary have two children*:

8.3.29   On the $1.50 dinner you get two vegetables.

When one is offered a package deal, one is not normally required to accept all the items in the package: in exchange for your money, you receive the entitlement to all the items in the package, but you still have the option of not exercising that entitlement in the case of items that you do not want. Thus, 8.3.28 reports a more generous offer than 8.3.27*a*: an offer in which the customer has all the options that are available to him in 8.3.27*a* plus the additional option of having both soup and dessert. While what is offered has the form of a proposition, the offer need not entitle the recipient to make that proposition true in whatever way he pleases: the generosity of the offer is only broad enough to make the recipient entitled to more than what linguistically simpler alternatives entitle him to. For example, 8.3.27*a* entitles the hearer to take a soup and entitles him to take a dessert (since if he were not entitled to one of them, a linguistically simpler alternative such as *On the $1.50 lunch you get a soup* would express the full generosity of the offer) but does not entitle him to take both, any more than it entitles him to take two soups or two desserts. The illusion of an exclusive *or* in sentences like 8.3.27 results from the fact they relate to the transfer of entitlements from one person to another and that entitlements do not change unless some act of the current owner causes them to change; only as little entitlement is transferred as is consistent with the statement of what is transferred, interpreted in light of the maxims of quantity, manner, and relevance.

Before closing this section, it is necessary to devote some discussion to another kind of 'implicature', which Grice contrasts with the 'conversational implicature' that has figured in the discussion so far. Grice applies the term CONVENTIONAL IMPLICATURE in cases where (i) from the fact that a person has uttered a given sentence, it follows that he accepts (if he is being sincere) a certain proposition p, (ii) the speaker has not 'said that p' in uttering the sentence, and (iii) p is not conversationally implicated by the utterance. Grice illustrates conventional implicature in terms of the contrast between 8.3.30*a* and 8.3.30*b*:

8.3.30   a. He is an Englishman; he is, therefore, brave.
          b. He is an Englishman, and he is brave.

By uttering 8.3.30*a*, the speaker commits himself to the proposition that all Englishmen are brave; however, Grice maintains that that proposition is not part of what the speaker is saying in uttering 8.3.30*a*. Indeed, Grice maintains that the speaker is saying the same thing as if he had uttered 8.3.30*b* in particular, that the falsehood of the proposition that all Englishmen are brave does not mean that the speaker has uttered a falsehood in uttering 8.3.30*a*. For Grice, one asserts exactly the same proposition in uttering 8.3.30*a* as in uttering 8.3.30*b*, but the word *therefore* serves to bring in an implicature that otherwise would be absent (or at least, need not be present); this implicature is conventional, since it depends on the use of the word *therefore* and not just on the content of the sentence and on the principles of cooperation. Grice takes a similar view of *but*: it makes the same contribution to meaning as does *and* but carries with it a conventional implicature, roughly, that the speaker finds the second conjunct remarkable, given the truth of the first conjunct.

It is in fact quite difficult to demonstrate that a putative conventional implicature is really that, particularly in view of the difficulty of establishing what has been 'said' and not just 'implicated'. For example, instead of analyzing *A, therefore B* as *A and B* plus a conventional implicature, one might treat it as *A, and if A then B*, without any conventional implicature. In classical logic, $\wedge AB$ and $\wedge(A, \supset AB)$ are deductively equivalent. However, sentences corresponding to those two logical forms need not have the same conversational implicatures, and $\supset AB$ would just as much conversationally implicate a causal or other connection between A and B when it is a covert part of a sentence as when it surfaces as a full-fledged conditional sentence. Sentences such as the following provide some evidence that this alternative is preferable to Grice's analysis:[16]

8.3.31   It's not the case that John is English and is therefore brave—
          a. He's Hungarian.
          b. Englishmen aren't all brave, though John in fact *is* brave.

In 8.3.31*b* the speaker is not denying the conjunction $\wedge$ (John is English, John is brave); rather, he is denying the proposition that if John is English, then he is brave. Of course, in saying that, I am assuming that denying a conditional proposition does not consist merely in asserting the antecedent and denying the consequent; see the discussion above of Cohen's objections to Grice's analysis.

But provides a more plausible case of conventional implicature. Note that in the following sentences one cannot deny the proposition by denying the implicature that the speaker expects rich people to be intelligent:

8.3.32   It's not the case that John is rich but stupid—
    a. indeed, he's quite smart.
    b. ?indeed, he doesn't have a lot of wealth.
    c. *indeed, I expect rich people to be stupid.
    c'. *indeed, rich people generally are stupid.

Even appears to contribute nothing but a conventional implicature to the meaning of sentences in which it is used. For example, 8.3.33a conventionally implicates that others besides Carter favor deregulating air transport and its 'meaning' in the narrow sense is simply that Carter favors deregulating air transport:[17]

8.3.33   a. Even Carter favors deregulating air transport.
    b. Does even Carter favor deregulating air transport?
      i. Yes, he favors it.
      ii. *No, he's the only one who favors it.
      iii. ?Yes, though no one else favors it.

Note that 8.3.33a is true or false depending on whether Carter favors deregulating air transport or not, as is shown by the preferred choices of *Yes* and *No* in the answers to 8.3.33b, and if no one else favors it, that makes 8.3.33a only inappropriate, not false.[18]

8.4. Exercises

1. In each of the following cases, identify whether the proposition indicated in parentheses is a logical implication, a conversational implicature, or a conventional implicature of the given sentence, or none of the preceding.

  a. There was a package on the table. (there was only one package on the table)
  b. There were packages on the table. (there was more than one package on the table)
  c. Tom is a linguist, but he doesn't smoke pot. (linguists usually smoke pot)

2. Could a proposition be simultaneously logically implied and conventionally implicated by a given sentence? If so, give an example; if not, show why.

3. What ought one to make of the fact that 7.5.2a (*The king and queen are an excellent battery*) is normally interpreted as implying that the king is the pitcher and the queen the catcher and not vice versa?

4. What is wrong with the following analysis (Grice 1975: 53), in which a conveyed proposition is treated as a conversational implicature resulting from exploitation of the maxim of quality:

'X, with whom A has been on close terms until now, has betrayed a secret of A's to a business rival. A and his audience both know this. A says *X is a fine friend*. (Gloss: It is perfectly obvious to A and his audience that what A has said or has made as if to say is something that he does not believe, and the audience knows that A knows that this is obvious to the audience. So, unless A's utterance is entirely pointless, A must be trying to get across some other proposition than the one he purports to be putting forward. This must be some obviously related proposition; the most obviously related proposition is the contradictory of the one he purports to be putting forward.)'

Compare Grice's example with the following two:

i. Tom is visiting Dick's new apartment. The apartment is warm but not extremely so. Dick has just been complaining about the many defects of the apartment. Tom says *Can you open the window*? intending thereby to get Dick to open the window.
ii. George and Martha are eating in a Chinese restaurant, talking about baseball. Tom says *I don't want any soy sauce*, intending thereby to get Martha to pass him the soy sauce, which is on Martha's side of the table.

9. Presupposition

9.1. Kinds of Presupposition

The word 'presupposition' has been used by both linguists and philosophers to cover a class of phenomena that is not obviously homogeneous. Sometimes one speaks of a proposition presupposing another proposition, sometimes of a sentence (in its surface form) presupposing a proposition, sometimes of a person presupposing something in uttering a sentence. Linguists also occasionally speak of a word as presupposing a proposition.

One notion of presupposition that has been studied fairly widely is that of SEMANTIC PRESUPPOSITION, which is a relation between two propositions and has to do with truth value assignments. It involves an important modification of the notion of assignment of truth values assumed so far, namely, giving up the assumption that a proposition is always either true or false. The possibility of a proposition being neither true nor false is not outlandish; indeed, it is fairly reasonable in the case of propositions like that expressed by 9.1.1a, for which the question of their truth does not arise unless some other proposition (in this case, 9.1.1b) is true:

9.1.1   a. Nixon$_i$ regrets that he$_i$ is a member of the SLA.
            b. Nixon is a member of the SLA.

Let us admit the possibility of valuations in which some propositions are assigned neither the value T nor the value F. As an aid to exposition, let us speak of a proposition having the value $\#$ (which I like to read as 'Tilt') when it has neither the value T nor the value F. Just as not all assignments of T and F to a set of propositions deserve to be given serious consideration, neither will all assignments of T, F, and $\#$. In particular, a proposition should only be assigned $\#$ for a reason, and the constraints on assigning T, F, and $\#$ must reflect the reasons for which a proposition could lack a truth value.

One obvious restriction to impose on assignments of T, F, and $\#$ is that a proposition is $\#$ if and only if its negation is $\#$, that is, that a proposition and its negation have the same presuppositions. Assuming that we are attempting to conform as much as possible to classical logic and thus to avoid assignments in which a proposition and its negation can be simultaneously true or simultaneously false, we arrive at the following truth table for negation:

9.1.2

A	$\sim$A
T	F
F	T
#	#

What further modifications must be made in the principles of truth value assignment and in the rules of inference will for the time being be left up in the air. For the moment, I will speak vaguely of 'coherent assignments of truth values', meaning roughly assignments of the truth values T, F, # for which (i) the previously presented rules of inference and principles of truth value assignment require only relatively minor modification in order that the rules of inference always lead from true premises to true conclusions even when truth value assignments involving # are allowed, and (ii) # is assigned precisely to those propositions for which there is a reason for them to lack a 'real' truth value.

The following definition of sematic presupposition has frequently been offered:

9.1.3   A semantically presupposes B if A ⊩ B and $\sim$A ⊩ B.

That is, A semantically presupposes B if whenever A is true, B is true, and whenever $\sim$A is true (that is, by virtue of 9.1.2, whenever A is false), B is true. 'A ≫ B' is used to symbolize 'A semantically presupposes B'. This definition allows for 'trivial presuppositions', that is, cases where B fits 9.1.3 only because B is true in every state of affairs. For example, if B is 'Either there is a Santa Claus or there isn't a Santa Claus', then no matter what A is, whenever A is true, B will be true, and whenever A is false, B will be true, and thus any proposition whatever presupposes that either there is a Santa Claus or there isn't a Santa Claus. For a proposition to have 'nontrivial' presuppositions, it must have TRUTH VALUE GAPS, that is, there must be states of affairs in which it is assigned #. This follows from the fact that if A ≫ B and in some coherent assignment of truth values, B is not true (i.e., is either F or #), then in that assignment of truth values, A can be neither true nor false, since if it were true, B would be true (since A ⊩ B), and if it were false, B would be true (since $\sim$A ⊩ B), contrary to hypothesis that B is not true. It should be noted, though, that before we can apply 9.1.3 to any concrete cases, we must specify what is to count as a 'coherent assignment of truth values'. 'A ⊩ B' means 'in all (coherent) truth value assignments in which A is true, B is also true', and to determine whether that condition is met one will have to be able to tell whether a given truth value assignment in which B is F or # is 'coherent'.

There are a variety of linguistic phenomena to which the term 'presupposition' has been applied which do not conform to the definition given for semantic presupposition. For example, 9.1.4 has been said to presuppose rather than assert that the neighbor is female:

9.1.4   My neighbor has hurt herself.

This is not a case of semantic presupposition, since the falsehood of the proposition that the neighbor is female does not make 9.1.4 lack a truth value, nor does it make 9.1.4 false. If the neighbor is a male transvestite whom the speaker takes to be a woman, 9.1.4 is still true or false, depending on whether the neighbor has hurt himself or not, despite the speaker's incorrect choice of a pronoun to refer to the neighbor. It neither asserts nor semantically presupposes that the neighbor is female: it rather PRAGMATIC-ALLY PRESUPPOSES it; that is, the neighbor's being female is a condition on the appropriateness of the use of 9.1.4 rather than a necessary condition for the proposition expressed by 9.1.4 to have a truth value.

The relationship between 9.1.5 and the proposition that the person addressed is called Sam is then also a case of pragmatic presupposition:

9.1.5   You know, Sam, China is industrializing rapidly.

If the addressee is not called Sam, the utterance is inappropriate, though the proposition which it expresses is true or false depending on whether China is or is not industrializing rapidly, regardless of the name of the person to whom the utterance is addressed. Similarly with the relationship between 9.1.6 and the proposition that the speaker has the authority to order the addressee to give him the tapes:

9.1.6   Mr. President, I order you to give me all your tapes.

The proposition that he has such authority is not a necessary condition for 9.1.6 to have a truth value, since only by stretching the terms 'true' and 'false' could one speak of 9.1.6 as having a truth value (even the truth value #). The way in which those terms might be stretched would be to speak of an occurrence of 9.1.6 as being true if the speaker did in fact thereby order the addressee to give him all the tapes (and either false or truth-valueless otherwise). However, such usage obscures the systematic difference between the presuppositions of 9.1.4–9.1.6 and the semantic presupposition of 9.1.1: semantic presupposition is a relationship between two propositions, whereas pragmatic presupposition is a relationship between an utterance and a proposition. In ordinary usage, utterances are not said to be true or false (though propositions involved in those utterances are said to be true or false: recall the discussion of 9.1.4). While one might respond to an utterance of 9.1.5 by saying *That's false*, the *that* would refer not to the utterance but to the proposition that China is industrializing rapidly. Note that according to what has just been said, the presupposition in 9.1.7 that Nixon is a member of the SLA is only a pragmatic, not a semantic presupposition:

9.1.7   Does Nixon$_i$ regret that he$_i$ is a member of the SLA?

This fact is somewhat disturbing in that the source of the pragmatic presupposition in 9.1.7 is exactly the same as the source of the semantic presupposition in the corresponding declarative 9.1.1*a*, namely, the 'factive' predicate *regret*. However, this need not be a cause for worry, since in general an utterance asserting a proposition with a semantic presupposition B will pragmatically presuppose B; for example, not only does the proposition that Nixon regrets that he is a member of the SLA semantically presuppose that Nixon is a member of the SLA, but an utterance in which one asserts that Nixon regrets that he is a member of the SLA will pragmatically presuppose that Nixon is a member of the SLA.

At least two distinct notions of 'pragmatic presupposition' can be distinguished. In addition to the notion that we have just been discussing ('proposition which must be true for the utterance to be "appropriate"'), there is a more restricted notion, which figures prominently in Karttunen 1974: an utterance presupposes a proposition if that utterance is acceptable only at a point in a discourse where that proposition is in the set of propositions that the parties to the discourse take as established. For example, an utterance of 9.1.1*a* pragmatically presupposes 9.1.1*b* in this sense, since it is only normal for a person to assert 9.1.1*a* if either 9.1.1*b* (or propositions entailing 9.1.1*b*) has been asserted by one of the parties to the discourse and assented to by the others, or 9.1.1*b* is something that the parties to the discourse recognize as common knowledge. By contrast, *My neighbor has hurt herself* does not presuppose that the neighbor is a woman, in Karttunen's sense of 'presuppose', since a person can say *My neighbor has hurt herself* even if he knows that the other parties to the discourse do not know the sex of his neighbor. If one of the parties to a discourse cannot assume that the other parties assume that Nixon is a member of the SLA, he can assert that Nixon regrets that he is a member of the SLA only if he first asserts (and gets at least tacit assent from the others) that Nixon is a member of the SLA. However, a person who wishes to say *My neighbor has hurt herself* to a person who does not know the sex of the neighbor not only does not have to first assert that the neighbor is a woman—indeed it would be rather bizarre behavior on his part if he did. Similarly with the presupposition that the addressee is called Sam in the case of 9.1.5: if the speaker knows that one of the parties to the discourse does not know Sam's name, the speaker is not obliged to introduce that person to Sam before addressing his remark to Sam.

9.2. Some Possible Cases of Semantic Presupposition

Sentences containing *regret*, *realize*, *surprise(d)*, *strange*, and a fairly large number of other verbs, predicate adjectives, and predicate nouns which take a clause as subject or object are widely held to presuppose that clause, as in the following pairs of sentences (9.2.1–9.2.4), where the proposition expressed by 9.2.1*a* can reasonably be held to semantically presuppose that expressed by 9.2.1*b*, that is, for the first sentence to be either true or false, the second sentence must be true:

9.2.1   a. Cecil is aware that Marcia is pregnant.
           b. Marcia is pregnant.

9.2.2   a. The Senator$_i$ didn't reveal that he$_i$ had spent the winter in Monaco.
           b. The Senator spent the winter in Monaco.

9.2.3   a. It's odd that Oliver didn't kiss Pauline.
           b. Oliver didn't kiss Pauline.

9.2.4   a. The public doesn't realize that Nauru threatens our security.
           b. Nauru threatens our security.

These elements are know as FACTIVE PREDICATES and are discussed in detail in Kiparsky and Kiparsky (1970) and Karttunen (1971*b*, 1971*c*).

These examples should be contrasted with parallel examples involving other predicates, where the falsehood of the complement sentence does not remove the whole sentence from the realm of truth and falsehood:

9.2.1′   Cecil is afraid that Marcia is pregnant.

9.2.2′   The Senator didn't state that he had spent the winter in Monaco.

9.2.3′   It's likely that Oliver didn't kiss Pauline.

9.2.4′   The public doesn't believe that Nauru threatens our security.

Cecil can be afraid that Marcia is pregnant regardless of whether Marcia actually is pregnant; the Senator can state that he spent the winter in Monaco regardless of whether he actually spent the winter there, and so on.

Thus the falsehood of the complement of *afraid*, *state*, and the like has no direct bearing on whether the whole proposition has a 'real' truth value.

Since the publication of Strawson 1950, 9.2.5 has been widely held to lack a truth value, given that there is at present no king of France:

9.2.5   The present king of France is bald.

Example 9.2.5 is then held to presuppose that there is one and only one king of France.

Example 9.2.5 is also widely held to be false, which is the position taken in Russell 1905 (whose analysis is discussed above in 7.1), the paper that made 9.2.5 one of the standard examples of the philosophical literature and which Strawson 1950 constituted an attack on. Strawson (1964) takes great care to point out that two distinct issues are raised by 9.2.5: first, is it defective in some way other than that for which the word 'false' is normally reserved? and, second, whatever other defects it may have, does it (also) have the defect of falsehood? Strawson recognized that in his initial critique of Russell's theory of definite descriptions he failed to keep those issues separate and incorrectly took his positive answer to the first question as implying a negative answer to the second; that is, he accepted in 1950 but rejected in 1964 the position that all presuppositions (at least in the case of declarative sentences) are semantic presuppositions.

Strawson (1964) observes that one can perfectly consistently say that 9.2.5 is false and in addition has the defect of having a false presupposition. He also points out a number of clear cases in which the existence presupposition that accompanies a definite description is false, yet the whole sentence is false rather than lacking a truth value. For example, suppose that 9.2.6 is uttered in a locality where there is no public swimming pool:

9.2.6   Fred spent yesterday afternoon at the public swimming pool.

The presupposition that there is a public swimming pool is false; yet 9.2.6 is clearly false rather than lacking in truth value. Similarly with 9.2.7, under the assumption that Jenny is a real person:

9.2.7   Jenny is dating the present king of France.

The fact that there is no king of France makes 9.2.7 false rather than lacking in truth value, though it still presupposes (in some sense) that there is a king of France.

What distinguishes cases like 9.2.5, which it is at least reasonable to say lack a truth value, from cases like 9.2.6 and 9.2.7 which are clearly false, cannot be just the fact that the relevant definite description is the subject in

9.2.5 but has another grammatical role in 9.2.6 and 9.2.7. Note that contrastive stress can change the behaviour of these examples; for example, in a context in which it has been established that someone is bald, 9.2.8 is false rather than lacking in truth value:

9.2.8   The kíng of Fránce is bald.

This point becomes even clearer if one notes that contrastive stress here has the same function as the 'cleft' construction, as in 9.2.9, which has a 'real' truth value (namely, false) provided that the presupposition contributed by the cleft construction (that someone is bald) is true:

9.2.9   It's the kíng of Fránce that is bald.

I conjecture that it is the notion of TOPIC rather than that of SUBJECT that determines whether the failure of a presupposition makes a proposition lack a truth value: in 9.2.5, one is saying of the present king of France that he is bald, whereas in 9.2.7, one is saying of Jenny that she is dating the king of France rather than of the king of France that Jenny is dating him, and in 9.2.9 and 9.2.8 one is saying of the propositional function 'x is bald' that the king of France is the one element of the given domain that satisfies it. In 9.2.5, one is predicating something of a nonexistent entity, whereas in 9.2.7 one is predicating something (a property which in fact no real object has) of the real person Jenny. However, I will drop this conjecture without making any concrete proposal on how the notion of 'topic' fits into logic.

It is worth remarking that the falsehood of the complement of a factive predicate likewise does not always make the whole sentence false:

9.2.10   What Nixon$_i$ regrets is that he$_i$ is a member of the SLA.

Under the assumption that Nixon regrets something and that Nixon is not a member of the SLA, 9.2.10 is false.[1]

Another presumable case of semantic presupposition is provided by IMPLICATIVE PREDICATES such as *manage, happen, have the foresight/ impudence, get to*, and the like (Karttunen 1971*b*, 1971*c*). Implicative predicates are predicates *f* having the property that $f(A)\Vdash A$ and $\sim f(A)\Vdash \sim A$; for example, if it is the case that John managed to open the window, it must be the case that he opened it, and if it is the case that John didn't manage to open the window, it must be the case that he didn't open it. However, this does not mean that 'X managed to do Y' and 'X did Y' always have the same truth value. 'X did Y' is a correct description of many states of affairs that could not correctly be described with 'X managed to do Y'. For example, if Mort is sound in mind and body and is not being subjected to constraints such as a straightjacket or hypnotism, 9.2.11*a* would be a weird thing to say even if 9.2.11*b* were true:

9.2.11   a. At 7:35, Mort managed to scratch his nose.
            b. At 7:35, Mort scratched his nose.

Manage carries with it a presupposition that the person will perform the action if and only if he overcomes some obstacle to performing it. Other implicative verbs have similar presuppositions; for example, *happen* is accompanied by the presupposition that the given event or state will come about if and only if chance brings it about, which is why 9.2.12*b* suggests a bizarre situation but 9.2.12*a* does not:

9.2.12   a. The waiter happened to give me the wrong change.
            b. The waiter happened to give me the right change.

Example 9.2.11*a* in the case where there is no obstacle to Mort's scratching his nose and 9.2.12*b* in the case where the waiter is willing and able to give the right change are somewhat less clear-cut cases of lack of truth value than were 9.2.5 and sentences in which the complement of a factive predicate is false, but it is still not at all unreasonable to treat them as lacking a truth value. The possibility of treating them as lacking a truth value raises important problems that will be touched on in the next section.

9.3. Supervaluations

Van Fraassen (1969) proposed a treatment of presuppositions based on the idea that valuations in which truth value gaps occur should agree as much as possible with classical valuations: for example, if A is false, then ∧ AB ought to be false no matter what truth value B has (thus, even if B is #), and ∨ (A, ∼A) ought to be true no matter what the truth value of A is (thus, even if A is #). As a means toward implementing this policy, van Fraassen introduced the notion of SUPERVALUATION. A supervaluation is an assignment of truth values according to which certain propositions are assigned 'classical' truth values (T and F) and the remaining propositions are assigned T, F, or # on the basis of what the classical truth tables plus the given partial assignment of T's and F's forces on one. Specifically, one considers the set of all classical valuations that assign to the given propositions the agreed upon values; for any other proposition, if those valuations all assign it the same value, we assign it that value, but if those valuations do not all assign it the same value (i.e., some of them make it T and others make it F), we assign it the value #. The formal definition of supervaluation given by van Fraassen is as follows: for any consistent set of propositions X, the supervaluation v_X induced by X (i.e., the assignment of truth values which makes the propositions of X true but makes only as much else true as is forced by the classical truth tables) is the assignment of truth values such that

9.3.1   a. $v_X A = T$ if $X \Vdash_c A$ (that is, if every classical valuation which all members of X true makes A true)

b. $v_X A = F$ if $X \Vdash_c \sim A$ (that is, if every classical valuation which makes all members of X true makes A false).

c. $v_X A = \#$ otherwise (that is, if some of the classical valuations that make all members of X true make A true and others of them make A false).

For example, to assign truth values in such a way that p is T, q is F, and r is $\#$, we use the supervaluation induced by $\{p, \sim q\}$. According to that supervaluation, $\lor pr$ will be T (since any classical valuation that makes p true will make $\lor pq$ true), $\land qr$ will be F (since any classical valuation that makes $\sim q$ T will make q F and thus will make $\land qr$ F), and $\supset pr$ will be $\#$ (since, of the classical valuations that make p T and q F, those which make r T will make $\supset pr$ T, and those which make r F will make $\supset pr$ F).

We could describe a supervaluation as an assignment of T, F, and $\#$ such that T or F is assigned to a complex proposition when those constituents of the complex proposition which are $\#$ 'don't matter', in the sense that if they were assigned T or F instead (in a manner consistent with the classical truth tables), the classical truth tables would assign the whole proposition the same truth value regardless of how the $\#$'s were replaced by T's and F's.

The notion of supervaluation is a generalization of the notion of classical valuation, in that every classical valuation is a supervaluation. Specifically, for any classical valuation v, define Y as $\{A : v(A) = T\}$. Then one can easily verify that v_Y, the supervaluation induced by Y, is identical to v: there is only one classical valuation that assigns the value T to all members of Y, namely, v, which means that $v_Y(A) = T$ if and only if $v(A) = T$, and $v_Y(A) = F$ if and only if $v(A) = F$. However, there are also supervaluations which are not classical valuations, that is, supervaluations in which there are truth value gaps; those will be the v_X for which, roughly speaking, X is not large enough to fix the truth values of all propositions.

Supervaluations give rise to truth tables for the propositional connectives, in the sense that if only supervaluations are allowed as assignments of truth values, only certain combinations of truth values for a complex proposition and for its pieces are possible. Trivially, van Fraassen's system yields the following truth table for negation:

9.3.2

A	~A
T	F
F	T
#	#

This follows from the fact that any classical valuation assigns A and ~A opposite truth values; thus, if all classical valuations that make all members of X true make A true, then all classical valuations that make all members of X true make ~A false.

The truth table for $\wedge$ is

9.3.3

$\wedge$ B			
A	T	F	#
T	T	F	#
F	F	F	F
#	#	F	F/#

Suppose that for some set X of propositions, all classical valuations that make all members of X true make A false; then all classical valuations that make all members of X true make $\wedge$ AB false, regardless of what B is (since a classical valuation makes an *and*-conjunction false whenever one of its conjuncts is false); thus any supervaluation that makes A false will also make $\wedge$ AB false, regardless of what B is, and thus F's appear is all three cells of the second row of the table. Consider the case where some supervaluation v_x makes A T and B #; all classical valuations that make all members of X true make A true, but some of them make B true and others of them make B false; the former valuations make $\wedge$ AB true and the latter ones make $\wedge$ AB false, which means that v_x makes $\wedge$ AB #. Thus there is a # as the entry in the last cell in the first row. In the case of A # and B #, $\wedge$ is non-truth-functional. Consider a supervaluation v_x which A # and B #; some of the classical valuations that make all members of X true make A true and some of them make A false, and some of them make B true and some of them make B false. It can't be the case that all classical valuations that make all members of X true will make $\wedge$ AB true, since that could happen only if they all made A true and all made B true, which is not the case here. Whether they all make $\wedge$ AB false will depend on details of A and B; if A happens to be inconsistent with B, for example, it is the negation of B, then $\wedge$ AB will be false under all classical valuations (even those which don't make all members of X true); however, if A and B are unrelated (e.g., if A is 'Ford regrets that he is a member of the SLA' and B is 'The commander-in-chief of the Nebraskan navy plays the bassoon'), some classical valuations will make both true (and thus make $\wedge$ AB true) and others will make one or both of them false (and thus make $\wedge$ AB false). Thus both F and $\#$ are possible values for $\wedge$ AB in supervaluations that make A $\#$ and B $\#$.

The truth tables for $\vee$ and $\supset$ that emerge from van Fraassen's treatment are as in 9.3.4, which the reader should verify for himself:

9.3.4

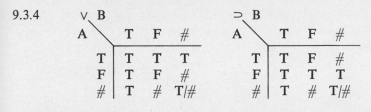

In the notion of supervaluation developed in the last couple of pages, no particular restriction has been placed on what propositions can fail to have a truth value: aside from tautologies (which will be true under any supervaluation, since they are true under any classical valuation) and contradictions (which will be false under any supervaluation, since they are false under any classical valuation), any proposition is a potential truth value gap. This may allow too free a use of truth value gaps. For example, there are certain propositions which are presupposition-free and which one could thus have no reason ever to want to say lacked a truth value (e.g., 'There are unicorns', 'Some isotopes of copper are radioactive', 'If all men are mortal, then Socrates is mortal'), and nothing so far rules out supervaluations in which some of those propositions lack a truth value; and there is nothing so far to rule out supervaluations in which 'Nixon is Jewish' is true but nonetheless 'Nixon regrets that he is Jewish' lacks a truth value.

One step toward eliminating such bizarre occurrences of $\#$ would be to supplement the apparatus of classical logic with a notion of what van Fraassen calls 'non-classical necessitation', that is, a relation A N B between propositions, which is to reflect the meanings of items of non-logical vocabulary (e.g., N might be such that Regret(x, A) N A), with only those classical valuations being taken into account which 'respect' the nonclassical necessitation relation, that is, for a classical valuation v to be taken into account in defining the admissible supervaluations, if A N B and v(A) = T, then v(B) must be T. We can then redefine v_x(A) so that it will be T if all ADMISSIBLE classical valuations that make all members of X T make A T. If N is such that Regret(x, A) N A, then supervaluations in which A is F but Regret(x, A) is T are excluded, since any admissible classical valuation which makes Regret(x, A) T will make A T.

What we have just said is not enough to insure that when A is T, Regret(x, A) will not be $\#$, and indeed there is no nonclassical necessitation relation that will accomplish that, other than one which conflicts with the meaning of *regret* (e.g., A N Regret(x, A) would exclude a supervaluation in which A is T and Regret(x, A) is $\#$; but such an N would be absurd, since in fact the truth of A does not insure the truth of 'x regrets that A'). To exclude such supervaluations and still have a reasonable N, one must allow only those supervaluations in which the truth value gaps are forced on one (rather than just permitted) by the relation N. For example, if A N B and $\sim$ A N B, then when B is F or $\#$, A must be $\#$ (i.e., if it were T or F, then B would be T); in this case, N forces a truth value gap on any supervaluation that makes B F or $\#$. Van Fraassen distinguishes between CONSERVATIVE presuppositional systems, in which only those truth value gaps are admitted which are forced on one by N,[2] and RADICAL presuppositional systems, in which all supervaluations that conform to N are allowed, even those which have more truth value gaps than are forced by N.

If all supervaluations are admitted, the same propositions are valid and the same entailments hold as in classical logic. Let $\Vdash_c$ stand for validity and entailment relative to the classical valuations (i.e., $\Vdash_c$ A means that A is true in all classical valuations—'is classically valid'—and X$\Vdash_c$ A means that in all classical valuations which make all propositions of X true, A is true—X 'classically entails' A), and let $\Vdash_s$ stand for validity and entailment relative to the set of all supervaluations. It can easily be shown that $\Vdash_c$ A if and only if $\Vdash_s$ A. Note first that it is trivially true that if $\Vdash_s$ A, then $\Vdash_c$ A (every classical valuation is a supervaluation, and thus, if every supervaluation makes A true, then in particular, every classical valuation does), so we need only prove that if $\Vdash_c$ A, then $\Vdash_s$ A. Suppose that $\Vdash_c$ A, and consider any supervaluation v_X. Every classical valuation makes A true, so in particular, every classical valuation that makes all propositions of X true makes A true; but that means that $v_X(A) = T$. Thus, every supervaluation makes A true, that is, $\Vdash_s$ A. It can be shown similarly that for any proposition A and any set of propositions X, X$\Vdash_c$ A if and only if X$\Vdash_s$ A. As before, it is trivially true that if X$\Vdash_s$ A, then X$\Vdash_c$ A, so all that needs to be shown is that when classical entailment holds, supervaluation entailments holds. Suppose that X$\Vdash_c$ A, and let v_Y be any supervaluation that makes all members of X true. Let v be any classical valuation that makes all members of Y true. Then v makes all members of X true (since any classical valuation that makes all members of Y true makes all members of X true—that's what it means to say that v_Y makes all members of X true), and hence $v(A) = T$ (since any classical valuation that makes all members of X true makes A true). But that implies that $v_Y(A) = T$, and thus all supervaluations that make all members of X true make A true, that is, X$\Vdash_s$ A.

Since the supervaluations of any radical presuppositional system are a subset of the set of all supervaluations, and the set of supervaluations of any conservative presuppositional system is a subset of the set of supervaluations of the corresponding radical presuppositional system, it is the case that if $\Vdash_s A$, then $\Vdash_{\mathbf{N}r} A$, and if $\Vdash_{\mathbf{N}r} A$, then $\Vdash_{\mathbf{N}c} A$, where $\Vdash_{\mathbf{N}r}$ means 'valid relative to the supervaluations of the radical presuppositional system defined by the necessitation relation $\mathbf{N}$', and $\Vdash_{\mathbf{N}c}$ means 'valid relative to the supervaluations of the conservative presuppositional system defined by the necessitation relation $\mathbf{N}$'. It is not obvious that the converses of either of these statements hold; that is, it is not obvious that validity in a conservative presuppositional system implies validity in the corresponding radical system or that validity in a radical system implies validity relative to presuppositions in general (and thus classical validity). However, it is difficult to show that those converses fail, since the most obvious candidates for propositions valid relative to a restricted system of supervaluations but not valid with respect to a broader system turn out in fact not to be valid in either system. For example, given a relation $\mathbf{N}$ for which Regret(x, A) $\mathbf{N}$ A and $\sim$ Regret(x, A) $\mathbf{N}$ A, one might propose that $\supset$(Regret(x, A), A) will will be valid in the (radical or conservative) presuppositional system but invalid relative to supervaluations in general. However, it turns out that $\supset$(Regret(x, A), A) is invalid relative to the conservative presuppositional system. This follows from the fact that the conservative presuppositional system allows for supervaluations such that A is F and Regret(x, A) is $\#$. However, relative to any supervaluation, a conditional whose antecedent is $\#$ and whose consequent is F is $\#$, not T, and hence $\supset$(Regret(x, A), A) is not assigned the value T by all supervaluations of the conservative system.

While it is hard to determine whether the same propositions are valid relative to a conservative presuppositional system, the corresponding radical system, and supervaluations in general, it is easy to show that the entailments in a presuppositional system are generally not the same as entailments relative to supervaluations in general. For example, given the above $\mathbf{N}$, we have Regret(x, A)$\Vdash_{\mathbf{N}c} A$, but not Regret(x, A)$\Vdash_s A$. This follows from the fact that while supervaluations in general are not constrained to make A T when Regret(x, A) is T (indeed, relative to supervaluations in general, those two propositions count as unrelated atomic propositions and thus could be assigned any combination of truth values at all), the nonclassical necessitation relation for the presuppositional system in question allows a supervaluation to make Regret(x, A) T only if it also makes A T.

There is such a discrepancy between what can be proven about validity and what can be proven about entailment because the relationship which linked entailment to validity in the classical case fails in presuppositional systems: $\Vdash_{Nc} \supset AB$ is a stronger condition than $A \Vdash_{Nc} B$ (and similarly with $\Vdash_{Nr}$), since for the conditional to be valid there must be no admissible valuation than makes A # and B F, whereas for A to entail B it is immaterial whether such a case exists. Put another way, to say that A entails B in a given presuppositional system is to say that the boxed cases in the following table never arise, whereas to say that $\supset AB$ is valid in that system is to say that neither the boxed cases nor the circled cases ever arise:

9.3.5

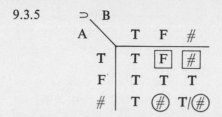

The kinds of considerations just discussed make it clear that there are significant discrepancies between classical logic and presuppositional systems with regard to what entailments follow from other entailments. For example, in classical logic, if $A \Vdash B$, then $\sim B \Vdash \sim A$. This follows from the facts that in classical logic the one entailment is equivalent to $\Vdash \supset AB$ and the other to $\Vdash \supset (\sim B, \sim A)$ and that in classical logic $\supset AB$ always has the same truth value as $\supset (\sim B, \sim A)$. However, in a presuppositional system (conservative or radical) with the relation N described above, there are formulas A and B such that A entails B but $\sim B$ does not entail $\sim A$. For example, we have seen that $\text{Regret}(x, B) \Vdash_N B$; however, it is not the case that $\sim B \Vdash_N \sim \text{Regret}(x, B)$, since (assuming that B is not a tautology) there will be a supervaluations for which B is F, and with respect to any such supervaluation, $\sim B$ is T, but $\sim \text{Regret}(x, B)$ is #, from which it follows that $\sim \text{Regret}(x, B)$ is not entailed (relative to the presuppositional system) by $\sim B$.

The last observation is important in understanding a set of facts that might at first glance seem to demand an analysis in which there is a pattern of truth value gaps other than what would correspond to a supervaluation. Recall the discussion of 'implicative verbs' in 9.2, where it was suggested that *manage* has a presupposition that an obstacle must be overcome for the subject to carry out the action, and thus that, for example,

9.3.6   a. John managed to put milk in his coffee.
             b. John didn't manage to put milk in his coffee.

would lack a truth value in a state of affairs in which there was no obstacle to John's putting milk in his coffee. The following combinations of truth values would then be possible, using A to stand for 'John put milk in his coffee' and *m*A for 'John managed to put milk in his coffee':

9.3.7

A	*m*A
T	T/#
F	F/#
#	#

(Note that when A is #, *m*A must be # also; if *m*A were T or F, then A would be T or F, respectively). The following sentence looks as if it expresses an unassailable proposition:

9.3.8 If John managed to put milk in his coffee, then he put milk in his coffee.

However, according to the truth tables for supervaluations, ⊃(*m*A, A) does not always come out true:

9.3.9

A	*m*A	⊃(*m*A, A)
T	T	T
T	#	T
F	F	T
F	#	#
#	#	#[3]

Moreover, if ⊃AB is true in a given supervaluation, so is ⊃(~B, ~A); this follows from the fact that that is true of classical valuations. However, 9.3.10 does not have the ring of truth to it that 9.3.8 does:

9.3.10 If John didn't put milk in his coffee, then he didn't manage to put milk in his coffee.

in that the antecedent can clearly be true without the consequent being true.

There are several ways that one might react to these observations. (i) One might reject the idea that *manage* carries with it a semantic presupposition, and thus maintain that the cases where *m*A is # do not arise. (ii) One might take the facts about implicative verbs as showing that T, F, and # must be assigned in ways other than those which a system of supervaluations allows: that ⊃(*m*A, A) must always be T but ⊃(~A, ~*m*A) need not always be T, in spite of the fact that in a supervaluation treatment, not only is ⊃(*m*A, A) not always T, but when it is T, so is ⊃(~A, ~*m*A). (iii) One might challenge the interpretation of 9.3.8 as ⊃(*m*A, A) and instead interpret it as meaning *m*A⊩A. I am inclined to rate the third as the most attractive of the three alternatives. Note that while the truth of ⊃(*m*A, A) insures the truth of ⊃(~A, ~*m*A) in a presuppositional system,

mA⊩A does not insure ~A⊩~mA. According to 9.3.9, mA⊩A is true (i.e., in the one case where mA is T, A is also T), but ~A⊩~mA is not true, since the two cases in which ~A is T (the third and fourth lines of 9.3.9) include a case in which ~mA is not T (the fourth line). Thus, the fact that mA⊩A but not ~A⊩~mA parallels the fact that one would more readily call 9.3.8 true than 9.3.10.

It is worth recalling that in the preceding chapter we also encountered considerations that suggested that *if* should be interpreted as ⊩ rather than as ⊃. Recall the discussion of example 8.3.15 and the suggestion that, to account for the fact that *It is not the case that if God is dead, then everything is permitted* is not normally taken to imply that God is dead, it may be appropriate to analyze the example as having an understood quantifier in it: 'It is not the case that for all states of affairs w, if God is dead in w, then everything is permitted in w'. But that suggestion is essentially identical to the suggestion that *if* be interpreted as ⊩: the suggested analysis is equivalent to 'It is not the case that in all states of affairs in which God is dead, everything is permitted'; that is, it is not the case that 'God is dead' semantically entails 'everything is permitted' (with the understanding, of course, that this entailment is with regard to some restricted class of possible states of affairs and not with regard to the whole set of classical valuations).

If one were to adopt position ii, however, it would be necessary not only to devise something other than supervaluations as the system for assigning T, F, and # to complex propositions, but also to change the rules of inference so that ⊃(~B, ~A) was not in general inferrable from ⊃AB. The most obvious derivation of ⊃(~B, ~A) from ⊃AB is the following:

9.3.11   1 ⊃AB

      2   ~B   supp

      3   A   supp

      4   B   1, 3, ⊃-elim
      5   ~B   2, reit
      6   ~A   3–5, ~-intro
      7 ⊃(~B, ~A) 2–6, ⊃-intro

The step in 9.3.11 that it seems most reasonable to disallow if nontrivial presuppositions are allowed is step 6, since under the assumptions about implicative verbs which go with proposal ii, there are coherent assignments of truth values fitting the following scheme:

9.3.12   ⊃AB   T
        ~B   T
        ~A   #

Steps 1 and 2 set up hypotheses that are true relative to such an assignment of truth values. However, step 6 derives a nontrue conclusion from those true premises. One obvious way to weaken the suspect rule of inference, $\sim$-intro, would be to change it from 9.3.13a to 9.3.13b:

9.3.13   a. $\begin{array}{|l} A \\ \;\ldots \\ B \\ \sim B \\ \hline \sim A \end{array}$ b. $\begin{array}{|l} A \\ \;\ldots \\ B \\ \sim B \\ \hline \sim tA \end{array}$

where tA means 'A is true' and has the truth table

9.3.14

A	tA
T	T
F	F
#	F

Note that $\sim t(\sim A)$ would have been innocuous as a deduction from lines 1 and 2: it would likewise be true. However, it would not have allowed the deduction of line 7, since there is no way to get from $\sim t(\sim A)$ to A if nontrivial presuppositions are allowed: $\sim t(\sim A)$ is true not only when A is T but also when it is #.

9.4. Pragmatic Presupposition

This section is devoted to the notion of a presupposition of a sentence as a proposition which the speaker 'takes for granted' when he utters the sentence, that is, a proposition which either has been established in the preceding discourse or the speaker can assume that the parties to the discourse will agree to. I will begin by describing an approach to presupposition which was in fact originally framed in terms of semantic presupposition (i.e., in terms of conditions under which a proposition will lack a truth value), but which developed in a natural way into an account of pragmatic presupposition which can be divorced entirely from considerations of truth value gaps.

Karttunen 1973 is devoted to the question of the conditions under which a proposition of the form $\wedge AB$, $\vee AB$, or $\supset AB$ shares the presuppositions of the constituent propositions A and B. Let us begin with Karttunen's treatment of $\wedge$. Karttunen claims that $\wedge AB$ shares any presuppositions of A; for example, 9.4.1a and 9.4.2a presuppose 9.4.1b and 9.4.2b, respectively:

9.4.1   a. John regrets that he beats his wife, and he intends to reform.
          b. John beats his wife.

9.4.2   a. The king of France is bald and the archbishop of Mt. Isa is
              deaf.
            b. There is a king of France.

However, Karttunen maintains that whether $\land$ AB shares the presuppositions of B depends on how A and B are related, as illustrated by the
difference between 9.4.3*a* and 9.4.4*a*:

9.4.3   a. Ford$_i$ belongs to the SLA, and Kissinger$_j$ regrets that he$_j$
              belongs to the IRA.
            b. Kissinger belongs to the IRA

9.4.4   a. Ford$_i$ belongs to the SLA, and he$_i$ is ashamed that he$_i$
              belongs to the SLA.
            b. Ford belongs to the SLA.

Example 9.4.3*a* clearly presupposes 9.4.3*b*, at least in the sense that it
would be improper to assert 9.4.3*a* in a context where one could not take
it for granted that Kissinger belonged to the IRA. Karttunen accordingly
claimed that 9.4.3*a* was # in any state of affairs in which Kissinger did not
belong to the IRA. (Note, of course, that in a supervaluation treatment,
the falsehood of the first conjunct of 9.4.3*a* would make the whole conjoined proposition false rather than lacking in truth value.) In contrast,
Karttunen held that 9.4.4*a* is false rather than # when 9.4.4*b* is false, despite
the fact that, just as in 9.4.3*a*, the first conjunct is false and the second
conjunct involves a factive predicate with a false complement. While it is
not clear that Karttunen is correct in holding that 9.4.3*a* and 9.4.4*a* differ
in truth value, they do clearly differ with regard to pragmatic presupposition: one could assert 9.4.4*a* even when the proposition that Ford belongs
to the SLA (the presupposition of the second conjunct) was new to the
discourse.

Karttunen notes that the behavior of examples like 9.4.4*a* is shared by
examples like 9.4.5*a*, in which the presupposition of the second conjunct
is not identical to but is merely entailed by the first conjunct:

9.4.5   a. Many people admire Nixon, and Nixon is happy that there
              are people who admire him.
            b. There are people who admire Nixon.

In accordance with his policy that the pragmatic presupposition of 9.4.3*a*
was also a semantic presupposition, Karttunen formulated the following
statement of the presuppositions of $\land$ AB:

9.4.6 $\land$ AB $\gg$ C if and only if either
            (i) A $\gg$ C or
            (ii) B $\gg$ C and it is not the case that A⊩C.

Karttunen accordingly speaks of *and* as a FILTER: it allows some, but not necessarily all, of the presuppositions of the constituent propositions to be presuppositions of the whole proposition. He contrasts 'filter' with 'holes' and 'plugs'. A HOLE is an element h of logical structure which combines with propositions and has the property that if $A \gg C$, then $hA \gg C$. Factive predicates and negation are clear examples of holes. PLUGS are elements p such that the presuppositions of A have no bearing on the presuppositions of pA. Karttunen gives verbs of saying as an example of plugs: *John says that Nixon regrets that he is Jewish* presupposes that John exists, but not that Nixon is Jewish or even exists. Karttunen's claim that these verbs are plugs will be disputed in 11.2.

The conditions 9.4.6 imply that $\wedge$ has the following truth table:

9.4.7

$\wedge$	B		
A	T	F	#
T	T	F	#
F	F	F	F/(#)
#	#	(#)	(#)

The encircled entries in 9.4.7 are those for which Karttunen's 1973 treatment of presuppositions implies different truth values than does a supervaluation treatment. The entry in 9.4.7 for A T, B # would have to be #, since for B to be #, some semantic presupposition of B would have to fail, and that presupposition would not be entailed by A, since A is true. Note that according to Karttunen's treatment, $\wedge$ is not truth-functional: when A is F and B is #, further details about A and B have to be known in order to tell what the truth value of $\wedge$ AB is. In a supervaluation treatment, $\wedge$ is also non-truth-functional, but the deviation from truth-functionality is in a different place: not the case of A F, B #, but the case of A #, B #. When A and B are both false but are mutually contradictory, supervaluations make $\wedge$ AB false (because every classical valuation does), but Karttunen's treatment makes it # because of the presuppositional failure in the first conjunct.

Karttunen argued that the same conditions determine what the presuppositions of $\supset$ AB are:

9.4.8 $\supset$ AB $\gg$ C if and only if either
  (i) A $\gg$ C or
  (ii) B $\gg$ C and it is not the case that A⊢C.

This is supported by the parallelism between 9.4.3*a*–9.4.5*a* and 9.4.9–9.4.11:

9.4.9   If Ford$_i$ belongs to the SLA, then Kissinger$_j$ regrets that he$_j$ belongs to the IRA.

9.4.10   If Ford belongs to the SLA, then he is ashamed that he belongs to the SLA.

9.4.11   If many people admire Nixon$_i$, then he$_i$ is happy that there are people who admire him$_i$.

Consequently, for Karttunen 1973, $\supset$ has the following truth table:

9.4.12

$\supset$ B			
A	T	F	#
T	T	F	#
F	T	T	T/#
#	#	#	#

Karttunen found it somewhat less clear what the presuppositions of $\vee$ AB were. If one were to hold that $\vee$ AB must have the same presuppositions as $\supset (\sim A, B)$, its presuppositions would be given by

9.4.13 $\vee$ AB $\gg$ C if and only if either[4]
(i) A $\gg$ C or
(ii) B $\gg$ C and it is not the case that $\sim A \Vdash C$.

This rule would imply that 9.4.14*a* does not presuppose 9.4.14*b* but that 9.4.14*a'* does:

9.4.14   a. Either Nixon belongs to the Elks or he regrets that he doesn't belong to the Elks.
        a'. Either Nixon regrets that he doesn't belong to the Elks or he belongs to the Elks.
        b. Nixon doesn't belong to the Elks.

However, $\vee$ AB does not show the striking asymmetry between the conjuncts that $\wedge$ AB does, with regard to presupposition: 9.4.14*a'* is not an extremely odd thing to say in a context where one cannot take it for granted that Nixon does not belong to the Elks, though 9.4.15 is an extremely strange thing to say in that (or indeed any other) context:[5]

9.4.15   Nixon regrets that he doesn't belong to the Elks, and he doesn't belong to the Elks.

In a later paper (1974), Karttunun leans more toward the policy that $\vee$ is symmetric with regard to presupposition (i.e., that in both 9.4.14*a* and 9.4.14*a'*, 'Nixon belongs to the SLA' filters out the presupposition of 'Nixon regrets that he doesn't belong to the SLA'). Karttunen gives the following example, which more clearly involves such symmetry:

9.4.16   a. Either Bill didn't write any letters, or all of his letters were intercepted.

> b. Either all of Bill's letters were intercepted, or he didn't write any.

(the presupposition at issue is the presupposition that there were letters from Bill: Karttunen takes *all* as carrying an existence presupposition). Accordingly, Karttunen gave the following alternative to 9.4.14:

9.4.17 $\vee$ AB $\gg$ C if and only if either
(i) A $\gg$ C and it is not the case that $\sim$ B$\Vdash$C, or
(ii) B $\gg$ C and it is not the case that $\sim$ A$\Vdash$C.

The truth tables corresponding to 9.4.13 and 9.4.17 are 9.4.18*a* and 9.4.18*b*, respectively:

9.4.18   a.

$\vee$ B A	T	F	#
T	T	T	T/#
F	T	F	#
#	#	#	#

b.

$\vee$ B A	T	F	#
T	T	T	T/#
F	T	F	#
#	T/#	#	#

The following sort of example, which Karttunen 1973 discusses briefly but which plays a more central role in his later papers, creates a problem for the approach just outlined that can be solved only by dealing more explicitly with the relationship of utterances to the contexts in which they are uttered. Given assumptions that the readers of this chapter are likely to share, 9.4.14*a* no more presupposes 9.4.19*b* than 9.4.5*a* presupposes 9.4.5*b*:

9.4.19   a. Carter has appointed Angela Davis Secretary of the Interior, and he regrets that he has appointed a black militant to the cabinet.
            b. Carter has appointed a black militant to the cabinet.

However, if the $\Vdash$ of 9.4.6 is 'classical entailment', then in 9.4.19*a* the condition for 'filtering out' the presupposition of the second conjunct is not met: the proposition that Carter has appointed Angela Davis Secretary of the Interior does not classically entail the proposition that he has appointed a black militant to the cabinet, since classical logic and the proposition that Carter has appointed Angela Davis Secretary of the Interior do not rule out states of affairs in which Angela Davis is white or is an Uncle Tom (Aunt Jemima?) or in which Secretary of the Interior is not a cabinet post, and in those states of affairs, it need not be the case that Carter has appointed a black militant to the cabinet. The reason that 9.4.19*a* is normally interpreted as not presupposing 9.4.19*b* is that people do not determine entailments in a vacuum but bring in any facts that it is reasonable to assume, in this case, the facts that Angela Davis is a black militant and that Secretary of the Interior is a cabinet post.

There are two closely related ways in which one might revise 9.4.6 (as well as 9.4.8 and 9.4.14 or 9.4.17 to accommodate the last observation. Either one replaces classical entailment by a more restricted relationship (say, restricting the valuations to those in which the assumed facts are all assigned the value T), or one replaces $A \Vdash C$ by the less stringent condition $X \cup \{A\} \Vdash C$, where X is the set of propositions that the parties to the discourse can take for granted at that point in the discourse.

Karttunen in fact adopted the latter of these alternatives, though he shortly revised it further by divorcing his account of presupposition from the notion of truth value gap. Specifically, in Karttunen 1974, he restates 9.4.6 and the other conditions in terms of the notion 'is acceptable relative to context X', which no longer commits him to saying that utterances with presuppositional failure must lack truth values; that is, his notion of 'acceptable relative to context X' is such that a sentence can be unacceptable relative to a context without necessarily lacking a truth value. Note that Karttunen's initial revision, in which he replaced $A \Vdash C$ by $X \cup \{A\} \Vdash C$, could hardly be an account of semantic presupposition anymore, since, depending on what the speakers take as 'established' when 9.4.19a is uttered, the revised condition can be met or fail to be met (and thus, if the account were one of semantic presupposition, 9.4.19a be respectively F or #) even though there is no difference in terms of who appointed whom to what post and who regrets what.

Karttunen (1974) also discusses cases which show that the rules 9.4.6, 9.4.8, and 9.4.14 or 9.4.17 fail to account for the presuppositions of more complex propositions (e.g., propositions in which a $\supset$ and a $\wedge$ are combined) but their failure is readily correctible in a treatment which makes explicit reference to 'context'. Note that 9.4.20 does not presuppose that Nixon is Jewish and loves his mother:

9.4.20   If Nixon is Jewish, then he loves his mother and he regrets that he is Jewish and loves his mother

However, according to 9.4.6 and 9.4.8 it ought to presuppose that: the consequent presupposes that Nixon is Jewish and loves his mother (since that is not entailed by the proposition that Nixon loves his mother), but the antecedent does not entail the presupposition of the consequent: the proposition that Nixon is Jewish does not entail that he is Jewish and loves his mother. The fact that 9.4.20 does not presuppose that Nixon is Jewish and loves his mother is due to the fact that the antecedent of a conditional provides 'extra context' for the consequent. With the term CONTEXT having the technical meaning of 'the set of propositions taken for granted by the participants in a discourse at a given point in the discourse', a sentence A will be acceptable relative to a context X if and only if X entails all propositions that must be taken for granted for it to be normal to utter A.[6] Using 'A/X' to indicate that this condition is met, one can restate 9.4.6, 9.4.8, and 9.4.17 as follows:

9.4.21   a. $\wedge$ AB/X if and only if A/X and B/X$\cup${A}.
           b. $\supset$ AB/X if and only if A/X and B/X$\cup${A}.
           c. $\vee$ AB/X if and only if A/X$\cup$$\{\sim$B} and B/X$\cup$$\{\sim$A}.

With 9.4.21 it is easy to show that 9.4.20 is acceptable relative to any context that contains (or entails) the propositions that Nixon exists and that Nixon has a mother. The condition $\supset$(A, $\wedge$BC)/X is met if and only if A/X and $\wedge$BC/X$\cup${A}, and $\wedge$BC/X$\cup${A} if and only if B/X$\cup${A} and C/X$\cup${A,B}. Here, A demands of a context only that it entail that Nixon exists, and the context X, by assumption, meets that demand; B demands of a context only that it entail that Nixon exists and that he has a mother, and the context X$\cup${A} meets that demand. Proposition C demands of a context only that it entail that Nixon exists and that Nixon is Jewish and loves his mother (this demand being by virtue of the 'basic presupposition' carried by *regret*), and the context X$\cup${A, B} meets those demands, since X meets the first demand and {A, B} meets the second.

The condition 9.4.21*a* corresponds to the observation that the first conjunct of an *and*-conjoined proposition 'provides context for' the second conjunct; that is, that what is at issue in considering the acceptability of the second conjunct is not acceptability relative to the context of the entire conjoined sentence (i.e., relative to the propositions that are taken for granted at the moment one begins to utter the sentence) but relative to that context supplemented by the first conjunct. Condition 9.4.21*b* corresponds to a similar observation about conditionals: that the antecedent 'provides context for' the consequent.

This is as good a place as any to remark on the distinction between 'indicative' and 'counterfactual' conditionals. In a counterfactual conditional, the antecedent is inconsistent with the context (i.e., it conflicts with what you are taking for granted). Condition 9.4.21*b* thus applies only to indicative, not to counterfactual conditionals. The closest analogue to 9.4.21*b* that would make sense in an account of counterfactual conditionals would be a condition B/Y$\cup${A}, where Y is a maximal subset of X that is consistent with A (i.e., Y is what you get by throwing out as little of X as is necessary to achieve consistency with A). Of course, there will generally be many nonequivalent ways of throwing out propositions so as to achieve consistency with A (for example, if X contains both $\sim p$ and $\sim q$, and A $=$ $\vee pq$, then one could either throw out $\sim p$ or throw out $\sim q$ to attain consistency with A), and how one chooses the Y can affect whether $B/Y\cup\{A\}$. In 11.1 I will briefly discuss an account of counterfactuals along these lines by Rescher (1964) in which the choice of Y is made on the basis of the 'degree of confidence' or 'degree of attachment' that the speaker has for the various propositions. In Rescher's account, Y is chosen so that not only is it a maximal subset of X consistent with A but the 'degree of confidence' in the propositions of Y is maximized (for example, if one had more confidence in $\sim p$ than in $\sim q$, then $\sim q$ would be thrown away and Y would contain $\sim p$).

The 'basic presuppositions' associated with the 'atomic propositions' may be but do not have to be semantic presuppositions. However, even if they are semantic presuppositions, the pragmatic presuppositions that they contribute to complex sentences need not also be semantic presuppositions; for example, one can take the truth conditions of conjoined sentences to be given by van Fraassen's tables and still take the pragmatic presuppositions of conjoined sentences to be determined by 9.4.21a. In addition, one can take items as contributing pragmatic presuppositions without being committed to ever allowing them to contribute semantic presuppositions; for example, one can take *The king of France is bald* to pragmatically presuppose that there is a king of France regardless of whether one takes it to be false or truth-valueless when there is no king of France. Moreover, while items that contribute semantic presuppositions generally also contribute pragmatic presuppositions, there is a class of factive verbs (the so-called semifactives) that not only are not accompanied by a pragmatic presupposition of the complement but indeed are commonly used to introduce that complement as 'new information':

9.4.22   a. I was about to get on the bus when I *realized* that I had left my briefcase in the office.
              b. After he graduated from college, Bill *discovered* that most of what he had been taught was nonsense.

9.5. Broad and Narrow Conceptions of Falsehood

In 3.2, we considered the possibility of nonstandard valuations, that is, assignments of truth values which do not conform to the standard truth tables. It was shown there that if a nonstandard valuation is to fit the rules of inference for propositional logic that were given in chapter 2, that is, if the rules lead to true conclusions (relative to the given valuation) whenever applied to premises that are true relative to the given valuation, then there must be false propositions whose negations are false relative to the valuation. I suggested there that the possibility of a proposition and its negation being simultaneously false was not at all outlandish and that it might be reasonable to assign 'F' to both a proposition and its negation when the proposition has a false semantic presupposition. That policy would amount to taking a broader conception of falsehood than is normally taken. Normally a proposition is taken to be false if and only if its negation is true; thus, under that policy, if neither a given proposition nor its negation is true, then neither it nor its negation is false, and both the proposition and its negation 'lack any truth value'. The policy suggested in 3.2 involved the broader conception of falsehood, according to which a proposition was false whenever it was not true. Under the narrow conception of falsehood, if a proposition and its negation both fail to be true, then both lack any truth value; under the broad conception of falsehood, if a proposition and its negation both fail to be true, then both are false.

There is thus a precise scheme for translating between valuations involving a narrow conception of falsehood (with possible 'truth value gaps') and valuations involving a broad conception of falsehood (where a proposition is false whenever it is not true, and a proposition and its negation may be simultaneously false). Using T, F, # to represent 'truth', 'falsehood', and 'lack of truth value', under the narrow conception of falsehood, and using t, f, to represent 'truth' and 'falsehood' under the broad conception of falsehood, the correspondence is given by:

9.5.1   Narrow   Broad

A	~A		A	~A
T	F		t	f
F	T		f	t
#	#		f	f

An interesting question can now be raised. If the truth tables for 'broad falsehood' that were established in 3.2 are translated into the narrow conception of falsehood, how will they compare with the truth tables that follow from van Fraassen's supervaluations? Alternatively, how does the set of valuations that conform to the rules of inference of chapter 2 compare with the set of supervaluations defined by the 'classical' valuations?

Let us start by translating the truth table for ∧ that was given in 3.2, using only the two truth values t and f,[7] into a truth table involving T/F/#. The 'narrow' truth table here takes the same form as the 'classical' table:

9.5.2   ∧ B

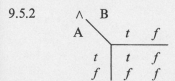

A	t	f
t	t	f
f	f	f

However, that appearance is slightly misleading, since this table covers a broader class of situations than the 'classical' table was envisioned as covering: it covers even cases where A and ~A are both assigned the value f. The 'translation' of this table will be a 3×3 matrix of the form

9.5.3

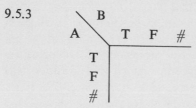

Filling in the nine blanks will involve determining for each situation not only whether $\wedge$ AB is 'true with a small t' or 'false with a small f' but also whether $\sim \wedge$ AB is 'true with a small t' or 'false with a small f'. The upper left cell will of course be filled by T, since a proposition is 'true with a small t' if and only if it is 'true with a capital T': when A and B are both T, they are both t, thus $\wedge$ AB is also t, and thus $\wedge$ AB is T. Let us now turn to the second cell in the top row, that is, the case where A is t, B is f, and $\sim$ B is t. The proposition $\wedge$ AB will then be f, which means that it will be either F or #, depending on whether $\sim \wedge$ AB is t or f, respectively. The proposition $\sim \wedge$ AB is deductively equivalent to $\vee(\sim A, \sim B)$. By assumption, $\sim$ B is t, which means that $\vee(\sim A, \sim B)$ will also be t (as a consequence of the rule of $\vee$-introduction) and hence also $\sim \wedge$ AB. Thus, the second cell in the top row must contain F. Now let us turn to the last cell in the top row, that corresponding to the case where A is t, B is f, and $\sim$ B is also f. Again, $\wedge$ AB is f, and thus will be F or # depending on whether its negation is t or f, respectively. At first glance it might appear that both possibilities can occur, since $\sim \wedge$ AB is deductively equivalent to $\vee(\sim A, \sim B)$ and an $\vee$-conjunction of f propositions can be either t or f. However, in this case it can't be t, since if it were, the following inference would lead from true premises to a false conclusion:

9.5.4

1	A	supp
2	$\vee(\sim A, \sim B)$	supp
3	$\quad \sim A$	supp
4	$\quad$ A	1, reit
5	$\quad \sim B$	3, 4, 2.2.8e
6	$\quad \sim B$	supp
7	$\quad \sim B$	6, reit
8	$\sim B$	2, 3–5, 6–7, $\vee$-expl

Thus, when A is T and B is #, $\wedge$ AB will be #.

The first line of the truth table under construction thus agrees with the corresponding line of van Fraassen's truth table. In fact the remaining entries also agree with van Fraassen's table; a proof of this is left as an exercise to the reader. Note in particular that both F and $\#$ are possible truth values for $\wedge$ AB in the case where both A and B are $\#$. This follows from the fact that among the cases where A, $\sim$A, B, and $\sim$B are all f, there are both instances in which $\sim \wedge$ AB is t (for example, cases where $\wedge$ AB is a contradiction and its negation is thus a theorem and hence true, for example, the case of $\wedge (p, \sim p)$) and instances in which $\sim \wedge$ AB is f (for example, under the valuation which assigns t to all theorems and f to everything else, $\sim \wedge (p, q)$ will be f if p and q are distinct atomic propositions).

In fact, the same is true of the truth tables for $\vee$ and $\supset$, as the reader should attempt to verify for himself. (The truth table for $\sim$ of course agrees with van Fraassen's since we set up the correspondence between T/F/$\#$ and t/f in such a way that the truth tables for negation would agree). Thus the notion of semantic presupposition that van Fraassen's system formalizes coincides exactly with the notion of semantic presupposition obtained by admitting all valuations that conform to the standard rules of inference and taking a proposition to have failure of semantic presupposition relative to a given valuation if and only if both it and its negation are false relative to that valuation. This perhaps surprising result becomes less surprising if one notes that the valuations that conform to the given rules of inference can be characterized in a way that is parallel to van Fraassen's characterization of supervaluations. Let X be any set of propositions. Define a valuation w_X as follows:

9.5.5   If X $\vdash$ A, then $w_X(A) = t$ (i.e., w_X assigns t to those propositions that can be inferred from the premises X by the given rules of inference). Otherwise $w_X(A) = f$.

Every valuation that conforms to the rules of inference is a w_X for some choice of X. Specifically, let v be any valuation that conforms to the given rules of inference, and define X as $\{A: v(A) = t\}$. It can easily be verified that $v = w_X$. If the above definition is translated into the T/F/$\#$ system, the result is:

9.5.6   If X $\vdash$ A, then $w_X(A) = $ T.
        If X $\vdash \sim$A, then $w_X(A) = $ F.
        Otherwise, $w_X(A) = \#$.

This definition is quite parallel to van Fraassen's definition of v_X. They differ only in that where the above definition has 'A is deducible from X by the standard rules of inference', van Fraassen's definition has 'A is true under all classical valuations that make all members of X true'. But the completeness theorem for propositional logic implies that those two conditions are equivalent and thus that $v_x = w_x$: the completeness theorem implies that a proposition is true whenever given premises are true, if and only if it is inferrable from them, where the admissible valuations are the 'classical' ones and the rules of inference are those of chapter 2.

9.6. Discourse Referents

Karttunen, in a paper originally circulated in 1969 but not published until 1976, proposed an important emendation to standard accounts of existential sentences. This proposal is in fact intimately connected with the notion of pragmatic presupposition, and it is thus appropriate that it be taken up at this point.

Karttunen notes that existential NP's have, in addition to the function of binding a variable in forming existential propositions, as in the analyses presented so far in this book, the function of bringing into being constants (which Karttunen christens DISCOURSE REFERENTS) that may figure in all or part of the subsequent discourse and which correspond to the entity that the existential proposition asserts to exist. The distinction between these two functions can easily be seen in the common practise of mathematicians, who will use the same letter for a bound variable in the existential proposition and for a corresponding constant in subsequent propositions, as in the following formulation of the postulates for the notion 'group':

9.6.1   A set G with a binary operation $\cdot$ is a group if and only if
   a. ('Closure') $(\forall x: x \in G)(\forall y: y \in G)(x \cdot y \in G)$
   b. ('Associativity') $(\forall x: x \in G)(\forall y: y \in G)(\forall z: z \in G)$
$$(x \cdot (y \cdot z) = (x \cdot y) \cdot z)$$
   c. ('Identity') $(\exists e: e \in G)(\forall x: x \in G)(x \cdot e = e \cdot x = x)$
   d. ('Inverses') $(\forall x: x \in G)(\exists x^{-1}: x^{-1} \in G)(x \cdot x^{-1} = x^{-1} \cdot x = e)$

Note that the quantifier that binds e in 9.6.1c has only 9.6.1c as its scope; the occurrence of e in 9.6.1d figures as a constant (if it were an instance of the same bound variable as in 9.6.1c, it would be a blatant violation of the coherency conditions on bound variables), though in some sense it corresponds to the bound variable of 9.6.1c.

More purist mathematicians will not accept 9.6.1 as it stands: they will insist that before a constant such as the e of 9.6.1d can be employed, a proper baptismal ceremony must be performed, in which defining characterisitics of the putative constant are given and it is proven that only one element has those characterisitics. In this case, the purist's demands can easily be satisfied: it is easy to show that if a set with an associative operation contains an identity element, then it contains only one identity element.

However, the informal practise of less purist mathematicians is of inherent interest, since it corresponds closely to the way that people (mathematicians or not) use existential propositions regardless of whether the uniqueness theorem that a purist would demand can be proven.

In 9.6.1*d*, the existence and identity of the item written as *e* are treated as known. The existence of such an element has in fact just been vouched for, that is, 9.6.1*c* asserts that there is such an element. The identity of that element need not, strictly speaking, be known, but the participants in a (mathematical) discourse containing 9.6.1 nonetheless take it as known. In doing so, they are doing essentially the same thing as when they participate in a discourse in which one of the participants says 9.6.2:

9.6.2   One day last week a strange person visited me at my office. He wanted me to give money to a home for unemployed philosophers.

The persons who hear 9.6.2 have no idea who the strange fund-raiser is, and the speaker might indeed be unable to identify that person in a police lineup. Nonetheless, the hearers cooperate with the speaker by acting as if he could provide a specific referent for his words if called upon to do so and the speaker in effect guarantees referential backing for the *he* of 9.6.2 even though he might not be able to supply it in a form satisfactory to a less charitable interrogator.

The use of the economic term 'backing' in the last paragraph is intentional. The relationship between discourse referents and entities is closely parallel to that between paper money and the gold or silver that it originally was redeemable for: discourse referents are issued by someone who commits himself (perhaps irresponsibly or insincerely) to redeem them on demand, they facilitate transactions, and they are traded on a par with the things that they purportedly are redeemable for. This section will be devoted principally to exploring ways in which discourse referents 'facilitate transactions' and indeed make possible a broad range of transactions that would otherwise be impossible. Specifically, we will explore ways in which discourse referents can serve to make sense out of certain logical formulas that we have hitherto dismissed as incoherent but which nonetheless are supported by linguistic evidence that goes against their logically coherent alternatives as well as a detailed proposal for the use of discourse referents in a comprehensive treatment of definite descriptions that avoids all of the more serious defects that Russell's treatment exhibits.

In 4.2, we considered the proposal (Quine 1960) that *any* is a universal quantifier with wide scope. In the alternative proposal of Klima 1964 and Horn 1972, the *any* that appears in conditional and negative clauses is an existential quantifier with 'narrow' scope and arises through a transformation of 'some-any conversation' that converts an existential quantifier into any if it is commanded by an appropriate 'triggering' element such as negation or if. Thus, according to Quine's proposal, 9.6.3a has the logical structure 9.6.3b, and according to Klima and Horn's the structure 9.6.3c:

9.6.3   a. If anyone objects, I'll resign.
          b. $(\forall x) \supset (x$ objects, I resign$)$
          c. $\supset ((\exists x)(x$ objects$)$, I resign$)$

That both 9.6.3b and 9.6.3c should be serious candidates for the title of logical structure of 9.6.3a is not surprising, since, as was shown in chapter 4, they are deductively equivalent. However, for sentences such as 9.6.4a, Quine's proposal appears to have a decisive advantage over Klima and Horn's, since the pronoun referring back to the quantified NP is inside the scope of the quantifier in Quine's proposal but outside the scope of the quantifier in Klima and Horn's proposal, which thus leads to a violation of the coherency conditions:

9.6.4   a. If *any student* asks me, I'll tell *him* the answer.
          b. $(\forall: \text{student } x)_x \supset (x$ asks me, I tell x the answer$)$
          c. $* \supset ((\exists: \text{student } x)_x(x$ asks me$)$, I tell x the answer$)$

There are, however, linguistic facts that provide support for the Klima and Horn analysis over Quine's and raise some question about whether formulas such as 9.6.4c should be admitted despite their violation of the coherency conditions. First, there are instances in which an anaphoric device demands as its antecedent the existential clause that figures as a constituent of the Klima and Horn analysis but does not appear in the Quine analysis:

9.6.5   If you find any copies of *Fanny Hill*, I'll give you \$10 for one,

but if $\left\{ \begin{matrix} \text{not} \\ \text{you don't} \end{matrix} \right\}$, I'll buy a copy of *Lady Chatterly's Lover*.

The deleted sentence in the first version of 9.6.5 must be 'You find copies of *Fanny Hill*', and the deleted VP in the second version must be 'find copies of *Fanny Hill*', and each of those constituents demands an existential quantifier in its logical structure.[8] Thus, if the ellipsis in the two versions of 9.6.5 is accomplished through transformations that delete constituents under identity, the two conjuncts of 9.6.5 must both contain occurrences of 'You find copies of *Fanny Hill*' in their underlying structure, in which case 9.6.5 has an underlying structure that conforms to Klima and Horn's proposal but not to Quine's. Second, consider such sentences as

9.6.6   a. If a war breaks out in Uganda, *it* will spread to Tanzania.
          b. If we have a son, we'll name *him* Oscar.

    c. Whenever Jack writes a story, he submits *it* to Playboy.
    d. If blisters develop on the patient's body, you should bandage *them*.

It makes no sense to speak of these sentences as being universal quantifications of 'If x breaks out in Uganda, x will spread to Tanzania', 'If we have x, we'll name x Oscar', and so on. In each of the sentences of 9.6.6, the *if*-clause involves a verb of coming into being and demands an analysis in which an existential clause ('There is a war', 'We have a son', with the stative sense of *have* that figures in *Tom and Betty have three sons*, etc.) is the complement of a predicate such as 'come about', and the existential quantifier of that complement clause does not even have the whole *if*-clause in its scope, let alone the consequent clause as well.[9] Karttunen's notion of discourse referent can be adapted to the analysis of sentences such as 9.4.4–9.4.6 by taking the pronoun in the consequents of these sentences to correspond not to a repetition of the bound variable of the antecedent but to a discourse referent associated with that variable. The discourse referent here is only a temporary addition to the set of constants, or CONTEXTUAL DOMAIN: it is available only in the consequent of the given conditional.[10] The contextual domain then behaves very much the way that the context did in Karttunen's treatment of pragmatic presupposition: the consequent of a conditional is interpreted relative to a temporarily augmented context (the antecedent is temporarily added to the context) and a temporarily augmented contextual domain (discourse referents corresponding to entities whose existence the antecedent asserts or implies are temporarily added to the contextual domain).

    Consider now some serious problems for Russell's analysis of definite descriptions. I take it as obvious that *the* plays exactly the same role in 9.6.7*a* as it does in 9.6.7*b–b'*:

9.6.7   a. The dog is hungry.
           b. The dog likes all dogs.
           b'. The dog was barking at another dog.

Adherents of Russell's analysis have generally felt happy analyzing 9.6.7*a* the same way that Russell analyzed *The king of France is bald*, and to the obvious objection that 9.6.7*a* does not imply that there is only one dog, they have responded that 9.6.7*a* is acceptable provided one assumes a suitably restricted universe of discourse, namely, one containing only one dog. This response is reasonable in that the user of 9.6.7*a* surely does restrict his attention to only one of the world's millions of dogs. However, 9.6.7*b–b'* show that this restriction of attention cannot be a restriction of the universe of discourse, that is, of the set that is to provide the domains of ALL variables: if 9.6.7*b* were used relative to a universe of discourse that contained only one dog, then it ought to convey the same thing as *The dog likes itself*, which it does not, and if 9.6.7*b'* were used relative to a universe of discourse containing only one dog, it ought to convey something guaranteed to be false, since there would be no other dog in that restricted universe for it to bark at. Clearly, *all* and *another* in 9.6.7*b–b'* demand universes of discourse that can contain as many dogs as you want, and thus *the dog* cannot pick out its referent simply by virtue of a restriction on the universe of discourse. In the analysis that I am about to propose, the interpretation of definite descriptions involves a search not through the universe of discourse but through the contextual domain.

Additional problems for Russell's analysis are provided by plural definite NP's. Russell's analysis does not carry over in any natural way to the case of plural NP's; for example, the uniqueness term of Russell's analysis, which is clearly inappropriate for plural NP's, cannot be simply deleted, since then the distinction between *The dogs are hungry* and *Some dogs are hungry* would be lost, and the quantifier of Russell's analysis cannot be turned into a universal, since then the difference between *The dogs are hungry* and *All dogs are hungry* would be lost. In addition, 9.6.8*a–b* present the same problems for any form of Russell's analysis as did 9.6.7*b–b'*:

9.6.8   a. The dogs like all dogs.
         b. The dogs were barking at another dog.

Let us now be more precise about what the contextual domain is. The contextual domain at any point of a discourse will be the set of entities whose existence and identity the participants in the discourse take as established. Entities will get into the contextual domain in the same ways that propositions get into the context: through explicit mention in the discourse in existential propositions and through background knowledge that will involve entities whose existence and identity the participants can regard as their common knowledge. We then can take the sentences in 9.6.7 as acceptable relative to any contextual domain that contains one dog: *the dog* in each of the sentences will refer to that dog, and 9.6.7*a*, 9.6.7*b*, and 9.6.7*c* will express a true proposition if and only if that dog is hungry, likes all dogs, or was barking at another dog, respectively. The contextual domain will have no bearing on the domains over which variables bound by ordinary quantifiers range, and thus 9.6.7*b* can be truthfully uttered by a person who realizes that there are millions of dogs in the world.

The referent of a plural definite NP, as in 9.6.8, is a set (here, a set of dogs). No restriction has so far been placed on the nature of the entities that are members of the contextual domain, and, in particular, there is nothing to prevent a set from being a member of the contextual domain. If 9.6.8*a* or 9.6.8*b* is uttered relative to a contextual domain having exactly one set of dogs among its members, that set is picked out as the referent of *the dogs*, and the proposition expressed by the sentence will be true or not depending on whether those dogs like all dogs or were barking at another dog, respectively. Note that a set may be a member of the contextual domain without all or even any of its members being a member of the contextual domain; for example, you can treat the existence and identity of your neighbor's dogs as established even though you may not even know how many dogs he has or be able to identify any one of them as an individual.

While the contextual domain has figured centrally in the discussion of the last couple of paragraphs, the context (in Karttunen's sense) has not. There is in fact one important respect in which the context may play a role in the interpretation of definite descriptions. I have spoken of the interpretation of the definite NP *the dog* as involving a search through the contextual domain for an entity that 'is a dog'. But does this mean 'is a dog really' or perhaps rather 'is a dog according to the context'? This difference will be important in cases where there is a discrepancy between what is the case and what is treated as established, as in Donnellan's (1966) celebrated example:

9.6.9   The man in the corner with the martini in his hand has just been hired at Stanford.

Example 9.6.9 could very well be interpreted as picking out a certain person and asserting that that person has just been hired at Stanford, even if that person really had a daiquiri or even a glass of chicken soup in his hand. It would in fact be so interpreted as long as the speaker and addressee(s) take as established (most likely, as background knowledge) that that person has a martini in his hand. If the utterer of 9.6.9 and his hearers later discover that Schwartz, the person whom they had taken to have a martini in his hand, was really drinking a daiquiri and that another person in the same corner, Gonzalez, whom they had taken to be drinking coffee, was really drinking a martini out of a coffee cup, they would not then take the speaker to have asserted that Gonzalez had been hired at Stanford, and the speaker would not be expected to recant 9.6.9. Thus, at least in some cases, for an element a of the contextual domain to be picked out as referent of a definite description $(\iota x : fx)$, what is necessary is not that fa be true but that $X \Vdash fa$, where X is the context. For the moment, subject to later revision, let us assume that that is always the case.

According to what was said about temporary augmentation of the contextual domain, it ought to be possible to get not only pronouns, as in 9.6.4–9.6.6, but also definite descriptions in the consequent of a conditional sentence that refer back to an existential NP in the antecedent, since the discourse referent temporarily added to the contextual domain is then there to be found in the search for a referent for a definite description. Sometimes the definite description is awkward, probably because a simple personal pronoun would have done as well, but in many cases it is perfectly natural, especially in cases where it would not be clear which of two or more NP's would be the antecedent if a pronoun were used, as in 9.6.10c:

9.6.10   a. ?If a student asks me, I'll tell the student the answer.
              b. If a war breaks out in Uganda, the war will spread to Tanzania.
              c. If a motorcycle collides with a truck, the motorcycle is usually damaged worse than the truck.

Suppose that 9.6.10c is uttered relative to a context X and a contextual domain O. Then the consequent clause is interpreted relative to the contextual domain $O \cup \{a, b\}$ and the context $X \cup \{a$ is a motorcycle, b is a truck, a collides with $b\}$, where a and b are the discourse referents corresponding to the two indefinite NP's. Assuming for the moment that O contains no motorcycle and no truck, the enlarged contextual domain contains exactly one motorcycle (namely, a) and one truck (namely, b), and those two individuals will be picked out by the NP's *the motorcycle* and *the truck*. The same is the case for 9.6.11:

9.6.11   If a Honda collides with a three-axle semi, the motorcycle is usually damaged worse than the truck.

Provided that X contains the proposition that Hondas are motorcycles and the proposition that three-axle semis are trucks, a and b will be the only elements of the enlarged contextual domain for which the enlarged context entails that the one is a motorcycle and that the other is a truck, and thus they will be picked out as the referents of the two definite descriptions.

There are a number of respects in which this discussion of 9.6.10 and 9.6.11 has been oversimplified. First, it is obviously possible to utter 9.6.10c in relation to a contextual domain that already contains a motorcycle and/or a truck (it could easily be a part of a discourse in which a parent is admonishing his biker son to be careful in riding his motorcycle, with that motorcycle belonging to the contextual domain) and have it interpreted exactly the same way as in the above discussion. Since the augmented contextual domain will then contain two motorcycles (and/or two trucks), an adequate account of definite descriptions must provide some means by which one of those motorcycles can be picked as the referent of the definite description, and I will accordingly impose more structure on the contextual domain than I have so far. Rather than being simply a set, the contextual domain must have different 'levels', with items on higher levels being, for the moment at least, more 'prominent' than items on lower levels. As long as the temporary additions to the contextual domain are put on a higher level than its previous contents, the temporarily added discourse referents will be picked as the referents of *the motorcycle* and *the truck*, just as before. I have at the moment no general account of principles determining the relative prominence of the various discourse referents. Lewis (1979) notes that relative prominence can change as the discourse proceeds and that in some cases the speaker is free to decide which of two discourse referents is the more prominent. For example, when one says *The dog was barking at another dog*, he is free to treat the new discourse referent (the one corresponding to *another dog*) as either more or less prominent than the given one; that is, in the next sentence he can use *the dog* to refer to either of the two dogs (though details of that sentence may render one of the two interpretations impossible or implausible).

A second respect in which the discussion has been oversimplified is that it has been confined to cases where the discourse referent corresponds directly to an existentially quantified variable. In fact, in many cases the discourse is related only very indirectly to entities that have been explicitly introduced into prior discourse. Consider, for example, the sentences

9.6.12   a. The last time I ate here, I had to wait 15 minutes before *the waiter* brought me *the check*.
           b. Whenever I teach freshman algebra, *the girls* do better than *the boys*.

To utter 9.6.12*a*, it is not necessary that there have been any prior mention of a waiter or of a check. The relevant background information relates not to the specific waiter and the specific check to which 9.6.12*a* refers but to the way in which a waiter and a check figure in typical events of eating in a restaurant. Such information is referred to by Schank and Abelson (1977) as a SCRIPT, and in many cases it does in fact take the form of a skeletal scenario, giving the normal sequence of events and a description of the roles of the various persons and objects that figure in those events. By virtue of one's knowledge of a 'restaurant script', one will know that a waiter and a check figured in the event described as *the last time I ate here*.[11] The reference to teaching freshman algebra in 9.6.12*b* makes available a discourse referent corresponding to the pupils in the class. The two NP's *the girls* and *the boys* refer to subsets of that set. The participants in the discourse need not have established yet that in any algebra class taught by the speaker of 9.6.12*b* there will be both boys and girls. By contrast, if 9.6.12*b* had ended with *the Zulus do better than the Lapps*, it would have to have been established previously that the classes contain both Zulus and

Lapps. Clearly the fact that it is 'normal' for a class to contain both girls and boys is largely the cause for the acceptability of 9.6.12*b*, though I am not prepared to say exactly what role that fact plays.

In addition, in this section I have ignored entirely those examples that seem to fit Russell's analysis best—those that involve no reference to an entity whose existence and identity have been established in the discourse but do involve commitment on the part of the speaker to the proposition that there is one and only one entity fitting the given description:

9.6.13   a. The solution to this equation is greater than 43 and less than 107.
              b. The person who wrote these instructions is an imbecile.
              c. I'm still looking for the person who stole my guitar.

There is a way of dealing with sentences like 9.6.13 within the framework of this chapter that is in some respects close to Russell's approach. Suppose that we treat the contextual domain as not only having multiple levels, as in the discussion of 9.6.10, but also having a fixed bottom level, namely, the universe of discourse. This does some violence to the notion of 'contextual domain', since the bulk of the entities in the universe of discourse will not be things whose existence and identity is taken as established. Nonetheless, we can take this suggestion as embodying a generalization of the notion of 'prominence' to take in the degenerate case of things that have no prominence at all. If a search for a referent for a definite description fails to yield one on any of the levels of the contextual domain that have some 'prominence', it will continue on the bottom level, and if there is exactly one element on that level having the given property, that element will be picked out as the referent of the definite description. This suggestion agrees with Russell's at least to the extent that, when the higher levels of the contextual domain do not provide a referent, a referent is found if and only if one and only one element has the given property; it differs from Russell's account in that it provides no truth value for the proposition in cases where that search fails, that is, where no element or more than one has the property (e.g., there is no king of France or there is more than one).

It should be remarked that the sketch of definite descriptions presented in this section is close to the spirit of much recent work in 'procedural semantics' (see Miller and Johnson-Laird 1976 for an excellent review of that area), in which meanings are given in the form of algorithms (not always deterministic algorithms) for identifying objects and determining truth values, typically algorithms involving searches through structured domains.

9.7. Exercises

1. In each of the following pairs, sentence *a* has at some time or other been claimed to 'presuppose' the proposition expressed by sentence *b*. In each case, identify what sort(s) of presupposition, if any, is/are involved, and justify your claim. (underlines indicate elements that have been held responsible for the alleged presupposition):

i. (a) John has stopped beating his wife.
    (b) John used to beat his wife.
ii. (a) The vacuum cleaner is working again.
    (b) The vacuum cleaner once was working and subsequently was not working.
iii. (a) Have you visited the Monet exhibition?
     (b) It is possible for you to visit the Monet exhibition.
iv. (a) Tom ordered Mary to shine his shoes.
    (b) Tom has the authority to give Mary orders.
v. (a) Mary accused Bill of writing the letter.
    (b) It was bad to write the letter.

2. It is sometimes stated (Horn 1969) that the following example presupposes that Muriel voted for Hubert:

Only Muriel voted for Hubert.

Write about 1 page on the question of what is presupposed by sentences involving *only*, mentioning all examples of *only* that appear in 7.1 and the exercises for chapter 7, with attention to the question of whether it is possible to give a uniform statement of what is presupposed by *only*-sentences.

3. A definition of 'presupposition' that figures in some linguistic literature is that a *sentence* S presupposes a proposition *p* if uttering S and uttering the negation of S both commit the speaker to *p*. Write 1 to 2 pages comparing this notion of presupposition with the others discussed in this chapter, with regard to (a) the circumstances in which the criterion can be applied, (*b*) which of the well-known supposed instances of presupposition it would classify as being presuppositions, and (*c*) any other important issues.

4. According to the supervaluation that assigns the values p T, q F, r #, what is the truth value of

a. $\supset(\wedge pr, \vee qr)$
b. $\wedge(\supset rq, \supset(\sim p, \sim r))$

5. For each of the following sentences, indicate a plausible set of propositions that a context X might contain that would make the sentence acceptable relative to X according to Karttunen's rules:

a. It rained this morning and the roads are <u>still</u> wet.
b. John has written a sonnet, and he's put a stupid pun in <u>the 13th line</u>.
c. If Bob has any children, it's <u>appalling</u> that none of them <u>visited him</u> while he was in the hospital.

In each case underline indicates the element whose presupposition is at issue (NB: *appalling* is a factive predicate).

10. Modal Logic

10.1. Introduction

The term 'modal logic' is often used rather vaguely. It takes in the logic of notions of 'necessity' and 'possibility', but there is no real consensus on what else it takes in; it is sometimes used so broadly as to take in the whole of logic that is not taken in by predicate logic and sometimes so narrowly as to take in nothing more than 'necessity' and 'possibility' (in combination with the expressive material of propositional logic and predicate logic). In any event, notions of necessity and possibility have been of central interest in everything that has been called modal logic, and it is thus fitting for us to start our treatment of modal logic by concentrating on those notions.

The terms 'necessity' and 'possibility' are in fact used in quite a large number of ways. The following is a sample of the notions of necessity that can be distinguished:

Logical necessity.—A proposition is logically necessary if the given system of logic insures that it will be true; for example, the proposition that there either is a planet made of green cheese or is no planet made of green cheese is logically necessary.

Epistemic necessity.—A proposition is epistemically necessary if it has to be true, given what we already know. Thus, the proposition that J.S. Bach was 40 years old in 1725 is epistemically necessary, given that we know that Bach was born in 1685 and did not die until 1750, though it is not logically necessary. If we consider the constraints imposed not by the whole of our knowledge but by some specific area of our knowledge, we obtain other notions of 'necessity' that are basically variants of 'epistemic necessity', such as 'physical necessity', which applies to propositions that have to be true, given what we know about the laws of physics and about the physical makeup of the world. The proposition that if a person jumps off the Empire State Building he will fall is physically necessary; the proposition that if a sane adult jumps off the Empire State Building he will expect to die from the fall is epistemically necessary but not physically necessary.

Moral necessity.—A proposition is morally necessary (for a given person) if he will be at fault unless he sees to it that that proposition is (or becomes) true.

Temporal necessity.—A proposition can be (though usually is not) called 'temporally necessary' if it is true at all times.

While these notions of necessity obviously are not equivalent, they nonetheless have a lot in common. If asked to say what they have in common, the best answer I could come up with at the moment would be: in each case, to say that the proposition is necessary is to say that something would be anomalous if that proposition were not the case. The different notions of necessity correspond to different notions of anomaly: the anomaly of a breakdown in the assumed system of logic, the anomaly of a proposition being true which conflicts with what we already know, the 'anomaly' of a state of affairs prevailing even though it conflicts with our code of morality, or the anomaly of something which is always true not being true. Any notion of 'anomaly' divides 'states of affairs' into two types: anomalous states of affairs and nonanomalous states of affairs. In 3.2 we have already made use of a distinction between anomalous and nonanomalous states of affairs: we considered an extremely broad notion of state of affairs (i.e., any assignment of the values T and F to all propositions of the given language was a 'state of affairs') and distinguished between those states of affairs which conformed to the given rules of inference (i.e., those states of affairs such that any conclusion obtained by applying the rules of inference to premises that are true in that state of affairs is also true in that state of affairs) from those that did not conform (i.e., those states of affairs in which there was a false conclusion that could be inferred from true premises by the given rules of inference). To say that some proposition fails to be true only in an anomalous state of affairs is to say that it is true in all nonanomalous states affairs. Thus, for example, a system R of rules of inference determines a notion of necessity N_R: a proposition is necessary relative to R if and only if it is true in all states of affairs that conform to R.

To say that a proposition is necessary if it is true in all nonanomalous states of affairs is essentially to repeat Leibniz's characterization of necessity: a proposition is necessary if it is true in all possible worlds. Our 'nonamomalous' corresponds to Leibniz's 'possible' and our 'state of affairs' corresponds to Leibniz's 'world'. Since the publication in 1959 of Saul Kripke's remarkable paper, "A completeness theorem in modal logic", the term 'possible world' has been reinstated in the normal vocabulary of logicians, and I will in fact from now on feel free to use the term, keeping in mind, however, that it is composed of the two words 'possible' and 'world' and that 'possible' means 'nonanomalous', and thus its interpretation varies, depending on what notion of 'anomaly' one might happen to be discussing.

Let us adopt the standard practise of writing □ to stand for 'necessary', irrespective of the specific kind of 'necessity' that is at issue. We can then form expressions containing □ and ask under what interpretations of □ those expressions will be true. For example, consider the formula

10.1.1   ⊃(□A, A).

If □ is 'logical necessity', then 10.1.1 will be true in any (logically non-anomalous) state of affairs, regardless of what A is: it could be false in a given state of affairs only if A were false in that state of affairs but A were true in all nonanomalous states of affairs, which is impossible since A is false in the given nonanomalous state of affairs. Suppose, however, that □ stands for 'moral necessity'; unless the assumed moral code is vacuous (or effectively vacuous, e.g., the only thing that is prohibited is trisecting a 30° angle with a compass and straightedge), 10.1.1 can be false, that is, there can be a state of affairs in which something morally necessary fails to be the case (e.g., I may fail to love all my fellow men even though I am morally obliged to do so). Thus, in the case of moral necessity, the actual state of affairs may be anomalous, though in the case of logical necessity, the actual state of affairs will not be anomalous.

But wait a minute—how can I get away with saying that? When I was talking about logical necessity, I considered all and only those states of affairs that were logically nonanomalous and said that in any such state of affairs 10.1.1 was true; but I ruled out by fiat any consideration of states of affairs that are logically anomalous (e.g., the state of affairs in which all 'atomic' propositions are true and all complex propositions are false). When I was talking about moral necessity, instead of restricting myself to morally nonanomalous states of affairs, I considered the broader[1] class of all *logically* nonanomalous states of affairs; but couldn't I just as well have exercised my fiat and ruled out of consideration all morally anomalous states of affairs? I could have, but in that case I would have ruled out of consideration a large part of the subject matter of moral philosophy, whereas in the case of my earlier fiat, I ruled out only states of affairs in which no one has any particular interest. The point is that one cannot always restrict one's attention to nonanomalous states of affairs. The question to ask about 10.1.1 is: for the given interpretation of □, how anomalous would a state of affairs have to be in order for 10.1.1 to be false? In the case of logical necessity, the answer is 'extremely', indeed, so anomalous that the states of affairs that would make 10.1.1 false can just as well be forgotten about, as indeed they usually are. In the case of 'moral necessity', however, 10.1.1 could be false in a state of affairs that had nothing much anomalous about it beyond the fact that some moral principle was being violated, and thus a huge class of states of affairs that make 10.1.1 false cannot very well be forgotten about.

10.2. Syntax and Semantics for Modal Propositional Logic

So far, for each of the notions of necessity under discussion, I have spoken of various states of affairs being anomalous and others non-anomalous. In some cases, however, it makes more sense to speak of a state of affairs as being anomalous relative to other states of affairs rather than absolutely. In the case of epistemic necessity, a state of affairs is anomalous if it is inconsistent with what is known. But one state of affairs can differ from another with regard to 'what is known'. For example, there might be two states of affairs such that in both there are nine planets, but in only one of the two states of affairs is it *known* that there are nine planets: in the other state of affairs it is only known that there are at least 6 planets. A state of affairs in which there are eight planets would be inconsistent with what is known in the one state of affairs but not with what is known in the other. Similarly with moral necessity. Suppose one takes a state of affairs to be morally anomalous relative to a given state of affairs if there is a violation of some moral principle in that state of affairs that does not occur in the given state of affairs. Let w_1 be a world in which Simon Legree owns slaves and beats his slaves, let w_2 be a world in which Legree owns slaves but does not beat them, and let w_3 be a world in which Legree owns no slaves and beats no one, assuming there to be no further differences of relevance to a moral code that forbids both slavery and beatings. Then w_2 would be morally anomalous relative to w_3 but not relative to w_1.

Thus, to distinguish between the different kinds of 'necessity', we will have to refer to more than just different ways of classifying worlds into 'anomalous' and 'nonanomalous' worlds. Rather, it will be necessary to bring in a relationship of 'relative nonanomaly' or (to use terms that have become fairly standard) ACCESSIBILITY or ALTERNATIVENESS among worlds. Suppose that we consider a binary relation R among the worlds that come into consideration. Rw_1w_2 is to mean 'w_2 is possible relative to w_1' (or, figuratively, 'from w_1 you can get to w_2'). In the case of logical necessity, the relation R is very simple: if w_1 and w_2 both conform to the rules of inference, then Rw_1w_2, and otherwise it is not the case that Rw_1w_2. In this case, R has the important properties:

10.2.1   Symmetry: if Rw_1w_2, then Rw_2w_1.
            Transitivity: if Rw_1w_2 and Rw_2w_3, then Rw_1w_3.

Whether it possesses the further property 10.2.2, the remaining criterion that it would have to fulfill to be an EQUIVALENCE RELATION, depends on a technicality, namely, whether we consider 'all worlds' to be literally 'all worlds' (i.e., all assignments of truth values to the propositions of the given language L, even assignments which fail to conform to the assumed rules of inference) or to be a more restricted class of worlds (such as the set of all worlds that conform to the assumed rules of inference, or the set of worlds that conform to the 'classical' truth tables):

10.2.2   Reflexivity: For all worlds w, Rww.

Since the only way that Rww could be false in this case is for w not to conform to the rules of inference, the only way that the R corresponding to the notion of logical necessity could fail to be an 'equivalence relation' is for worlds to be allowed that do not conform to the rules of inference.

The accessibility relation R appropriate to other notions of necessity may fail to be symmetric or to be transitive or to be reflexive. For the notions of necessity that are most widely discussed, it will be reasonable to take R to be reflexive. However, it is not clear that it should be taken as reflexive if it is to be appropriate to a notion of moral necessity. Two possibilities suggest themselves for that case: one could either take Rw_1w_2 to mean that w_2 is morally no worse than w_1, in which case R would be reflexive, or take Rw_1w_2 to mean that bringing about (or maintaining) the state of affairs w_2 is morally desirable if one is in the state of affairs w_1, in which case R would not be reflexive.

Let us allow ourselves the power of fiat to decide what set of worlds we will allow into consideration in a particular discussion. We can then consider the full range of necessity relations that can be defined by choosing a set of worlds and an accessibility relation among those worlds, where $\Box A$ is to be true in a world w provided that A is true in all worlds accessible from w. We thus require the following definition and condition of truth value assignment:

10.2.3   A modal system M consists of
  (i) a language L,
  (ii) a set W of 'worlds' (= assignments of truth values to the propositions of L), and
  (iii) a binary relation R between the worlds of W.
  $\Box A$ is true in a world w of a modal system M if and only if for all w' such that Rww', A is true in w'.

For the purposes of this chapter, we will also stipulate that L must contain the propositional connectives $\wedge$, $\vee$, $\supset$, $\sim$, and that only worlds that conform to the classical truth tables will be admitted.

Note that according to this truth condition, $\Box$A may be true in one world and false in another world of the given system. That characteristic is all to the good: otherwise we could not adequately accommodate the notions of epistemic necessity and moral necessity within the framework of modal systems. It will be useful to define a notion of VALIDITY in a modal system M: A is valid in M (symbolized $\Vdash_M$A) if A is true in every world of M. Note that if a formula does not contain the modal operator $\Box$, whether it is true in a particular world will depend only on what is true in that world, but if it does contain $\Box$, its truth in a particular world will generally depend at least in part on what is true in other worlds. We are now in a position to prove some theorems about modal systems.

Theorem. For any modal system M and any formulas A and B, 10.2.4 is valid in M:

10.2.4 $\supset(\Box \supset AB, \supset(\Box A, \Box B))$

Proof. Pick any world w of any modal system M; what we must show is that 10.2.4 is true in w. Suppose that $\Box \supset AB$ is true in w. We must now prove that $\supset(\Box A, \Box B)$ is true in w. Suppose that $\Box A$ is true in w, and let w' be a world such that Rww'. Since $\Box \supset AB$ is true in w, $\supset AB$ is true in w', and since $\Box A$ is true in w, A is true in w'; consequently (by $\supset$-exploitation), B is true in w'. But that establishes that B is true in all worlds accessible from w, that is, that $\Box B$ is true in w. We have thus established that $\supset(\Box A, \Box B)$ is true in w. But this establishes that 10.2.4 is true in w.

Formula 10.2.4 is one of a number of formulas that have appeared among axioms for some variety or other of modal logic. Certain other formulas which have appeared in axiomatizations of modal logics are not valid in all modal systems, though they are valid in those modal systems whose accessibility relations have certain characteristics. For example, 10.2.5 is valid in all modal systems in which R is reflexive:

10.2.5 $\supset(\Box A, A)$.

Suppose that R is reflexive, and pick some world w in which $\Box A$ is true. Thus A is true in all worlds w' for which Rww'. But, by assumption, R is reflexive, and thus we have Rww. Consequently, A is true in w. But this establishes that 10.2.5 is true in any world of the modal system.

It is easy to find examples of modal systems in which R is not reflexive and 10.2.5 fails to be valid. For example, consider the trivial case of a modal system in which no world is accessible from any world. Then $\Box A$ will be (vacuously) true in every world, no matter what A is (since for any given world w, A is true in all of the no worlds that are accessible from w);

but any world has false propositions, and by choosing A such that A is false in w, we will have chosen A such that $\supset(\Box A, A)$ is false in w. In appendix 10.5, a proof is given that under certain conditions, the validity of 10.2.5 in a modal system implies that its accessibility relation is reflexive, and thus that, under those conditions, the validity of 10.2.5 is equivalent to reflexiveness of R.

The following formula is valid in any modal system whose accessibility relation is transitive:

10.2.6 $\supset(\Box A, \Box\Box A)$.

Suppose that R is reflexive and that $\Box A$ is true in world w. Let Rww'. If we can show that $\Box A$ is true in w', we will have established that $\Box A$ is true in any world accessible from w and thus that $\Box\Box A$ is true in w, which will establish that 10.2.6 is true for any world w. Consider any world w'' such that $Rw'w''$. Because Rww' and $Rw'w''$ and R is transitive, we have Rww''. But A is true in all worlds accessible from w, and we thus have that A is true in w''. Thus A is true in all worlds accessible from w', and hence $\Box A$ is true in w', as we were attempting to prove. In the appendix, we will prove a converse of this result: under certain conditions, if 10.2.6 is valid in a modal system, then the accessibility relation of that system is transitive.

So far I have been speaking only of notions of 'necessity'. Corresponding to any notion of 'necessity' there is a related notion of 'possibility'; for example, there is a notion of 'logical possibility' (something is logically possible if the rules of inference do not force it to be assigned the value 'False'), 'epistemic possibility' (something is epistemically possible if it is consistent with what is known), 'moral possibility' (something is 'morally possible' if it does not conflict with the moral code in question; in this case one usually says 'permissible' rather than 'possible'). Let us use the symbol $\Diamond$ to denote the notion of 'possibility' that goes along with whatever notion of necessity that we happen to be using $\Box$ as a symbol for. I will assume that $\Box$ and $\Diamond$ are related by the conditions:

10.2.7   a. $\Box A$ if and only if $\sim\Diamond\sim A$.
            b. $\Diamond A$ if and only if $\sim\Box\sim A$.

(Think about each of the notions of possibility in turn, and verify for yourself that 10.2.7 is reasonable in each case). The following is a reasonable way to set up truth conditions for $\Diamond$ so that 10.2.7 comes out true:

10.2.8 $\Diamond A$ is true in a world w of a modal system M if and only if there is a world w' of M such that Rww' and A is true in w'.

That is, $\Diamond A$ is true if A is true in some 'possible world'—possible, that is, in the sense of accessible from the world that you are talking about. You should verify for yourself that under the assumption 10.2.8, the conditions of 10.2.7 come out true.

The following formula is equivalent to 10.2.5 and is thus valid in any modal system whose alternativeness relation is reflexive:

10.2.9 $\supset(A, \Diamond A)$.

If 10.2.5 is true in every world of a modal system, for every formula A, then so is $\supset(\Box \sim A, \sim A)$ (the result of substituting $\sim A$ for A in 10.2.5), and thus so is $\supset(A, \sim \Box \sim A)$, which (by virtue of 10.2.7*b* and the principle of substitution of deductive equivalents) is true under the same circumstances as $\supset(A, \Diamond A)$. This establishes that if 10.2.5 is valid, then 10.2.9 is. All of the steps in this argument can be reversed, yielding a proof of the converse: that if 10.2.9 is valid, 10.2.5 is also. Of course, 10.2.9 can fail to be valid in a modal system, as in the trivial case of a system whose alternativeness relation does not hold of any pair of worlds: in that system, $\Diamond A$ will always be false, and if we choose A so that it is true in a given world w (which is always possible, since in any world there are true propositions), $\supset(A, \Diamond A)$ will be false in w for that choice of A.

Consider now whether the formula 10.2.10 could be false under any conditions:

10.2.10 $\supset(\Box A, \Diamond A)$.

For 10.2.10 to be false in a world w, $\Box A$ would have to be true and $\Diamond A$ false in w; that is, A would have to be true in all worlds that are accessible from w but not be true in any world accessible from w. The only way in which that could be the case would be for there to be no worlds that are accessible from w. Thus 10.2.10 is valid in all modal systems that meet the condition 10.2.11:

10.2.11   For any world w, there is a world w' such that Rww'. (NB: w' need not be distinct from w.)

In talking about ethics, one might want to consider modal systems that do not meet condition 10.2.11. For example, if one took the accessibility relation R to be such that Rww' whenever w' is a morally more acceptable state of affairs that can be reached from a state of affairs w by performing a physically possible act, one might have to admit situations in which 10.2.11 was violated—situations in which one had painted himself into a moral corner: immoral situations from which one could do nothing to extricate himself. However, in the case of logical possibility and epistemic possibility, 10.2.11 will hold, since in that case an even stronger condition than 10.2.11 holds: the R for logical possibility or epistemic possibility is reflexive.[2]

The following formula, the so-called Brouwer formula,[3] is valid in modal systems whose alternativeness relation is symmetric:

10.2.12 $\supset$(A, $\square\lozenge$A).

To see this, suppose that A is true in some world w of a modal system whose alternativeness relation is symmetric. Let Rww'. By the symmetry of R, we then have R$w'w$. But A is true in w, and thus A is true in a world accessible from w', that is, $\lozenge$A is true in w'. But since w' can by any world accessible from w, this establishes that $\square\lozenge$A is true in w. We have thus established that 10.2.12 is valid in any modal system whose R is symmetric. In the appendix to this chapter we will prove a converse of this result: under certain conditions, if 10.2.12 is valid in a modal system, then the R of that system is symmetric.

Suppose that we restrict ourselves for the moment to systems in which 10.2.9 is valid. Then the following, since it has a 'weaker' antecedent than does Brouwer's formula, will be valid only under more stringent conditions than those under which Brouwer's formula is valid:

10.2.13 $\supset$($\lozenge$A, $\square\lozenge$A).

One clear set of circumstances under which 10.2.13 would be valid in a modal system is that in which the alternativeness relation is symmetric *and* transitive. Suppose that $\lozenge$A is true in some world w of a modal system whose alternativeness relation is both symmetric and transitive. Then there is a world w' such that Rww' and A is true in w'. Let us now try to prove that $\square\lozenge$A is true in w, that is, that $\lozenge$A is true in all worlds accessible from w. Let w'' be accessible from w, that is, Rww''. Then, since R is symmetric, we have R$w''w$. But since Rww' and R is transitive, we then have R$w''w'$, and since A is true in w', we have A true in a world that is accessible from w'', that is, $\lozenge$A is true in w''. Since this is true of any world w'' that is accessible from w, $\lozenge$A is true in all worlds accessible from w, that is, $\square\lozenge$A is true in w, as we set out to prove.

So far I have been talking about 'semantics' of modal systems, that is, about the assignment of truth values to propositions involving 'modal operators'. Let us turn now to 'syntactic' treatments of modal logic, that is, to systems of rules of inference[4] that have been proposed for various kinds of modal logics. There are in fact a bewildering array of axiomatic systems of modal logic and an extremely rich literature on their logical properties and their mutual relationships. Most of these systems relate to notions of necessity that 'include' logical necessity, that is, they have a rule of inference that if A is provable, then $\square$A is a theorem of the modal system;[5] this rule of inference is known as NECESSITATION. One particularly rudimentary axiomatic system is the system (variously called 'T', 't', and 'M';

'T' seems to be the most popular name) that has as its rules of inference the rules of inference of propositional logic plus the rule of necessitation and axioms corresponding to the formulas discussed above as 10.2.4 and 10.2.5:

10.2.14   System T. Rules of inference:
              The rules of propositional logic.
              Necessitation: if ⊢A, then ⊢□A.
              ⊢⊃(□A, A)
              ⊢⊃(□⊃AB, ⊃(□A, □B)).

The following are some of the theorems that can be proved in T:

10.2.15   a. ⊃(A, ◊A)
              b. ◊(∨AB) if and only if ∨(◊A, ◊B)
              c. ⊃(◊∧AB, ∧(◊A, ◊B))
              d. ⊃(∧(□A, ◊B), ◊∧AB)

An extensive hierarchy of systems of axioms for modal logic was developed by C. I. Lewis (Lewis 1918, Lewis and Langford 1932) and expanded by numerous subsequent logicians. The various sets of axioms have names like S2, S4, S4.2, and S4.3.3; S1, S2, S3, S4, and S5 are Lewis's original hierarchy, and the others are later interpolations into the hierarchy.[6] The most widely known of these systems are S4 and S5. They each differ from T by the addition of an axiom:

10.2.16   System S4. Rules of inference:
              The rules of T.
              ⊢⊃(□A, □□A)   (= 10.2.6)
           System S5. Rules of inference:
              The rules of T.
              ⊢⊃(◊A, □◊A)   (= 10.2.13)

Strictly speaking, something is missing in 10.2.16, namely, rules of inference for ◊. Note that ◊ does not appear at all in the description of S4 and it appears only in one axiom of S5 that could not provide any basis for a proof of a result of the form ◊B. Modal logicians have generally accepted 10.2.7*b* as a definition of ◊ (or, alternatively, have given their axioms in terms of ◊ and adopted 10.2.7*a* as a definition of □). Despite my strong reservations about taking one of ∧, ∨, and ⊃ as basic and defining the other two in terms of it and negation, I do not feel it to be at all counterintuitive to define ◊ in terms of □ and negation (i.e., to say that 'possible' means 'doesn't have not to be the case'), and I will henceforth treat 10.2.7*b* as a definition of $\lozenge$. It is then easy to establish the following:

10.2.17   a. $\square\sim A \dashv\vdash \sim \lozenge A$.
         b. $\lozenge\sim A \dashv\vdash \sim \square A$.

For example, $\sim\lozenge A$ is an abbreviation for $\sim\sim\square\sim A$, which is deductively equivalent to $\square\sim A$, on the basis of the deductive equivalence of B and $\sim\sim B$.

S5 has the interesting property that from a string of modal operators ($\square$'s and $\lozenge$'s) one can cancel all but the last; that is, the following are theorems of S5:

10.2.18   a. $\supset(\square\square A, \square A)$ a'. $\supset(\square A, \square\square A)$
         b. $\supset(\square\lozenge A, \lozenge A)$ b'. $\supset(\lozenge A, \square\lozenge A)$
         c. $\supset(\lozenge\square A, \square A)$ c'. $\supset(\square A, \lozenge\square A)$
         d. $\supset(\lozenge\lozenge A, \lozenge A)$ d'. $\supset(\lozenge A, \lozenge\lozenge A)$

The proofs of 10.2.18*a* and 10.2.18*b* are trivial, since both theorems are special cases of the first axiom of T: 10.2.18*a* is what one gets from the axiom $\supset(\square A, A)$ by substituting $\square A$ for A, and one gets 10.2.18*b* by substituting $\lozenge A$ for A. Thus, 10.2.18*a* and 10.2.18*b* are theorems not only of S5 but also of T and of S4. To establish some of the other parts of 10.2.18, it will be necessary first to demonstrate that the principle of 'substitution of deductive equivalents' applies in S5; that is, that if X is a constituent of A, $X \dashv\vdash X'$, and A' is something obtained by substituting X for X' in A, then $A \vdash A'$, where the $\vdash$'s refer to proof in S5. Since the propositional connectives allow substitution of deductive equivalents for constituent propositions (which remains the case even if the extra deductive machinery of S5 is added to propositional logic), it suffices to show that such substitutions can be made in the scope of $\square$, that is, that if $X \dashv\vdash X'$, then $\square X \dashv\vdash \square X'$. This can be established as follows:

10.2.19   1 $X \vdash X'$ supp
         2 $\vdash \supset XX'$ 1, $\supset$-intro
         3 $\vdash \square \supset XX'$ 2, necessitation
         4 $\vdash \supset(\square X, \square X')$ 3, T axiom
         5 $\square X \vdash \square X'$ 4, $\supset$-expl

By the same derivation, if $X' \vdash X$, then $\square X' \vdash \square X$, and thus if $X \dashv\vdash X'$, then $\square X \dashv\vdash \square X'$. Substituting X' for X in more complicated expressions such as $\sim\square X$ or $\square\supset(\vee XY, \square \wedge XZ)$ will also produce a result that is deductively equivalent to the original. For example, the deductive equivalence of $\sim\square X$ and $\sim\square X'$ follows from the deductive equivalence of $\square X$ and

$\Box X'$ and the fact that the negations of deductive equivalents are deductively equivalent. We are now able to prove 10.2.18c:

10.2.20   1 $\supset(\Diamond \sim A, \Box \Diamond \sim A)$ 10.2.13 with $\sim A$ for A
           2 $\supset(\sim \Box A, \sim \Diamond \sim \Diamond \sim A)$ 1, 10.2.17a, 10.2.17b, SDE
           3 $\supset(\Diamond \sim \Diamond \sim A, \Box A)$ 2, contraposition
           4 $\supset(\Diamond \Box A, \Box A)$ 3, SDE

Let us now turn to the proof of 10.2.18d. Since 10.2.18d is obviously equivalent to the S4 axiom, proving that it is a theorem of S5 will establish a point that had been implicit in our choice of terminology, namely, that S5 is a special case of S4. To prove 10.2.18d, I will substitute a proof of the S4 axiom. First, however, I must justify a couple of steps that appear in the proof. Since 10.2.18b' is the S5 axiom, it is trivially a theorem of S5, and thus we have

10.2.21 $\Box \Diamond A$ and $\Diamond A$ are deductively equivalent in S5.

One can also easily establish 10.2.18c': substitute $\sim A$ for A in 10.2.18b and then perform a couple of obvious steps. Thus we have:

10.2.22 $\Diamond \Box A$ and $\Box A$ are deductively equivalent in S5.

Finally, the following is a theorem of T and thus also of S5:

10.2.23   Theorem (T): $\supset(A, \Diamond A)$
               1 $\supset(\Box \sim A, \sim A)$ T axiom with $\sim A$ for A
               2 $\supset(\sim \sim A, \sim \Box \sim A)$ 1, contraposition
               3 $\supset(A, \sim \Box \sim A)$ 2, SDE
               4 $\supset(A, \Diamond A)$ 3, 10.2.7b

We are now ready to prove the S4 axiom, and then 10.2.18d.

10.2.24   1 $\supset(\Box A, \Diamond \Box A)$ 10.2.23 with $\Box A$ for A
           2 $\supset(\Box A, \Box \Diamond \Box A)$ 1, SDE (10.2.21 with $\Box A$ for A)
           3 $\supset(\Box A, \Box \Box A)$ 2, SDE (10.2.22)

10.2.25   1 $\supset(\Box \sim A, \Box \Box \sim A)$ 10.2.24 with $\sim A$ for A
           2 $\supset(\sim \Box \Box \sim A, \sim \Box \sim A)$ 1, contraposition
           3 $\supset(\Diamond \Diamond A, \Diamond A)$ SDE, applied several times

Theorem 10.2.18a' has been proven in the course of proving 10.2.18d. Theorem 10.2.18b' is, as noted before, the S5 axiom and thus trivially a theorem of S5. Theorems 10.2.18c' and 10.2.18d' are both special cases of 10.2.15a, which is a theorem of T and thus also a theorem of S5. These theorems imply that any formula beginning with a sequence of modal operators is deductively equivalent in S5 to the formula obtained by deleting all but the last of the modal operators; for example, $\square\square\lozenge\square\lozenge A$ is deductively equivalent to $\lozenge A$ in S5.

10.3. Modal Predicate Logic

The formulas of modal logic that were discussed in the last section involved no quantifiers. This deficiency will have to be remedied, since modal logic will have to contend with perfectly ordinary sentences in which both modal operators and quantifiers appear, for example,

10.3.1   a. All men are necessarily mortal.
                b. Many linguists may beat their wives.

These examples are in fact ambiguous as regards the scope of the quantifier and the modal operator. The different interpretations possible for each could be expressed as follows:

10.3.2   a. (All x: Man x)$\square$Mortal x.
                a'. $\square$(All x: Man x)(Mortal x).

                b. (Many x: Linguist x)$\lozenge$(x beats x's wife)
                b'. $\lozenge$(Many x: Linguist x) (x beats x's wife).

Note that 10.3.2a and 10.3.2a' (likewise, 10.3.2b and 10.3.2b') need not have the same truth values: if one allows for alternative states of affairs in which there are not only ordinary men but also supermen who, unlike actual human beings, will live forever, then one could reasonably hold 10.3.2a to be true and 10.3.2a' to be false: every actual man has the property that of (physical) necessity he will die, but there are alternative worlds in which there are men who will not die and in which it is thus not the case that 'all men are mortal'.

There are two important respects in which 10.3.2a' and 10.3.2b' are less problematic than 10.3.2a and 10.3.2b. First, 10.3.2a and 10.3.2b involve the propositional functions ' $\square$(Mortal x)' and '$\lozenge$(x beats x's wife)'. In both of those propositional functions, a modal operator is applied not to a self-contained expression but to an expression containing a variable. It thus associates to each object the property 'is necessarily mortal' or 'possibly beats his wife'. At least some doubt can reasonably be entertained about whether an *object* can coherently be said to have (or lack) that sort of property. For example, Quine (1943, 1953) has maintained that it makes no sense to speak of ' $\square(x > 7)$' as being true or false of particular objects; rather, Quine holds that only expressions such as ' $\square(9 > 7)$' (presumably true) or ' $\square$(the number of planets > 7)' (presumably false), in which particular linguistic expressions appear in place of the variables inside the scope of the modal operator, can reasonably be assigned truth values and that different names for the same object (e.g., '9' vs. 'the number of planets') can yield different truth values when employed in a given modal context. Second, if one is to analyze 10.3.2*a* and 10.3.2*b* in terms of systems of possible worlds, it will be necessary to identify individuals in one world with individuals in another: to decide whether '□(Mortal *x*)' is true of Evel Knievel, it is necessary to identify the Evel Knievel (if any) in each alternative world and determine whether he is mortal. But how do you tell which individual in an alternative world is Evel Knievel and not just another individual who happens, confusingly, to have the same name and to practise the same trade as the Evel Knievel that we all know? This problem also arises in connection with '9' and 'the number of planets': if the number of planets in *w'* is smaller than the number of players on a baseball team in *w'*, can we identify either of those numbers nonarbitrarily with the number 9 of *w*? We might attempt to do it by looking at the arithmetic properties of these numbers, for example, the number of planets in *w'* is prime, so it can't be 9; but why does that show that that number can't be identified with 9 and not just that 9 has different arithmetic properties (such as being a prime number) in *w'* than in *w*?

One can react to the problems just mentioned either by avoiding them or by meeting them head on. Quine has chosen the former course and has rejected formulas such as 10.3.2*a* and 10.3.2*b* on the grounds that one can do philosophy adequately without making use of such formulas and that the philosopher has no compelling reason to get his hands (and mind) dirty wrestling with the problems that they raise. I am not convinced that one in fact *can* do philosophy adequately without allowing logical structures in which a quantifier outside the scope of a modal operator binds a variable inside the scope of that operator, as in 10.3.2*a* and 10.3.2*b*. However, be that as it may, it is at least clear that one cannot do linguistics adequately without recourse to such formulas, since they correspond to real meanings that may be exactly what the speaker intends in the given utterance. For example, 10.3.1*b* can perfectly well occur in a context where it is parallel to a sentence with a meaning of the form (Many *x*: F*x*)G*x* and thus itself demands a meaning of that form:

10.3.3   a. A: Chomsky beats his wife, Hockett beats his wife, Labov beats his wife, . . .
          B: Yeah, many linguists beat their wives.

          b. A: Chomsky may beat his wife, Hockett may beat his wife, Labov may beat his wife, . . .
          B: Yeah, many linguists may beat their wives.

Example 10.3.4*a*, which figures importantly in Quine's discussion of his doubts about formulas like 10.3.2*a*, appears to be ambiguous between 10.3.4*b* and 10.3.4*c*, as was pointed out in Smullyan's (1948) reply to Quine 1943:

10.3.4   a. □(the number of planets > 7).
             b. □(ιx: x is the number of planets) ($x > 7$)
             c. (ιx: x is the number of planets)□($x > 7$)

Example 10.3.4*b* is false, since there are alternative worlds in which there are 7 or fewer planets, but 10.3.4*c* is presumably true, since the number of planets is 9 and 9 is necessarily greater than 7. Quine was worried about the possibility that a propositional function '□($x > 7$)' might make no sense, since one could have $a = b$ and yet '□($a > 7$)' true but '□($b > 7$)' false, with '□($9 > 7$)' being an instance of the former and 10.3.4*a* an instance of the latter. However, 10.3.4*a* is ambiguous and neither of its interpretations has 'the number of planets' in the position of the variable in the suspect propositional function.

Nonetheless, one of the interpretations of 10.3.4*a* does involve a constituent □($x > 7$), and Quine (1969) has contested the claimed ambiguity of 10.3.4*a* on the grounds that one of the putative two interpretations of 10.3.4*c* is something whose coherence has not been adequately established.[7] Let us thus take up the question of whether 10.3.4*c* allows a coherent assignment of truth conditions (or, more generally, whether a coherent assignment of truth conditions can be achieved without incorrigible arbitrariness). The scheme for assigning truth conditions that is developed in this section provides a way of determining the truth value of 10.3.4*c* in any modal system whose language includes the vocabulary of 10.3.4*c*. However, that is not saying much, since we have so far left wide open the question of what modal systems are to be admitted. If we admit a modal system in which 9 is the prime minister of Ethiopia (and Spiro Agnew is the square root of Mickey Mantle, though 9 is still the number of planets), and that world is accessible from the real world, sure enough that will make 10.3.4*c* false in the real world. But is there any way of ruling out such bizarre modal systems which will in a nonarbitrary way make 10.3.4*c* come out true, as I said it should be? For example, if we are admitting an alternative world in which there are only 6 planets (or better, in which there are $1 + 1 + 1 + 1 + 1 + 1$ planets, since it is at issue whether we should call that number 6 in the alternative world), should we identify the $(1 + 1 + 1) \times (1 + 1 + 1)$ of that world with the 9 of the real world, or should we identify the number of the planets of that world with the 9 of the real world? If we can find a principled basis for rejecting the latter identification and accepting the former, we will then have a basis for calling 10.3.4c true. But if not, then we do not.

Thus, the question of what sense can be made of formulas like 10.3.4c is intimately connected with the question of how one can identify the individuals of one world with the individuals of another world. Quine (1953) observed that if one allows formulas like 10.3.4c, one must distinguish between ESSENTIAL PROPERTIES (properties an individual must have if it is to retain its identity) and ACCIDENTAL PROPERTIES (properties an individual could acquire or lose without changing its identity). For example, the property of being $1 + 1$ would be an essential property of 2, but the property of being the maximum number of terms that a person may serve as president of the United States is an accidental property of 2. In a context where it makes sense to speak of events affecting properties of the individual in question, one can distinguish between essential and accidental properties by asking oneself whether the individual would continue to exist (and retain its identity) after some possible or imaginable change had taken place. We can imagine a wicked witch turning a handsome prince into a frog, an ameba, or even an electron; in those cases, we regard the frog/ameba/electron as continuing to be the prince only if it serves as a repository for the prince's mind or soul (e.g., if the prince continues to be conscious and his perceptions are now from the vantage point of the frog/ameba/electron, or if the prince's consciousness is potentially recoverable from the frog/ameba/electron through another magical event which will occur when, say, a princess kisses the frog or provides a positive ion for the electron-prince to combine with). However, I am not up to the task of constructing a fairy tale in which a wicked witch turns a handsome prince into March the 21st or Planck's constant or the Tübingen dialect of German, or turns any of those three objects into a handsome prince. Thus, such properties as having a mind, being a period of time, being a number, and being a variety of language appear to be reasonable candidates for being essential properties.

I am sufficiently satisfied with the notion of 'essential property' as a means of restricting the classes of modal systems that come into consideration that I will henceforth assume that the notion makes sense and, accordingly, feel no qualms about writing formulas such as 10.4.2a'. One reasonable restriction on what properties can be 'essential', attributed to G. H. von Wright, is that a property which is essential anywhere is essential everywhere; that is, if there is any element a such that fa is an essential property of a, then for any element b, if fb, then fb is an essential property of b, and if $\sim fb$, then $\sim fb$ is an essential property of b.

'Verbs of propositional attitude' provide a more compelling case than do 'modal operators' for the sorts of worries that Quine voiced about formulas such as 10.3.4c. Consider example 10.3.5a (from Quine 1956), and the similar 10.3.5b:

10.3.5   a. John realizes that Bernard Ortcutt is a spy.
           b. Commissioner Gordon knows that Batman is a millionaire.

John may have realized that the sinister-looking bearded man that he has seen lurking near the Institute of Strategic Seismology is a spy, without realizing that that person is identical to the charming, clean-shaven pillar of the community, Bernard Ortcutt, who lives down the block from John. Is 10.3.5a true or false in that case? And does one's difficulty in deciding imply that '*x* realizes that *y* is a spy' is not a well-formed propositional function? Commissioner Gordon knows that Bruce Wayne is a millionaire but does not know that Batman and Bruce Wayne are the same person and has no information about Batman's financial status. Does this mean that '*x* knows that *y* is a millionaire' is not a proper propositional function, since substituting different proper names of the same individual in place of *y* can result in different propositions? Suppose that Batman/Wayne is lying on the ground, totally naked and with his head in a brown-paper bag, and someone points at him and says,

10.3.6   Commissioner Gordon knows that that man is a millionaire.

Has he expressed a true proposition? Is it even clear what proposition he has expressed?

It should be noted that the problems raised by 10.3.5–10.3.6 do not involve quantifiers. The problem rather is that of interpreting a propositional function $f(x)$ for which some occurrences of the *x* are in a 'referentially opaque' context such as the complement of *realize* or *know*. There are a number of possible approaches to the problems raised by 10.3.5–10.3.6. One possibility would be to take proper names to be some kind of definite description and thus allow 10.3.5a–b to be interpreted as having the same kind of ambiguity that 10.3.4a has. Undoubtedly proper names will sometimes have to be treated as definite descriptions if any sense is to be made of example 10.3.7a (called to my attention by George Lakoff), which has an interpretation that seems to demand an analysis along the lines of 10.3.7b:

10.3.7   a. Sam didn't realize that Kissinger was Kissinger.
           b. (ιx: *x* is Kissinger)(Sam didn't realize (*x* is Kissinger)).

That is, Sam failed to identify Kissinger correctly; 10.3.7a of course allows another interpretation, namely 'Sam didn't realize that Kissinger is the genius/bastard/megalomaniac/ . . . that he is'. However, that analysis raises problems of its own. The interpretation of the propositional function

'x is Kissinger' is more problematic than might at first seem to be the case. What exactly is it that Sam did not realize in 10.3.7b? Evidently, it is a proposition '$a = k$', where k is a constant denoting the real Kissinger, and a is some constant. In that case, Sam distinguishes two individuals that are in fact not distinct: Kissinger and the unidentified (or mis-identified) individual that in fact is Kissinger. My present feeling about the problems raised by 10.3.5–10.3.6 is that, just like that of 10.3.7, they revolve about a mismatch between two sets of individuals, where one of the two sets is the domain involved in the knowledge and beliefs of the in-dividual referred to. In Commissioner Gordon's mind, there are two dis-tinct individuals, one of whom he identifies as Bruce Wayne and the other as Batman. He has one set of beliefs about the one individual and another set of beliefs about the other, and he no more identifies those two in-dividuals with each other than he identifies either of them with Yogi Berra. *That man* in 10.3.6 thus corresponds to an individual that does not exist in the world of Commissioner Gordon's knowledge and beliefs: an individual that is Batman some of the time and Bruce Wayne at other times. But then what about an occurrence of 10.3.6 in which the speaker is pointing at Batman/Wayne dressed in his Bruce Wayne clothes and appearing at a public function at which he is clearly identified as Bruce Wayne? Two possibilities suggest themselves here: (i) *that man* in 10.3.6 is interpreted as referring to an individual of Commissioner Gordon's belief world, and that individual can be identified with the Wayne role of Batman/Wayne in the speaker's belief world; (ii) *that man* is interpreted as referring to the Wayne role in the speaker's belief world. Either way, Wayne in the Wayne role and Wayne in the Batman role would be distinguished in the speaker's belief world, though both would be 'mani-festations' of a single individual (another individual, strictly speaking) in the world of the speaker's knowledge and beliefs. In the case of Batman/Wayne appearing in the Wayne role, *that man* can be interpreted as refer-ring to an individual in the speaker's belief world that can be identified with an individual of the Commissioner's belief world, whereas in the case of Batman/Wayne without clothes and with his head in a bag, the individual in the speaker's belief world that *that man* must be interpreted as referring to does not have a unique counterpart in the Commissioner's belief world.

The need to distinguish between two manifestations of a single object is something that we will have to live with anyway, if we are to cope with sentences involving the expressions *the morning star* and *the evening star*. While the morning star and the evening star are generally both manifesta-tions of the planet Venus,[8] they still have to be distinguished in reference as well as in sense, since 10.3.8a is a bizarre thing to say when one is pointing at the evening manifestation of Venus,[9] and 10.3.8b, which involves a comparison between the morning star and the evening star, is perfectly intelligible:

10.3.8   a. Look at the morning star!
          b. The morning star is more beautiful than the evening star.

The intelligibility of 10.3.8*b* is not surprising when one considers that *beautiful* is normally predicated not of an object but of a manifestation of the object (or better, a class of manifestations of it). Thus, there is no contradiction in the following set of propositions:

10.3.9   a. Dr. Jekyll is handsome.
          b. Mr. Hyde is ugly.
          c. Dr. Jekyll and Mr. Hyde are the same person.

What *beautiful* and *ugly* are predicated of is not that one person, but two different 'aesthetic objects' that that one, person can turn himself into. Similarly, a person who utters 10.3.10*a* and a person who utters 10.3.10*b* are not contradicting each other:

10.3.10   a. God, is Mount Fuji beautiful! Look at this marvelous photograph of it that I took from Misaka Pass.
           b. God, is Mount Fuji ugly! I climbed it last year, and there's nothing to see—just cinders and the garbage left by the idiots that climb it.

Mount Fuji viewed from 20 miles away isn't the same aesthetic object as Mount Fuji viewed from its own slopes, though both are manifestations of the same mountain.

Let us return to the problem of how to identify individuals in different worlds. One obvious proposal for a criterion of identity between individuals in the domains of different worlds turns out to be grossly unsatisfactory, namely, the proposal that the individual in w' that one identifies with a given individual a of w is that individual of w' that is most similar to a. Over and above the objection that any measure of similarity is doomed to arbitrariness, this proposal is open to two fatal objections. First, there are perfectly intelligible sentences which presuppose cross-world identities between an individual of the one world and some individual other than the one most like him in the other world. Consider, for example, the sentences

10.3.11   If Nixon had received the education that I did and I had received the education that Nixon did, I would be a ruthless megalomaniac and Nixon would be a pure-hearted anarchist.

10.3.12   If I had been brought up by your parents and you had been brought up by my parents, I'd be just like you and you'd be just like me.

In either case the speaker is comparing the real world with an alternative world in which he is not the person in that world who has the most in common with the real him. Second, if an individual in the one world had to be identified with the individual in the other world that is most similar to him, the notion of identity would be neither symmetric nor transitive.[10] Suppose, for sake of concreteness, that we measure similarity between individuals by the number of properties that they have in common on a fixed checklist of properties, and that we have individuals as follows in three worlds:

	$Waldo_1$	$Oscar_1$	$Walter_2$	$Otto_2$	$Otokar_3$	$Waldemar_3$
trustworthy	+	−	+	+	−	+
loyal	+	−	−	−	−	+
brave	+	−	−	−	−	+
reverent	+	+	+	−	+	+
kind	+	+	+	+	−	−
etc.						

Here the subscript indicates the world to which the individual belongs. The names are purely for our convenience—it is not to be assumed that 'Waldo$_1$' is called 'Waldo', and I will indeed assume that all of these individuals are called 'Charlie'. Let us suppose that these individuals agree on all the other properties on the checklist (including the property of being called Charlie) and that there are no other individuals that are 'closer' to any of them. Then the individual of w_2 who is most similar to Waldo is Walter, but the individual of w_1 who is most similar to Walter is not Waldo but Oscar, and thus identity is not symmetric if an individual of one world is identified with the most similar individual of another world. The individual of w_2 who is most similar to Waldo is Walter, and the individual of w_3 who is most similar to Walter is Otokar, but the individual of w_3 who is most similar to Waldo is not Otokar but Waldemar; thus identity is not transitive if an individual of one world is identified with the most similar individual of another world.

Why then is 10.3.13a a reasonable thing to say but 10.3.13b totally bizarre?

10.3.13   a. Gerald Ford could have been an insurance executive.
           b. Gerald Ford could have been the daughter of a Nigerian goatherd.

Shouldn't both be trivially true, on the grounds that there is nothing to prevent your identifying Gerald Ford with any individual you like of another world, regardless of the degree of similarity to the real Gerald Ford? I maintain that there is a difference because of the particular principle of cross-world identification that figures in examples like 10.3.13, which I claim to be part of the meaning of the particular construction, rather than something deducible from characteristics of the alternative worlds. The most common use of sentences like 10.3.13a is to describe alternative present situations which would have come about had certain past events turned out differently, though with other things being as they were in the actual history of the world. What 10.3.13a means is that one could trace back in the real history of the world to some point (say, Ford's graduation from the University of Michigan) and then trace forward again along a different chain of events (though with the events being restricted to what we take to be possible events), with individuals retaining their identities through these changes, except where events bring new individuals into existence, eliminate old individuals, or bring about the fission or fusion of old individuals. For example, one can make sense of 10.4.14 by saying that it means that Gerald Ford can be traced back to a point when he could have undergone fission (i.e., he consisted of a single cell, and that cell split into two separate individuals, giving rise to identical twins):

10.3.14   Gerald Ford could have been identical twins.

The reason that 10.3.13b is so bizarre is that to trace Gerald Ford back to a point in time when different events could have given rise to a daughter of a Nigerian goatherd, you would have traced back to a point when there was no Gerald Ford and thus nothing to identify with the Nigerian goatherd's daughter that came into being later: from the moment that Gerald Ford first existed, he was the son of two Americans. (Of course, different assumptions about how persons come into existence would change things: if you believe in reincarnation, with a free-floating soul being incorporated into each new body at the moment of conception, 10.3.13b would become intelligible: you could interpret it as meaning that if the actual conception of Gerald Ford had not taken place, Ford's present soul might have been infused into the body of a Nigerian goatherd's daughter.)

     There is no reason to expect that any general criterion of identity of elements in different worlds will make sense for all the kinds of quantified modal logic that one might want to do. The theory of quantified modal logic developed in this section can be combined with any system of identifying elements in different worlds. Whether one must operate with a modal system in which 10.3.13b comes out true will depend on what kind of modal logic one is doing (and on what auxiliary nonlogical assumptions one makes, for example, the assumption that a person starts to exist at the moment of conception). Any 'modal' sentence must be supplied with an indication of what notion of necessity or possibility it involves. For a particular modal system to be of any use in analyzing the given sentence, one will have to establish that that system (including the way that elements of different worlds are identified) adequately represents the particular notions of possibility and necessity that play a role in the given sentence.[11]

If 10.3.14 is interpreted the way that I have suggested (that is, as meaning that Ford could have BEEN identical twins, rather than that he could have HAD an identical twin), we will have a case where one individual of one world is identified with more than one individual of another world. In that case, we do not have, strictly speaking, identity between individuals of different worlds—we have instead a relation of 'is a counterpart of'. Lewis (1968) has explored a version of modal predicate logic in which a relation of 'counterparthood' is one of the primitive notions of the theory. Lewis takes the domains of different worlds to be disjoint, that is, he takes individuals of one world never to be, strictly speaking, identical to their counterparts in other worlds,[12] a policy comparable to that of treating the Gerald Ford of 30 November 1975 and the Gerald Ford of 11 April 1937 as distinct individuals, though connected by an important relation, namely, that the latter individual is a 'temporal ancestor' of the former. He restates the truth conditions in terms of the counterpart relation. For example, whereas in the modal predicate logic developed in the preceding paragraphs, $\Box fa$ would be true under the conditions 10.3.15a, for Lewis the condition would be 10.3.15b, where a is an element of the domain of w:

10.3.15   a. $\Box fa$ is T in w if and only if for all w' such that Rww', fa is T in w'.

b. $\Box fa$ is T in w if and only if for all w' such that Rww' and all a' such that a' is a counterpart in w' to a, fa' is T in w'.

Condition 10.3.15b implies, incidentally, that if there is a world accessible from the real world in which Gerald Ford has two counterparts, then both of them would have to like sports for *Necessarily, Gerald Ford likes sports* to be true in the real world.

A need for speaking in terms of counterparts rather than in terms of identity arises precisely when more than one element of one world can correspond to one element of another world. For the remainder of this chapter, let us forget that such a need sometimes arises, and operate in terms of worlds whose domains may have elements in common or even be identical. Whether formula 10.3.2a, repeated below as 10.3.16a, should count as true depends on an important technicality. According to what I have said, the conditions under which 10.3.16a is true in w are given by 10.3.16b:

10.3.16 a. ($\forall x$: man x) $\square$(mortal x).
b. For every element a of the domain of w, and every world w' such that Rww', (mortal a) is true in w'.

What if some men in the real world do not belong to the domains of all alternatives to the real world? For example, suppose that w_{89} has for its domain all men of the real world except Evel Knievel. In that case, should (mortal EK) count as true in w_{89}? And if it doesn't, should that be grounds for saying that 10.3.16a is not true in the real world? There are three sets of answers to these questions that immediately spring to mind as worth considering: (i) The proposition (mortal EK) should be held not to be true (whether F or $\#$ is immaterial) in w_{89}, and that fact should be sufficient to make 10.3.16a false in w, since what the truth conditions for 10.3.16a require to be true for every element of the domain of w and every accessible w' is not true for every element and every accessible world. (ii) It should be taken to lack a truth value in w_{89}, and 10.3.16a should be considered $\#$ in the real world (assuming that no real man is immortal in any alternative world) on the grounds that $\#$ is the lowest truth value that 'mortal EK' takes in any world accessible to the real world. (iii) In interpreting $\square$(mortal EK), one should ignore worlds in which there is no Evel Knievel, and accordingly one should take 10.3.16a to be true on the grounds that, for any real world man, in any alternative world in which he exists, he is still mortal.

I lean strongly to the last alternative on the grounds that under the other two alternatives an object would have to have necessary existence before it could have any other necessary atomic properties.[13] Under either i or ii, $\square fa$ could be true in w only if $\square$(a exists) were true in w. However, necessary existence is too stringent a prerequisite to impose on anything—it would make $\square fa$ virtually always F or $\#$ for a rather uninteresting reason. It should be noted, though, that policy iii may amount to a special case of a proposal that I made in connection with the problem of whether universally quantified propositions with empty domains should always be considered (vacuously) true. In connection with examples 6.1.3. I suggested that it may not be possible to impose a general policy on whether 'vacuously true' instances should contribute to the truth value of a complex proposition and that the only thing common to the interpretation of the examples discussed there was that in each case only those elements that were relevant to the presumable purpose of the utterance were taken into consideration.

Which of these three policies one adopts will affect whether 10.3.17, which is known as the CONVERSE BARCAN FORMULA[14] is valid in the modal system:

10.3.17 $\supset(\Box(\forall x)fx, (\forall x)\Box fx)$

The only way that 10.3.17 could fail to be true in a world w would be for $(\forall x)fx$ to be true in every world accessible from w, but for $\Box fa$ not to be true in w for some choice of a in the domain of w; but that could be the case only if $\Box fa$ failed to be true by virtue of a not existing in some world accessible to w, since (by assumption) $(\forall x)fx$ is true in every such world, and thus fa is true in every world in which a exists. Note that the restricted-quantifier analogue to the Barcan formula, $\supset((\forall: fx)\ \Box gx,$ $\Box(\forall: fx)gx)$, will not be valid in any modal system in which a world has an accessible alternative in which the predicates are true of different things than in the given world. For example, if all the real world philosophers are dangerous in every alternative world but there is a real world television repairman who is a philosopher in w' and not dangerous in w', then $(\forall:$ philosopher $x)$ $\Box$(dangerous x) is true in the real world but $\Box(\forall:$ philosopher $x)$ (dangerous x) is false. Note that such counterexamples to the restricted-quantifier Barcan formula do not depend on alternative worlds having extra objects, only on the possibility of alternative worlds in which real world individuals have different properties than in the real world.

10.4. Strict Implication and Relevant Entailment Logic

The development of the hierarchy of systems of modal logic associated with the name of C. I. Lewis is intimately connected with Lewis's development of a notion of 'strict implication'. Lewis attempted to develop a connective that corresponded to such ordinary language words as *if* and *implies* better than the 'material implication' ($\supset$) of Russell and Whitehead's *Principia Mathematica* did. Lewis's strict implication (written $\dashv$) was to be related to necessity by virtue of A$\dashv$B being equivalent to $\Box \supset$ AB, or alternatively, to $\Box \lor (\sim A, B)$. In the earlier works, $\dashv$ played the major role, $\Box$ and $\Diamond$ only a peripheral role, though the balance reversed in the 1930s and 1940s.[15]

Some of the more bizarre theorems involving $\supset$ (bizarre, that is, if $\supset$ is identified with *if*) do not have analogues with $\dashv$ as theorems in any of the Lewis systems. For example, while $\lor(\supset AB, \supset BA)$ is a theorem of standard propositional logic, $\lor(\dashv AB, \dashv BA)$ is not a theorem of S1, S2,

S3, S4, or S5. However, in even the weakest of the Lewis systems, S1, the following so-called paradoxes of strict implication are theorems:

10.4.1   a. $\supset(\Box B, \dashv 3AB)$
           b. $\supset(\sim\Diamond A, \dashv 3AB)$
           c. $\dashv 3(\wedge(A, \sim A), B)$
           d. $\dashv 3(A, \vee(B, \sim B))$

These results are reminiscent of some of the so-called paradoxes of material implication, namely, the following theorems of standard propositional logic:

10.4.2   a. $\supset(B, \supset AB)$
           b. $\supset(\sim A, \supset AB)$
           c. $\supset(\wedge(A, \sim A), B)$
           d. $\supset(A, \vee(B, \sim B))$

Theorems 10.4.1a and 10.4.1b at least are quite different in content from their counterparts in 10.4.2: Theorem 10.4.1a can be paraphrased as 'a necessary proposition is implied by anything' and 10.4.1b as 'an impossible proposition implies anything', whereas it is only by quite misleading equivocation that one can give at all similar paraphrases to 10.4.2a and 10.4.2b (the common paraphrases of 10.4.2a and 10.4.2b as 'a true proposition is implied by anything' and 'a false proposition implies anything' are incorrect since neither says anything about implication). Hughes and Cresswell (1968:335–39) dismiss all allegations of 'paradoxicality' of 10.4.1a–d: 'the "paradoxes" seem to us on reflection not to be tiresome (though harmless) eccentricities which we have to put up with in order to have the disjunctive syllogism, transitivity of entailment, and the rest, but sound principles in their own right: a logic of entailment *ought*, for example, to contain some principle which reflects our inclination to say to someone who has asserted something self-contradictory, "If one were to accept *that*, one could prove anything at all"— and the principle that $(p \cdot \sim p)$ entails q expresses this in just the way that a formal system might be expected to' [pp. 338–39].

Anderson and Belnap (1975), by contrast, reject 10.4.1a–d, especially 10.4.1c–d, as perversions of the notion of 'entailment', maintaining instead that a proposition follows only from propositions that are relevant to it, and hold that the antecedents in 10.4.1c–d are blatantly irrelevant to the consequents (and that there is a less blatant fallacy of relevance in 10.4.1a–b); they would undoubtedly accuse Hughes and Cresswell of overkill: to squelch a person who has contradicted himself, it is enough to say that if one were to accept the contradiction one could prove anything to which it is relevant, not necessarily anything at all. Anderson and

Belnap hold 10.4.1a–b to be false on the grounds that the necessity of B or the impossibility of A is irrelevant to whether B follows from A: if A is irrelevant to B (say, if no atomic proposition is a constituent of both), then B does not follow FROM A, regardless of whether B is necessary and whether A is impossible.

Whether the 'paradoxes of strict implication' are things that one can live with depends mainly on whether one shares the depth of Anderson and Belnap's concern for 'relevance'; at least the 'paradoxes' do not lead one from uncontroversially true premises to uncontroversially false conclusions (the controversial cases being arguments whose premises or conclusion are of the form 'If X, then Y '). Other results that are sometimes considered paradoxical, though they are much easier to live with than 10.4.1a–d, for example, are the following theorems, which hold in T and stronger systems such as S4 and S5:

10.4.3   a. $\dashv(\sim A, A) \dashv\vdash \Box A$
          b. $\wedge(\dashv AB, \dashv(\sim A, B)) \dashv\vdash \Box B$

Theorem 10.4.3a follows from the fact that $\supset(\sim A, A) \dashv\vdash A$ in propositional logic, and hence $\dashv(\sim A, A)$ (i.e., $\Box \supset(\sim A, A)$) is deductively equivalent to $\Box A$ in T, since a principle of substitution of deductive equivalents is valid in T. Theorem 10.4.3b is based in a similar way on the fact that $\wedge(\supset AB, \supset(\sim A, B)) \dashv\vdash B$ in propositional logic. Theorem 10.4.3b can be thought of as a variant of the idea that a proposition is necessary if and only if it follows from everything, an idea that Anderson and Belnap of course reject.

Anderson and Belnap's (1975) treatment of 'strict implication' deviates far more radically from standard logic than does Lewis's. They dismiss the rationalizations usually given for identifying $\supset$ with *if* as characterized by 'perversity, muddle-headedness, and downright error' (p. 5) and argue for an alternative treatment of conditional propositions that rests on two ideas that play no role in the foundations of $\supset$: the idea of 'relevance' (i.e., that a conditional 'if A, then B' should be true only if A is relevant to the drawing of the conclusion B) and the idea of 'entailment' (i.e., that a conditional 'if A, then B' expresses that A is grounds for drawing the conclusion B, or that B follows from A). Anderson and Belnap thus dismiss $\supset(A, \vee(B, \sim B))$ as embodying a fallacy of relevance (its antecedent is irrelevant to its consequent, regardless of the fact that the consequent is guaranteed to be true), as does $\supset(A, \supset BA)$, which also blatantly conflicts with an interpretation of $\supset$ as involving 'entailment': from A it doesn't follow that A follows from B; for example, from '2 + 2 = 4' it does not follow that '2 + 2 = 4' follows from the proposition that Beethoven's 18th piano sonata is in E$^\flat$ major.

They propose a system of rules of inference that is set up so as to respect these two characteristics that they attribute to conditionals. Their accommodation of the notion of relevance is straightforward: each supposition in a proof is provided with an index, in the proof one must keep track of the indices corresponding to the suppositions that have been used in deriving the given line, and subproofs can be made use of only if the supposition of the subproof is used in establishing the conclusion of the subproof. Their rules of inference for 'entailment' (which, following Anderson and Belnap, I will write as $\rightarrow$ rather than as $\supset$ or $\dashv$) are identical to the rules for $\supset$ in chapter 2 except for the way that the indices fit in:

10.4.4 $\rightarrow$-introduction $\begin{array}{ll} A & k \\[2pt] \dots & \\ B & M\ (k{\in}M) \\ {\rightarrow}AB & M\text{-}\{k\} \end{array}$

$\rightarrow$-exploitation $\begin{array}{ll} {\rightarrow}AB & M \\ A & N \\ B & M{\cup}N \end{array}$

Here k is an index on a supposition and M and N are sets of indices that are built up in the process of keeping track of suppositions; here, as in general, in a rule involving a subproof, the set of suppositions from which the conclusion is deduced must include the supposition of that subproof (note the condition '$k{\in}M$' in $\rightarrow$-intro). The conclusion that is established BY the subproof depends on those suppositions other than the supposition of the subproof (i.e., the supposition of the subproof is 'discharged'). In a rule in which a conclusion is drawn from formulas on the same 'level' in the hierarchy of subproofs, the set of suppositions that the conclusion depends on is the union of the sets of suppositions on which the premises depend. There is in addition a rule of reiteration, which allows one to repeat an earlier superordinate line, preserving the set of indices of that line. Let us use $E_{\rightarrow}$ to denote the logical system having only the connective $\rightarrow$ plus the rules of inference in 10.4.4 and the rule of reiteration.[16] It can easily be seen that the most obvious proof of $\supset(A, \supset BA)$ fails to yield an analogous proof of the (for Anderson and Belnap) fallacious $\rightarrow(A, \rightarrow BA)$. Consider the proof of $\supset(A, \supset BA)$ given in chapter 2:

10.4.5 $\begin{array}{lll} 1 & A & \text{supp} \\ 2 & \quad B & \text{supp} \\ 3 & \quad A & 1,\ \text{reit} \\ 4 & {\supset}BA & 2\text{--}3,\ {\supset}\text{-intro} \\ 5\ {\supset}(A, {\supset}BA) & & 1\text{--}4,\ {\supset}\text{-intro} \end{array}$

Suppose we try to construct a parallel proof using → and the →-intro of
10.4.4. Call the indices of lines 1 and 2 simply 1 and 2. Line 3 will also have
the index 1, since reiteration preserves indices. But then a line 4 in which
→BA is inferred will not be admissible: the index of line 2 is not a member
of the set of indices of line 3, and thus →-intro is not applicable.

   It is in fact possible to show that E→ does not allow any proof of
→(A, →BA). The impossibility of proving that formula in E→ is a special
case of the result (proven in Anderson and Belnap 1975:34) that a formula
built up from atomic propositions using only → is provable only if every
atomic proposition that appears in the formula appears both as an
'antecedent part' and as a 'consequent part', where the notions of
'antecedent part' and 'consequent part' are defined as follows: (i) any
formula is a consequent part of itself; (ii) if →XY is a consequent part of
Z, then X is an antecedent part of Z and Y a consequent part; (iii) if →XY
is an antecedent part of Z, then X is a consequent part of Z and Y is an
antecedent part. The use of these terms is illustrated informally on the
following:

10.4.6   a.

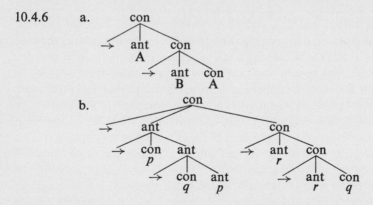

Since B occurs only as an antecedent part of →(A, →BA), the result implies
that that formula cannot be proven in E→. For the same reason, the formula
in 10.4.6*b* cannot be proven either: *r* occurs only as an antecedent part and
q only as a consequent part. Anderson and Belnap also prove (p. 33) that
→XY is not provable in E→ unless X and Y share an atomic proposition
among their constituents. This result supports their claim that E→ provides
an account of relevance: absence of any shared atomic constituent would
be a blatant instance of X being irrelevant to Y. This result also shows that
there are instances in which Y is a theorem of E→ but →XY is not, for
example, it shows that →(A, →BB) is not a theorem, even though →BB
obviously *is* a theorem; thus at least some of the 'paradoxes of strict
implication' are demonstrably not theorems of E→.

Anderson and Belnap's treatment of → provides the basis of a novel treatment of necessity. They propose defining □A as →(→AA, A). Given the interpretation that they put on →, it is not too hard to get used to this at first startling formula. The proposition →AB is to be true only when B follows from A. It is occasionally held that necessary propositions follow from all other propositions, as they do in some sense in all of the Lewis systems. For Anderson and Belnap, a formula can only follow from a formula that is relevant to it, and thus a formula could follow from everything only if everything were relevant to it. Only such formulas as the blatantly false (∀p)p (which might be read 'Everything is the case') and the trivially true (∃p)p meet that condition. If less outlandish propositions are to have a chance of being necessary, a weaker criterion of necessity must be accepted. The proposition →AA is relevant to A (i.e., it contains exactly the same atomic propositions), it is a theorem of E_, and it is indeed the most trivial theorem of that system (in the sense of being both the shortest theorem and the one with the shortest proof). The Anderson and Belnap analysis of □A thus says that A follows from the most trivial necessary truth that is guaranteed to be relevant to it. They demonstrate that necessity so defined has many of the properties that they would want it to have. For example, they prove a theorem that can be paraphrased as 'anything that follows from a true entailment is necessary' (they would want this to be a theorem since for them a formula →XY expresses that Y follows from X and thus ought to be true by necessity if it is true at all, and the same ought to be true of anything that follows from it). Their proof of this result is as follows:

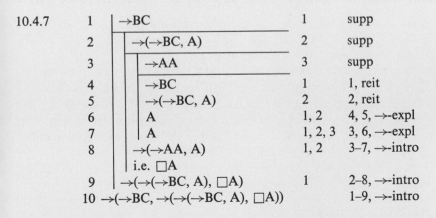

10.4.7	1	→BC	1	supp
	2	→(→BC, A)	2	supp
	3	→AA	3	supp
	4	→BC	1	1, reit
	5	→(→BC, A)	2	2, reit
	6	A	1, 2	4, 5, →-expl
	7	A	1, 2, 3	3, 6, →-expl
	8	→(→AA, A)	1, 2	3–7, →-intro
		i.e. □A		
	9	→(→(→BC, A), □A)	1	2–8, →-intro
10	→(→BC, →(→(→BC, A), □A))			1–9, →-intro

Note the importance of step 7: while it appears to duplicate step 6, the use of →AA in establishing it enlarges the set of indices, and that enlargement of the set of indices is essential if the subproof beginning at line 3 is to establish anything, since the conclusion of the subproof must involve the index 3 if the subproof is to terminate.

Anderson and Belnap (1975:29) credit Prior with calling their attention the fact that if $E_\rightarrow$ is supplemented by certain axioms that from their point of view express plausible relations between $\square$ and $\rightarrow$, $\square A$ can be shown to be deductively equivalent to $\rightarrow(\rightarrow AA, A)$. The axioms in question are

10.4.8   i. $\rightarrow(\square A, A)$
          ii. $\rightarrow(\rightarrow AB, \square(\rightarrow AB))$
          iii. $\rightarrow(\square A, \rightarrow(\rightarrow AB, \square B))$

(The axiom of this set that is most controversial but also most characteristic of Anderson and Belnap's approach is ii, which expresses the idea that any true entailment is true by necessity). The proof of $\rightarrow(\rightarrow(\rightarrow AA, A), \square A)$ is as follows; see Anderson and Belnap (1975:29) for a proof of its converse:

10.4.9   1 $\rightarrow AA$ theorem of $E_\rightarrow$
           2 $\rightarrow(\rightarrow AA, \square(\rightarrow AA))$ axiom ii, with A in
                                            place of B
           3 $\square(\rightarrow AA)$ 1, 2, $\rightarrow$-expl
           4 $\rightarrow(\square(\rightarrow AA), \rightarrow(\rightarrow(\rightarrow AA, A), \square A))$ axiom iii, with $\rightarrow AA$
                                            in place of A, A in
                                            place of B
           5 $\rightarrow(\rightarrow(\rightarrow AA, A), \square A)$ 3, 4, $\rightarrow$-expl

Thus, the effect of Anderson and Belnap's definition of $\square$ could be obtained equivalently by taking $\square$ as a primitive and adding the axioms 10.4.8 to the deductive apparatus of $E_\rightarrow$.

In subsequent chapters of their book, Anderson and Belnap investigate systems less rudimentary than $E_\rightarrow$. Their system $E_{\sim}$, in which both $\sim$ and $\rightarrow$ are available as connectives and the rules of inference of $E_\rightarrow$ are supplemented by rules of inference for $\sim$, allows further development of the modal logic based on $\rightarrow$, since $E_{\sim}$ has the means available to define $\diamondsuit$ as well as $\square$ ($\diamondsuit A$ is defined as $\sim\square\sim A$, that is, as $\sim\rightarrow(\rightarrow(\sim A, \sim A), \sim A)$). They are able to demonstrate a large number of deductive equivalences between formulas involving $\square$ and $\diamondsuit$, for example,

10.4.10 $\square\square A \dashv\vdash \square A$
            $\square\diamondsuit\square\diamondsuit A \dashv\vdash \square\diamondsuit A$

Using the term 'modality' to denote a concatenation of $\square$, $\diamondsuit$, and $\sim$, it it can be shown that $E_\approx$ has the following 14 mutually nonequivalent modalities:

10.4.11   Positive modalities:

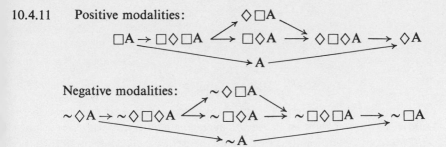

Negative modalities:

These are the same 14 'modalities' that are distinguished in Lewis's S4, though there is some problem in interpreting the word 'same' here. In an extended digression into the relationship between their modal logic and the various Lewis systems, Anderson and Belnap point out that one's picture of the relationship among the various systems depends heavily on what one takes the relationship between necessity and 'strict implication' to be. Regardless of whether one is operating in terms of Lewis's 'strict implication' or Anderson and Belnap's 'entailment', both the possibility of defining 'necessary' as 'implied by the proposition that it implies itself' and that of defining it as 'implied by its negation' are available. Calling the first kind of necessity $\Box$ and the second kind $\Box'$, one can separate the problem of determining what $\Box$-modalities a system has from that of determining what $\Box'$-modalities it has. $E_\approx$ has the 14 $\Box$-modalities listed in 10.4.11 but has 42 $\Box'$-modalities. When it is stated that S3 has 42 modalities, what is meant is $\Box'$-modalities, and in this respect S3 and $E_\approx$ agree completely. However, if one takes the trouble to determine what $\Box$-modalities S3 has, as apparently Anderson and Belnap were the first to do, one finds that S3, like $E_\approx$ and S4, has the 14 modalities listed in 10.4.11. In S4 the $\Box$-modalities and the $\Box'$-modalities coincide, as a result of the fact that in S4 (though not in S3 or $E_\approx$) $\Box'$A implies $\Box$A.

There is a large and important class of formulas X for which $\Box$X is provable in $E_\approx$ but $\Box'$X is not provable, namely, theorems of the form →AB. Anderson and Belnap (1975:120–21) establish that NO formula of the form →(~→AB, →CD) is a theorem of $E_\approx$. Thus, in particular, →(~→AB, →AB); that is, $\Box'$(→AB) is never a theorem, even though for many choices of A and B, →AB is a theorem (e.g., →AA is a theorem).

One important rule of inference Anderson and Belnap are forced to give up in order to accomplish their goal is the DISJUNCTIVE SYLLOGISM: the rule allowing one to infer B from ∨AB and ~A.[17] Note that that rule plays a crucial role in a standard proof of one of the results that they find most obnoxious:

10.4.12	1	$\wedge(A, \sim A)$	1	supp
	2	A	1	1, $\wedge$-expl
	3	$\sim A$	1	1, $\wedge$-expl
	4	$\vee AB$	1	2, $\vee$-intro
	5	B	1	4, 3, disj-syll
	6	$\supset(\wedge(A, \sim A), B)$		1–5, $\supset$-intro

The only other questionable step is 4, but Anderson and Belnap wish to allow free application of $\vee$-intro, even when it introduces 'irrelevant' disjuncts (their rationale presumably being that all they ought to be accountable for is relevance relations *among* the lines of the proof, and the line from which 4 is derived is surely relevant to it). Thus, only by giving up the disjunctive syllogism can they avoid having $\rightarrow(\wedge(A, \sim A), B)$ as a theorem. More generally, if they have a rule of $\vee$-introduction that gives a conclusion $\vee AB$ with the same set of indices as the premise A from which it is derived, the disjunctive syllogism will have to be excluded if one is to avoid fallacies of relevance: one will otherwise be able to deduce B from premises whose set of indices reflects only the derivational history of A and $\sim A$.

The closest analogue to the disjunctive syllogism 10.4.13*a* that Anderson and Belnap have is the derived rule of inference 10.4.13*b*:

10.4.13   a. $\{\vee AB, \sim A\} \vdash B$
         b. If $\vdash \vee AB$ and $\vdash \sim A$, then $\vdash B$.

Rule 10.4.13*b* will of course not justify step 5 in 10.4.12, since the premises from which line 5 is derived are not theorems. Note that 10.4.13*b* is much weaker than 10.4.13*a*: rule 10.4.13*b* is only applicable in the 'main' proof, whereas 10.4.13*a* is applicable at any depth of subordination, that is, for 10.4.13*a*, $\vee AB$ and $\sim A$ need not be things proven absolutely but can be consequences deduced from whatever set of suppositions is 'operative' at the given point of the proof. The difference between 10.4.13*a* and 10.4.13*b* is the same as the difference between the ludicrous 'rule' 10.4.14*a* and the perfectly respectable 'law of necessitation' 10.4.14*b*:

10.4.14   a. $A \vdash \square A$
         b. If $\vdash A$, then $\vdash \square A$.

Rule 10.4.14*a* would wipe out the difference between A and $\square A$ in most systems of modal logic, and no one but the most extreme fatalist could seriously propose it. Rule 10.4.14*b*, on the other hand, embodies merely the claim that the given notion of necessity includes logical necessity as a special case, which is a reasonable condition to impose on a number of notions of necessity, for example, epistemic necessity.

While $\rightarrow(\wedge(A, \sim A), B)$ is not a theorem of Anderson and Belnap's general system E, certain special cases of it are theorems; for example, $\rightarrow(\wedge(A, \sim A), A)$ is a theorem, being a special case of the theorem $\rightarrow(\wedge AB, A)$. Anderson and Belnap prove a result that establishes a limited realm of formulas for which something akin to the dread $\rightarrow(\wedge(A, \sim A), B)$ is a theorem of E. Following Anderson and Belnap, let us call a formula a MANIFEST REPUGNANCY if it is of the form $\wedge(p_1, \sim p_1, p_2, \sim p_2, \ldots, p_n, \sim p_n)$, that is, if it is a conjunction of atomic propositions and their negations, with every atomic proposition that appears in it appearing both negated and unnegated. They prove the following theorem (p. 163):

10.4.15   If X is a manifest repugnancy and Y contains no atomic propositions other than those that appear in X, then $\rightarrow$XY is a theorem of E.

A manifest repugnancy thus entails every formula made up entirely of things to which it is relevant. Note that 10.4.15 is a good deal weaker than $\rightarrow(\wedge(A, \sim A), B)$, since not only is Y restricted in the way indicated, but X must be of a form 'stronger' than $\wedge(A, \sim A)$: X is not simply $\wedge(\wedge(p_1, \ldots, p_n), \sim \wedge(p_1, \ldots, p_n))$ but has all the $\sim p_i$ among its conjuncts.

10.5. Appendix: Converses of the Theorems about Reflexivity, Symmetry, and Transitivity of the Accessibility Relation R

It was proven in 10.2 that for any modal system M with accessibility relation R, and any formula A,

10.5.1   If R is reflexive, then $\supset(\Box A, A)$ is valid in M; (10.2.5)

10.5.2   If R is symmetric, then $\supset(A, \Box \Diamond A)$ is valid in M; (10.2.12)

10.5.3   If R is transitive, then $\supset(\Box A, \Box \Box A)$ is valid in M. (10.2.6)

Under the assumptions that M has only finitely many worlds and that any two worlds of M are 'distinguishable', in the sense that for any two worlds there is a proposition that is true in one and false in the other, the converses of these three results can also be proven.

Theorem. Let M be a modal system such that M contains only finitely many worlds and any two worlds of M are distinguishable; let R be the accessibility relation of M. Then if $\supset(\Box A, A)$ is valid in M for all formulas A, R is reflexive.

Proof. Suppose that we had a modal system M which met those conditions, but in which R was not reflexive. Since R is not reflexive, there is a world w such that $\sim Rww$. There must be some world w_1 accessible from w, since if there were not, $\Box A$ would be vacuously true for any A, and thus, since $\supset(\Box A, A)$ is valid in M, all propositions A would be true in w, contrary to the standing assumption that only a classical valuation can be a world. Since $\sim Rww$, we have $w_1 \neq w$. There is some proposition A_1 such that A_1 is true in w_1 and false in w.[18] Since A_1 is false in w and $\supset(\Box A_1, A_1)$ is true in w (being a substitution instance of a formula that is valid in M), $\Box A_1$ will be false in w. That means that there is then a world w_2 such that Rww_2 and A_1 is false in w_2. That world B is not w, since $\sim Rww$, and it is not w_1, since A_1 is true in w_1 but false in w_2. There then is some proposition A_2 which is true in w_2 but false in w. Let us summarize what we have so far, using arrows to indicate the accessibility relation:

10.5.4

	w	w_1	w_2
A_1	F	T	F
$\Box A_1$	F		
A_2	F		T
$\lor A_1 A_2$	F	T	T

Since $\lor A_1 A_2$ is false in w, $\Box \lor A_1 A_2$ will also be false in w (by the assumption that $\supset(\Box A, A)$ is valid in M for any A), and thus there is some world w_3 such that Rww_3 and $\lor A_1 A_2$ is false in w_3. Since $\lor A_1 A_2$ is true in w_1 and w_2, w_3 cannot be the same world as w_1 or w_2, and since $\sim Rww$, w_3 cannot be the same world as w. Let A_3 be a proposition which is false in w and true in w_3. We then have the following more complete description of M:

10.5.4'

	w	w_1	w_2	w_3
A_1	F	T	F	
$\Box A_1$	F			
A_2	F		T	
$\lor A_1 A_2$	F	T	T	F
$\Box \lor A_1 A_2$	F			
A_3	F			T
$\lor A_1 A_2 A_3$	F	T	T	T

It is now apparent that the method used in constructing w_1, w_2, w_3 can be continued indefinitely. Each time that we construct another world w_i in this sequence, we find a proposition A_i which is true in w_i but false in w. Since

$\vee (A_1, A_2, \ldots, A_i)$ will be false in w, $\square \vee (A_1, A_2, \ldots, A_i)$ will be false in w, and there is then a world w_{i+1} such that Rww_{i+1} and $\vee (A_1, A_2, \ldots, A_i)$ is false in w_{i+1}. The world w_{i+1} will be distinct from $w_1, w_2, \ldots, w_i$, since $\vee (A_1, A_2, \ldots, A_i)$ is true in all of those worlds, and it will be distinct from w, since $\sim Rww$ but Rww_{i+1}. Thus, M will have to contain infinitely many worlds, contrary to the assumption that it contains only finitely many.

Theorem. Let M be a modal system such that M contains only finitely many worlds and any two worlds of M are distinguishable. Let R be the accessibility relation of M. Then if $\supset(A, \square \Diamond A)$ is valid in M for all formulas A, R is symmetric.

Proof. Suppose that we have a modal system M which meets those conditions but in which R is not symmetric. Then there are two worlds w and w_1 such that Rww_1 but $\sim Rw_1w$. There is then a proposition A_1 such that A_1 is true in w and false in w_1. Then $\square \Diamond A_1$ is true in w (since both A_1 and $\supset(A_1, \square \Diamond A_1)$ are), which means that $\Diamond A_1$ is true in all worlds accessible from w, thus in particular in w_1. Thus A_1 is true in some world w_2 which is accessible from w_1. World $w_2 \neq w_1$, since A_1 is false in w_1 and true in w_2, and $w_2 \neq w$, since Rw_1w_2 but $\sim Rw_1w$. There is then a proposition A_2 which is true in w and false in w_2. We then have the following partial description of M:

10.5.5

	w	w_1	w_2
A_1	T	F	T
$\square \Diamond A_1$	T		
$\Diamond A_1$		T	
A_2	T		F
$\wedge A_1 A_2$	T	F	F
$\square \Diamond \wedge A_1 A_2$	T		

Since $\square \Diamond \wedge A_1 A_2$ is true in w, $\Diamond \wedge A_1 A_2$ is true in all worlds accessible from w, thus in particular in w_1, which means that $\wedge A_1 A_2$ is true in some world w_3 accessible from w_1. World w_3 is distinct from both w_1 and w_2, since $\wedge A_1 A_2$ is false in both of those worlds but true in w_3, and w_3 is distinct from w, since Rw_1w_3 but not Rw_1w. Let A_3 be a proposition that is true in w and false in w_3. Then $\wedge (A_1, A_2, A_3)$ will be true in w but false in w_1, w_2, and w_3. Proposition $\square \Diamond \wedge (A_1, A_2, A_3)$ is then true in all worlds accessible from w, thus in particular in w_1, which means that $\wedge (A_1, A_2, A_3)$ is true in some world w_4 accessible from w_1. By the same argument as before, w_4 is distinct from w, w_1, w_2, and w_3. It is clear that this construction can be continued without limit. Having found a world w_i which is accessible from w_1 and distinct from $w, w_1, \ldots, w_{i-1}$, we know that there is a proposition A_i that is true in w and false in w_i, and $\wedge (A_1, A_2, \ldots, A_i)$ will be true in w

but false in $w_1, w_2, \ldots, w_i$. The proposition $\Box \Diamond \wedge (A_1, A_2, \ldots, A_i)$ is then true in w, which means that $\wedge (A_1, A_2, \ldots, A_i)$ is true in some world w_{i+1} which is accessible from w_i and which (by the same arguments as before) will be distinct from $w, w_1, \ldots, w_i$. Since this construction can be carried on indefinitely, M will have to contain infinitely many worlds, contrary to the assumption that M contains only finitely many.

Theorem. Let M be a modal system such that M contains only finitely many worlds and any two worlds of M are distinguishable, with accessibility relation R. Then if $\supset (\Box A, \Box \Box A)$ is valid in M for all formulas A, R is transitive.

Proof. Suppose that M meets the above conditions and that R is not transitive. Since R is not transitive, there are worlds such that Rww', $Rw'w''$, but $\sim Rww''$. Since M contains only finitely many worlds, there are only finitely many worlds accessible from w. Call those worlds $w_1, w_2, \ldots, w_n$. Since w'' is not accessible from w, w'' is not among the w_i's. For each $i (1 \leq i \leq n)$ there is a proposition A_i such that A_i is true in w_i but false in w''. Let B stand for $\vee (A_1, A_2, \ldots, A_n)$. We have chosen B in such a way that it is true in $w_1, w_2, \ldots, w_n$ but false in w''. Since $w_1, \ldots w_n$ are all the worlds that are accessible from w and since B is true in all of those worlds, $\Box B$ is true in w. Since $\supset (\Box B, \Box \Box B)$ is valid in M, $\Box \Box B$ will then be true in w, which means that $\Box B$ is true in all worlds accessible from w, thus in particular in w'. But that means that B is true in all worlds accessible from w', thus in particular in w''. However, we chose B in such a way that it would be false in w''. Thus the given premises lead to a contradiction, and the theorem is established.

The assumption that the worlds of M are distinguishable is essential only to the result about reflexivity. It is possible for $\supset (\Box A, A)$ to be valid in a modal system without the accessibility relation being reflexive, provided some world has a 'doppelgänger', in which the same propositions are true and which stands in the same accessibility relations to other worlds, except that the given world is accessible to its doppelgänger but not to itself. For example, compare the 'normal' system of worlds 10.5.6a with its close relative 10.5.6b, which has a doppelgänger w_1' for the world w_1:

10.5.6   a. $\overset{\frown}{w_0} \longleftrightarrow \overset{\frown}{w_1}$ b. $\overset{\frown}{w_0}$ with w_1 and w_1'

In either modal system, $\Box A$ is true in a particular world if and only if A is true in all worlds, and thus $\supset (\Box A, A)$ is valid in either system, despite the fact that in 10.5.6b the accessibility relation is not reflexive.

It is possible to replace a given modal system M in which some worlds have doppelgängers by an alternative modal system M* in which there are no doppelgängers and things are otherwise essentially the same. Specifically, let the worlds of M* be equivalence classes of worlds of M under the equivalence relation $\equiv$ that is defined by: $w \equiv w'$ if the same propositions are true in w as in w'. Using w^* to denote the equivalence class containing w (i.e., w^* consists of all worlds equivalent to w), let $R^*w_1^*w_2^*$ hold if w_1^* contains a world w_{1a} and w_2^* contains a world w_{2a} such that $Rw_{1a}w_{2a}$. Finally, let those propositions be true in w^* that are true in w. We have then set things up in such a way that no world of M* has a doppelgänger, but M* is 'essentially the same as' M, in that truth and accessibility in M* exactly parallel truth and accessibility in M. In particular, each of the three formulas that figure in the above theorems is valid in M is and only if it is valid in M*. R is symmetric if and only if R* is symmetric, and R is transitive if and only if R* is transitive; thus the distinguishability requirement can be dropped from the second and third theorems. However, it is not the case that R is reflexive if and only if R* is reflexive; in fact, if R is as in 10.5.6b, then R* will be as in 10.5.6a, and thus it is possible for R* to be reflexive without R being reflexive. Thus, the construction of M* from M allows one to prove a more general form of the symmetry and transitivity theorems, though not of the reflexivity theorem.

10.6 Exercises

1. Assume a system of possible worlds as follows (ⓘ→ⓙ means Rw_iw_j):

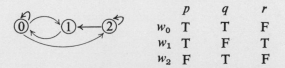

	p	q	r
w_0	T	T	F
w_1	T	F	T
w_2	F	T	F

For each of the three worlds, determine the truth value of

a. $\Box p$

b. $\Box \supset (r, \Box \wedge pq)$

2. If $\Box$ and $\Diamond$ are equivalent to 'in all accessible worlds, ...' and 'in some accessible worlds, ...', then the various valid formulas of predicate logic will correspond to valid formulas of modal logic, for example,

$\supset((\forall x) \wedge (fx, gx), \wedge ((\forall x)fx, (\forall x)gx))$ will correspond to
$\supset(\Box \wedge AB, \wedge (\Box A, \Box B))$

What are the modal analogues of each of the following valid formulas of predicate logic?

   a. $\supset ((\exists x) \vee (fx, gx), \ \vee ((\exists x)fx, (\exists x)gx))$
   b. $\supset (\wedge ((\forall x)fx, (\exists x)gx), (\exists x) \wedge (fx, gx))$
   c. $\vee ((\exists x)fx, (\exists x) \sim fx)$

3. Why is *b* more difficult to interpret than *a*:

   a. World War I could have ended a year earlier.
   b. World War I could have begun a year earlier.

4. i. Fill in the details of the proof (sketched in the text) that the restricted quantifier analogue of the Barcan formula is invalid in all but the most trivial modal systems.

   ii. Formulate the restricted-quantifier analogue to the converse Barcan formula and give an example of a modal system in which that formula is not valid.

11. Applications of Possible Worlds

11.1. Counterfactual Conditionals

The conditional propositions that we have considered so far have been of the kind that are expressed with the indicative mood, as in 11.1.1, rather than the subjunctive mood (11.1.2):

11.1.1   If Bill left at 2:00, he's in Pittsburgh by now.
          If Susan was born in Iceland, she can't run for President of the U.S.

11.1.2   If Solti had been conducting, I would have gone to the concert.
          If Kennedy hadn't been assassinated, he would have been impeached.

COUNTERFACTUAL CONDITIONALS, as in 11.1.2, have quite different logical properties from the INDICATIVE CONDITIONALS of 11.1.1. For example, as noted by Stalnaker (1969), indicative conditionals satisfy a law of transitivity but counterfactuals do not; that is, inferences like 11.1.3 are valid but inferences like 11.1.4 are invalid:

11.1.3   If Bill left at 2:00, he is in Pittsburgh by now.
          If Bill is in Pittsburgh by now, Lefty has tipped off the feds.
          Therefore, if Bill left at 2:00, Lefty has tipped off the feds.

11.1.4   If Carter had been born in Russia, he would be a communist.
          If Carter were a communist, he would be sending American defense secrets to the Kremlin.
          Therefore, if Carter had been born in Russia, he would be sending American defense secrets to the Kremlin.

The reason that 11.1.4 is invalid is that the two premises do not relate to the same states of affairs. The first premise has to do with states of affairs in which, other things being as close to equal as possible, Carter was born in Russia rather than in the U.S. The second premise has to do with

311

states of affairs in which, other things being as close to equal as is possible, Carter was a communist rather than a Democrat. But the 'other things' aren't the same in the two cases, and as a result, the states of affairs that the first premise has to do with do not overlap with those that the second premise has to do with: if Carter had been born in Russia, he wouldn't be president of the United States and thus presumably would not have access to American defense secrets.

Similarly, while indicative conditionals allow one to conjoin material to the antecedent, as in 11.1.5, counterfactual conditionals do not, as illustrated by such clearly invalid inferences as 11.1.6:[1]

11.1.5   If Betty was at the party, Bill enjoyed the party.
          Therefore, if Betty was at the party and they served guacamole, Bill enjoyed the party.

11.1.6   If Betty had been at the party, I'd have enjoyed myself.
          Therefore, if Betty had been at the party and I had broken my leg, I would have enjoyed myself.

The reason is similar to that for the invalidity of 11.1.4: the states of affairs that the premise in 11.1.6 has to do with, namely, those in which Betty came to the party but otherwise things are as close to the way they really are as is possible, are not the states of affairs that the conclusion has to do with, in which some of those other things are otherwise, in particular, that I have broken my leg.

David Lewis's treatment (1973) of counterfactuals involves imposing additional structure on modal systems such as were discussed in chapter 10. Instead of merely an accessibility relation connecting different worlds, there must be some relation of 'relative closeness', so that one can speak of w_1 being closer to w than w_2 is. This notion of relative closeness could be expressed through a numerical measure of 'distance' between worlds. However, it is not really necessary to treat closeness in terms of 'distance': it suffices to assume that there is a three-place relation $Cxyz$ ('y is at least as close to x as z is') which satisfies the conditions

11.1.7   For all worlds w, w', w'', w''' of the given system,
          a. ('connectedness') If Rww' and Rww'', then either $Cww'w''$ or $Cww''w'$.
          b. ('transitivity') If $Cww'w''$ and $Cww''w'''$, then $Cww'w'''$.
          c. ('centering') If Rww' and $w' \neq w$, then $Cwww'$ and $\sim Cww'w$.

Condition 11.1.7a says that for any two worlds that are accessible from the given world, one of them is at least as close to the given world as the other one is[2] (of course, it might be that both $Cww'w''$ and $Cww''w'$, which would be the case where w' and w'' are 'equally close to' w). Condition 11.1.7*b* says that if one world is at least as close to the given world as is a second world, which is in turn at least as close to the given world as is a third world, then the first world is at least as close to the given world as is the third world. Condition 11.1.7*c* says that the world closest to any world is that world itself.[3]

Lewis adds to the language of modal propositional logic a connective $\square\!\!\rightarrow$ (which, for reasons that will soon be obvious, can be read 'locally entails') that is to represent the content of counterfactual conditionals. The truth conditions for $\square\!\!\rightarrow$AB are given by Lewis as:

11.1.8 $\square\!\!\rightarrow$AB is true in a world w if either (i) there is a world w' such that A is true in w', B is also true in w', and there is no world w'' for which A is true in w'', C$ww''w'$, and B is false in w''; or (ii) there is no world in which A is true.

That is, for $\square\!\!\rightarrow$AB to be true in w, it is necessary and sufficient that if there are worlds in which A is true, B is true in those which are closest to w. Lewis formulates the truth conditions as in 11.1.8 rather than in terms of 'the closest world to w in which A is true', since he wants to allow for the possibility that no world is the closest of all those in which A is true. This will cover both the case where several worlds in which A is true are equally close to the given world and the case where there is an infinite series of worlds that 'converge on a limit'; for example, if A is 'David Lewis is over 7 feet tall' and worlds in which Lewis's height is closer to his real height are closer to the real world (other things being equal), there could be an infinite series of worlds (one in which his height is $7'1''$, one in which it is $7'0.1''$, one in which it is $7'0.01''$,...), where A is true in all of them but none of them is the closest such world to the real world.

Note that this analysis accords with the failure of transitivity noted in 11.1.4 and the failure of the argument form that figured in 11.1.6. If the closest worlds to the real world in which A is true are pretty remote worlds and the closest worlds to the real world in which B is true are relatively close worlds, then it could perfectly well be the case that B was true and C false in the former worlds while C was true in the latter worlds (see diagram). The plane represents the whole set of worlds of the given modal system, distances in the diagram are to correspond to the relative closeness of the worlds, and the regions marked represent sets of worlds in which the various propositions are true. In this case, $\square\!\!\rightarrow$AB is true (i.e., in the closest worlds to w in which A is true, B is also true), $\square\!\!\rightarrow$BC is true (i.e., in the closest worlds to w in which B is true, C is also true), but $\square\!\!\rightarrow$AC is not true (i.e., in the closest worlds to w in which A is true, C is false). The same diagram illustrates the failure of the argument in 11.1.6: here B

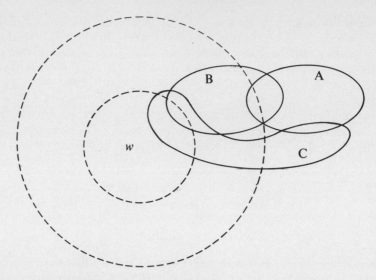

is true in the closest worlds to w in which A is true but not in the closest worlds to w in which $\wedge$ AC is true.

The diagram also makes clear the reason for the term 'local entailment': for $\Box\!\!\rightarrow$AB to be true, it need not be the case that A entails B (i.e., there can be worlds in which A is true and B false, as in the diagram)—all that is necessary is that within some 'neighborhood' of w (as indicated by the dotted circles) A entail B: while B is not true in all worlds in which A is true, it is true in all worlds in the larger dotted circle in which A is true.

There are a number of cases in which $\Box\!\!\rightarrow$AB turns out to be true (relative to a reasonable 'closeness' relation among the worlds) but where 'If A were the case, B would be the case' (and similar sentences of the same content) sound bizarre. Let us see what these cases are and determine whether they point to defects in Lewis's proposal or merely to interactions between natural language, Lewis's system of logic, and some third factor such as conversational implicature. The first case is that in which A is true in the given world. Since (by 11.1.7c) w is the closest world to w, if A is true in w, then $\Box\!\!\rightarrow$AB will be true in w if B is also true in w. However, corresponding sentences are bizarre:

11.1.9   a. ?If 6 were an even number, 12 would be a multiple of 4.
          b. ?If London were in England, the Queen of England would live in London.
          c. ?If Nixon had resigned in 1974, Ford would have become president.
          d. ?If 6 were an even number, Kathmandu would be in Nepal.

An attempt to explain the bizarreness of 11.1.9 in terms of conversational

implicature will have to contend with the important problem of distinguishing between indicative and counterfactual conditionals, in that the
corresponding indicative conditionals exhibit a gradation of normalness
that is not found in the counterfactuals:

11.1.10   a. If 6 is an even number, 12 is a multiple of 4.
             b. (?) If London is in England, the Queen of England lives in
                London.
             c. ?If Nixon resigned in 1974, Ford became president.
             d. ?If 6 is an even number, Kathmandu is in Nepal.

When a person asserts a counterfactual conditional, just as when he
asserts an indicative conditional, he is normally taken to believe that there
is some connection between antecedent and consequent, since if he did not
so believe, he could be more cooperative by asserting something else (e.g.,
the consequent). However, the kind of connection that he is taken to believe
exists is not the same in the two cases. In the case of the indicative conditional, the connection is a connection between partial knowledge of a state
of affairs (such as the physical world as it really is) and more complete
knowledge, mediated by whatever means are available for one to augment
his knowledge. The gradation of acceptability in 11.1.10 parallels the gradation of ease with which one could imagine a person getting from the
proposition expressed in the antecedent to that expressed in the consequent,
via normal methods of augmenting knowledge, and starting from a reasonable set of 'known' propositions. In 11.1.10a, there is no oddity, since the
knowledge that twice any even number is a multiple of 4 gets you from the
antecedent to the consequent. Example 11.1.10b is slightly less plausible,
since it is somewhat harder to see what prior knowledge one would have to
get from the antecedent to the consequent, though plausible possibilities
can be found (e.g., that monarchs live in the capitals of their respective
countries, that the capital of a country is in that country, and that London
is the capital of some country or other, though the speaker doesn't remember which one). If 11.1.10c is less plausible than 11.1.10b, it is probably
because it is harder to imagine someone, years after the events of 1974,
using the proposition that Nixon resigned as a means of arriving at the
proposition that Ford became president; of course, a few hours after the
resignation there was nothing odd in saying *If Nixon has resigned, Ford is
president*, since at that time the proposition that Ford was president was
not yet a full-fledged member of the set of 'known propositions'. Note, by
the way, that both in that case and in the case of a person in the present
uttering 11.1.10c, there is a connection between the antecedent and the
consequent (indeed, the same connection), but only in the case of the
utterance in 1974 is the utterance normal. Example 11.1.10d is so bizarre

because it would take such bizarre knowledge to allow one to get from the proposition that 6 is an even number to the proposition that Kathmandu is in Nepal; the least bizarre context may be of the type suggested by Grice (1967): the sentence is part of the instructions in a puzzle (though it would be a meaningful puzzle only if directed at persons who were ignorant of arithmetic and geography).

With counterfactual conditionals, however, the connection between antecedent and consequent involves the relationship between the real world and alternative worlds that differ enough from the real world to 'make' the antecedent true. The oddity of 11.1.9 may then be attributed to the fact that nothing need be done to 'present knowledge' to make the antecedent consistent with it. However, that fact need not prevent one from calling all of 11.1.9 true, in accordance with Lewis's proposals. I will tentatively accept Lewis's conclusion that $\square\!\!\rightarrow AB$ should be considered true even in the case where A and B are both true in the world in question, and take the oddity of corresponding counterfactual sentences such as 11.1.9 to reflect the uncooperativeness that would accompany the assertion of any of them. This policy is confirmed (albeit weakly) by the facts about the use of *Yes* and *No* in answers to questions:

11.1.11   a. If London were in England, would the Queen of England
                   live in London?
                Yes, and as a matter of fact, London *is* in England.
              b. If London were in England, would the Queen of England
                   live in Instanbul?
                No/*Yes—London *is* in England, and the Queen lives in
                   London.
              c. If 6 were an even number, would Kathmandu be in Nepal?
                Yes, and of course, 6 *is* an even number.

However, there is a possibility that 11.1.11*c* (similarly, 11.1.11*a*) is being interpreted as 'If 6 were an even number, would Kathmandu *still* be in Nepal?' and that the understood *still* improves the acceptability of *Yes*.

A second class of cases where an English counterfactual sentence sounds bizarre while the corresponding proposition $\square\!\!\rightarrow AB$ comes out true according to 11.1.8 was discovered by Dowty in unpublished investigations of the notion of causation. Specifically, Dowty noted that in situations where one would normally speak of one event having caused another, as in 11.1.12*a*, two counterfactuals generally come out true (11.1.12*b*–*c*), while only one of the corresponding English counterfactual sentences (11.1.12*b'*–*c'*) is a normal thing to say:

11.1.12   a. George's eating those mushrooms caused him to die.
              b. $\square\!\!\rightarrow (\sim$(George ate those mushrooms), $\sim$(George died))

     b′. If George hadn't eaten those mushrooms, he wouldn't have died.

     c. $\Box\!\!\rightarrow\!(\sim$ (George died), $\sim$ (George ate those mushrooms))
     c′. ??If George hadn't died, he wouldn't have eaten those mushrooms.

Example 11.1.12c′ reverses the normal temporal and causal connections: while 11.1.12a implies that the eating of the mushrooms preceded and was the cause of the death, 11.1.12c′ implies that the death preceded the eating of the mushrooms and suggests that it caused George to eat them. Nonetheless, 11.1.12c would come out true for a reasonable possible world structure that makes 11.1.12a true: 11.1.12c implies that in the closest-to-real states of affairs in which George did not die, he did not eat the mushrooms, and one would not normally say that George's eating the mushrooms caused him to die unless that condition were met.

This observation points out a respect in which Lewis's $\Box\!\!\rightarrow$ is more general than the English counterfactual construction. The English counterfactual construction, like all conditional constructions in English, is normally used only when the antecedent is temporally and/or causally and/or epistemologically prior to the consequent, as in the examples discussed in 2.6 such as

11.1.13   a. If you touch me, I'll scream.
          a′. You'll touch me only if I scream.

The *if*-clause must be temporally/causally/epistemologically prior even if it is modified by *only*, contrary to the usual claim of introductory logic texts that 'If A, B' and 'A only if B' are 'equivalent'. As Lewis has set up $\Box\!\!\rightarrow$, it has no such restriction on the antecedent, and there is thus nothing to prevent its being used in expressions like 11.1.12c, in which the antecedent is not temporally or causally prior to the consequent. Or rather, 11.1.12c, as it stands, says nothing about whether the antecedent is prior to the consequent, and it could be used for either case; however, the corresponding English sentence 11.1.12c′ is reserved for cases where the antecedent is causally or temporally prior to the consequent. See McCawley 1976a for arguments that one sense of '*x* caused *y*' should be analyzed as $\Box\!\!\rightarrow\!(\sim(y$ occurred), $\sim(x$ occurred)) and that the other senses of *cause* all at least imply something of the form $\Box\!\!\rightarrow\!(\sim B, \sim A)$, where A is a certain proposition (exactly what depends on the sense in which *cause* is being used) associated with the cause; one main reason for proposing an analysis in terms of $\Box\!\!\rightarrow\!(\sim B, \sim A)$ rather than in terms of $\Box\!\!\rightarrow\!(\sim A, \sim B)$ is that the truth of 11.1.12a has more to do with the question of how easily George could have avoided death (i.e., with what is the case in the closest worlds in which ~(George died) is true) than with the question of how easily George could have avoided eating the mushrooms.

Lewis formulated the truth conditions 11.1.8 in such a way that □→AB comes out 'vacuously true' if there is no accessible world in which A is true. If condition ii had been omitted from 11.1.8, □→AB would have come out false in all such cases. It is not clear that either Lewis's policy of making all such counterfactuals true or a policy that makes them all false is really justified. Consider the following examples:

11.1.14   a. If 3 were an even number, 6 would be a multiple of 4.
            b. If 3 were an even number, 6 would be a multiple of 5.
            c. If 3 were an even number, Charles de Gaulle would be the bastard son of Chester Alan Arthur.
            d. If 3 were an even number, Charles de Gaulle would be the square root of Mozart's quintet for piano and winds.

These sentences are arranged in decreasing order of acceptability, ranging from the fairly normal 11.1.14a to the totally outlandish 11.1.14d. Such examples raise the question of whether one must allow 'possible worlds' in which '3 is an even number' is true and allow some such worlds (e.g., those in which all even multiples of 3 are multiples of 4 but only the actual multiples of 5 are multiples of 5) to be closer to the real world than others (e.g., worlds in which every integer is a multiple of every other integer). Here the question of cross-world identification arises with a vengeance: in what is supposedly a world in which 3 is an even number, how do we know we aren't just applying the name '3' to something that doesn't deserve to be called '3'? Is there any coherent way of assigning truth values to propositions in such a way that '3 is even' comes out true which is consistent with what we mean by '3' and by 'even'? If not, then should 11.1.14a–d all be rejected as semantically screwed up, with the gradation in acceptability to be explained in terms of the grossness of the semantic screw-up?

I don't claim to be able to answer these questions here, and I won't attempt to. I will confine myself to just mentioning an alternative approach to counterfactuals that makes 11.1.14a–d somewhat less problematic and allows one to call some of them true and others false without any necessity of admitting worlds in which '3 is an even number' is true. I refer to the approach by Rescher (1964), which elaborates ideas by Nelson Goodman (1947). According to Rescher, the determination of the truth value of 'If A were the case, B would be the case' is as follows. The determination is carried out relative to a set of propositions M that a person holds to be true, ranked according to his confidence in or attachment to them. If M∪{A} is inconsistent (as it is in ordinary counterfactual propositions), then a subset M' of M is found such that (i) M'∪{A} is consistent, (ii) M' is maximal (i.e., there is no larger subset M″ such that M″∪{A} is consistent), and (iii) M–M′ involves propositions of minimum 'confidence level'; that is, if $C_{M'}$ is the proposition in M–M′ that has the highest 'confidence level', then $C_{M'}$ is of lower confidence level than $C_{M''}$ for any M″ for which M″∪{A} is consistent and M″ is maximal. 'If A were the case, B would be the case' is assigned the value T if M′∪{A}⊢B, and is assigned the value F otherwise, where ⊢ refers to provability in whatever system of rules of inference is assumed. Thus, for Rescher, a counterfactual is true if the consequent is implied by the consistent set of propositions that includes the antecedent and is otherwise 'closest to' the previously assumed knowledge, in the sense that as few propositions as possible, and propositions of as low a confidence level as possible, have been discarded in constructing the new consistent set. This informal statement is not precise enough to allow one to deal with any but the simplest cases, since it does not make clear how one chooses among different ways that one might delete several propositions so as to achieve consistency (which is worse—giving up one high-confidence proposition and three low-confidence ones or giving up two medium-confidence ones?). The following algorithm will remedy that defect:

11.1.15   Given a set M of propositions ranked in the order $p_1, p_2, p_3, \ldots$
            and given a proposition A, the maximal subset M′ of M con-
            sistent with A is the limit of the sequence $M_1, M_2, \ldots$, where
            the M_i are defined as follows:
            (i) If $\{p_1, A\}$ is consistent, then $M_1 = \{p_1\}$; otherwise $M_1 = \varnothing$;
            (ii) for i > 1, if $M_{i-1} \cup \{p_i, A\}$ is consistent, then
            $M_i = M_{i-1} \cup \{p_i\}$; otherwise $M_i = M_{i-1}$.

Put more informally, one checks the p_i, starting from the one in which one is most confident and working downwards; a p_i is retained for inclusion in M′ if it plus the earlier p's that have not been discarded is consistent with A but is discarded otherwise. In this scheme, propositions near the top of the confidence ranking will stand a better chance of being retained than will propositions further down, since they have to pass a less stringent test for inclusion in M′ (i.e., the set of propositions that they must be consistent with is smaller). For example, suppose M consists of the propositions ∨pq, ∨(~p, r), p, q, ranked in the order given, and that A is ~q. (Note that it is reasonable for disjunctive propositions to appear at the top of the list; e.g., you will be more certain that physical space is either Newtonian or Einsteinian than that it is Einsteinian.) M′ will then contain ∨pq (since {∨pq, ~q} is consistent); it will contain ∨(~p, r) (since {∨pq, ∨(~p, r), ~q} is consistent); and it will contain p (since {∨pq, ∨(~p, r), p, ~q} is consistent); but that is all it will contain, since ~q is inconsistent with any set containing q. Relative to this M, 'if $\sim q$ were the case, r would be the case' is true, since $M' \cup \{\sim q\} \vdash r$.

Rescher's approach to counterfactuals makes it easier for a counterfactual to come out false than does Lewis's approach. The set M of 'accepted' propositions can be 'incomplete'; that is, there can be propositions such that neither $M \vdash B$ nor $M \vdash \sim B$, and the deletions needed to obtain M' may leave $M' \cup \{A\}$ even more 'incomplete' than was M, thus making both 'if A were the case B would be the case' and 'if A were the case, $\sim B$ would be the case' false if B is one of the propositions such that neither it nor its negation is implied by $M' \cup \{A\}$. For a trivial example of this, note that if M contains no propositions having a bearing on whether Gilyak has VSO word order, then both of 11.1.16a and 11.1.16b come out false:

11.1.16   a. If Kennedy hadn't been assassinated, Gilyak would have VSO word order.
          b. If Kennedy hadn't been assassinated, Gilyak would not have VSO word order.

For Lewis, one of these would generally be true, since if there is a closest world to the real world in which Kennedy was not assassinated, then depending on whether Gilyak does or does not have VSO word order in that world, 11.1.16a or 11.1.16b, respectively, would be true in the real world. By the same token, Lewis's approach makes it easier for a counterfactual to come out true, and it takes a less restrictive condition to make $\square \rightarrow AB$ and $\square \rightarrow (A, \sim B)$ simultaneously true for Lewis (namely, that A is true in no world) than to make the corresponding counterfactuals both true for Rescher (which would happen only if A were self-contradictory). Thus, if one requires the true propositions of arithmetic to be true in all worlds (i.e., to be necessary truths), then both of 11.1.17a and 11.1.17b will be true in Lewis's system, whereas at most one would be true for Rescher:

11.1.17   a. If 7 were an even number, 8 would be prime.
          b. If 7 were an even number, 8 would not be prime.

Note that Rescher's approach thus allows for truth distinctions among 11.1.14a–d, which Lewis's treatment makes all true. The propositions you'll have to delete from M to make the remainder consistent with '3 is an even number' will be propositions of arithmetic, and thus $M' \cup \{3$ is an even number$\}$ won't imply that de Gaulle was Chester Alan Arthur's son if M didn't imply it to begin with. And while it is easy to find 'high confidence' propositions that, added to '3 is an even number', would imply that 6 is a multiple of 4 (e.g., $6 = 2 \times 3$, twice any even number is a multiple of 4), it is hard to think of propositions worthy of that degree of confidence that, added to '3 is an even number', would imply that 6 is a multiple of 5.

Still, the Lewis and Rescher approaches are not all that different. If one broadens the conception of 'world' and weakens the assumptions about the 'closeness' relation, one can reinterpret Rescher's scheme in Lewis's terms. Specifically, suppose that we take each world not necessarily to involve an assignment of values 'true' and 'false' to all propositions (a 'valuation') but allow some propositions to have no truth value in a given world (say, by taking the assignment of truth values to be a 'super-valuation'), and suppose that we give up assumption 11.1.7a, thus allowing the possibility of worlds that are incomparable (i.e., $Cww'w''$ and $Cww''w'$ might both be false). For a given ranked set of propositions M, we can then define worlds as follows: for every proposition A, determine the corresponding M' according to 11.1.15, and take the world w_A to be the assignment of truth values such that B is true if $M'\cup\{A\}\vdash B$, B is false if $M'\cup\{A\}\vdash \sim B$, and B is # otherwise. The closeness relation can then be defined as follows: $Cww'w''$ if and only if $T(w'')\subseteq T(w')\subseteq T(w)$, where $T(w)$ is the set of propositions that are true in w. A counterfactual will then be true according to Lewis's truth conditions, relative to this system of worlds, if and only if it is true according to Rescher's scheme.

In the worlds of such a system, necessary truths may lack truth values; for example, '$6 = 4 + 2$' might well lack a truth value in a world from which most of one's arithmetic information had been deleted, as in a Rescher treatment of 'If 3 were an even number, 6 would be a multiple of 4'. This need not be disconcerting. The worlds that one allows for the purpose of analyzing counterfactuals need not be the same worlds that figure in a treatment of epistemic necessity. To each notion of necessity there will correspond a different accessibility relation, and many of the worlds that figure in the analysis of counterfactuals can perfectly well be 'inaccessible from the real world' with regard to the accessibility relation for epistemic necessity.

In the remainder of this section, I will discuss a number of deficiencies that are shared by Lewis's and Rescher's approaches to counterfactuals and will make suggestions for how these deficiencies might be remedied. The first deficiency is that both analyses cover only counterfactuals whose consequents contain *would*, as in 11.1.18a, and are not directly applicable to counterfactuals with *might*, like 11.1.18b:

11.1.18   a. If Rosalyn had had an affair with Kennedy, Jimmy would have divorced her.
           b. If Rosalyn had had an affair with Kennedy, Jimmy might have divorced her.

The most obvious way to accommodate *might* counterfactuals in Lewis's framework (and locate the difference between them and *would* counterfactuals) would be to treat a *might* counterfactual as true if, among the closest worlds in which the antecedent is true, there are some in which the consequent is true. For example, suppose that there are three worlds in which Rosalyn had an affair with Kennedy that are the same distance from the real world and are closer to the real world than any other worlds in which Rosalyn had an affair with Kennedy:

Then for 11.1.18*b* to be true, it is necessary and sufficient that Jimmy divorced Rosalyn in at least one of those worlds, whereas for 11.1.18*a* to be true, he must have divorced her in all three of those worlds. The only problem with this proposal is that, if made precise in terms parallel to the conditions given in 11.1.8 for the truth of *would* counterfactuals, it imposes too loose a criterion of truth on *might* counterfactuals. Suppose that we introduce a connective $\diamondsuit\!\!\rightarrow$ that is to stand in the same relation to *might* counterfactuals as $\square\!\!\rightarrow$ does to *would* counterfactuals. The truth conditions for the two connectives, if they are stated in maximally parallel terms and the troublesome case where A is true in no world is ignored, are then:

11.1.19   a. $\square\!\!\rightarrow$AB is true in w if and only if there is a world w' such that Rww', A is true in w', and for every world w'' for which C$ww''w'$ and A is true in w'', B is also true in w''.

         b. $\diamondsuit\!\!\rightarrow$AB is true in w if and only if there is a world w' such that Rww', A is true in w', and for some world w'' for which C$ww''w'$ and A is true in w'', B is also true in w''.

What makes 11.1.19*b* too lax a condition on the truth of $\diamondsuit\!\!\rightarrow$AB is that it allows conditions in an extremely remote world to make $\diamondsuit\!\!\rightarrow$AB true. In fact, as 11.1.19*b* is formulated, C is irrelevant to the truth of $\diamondsuit\!\!\rightarrow$AB: it makes $\diamondsuit\!\!\rightarrow$AB true just as long as there is some world in which A and B are both true, regardless of the closeness relations among worlds. While 11.1.19*b* is a close analogue to 11.1.19*a*, it does not successfully incorporate any analogue to the rationale for 11.1.19*a*, namely, that the truth of counterfactuals should depend on conditions in the closest worlds in which the antecedent is true. But a reformulation in terms of 'closest worlds' will impose too stringent a criterion of truth on $\diamondsuit\!\!\rightarrow$. If there is one single world in which A is true that is closer to the real world than any other such world, a requirement that B be true in the closest worlds to the real world in which A is true would be equivalent to a requirement that B be true in that single world. But that requirement misrepresents the meaning of a *might* counterfactual like 11.1.18b: if the worlds in which Rosalyn had an affair with Kennedy were as in the following diagram, with all of them fairly close to the real world, and with Jimmy divorcing Rosalyn in w_2 and w_3 but not w_1, 11.1.18b should count as true, even though in the closest world in which it is true that Rosalyn had an affair with Kennedy (w_1), it is false that Jimmy divorced Rosalyn.

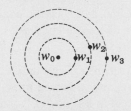

The only way out of this dilemma that I can see is to bring in an extra factor: a 'threshold of relevance' of worlds, which will serve as a limit on the set of worlds over which the variable w' ranges in 11.1.19b. If w_2 is close enough to the real world to be within this limit, then the truth of 'Jimmy divorced Rosalyn' in that world will be sufficient to insure the truth of the *might* counterfactual, regardless of whether 'Jimmy divorced Rosalyn' is true in w_1. The threshold, of course, would have to vary depending on the antecedent of the counterfactual.[4] Introduction of this threshold into the truth conditions for *might* counterfactuals destroys the parallelism with those for *would* counterfactuals unless the threshold is also brought into the latter. It has in fact been argued by Nute (1975a, 1975b) that a threshold is required in the truth conditions for *would* counterfactuals. For Nute, the truth conditions for *would* counterfactuals are paraphraseable not as 'in the worlds in which A is true that are closest to the real world, B is true' but as 'in all worlds in which A is true that are sufficiently close to the real world, B is true'. Nute's truth conditions and Lewis's agree to a large extent, since there is a fair degree of overlap in the set of worlds in which, under each analysis, the truth of B is at issue: Nute's threshold must be far enough from the real world to take in some worlds in which A is true, thus it takes in the closest worlds in which A is true, and it excludes the more remote worlds in which A is true. However, Nute's truth conditions differ from Lewis's in that the threshold takes in all of the less outlandish worlds in which A is true, regardless of their relative distance from the real world. In particular, when one world in which A is true is closer to the real world than all others, Lewis's truth conditions make truth of the *would* counterfactual amount to truth in that world of the consequent, whereas Nute's truth conditions let it depend on the truth of the antecedent in other worlds that are not quite so close to the real world; for example, if 'Jimmy divorced Rosalyn' is true in w_1 and false in w_2 in the last diagram and w_2 is within the threshold, then 11.1.18a is true by Lewis's truth conditions and false by Nute's. To make this precise, let us introduce a function $\psi(w, A)$, which picks out a 'neighborhood' of w large enough to include worlds in which A is true, and conceivably large enough to include many worlds in which A is true. (To say that $\psi(w, A)$ is a neighborhood of w is to say that, for any world $w' \in \psi(w, A)$, $\psi(w, A)$ also contains all worlds that are closer to w than w' is). Nute's truth conditions for *would* counterfactuals and the corresponding truth conditions for *might* counterfactuals can then be stated as follows:

11.1.20   a. $\Box \rightarrow AB$ is true in w if and only if in all worlds w' for which $w' \in \psi(w, A)$ and A is true in w', B is true in w';

b. $\Diamond \rightarrow AB$ is true in w if and only if in some world w' for which $w' \in \psi(w, A)$ and A is true in w', B is true in w'.

The characterization of ψ is intentionally vague: it will vary from one context to another depending on how broad a class of worlds comes into the picture.[5]

The truth conditions 11.1.20 provide a partial remedy to another deficiency in the Lewis and Rescher treatments of the counterfactual conditional, namely, that their analyses do not distinguish between the contribution to the meaning made by the *would* and the contribution made by the counterfactual construction. The *would* can here be identified with the universal quantifier expression 'in all worlds w'' and the *might* with the existential quantifier expression 'in some worlds w''. There still remains the problem of identifying a specific part of 11.1.20a–b with the counterfactual conditional construction, or better, of identifying some part(s) of them with the counterfactuality of the construction and identifying other parts as comprising a conditional construction that recurs in indicative conditionals. I will return to this problem later in this section.

The remaining deficiency in the Lewis and Rescher accounts of counterfactuals is that they ignore counterfactual constructions in which the *if* is modified by the sorts of things that *if* can be modified by in indicative conditionals:

11.1.21   a. Carter would fire Powell *only if* Powell killed someone.

b. Carter wouldn't fire Powell *even if* Powell killed someone.

To argue that 11.1.21a was false, one would have to argue that there was a not too bizarre situation in which Carter fires Powell but Powell hasn't killed anyone (it would have to be a not too bizarre situation: it isn't enough to argue that Carter would fire Powell if Powell kidnapped all nine Supreme Court justices and threatened to keep all of them stoned on peyote until he was made pope). Within Nute's approach, a plausible analysis of such sentences can readily be constructed: 'B would be the case only if A were the case' is true in w if and only if, among the worlds within a threshold around w determined by A, in those worlds in which $\sim$A is the case, $\sim$B is the case. That is, the set of worlds that come into the picture deviate from the real world by as much as do those that came into the picture in evaluating 'If A were the case, B would be the case', but this time we are concerned with the ones in which A is false.

11.1.22   'B would be the case only if A were the case' is true in w if and only if in all worlds w' for which $w' \in \psi(w, A)$ and $\sim$A is true in w', $\sim$B is true in w'.

Note that under 11.1.22, 'B would be the case only if A were the case' is equivalent neither to $\square\!\!\rightarrow$BA nor to $\square\!\!\rightarrow(\sim A, \sim B)$, since the domain of the world variable is different in the three cases: for 'B would be the case only if A were the case', w' ranges over $\psi(w, A)$, for $\square\!\!\rightarrow$BA it ranges over $\psi(w, B)$, and for $\square\!\!\rightarrow(\sim A, \sim B)$ it ranges over $\psi(w, \sim A)$. These three sets of worlds will generally be different; in particular, $\psi(w, A)$ and $\psi(w, \sim A)$ will generally be different in that whichever of A and $\sim$A is true in w, the corresponding ψ will be a smaller set of worlds.

The obvious candidate for truth conditions for *would even if* counterfactuals such as 11.1.21*b* is 11.1.23:

11.1.23   'B would be the case even if A were the case' is true in w if and and only if for every world w' in $\psi(w, A)$, even those in which A is true, B is true in w'.

As Lycan (1977) has pointed out, conditionals with *even if* differ from simple assertions of their consequents in that the antecedent limits the class of worlds that come into the picture: note that the only role that A plays in distinguishing true from false *would even if* sentences is in specifying how large a class of worlds B must be true in. The analysis of *might even if* counterfactuals such as 11.1.24 is somewhat less obvious.

11.1.24   Carter might lose the election even if Reagan were his opponent.

There is no coherent direct analogue to the parenthetical interpolation in 11.1.23; leaving out that interpolation, the closest analogue to 11.1.23 would be 11.1.25:

11.1.25   'B might be the case even if A were the case' is true in w if and only if for some world w' in $\psi(w, A)$, B is true in w'.

But 11.1.25 as it stands misrepresents the truth conditions of *might even if* counterfactuals: it would allow 11.1.24 to be true by virtue of Carter losing in some extra close world in which someone other than Reagan is his opponent, whereas the truth of 11.1.24 clearly hinges on the existence of a not too outlandish world in which Carter loses and Reagan is his opponent. The best I can suggest in the way of an analysis that localizes the difference between *might even if* and *would even if* in a constituent that can be identifiable with *might* or *would* is to admit a redundant clause in the analysis of *would even if*:

11.1.26   a. 'B would be the case even if A were the case' is true in w if and only if for every world w' in $\psi(w, A)$, including worlds in which A is true, B is true.

    b. 'B might be the case even if A were the case' is true in w if and only if for some worlds w' in $\psi(w, A)$, including worlds in which A is true, B is true.

The conditional construction, whether indicative or counterfactual, can be identified as a specification of a set of relevant worlds. In counterfactual conditionals, this set is $\psi(w, A)$, the worlds that differ from the real world by not much more than what it would take to make A true (though, NB, $\psi(w, A)$ also includes worlds in which A is false that are no further from the real world than the closer worlds in which A is true). For indicative conditionals, the set of worlds will be a set of epistemically possible worlds: worlds that, for all we know, may be the actual world. Quantifiers may range over domains within that set of worlds; for example, the *only* of *only if* corresponds to a universal quantifier ranging over the worlds in which the antecedent is false (just as the *only* of *only John* ranges over the set of individuals other than John). The difference between *might* and *would* in the counterfactual case and between *may* and either *will* or a modally unmarked form in the indicative case corresponds to the difference between existential and universal quantifiers binding a world variable w' and applying to the propositional function 'B is true in w'' ('$\sim$ B is true in w'', in the case of *only if*), where B is the consequent of the conditional.

11.2. 'World-creating' Predicates

An informal practise has developed among linguists of speaking of certain verbs and adjectives as 'world-creating' and of speaking of the complements of those predicates as referring to various alternative worlds, for example, speaking of the complement of *believe* in 11.2.1*a* (i.e., the clause *I have an elder sister*) as referring to a 'world of John's beliefs' rather than to the 'real world' and speaking of the complement of *want* in 11.2.1*b* (i.e., the underlying clause *Someone helps John*) as referring to a 'world of John's wants':

11.2.1   a. Oscar believes that I have an elder sister.
          b. John wants someone to help him.

I will attempt in this section to develop this informal way of speaking into something more precise and in the process deal with some of the syntactic and semantic problems that have been discussed in terms of such 'worlds'.

I will begin by mentioning briefly some of these problems and the reasons why they are of interest. First, there is the problem of specifying where pronouns can be relative to their antecedents. It is possible for a NP inside the complement of a world-creating predicate to be the antecedent of a pronoun that is not inside the complement of that predicate, even of a pronoun that is in the complement of some other world-creating predicate:

11.2.2   Tom expects to catch *a fish* and intends to fry *it* for dinner.

The interpretation of 11.2.2 that is at issue here is the 'nonreferential' one, which does not imply that there is a (specific) fish that Tom expects to catch. The usual treatment of nonreferential NP's (e.g., Quine 1960: 154–56), in which they are bound by existential quantifiers with narrow scope (in this case, 'Tom catch x' would have to be the scope of the existential quantifier) is doomed to failure here, since the pronoun, which should presumably be just a repetition of the bound variable, is outside the scope of the quantifier that binds it. Moreover, whether a pronoun can have a given antecedent depends on what predicates are used and not just on gross syntactic structure:[6]

11.2.3   a. Tom expected to inherit *$50,000* and hoped/*managed to buy a house with *it*.
          b. It's certain that you'll find *a job*, and it's conceivable that *it* will be a good-paying one.
          b'. ??It's conceivable that you'll find *a job*, and it's certain that *it* will be a good-paying one.
          c. Gladys intends to buy *an apartment building* and is considering turning *it* into a condominium.
          c'. *Gladys is considering buying *an apartment building* and intends to turn *it* into a condominium.

Following Lakoff (1972*a*: 615ff.), I will present an analysis below in which the differences are ascribed to differences in the relationships that the various predicates allow between their complements and the various 'worlds' that come into consideration.

A second problem that has led linguists to discuss world-creating predicates in terms of 'worlds' is that of determining the presuppositions of a complex sentence, especially determining the relationship between presuppositions of the constituents of a sentence and the presuppositions of the entire sentence. This includes such questions as why the presupposition of the *regret* clause (that Mary's parents have only one child) is a presupposition (in some sense) of the main clause in 11.2.4*a* but not in 11.2.4*b*:

11.2.4	a. Mary thinks her parents regret that they have only one child.
	b. Mary thinks that she has no brothers and sisters and that her parents regret that they have only one child.

I will sketch below an extension of Karttunen's (1974) treatment of pragmatic presuppositions that is suggested by ideas of Morgan (1973) and use it to provide an account of presuppositional phenomena in relation to world-creating predicates.

In addition, there is an important problem relating to the grammatical feature of person that has occasionally been analyzed in terms of worlds. Normally, two occurrences of *I/me/myself* in the same sentence must be coreferential, and, accordingly, processes such as reflexivization that are contingent on coreferentiality are obligatory when the items in question are both first person singular:

11.2.5	a. I kicked myself/*me.
	b. Marge asked me about myself/*me.

However, it is possible to get noncoreferential first-person singular pronouns in such sentences as 11.2.6:

11.2.6	a. I dreamed that I was Brigitte Bardot and that I kissed me.
	b. If I were you, I'd kiss me.
	c. While I was stoned out of my head on peyote last week, I thought I was Geraldine and I kept telling everyone that I loved me.

The reason that I have put the word 'world' in quotation marks in much of the above discussion is that the so-called belief worlds, wish worlds, dream worlds, and the like are not single worlds but entire modal systems. Mark's beliefs have to do not only with what he takes to be the real world but with his conception of what the alternatives to that world are. When I ascribe to Mark belief in a modal proposition, I am ascribing to him a belief about what for him are the alternatives to his 'real world',

not a belief about what for me are the alternatives to my 'real world'. This
point is brought out by such examples as

11.2.7   a. Mark believes that Bill, whom I know to already be in
                Pittsburgh, can't possibly be in Pittsburgh yet.
            b. Pythagoras though that π was a rational number.
            c. Oliver thinks it's possible that John F. Kennedy, who we all
                know was killed in 1963, is still alive in a secret location
                in Texas.

The 'belief worlds' may involve objects that the speaker not only does not
take as existing in the real world but may take as not existing in any
alternative worthy of consideration:

11.2.8   a. Larry thinks I have an elder sister named Mary.
            b. Janet is convinced that there is a largest prime number.
            c. My neighbor's son is worried that there may be a three-
                headed fire-breathing monster that devours little boys
                lurking under his bed.

   The belief worlds may also lack objects that exist in the real world, and a
belief proposition may be false simply by virtue of the alleged belief being
about an object that the person does not have in his belief world for him to
have a belief about. Thus, since Plato (like ancient Greeks in general) had
no conception of zero as a number, 11.2.9a is false and, indeed, is false for
exactly the same reason that 11.2.9b is false, namely, that neither Chomsky
nor the proposition that $0 \times 7 = 0$ existed for Plato:

11.2.9   a. Plato believed that $0 \times 7 = 0$.
            b. Plato admired Chomsky.

This does not mean that '$0 \times 7 = 0$' was false in the world of Plato's
beliefs: the proposition simply did not exist for him. This observation casts
doubt on the treatment of belief by Hintikka (1969a), according to which
'a believes S' is true if and only if S is true in all 'worlds' in which a's
beliefs are true. Since for Hintikka (in contrast with this section), a world
involves a COMPLETE specification of truth values of propositions, the only
way that 11.2.9a could be false for Hintikka would be for there to be a
world in which all of Plato's beliefs are true but '$0 \times 7 = 0$' is false. But
the falsehood of 11.2.9a results not from its being possible as far as Plato
is concerned for 0×7 not to equal 0, but rather from the fact that the
proposition that $0 \times 7 = 0$ is in a different ballpark.

   Belief worlds may even conform to a different version of logic than the
real world is taken to be subject to; such worlds would be appropriate
devices for analyzing such sentences as those in which an adherent of
standard logic accurately attributes beliefs to an intuitionist (or vice versa).

The problem of establishing the logical properties of sentences involving world-creating predicates is complicated by the fact that the use of such sentences is subject to a principle of cooperativity: the speaker is taken as implying that the belief worlds, and so on, to which he refers agree with the real world in all relevant respects except those in which he has given the addressee reason to believe that they may differ from the real world. For example, the reason why 11.2.10*a* is so much more normal than 11.2.10*b* is that the clause *Beethoven died at the age of forty* tells us that the dream world is one in which the events subsequent to Beethoven's fortieth year (such as his writing three more symphonies) did not occur, but provides us with no information about Beethoven's tastes in food (for present purposes, I assume that Beethoven in fact liked gebratene Leberkäse).

11.2.10   a. Sam dreamed that Beethoven died at the age of forty and that Bernstein regretted that Beethoven had composed only six symphonies.
            b. Sam dreamed that Beethoven died at the age of forty and that Bernstein regretted that Beethoven disliked gebratene Leberkäse.

The understanding of a sentence with a world-creating predicate is thus rather like the understanding of a counterfactual conditional; that is, 11.2.10*a* is acceptable for essentially the same reason that one would agree that if Beethoven had died at the age of forty he would have composed only six symphonies but would not agree that if he had died at the age of forty he would have disliked gebratene Leberkäse. The same point can be made about the relationship of 11.2.11*a* to 11.2.11*a'*:

11.2.11   a. I dreamed that the Red Sox had won the 1977 American League pennant and that Billy Martin regretted that the Yankees had finished second.
            a'. If the Red Sox had won the 1977 American League pennant, the Yankees would have finished second.

One will hold 11.2.11*a'* to be true if one believes that the Yankees and the Red Sox were bound to be the two top teams, and that proposition plus the counterfactual proposition that the Red Sox won the pennant implies that the Yankees finished second.

The fruitlessness of much of the discussion of whether various world-creating predicates are presuppositional 'holes' (as claimed by Langendoen and Savin 1971) or presuppositional 'plugs' (Karttunen 1973) is due to the failure on the part of most authors to recognize that both the context and considerations of cooperativity affect what a sentence involving a world-creating predicate conveys. The fact that world-creating predicates are neither unequivocal plugs nor unequivocal holes was first observed by Morgan (1973), who noticed that while 11.2.12*a* normally commits the speaker to the proposition that Alice's house is on fire, it will not so commit him if it appears in a context like that in 11.2.12*b*:

11.2.12   a. Tom thinks Alice doesn't know her house is on fire.
            b. Betty: Tom thinks Alice's house is on fire.
               Marvin: How on earth could he think that? Surely if Alice's house was on fire, she wouldn't just be sitting in the next room doing a crossword puzzle—she'd be trying to save her collection of James Joyce manuscripts from the fire.
               Betty: Tom thinks Alice doesn't know her house is on fire.

In 11.2.12*a*, it is not so much that the presupposition of the complement clause is passed on to the whole sentence as that, without additional context as in 11.2.12*b*, the world of the main clause (or better, the 'context' of the main clause, in the sense of the work by Karttunen summarized in 9.4) is the only available source of information about Tom's belief world. Example 11.2.12*a* clearly does not semantically presuppose that Alice's house is on fire: it is true or false depending only on whether the proposition that Alice doesn't know her house is on fire is included in (or perhaps, implied by) the propositions that Tom believes, regardless of whether Alice's house is actually on fire; and if Tom doesn't believe that Alice's house is on fire, it is false that he thinks she knows her house is on fire, regardless of whether it really is on fire. Any presupposition embodied in 11.2.12*a* is a pragmatic presupposition, that is, a demand that the sentence makes on its context, and in the following pages I will develop Karttunen's conception of presupposition in a direction that will allow it to accommodate the presupposition embodied in 11.2.12*a*.

The fact that the context in 11.2.12*b* appears to 'filter out' the apparent presupposition of 11.2.12*a* is a result of the fact that Betty's first remark provides the addressee with information about the same alternative world that her second remark relates to. The fact that both of her remarks begin with *Tom thinks* is immaterial; distinct predicates can refer to the same world, as in such examples as

11.2.13   Larry thinks I have a sister named Mary. He is convinced that my sister Mary is working for a Ph.D. in anthropology.

The two world-creating predicates in 11.2.13 both refer to the same 'world of Larry's beliefs'. The first sentence in 11.2.13 informs the addressee that in that world the speaker has a sister named Mary, and the second sentence informs him that in that same world the speaker's sister Mary (not a real world person, but an individual in Larry's belief world) is working for a Ph.D. in anthropology. If the second sentence in 11.2.13 were used in a different context (say, one in which nothing has yet been said about Larry's beliefs), it would be interpreted as ascribing to Larry a belief about a real world individual and would take for granted that the speaker actually has a sister named Mary. In either case the definite description *my sister Mary* picks out an individual of Larry's belief world; that individual will be identified with a real world individual unless the context establishes the existence in the belief world of a nonreal individual that is the speaker's sister and is named Mary.

In subordinate clauses, even in complements of world-creating predicates, definite descriptions and factive verbs function the same way that they do in main clauses. If the account of presuppositional phenomena in terms of 'context' and 'contextual domain' given in 9.6 is correct, then the contexts and contextual domains with respect to which items in the complements of world-creating verbs are interpreted cannot be the same as the contexts and contextual domains of the main clauses; for example, the individual picked out by *my sister Mary* in 11.2.13 is not a real world individual whose existence and identity are taken for granted by speaker and addressee. Moreover, that individual is not merely a temporary increment to the real world contextual domain, since the discrepancy between the real world contextual domain and the belief world contextual domain is not localized to the complement clause in which the discrepancy is introduced but can extend arbitrarily far into the subsequent discourse, as long as reference to the same alternative world is maintained, as in 11.2.12*b*, where Betty's first remark adds 'Alice's house is on fire' to the belief world context and her second remark puts into the belief world a proposition whose acceptability is contingent on the belief world context (not the real world context) entailing that Alice's house is on fire, which it does, given Betty's remark. Note that there is no limit to the amount of discourse that could in principle intervene between Betty's first and second remarks, none of which need refer to Tom's belief world. In addition, the discrepancy between the real world contextual domain and the belief world contextual domain may consist in the absence from the latter of certain members of the former:

11.2.14   Agnes thinks I have only one elder brother and that my elder brother regrets that I am a second son.

If 11.2.14 is spoken in a context containing the proposition that the speaker has two elder brothers, with both of the brothers belonging to the contextual domain, *my elder brother* will pick out a referent not from the real world contextual domain but rather from an alternative contextual domain in which either a real world brother is missing or a single alternative world brother corresponds equally to the two real world brothers.

What desires, intentions, and beliefs a person can have and what he can order or request depend directly not on the real world but on his beliefs. I will accordingly speak of worlds corresponding to fulfillment of a person's desires, compliance with his requests, and the like as having his belief world as a REFERENCE WORLD. The context and contextual domain corresponding to the complement of a verb such as *want* or *order* will be based on those for the stratum of discourse referring to the person's beliefs. Thus, in 11.2.15, the acceptability of *it* is due to the presence in the belief contextual domain of an object a such that 'a is a unicorn' and 'a has been eating Arthur's roses' are in the belief context, and the acceptability of *its horn* is due to the same considerations plus the presence in the belief context of the proposition 'every unicorn has exactly one horn', which was carried over to the belief context from the real world context:

11.2.15   Arthur stupidly thought that a unicorn had been eating his roses, and he wanted to catch it by throwing a rope around its horn.

The difference between 11.2.15 and 11.2.16 is that with implicative verbs such as *manage*, the reference worlds of the superordinate clauses are the same:

11.2.16   *Arthur stupidly thought that a unicorn had been eating his roses, and he managed to catch it by throwing a rope around its horn.

The reference world of a main clause is the real world, which means that the complement of *manage* also has the real world as its reference world, and the real world context and contextual domain provide no referents for *it* and *its horn*. I conjecture that the sameness of reference world for the *manage* clause and its complement is part of a more general point about implicative verbs, namely, that the complement clause shares ALL reference points with the clause of the implicative verb, for example, as Karttunen (1971*b*) has observed, they share the same time reference: the time at which Brenda manages to open the jar is the time at which Brenda opens the jar, and the time at which Oscar has the impudence to tell you to shine his shoes is the time at which Oscar tells you to shine his shoes.

The differences in acceptability between some of the examples in 11.2.3 can be attributed to considerations of reference world. For example, in 11.2.3*c*, what Gladys is considering is contingent on fulfillment of her intention, that is, the world corresponding to what she is considering takes as reference world the world specifying fulfillment of her intention. The unacceptability of 11.2.3c' reflects a restriction on what an intention can take as a reference world: one's intentions can be based only on what one is sure of, not on ideas that one is merely entertaining:

11.2.17   a. Gladys intends to buy an apartment building and is considering turning *it* into a condominium.
            b. *Gladys is considering buying an apartment building and intends to turn *it* into a condominium.

The terms 'belief world' and 'dream world' have been convenient in the discussion so far, largely because of the relative stability of beliefs and dreams: one has a single set of beliefs at a time (possibly inconsistent beliefs, but a single set nonetheless), and one has dreams one at a time, with a second dream not beginning until the first dream has come to an end. There is no equally convenient analogous terminology for worlds having to do with wishes and orders, since one may have independent sets of wishes or independent sets of orders in effect simultaneously. For example, you can both want to spend the summer in Greece and want to spend the summer in Mexico without necessarily having the contradictory wish to spend the summer both in Greece and in Mexico. Likewise, one can both order Patricia to play the piano and order Stan to prevent anyone from playing the piano, and one must separate the question of whether the one order is complied with from the question of whether the other one is complied with, rather than lumping those two questions together by talking about a world in which your orders are complied with. It thus makes no sense to speak of 'Alice's wish world' or 'Oscar's order world', although it does make sense to speak of wishes and orders in terms of alternative worlds. A treatment in terms of alternative worlds seems to be called for in view of the fact that pronouns and definite descriptions can be used that refer not to real world entities but to entities that will be identifiable only if the wish or order is fulfilled, and they can appear in the complements of separate predicates:

11.2.18   a. Nancy wants to write a short story and hopes she can get *Playboy* to accept *it*.
            b. Morris ordered me to write a piano sonata and suggested that I put lots of modulations in *the slow movement*.

It will probably be clearest if one simply avoids such terms as 'wish world', which misleadingly suggests that there is a single system of wishes whose simultaneous fulfillment is at issue, and instead simply use circumlocutions that say that a particular world corresponds to the fulfillment of a particular wish or order on the part of a given person. These worlds may serve as reference worlds for other worlds that correspond to, say, the fulfillment of wishes, hopes, and so forth, that are contingent on the fulfillment of a given wish, as in 11.2.18*a*, where the complement of *hope* refers to a world in which the want in the first conjunct is fulfilled.

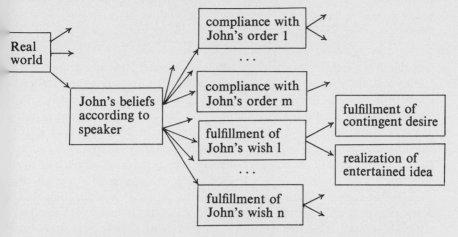

Details of the meanings of various predicates can impose various restrictions on what their complements can have as reference world. Consider, for example, what is responsible for the oddity of the sentence obtained from 11.2.18*b* by interchanging the two main verbs:

11.2.19   Morris suggested that I write a piano sonata and ordered me to put lots of modulations in the slow movement.

An order creates an obligation on the addressee's part to perform the action in question. But the addressee's action is performed in the real world, not in a fictitious alternative to it, and in the fictitious world in which I do not carry out Morris's suggestion that I write a piano sonata, there is no slow movement for me to put any modulations in to comply with his order. Taking the world corresponding to the complement of *suggest* as the reference world for the complement of *order* would result in an ill-formed order: an order such that whether the notion of complying with it is intelligible depends on a choice that one is ostensibly free to make. (Note that the oddity of the order in 11.2.19 is of a quite different kind from the oddity of an order such that compliance with it is impossible even though there is no problem determining what would constitute compliance, for example, ordering someone to turn a lump of lead into gold by saying magic words or to write a ten-volume history of China in half an hour.)

I have so far been describing what I want to take as the 'normal' way that propositions and objects get into the contexts and contextual domains associated with the various worlds that figure in a discourse. An important class of cases in which propositions and objects get into contexts and contextual domains by other than the 'normal' route was first discussed in a remarkable paper by Peter Geach (1967), which dealt with the coreferentiality relation between the emphasized NP's in such sentences as

11.2.20   Jake believes that *a witch* has ruined his crops, and Zeke is convinced that *she (the selfsame witch)* has cursed his cows.

Geach's main point was that the means of standard predicate logic are insufficient to account for this coreferentiality: standard quantification theory allows *she* in 11.2.20 only to correspond to an instance of a bound variable, bound by a quantifier that both it and its antecedent are in the scope of. But since it and its antecedent are in separate conjuncts of 11.2.20, the only way that a single quantifier could bind both of them would be for the quantifier to have the entire coordinate structure for its scope, and the resulting formula could only correspond to the referential reading of 11.2.20 (the interpretation paraphraseable as 'There is a witch such that Jake believes she has ruined his crops and Zeke is convinced that she has cursed his cows'), which leaves the nonreferential interpretation unaccounted for. The proposals of 9.5 avoid that particular difficulty, since a pronoun with an existentially quantified NP as antecedent no longer need be in the scope of the existential quantifier: it can merely be a repetition of the 'discourse referent' that that quantified NP makes available. But a related difficulty immediately appears: the discourse referent here should be available only in those parts of the discourse that have Jake's belief world as reference point, and the pronoun in 11.2.20 has Zeke's belief world rather than Jake's as reference point.

The problem presented by 11.2.20 in fact arises daily in the conduct of normal science, as witness 11.2.21 and parallel examples that can easily be constructed using controversial notions of particle physics or radio astronomy or even linguistics:

11.2.21   Halle believes that English has a productive rule of trisyllable laxing and that that rule is responsible for the vowel alternation in *divine/divinity*, and Keyser is convinced that the same rule is the reason for the shortness of the vowel in such words as *develop*; but Stampe has pretty convincingly demonstrated that English has no such rule.

The plausibility of these examples depends on the ease with which we can imagine the beliefs of the one person being communicated to and accepted by the other. For example, 11.2.20 becomes quite strange if one inserts *secretly* before *believes*. It is indeed such migration of beliefs and supposed objects from one person's belief world to those of others that makes it possible for scientific communities to exist. The acceptability of 11.2.20 reflects not merely the scheme of worlds and contexts developed here but also knowledge on the part of those accepting 11.2.20 and 11.2.21 of a basic mechanism in the sociology of science. Of course, 11.2.20 still fails to conform to the scheme of this section, since this principle of the sociology of science only tells one that the witch and the proposition that she ruined Jake's crops CAN migrate to Zeke's belief world: nothing in that principle or in the first conjunct of 11.2.20 tells us that they HAVE migrated there.

Many world-creating predicates have negative counterparts; for example, one sense of *deny* is a negative counterpart of *think* or *believe*, and *forbid* is a negative counterpart of *order*. These items take complements involving nonreferential NP's but do not allow those nonreferential NP's to serve as antecedents for pronouns in subsequent sentences the way that 'positive' world-creating predicates do:

11.2.22   a. Arthur thinks that *a unicorn* has been eating his roses. He
                   hopes he can catch *it*.
           a'. Arthur denies that *a unicorn* has been eating his roses. *He
                   hopes he can catch *it*.
           b. Mary ordered John to paint *a portrait of her* and suggested
                   that he hang *it* in the living room.
           b'. *Mary forbade John to paint *a portrait of her* and suggested
                   that he hang *it* in the living room.

This can be accounted for by treating these verbs as if they were combinations of the corresponding 'positive' verb and a negation: they will refer to a belief world (or an order world) rather than a 'denial world' (or a 'prohibition world'), and the propositions that they will cause to be added to the belief context will be the negations of the complement propositions; for example, the first sentence in 11.2.22a' will cause the addition to Arthur's belief context of the proposition that it is not the case that a unicorn has been eating Arthur's roses; since that proposition does not imply the existence of a unicorn that has been eating Arthur's roses, no individual matching that description will be added to the contextual domain for Arthur's belief world. Of course, the negative propositions that are added to the belief context can satisfy the contextual demands made by factive predicates that refer to the belief (or other) world in question:

11.2.23   a. Arthur denies that Jennie loves him and regrets that no one
                   but his mother loves him.
           b. Mary forbade John to paint a portrait of her and requested
                   that he try not to regret not being allowed to paint a
                   portrait of her.

World-creating predicates can of course appear within the complements of world-creating predicates, for example,

11.2.24   a. Doreen dreamed that Bruno thought she admired him.
               b. Jonathan hopes that I'll want to try to believe that he has reformed.
               c. Maxine thinks Billy believes that peanut butter is a carcinogen.

Just as Maxine's beliefs about Henry Kissinger need not agree with the facts about Kissinger, her beliefs about Billy's belief world need not agree with the facts about Billy's belief world: Billy may in reality have no opinion on whether peanut butter is a carcinogen or may believe that it is not a carcinogen. It is thus necessary (as proposed by Morgan 1973) to distinguish the real belief world of Billy from Billy's belief world according to Maxine, Billy's belief world according to Jake according to Samantha, and so on. It is possible to construct sentences in which several such versions of 'Billy's belief world' coexist and figure in the satisfaction of the contextual demands made by different definite descriptions and factive predicates later in the discourse:

11.2.25   a. Samantha is convinced that Jake believes that Billy thinks she snorts coke and is sure that Jake regrets that someone who thinks she uses illegal drugs is a friend of the Chief of Police, but actually Jake thinks Billy believes no one in town uses any drugs and is ashamed that Billy hasn't realized that Samantha is taking coke, when in fact Billy believes that everyone but Samantha is taking drugs.
               b. Tom thinks that Alice doesn't know me and that she regrets that none of her friends are anarchists; but Alice and I are actually very good friends and she's delighted that at least one of her friends, namely me, is an anarchist.

I will conclude this section by saying a little about an important class of cases in which sentences not necessarily involving complement clauses can refer to multiple worlds, namely, sentences making reference to 'fictions', taken in the broad sense that includes pictorial representations.[7] Neither Santa Claus nor Batman exists. Nonetheless, one must distinguish between Santa Claus and Batman, since a picture of Santa Claus is not a picture of Batman. One must indeed even distinguish between a picture of Santa Claus and a picture of Batman disguised as Santa Claus. The context 'a picture of _____' has often been held to be an 'opaque context' because

∃-introduction would derive the supposedly false 11.2.26*b* from 11.2.26*a* when 11.2.26*a* was true:

11.2.26   a. This painting is a picture of Santa Claus.
            b. There is someone of whom this painting is a picture.

I maintain that the fallacy in going from 11.2.26*a* to 11.2.26*b* is not really in the inferential step but in the interpretation that one tends to (but really need not) put on the conclusion, in which the variable is interpreted as ranging over an irrelevant domain, namely, that of real world persons. The blank in 'a picture of _____' need not be filled by real world persons.[8] The domain over which the variable bound by *someone* ranges is a gloriously open-ended one: it encompasses all persons, past, present, or future, real or fictitious, perhaps even from fictitious fictions (fictions that have not actually been composed, such as the play within *Hamlet*) as well as from real fictions (such as *Hamlet* or the myth of Orpheus). *Someone* is in fact ambiguous in terms of whether it ranges over that gloriously open-ended domain or only over real persons. If interpreted the former way, 11.2.26*b* is true, if interpreted the other way, it is false. The same ambiguity may be seen more clearly in the range of possible answers to questions like 11.2.27*a*; the choice between *yes* and *no* indicates that on one interpretation *This painting is a painting of someone* is true and on another interpretation is false:

11.2.27   a. Is this painting a picture of someone?
            b. Yes, it's a picture of Santa Claus.
            c. No, it's a picture of Santa Claus.

As with belief worlds and dream worlds, fictional worlds take over propositions and objects from the real world (or better, from the reference world—you can have thoughts or dreams about fictions, too). Thus, a painting can depict real world events involving real world participants, fictitious events involving real world participants, or fictitious events involving fictitious participants (or a mixture of real world and fictitious ones):

11.2.28   a. He painted a picture of Warren Burger administering the oath of office to Jimmy Carter.
            b. He painted a picture of Warren Burger throwing Jimmy Carter into a vat of peanut butter.
            c. He painted a picture of a nineteenth-century American president named Simon Saddlesores leading an invasion of a Central American republic called Molcajetillo.

Kripke (1973 lecture at the University of Western Ontario) has made the important point that fictions exist in specific worlds rather than by themselves in some limbo, and thus it makes sense to speak of paintings by Rembrandt and by Picasso as depicting the same myth. Here there is a bound variable ranging over real myths (that is, myths that exist as myths in the real world, which is not to say that the things that figure in the myths exist in the real world: there is a real myth of Sisyphus but no real person Sisyphus). A bound variable ranging over real myths is no more objectionable than a bound variable ranging over real languages: the problems involved in individuating myths (i.e., in deciding whether two actual instances of myth are instances of the same myth) are of essentially the same type and complexity as the problems involved in individuating languages.

Persons, objects, and events in fictions may be represented by real world items (e.g., by actors, props, and actions in the staging of a play). The real items and the fictitious items need not be individuated the same way; for example, a single actor may play several roles, a single fictitious person may be played by a different actor in each act, and a single fictitious event may be represented by several different real world events (as in *Rashomon*, where the killing of the husband is enacted several times). Bound variables may range over either the fictitious objects or the real objects that represent fictitious objects:

11.2.29   a. In the banquet scene, the king promises a fortune to the same woman that he had insulted in the battle scene.
           b. In the banquet scene, the same actor is slapped as is slapped in the battle scene.

In 11.2.29a, the variable ranges over characters of the particular play, and it is immaterial whether the same character might be played by different actors in different scenes; in 11.2.29b, the variable ranges over actors in a given performance, and it is immaterial whether a given actor might have played a different role in the battle scene than in the banquet scene. There is no need to deny that the lines in a play are the orders, questions, statements, and curses that they purport to be, though one must be careful to distinguish between the speech acts in the world of the play and the real world representations of those acts: it is the fictional Richard III and not the real Laurence Olivier who is offering to exchange his kingdom for a horse (thus, the words that Olivier utters in that scene do not entitle you to present him with a horse the next day and say 'Okay, Larry baby, where's that kingdom you have for me?').[9]

11.3. Tense Logic

In discussing the various examples taken up so far, we have paid no attention to the tenses of the verbs or to auxiliary verbs such as *have* and *will* that have some relation to time. In this section I wish to remedy this omission partially and to suggest ways that considerations of time reference may be incorporated into logical structure and related to linguistic means of indicating time reference.

The most basic time notion is probably that of 'preceding' or 'being earlier than'. One time precedes another time if the passage of time 'takes one' from the former time to the latter. A second, almost equally central notion is that of 'now' or 'the present'. The notions of 'past' and 'future' are put together out of these two more basic notions: the past is what is prior to now and the future is what now is prior to. It is common for languages to express propositions differently, depending on whether they refer to the present, to the past, or to the future. However, there is not a straightforward correspondence between linguistic forms and the present, past, or future time reference of sentences in which they are used. For example, the present tense in English often refers to future events (*Bill's plane arrives at 2:00*; *I'm cooking red-cooked pig tripe tomorrow*) and *will* may be used with reference to past or present events (*Bill will be in Baltimore by now*). The conditions under which the various tenses and auxiliary verbs may be used involves not only temporal factors but notions such as necessity and possibility and the current information of the speaker and addressee.

There are a number of ways that time considerations might be brought into logical structure. A first possibility is simply to have time appear as an extra argument in the various propositional functions that we have so far considered; for example, instead of having a predicate 'Bald(x)' we would have a two-place predicate 'Bald(x, t)' expressing that x is bald at time t. A second possibility is to have 'operators' R_t expressing that the proposition they are combined with is true at the indicated time; for example, we would have R_t(Bald(x)) instead of Bald(x, t). A third possibility is to treat times as 'indices': just as a proposition is not flatly true or flatly false but is true in certain worlds and false in others, a proposition would be true at some times and false at other times. 'Now' would have the same special role among the time indices that 'the actual world' has among the world indices; that is, unless something indicates the contrary, a proposition is 'evaluated' relative to the 'actual' indices: it is taken as referring to the present time, to the actual world, to the place where it is uttered, and so forth. These three possibilities can of course be combined with each other. For example, one can treat propositions as being evaluated at times, rather than always involving times as arguments, and still employ R_t in formulating propositions that refer to times other than 'now'.

Under the third approach, moments in time assume a status like that of worlds in modal logic, and both the relation of temporal precedence and its converse (the relation of temporal subsequence) assume a status like that of an alternativeness relation. For example, if 't_1 precedes t_2' (henceforth written Pt_1t_2) were taken as an alternativeness relation, then according to the truth conditions for modal operators, 'necessary' would amount to 'at all future times' and 'possible' to 'at some future time'. The bulk of work done on tense logic since the 1950s has in fact developed tense logic as a variety of modal logic, with temporal relations playing the role of 'alternativeness'.[10] What I propose to do in this section is not to survey 'standard' tense logic but rather to survey the various linguistic considerations that I regard as important and sketch a specific variant of tense logic that ties in with them as closely as possible.

The first of these considerations is that English[11] normally separates factors of time from factors of modality; for example, in 11.3.1, *possible* relates to a choice among alternative future histories, whereas *will* relates to future time within a given future history:

11.3.1   It is possible that Bill will finish his novel.

In existing work on tense logic, 'branching time' is generally allowed by letting the relation P of temporal precedence be a partial ordering rather than a strict ordering: there can be distinct worlds w' and w'' such that Pww' and Pww'', with w' and w'' not standing in any temporal relation to one another (i.e., $w' \neq w''$, yet neither $Pw'w''$ nor $Pw''w'$):

11.3.2

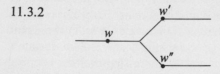

With P taken to represent a relation as in 11.3.2 and used as the alternativeness relation of a modal system, the truth conditions for $\Diamond$ will not strictly speaking define a temporal notion but will rather conflate the notions that are separated into the *possible* and the *will* of 11.3.1. If we wish to have an element of logical structure that can be identified with a linguistic notion of futurity and to define that element in terms of an alternativeness relation, we will have to require that it deal with time branches one at a time: *possible* in 11.3.1 will have to be taken as saying that there is a time branch in which . . ., and the *will* of the proposition that *possible* is combined with will have to be taken as saying simply that 'Bill finish his novel' is true at some future point on that time branch.

Suppose that the embedded sentence in 11.3.1 is used as an independent sentence:

11.3.3   Bill will finish his novel.

The meaning of 11.3.3 is clearly not that in some world w' such that Pww' (with P as in 11.3.2 and w taken to be the actual present world) Bill finishes his novel, since then it would only mean that there is SOME time branch containing a future point at which Bill finishes his novel, which is not the meaning of 11.3.3 but of 11.3.1 or of *Bill may finish his novel*. Nor does 11.3.3 mean that on ALL branches leading into the future from the present there is a point at which Bill finishes his novel, since 11.3.3 does not embody such a strong assertion: it only says that at some point in the ACTUAL future Bill will finish his novel and leaves it open whether there are other possible but nonactual futures in which Bill does not finish the novel. I thus maintain that an extra index must be brought into the analysis of future sentences: one must evaluate the sentence relative not only to the actual world and the actual time but also to the actual future. The notion of 'actual future' may give one a queasy feeling, in view of the fact that one normally has very little conception of which of the infinitely many possible futures is the actual one; one's knowledge of the past, which involves knowledge of innumerable details that could have turned out otherwise but in fact did not, is far richer than one's knowledge of the future, which consists merely in what can be predicted from one's knowledge of the present via general laws. Nonetheless, speakers of natural languages frequently indulge in the rashness of making statements that purport to describe the actual future. That such statements as 11.3.3 are interpreted as referring to the actual future is confirmed by a consideration of how one applies words like *right, wrong, true,* and *false* in talking about previous statements about the future. For example, 11.3.4 can be a report of George's having said *Mary will finish her thesis by January,* and the speaker's use of *wrong* indicates that the actual future was not what George said it would be:

11.3.4   George said in June that Mary would finish her thesis by January, but he was wrong.

The speaker is not attributing to George the proposition that Mary would not finish her thesis by January in any possible future; for example, if Mary actually finished her thesis by January but was in grave danger of not finishing it by then, one could not say 11.3.4 to indicate that George made a rash assertion: 11.3.4 is a remark about the correctness of a statement about the actual future, not a comment on a statement about all possible futures. I accordingly take 11.3.3, both as an independent sentence and when it appears embedded in a larger sentence as in 11.3.1, as involving a time variable that ranges over only one time branch at a time, with the time branch over which it ranges being either the actual time branch (if it is an independent sentence) or a variable time branch bound by a quantifier such as I would suggest is involved in the *possible* of 11.3.1 ('there is a time branch in which . . .').

So far it appears that the best temporal analogues to $\Diamond$ and $\Box$ will be operators $\Diamond_f$, $\Box_f$, $\Diamond_p$, $\Box_p$ with the following truth conditions:

11.3.5 $\Diamond_f$A is true at t on time branch B if and only if there is a t' such that Ptt' for which A is true at t' on branch B.

$\Box_f$A is true at t on time branch B if and only if for all t' such that Ptt', A is true at t' on branch B.

$\Diamond_p$A is true at t if and only if there is a t' such that P$t't$ for which A is true at t'.

$\Box_p$A is true at t if and only if for all t' such that P$t't$, A is true at t'.

However, these four operators do not fit at all closely any devices of the English language. First of all, the bound variables that figure in the meanings of English sentences typically range over restricted segments of time, rather than over the whole past or the whole future; the language provides a great profusion of devices for indicating the limits of the domains of bound time variables (*since he was three years old* or *until November*, and so on), and such devices are of very frequent use. Second, in sentences referring to the future, *will* (or *'ll*) is used regardless of whether the future time is constant, existentially quantified, or universally quantified:

11.3.6   The concert will begin at 2:00.
I'll phone you some time before I leave.
There'll always be an England.

Third, the conditions for the use of the devices for referring to the past, namely, the past tense, the present perfect, and the past perfect, are in terms of factors other than the one ($\exists$ vs. $\forall$) that distinguishes $\Diamond_p$ from $\Box_p$: they have to do with what the 'reference point' is and what relevance the past event has to the present (e.g., it is normal to say *I've sprained my ankle* only as long as the injury still interferes with your activities). Thus, if we are to use temporal analogues of $\Diamond$ and $\Box$ in logical structures, we will have to expect that (i) in addition to the operators defined in 11.3.5 we will need 'restricted' versions of those operators, for example, an operator $\Diamond_f{}^t$ such that $\Diamond_f{}^t$A is true if and only if there is a future time between now and t at which A is true; and (ii) it will be necessary to go beyond what can be expressed with these temporal operators in order to distinguish among the relevant natural language devices.

Before I take up in some detail these natural language devices, it will be useful if I first bring in an important notion that had been missing from the above discussion, namely, that of an INTERVAL in time. There are many predicates or combinations of predicates and arguments that refer to things that are spread over time rather than concentrated at an instant:

11.3.7   a. John has read *War and Peace*.
          b. Elsa hitchhiked across Europe last summer.
          c. J. Paul Getty amassed one of the finest art collections in the world.

To express the meaning of 11.3.7*a*, it is not satisfactory to say that there is a time instant at which John's reading of *War and Peace* took place, since it is physically impossible for there to be such an instant—reading *War and Peace* isn't something that can be accomplished in an instant. Nor can one reduce the analysis of 11.3.7*a* to sentences referring to instantaneous events such as that of finishing reading *War and Peace*, since any time adverbs combined with the sentences in 11.3.7 refer to the entire process and not to, say, its termination. For example, 11.3.8*a* implies that the entire reading took place yesterday, whereas 11.3.8*b* strongly suggests that the reading did not begin yesterday—John could have read *War and Peace* one sentence a day and have read only the last sentence yesterday:

11.3.8   a. John read *War and Peace* yesterday.
          b. John finished reading *War and Peace* yesterday.

Nor can one analyze *read 'War and Peace'* as a conjunction such as 'begin reading *War and Peace* and finish reading *War and Peace*', since in 11.3.9 the reading that began yesterday need not be the same reading that finished yesterday—John might have begun a second reading of the book in the morning and then devoted the evening to finishing his first reading:

11.3.9   John began reading *War and Peace* and finished reading *War and Peace* yesterday.

I would like to propose that not only points in time but also intervals figure in the logical structures of sentences and that the logical structures of examples like 11.3.7 all involve time intervals. Example 11.3.7*a* will then not say that there is a past time at which John read *War and Peace* but that there is a past time interval such that he read it on that interval. I maintain, though, that propositions that must be evaluated on intervals do not comprise whole sentences but are only constituents of larger sentences that are evaluated at points in time, as in the case of 11.3.7*a*, in which 'John read *War and Peace*' is embedded in the scope of a generalized version of $\Diamond_p$, which is evaluated at the present moment.

The progressive aspect is another common device for deriving point propositions from interval propositions. For example, 11.3.10*a* can be taken as saying that the point at which Tom enters Agnes's office is contained in an interval occupied by Agnes's writing a letter, formalized provisionally in 11.3.10b:

11.3.10   a. When Tom entered Agnes's office, she was writing a letter.
                b. (ιt: R_t (Tom enter Agnes's office))
                   ($\exists I$: $\in tI$)R_I(Agnes write a letter)

The interval need not be wholly within the actual time branch; for example, Agnes might have stopped writing when Tom entered and never resumed the task. However, not just any interval leading into a possible future will do, since in describing a roll of fair dice that was interrupted (say by a police raid or an earthquake), it is not correct to say any of *I was rolling 2/3/4/ ... /12*, even though there were possible futures in which the dice turned up 2, 3, ..., or 12. The interval must lead into either the actual future or a 'normal' future: one in which things turn out as they were supposed to. If we introduce an operator PR (= 'progressive') such that PR(A) is true at t if and only if A is true on an interval that contains t and is an actual or 'normal' continuation of events then in progress, then 11.3.10b can be restated as

11.3.11   (ιt: R_t(Tom enter Agnes's office))R_t(PR(Agnes write a letter))

One important thing is still missing from 11.3.11, namely, any indication that the event of Tom's entering Agnes's office is in the past rather than the future. Note that there is no way of employing $\Diamond_p$ or $\Box_p$ to incorporate that information into 11.3.11: there are no more time variables available for them to bind. The minimum application for brute force that would fit in the information that the value of t is past is probably to conjoin Ptn, where n stands for 'now' with R_t(I enter Agnes's office) in the definite description operator.

   Intervals figure in the logical structure not only of propositions involving events and states that are spread over time but also in propositions in which an instantaneous event is located inexactly. It is often either impossible or not worth the effort to specify the exact moment of an event's occurrence, and one will be satisfied with sentences such as 11.3.12 as specifications of the time at which something happened:

11.3.12   a. Mozart died in 1791.
                b. I ran into Marge yesterday.

The use of *in* in 11.3.12a is directly analogous to spatial uses of *in*: the point at which Mozart died is in the interval 1791; indeed, except for the idiosyncracy of *on* rather than *in* being used with days (*on/*in Tuesday*), the use of prepositions for temporal relations matches very closely the use of the same prepositions for spatial relations (see Bennett 1975).

Natural languages provide a great profusion of devices for referring to times. Besides expressions referring to the present time (*now, at present*), there is a system of 'dates' that are in effect proper names for points and periods in time (11.3.13*a*), there are devices for describing times in terms of things that happened or were the case at those times (11.3.13*b*), and there are devices for describing times in terms of their distances from other times (11.3.13*c*), and these devices can be combined in numerous ways:

11.3.13   a. Darwin was born on February 12, 1809.
            a'. The explosion occurred at 4:22 P.M. Eastern Daylight
                Time.
            b. When I started teaching here, housing was fairly easy to
                find.
            b'. Darwin was born on the day that Lincoln was born.
            c. Bill left the party one hour after he arrived.
            c'. I'll phone you five minutes before I leave.
            c". Janet left ten minutes ago. (= ten minutes before now)

These can be analyzed as combinations of R_t with either a constant or a definite description operator, provided one enriches the formal language by the addition of n for 'now' and machinery for referring to lengths of time intervals (here rendered by the informal practise of writing '$t' - t = 1$ hour' for 't is 1 hour before t'''):

11.3.14   b. $(\iota t: R_t(\text{I start teaching here}))$
                $R_t(\text{housing be fairly easy to find})$
            c'. $(\iota t: (\iota t': R_{t'}(\text{Bill arrive}))(t - t' = 1 \text{ hour}))$
                $R_t(\text{Bill leave the party})$
            c". $(\iota t: n - t = 10 \text{ minutes})R_t(\text{Janet leave})$

The same devices are used in specifying the endpoints of intervals in time:

11.3.15   a. Since 1 January 1971, it has been illegal to broadcast
                cigarette commercials.
            a'. Genevieve worked here from 20 October 1968 until 19 May
                1974.
            b. The job will be ready by Tuesday.
            b'. Since I started teaching here, I've gone to the opera many
                times.
            b". The office will be closed until the radiator is repaired.
            c. I'll be here until an hour from now.
            c'. Between graduating from high school and getting his Ph.D.,
                Bill made three trips to Europe.

When only one endpoint of the interval is mentioned, either the interval extends indefinitely far away from the present (*until last Wednesday*) or the other endpoint is the present (or rather, the 'reference time': in such examples as *When I ran into Bill, he had been out of work since the previous April*, it is not up to the present but only up to the time when you ran into Bill that you are saying he was out of work; the sentence is noncommittal about whether he remained out of work after that).

In this discussion, Reichenbach's (1947) notion of 'reference point' or 'reference time' has raised its head a couple of times. It would be worthwhile at this point to say something about that notion and to sketch Reichenbach's justly influential analysis of tense and time reference. Since the notion of reference point is manifested most clearly in the past perfect, I will begin with a discussion of that relatively uncommon form. A past perfect typically involves a time adverb referring to some past time, combined with a clause that refers to a still earlier time:

11.3.16   a. When John married Sue, he had met Cynthia five years earlier.
           b. When John married Sue, he had already read *War and Peace* three times.

Example 11.3.16*a* is the past of a past and 11.3.16*b* the past of a present perfect, in the sense that the content of the main clause, if expressed at the time of John's marriage to Sue, would be expressed by a past tense (*John met Cynthia five years ago*) or a present perfect (*John has already read War and Peace three times*), respectively. The time referred to by the time adverb serves as a 'reference point' for the main clause, in the sense that the choice of time adverbs and auxiliary verbs and their interpretation depends on relations to that 'reference time'; for example, *earlier* in 11.3.16*a* means 'earlier than [reference time]', and *already* in 11.3.16*b* means 'in the interval ending at [reference time]'. Reichenbach represented the various combinations of tense and auxiliary verb in terms of diagrams that specified the relative positions of the speech time, the reference time, and the event reported (S, R, and E, respectively) and took the simple past and the present perfect to differ from the past perfect by virtue of two of the times coinciding that are kept separate in the past perfect:

11.3.17   past perfect   present perfect   past

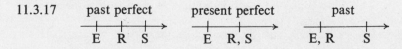

Reichenbach's assignment of reference points in present perfect and past clauses is easiest to justify when one considers not isolated sentences but entire stretches of narrative or other text, in which a single reference point extends over several sentences that differ in time reference:

11.3.18   a. When Mark got off the plane, he felt apprehensive. He hadn't seen Geraldine since her wedding and had no idea how she felt about him. . . .

b. Tom is in a lot of trouble. He $\left\{\begin{array}{l}\text{has received}\\ \text{?received}\end{array}\right\}$ several complaints about his party, and the landlord is threatening to evict him.

In 11.3.18*a*, *when Mark got off the plane* provides the reference time for the entire stretch of discourse, both the past tense clause of the first sentence and the past perfect clause of the second sentence. (But why is *Mark got off the plane* itself in the past tense? What is ITS reference point? See below for an attempt at an answer to these questions, which raise serious problems for Reichenbach's approach.) In 11.3.18*b*, there is a constant present reference point, covering both sentences.

In view of the fact that Reichenbach's book is filled with formal analyses of sentences of ordinary language, it is remarkable that in his entire section on 'The tenses of verbs' (pp. 287–98), he gives only diagrams in the style of 11.3.17 and does not present a single formula in which the content of such a diagram is incorporated into a logical structure. To a large extent, the machinery developed so far in this section allows us to fill that gap in Reichenbach's presentation. For example, both 11.3.16*a* and 11.3.16*b* can be assigned logical structures in which the reference time appears as a superstructure in which the remainder of the sentence is embedded:[12]

11.3.19   a. $(\iota t: R_t(\text{John marry Sue}))R_t(\iota t': t - t' = 5 \text{ years})$
            $R_{t'}(\text{John meet Cynthia})$
         b. $(\iota t: R_t(\text{John marry Sue}))R_t((\exists 3I: PI t)$
            $R_I(\text{John read } War \text{ and } Peace))$

As a first approximation, one could take '*t* is reference time for φ' to be equivalent to '*t* and φ appear in the combination $R_t(\varphi)$ in the logical structure of the given sentence'. This would greatly enlarge the class of things that would count as reference times (e.g., in 11.3.19*a*, *t'* would be a reference time for 'John meet Cynthia' and *t* would be a reference time for 'John marry Sue'), but that seems unobjectionable; indeed, it would bring the past tense of *when John married Sue* under Reichenbach's generalization about when the simple past can be used. A more serious problem with it is that we have not adopted any firm policy on when R_t must appear in a logical structure, and thus arbitrary decisions in formalization could affect whether something counts as a reference point. For example, nothing I have said so far forces us to have the second R_t that appears in 11.3.19a: if we were to omit it, we would have a logical structure having exactly the same truth conditions as 11.3.19a but not meeting the proposed criterion for t to be reference time for 'John meet Cynthia 5 years earlier'.

We could no doubt avoid this obstacle to a fixed correlate in logical structure to Reichenbach's notion of 'reference time' by imposing some restriction on logical form that would require the apparently superfluous R_t in 11.3.19 to appear there. I choose instead to revise the system of logical structures in a more radical fashion. Specifically, I wish to incorporate notions of 'past' and 'future' directly into logical structure, with both 'past' and 'future' interpreted relative to the context in which they appear rather than relative to the present (thus, 11.3.16a is to involve literally a past of a past). Let us introduce the following elements into our system of logical structure:[13]

11.3.20 $T_p(A)$ = 'at the past time at which A', for example, T_p(John meet Cynthia)(John be a student) will represent 'John was a student when he met Cynthia'.

$T_f(A)$ = 'at the future time at which A', for example, T_f(Bill arrive)(Bill call you) will represent 'When Bill arrives, he'll call you'.

$D_p(m)(A)$ = 'A m units into the past', for example, D_p(5 years) (Mary buy a piano) will represent 'Mary bought a piano 5 years ago'.

$D_f(m)(A)$ = 'A m units into the future', for example, D_f(2 years)(Fred get out of prison) will represent 'Fred will get out of prison in 2 years'.

$C_p(a)(A)$ = 'A at the past time a', for example, C_p(2:00)(I take the cake out of the oven) will represent 'I took the cake out of the oven at 2:00'.

$C_f(a)(A)$ = 'A at the future time a', for example, C_f(Christmas) (Uncle George visit us) will represent 'Uncle George will visit us on Christmas'.

The notion of 'reference point' will come in indirectly in giving truth conditions for the expressions in 11.3.20. The following can serve as rules for translating expressions involving the items in 11.3.20 into expressions involving P ('prior') and R_t that will give the conditions under which the given expression is true at a given time a. I will follow the practise of using a superscript to indicate the time at which an expression is to be evaluated;

the rules allow one to move the superscripts onto even smaller expressions and ultimately eliminate them entirely:

11.3.21 $[T_p(A)(B)]^a$ $\rightarrow$ $(\iota t: \wedge (Pta, A^t))\, B^t$

$[T_f(A)(B)]^a$ $\rightarrow$ $(\iota t: \wedge (Pat, A^t))\, B^t$

$[D_p(m)(A)]^a$ $\rightarrow$ $(\iota t: a - t = m)\, A^t$

$[D_f(m)(A)]^a$ $\rightarrow$ $(\iota t: t - a = m)\, A^t$

$[C_p(b)(A)]^a$ $\rightarrow$ A^b if Pba, undefined otherwise

$[C_f(b)(A)]^a$ $\rightarrow$ A^b if Pab, undefined otherwise

A^a $\rightarrow$ $R_a(A)$ if A is not of one of the above forms

(The arrow here means 'is translated into' or 'is reduced to'; the notation is borrowed from Montague grammar and will recur in chap. 13.)
These rules allow 11.3.16a to be assigned the logical structure 11.3.22a and for what is essentially 11.3.19a to be derived by the steps in 11.3.22b:

11.3.22   a. T_p(John marry Sue) D_p(5 years)(John meet Cynthia)

b. $[T_p$(John marry Sue) D_p(5 years)(John meet Cynthia)$]^a$

$\rightarrow$ $(\iota t: \wedge (Pta, $(John marry Sue)$^t))$

$[D_p$(5 years)(John meet Cynthia)$]^t$

$\rightarrow$ $(\iota t: \wedge (Pta, R_t$(John marry Sue)$))(\iota t': t - t' = 5$ years$)$

[John meet Cynthia]$^{t'}$

$\rightarrow$ $(\iota t: \wedge (Pta, R_t$(John marry Sue)$))(\iota t': t - t' = 5$ years$)$

$R_{t'}$(John meet Cynthia)

The symbols introduced in 11.3.20 are direct analogues of the natural language devices for referring to times, as sketched in connection with 11.3.13. The notion of reference point falls naturally out of the translation scheme in 11.3.21: the reference point for a constituent of logical structure is simply the time that it is evaluated at; that is, t is the reference point for A if A^t appears in the course of the translation according to the rules 11.3.21. This does not fit Reichenbach's use of the term 'reference point' very closely; for example, t' and not t will be the reference point for 'John meet Cynthia' in 11.3.22, whereas Reichenbach used his symbols E and R in such a way that when E is John's meeting Cynthia in 11.3.22a, the corresponding R is t. Nonetheless, the relationships that Reichenbach talked about are recoverable from 11.3.22, that is, t' is dependent on t, in the sense that the range of values for t' depends on the value for t, which can be said to make t 'indirectly' a reference point for 'John meet Cynthia'.

The proposal embodied in 11.3.20 and 11.3.21 provides an explanation for a lack of correspondence between Reichenbach's diagrams and the English tense system that would otherwise appear (and to Reichenbach apparently did appear) to be simply an idiosyncracy of English, namely, that while the relationship between S and R and the relationship between R and E are relevant to the choice among linguistic expressions, the relation between S and E is not. Reichenbach remarks (1947:297) that the 'posterior past' as in 11.3.23*a* and the 'anterior future' as in 11.3.23*b* cover all possible relationships between S and E, though for each the relationship between S and R and between R and E is fixed:

11.3.23   a. I didn't expect that he *would win* the race.

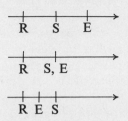

b. Mary *will have finished* her novel by the time you read this.

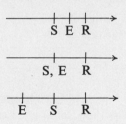

The clause expressing E is embedded in a structure that provides R, and it is evaluated relative to R; it is only the entire structure (which provides both R and E) that is evaluated relative to S, and the steps that evaluate the whole structure relative to S yield intermediate stages in which the E clause is evaluated relative to R (or relative to one of a chain of R's), as can be seen from the superscript *t*'s and *b*'s (never *a*) that appear to the right of the arrows in 11.3.21.[14]

My discussion of Reichenbach's analysis has been in terms that suggest that S, R, and E are all constant times. I wish to take up at this point the question of how Reichenbach's scheme and the formalization of it proposed above can be extended to cases in which the time reference of a clause is a bound variable. One of the examples discussed in fact involved a bound time variable, namely 11.3.16*b*, and a bound time variable appeared in the analysis of it given in 11.3.19*b*. I spoke of 11.3.16*b* as being the past of a present perfect, and so presumably the sentence of which it is a past

(11.3.24a) will have an analysis (11.3.24a') that also involves a bound time variable:

11.3.24   a. John has (already) read *War and Peace* three times.
           a'. ($\exists 3$I: PIn)R$_I$(John read *War and Peace*)

(Here n stands for 'now' and thus PIn corresponds to 'I is prior to now'.) If we wish to revise 11.3.24a' to bring it into closer agreement with the spirit of 11.3.20, in which P and R were avoided in terms of operators that were specified as 'past' or 'future', the best we can do is probably

11.3.25   ($\exists 3$I)C$_p$(I)(John read *War and Peace*)

That is, we can make the quantifier that binds the time variable an unrestricted quantifier but combine it with a device that is restricted to past times. The present perfect is in fact frequently used for quantified past time variables, not only for existentially quantified variables, as in 11.3.24a, but also for universally quantified variables, as in 11.3.26:[15]

11.3.26   a. Mary has always lived in Milwaukee.
           b. Mary has lived in Milwaukee since she was six years old.

However, finding formulas in the descriptive apparatus of 11.3.20 to represent the meanings of these sentences is not as easy as it was for 11.3.24a; indeed, as far as I can see, it is impossible without adding more operators to the list in 11.3.20. The most obvious additions to 11.3.20 to allow one to formalize 11.3.26 (and future analogues such as *Mary will always love Roger*) are operators 'Past' and 'Future', allowing 11.3.26a–b to be formalized as follows:

11.3.27   a. ($\forall t$: past t)R$_t$(Mary live in Milwaukee)
           b. ($\forall t$: $\wedge$ (past t, ($\iota t'$: C$_p$(t')(Mary be 6))(future t))
               R$_t$(Mary live in Milwaukee)

But clauses involving a quantified past time variable are not always in the present perfect; note sentences such as the following, with a simple past, in which a present perfect would be quite unacceptable:

11.3.28   a. George Washington (*has) slept in this house several times.
           b. George Washington $\left\{ \begin{array}{l} \text{drank} \\ \text{*has drunk} \end{array} \right\}$ Madiera every day until
               he died.

One attractive proposal for distinguishing cases like 11.3.24 and 11.3.26 in which a quantified past time variable requires a present perfect from those like 11.3.28 that require a simple past is in terms of the domain of the bound variable: that it includes the present in cases like 11.3.24 and 11.3.26 but does not include the present in cases like 11.3.28. Note that 11.3.28b in fact involves an expression that explicitly puts the domain over which the variable ranges well away from the present (*until he died*). And while, strictly speaking, one could take the variable in 11.3.28a as ranging over a domain that includes the present (i.e., if there are occasions between 1732 and 1799 when Washington slept in this house, they are also occasions between 1732 and 1999 when Washington slept in this house), cooperativity could be held to demand that only 'relevant' values be included in domains of variables, which would exclude from the domain of the variable in 11.3.28a all times after Washington's death. The acceptability of 11.3.24a in a given context will depend on whether that context still allows for the possibility of John reading *War and Peace*; for example, the past tense would have to be substituted for the present perfect if the parties to the discourse take it as established that John is dead, or that John is suffering from a degenerative disease that will prevent him from reading again. Leech (1969) and McCawley (1971) make similar observations on the conditions under which 11.3.29a or 11.3.29b is acceptable:

11.3.29   a. Have you seen the Monet exhibition?
           b. Did you see the Monet exhibition?

For 11.3.29a to be acceptable, it is necessary that the context still allow for the possibility of your seeing the Monet exhibition; it would be unacceptable (and 11.3.29b acceptable) if the speaker knows that the exhibition has already closed or if the speaker and addressee take it for granted that the addressee is incapacitated from seeing the exhibition (e.g., he has broken his leg and will not be able to walk again until after the exhibition has closed). Both 11.3.29a and the relevant interpretation of 11.3.29b (there is another interpretation, that in which the past tense refers to an already established reference point and the speaker is asking whether you saw the exhibition at that time) involve an existential quantifier binding a time variable; they differ on whether the domain of that variable includes the present, and contextual conditions determine what one may take to be the domain of the variable.

I feel uneasy speaking of 11.3.28a as having a past reference time. Indeed, it fits quite naturally into a discourse that is not set in the eighteenth century but deals with the house as it exists at present. In the case of quantified time variables, the closest thing to a reference time may often not be a single point in time but rather the interval over which the bound variable ranges; for example, the appropriate diagram for 11.3.28a may not be the one given for 'past' in 11.3.17 but rather the following:

11.3.30

This is not to say that a bound variable ranging over past times never involves a reference POINT; indeed, I take 11.3.16b to have a 'reference point' over and above the interval over which the bound variable ranges. Note that in 11.3.28a the end of the interval over which the bound variable ranges (presumably, the time of Washington's death) does not have the special role in the meaning of the sentence that the time of John's marriage has in 11.3.16b. If we allow R to be an interval, there is no reason why it could not be an interval containing the present, and we thus come up with 11.3.31 as a possible Reichenbach diagram, one that, given what we have said about the implications of whether the present is included in the domain of a bound variable, ought to be a possible diagram for some uses of the present perfect:

11.3.31

A generalization could then be made that would cover both quantified pasts as in 11.3.28 and constant pasts as in *John left at 2:00*: the past is used if E is contained in R (not necessarily as a proper part) and S is not contained in R.

There is another use of the present perfect that does not conform to the discussion of 11.3.24 and 11.3.26, namely, the so-called stative present perfect of

11.3.32   a. I've sprained my ankle (so I can't go skiing with you).
          b. John's gone to the library (but he should be back by 8:00).
          c. The reason you can't say "The Brooklyn Dodgers have won several pennants" is that we all know that the Dodgers have moved to Los Angeles and so the Brooklyn Dodgers can't win any more pennants.

Here the sentence refers to a change and the present perfect conveys that the change remains in effect (e.g., my ankle is not yet healed; John is not here); the difference between the 'stative' and 'existential' present perfects is brought out in such pairs as

11.3.33   a. Why are you limping? Have you sprained your ankle?
          b. I wonder if you know what discomfort I'm going through. Have you ever sprained your ankle?

Stative present perfects involve a present reference point, in that they fit naturally into discourses in which everything else is about the present, but they involve a bound time variable whose domain need not include the present. One can easily form pasts of stative present perfects, in which a past reference point plays the same role that the present reference point plays in 11.3.32:

11.3.34   a. When I talked to John, he had sprained his ankle and so he couldn't come along on the skiing trip.
            b. I phoned Mary at 2:00, but she had gone to the library and so I wasn't able to talk with her.

That stative present perfects involve an existentially quantified time variable is shown by the fact that, like existential present perfects, they allow time adverbs that place lower limits on the domain over which a variable ranges but exclude adverbs that mark a specific past time:[16]

11.3.35   a. I've sprained my ankle recently/*yesterday, so I can't join you.
            b. I've gotten married $\left\{\begin{array}{l}\text{since I last saw you}\\ \text{*last month}\end{array}\right\}$, so I can't go to Acapulco with you like I said I would.

Not having anything approaching a satisfactory analysis of stative present perfects (or even an unsatisfactory analysis that is worth the space it would take to exhibit it), I will leave the discussion up in the air at this point, noting only that the logical structure must involve both a reference point and an existentially quantified variable.

It has long been recognized that sentences referring to past or future time that include a quantifier can be ambiguous in terms of the relative scopes of the quantifier and the time operator and that furthermore the ambiguity can be correlated with a difference in the domain over which the variable bound by the quantifier ranges. For example, Buridan discussed the ambiguity of the Latin equivalent of

11.3.36   Everything at some time was God.

In the interpretation in which *everything* has higher scope than *some time*, the variable bound by *everything* ranges over all objects now existing, for example, it would imply that the World Trade Center was once God, that Prince Charles was once God, and that all the pornographic movie houses on 42d Street were once God. In the other interpretation, in which *some time* has higher scope, 11.3.36 says only that there was a past time such that everything that existed THEN was God, that is, that there was a past time at which only God existed.

The rules 11.3.21 can be extended in a fairly natural way to quantifiers, with this relationship between domain and scope as a natural consequence.

It will be necessary to distinguish between quantifiers binding time variables and quantifiers binding other variables (alternatively, quantifiers binding time variables could be avoided in favor of operators such as $\Diamond_f$, with separate rules given for those operators). Specifically, I propose the following rules:

11.3.37   a. $[(Qt: At)B]^a \to (Qt:(At)^a)\ B^t$, for any quantifier Q.
            b. $[(Qx: Ax)Bx]^a \to (Qx: (Ax)^a)\ B^a$

The rationale for these rules can be seen by going through their application to logical structures for the two interpretations of 11.3.36:

11.3.38   a. $[(\forall x: \text{thing } x)(\exists t: \text{Past } t)(\text{God } x)]^a$
               $\to (\forall x: (\text{thing } x)^a)(\exists t: (\text{Past } t)^a)(\text{God } x)^t)$
               $\to (\forall x: R_a(\text{thing } x))(\exists t: Pta)R_t(\text{God } x)$
           b. $[(\exists t: \text{Past } t)(\forall x: \text{thing } x)(\text{God } x)]^a$
               $\to (\exists t: (\text{Past } t)^a)[(\forall x: \text{thing } x)(\text{God } x)]^t$
               $\to (\exists t: Pta)(\forall x: (\text{thing } x)^t)(\text{God } x)^t)$
               $\to (\exists t: Pta)(\forall x: R_t(\text{thing } x))R_t(\text{God } x)$

Thus, when a quantifier binds a time variable, the proposition to which it applies is evaluated at each value of the variable, as in the second reading of 11.3.36, where what is at issue is whether there is a past time such that *Everything is God* is true of that time.

Similar ambiguities are found in the following slightly less contrived examples:

11.3.39   a. The Pope has always been a Catholic.
            b. Many linguists have always been insane.

These sentences have readings formalizable as follows, and convertible as indicated into formulas involving P and R_t:

11.3.40   a. $(\iota x: \text{Pope } x)(\forall t: \text{Past } t)(\text{Catholic } x)$
               $\to (\iota x: R_a(\text{Pope } x))(\forall t: Pta)R_t(\text{Catholic } x)$
           a'. $(\forall t: \text{Past } t)(\iota x: \text{Pope } x)(\text{Catholic } x)$
               $\to (\forall t: Pta)(\iota x: R_t(\text{Pope } x))R_t(\text{Catholic } x)$
           b. $(\text{Many } x: \text{Linguist } x)(\forall t: \text{Past } t)(\text{Insane } x)$
               $\to (\text{Many } x: R_a(\text{Linguist } x))(\forall t: Pta)R_t(\text{Insane } x)$
           b'. $(\forall t: \text{Past } t)(\text{Many } x: \text{Linguist } x)(\text{Insane } x)$
               $\to (\forall t: Pta)(\text{Many } x: R_t(\text{Linguist } x))R_t(\text{Insane } x)$

Thus, the first interpretation of 11.3.39*a* implies that John Paul II has always been a Catholic (even before he was ordained, let alone crowned pope) but says nothing about Innocent V or Pius IX; the second interpretation implies that John Paul II, Innocent V, and Pius IX were Catholics while they were pope but implies nothing about their religion before becoming pope (e.g., it is consistent with the proposition that John Paul II was a Buddhist until he was 18). The first interpretation of 11.3.39*b* is a proposition that could be argued for by showing that Chomsky has always been insane, that Hockett has always been insane, that Karttunen has always been insane, and so on through a large number of current linguists, but the insanity of persons who were linguists in 1950 but are not linguists any longer would be irrelevant to establishing that proposition. The second interpretation of 11.3.39*b* could be argued for by showing that many of those who were linguists in 1935 were insane in 1935, that many of those who were linguists in 1945 were insane in 1945, and so on, but whether Chomsky was insane before he became a linguist would be irrelevant. It is interesting to ask whether these sentences have any additional interpretations. For example, if we were to replace the first occurrence of R_t in 11.3.40*b'* by R_a, would the resulting formula be a possible interpretation of 11.3.39*b*?

11.3.41 $(\forall t: Pta)(\text{Many } x: R_a(\text{Linguist } x))R_t(\text{Insane } x)$

This would say that at every past time, many of those who now are linguists were insane. I am inclined to say that this is not a possible interpretation of 11.3.39*b*, but my judgment is not clear here and I have not found other examples in which it is easier to say whether an interpretation like 11.3.41 is possible. It will be of considerable interest if such interpretations are systematically excluded, since that would mean that the narrower expressive possibilities of the system of logical structures with $T_p, \mathbb{D}_{p}$, and the like were sufficient to specify the meanings of English sentences, rather than the broader expressive capacity of the system with P and R_t, which allows distinctions in the subscripts on R that cannot be drawn purely in terms of the notions of 'past' and 'future' that are the basis of the system with operators such as T_p (11.3.20).

11.4. Exercises

1. Show that $\square \supset AB$ doesn't have the same truth conditions as $\square \rightarrow AB$.

2. For each of the following verbs, discuss whether it is in any sense 'world-creating', bringing in any considerations relevant to how similar to or different from the examples given in 11.2 of 'world-creating verbs' it is.

a. *ask* (as in "He asked me to open the door")
b. *say*

c. *see* (as in "I saw him open the window")
d. *seem*

3. Write a short paragraph giving some reason why *dream/imagine/* ... more easily allow items in their complements to be made heads of definite NP's with relative clause than do the other kinds of world-creating verbs, for example,

The woman I dreamed about last night had red hair.
*The witch I hope curses Sam's cow has bony fingers.

12. Many-valued and Fuzzy Logic

12.1. Values between 'True' and 'False'

While the vast bulk of the literature of logic adheres to the traditional idea that there are only two truth values, 'true' and 'false', with occasional deviations to the extent of allowing some propositions to 'have no truth value' and thus in effect have a third truth value, there also exists a sizeable though not widely known literature in which more than two truth values are assumed, and rules of inference and principles of truth value assignment are formulated and investigated for the set or sets of truth values in question. An excellent survey of this literature is given by Rescher 1969.

Before I begin a survey of some ideas and results in the area of 'many-valued logic', I should point out that the term 'truth value', while firmly established and thus hard to avoid, is misleading in one important respect, namely, that the 'values' assigned to propositions need not be TRUTH values per se but can be values for other parameters or combinations of parameters. For example, Belnap (1977) has recently been investigating a four-valued system of logic in which the four values are the four possible information states that one could be in with respect to a proposition P:

12.1.1   0 (I have not been informed that P; I have not been informed that not P)
            T (I have been informed that P; I have not been informed that not P)
            F (I have been informed that not P; I have not been informed that P)
            B (I have been informed both that P and that not P)

This system of four values is of practical importance in designing a computer question-answering system, since the information that has been provided to the computer could put it into any of these four states with respect to a given proposition; in particular, it might be given inconsistent inputs and thus be in state B with respect to certain propositions. Another example of values that, strictly speaking, are not truth values would be an assignment to each proposition of a real number (greater than or equal to 0 and less than or equal to 1) which expresses one's degree of confidence that that proposition is true. A third such example is the treatment of tense logic in which the 'value' of a proposition in a given temporal model is the set of times at which it is true in that model; the set of 'values' in this case is a partially ordered set whose maximum member is the set of all times and whose minimal member is the empty set. Many-valued logic is concerned with assignments of 'values' to propositions, without regard to whether those values are appropriately called truth values, though the 'values' will normally have some relation to inference (for example, if the 'values' are degrees of confidence in the propositions, one would be interested in developing rules of inference such that the conclusions deserve at least the degree of confidence that the premises do, or perhaps, such that each rule of inference yields conclusions whose confidence level can be only a limited amount below that of the premises). Of course, it will often not particularly matter whether one considers the 'values' to be truth values. For example, there need be no formal difference between the 'logic' with which one formalizes a 'conservative' approach in which every proposition is either true or false and one assigns a 'confidence level' to propositions about whose truth he is not completely sure, and the 'logic' with which one formalizes an 'avant garde' approach in which there are only degrees of truth, with no particularly privileged place assigned to the maximum degree of truth.

One of the best known three valued logics is that proposed by Łukasiewicz in 1920 (described in Rescher 1969:22ff.). Łukasiewicz held that future contingent propositions (such as Aristotle's celebrated example of the proposition that there will be a sea battle tomorrow) cannot properly be called either true or false (at least, not by someone speaking now) and thus deserve a different truth value, intermediate between truth and falsity. He proposed the following assignments of truth values, where 'I' denotes the 'intermediate' truth value:

12.1.2

A	~A
T	F
I	I
F	T

∧ B			
A	T	I	F
T	T	I	F
I	I	I	F
F	F	F	F

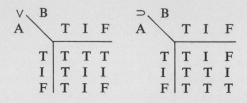

∨ \ B	T	I	F		⊃ \ B	T	I	F
A					A			
T	T	T	T		T	T	I	F
I	T	I	I		I	T	T	I
F	T	I	F		F	T	T	T

Łukasiewicz sought to fit 'I' into a system of truth value assignment which was truth-functional and which agreed as closely as possible with the classical truth tables. The rationale for his table for ∼ is obvious: the cases where A is T and where A is F agree with the classical truth table, and in the case where A is I, ∼A must also be I, since the negation of a future contingent proposition is equally future and equally contingent. The rationale for most of the entries in the tables for ∧ and ∨ is also obvious. The falsehood of one conjunct of an ∧-conjunction suffices to make the conjunction false, thus the F's in the bottom line and rightmost column; the truth of one conjunct of an ∨-conjunction suffices to make the conjunction true, thus the T's in the top line and the leftmost column of the table for ∨. If one conjunct of an ∧-conjunction is true and the other future contingent, then the whole thing is future contingent (e.g., *Goethe is buried in Weimar and the Anchorage Braves will win the 1989 World Series*); if one conjunct of an ∨-conjunction is false and the other one future contingent, then the whole thing is future contingent (e.g., *Either Goethe is buried in Zanzibar or the Anchorage Braves will win the 1989 World Series*). However, the entry in the middle of both tables is problematic. If both conjuncts are future contingent, then normally their ∧-conjunction and their ∨-conjunction will also be future contingent 12.1.3*a–b*; however, if the conjuncts are mutually contradictory, the ∧-conjunction would generally be held to be not contingent at all but out and out false (12.1.3*c*), and the ∨-conjunction true (12.1.3*d*):

12.1.3   a. There will be a sea battle tomorrow, and the Anchorage Braves will win the 1989 World Series.
           b. Either the United States will annex Israel, or Saudi Arabia will invade Burma.
           c. There will be a sea battle tomorrow and there won't be a sea battle tomorrow.
           d. Either the United States will annex Israel or it won't annex Israel.

To accept Łukasiewicz's truth tables, one must treat even ∧-conjunctions such as 12.1.3*c* and ∨-conjunctions such as 12.1.3*d* as future contingent, which conflicts blatantly with the normal understanding of the term 'contingent'. Or at least, one must if one interprets 'I' as 'future contingent'. Below we will consider other possibilities such as interpreting it as meaning 'sort of true', with the grounds for assigning 'I' as the truth value of a proposition being not future contingency but vagueness (e.g., 'Dick Cavett is tall' might be 'sort of true', whereas 'There will be a sea battle tomorrow' is either 'true' or 'false', though you don't at the moment know which, rather than 'sort of true'). Under that interpretation of 'I', Łukasiewicz's truth tables for ∧ and ∨ are much less counterintuitive. In any event, if one is to retain the interpretation of 'I' as 'future contingent', then the closest one could get to Łukasiewicz's tables for ∧ and ∨ would be tables that were non-truth-functional in the case where both conjuncts are I, that is, allow some instances of ∧ II to be I and others F, and allow some instances of ∨ II to be I and others T.

Łukasiewicz's table for ⊃ has T's in the leftmost column and the bottom row, following the classical tables, in which falsehood of A or truth of B is sufficient to make ⊃ AB true. The I's that he has in the cases of ⊃ TI and ⊃ IF are reasonable if one identifies 'future contingent' with 'could turn out either true or false, depending on future events'. If A is T and B is I, then if B turns out to be true, ⊃ AB also turns out to be true (by the classical truth table), and if B turns out to be false, ⊃ AB also turns out to be false. The case of ⊃ IF works similarly. However, by that rationale, Łukasiewicz ought to have had I rather than T for the case of ⊃ II: if A and B are both I, then either could turn out to be either true or false; if A turns out true and B false, then ⊃ AB will turn out false, but otherwise ⊃ AB will turn out true.

Łukasiewicz's reason for having T rather than I is that he wanted both for the truth tables to be truth-functional and for ⊃ AA to remain a valid formula, and the only way he could do that was to take all instances of ⊃ II to be T. In order to deal properly with that part of the rationale for the tables, I must digress into the notion of 'validity'. Łukasiewicz was operating with a notion of validity according to which a formula is valid if and only if it receives the value T under all admissible assignments of truth values (in this case, all assignments that conform to the given truth tables). This, however, is not the only way of extending the notion of validity to the many-valued case: one can allow a set of truth values to be 'designated' and take a formula to be valid if and only if it receives a designated truth value under all admissible assignments of truth values. (In the two-valued case, one need not distinguish between 'true' and 'designated': if there are only two truth values and if one but not all truth values are to be 'designated', then one truth value must be designated and the other nondesignated, and those values can be referred to as 'true' and 'false', respectively). Allowing more than one truth value to be 'designated' does not lead to quite as perverted a conception of 'validity' as one might think: as Dummett (1958:61) points out, the different designated values can be conceived of as 'different ways in which a statement may be true' and the different nondesignated values as 'different ways in which it may be false'. Thus, one could make ⊃AA be valid while having I as the value for ⊃II if one took I as well as T to be designated. However, in this case it is counterintuitive to recognize more than one value as designated, since a proposition and its negation could then simultaneously be 'true' in one of the 'ways of being true', since the negation of an I proposition is I. Thus, Łukasiewicz had in fact assumed the only plausible notion of validity for the system of three values with which he was operating.

Note that it is not possible to preserve ALL valid formulas under Łukasiewicz's approach; for example, ∨(A, ∼A) will not be valid, since its value is I whenever A is I. Thus, Łukasiewicz appears to have been more attached to some formulas of classical propositional logic than to others. His preferences among the valid formulas are quite reasonable; or at least, I could live more easily without ∨(A, ∼A) than without ⊃AA. However, to get ⊃AA to be valid, one must accept a truth table which is at odds with the interpretation of I as 'future contingent'. As before, a possible way out of the dilemma would be to allow the connective to be non-truth-functional, for example, allow ⊃II to be T in some instances and I in others.[1]

Let's try reinterpreting 'I' as 'sort of true'. In that case, some of the oddities of Łukasiewicz's tables become less odd. Note that 12.1.4 is nowhere near as outlandish as 12.1.3c:

12.1.4   Richard Burton is fat and he isn't fat.

Indeed, 12.1.4 is a perfectly normal way of expressing the idea that Burton is sort of fat (though not extremely fat). If we do not take 12.1.4 as being just a strange idiomatic expression but interpret it literally, and take 'Richard Burton is fat' as having the truth value I, 12.1.4 will also get the truth value I. The only oddity about 12.1.4 is that it is used to convey the true proposition that Burton is sort of fat, not the sort-of-true proposition that Burton is and isn't fat. Presumably that oddity has an explanation in the realm of conversational implicature, though I am not completely clear how to explain why 12.1.5 cannot be used the way 12.1.4 is to assert that Burton is sort of fat:

12.1.5   Either Richard Burton is fat or he isn't fat.

Indeed, 12.1.5 conveys an unwillingness on the speaker's part to admit any intermediate truth values.

The only entry in Łukasiewicz's tables that is pretty unreasonable if I is interpreted as 'sort of true' is the value of I for ⊃IF. That assignment of truth values implies that 'If Richard Burton is fat, then $2 + 2 = 85$' is 'sort of true'. I find that result sufficiently bizarre that for the remainder of the discussion I will replace Łukasiewicz's table by one that has F rather than I in that case:[2]

12.1.6

⊃ B A	T	I	F
T	T	I	F
I	T	T	F
F	T	T	T

Note that neither 12.1.6 nor Łukasiewicz's original table assigns exactly the same values to ⊃AB as to ∨($\sim$A, B): under either truth table, when A and B are both I, ⊃AB is T but ∨($\sim$A, B) is I. Under either truth table for ⊃, one important valid formula of classical logic will cease to be valid, namely, ⊃(⊃AB, ∨($\sim$A, B)): when A and B are both I, that formula will have the value I both according to Łukasiewicz's original truth tables and according to 12.1.6.

The reinterpretation of I as 'sort of true' can be generalized in a natural way to systems in which there is more than one 'degree of truth' between T and F. In particular, it can be generalized to allow arbitrary numbers in the interval from 0 to 1 as truth values (0 corresponds to F, 1 to T, and the numbers in between to various greater and lesser degrees of truth). A system with this range of truth values is useful in coping with inexact concepts such as 'fat', 'obnoxious', and 'uncomfortable'. Rather than having to draw arbitrary distinctions by assigning to every proposition of the form 'x is fat' either the value T or the value F, even in 'borderline' cases, one can assign the value 1 to propositions in which the inexact concept is applied to something that is in its 'core' of applicability, and smaller truth values to propositions in which the concept is only 'peripherally' applicable. For example, one might assign truth values as follows, where $|p|$ is used to indicate the truth value of p in the given assignment:

12.1.7   /Robert Morley is fat/ $= 1$
            /Quine is fat/ $= 0.8$
            /Richard Burton is fat/ $= 0.5$
            /Elizabeth Taylor is fat/ $= 0.2$
            /Chomsky is fat/ $= 0$

Note that 'the extent to which it is true that x is fat' is not the same thing as 'the extent to which x is fat' (cf. 7.3): to say that 'x is fat' has the truth value 0 is to say that x is not at all fat, not that x is at the extreme lower end of the fat/thin scale. This point is clearer in the case of 'x is tall': you can speak of one person being taller than another (i.e., of the extent to

which the one is tall exceeding the extent to which the other is tall) even
when neither is at all tall, that is, when neither is at or above 'normal
height'. Thus I spoke of 'Chomsky is fat' as having the truth value 0 rather
than some positive truth value, even though Chomsky is nowhere near the
limit of thinness.

Let us try to generalize Łukasiewicz's truth tables so as to get something
applicable to the case where the truth values are numbers on the interval
from 0 to 1. Suppose that we replace 'T', 'I', and 'F' by '1', '1/2' and
'0', respectively (which in fact is what Łukasiewicz originally called them).
Then Łukasiewicz's truth tables for $\sim$, $\wedge$, and $\vee$ can be summarized as
follows:

12.1.8 $/\sim A/ = 1 - /A/$
$/\wedge AB/ = \min(/A/, /B/)$ (i.e., the lesser of $/A/$ and $/B/$)
$/\vee AB/ = \max(/A/, /B/)$ (i.e., the greater of $/A/$ and $/B/$)

There does not seem to be any single formula that would express the truth
table 12.1.6 for $\supset$; it must be divided into two cases along the lines of[3]

12.1.9 $/\supset AB/ = 1$ if $/A/ \leq /B/$
$= /B/$ if $/A/ > /B/$

Suppose that we allow arbitrary numbers from 0 to 1 as truth values and
assign them according to the formulas 12.1.8 and 12.1.9. For example, if A
and B have the truth values given below, $\wedge AB$, $\vee AB$, and $\supset AB$ will have
the indicated truth values:

12.1.10

$/A/$	$/B/$	$/\wedge AB/$	$/\vee AB/$	$/\supset AB/$
1	0.5	0.5	1	0.5
0.3	0.5	0.3	0.5	1
0.9	0.2	0.2	0.9	0.2
0	0.3	0	0.3	1

Let us then see what formulas will be 'valid', in the sense of being assigned
the value 1 ($=$ T) under all assignments of truth values that conform to the
constraints given by 12.1.8 and 12.1.9. As we have noted above for the
special case of three-valued logic, not all of the valid formulas of classical
logic remain valid. For example:

12.1.11   Classically valid formulas that are valid with respect to 12.1.8
and 12.1.9

a. $\supset AA$
b. $\supset(A, \supset BA)$
c. $\supset(\sim \wedge AB, \vee(\sim A, \sim B))$, and the other de Morgan laws.
d. $\vee(\supset AB, \supset BA)$

12.1.12   Classically valid formulas that are not valid with respect to
           12.1.8 and 12.1.9

    a. $\vee(A, \sim A)$
    b. $\sim \wedge(A, \sim A)$
    c. $\supset(\wedge(A, \sim A), B)$
    d. $\supset(B, \vee(A, \sim A))$
    e. $\supset(\supset AB, \supset(\sim B, \sim A))$
    f. $\supset(\wedge(\vee AB, \sim B), A)$
    g. $\supset(\supset AB, \vee(\sim A, B))$
    h. $\supset(\vee(\sim A, B), \supset AB)$

For example, 12.1.11*b* can be shown to be valid as follows. The only way a
conditional formula can fail to be valid is for there to be cases where its
antecedent has a greater truth value than its consequent. Thus 12.1.11*b* is
invalid only if a case can arise in which $/A/ > /\supset BA/$. In such a case,
$/\supset BA/$ would have to be less than 1 (since $/A/$ can be at most 1), which
would mean that $/\supset BA/ = /A/$ (i.e., the only way that the truth value of a
conditional can fail to be 1 is for it to equal the truth value of the consequent). This means that $/\supset(A, \supset BA)/$ can be less than 1 only if
$/A/ > /A/$; thus $/\supset(A, \supset BA)/$ always equals 1. Demonstrations of the
other claims embodied in 12.1.11 and 12.1.12 are left as an exercise. It
is interesting to note that under the truth conditions adopted here,
$\supset AB$ and $\vee(\sim A, B)$ not only do not always have the same truth value but
indeed generally differ in truth value. In the following diagram, the
vertically cross-hatched area is the region in which the truth value of
$\supset AB$ exceeds that of $\vee(\sim A, B)$ (the former equals 1, the latter is less than
1 in that region), and the horizontal cross-hatching indicates the region
where $\supset AB$ is lower in truth value than $\vee(\sim A, B)$ (in that region,
$/\supset AB/ = /B/$ and $/B/ < 1 - /A/$):

12.1.13

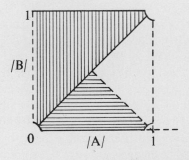

(The diagonal and the upper edge belong to the vertically cross-hatched
region, the lower edge to the horizontally cross-hatched region.)

If fewer formulas are going to be valid than in classical propositional logic, then a different system of rules of inference will have to be developed to fit the 'fuzzy logic' whose truth conditions are given by 12.1.8 and 12.1.9, since otherwise we would be in the anomalous position of having theorems that need not always be true. Before we can say anything further along these lines, however, we must reexamine the question of what it means to say that a system of rules of inference and a set of conditions on truth value assignment 'fit'. The criterion of 'fit' in the two-valued case was that, for any admissible assignment of truth values, the conclusions that can be inferred from premises that are true (in that assignment) are also true. This criterion, in conjunction with the specific rules of inference that we considered in chapter 2, imposed very heavy constraints on how truth values could be assigned to complex propositions. The constraints were so heavy largely because we had only two truth values. For example, we noted that since $\wedge$-elimination allows you to infer A from $\wedge$AB, $\wedge$AB has to be false if A is false, since if it were true you would be able to infer a false conclusion (A) from a true premise ($\wedge$AB). However, if truth values can be any number from 0 to 1 and 'true' is identified with 1, then the most that $\wedge$-exploitation would force on us is that if $|A| < 1$ (likewise, if $|B| < 1$), then $|\wedge AB| < 1$. Or at least, that is the most that it would force on us if our criterion of fit is merely that conclusions inferred from true premises must be true. Suppose we were to adopt a more stringent criterion of fit, namely, that the conclusion of an inference can't be less true than the premises, or more precisely, that the conclusion must be at least as true as at least one of the premises. In that case, $\wedge$-elimination would impose a much tighter constraint on truth value assignment, namely, that $|\wedge AB| \leq \min(|A|, |B|)$. Since you can infer A from $\wedge$AB, its truth value must be greater than or equal to that of $\wedge$AB; since you can infer B from $\wedge$AB, its truth value must also be greater than or equal to that of $\wedge$AB. Since $|A|$ and $|B|$ are both greater than or equal to $|\wedge AB|$, the lesser of them is greater than or equal to $|\wedge AB|$, that is, $|\wedge AB| \leq \min$ $(|A|, |B|)$. The rule of $\wedge$-introduction imposes the constraint that $|\wedge AB| \geq \min (|A|, |B|)$: since you can infer $\wedge$AB from the premises A and B, $\wedge$AB must have a truth value at least that of the weaker premise. Putting these two results together, we reach the conclusion that in fuzzy logic with a system of rules of inference that includes both $\wedge$-exploitation and $\wedge$-introduction, $|\wedge AB|$ must be exactly what 12.1.8 says it is: it is neither greater than nor less than $\min(|A|, |B|)$ and thus must be equal to it. Note that according to this criterion of fit, Łukasiewicz's original truth table for $\supset$ would be inconsistent with $\supset$-exploitation: by $\supset$-exploitation, from $\supset$AB and A you can infer B; but Łukasiewicz's table makes $|\supset AB| = 1$ when $|A| = 0.5$ and $|B| = 0$, thus allowing you to infer a conclusion with truth value 0 from premises, none of which has a truth value less than 0.5. Since $\supset$-exploitation is something that we could not possibly give up if our account of ⊃ is to fit a normal understanding of 'if', Łukasiewicz's table cannot be admitted unless a less stringent criterion of fit is adopted.

The truth conditions given in 12.1.8 and 12.1.9 are clearly consistent with the rules of ∧-introduction, ∧-exploitation, ∨-introduction, ⊃-exploitation, and ~-exploitation. One rule that 12.1.8 is clearly not consistent with, under this criterion of 'fit', is ~-introduction. Note that if $|A| = 0.5$ and $|B| = 1$, ~-introduction would allow one to perform the following inference, in which a conclusion with truth value 0 is deduced from premises with truth value 0.5:

12.1.14   1 A   0.5
            2 ~A   0.5

            3 │ B   supp   1

            4 │ A   1, reit
            5 │ ~A   2, reit
            6 ~B   3–5, ~-intro   0

It should be noted that ~-introduction plays a role in the most obvious proofs of all of the nonvalid formulas listed in 12.1.2. Thus, if a system of rules of inference is to be developed which will make the present version of fuzzy logic 'semantically complete' (i.e., which will insure that what is provable is exactly what is valid), it ought to differ from the rules of chapter 2 at least to the extent of having a weaker form of ~-introduction.

The remaining rules from chapter 2 (∨-exploitation and ⊃-introduction) also fit 12.1.8 and 12.1.9 in that if they are involved in a 'bad' inference, that is, an inference in which a conclusion is drawn that is less true than any of the premises, some other rules of inference must be responsible for that anomaly. For example, suppose that ∨-exploitation were to yield a conclusion that had a truth value less than that of any of the premises. Let $|A| = a$, $|B| = b$, $|C| = c$, and let d be the minimum truth value of any other premises:

12.1.15   . . .
            ∨ AB $\max(a, b)$
            │ A a

            │ . . .
            │ C c
            │ B b

            │ . . .
            │ C c
            C c

Suppose that C has a lower truth value than any of the premises, that is, $c < \min(d, /\vee AB/)$. Then one of the steps in the subproofs must lead to a conclusion with truth value less than that of all the operative premises. Since $c < \min(d, /\vee AB/) = \min(d, \max(a, b)) = \max(\min(d, a), \min(d, b))$, we have either $c < \min(d, a)$ or $c < \min(d, b)$. But that means that one of the steps either in the inference of C from A or the inference of C from B yielded a conclusion whose truth value was less than that of all the operative premises, since $\min(d, a)$ is the truth value of the weakest premise operative in the one subproof, and $\min(d, b)$ the truth value of the weakest premise operative in the other. Thus, some step other than the $\vee$-exploitation is responsible for the failure of 12.1.15 to fit the principles of truth value assignment in 12.1.8 and 12.1.9. A similar argument can be given to show that $\supset$-introduction is not responsible for any inferences in which conclusions are 'worse than' premises. Thus, a system of rules of inference that 'fits' 12.1.8 and 12.1.9 can include all of the rules of chapter 2 except for $\sim$-introduction.

12.2. Fuzzy Predicate Logic

Let us turn to the question of how logic may be extended to cover combinations of 'fuzzy predicates' with quantifiers, as in

12.2.1   a. All fat persons are jolly.
              b. Some tall persons are obnoxious.

If these are analyzed in terms of unrestricted quantifiers, we must find a way to extend the classical truth conditions for $(\forall x)fx$ and for $(\exists x)fx$ so as to make them cover the fuzzy case. The most obvious such proposal, and the one which is in fact adopted in Lakoff (1972b), is to take the truth value of $(\forall x)fx$ to be the minimum truth value that fx has (allowing x to range over the universe of discourse) and to take the truth value of $(\exists x)fx$ to be the maximum truth value that fx has:[4]

12.2.2   a. $/(\forall x)fx/ = \min_x /fx/$
              b. $/(\exists x)fx/ = \max_x /fx/$

If these are the truth values for quantified expressions, and if $\supset$ and $\wedge$ have the truth values proposed in 12.1, then in an analysis with unrestricted quantification, the truth values of 12.2.1 will be given by:[5]

12.2.3   a. $\min_x /\supset(\text{fat } x, \text{ jolly } x)/$
              b. $\max_x /\wedge(\text{tall } x, \text{ obnoxious } x)/$

The truth values that the expressions in 12.2.3 yield are often counter-intuitive. Suppose that /Kissinger is fat/ = 0.3 and /Kissinger is jolly/ = 0.2. Then /⊃(Kissinger is fat, Kissinger is Jolly)/ = 0.2, and hence 12.2.3*a* can be at most 0.2. But this is counterintuitive: Kissinger is at most a weak counterexample to the proposition that all fat persons are jolly, yet under the proposal considered here, his existence would take an enormous bite out of the truth value of that proposition. Moreover, as things are set up here, a weak counterexample like Kissinger does not reduce the truth value of that proposition any more than does a strong counterexample, such as a person (the name of Marlon Brando comes to mind) for whom /fat x/ = 0.9 and /jolly x/ = 0.2. In this case, just as in the case of Kissinger, /⊃(fat x, jolly x)/ comes out to be 0.2, and thus Brando makes no more of a dent in the truth value of *All fat persons are jolly* than does Kissinger.

The truth values given in 12.2.2*b* for the existential quantifier create a similar problem. Suppose there are three persons whose tallness and obnoxiousness are as in 12.2.4:

12.2.4	Bill	Sam	Mike
/tall x/	0.9	0.6	0.6
/obnoxious x/	0.6	0.6	0.9

The truth value of /∧(tall x, obnoxious x)/ in each of the three cases is 0.6, and thus each of the three persons should make the same contribution to the truth value of the proposition that some tall persons are obnoxious. However, the three persons in fact differ in how well they illustrate the proposition that some tall persons are obnoxious: Bill is the best example of the three, Sam the worst example, and Mike somewhere in between. Bill's tallness makes him more relevant to the proposition that some tall persons are obnoxious than either Sam and Mike, and Mike's obnoxiousness does not counterbalance his relative irrelevance to the proposition.

It thus appears that the truth values of quantified expressions ought to take account of the relevance of various members of the domain to the proposition: in the case of a universally quantified proposition, an item should reduce the truth value only to the extent that it is a real counter-example to the proposition (thus, Brando ought to reduce the truth value of 12.2.2*a* more than Kissinger does), and in the case of an existentially quantified proposition, an item should count more heavily as an instance of the proposition if it partakes more strongly of the property defining the domain of the quantifier.

One possible way of coping with these difficulties is to do fuzzy predicate

logic in terms of restricted rather than unrestricted quantification, and set
up the truth values so as to accord with some reasonable measure of
'degree of counterexamplehood' or 'degree of relevance'. As a first
approximation to a measure of counterexamplehood, I propose that an
element be a counterexample to 'all f's and g's' (i) in proportion to the
degree to which it is an f, and (ii) in proportion to the degree to which its
f-ness exceeds its g-ness. Thus, we can propose that the degree to which
a is a counterexample to $(\forall x: fx)gx$ is given by $|fa|(|fa| - |ga|)$. This
measure is reasonable [6] in that it rates as the best counterexamples those
elements for which $|fa| = |fa| - |ga| = 1$, that is, $|fa| = 1$ and $|ga| = 0$,
and those elements are in fact the best possible counterexamples (e.g.,
persons who are unqualifiedly fat but are not at all jolly). In the case
discussed above, Kissinger would be a counterexample to degree
$0.3 \times 0.1 \ (= 0.03)$ to the proposition that all fat persons are jolly, whereas
Brando would be a counterexample to degree $0.9 \times 0.7 \ (= 0.63)$. This
sounds pretty reasonable: it would mean that the existence of Kissinger
would be consistent with *All fat persons are jolly* having a truth value as
high as 0.97, whereas the existence of Brando would mean that it could
have at most the truth value 0.37.

The truth value of a universally quantified proposition could then be
given as

12.2.5 $|(\forall x: fx)gx| = 1 - \max_x(|fx|(|fx| - |gx|))$
$$= \min_x(1 - |fx|(|fx| - |gx|))$$

That is, the truth value of a universal proposition is 1 minus the maximum
extent to which anyone is a counterexample to it. Note that 12.2.5 requires
that the analysis of quantified propositions be in terms of restricted rather
than unrestricted quantification, in that the expression given in 12.2.5
cannot be resolved into the contributions of a universal quantifier and a
conditional. At least, if '$\min_x$' were to be the contribution of the universal
quantifier, the remainder could not be identified with the contribution of
$\supset$, since if $|\supset AB|$ were $1 - |A|(|A| - |B|)$, then $\supset$-exploitation could
lead to conclusions weaker than the premises:

12.2.6 $\supset AB$ $0.86 \ (= 1 - 0.7(0.7 - 0.5))$
A   0.7
B   0.5

Condition 12.2.5 has the desired property of being an extension of the
classical truth conditions: if we apply 12.2.5 to a 'classical case' (i.e., a
case in which $|fx|$ and $|gx|$ can only take on the values 0 and 1), then a

universal proposition will have the value 0 if there is a counterexample (i.e., an instance in which $|fx| = 1$ and $|gx| = 0$) and will have the value 1 otherwise, which is precisely the classical truth conditions.

Let us now turn to the existential quantifier. If we want the truth conditions for existential propositions and for universal propositions to remain connected by the de Morgan laws (e.g., if the truth value of *All fat persons are jolly* is to be the same as that of *There isn't any fat person who isn't jolly*), then the truth conditions for the existential quantifier will have to be chosen in a way that conforms to the truth conditions that we have assigned to the universal quantifier. Specifically, $\max_x |fx|(|fx| - |gx|)$ would have to be the truth value of 'Some f's are not g's', and, by replacing gx by $\sim gx$, we would get 12.2.7 as the truth value of 'Some f's are g's':

12.2.7 $|(\exists x: fx)gx| = \max_x |fx|(|fx| + |gx| - 1)$

This proposal distinguishes between Bill, Sam, and Mike in the case discussed in 12.2.4 above: for Bill, $|fx|(|fx| + |gx| - 1) = 0.9(1.5 - 1) = 0.45$, for Sam it is $0.6(1.2 - 1) = 0.18$, and for Mike it is $0.6(1.5 - 1) = 0.3$, which means that Bill makes the most contribution to the truth of the existential proposition and Sam makes the least contribution, which is in accordance with the considerations of the earlier discussion.

Condition 12.2.7 has the noteworthy feature that it allows *Some f's are g's* to have a different truth value than *Some g's are f's*. Note that in the last example, Bill would make more of a contribution to the truth value of *Some tall persons are obnoxious* (namely, 0.45) than he would to the truth value of *Some obnoxious persons are tall* (namely, 0.12); thus, in a world peopled by Bills and Sams but not by Mikes, *Some tall persons are obnoxious* would be more true than *Some obnoxious persons are tall*. On reflection, I find this difference reasonable: Bill is of much more relevance to a statement about tall persons than to a statement about obnoxious persons. Like 12.2.5, 12.2.7 includes the classical truth conditions as a special case: in the classical case, $\max_x |fx|(|fx| + |gx| - 1)$ has the value 1 when there is an individual such that $|fx| = |gx| = 1$ and has the value 0 otherwise.

Of the four rules of inference for quantifiers given in chapter 7, only two, namely, ∃-expl and ∀-intro, fit the truth conditions 12.2.5 and 12.2.7, in the sense that if they yield a conclusion that is less true than all of the operative premises, then the same will also be true of the subordinate proof, and thus the blame for the 'unsoundness' of the inference can be shifted onto some step of the subordinate proof and thus off of the application of ∃-expl or ∀-intro. The rules of ∃-intro and ∀-expl obviously do not fit the truth conditions, as is shown by picking truth values that make the conclusion have lower truth value than either premise:

12.2.8   a. Let $|fa| = 0.8$, $|ga| = 0.8$, and a be the best example of 'an
              f which is a g'.

fa	0.8
ga	0.8
$(\exists x : fx)gx$	0.48

              b. Let $|fb| = 0.4$, $|gb| = 0.2$, and b be the best example of 'an
              f which is not a g'

$(\forall x : fx)gx$	0.92
fb	0.4
gb	0.2

It is dismaying that of the four rules for quantifiers, the two that clearly do not fit the truth conditions proposed above are the two that a logician would be most willing to stake his life on. A dilemma now arises. If $\forall$-expl is to yield conclusions of truth value not less than that of any premise, then a universal proposition can have at most the value that Lakoff's proposal (see 12.2.3) would assign to it. If $|fa| > |ga|$, then for the truth conditions to fit $\forall$-expl, $|(\forall x : fx)gx|$ can be at most $|ga|$, since otherwise both premises in the inference via $\forall$-expl would have a greater truth value than the conclusion. Since in that case $|\supset(fa, ga)| = |ga|$, and since $|\supset(fa, ga)| = 1$ when $|fa| \le |ga|$, the truth value of the universal $\le |\supset(fa, ga)|$, no matter what a is, which is to say

12.2.9 $|(\forall x : fx)gx| \le \min_x |\supset(fx, gx)|$.

But then $\forall$-expl can only fit truth conditions that make a universal proposition less true than I've argued it ought to be in cases like the Kissinger case. This means that if universal propositions are to have as high a truth value as I have argued for, I will have to either give up $\forall$-expl in favor of some weaker rule of inference or accept some less stringent criterion of fit between rules of inference and principles of truth value assignment than the criterion that the conclusion must be at least as true as the weakest premise. While I find giving up $\forall$-expl by far the less attractive of these alternatives, I also feel quite uneasy about the other alternative, especially in view of the fact that it was not particularly difficult to find truth conditions for the propositional connectives which fit virtually all of the natural deduction rules of classical propositional logic, under this stringent criterion of fit.

Propositions $(\forall x : fx)gx$ in which f can take on nonclassical truth values constitute one of the few cases where I can see some point in a 'normative' attitude which would either condemn some natural language usages as logically incoherent or maintain that in all supposed instances of those usages the speaker really means something else. The difficulty with applying ∀-exploitation or ∃-introduction is that both rules hinge upon the notion of 'special case' or 'particular instance', but when f is a fuzzy predicate it is not clear what should count as 'instances' of fx for which gx. Here a striking difference between quantification and conjunction appears. Quantifiers are often thought of as 'big conjunctions' (or conjunctions are thought of as little quantifiers). However, in any conjunction, no matter how fuzzy the constituent propositions are, there is no fuzziness in what constituent propositions the conjoined proposition is made up of: any particular proposition either is one of the conjuncts or is not one of the conjuncts, and the possibility of its being 'sort of a conjunct' does not arise. By contrast, in the case of $(\forall x: fx)gx$ or of $(\exists x: fx)gx$, where fx is 'fuzzy', the proposition can be regarded as a 'big conjunction' only by admitting fuzziness in what the conjuncts are. Does *All fat persons are jolly* cover the case of Marlon Brando? Of Kissinger? Not only can an absolute answer of *yes* or *no* not be given here, but an answer of *sort of* or *somewhat* would be quite bizarre, as well as not being true. Whether a given special case a for which $|fa| < 1$ is taken in depends on what the speaker intended to be taken in. If he intends the universal proposition to be taken broadly enough to include Brando, fine. If he intends it to be taken even more broadly, so as to include Kissinger, also fine. However, it is up to him to make clear what is to be taken in, and for any particular decision on his part, the truth value of the quantified proposition will be determined by the values that $|gx|$ takes within the domain that he has taken the quantified proposition to cover. If the truth value of the quantified proposition is taken to be $\min_x |gx|$ for the universal, and $\max_x |gx|$ for the existential, we will have the truth conditions that would arise were we to replace $|fx|$ by a function that takes the values 0 and 1 in accordance with the broadness of the speaker's conception of 'special case' and then assign truth values in accordance with Lakoff's proposal. This treatment is merely a terminological variant of the normative logician's suggestion that a person who says *All fat persons are jolly* really means something else, namely, that all persons whose fatness exceeds some fixed degree are jolly. (It should be emphasized that fuzziness in gx creates no problems whatever: thus a normative logician can demand that *All fat persons are jolly* be supplied with something more precise than *fat person* as a specification of the domain of the quantifier, without his necessarily having any scruples about fuzzy predicates in general). Under this approach, the difference between Marlon Brando and Kissinger is not that they reduce the truth value of *All fat persons are jolly* by different amounts. In any case in which they both affect its truth value (i.e., in any case in which the speaker interprets *all fat persons* so broadly as to take in not only Brando but also Kissinger), they place the same upper limit on its truth value. The difference is that it takes a much less broad interpretation of *all fat persons* for Brando to have this effect than for Kissinger to have it.

This approach differs from those discussed previously with regard to cases such as that of /Kissinger is fat/ $= 0.5$ and /Kissinger is jolly/ $= 0.6$. In that case, for $x =$ Kissinger, $/\supset(fx, gx)/ = 1$ and $/fx/(/fx/ - /gx/) = -0.05$. Thus, under both of the proposals considered earlier, Kissinger would not reduce the truth value of *All fat persons are jolly* (i.e., it could still have the value 1 despite the existence of Kissinger). Under the proposal sketched in the last paragraph, either the intended domain is so narrow as to exclude Kissinger and he thus plays no role in the determination of the truth value of the universal proposition, or it would be broad enough to include him, and since he would then be a member of the domain for which $/gx/ = 0.6$, the truth value of the universal would be at most 0.6. This approach also is consistent with the approach to variables sketched in 6.3, unlike the proposal embodied in 12.2.5 and 12.2.7, where the variable bound by $\max_x$ and $\min_x$ must range over the entire universe of discourse, since for /fat x/ (/fat x/ - /jolly x/) always to have a determinate maximum, it must have a value even when x is the number 91 or Beethoven's triple concerto.

The problems discussed in this section in connection with fuzzy predicate logic also arise in fuzzy modal logic. Suppose we allow the alternativeness relation to be fuzzy, that is, allow Rww' to have truth values between 0 and 1.[7] I do not intend for the degree to which w' is an alternative to w to be a measure of its similarity to w. It might be, say, a measure of the extent to which the history leading up to w would have to be different for it to have resulted in w' rather than w being 'the present world', given that a minor change in the past (such as better aim by an assassin) can result in major differences in the present. The truth value of $\Box$A in w might be taken to be the minimum truth value of A in the worlds w' that are alternatives to w. But how much of an alternative to w does a world w' have to be for a low truth value of A in w' to force a low truth value on $\Box$A in w? Suppose, for example, that in all worlds that are unqualified alternatives to the real world, the truth value of *Chomsky is a genius* is 1, but in some world which is only weakly alternative to the real world, /Chomsky is a genius/ $= 0.2$. Should that mean that /Necessarily Chomsky is a genius/ in the real world must be 0.2 or less? If not, then we have essentially the same problem as with the status of Kissinger as a counterexample to the proposition that all fat persons are jolly, and the range of solutions to that problem will be essentially parallel to the range of solutions to the Kissinger problem.

PROOF THAT ∀-INTRO FITS THE TRUTH CONDITION 12.2.5. Suppose we have a proof whose conclusion is drawn by ∀-intro and whose conclusion is of lower truth value (according to 12.2.5) than the weakest operative premise:

12.2.10   Premises
               ————————
               ...
               | fu
               |—————————
               | ...
               | gu
               $(\forall x : fx)gx$

Let d be the truth value of the weakest of the premises, and let a be the value of x which maximizes $|fx|(|fx| - |gx|)$.[8] Let $b = |fa|$ and $c = |ga|$. Then the truth value of the conclusion is $1 - b(b - c)$, and that is by assumption less than d. Suppose that the steps of the proof other than its last step are 'sound' in the sense that no instance of that step leads to a conclusion of lower truth value than the weakest premise that is operative in that step. Then the following proof is 'sound':

12.2.11 fa b
           Premises d
           ————————
              ...
              ...
           ga c

and thus $c \geq \min(b, d)$. *Case 1*. Suppose that $c \geq b$. Then $b - c \leq 0$, and so $1 - b(b - c) \geq 1$. But $d > 1 - b(b - c)$, and thus $d > 1$, which is impossible, since d is a truth value. *Case 2*. Suppose that $c < b$. Then $c \geq d$ (since $c \geq \min(b, d)$). Since $d > 1 - b(b - c)$, we then have

12.2.12 $c > 1 - b^2 + bc$
             $c - bc > 1 - b^2$
             $c(1 - b) > (1 + b)(1 - b)$

Let us separate two subcases. *Case 2a*: Suppose $b < 1$. Then we can cancel $1 - b$ from both sides of the inequality and obtain $1 + b < c$. But $c < b$ and thus $1 + b < b$, which is impossible. *Case 2b*: Suppose $b = 1$. Then $d > 1 - b(b - c)$ becomes $d > 1 - 1 + c$, that is, $d > c$. But that contradicts our conclusion that $c \geq d$. Thus, the assumption that unsoundness comes in only in the final step of the proof leads to a contradiction, hence there must have been an unsound step somewhere earlier in 12.2.10.

PROOF THAT ∃-EXPL FITS THE TRUTH CONDITIONS 12.2.7. Suppose we have a proof whose conclusion is inferred by ∃-expl and whose conclusion is of lower truth value than any of the operative premises:

12.2.13   Premises

. . .

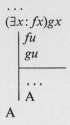

$(\exists x : fx)gx$
| fu
| gu
|
| . . .
| A
A

Let e be the element which maximizes $|fx|/(|fx| + |gx| - 1)$, and let $a = |A|$, $b = |fe|$, $c = |ge|$, and $d = $ the truth value of the weakest of the premises. Then the truth value of the existential is $b(b + c - 1)$, and if the application of ∃-expl is what is responsible for the unsoundness of the whole argument, we have $a < d \le b(b + c - 1)$. If the unsoundness of the whole proof is due only to the final step, then the following proof is sound:

12.2.14   Premises d
     fe b
     ge c
   ——————

. . .

. . .

    A a

Since b and c are both at most 1, $b(b + c - 1)$ is less than or equal to both b and c. Since we have $d \le b(b + c - 1)$, we thus have $d \le b$ and $d \le c$, and hence the weakest premise of 12.2.14 has truth value d. But since $a < d$, that means that 12.2.14 has a conclusion of lower truth value than its weakest premise and is thus unsound. Since the steps in the latter argument are merely the steps prior to the final step in 12.2.13, we have shown that any unsoundness in 12.2.13 must be attributable to some step other than its final step.

12.3. Fuzzy Sets

A predicate in fuzzy logic can be said to have as its extension a 'fuzzy set': an entity that has not only unqualified members but also members that belong to it to varying degrees between 0 and 1. The notion of 'fuzzy set'[9] can be made more precise by defining it in terms of the notion of CHARACTERISTIC FUNCTION. In ordinary (nonfuzzy) set theory, any set A can be characterized in terms of a function μ_A that specifies what its members are:

12.3.1 $\mu_A(x) = 1$ if $x \in A$
$= 0$ if $x \notin A$

Suppose we take characteristic functions rather than sets as basic. Then a fuzzy set A will be identifiable with a function μ_A whose values are real numbers in the interval from 0 to 1; for any object x in the universe, $\mu_A(x)$ will be the degree to which x is a member of A.

To describe a fuzzy set is to specify what its characteristic function is. Thus, to specify what the complement of a fuzzy set is or to specify what the union or intersection of two or more fuzzy sets is, it suffices to say how the characteristic function of the complement or union or intersection is related to the characteristic function(s) of the fuzzy set(s) from which it is derived. The following definitions are widely accepted

12.3.2   a. $\mu_{\bar{A}}(x) = 1 - \mu_A(x)$
b. $\mu_{A \cup B}(x) = \max(\mu_A(x), \mu_B(x))$
c. $\mu_{A \cap B}(x) = \min(\mu_A(x), \mu_B(x))$

These definitions are generalizations of the relationship of nonfuzzy sets to their complements, unions, and intersections; for example, if A and B are nonfuzzy sets, then $x \in A \cup B$ if and only if $x \in A$ or $x \in B$, that is, if and only if $\mu_A(x) = 1$ or $\mu_B(x) = 1$, that is, if and only if the greater of $\mu_A(x)$ and $\mu_B(x)$ is 1; and $x \notin A \cup B$ if and only if neither $x \in A$ nor $x \in B$, that is, if and only if $\mu_A(x) = \mu_B(x) = 0$, that is, if and only if the greater of $\mu_A(x)$ and $\mu_B(x)$ is 0. The notion of subset can be extended to fuzzy sets as follows:

12.3.3 $A \subseteq B$ if and only if for all x, $\mu_A(x) \leq \mu_B(x)$.

That is, A is a subset of B if and only if, to whatever extent any object is a member of A, it is to at least that extent a member of B.

Just as a relation can be identified with a set of ordered pairs, a fuzzy relation can be identified with a fuzzy set of ordered pairs; if R is a fuzzy relation, then $\mu_R(a, b)$ will be the extent to which the pair (a, b) stand in the relation R, that is, the extent to which a stands in the relation R to b. Various notions having to do with relations can be generalized so as to cover fuzzy relations. For example, the notion of 'fuzzy partial ordering' can be defined as follows:

12.3.4   A fuzzy relation R on a domain U is a fuzzy partial ordering if and only if
i. R is antisymmetric: for all $x, y \in U$, if $\mu_R(x, y) > 0$, then $\mu_R(y, x) = 0$, and
ii. R is transitive: for all $x, y, z \in U$, $\mu_R(x, z) \geq \min(\mu_R(x, y), \mu_R(y, z))$.

If U is the positive integers and R is the relation of 'much greater than' and μ_R is defined so that $\mu_R(x, y)$ is 0 if $x \leq y$ and $\mu_R(x, y)$ comes closer to 1 the more that x exceeds y, then R will be a fuzzy partial ordering.

The COMPOSITION R°S of two nonfuzzy relations R and S has the definition: $x(R°S)y$ if and only if there is a z such that xRz and zRy; for example, if R is 'is mother of' and S is 'is parent of', then R°S is 'is grandmother of'. The fuzzy version of composition will then be defined as follows:

12.3.5 $\mu_{R°S}(x, y) = \max_z(\min(\mu_R(x, z), \mu_S(z, y)))$.

The extent to which x has the relation R°S to y is the maximum extent to which x has the relation R to some individual and that individual has the relation S to y. If we compare 12.3.4ii and 12.3.5, we can easily see that R is transitive if and only if R°R $\subseteq$ R.

12.4. Degrees of Truth

Truth values between 0 and 1 have been proposed in a number of works as an appropriate device for dealing with inexact concepts. With inter-mediate truth values one is not forced to draw an arbitrary distinction between tall individuals and not-tall individuals but can recognize in-dividuals who are somewhat tall, slightly tall, and so on without being unqualifiedly tall or unqualifiedly not tall. There are still arbitrary decisions (e.g., it will be arbitrary how one distinguishes between those who are unqualifiedly tall and those who are not so tall as to be unqualifiedly tall), but the effects of these arbitrary decisions are more attenuated: they affect whether the truth value of p will be 1.0 or 0.9, not whether it will be 1 or 0.[10]

In the case of adjectives that refer to a magnitude, such as *tall* or *heavy* or even *obnoxious*, there is no direct correspondence between values of that magnitude and truth values of propositions 'x is tall', and the like. What 'x is tall' expresses depends on what x is being judged as: a tall six-year-old is shorter than most short adults, and a tall Japanese may be at the same time a short basketball player. An entity is thus not tall absolutely but only relative to a 'standard' for a class to which it belongs, and different standards may prevail for different classes to which something belongs. Each standard for tallness provides a standard for being very tall, for being somewhat tall, for being a little tall; given the relationship between x's height and the truth value of 'x is tall' relative to a given standard, one is in a position to know also the relationship between x's height and the truth value of 'x is very tall' relative to that standard.

There are a number of ways that the truth value of 'x is very tall' could conceivably be related to the given standard. One possibility is that the truth value of 'x is very tall' might be completely determined by the truth value of 'x is tall' without any direct reference to x's height, as in Zadeh's proposal (1972) that

12.4.1 $/x$ is very tall$/ = /x$ is tall$/^2$.

This particular suggestion has the desirable feature that $/x$ is very tall$/ \leq /x$ is tall$/$; that is, you can't be very tall to a greater degree than you're tall. However, it has the counterintuitive characteristic of making exactly the same individuals unqualifiedly very tall as are unqualifiedly tall and making exactly the same individuals unqualifiedly not very tall as are unqualifiedly not tall, since $1^2 = 1$ and $0^2 = 0$. Another possibility would be to make the truth value of 'x is very tall' depend both on heights and on truth values in some fashion such as the following:

12.4.2 $/x$ is very tall$/ = /x'$ is tall$/$, where height$(x') =$ height$(x) - 3''$.

This proposal avoids the last difficulty: to be unqualifiedly very tall, you would have to be at least $3''$ taller than is needed in order to be unqualifiedly tall. The arbitrarily chosen figure of $3''$ could of course be replaced by some characteristic of the height distribution, say, some fixed multiple of the standard deviation from the mean, so as to allow 12.4.2 to be generalized to adjectives referring to magnitudes other than heights. A third possibility is that the truth values for 'x is very tall' depend directly on the distribution of magnitudes and not on the truth values, as in 12.4.3a or some 'fuzzified' analogue of it such as 12.4.3b:

12.4.3   a. $/x$ is very tall$/ = 1$ if x's height exceeds the median height
                    by more than $3''$, $/x$ is very tall$/ = 0$ otherwise.

             b. $/x$ is very tall$/ = \begin{cases} 0 \text{ if } t(x) \leq 0.7 \\ 5(t(x) - 0.7) \text{ if } 0.7 < t(x) < 0.9 \\ 1 \text{ if } t(x) \geq 0.9, \end{cases}$

                    where $t(x)$ is the fraction of members of the domain that x
                    is at least as tall as (e.g., $t(x) = 1$ if x is the tallest in-
                    dividual in the domain; $t(x) = 1/2$ if x has median
                    height).

   The ideas embodied in the different proposals have different implications for what *very* can be combined with in a semantically coherent way. According to 12.4.1, *very* should be combinable with all inexact concepts, according to 12.4.3 it should be combinable with all adjectives that express magnitudes, and according to 12.4.2 it should be combinable with those adjectives that are both inexact and express magnitudes. A test case for choosing among these approaches will be inexact concepts that do not represent magnitudes. A good example of this type is notions like 'very tall' themselves: 'very tall' is an inexact concept (any sharp distinction on who is 'very tall' is arbitrary) but there is no corresponding scale of very-tall-ness. Thus the proposals in 12.4.2 and 12.4.3 (or better, 12.4.2 and 12.4.3*b*, since a 'fuzzy' version of 12.4.3 is called for here) imply that *very* should not be combinable with *very tall*, whereas the proposal in 12.4.1 implies the opposite. The fact that we can say things such as *very, very tall* or *very, very, very stupid* seems at first to support approaches like 12.4.1 and refute those like 12.4.2 and 12.4.3. But that conclusion is premature. Here *very* does not modify *very tall* or *very, very stupid* but rather combines with the other *very* to yield a complex degree expression, as can be seen from the fact that the relationship of *very tall* to *tall* is not mirrored in the relationship of *very, very tall* to *very tall*:

12.4.4   a. How tall is Fred? Véry tall.
                        Very, véry tall.
           b. *How very tall is Fred? *Véry very tall.
                        (Cf. *Extrémely very tall, *Quíte
                        very tall.)

These facts suggest that for *very* an approach like 12.4.2 or 12.4.3 stands a chance of being correct whereas one like 12.4.1 must be wrong. The same is the case for many other 'hedges', including *quite, somewhat, rather, pretty*, and *a little*. Further reason for preferring an analysis along the lines of 12.4.2 or 12.4.3 to one like 12.4.1 is provided by the fact that these hedges normally combine only with adjectives referring to magnitudes:[11]

12.4.5
$$\left\{\begin{matrix} \text{*very} \\ \text{*quite} \\ \text{*somewhat} \\ \text{*rather} \\ \text{*pretty} \\ \text{*a little} \\ \text{*a bit} \end{matrix}\right\} \left\{\begin{matrix} \text{dead} \\ \text{striped} \\ \text{two-legged} \end{matrix}\right\}$$

There are other hedges that combine with nonmagnitude adjectives:

12.4.6   more or less dead
           pretty well impossible

Combinations of *more or less* with hedged adjectives are marginally possible:

12.4.7   ?John is more or less very tall.

Combinations of *pretty well* with hedged adjectives make no sense, but that is because *pretty well* can only be combined with expressions referring to the end of a scale:

12.4.8   a. *John is pretty well very tall.
          b. John is pretty well exhausted/*tired.

In making proposals along the lines of 12.4.2 or 12.4.3 for the semantics of hedges, it is important to separate the semantic content of the sentences from what they convey by virtue of cooperativeness. The fact that '*x* is pretty tall' conveys that *x* is tall but not very tall does not imply that '*x* is pretty tall' should have a low truth value when *x* is very tall. *Wilt is pretty tall* will convey that Wilt is not extremely tall by virtue of the fact that if he were extremely tall there would be more informative alternatives to *pretty tall* that involve the same amount of linguistic effort (*very tall*) or less (*tall*). The conjecture that *pretty tall* conversationally implicates but does not logically imply that the individual is not extremely tall is confirmed by question and answer pairs such as:

12.4.9   Is Wilt pretty tall?
          Yes/*No, he's over 7 feet tall.

Thus the relation between heights and the truth value of '*x* is pretty tall' relative to a given standard should not correspond to a curve that rises and then falls, as in Zadeh's 1972 proposal (the lower branch of the barbed curve), but to one that rises and remains at its maximum point (the upper branch):

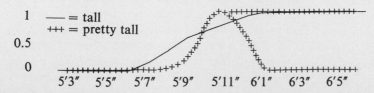

By contrast, *a little* not merely conveys but really *implies* that the truth value of the predicate is greater than 0 and less than 1 (in fact, is much less than 1). For example, if Jane weighs 400 pounds, it is not only misleading but outright false to say that she is a little fat:

12.4.10   Is Jane a little fat?
           ??Yes/?No, she weighs over 400 pounds.

Sadock (1977) gives a detailed account of what is conveyed by another important class of hedges, namely APPROXIMATIONS, and argues that most of what is conveyed is a matter of conversational implicature. Sadock notes that the correctness of a sentence involving *approximately n* depends not simply on the difference between *n* and the real value but on the amount of precision suggested by the expression by which *n* is specified and the amount of precision that the context calls for. Thus, if the population of Odessa is 979,793, example 12.4.11*a* is more 'correct' than 12.4.11*b* even though in 12.4.11*b* the number given is closer to the actual population of Odessa:

12.4.11   a. The population of Odessa is approximately one million.
b. The population of Odessa is approximately 990,000.

The use of 990,000 in 12.4.11*b* suggests that the figures are given to two significant digits, and with that standard of precision 980,000 is a closer approximation that is no more costly in linguistic effort than the figure actually mentioned, and thus cooperativity would demand that one say *approximately 980,000* in preference to *approximately 990,000*. By contrast, *one million* requires a minimum of linguistic effort and is closer to the actual population figure than is the next cheapest alternative, 900,000. Thus 12.4.11*a* is not misleading whereas 12.4.11*b* is. *Approximately 6 feet tall* is less correct when applied to a 5'8" man than when applied to a 5'8" tall fence or (to use Sadock's example) a 5'8" tall mutant cockroach, and it is less correct with reference to a 5'8" man than *approximately 8 feet tall* is with reference to a 7'8" man. Normal adult human beings have heights in a fairly narrow range, within which we normally expect estimates to be accurate within a couple of inches; but those standards of precision are dropped when one is talking about things other than human beings or about human beings of abnormal (not just unusual) height.

Sadock proposes that simple sentences containing *approximately n*, *roughly n*, and the like are true under virtually all conditions, that is, that *John is approximately 6' tall* is true as long as John's height is greater than 0, even if it is 4' or 8', and that what it conveys about John's height is determined purely by considerations of cooperativity. Some doubt is shed on that proposal by the fact that *no* can be an appropriate answer to questions about approximations:

12.4.12   Is John approximately 6 feet tall?
No/*Yes, he's four foot eight.

However, considerations of cooperativity suggest that the *yes-no* test might be inappropriate here: if a proposition is guaranteed to be true, a yes-no question ostensibly about that proposition may be reinterpreted as a question about something else (here, about the proposition conveyed by the given sentence) since otherwise the question would be pointless. I accordingly suspend judgment on Sadock's suggestion. The most viable alternative to Sadock's proposal is probably the treatment in which propositions involving approximations are assigned truth values that reflect not only the discrepancy between the actual value and the approximation but also the standards of accuracy being observed (which is to say that a sentence involving an approximation expresses different propositions depending on the assumed standards of accuracy). The proposition involving the best approximation relative to the given standards should receive the truth value 1, and those involving other approximations should receive other truth values, perhaps even 0 in all cases. I know of no knockdown argument supporting any of the three candidates for the truth values of approximation sentences with less than optimal approximations: (i) that they have the truth value 1, (ii) that they have the truth value 0, (iii) that they have truth values that are lower the more that the approximation differs from the best approximation at the given standard of accuracy. One consideration pointed out by Sadock may ultimately provide an argument against (iii), namely, the fact that words like *approximately* cannot be iterated:

12.4.13   *The population of Odessa is roughly approximately one million.

Whether it does provide such an argument will depend on whether iii, when worked out as best as it can be, will provide a scale of 'approximate one million-hood' that *roughly* could be combined with.

12.5. Dimensions of Truth

Let us suppose that *some* and *most* make the same contribution to the meanings of the sentences in 12.5.1 as they do to sentences such as *Some/ Most linguists are insane*:

12.5.1   a. In some respects, Warren Harding was a good president.
          b. In most respects, FDR was an atrocious president.

What then is the variable that the quantifiers in 12.5.1 bind? The only plausible answer that I can think of to this question is that the 'respects' over which the variable ranges are dimensions of truth (in this case, particular criteria of what a good president is). Example 12.5.1a then says that there are criteria of being a good president on which Harding was a good president, and 12.5.1b that on most criteria of being a good president, FDR was atrocious. If this conjecture is correct, then to such a sentence as 12.5.2 there should correspond not a single truth value but rather a complex of truth values, one for each of the criteria (or at least, each of the ones that come into consideration in the discourse in question) of what a good president is:

12.5.2   Warren Harding was a good president.

But wait, doesn't 12.5.2 have just a single truth value rather than some complex of truth values? Or at least, don't we treat it that way when someone utters it? I conjecture that the relation of 12.5.2 to a normal (one-dimensional) truth value is the same as that of 12.5.3 to such a truth value:

12.5.3   Scandinavians are tall.

In the type of 'generic' construction illustrated by 12.5.3, in which the bound variable corresponds to a plural indefinite noun phrase, the speaker is not asserting the corresponding universal proposition (i.e., he is not saying something that you could refute by exhibiting a Scandinavian who wasn't tall) but is rather asserting that it is 'typical' of Scandinavians to be tall. Example 12.5.2 is given a similar interpretation: not that in every respect Harding was a good president, but only that the values for Harding on the dimensions of goodness as a president are typically high. I thus conjecture that when 12.5.2 is a constituent of a larger proposition it has a complex of truth values rather than a one-dimensional truth value, but a sentence in which it appears to be used as an independent proposition is actually interpreted as a generic construction, with 'dimensions of goodness as president' as the domain over which the bound variable ranges.

Lakoff 1972b has discussed a number of words that serve to pick out particular dimensions of propositions that have multiple dimensions of truth. Consider the sentences

12.5.4   a. *Technically*, Richard Nixon is a Quaker.
          b. Esther Williams is a *regular* fish.
          c. *Strictly speaking*, the tomato is a fruit.
          d. *Loosely speaking*, whales are fish.

Someone who is a regular fish is not a fish but possesses some property popularly associated with fish, particularly that of swimming with such naturalness that one seems 'at home' in the water.[12] *Technically*, by contrast, excludes such 'connotational' dimensions of meaning in favor of precise definitional dimensions. *Technically* is thus inappropriate where no precise definition has any status:

12.5.5   a. ?Technically, this soup is icky.
          b. ?Technically, your brother is a creep.
          c. ?Technically, Kissinger is an ass.

While the examples given so far have involved combinations of *technically* with something of the form 'NP be Adj/NP', it is possible to combine it with more complex sentences:

12.5.6   a. Technically, Nixon isn't a criminal.
        b. Technically, any student using profanity can be expelled.
        c. Technically, you're related to every other human being.
        d. Technically, there are infinitely many nouns in English.

These sentences allow analyses in which *technically* imposes a 'precise definitional' interpretation on one of the predicates, though in the case of 12.5.6*b* the only apparent such analysis (that in which *technically* qualifies *can*) may be somewhat counterintuitive, and in 12.5.6*d* it is not clear whether *technically* qualifies *infinite* or *noun* or both. In fact it strongly suggests that *technically* really qualifies the whole sentence rather than some particular predicate or predicates in it; after all, there really isn't any nontechnical interpretation of *infinite* or of *noun* that 12.5.6*d* could be taken as contrasting with, given that 12.5.6*d* is used as a way of expressing that the means for forming compound nouns in English can be iterated without limit. Note, though, that the use of *technically* does not force all words in the sentence to be given a 'technical' interpretation:

12.5.7   Technically, any ass who shoots his mouth off in public can get
           pushed around by the cops.

Here clearly no 'technical' interpretation is imposed on *ass, shoot one's mouth off,* or *push around.* Perhaps *technically* merely warns the hearer that he is to give a 'precise' interpretation to all terms in the sentence that allow a precise interpretation.

    Lakoff has observed that *technically* and *strictly speaking* are far from being synonymous. For example, given that Ronald Reagan owns cattle and is able to deduct their expenses on his income tax but is not actively concerned with their breeding and feeding, 12.5.8*a* but not 12.5.8*b* would be an appropriate thing to say:

12.5.8   a. Technically, Reagan is a cattle rancher.
        b. Strictly speaking, Reagan is a cattle rancher.

By contrast, for a person who thinks that Chomsky's research on language is more philosophy than linguistics, 12.5.9*b* would be a more appropriate thing to say than 12.5.9*a*:

12.5.9   a. Technically, Chomsky is a philosopher.
        b. Strictly speaking, Chomsky is a philosopher.

Lakoff observes that while *technically* picks out 'definitional' criteria,

strictly speaking picks out 'important' criteria, and for a criterion of
X-hood to be 'important', it is neither necessary that it be 'definitional', as
is illustrated by 12.5.10, nor is it sufficient, as illustrated by the contrast
between 12.5.8*a* and 12.5.8*b*:

12.5.10   Strictly speaking, Kissinger is an ass.

Pinning down the contribution of *loosely speaking* to a sentence is
somewhat more problematic than was the case with *strictly speaking*. It is
not the case that *loosely speaking* picks out the 'unimportant' criteria,
since examples 12.5.11 do not express true propositions, notwithstanding
the fact that Esther Williams and Lou Brock possess properties (though
not definitional criteria) that are associated with fish and gazelles, respectively.

12.5.11   ? Loosely speaking, Esther Williams is a fish.
            ? Loosely speaking, Lou Brock is a gazelle.

While *regular* picks out 'connotational' criteria to the exclusion of anything else, *loosely speaking* gives 'secondary' criteria more than usual
weight relative to 'important' criteria. For something to be loosely speaking
a fish, it has to be a fish under a permissive interpretation of that term, that
is, an interpretation that makes it easier for something to qualify as a fish
than would normally be the case, though an interpretation that still leaves
fish being interpreted as a 'natural kind': a class of objects that go together
in a category for reasons that depend on their nature rather than on the
technicalities of legal systems and the like. Connotations such as those
picked out by *regular* are irrelevant to membership in a natural kind and
are thus ignored by *loosely speaking*.[13] *Loosely speaking* also lowers
'thresholds' for primary criteria. For example, while there is nothing that
could be called a 'secondary' criterion for being a rectangle, still one can
say 12.5.12:

12.5.12   Loosely speaking, this is a rectangle.

The reference here is presumably to something that counts as a rectangle if
one lowers one's standards of when lines are perpendicular (i.e., a four-
sided figure whose angles are loosely speaking right angles) or of when the
sides are coplanar or of whether the sides are straight line segments (i.e., a
four-sided figure with crooked sides could be loosely speaking a rectangle)
or of whether the sides are continuous and intersect (e.g., a four-sided
figure with a gap in one side or a missing corner could be loosely speaking a
rectangle; Gestalt psychologists have shown that figures of this type are
usually perceived *as* rectangles). Note that this discussion raises the
possibility of combining multidimensional truth values with 'fuzziness',

that is, of allowing the component truth values of a multidimensional truth value to be intermediate between truth and falsehood.

So far, I have avoided the question of how the complexes of truth values that I have been alluding to so vaguely relate to traditional questions of logic such as how the truth values of $\wedge AB$, $\vee AB$, and $\supset AB$ depend on those of A and B. There is in fact no clearly satisfying answer to the question of how propositions having complex truth values determine truth values of larger propositions of which they are constituents. We have already noted that different elementary propositions need not have the same dimensions of truth: a predicate may have no 'technical' criteria of applicability or may have no 'secondary' criteria. Also, there is no reason to expect any one-to-one match between criteria of being a good president and criteria of being a good Catholic. We could, of course, render the various propositions comparable by giving them 'vacuous' values for any missing dimensions and then set up truth conditions such as, say, that if $|A| = (a_1, a_2, \ldots, a_n)$ and $|B| = (b_1, b_2, \ldots, b_n)$, then $|\wedge AB| = (\min(a_1, b_1), \min(a_2, b_2), \ldots, \min(a_n, b_n))$; that is, you compute the truth value 'component by component'. However, I will refrain from presenting a detailed proposal of that type here, since it is not clear that the truth values of complex propositions work that way. It might very well be, for example, that each of the conjuncts of a conjoined proposition is assigned a 'one-dimensional' truth value (either by interpreting it as a generic proposition about the various dimensions of truth, or on the basis of an explicit or implicit hedge) and the truth values of the complex propositions are computed via the truth conditions proposed in 12.1.

The treatment of 'dimension hedges' sketched in this section provides an explanation of some of their combinatory restrictions. For example, 12.5.13a is deviant because *regular fish* has no connotative dimensions for another occurrence of *regular* to pick out (the connotative dimensions of *fish* are literal dimensions of *regular fish*) and 12.5.13b is deviant because combinations with *regular* are nontechnical:

12.5.13   a. *Esther Williams is a regular regular fish.
           b. *Technically, Esther Williams is a regular fish.

Certain 'degree hedges' can be taken to have an effect on various dimensions of truth; for example, regardless of what dimensions an adjective A has, *very A* and *quite A* will have no 'technical' dimension. Thus, while *strictly speaking* can be combined with such expressions, *technically* cannot:

12.5.14   a. Strictly speaking, Lyndon Johnson was very tall.
           b. *Technically, Lyndon Johnson was very tall.

Certain combinatory restrictions are grammatical in nature, for example, each of the various hedges belongs to a particular morphological category and can only appear where items of that category are permitted by the syntax of the language:

12.5.15   a. Sam is a regular pig.
            b. *Sam is regular(ly) filthy. (acceptable only with irrelevant sense)
            c. *Regular(ly) Sam is filthy.

However, there remain several combinatory restrictions that do not appear to be grammatical in nature and do not seem to follow from the rough account given above of the semantics of dimension hedges:

12.5.16   a. Sam is a regular (*stingy) bastard.
               Sam is a regular tightwad.
               (Cf. Sam really is a stingy bastard)
            b. Nixon is virtually a criminal.
               Technically/*Virtually, Gandhi was a criminal.
            c. Technically/Nominally, Asimov is a professor.
               Technically/*Nominally, Nixon isn't a crook.

The literature includes a number of works in which other uses of multidimensional truth values are proposed. Herzberger (1975a, 1975b) has proposed treating semantic presuppositions in terms of two-dimensional truth values, where the first component of a truth value evaluates the proposition on the dimension true versus false and the second component evaluates it on the dimension of satisfaction versus failure of presuppositions. Suppose that each of these components can take the value 1 or 0 and that we define symbols T, F, t, f as follows:

12.5.17 $T = (1, 1)$ $t = (1, 0)$
            $F = (0, 1)$ $f = (0, 0)$

Note that there are then two different truth values, t and f, for the case of presuppositional failure, rather than the single truth value $\#$. There are a number of ways that truth tables might be set up involving these four values. We would presumably want the first component to obey the classical truth tables (e.g., $\wedge$AB should have 1 as the first component of its value if both A and B have 1 as first component, and should have 0 as its first component if either A or B has 0 as first component). What the second component should be depends on what the relationship is between the presuppositions of complex sentences and the presuppositions of their pieces. Suppose, for the moment, that we take all the propositional connectives to be 'holes', that is, we take a complex proposition as having presuppositional failure whenever any of its constituents has presuppositional failure. We then obtain the following truth tables.

12.5.18

A	~A
T	F
F	T
t	f
f	t

∧ B / A	T	F	t	f
T	T	F	t	f
F	F	F	f	f
t	t	f	t	f
f	f	f	f	f

∨ B / A	T	F	t	f
T	T	T	t	t
F	T	F	t	f
t	t	t	t	t
f	t	f	t	f

⊃ B / A	T	F	t	f
T	T	F	t	f
F	T	T	t	t
t	t	f	t	f
f	t	t	t	t

These truth tables have certain nice properties. For example, they assign reasonable truth values to $\wedge(A, \sim A)$ and to $\vee(A, \sim A)$ in the cases where A suffers presuppositional failure: there $\wedge(A, \sim A)$ comes out f and $\vee(A, \sim A)$ comes out t. Thus, $\wedge(A, \sim A)$ will always have one of the 'false' values (F or f), and $\vee(A, \sim A)$ will always have one of the 'true' values (T or t). It is not quite so nice that $\supset AA$ will have the value t whenever A is t or f; thus, $\supset AA$, the formula which ought to be a tautology if anything is, can have a value less than T.[14] Obviously, if a tautology is to be a formula that can take only the value T, no matter how truth values are assigned to its constituents, then in the system described by 12.5.18 there are no tautologies: assigning a value of t or f to one of the constituent propositions will result in the whole formula receiving a value whose second component is 0, that is, t or f.

Lakoff (1972b) has proposed a somewhat different multidimensional treatment of presupposition, namely, one in which a truth value is a complex (a, b, c) of three nonnegative numbers such that $a + b + c = 1$, where a represents the degree to which the proposition is true, b the degree to which it is false, and c the degree to which it is 'nonsense'. Note that this proposal does not merely amount to a fuzzy analogue of Herzberger's treatment, since Herzberger allows different truth values to be assigned to propositions that have 'total' presuppositional failure, whereas for Lakoff, if $c = 1$, then $a = b = 0$ and thus there is only one truth value having 'total' presuppositional failure.

Lakoff notes that there are expressions which 'cancel out' failing presuppositions. For example, he maintains that 12.5.19*a* lacks a failing presupposition that is manifested in 12.5.19*b*:

12.5.19   a. To the extent that J. L. Austin was a linguist, he was a good
            linguist.
            b. J. L. Austin was a good linguist.

J. L. Austin was not really a linguist, but some of his research on language could be regarded as linguistics, indeed as very good linguistics. Lakoff accordingly assigns to 12.5.19*b* a truth value such as (0.3, 0, 0.7) and to 12.5.19*a* a truth value (1, 0, 0), in which the 'nonsense value' of 12.5.19*b* has been reduced to zero and the 'truth' and 'falsity' values have been multiplied by a factor that will keep the sum of the components equal to 1. A similar treatment is available in a fuzzy analogue to Herzberger's two-dimensional truth values: 12.5.19*b* would have a truth value such as (1, 0.3), and 12.5.19*a* would have a truth value in which the first component remains the same but the second component is increased (thus, (1, 1)).

The system of 'information values' (Belnap 1977) discussed at the beginning of 12.1 can also be viewed as two-dimensional values. Taking the first component to indicate whether you have been told that the proposition is true and the second component to indicate whether you have been told that it is false (and using square brackets, to avoid confusion with the two-dimensional truth values discussed so far), we can represent the four 'information values' as

12.5.20   B = [1, 1] (= you have been told that A and have been told
            that ~A)
            T = [1, 0] (= you have been told that A but not that ~A)
            F = [0, 1] (= you have been told that ~A but not that A)
            0 = [0, 0] (= you have been told neither that A nor that ~A)

Belnap's system is, like the 'relevant entailment logic' that he and Anderson have developed (see 10.4 and Anderson and Belnap 1975), an attempt to set logic up in such a way that the effects of contradictions are localized: instead of a contradiction causing all hell to break loose (i.e., forcing all propositions to be assigned the value T), it should only cause some hell to break loose. Belnap's treatment, which is framed in terms of a computer system for storage and retrieval of (not necessarily consistent) information, allows a proposition to have the value B without all propositions having to receive that value. Consider, for example, two atomic propositions p and q, where you have been told both that p is true and that it is false and have been told that q is false but not that it is true. The conflicting information that you have been given about p has no bearing on the information you have been given about q: p has the value B and q the value F in this case.

Moreover, $\wedge pq$ should be assigned the value F: your information about q is sufficient to make $\wedge pq$ F regardless of which of your contradictory pieces of information about p you believe.

Belnap's information values are non-truth-functional with a vengeance. They are sensitive to the order in which pieces of information are acquired, and to whether two pieces of information come in together or separately. For example, suppose that an information-gathering system is in state F with regard to p and state T with regard to q, and that the information that p is true and $\sim q$ is true come in together. Prior to this input, the system was in state F with regard to $\wedge pq$: we had information that p was false and no information to the contrary, and that was enough to make $\wedge pq$ false. The new information puts us into state B with regard to both p and q. That might seem to put us into state B with regard to $\wedge pq$: our information that p is false and our information that q is false are each sufficient to make $\wedge pq$ false, but our information that p is true and that q is true would make it true. However, the old information had p false and q true, making $\wedge pq$ false, and the new information has p true and q false, again making $\wedge pq$ false, and there is no reason to allow the combination of 'p true' from the new information and 'q true' from the old information to come into the picture. Thus, we can take $\wedge pq$ to be F in this case, though in other circumstances in which p is B and q is B, $\wedge pq$ will be B.

In addition, there are cases in which none of the four values provides an adequate statement of the state that you are in with regard to information about the proposition in question. Consider, for example, the case where you have been told both that p is true and that it is false but have been given no information about q. What then is the information value of $\wedge pq$? Since the information that p is false suffices to make $\wedge pq$ false even in the absence of information about q and since the information that p is true does not suffice to give any conclusion about the truth value of $\wedge pq$ unless one has the information that q is true, one might conclude that our information about $\wedge pq$ is F: we have been given information implying that it is false, but we have not been given information implying that it is true. Yet our information that p is true, combined with our lack of information about q, is consistent with $\wedge pq$ being true and indeed puts us halfway to the information that $\wedge pq$ is true; thus we are not in the same position with regard to $\wedge pq$ as if we had only been told that p is false (and had no information about q), in which case our information would be unequivocally that $\wedge pq$ is false. Ought we to distinguish between these two situations by admitting extra values? We might, for example, allow the components to range over not two but three values, say, 1 (= we have been told the proposition is true), 1/2 (we have information relevant to it, but not enough to tell whether it is true or false), and 0 (we have no information relevant to it). Or ought we just to be happy calling the information value F in both cases? Or perhaps say that the value is 0 when p is B and q 0, on the grounds that we do not have enough of an asymmetry in our information about $\wedge pq$ to justify giving it a value in which the two components differ? I will not attempt to choose among these alternatives here.

12.6. Exercises

1. Assume the truth conditions given in 12.1.8–9. What range of truth values would have to be 'designated' for $\vee(A, \sim A)$ to be valid? Would that choice of 'designated' truth values have any undesirable consequences for what counts as valid?

2. Assume the truth conditions given in 12.1. State informally how the truth value of each of the following expressions is related to the truth values of its constituents:

  a. $\supset(A, \sim A)$
  b. $\supset(\wedge(A, \sim A), B)$
  c. $\wedge(\vee(A, \sim B), \vee(B, \sim A))$

3. If /x is very tall/ is /x is tall/^{2} (and similarly for all expressions of the form *very* + Adjective), how can the notion of conversational implicature be used to show why *very pregnant* or *very prime* is a strange thing to say?

4. Suppose we take the following as our set of truth values:

1 = true today and true tomorrow
2 = true today and false tomorrow
3 = false today and true tomorrow
4 = false today and false tomorrow

Give truth tables for $\wedge$, $\vee$, $\supset$, and $\sim$ in terms of these four values, assuming that 'true' and 'false' in the descriptions given above of the four values are to conform to the classical tables.

13. Intensional Logic and Montague Grammar

13.1. The λ-Calculus

In this section we introduce a notational device that allows one to construct functions galore. Let A be an expression of any type (say, a sentence) and x a variable of any type (say, an individual variable) that occurs in A. Then (λx)A denotes a function that maps objects of the type over which x ranges into objects of the type of A and is defined as follows: for any object a that can be a value of x, $[(\lambda x)$A$](a) =$ the result of substituting a for all occurrences of x in A. For example,[1] $[(\lambda x)(x$ is bald)](Aristotle) = (Aristotle is bald). The λ-notation provides an easy way of expressing PROPERTIES. Thus, one could represent the property of having a spouse who is older than one as $(\lambda x)((\exists y) \wedge ($spouse$(y, x)$, older$(y, x)))$.

The variable that is bound by the λ need not be an individual variable. For example, one could express the property of being a property of John as $[(\lambda P)P(John)]$. This expression is a function that maps properties into propositions. The property that it is applied to can perfectly well be expressed by a λ-expression itself. Thus, one might express by 13.1.1 the proposition that 'having a spouse older than oneself' is a property of John:

13.1.1 $[(\lambda P)P(John)](\lambda x)(\exists y) \wedge ($spouse$(y, x)$, older$(y, x)))$.

The two λ's can be eliminated by first replacing P by the expression of which the first λ-expression is predicated, yielding 13.1.2a, and then replacing x by the expression of which the other λ-expression is predicated, yielding 13.1.2b:

13.1.2   a. $(\lambda x)((\exists y) \wedge ($spouse$(y, x)$, older$(y, x)))$(John)
            b. $((\exists y) \wedge ($spouse$(y$, John), older$(y$, John)))

Note that the elimination of λP must precede the elimination of λx, since until λP has been eliminated, nothing appears as argument of the λx

395

expression. The process of eliminating λ's by substituting the argument for the bound variable is called λ-CONVERSION.

By use of λ's, one can reinterpret many-place functions as functions of a smaller number of variables. For example, let f be a two-place propositional function of individual variables. The expression $(\lambda y)[(\lambda x)f(x, y)]$ then denotes a one-place function whose values are one-place propositional functions; for example, if f expresses the predicate *loves*, then the values of $(\lambda y)[(\lambda x)f(x, y)]$ are the various propositional functions obtained by substituting constants for y in $(\lambda x)f(x, y)$, such as the propositional function 'loves John' and the propositional function 'loves Evel Knievel'.

There are thus two roughly equivalent ways that one can express a two-place property by means of λ's: the property of being the father of the mother of can be expressed either as a predicate of ordered pairs, as in 13.1.3*a*, or as a one-place predicate whose values are one-place predicates, as in 13.1.3*b*:

13.1.3   a. $(\lambda(x, y))[(\exists z) \wedge (\text{father } x\, z, \text{mother } z\, y)]$
           b. $(\lambda y)(\lambda x)[(\exists z) \wedge (\text{father } x\, z, \text{mother } z\, y)]$

An extremely interesting application of the λ-notation is found in recent work by Sag (1976), who uses representations involving λ's as a central part of an explanation of a number of previously problematic exceptions to the rule of VP-deletion. VP-deletion is the transformation that deletes one of two identical VP's (subject to the usual constraints on the relationship of anaphoric devices to their antecedents, for example, the antecedent VP must precede or command the deleted VP), as in[2]

13.1.4   a. John didn't win a prize, but Mike did $\varnothing$ ($<$ win a prize).
           b. If Macy's lowers the price on platinum backscratchers, Gimbel's will $\varnothing$ ($<$ lower the price on platinum back-scratchers).
           c. Peter is easy to talk to, and Betsy is $\varnothing$ ($<$ easy to talk to) too.

Sag notes that in a number of cases, the deletion does not go through even though all relevant conditions appear to be met:

13.1.5   a. *Peter is easy to talk to, and Betsy is easy to $\varnothing$ ($<$ talk to) also.
           b. The steak is ready to eat, and the chicken is
$$\left\{\begin{array}{l} \varnothing \ (< \text{ready to eat}) \\ \text{*ready to } \varnothing \ (< \text{eat}) \end{array}\right\} \text{also.}$$

He notes that one cannot just rule out deletion of a VP that is contained in a larger potentially deletable VP (as *talk to* is contained in *easy to talk to* in

13.1.5*a*), since deletion of the smaller VP under identity is permissible in such examples as

13.1.6   a. Peter is ready to give up, and Betsy is
$$\begin{cases} \varnothing \ (< \text{ready to give up}) \\ \text{ready to } \varnothing \ (< \text{give up}) \end{cases} \text{also.}$$
         b. Sam wants to write a novel, and Larry
$$\begin{cases} \text{does } \varnothing \ (< \text{want to write a novel}) \\ \text{wants to } \varnothing \ (< \text{write a novel}) \end{cases} \text{also.}$$

Sag also notes that in many cases VP-deletion in an ambiguous clause is possible only on certain readings of that clause:

13.1.7   a. Sam claimed he was taller than he was, and Bill claimed he was taller than he was too.

       a'. Sam claimed he was taller than he was, and Bill claimed he was too.

       b. Alan said Betsy had hit him, and Peter also said Betsy had hit him.

       b'. Alan said Betsy had hit him, and Peter also said she had.

Each of the conjoined caluses in 13.1.7*a* is ambiguous between an interpretation that attributes a contradiction to Sam or Bill (i.e., the contradictory claim that his height exceeds itself) and an interpretation that attributes a falsehood but not a contradiction to him (i.e., the claim that his height exceeded *h*, where *h* is his actual height).[3] However, 13.1.7*a'* allows only the interpretation in which a contradiction is attributed to both Sam and Bill. Note, though, that if *claim he was taller than he was* is deleted rather than *taller than he was*, the ambiguity reappears: 13.1.8 can be interpreted either as attributing to each person an overestimate of his height or as attributing a contradiction to him:

13.1.8   Sam claimed he was taller than he was, and Bill did too.

Likewise, if the first *him* in 13.1.7*b* refers to Alan, the second *him* can refer to either Alan or Peter; however, in 13.1.7*b'*, the deleted VP can only be interpreted as referring to Betsy hitting Alan, not to her hitting Peter.[4] Again, if deletion of the higher VP is performed, the ambiguity reappears: 13.1.9 allows both the STRICT IDENTITY interpretation, in which Peter said that Betsy hit Alan, and the SLOPPY IDENTITY[5] interpretation, in which Peter said that Betsy hit Peter:

13.1.9   Alan said that Betsy had hit him, and Peter did also.

Sag proposed an explanation of these facts in terms of logical structures in which, as in Montague grammar, a VP is taken as corresponding to a constituent of semantic structure consisting of a λ-expression, for example, the VP *love Betsy* in *Peter loves Betsy* would be represented as $(\lambda x)(x$ love Betsy). This apparently trivial notational proposal shows remarkable descriptive possibilities when it is applied to sentences involving complex VP's. Consider the unreduced counterpart 13.1.10*a* of 13.1.4*c* and 13.1.5*a*, and the logical structure that would correspond to it according to Sag:

13.1.10   a. Peter is easy to talk to, and Betsy is easy to talk to also.

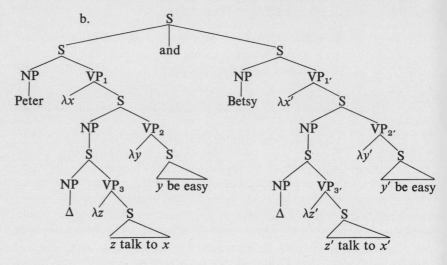

Sag proposes that the reason why $VP_{1'}$ can be deleted under identity with VP_1 but $VP_{3'}$ cannot be deleted under identity with VP_3 is that VP_1 and $VP_{1'}$ express the same property: they differ only to the extent that variables bound by operators WITHIN VP_1 and $VP_{1'}$ are labeled differently; but VP_3 and $VP_{3'}$ do not, strictly speaking, express properties (one forms properties by the use of the λ operator, and the λ's that bind z and z' are not within VP_3 and $VP_{3'}$, respectively), nor are they identical constituents of some larger property (i.e., there is no basis for identifying z with z').

The notion described informally in the last sentence can be made more precise by introducing the notion of ALPHABETIC VARIANT: a coherent formula α is an alphabetic variant of a coherent formula β if α differs from β at most in that there are variable-binding operators in α that correspond to occurrences of the same operator (but with a different variable) in β. Sag's proposal is then that VP-deletion is possible only if the logical structures of the two VP's are alphabetic variants of each other. To get this proposal to work, it is necessary that all variables be given distinct names, as in 13.1.3*b*, even though the coherency conditions would not be violated if, for example, *x* and *x'* were given the same name; let us assume henceforth that different variables will be given different names. What makes VP$_3$ and VP$_{3'}$ fail to be alphabetic variants is that VP$_3$ contains a variable *x* bound by an operator that is not within that VP, and VP$_{3'}$ contains in the corresponding position a variable bound by another operator (another operator-occurrence, that is—the fact that both operators are λ's doesn't make VP$_3$ and VP$_{3'}$ alphabetic variants).[6]

Note that the definition of alphabetic variance allows two VP's to be alphabetic variants if both are in the scope of some operator and both contain occurrences of the variable that that operator binds. Example 13.1.11 illustrates that VP-deletion is applicable in that situation:

13.1.11   Betsy greeted everyone when Sandy did.

One interpretation of 13.1.11 presents no problems: the one that refers to two acts of greeting everyone (say, by saying 'Hello, everybody'), one performed by Betsy and one by Sandy. We are interested here in the other reading of 13.1.11, which says that, for every person, Betsy greeted him when Sandy did (e.g., when George entered, Betsy and Sandy both said 'Hello, George', when Ellen entered, Betsy and Sandy both said 'Hello, Ellen', and so forth). The latter reading of 13.1.11 could be expressed by a formula along these lines:

13.1.12 $(\forall x)$([Betsy, $(\lambda y)(y$ greet $x)$] when [Sandy, $(\lambda w)(w$ greet $x)$]).

Note that here the two VP's are alphabetic variants: $(\lambda y)(y$ greet $x)$ contains two variables, one bound and one unbound (at least, not bound by anything within the VP's under consideration); $(\lambda w)(w$ greet $x)$ likewise contains two variables, one bound and one unbound, and the bound one differs only alphabetically from the corresponding variable in the first VP, while the unbound one is identical to the unbound one in the first VP.

The difference between 13.1.5*a* and 13.1.6*a* is that 13.1.5*a* demands a logical structure like 13.1.10*b*, in which the VP whose deletability is at issue contains a variable bound by the λ of a higher VP, whereas such is not the case with 13.1.6*a*:

13.1.13   a. Peter is easy to talk to.
                  (Peter, $(\lambda x)[(\Delta, (\lambda z)(z$ talk to $x))$, $(\lambda y)(y$ be easy)])
              b. Peter is ready to give up.
                  (Peter, $(\lambda x)[x$ ready for $(x, (\lambda z)(z$ give up))])

The explanation of why 13.1.7b' lacks the ambiguity that both 13.1.7b and 13.1.9 have is that the logical structures for the two readings, according to Sag, will be:[7]

13.1.14   a. 'Strict identity' reading:
            $(\text{Alan}_i, (\lambda x)(x \text{ said } [\text{Betsy}_j, (\lambda y)(y \text{ hit him}_i)]))$ and
            $(\text{Peter}, (\lambda w)(w \text{ said } [\text{she}_j, (\lambda z)(z \text{ hit him}_i)]))$
            b. 'Sloppy identity' reading:
            $(\text{Alan}_i, (\lambda x)(x \text{ said } [\text{Betsy}_j, (\lambda y)(y \text{ hit } x)]))$ and
            $(\text{Peter}, (\lambda w)(w \text{ said } [\text{she}_j, (\lambda z)(z \text{ hit } w)]))$

In 13.1.14a, $(\lambda y)(y \text{ hit him}_i)$ and $(\lambda z)(z \text{ hit him}_i)$ are alphabetic variants—each contains only one variable (here *him*$_i$ is a constant, not a variable)—and are identical aside from the naming of that variable. Thus, when the logical structure is 13.1.14a, $(\lambda z)(z \text{ hit him}_i)$ can be deleted under identity with the corresponding VP of the first conjunct, and 13.1.7b' is derived. However, in 13.1.14b, $(\lambda y)(y \text{ hit } x)$ and $(\lambda z)(z \text{ hit } w)$ are not alphabetic variants: the x in the former is an unbound variable and is not identical to the w that appears in the corresponding position of the latter. Thus, VP-deletion cannot delete $(\lambda w)(w \text{ hit } z)$, which means that 13.1.7b' can only be derived with the 'strict identity' interpretation, which is exactly the factual observation that we set out to explain. By contrast, $(\lambda x)(x \text{ said } [\text{Betsy}_j, (\lambda y)(y \text{ hit } x)])$ and $(\lambda w)(w \text{ said } [\text{she}_j, (\lambda z)(z \text{ hit } w)])$ are alphabetic variants, and thus in the derivation of 13.1.9 the sloppy identity reading may serve as the logical structure. The explanation of the difference in interpretation between 13.1.7a' and 13.1.8 is along the same lines.

Sag's proposal provides a solution to the problem raised in 4.7: why can conjunction reduction apply to 13.1.15a to yield 13.1.15a' when it cannot apply to 13.1.15b to yield 13.1.15b'?

13.1.15   a. Tom admires few authors, and Dick admires few authors.
            a'. Both Tom and Dick admire few authors.

            b. Few rules are correct and few rules are easy to read.
            b'. Few rules are both correct and easy to read.

Suppose that the identity condition for conjunction reduction is the same as that for VP-deletion: two constituents count as identical for conjunction reduction only if they correspond to parts of logical structure that are alphabetic variants of each other. Then conjunction reduction can apply in 13.1.15a because the underlined VP's in 13.1.16 are alphabetic variants:

13.1.16 $(\text{Tom}, \underline{(\lambda x)(\text{few author } y)(x \text{ admire } y)})$ and
            $(\text{Dick}, \underline{(\lambda z)(\text{few author } w)(z \text{ admire } w)})$

We will be able to explain its inapplicability in 13.1.15*b* if we can show that the constituents that must be identified (the two occurrences of *Few rules*) are not alphabetic variants. It is not completely clear how the definition given above of alphabetic variant should apply to a pair of constituents such as (few rule x) and (few rule u) in 13.1.17:

13.1.17   (few rule x)(x, (λy)(y be correct)) and
            (few rule u)(u, (λv)([Δ, (λz)(z read v)], (λw)(w be easy))

However, it appears that we should not take them to be alphabetic variants, since the essential idea in 'alphabetic variant' appears to be: two expressions are alphabetic variants if we could rename their bound variables (otherwise leaving things unchanged) and make them identical without changing meaning. Note that one could not change the variables in (few rule x) and (few rule u) and preserve the meaning unless one made further changes in the formula. On this understanding of 'alphabetic variant', then, conjunction reduction cannot identify the two occurrences of *few rules* in 13.1.15*b*. More generally, two occurrences of a quantified NP will not count as identical, though (as in 13.1.15*a* and *a'*), two expressions containing a quantified NP may count as identical. I note that this conception of identity is appropriate only for some syntactic rules; for example, the rule of RIGHT NODE RAISING must be allowed to identify the two occurrences of *all operas* in 13.1.18*a* so as to yield 13.1.18*b*, even though they are not alphabetic variants according to what has just been said:

13.1.18   a. Schwartz loves all operas, and Morgenstern hates all operas.
            b. Schwartz loves, and Morgenstern hates, all operas.

13.2. Intensional Logic

The notion of INTENSION that figures in much modern work in logic is, in a sense, a compromise between the traditional notions of meaning and reference. The notion is framed in set-theoretic terms rather than in terms of 'concepts'; however, it is set up in such a way as to distinguish between many expressions that have the same reference, such as *the morning star* and *the evening star*, or *the first pope* and *Saint Peter*. The intension of an expression is a function giving the reference of that expression in any world; that is, the intension of an expression is a function that associates to each world the EXTENSION of that expression in that world.[8] Thus, expressions differ in intension if and only if it is POSSIBLE for them to differ in extension, whether or not they actually do.

The truth value of a proposition is taken to serve as the extension of the proposition. The intension of a proposition is thus a function that associates to each world a truth value: the truth value that the proposition has in that world. For any two sets A and B, it is customary to write A^B to stand for the set of all functions having B as domain and having values in A. (The reason for the notation A^B is that if A has m elements and B has n elements, the number of functions that belong to A^B is m^n; for example, there are $2^3 = 8$ different functions that have the domain $\{a, b, c\}$ and have the values in the set $\{0, 1\}$). Thus, the intension of a proposition is a member of the set V^I, where I is the set of worlds under consideration and V is the set of truth values, here assumed to be $\{T, F\}$. The intension of an individual constant symbol is a function that associates to each world the individual that that constant refers to in that world. Suppose that we use U to indicate the set of all individuals that figure in any of the worlds. Then the intension of an individual constant symbol is a member of U^I, since, for any world i, the extension of the constant symbol in i is a member of U.

The extension of a one-place predicate in a given world can be taken to be the set of individuals of which it is true in that world. Alternatively, it can be taken to be the CHARACTERISTIC FUNCTION of that set: the function associating to each element a truth value indicating whether that element belongs to the set. It is customary in intensional logic to take the latter interpretation, and we will do so here. Accordingly, for any world i, the extension of the predicate in i is a member of V^{A_i}, where A_i is the domain of i: the set of individuals that figure in determining what universal or existential propositions are true in i. The intension of a one-place predicate is thus a function that maps each i onto a member of V^{A_i}. Since A_i will generally vary from one world to the next, and since the functions in V^{A_i} will generally not belong to V^U (U will generally contain elements that are not in A_i, and a function belonging to V^{A_i} will thus not be defined on all elements of U), we cannot say that the intension of a one-place predicate belongs to $(V^U)^I$, nor to any other such expression that we can construct. Suppose, however, that to simplify our discussion we assume that the same individuals figure in each world. Then, calling that set of individuals U, we can say that the intension of a one-place predicate belongs to $(V^U)^I$.

I have been assuming so far that what a predicate is predicated of is an individual. In various works, Montague argued that predicates are predicated of the kind of thing that we have taken to be the intension of an individual constant. For Montague, thus, the extension of a one-place predicate is a member not of V^U but of $V^{(U^I)}$, and the intension of a one-place predicate belongs to $(V^{(U^I)})^I$.

The extension of a two-place predicate will be a function that associates a truth value to each PAIR of elements of U, or (if one accepts Montague's conclusions) each pair of elements of U^I. Using the notation $A \times B$ to stand for the set of all ordered pairs of elements, the first from A and the second from B,[9] we can say that the extension of a two-place predicate will belong to $V^{U \times U}$ (or to $V^{U^I \times U^I}$, if one accepts Montague's conclusions; let us for the moment ignore this alternative and take predicates to be predicated of elements of U). Consequently, the intension of a two-place predicate will belong to $(V^{U \times U})^I$: the intension of a two-place predicate is a function that associates to each world the function that specifies which pairs of elements the predicate is true of in that world.

A two-place predicate can also be thought of as a one-place predicate whose values are one-place predicates, for example, the two-place predicate 'love(x, y)' can be reinterpreted as $(\lambda y)[(\lambda x)\text{love}(x, y)]$, which associates with any individual a the propositional function 'x loves a'. Under the reinterpretation, the extension of a two-place predicate is a member of $(V^U)^U$, and the intension of a two-place predicate is a member of $((V^U)^U)^I$.

The notion of intension can also be applied to 'higher-order' expressions, in which variables range over predicates or over sets. If F(P) stands for 'P is true of Henry Kissinger', then the extension of F will be a function that associates a truth value to the extension of each one-place predicate. Suppose we take a permissive view of what can be an extension of a one-place predicate and allow it to be any member of V^U. It should be noted that this will allow not only functions that might be the extensions of normal predicates such as 'has long hair' or 'knows the *Philosophical Investigations* by heart', but also such bizarre functions as the one that associates Richard Nixon, the number 94, and Mozart's C Minor Mass with the value T and everything else with the value F. Then the extension of F will belong to $V^{(V^U)}$, and the intension of F will be a member of $(V^{(V^U)})^I$. It is customary in intensional logic to apply the term 'property' not to the extension of a predicate but to its intension; that is, a 'property' of individuals denotes a member of $(V^U)^I$: a function that associates to each world the extension of a predicate. Under this terminology, an object a has a property P if and only if the extension of P is true of a.

In work by or inspired by Montague, it is essential to distinguish expressions according to their semantic TYPES. There are two "atomic" types: t ('truth value') and e ('entity'). To any two types, a and b, there corresponds a type $\langle a, b \rangle$, and to any type a there corresponds a type $\langle s, a \rangle$, s standing here for 'world'.[10] For any given type, one can speak of the 'meaningful expressions' of that type and of the 'possible denotations' of meaningful expressions of that type. The meaningful expressions of type t have truth values as their possible denotations, and those of type e have entities as their possible denotations. The meaningful expressions of type $\langle a, b \rangle$ have as possible denotations functions whose argument ranges over possible denotations of type a and whose values are possible denotations of type b; for example, an expression of type $\langle e, t \rangle$ denotes a function that associates a truth value to each entity. A meaningful expression of type $\langle s, a \rangle$ denotes a function that associates to each world a possible denotation of type a; for example, an expression of type $\langle s, \langle e, t \rangle \rangle$ denotes a function that associates to each world a function from entities to truth values. A variable ranging over objects of a given type is also a meaningful expression of that type; for example, a variable ranging over individuals is a meaningful expression of type e. In the Montague tradition, variables of type $\langle a, b \rangle$ or $\langle s, a \rangle$ have generally been taken to range over ALL objects of the given type. This means that variables of types other than e generally have far more possible values than an outsider would be likely to expect them to have, for example, a variable of type $\langle s, e \rangle$ has as values not only 'ordinary' objects of that type (such as the function that associates to each world the person who is pope in that world) but also bizarre functions such as one that associated a prime number to w_1, an archbishop to w_2, a Mozart string quintet to w_3, and an attack of diarrhea to w_4.

We can thus restate some of the conclusions of the earlier paragraphs. An individual constant or variable is of type e. The intension of such an expression is of type $\langle s, e \rangle$. Montague's position on intransitive verbs is that their arguments are of type $\langle s, e \rangle$ (i.e., they are predicated of 'objects in intension' rather than of objects pure and simple); thus, for Montague, the translation of an intransitive verb into intensional logic must be an expression of type $\langle \langle s, e \rangle, t \rangle$. Or at least, the denotation in any world of an intransitive verb is of type $\langle \langle s, e \rangle, t \rangle$; if intransitive verbs are taken to denote functions associating denotations of that type to each world, as they are by Montague, intransitive verbs are of type $\langle s, \langle \langle s, e \rangle, t \rangle \rangle$.

If u is a variable of type a and φ is an expression of type b, then $(\lambda u)\varphi$ will be of type $\langle a, b \rangle$: it can be combined with things of type a (i.e., of things that can be substitued for u), and the result of substituting anything of the appropriate type for u will still denote something of type b. 'Being true of Kissinger' can be expressed by $(\lambda P)P(k)$, for an appropriately chosen constant k. Taking k to be of type $\langle s, e \rangle$ (i.e., a function giving a denotation of *Kissinger* in every possible world), P is then of type $\langle \langle s, e \rangle, t \rangle$, $P(k)$ is of type t, and thus $(\lambda P)P(k)$ is of type $\langle \langle \langle s, e \rangle, t \rangle, t \rangle$.

In the next section, we will consider a number of analyses in which it is held that the extension of a complex expression depends on the intension of one or more of its constituents. In discussing such cases, it will be convenient to be able to use an expression whose extension in every world is the intension of the given constituent. In addition, it will often be convenient, when an expression of intensional logic denotes an intension, and thus is of some type $\langle s, a \rangle$, to have a way of referring to the entity of type a that that intension associates to a given world. Thus, we wish to introduce operators ^{in} and ^{ex} such that, for example, ^{in}(the pope) will be a function mapping worlds onto individuals, with $[^{in}$(the pope)](i) = the individual that is the pope in i, for each world i; and if f is the intension of *dog* (i.e., if f associates to each world i a function $f(i)$ such that for any individual u, $f(i)(u)$ = T if and only if u is a dog in i), then ^{ex}f must be a function mapping individuals onto truth values, such that for any individual u and any world i, $(^{ex}f)(u)$ = T in i if and only if $f(i)(u)$ = T, that is, if and only if u is a dog in i.[11]

The last sentence makes it hard to tell the difference between ^{ex}f and f. To clarify the difference, and to put the informal definitions of the last paragraph on a somewhat firmer footing, we must get slightly more precise about the systems that we are discussing. By a SYSTEM OF INTENSIONAL LOGIC, let us understand a formal language which includes (i) the operators, quantifiers, and variables of predicate logic (not necessarily first-order predicate logic—we will allow for variables that range over predicates, and for quantifiers that bind such variables), (ii) well-formed λ-expressions, as outlined in 13.1, and (iii) further modal and intensional operators (such as □, ^{in}, and ^{ex}) as needed. By an INTERPRETATION of a system of intensional logic, we will mean something consisting of (i) a set I of possible worlds, (ii) a set of U of possible individuals, and (iii) an assignment of a denotation in each world of I to each individual constant or predicate constant of the system. For any interpretation Q and any world i, it is possible to determine the denotation in i, relative to the interpretation Q, of any expression X of the system of intensional logic. Using $X^{Q,i}$ to stand for the denotation of X in i relative to Q, we see from iii what $X^{Q,i}$ is in case X is either an individual constant or a predicate constant. In case X is a more complex complex expression, $X^{Q,i}$ can be determined from the denotations of the constituents of X by means of various rules. For example, if X is a conjoined proposition $\wedge X_1 X_2 \ldots X_n$, then $X^{Q,i}$ = T if $X_1^{Q,i} = X_2^{Q,i} = \ldots = X_n^{Q,i}$ = T, and $X^{Q,i}$ = F otherwise (i.e., if one or other of $X_1^{Q,i}, \ldots, X_n^{Q,i}$ is F). I will not go through the details of the rules for determining $X^{Q,i}$ from the denotations of the constituents of X for all the other possibilities of what X might be; any one who wishes to see the details spelled out should consult Montague 1973:§2. I will confine myself to giving the rules for the case where X is of the form ^{in}Y or ^{ex}Y.

Let Y be any expression of the system of intensional logic. We have to determine $(^{in}Y)^{Q,i}$ for every i. This can be done as follows:

13.2.1 $(^{in}Y)^{Q,i}$ is the function mapping worlds onto things of the type of Y, such that for every world j, $(^{in}Y)^{Q,i}(j) = Y^{Q,j}$

Note that i does not appear on the right-hand side of this equation. Thus, $(^{in}Y)^{Q,i}$ is the same no matter what i is. This is as it should be: the reason for having such expressions as $^{\text{in}}Y$ is to allow one to refer in one fell swoop to what goes on in all worlds, independently of what world one is operating in at the moment. The denotation of $^{\text{ex}}Y$ in any world with respect to any interpretation can be determined as follows. Let Y be of type $\langle s, a \rangle$ for some a. (If Y is not of such type a, then $^{\text{ex}}Y$ will make no sense.) Then,

13.2.2 $(^{\text{ex}}Y)^{Q,i} = Y^{Q,i}(i)$

It is fairly easy to show that for any expression X, $^{\text{ex}}(^{\text{in}}X) = X$. For any interpretation Q, any world i, and any expression X, $(^{\text{ex}}(^{\text{in}}X))^{Q,i} = (^{\text{in}}X)^{Q,i}(i) = X^{Q,i}$. Thus, $^{\text{ex}}(^{\text{in}}X)$ and X have the same denotations in any world, relative to any interpretation, that is, $^{\text{ex}}(^{\text{in}}X) = X$. It is not true in general that $^{\text{in}}(^{\text{ex}}X) = X$. First of all, unless X is of type $\langle s, a \rangle$ for some a, $^{\text{ex}}X$ makes no sense and thus the equality fails. However, even if X is of a type that allows one to form $^{\text{in}}(^{\text{ex}}X)$, that expression denotes what X does only under a very stringent condition, namely, that X is of the form $^{\text{in}}Y$. A simple example will illustrate how $^{\text{in}}(^{\text{ex}}X)$ can fail to be identical with X. Consider a rudimentary system of intensional logic in which there is a constant c of type $\langle s, e \rangle$ and two worlds 1 and 2 (it won't matter what happens in any other worlds, so we can act as if these were the only worlds). Suppose that a and b are two distinct objects and that in 1 c denotes the function mapping 1 onto a and 2 onto b, but in 2 c denotes the function mapping 1 onto b and 2 onto a. Then $^{\text{ex}}c$ denotes a both in 1 and in 2, which means that $^{\text{in ex}}c$ (in either world) will designate the function mapping both 1 and 2 onto a. But since c does not designate that function in either world, $^{\text{in ex}}c \neq c$.

It is easy to show that $^{\text{in ex}}X = X$ if and only if $X = {}^{\text{in}}Y$ for some Y. That X's being of the form $^{\text{in}}Y$ is a nesessary condition for $^{\text{in ex}}X$ to equal X is trivial: if $X = {}^{\text{in ex}}X$, then X is the intension of $^{\text{ex}}X$. To show that it is a sufficient condition, let $X = {}^{\text{in}}Y$ and let us see what $^{\text{in ex}}X$ is. Let i and j be any two worlds and Q any interpretation. Then $(^{\text{in}}(^{\text{ex}}X))^{Q,i}(j) = (^{\text{ex}}X)^{Q,j} = X^{Q,j}(j) = (^{\text{in}}Y)^{Q,j}(j) = (^{\text{in}}Y)^{Q,i}(j)$ (since an intension has the same denotation in every world), and that equals $X^{Q,i}(j)$. Thus $(^{\text{in}}(^{\text{ex}}X))^{Q,i}$ and $X^{Q,i}$ denote the same mapping of worlds into objects, and since this is the case for any interpretation Q and any world i, we have $^{\text{in}}(^{\text{ex}}X) = X$.

13.3. Montague's Approach to Syntax and Semantics

An important tradition of logical and linguistic research has developed out of work by Richard Montague.[12] Montague's approach is characterized by the following features: (i) the goal of research on a given language is to provide truth conditions for all the sentences of that language, that is, to provide the conditions under which each sentence is true in any given possible world relative to any given choice of denotations for INDEXICAL elements such as *here*, *you*, and *this*; (ii) this goal is accomplished by providing a SYNTAX and a SEMANTICS for the language; (iii) the syntax is formulated in terms of a system of CATEGORIES, a LEXICON listing the BASIC members (if any) of each category, and a system of SYNTACTIC RULES, which specify how derived members of a given category can be constructed from members (basic or derived) of various categories; (iv) the semantics for the language is formulated not directly in terms of the sentences of the language but in terms of the ANALYSES that the syntax provides for each sentence; (v) the semantics consists of an intensional logic, which provides means of determining the intension of any expression of the intensional logic, and TRANSLATION RULES, which associate an expression of intensional logic to each expression that appears in a syntactic analysis; (vi) the translation rules construct the translation of any derived expression out of the translations of the constituents from which it is derived; and (vii) the preferred syntactic analyses are in terms of categories that correspond to surface phrase structure types of the given language.

For example, in terms of the rules given in Montague (1973), Montague would assign to the sentence *Every man loves a woman* the following syntactic analysis (as well as a couple of other possible analyses):

13.5.1   Every man loves some woman [S; 3, 0]

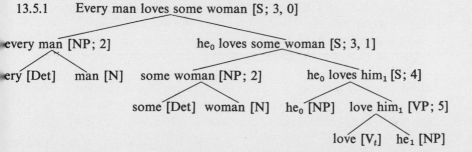

The material given in square brackets at the end of each constituent indicates the syntactic category of the constituent and (in the case of 'derived' expressions) the rule of Montague's syntax which derives it from the expressions that it directly dominates in the tree. The category names that appear in 13.3.1 are not Montague's: for clarity's sake, I have substitued more familiar category names that correspond fairly closely to Montague's categories.

Some of Montague's syntactic rules amount to phrase structure rules. For example, his rule 5 amounts to the statement that a VP may be formed by putting a V_t before a NP, and thus it has the content of the phrase structure rule VP: V_t NP. However, some of his syntactic rules correspond to transformations or to combinations of a transformation and a phrase structure rule. For example, his rule 4 says not merely that a S may be formed by putting a NP before a VP but also that the V of the VP must be put into the appropriate person and number: thus, it is a composite of the phrase structure rule S: NP VP and an agreement transformation. Likewise with his rule 3, which forms a S by replacing an occurrence of he_i or him_i in a given S by a given NP.[13] Its effect is thus a composite of the phrase structure rule S: NP S and the transformation of Quantifier-lowering (discussed in chapter 4), which applies to a S of the form [[Quantifier S] S] and inserts the Quantifier + S constituent in place of an occurrence of a variable in the remaining S; for example, it converts (every: man x)(mortal x) into (mortal (every: man x)).

Let us now sketch the parts of Montague's semantics that figure in his treatment of 13.3.1. He_0 and he_1 correspond to individual variables. For Montague, a basic member of the category V_t, such as *love*, corresponds to a two-place predicate[14]—a function love'(x, y) that in any world associates a truth value to each pair of individuals (x, y). For the sake of making the predicate-argument structure completely clear, I will in fact take the translation of *love* into intensional logic to be not that two-place propositional function but the related function $(\lambda y)(\lambda x)$love'(x, y), which in any world associates with each individual a one-place propositional function. The translation of a VP that is formed from a V_t and a variable can be taken from combining the translations of the two constituents. The V_t in 13.3.1 is translated as $(\lambda y)(\lambda x)$love'(x, y) and the NP that is combined with is translated as the variable x_1, and thus the VP is translated as $[(\lambda y(\lambda x)$love'$(x, y)](x_1)$, which is convertible into (λx)love'(x, x_1), The translation of the S formed by rule 4 is constructed similarly: the translation of the VP, here (λx)love'(x, x_1) is applied to the translation of the NP, here x_0, and the result, (λx)love'$(x, x_1)(x_0)$, is converted into love'(x_0, x_1).

This may seem like a round-about way of arriving at love'(x_0, x_1)—you could have obtained that just by plugging x_0 and x_1 directly into love'(x, y), without bringing in all those λ's. However, the use of λ's in deriving love'(x, y) is dictated by condition vii: in English there is a surface phrase consisting of a verb and its object(s), and Montague's approach allows one to treat such phrases as making direct semantic contributions themselves, rather than being purely syntactic constituents that have no direct role in semantics.

As we continue with the translation of 13.3.1 into intensional logic, we encounter a much less trivial use of this ploy. A quantified NP, such as *every man*, must make its own semantic contribution to the sentence, and that contribution must be something that can be combined with the translation of the expression that the quantified NP is combined with. Here Montague's solution is to take the quantified NP to represent a propositional function not of individuals but of propositional functions; that is, *every man* is translated as the propositional function $f(P)$ which is true when P is a property that every man has and false when P is a property that not every man has. Specifically, he takes the translation of *every man* to be[15] $(\lambda P)(\forall x) \supset (man'(x), Px)$. The propositional function which that expression is combined with is the propositional function obtained by prefixing (λx_i) to the S that the quantified NP is combined with, where x_i is the bound variable (thus, here x_0). Similarly, the translation of *some woman* is $(\lambda P)(\exists x) \wedge (woman'(x), Px)$. Thus, the translation of *he$_0$ loves some woman* is 13.3.2a, which is convertible to 13.3.2b and then to 13.3.2c:

13.3.2   a. $[(\lambda P)(\exists x) \wedge (woman'(x), Px)][(\lambda x_1)love'(x_0, x_1)]$
            b. $(\exists x) \wedge (woman'(x), (\lambda x_1)love'(x_0, x_1)(x))$
            c. $(\exists x) \wedge (woman'(x), love'(x_0, x))$

The translation of *Every man loves some woman* will then be 13.3.3a, which is convertible to 13.3.3b, and then to 13.3.3c:

13.3.3   a. $[(\lambda P)(\forall y) \supset (man'(y), Py)][(\lambda x_0)(\exists x) \wedge (woman'(x),$
               $love'(x_0, x))]$
            b. $(\forall y) \supset (man'(y), [(\lambda x_0)(\exists x) \wedge (woman'(x), love'(x_0, x)](y))$
            c. $(\forall y) \supset (man'(y), (\exists x) \wedge (woman'(x), love'(y, x)))$

Let us now start to correct a number of oversimplifications that were made in the above illustrative sketch. The categories that figure in Montague grammar are not those of linguistic syntax but derive from the CATEGORIAL GRAMMAR of Ajdukiewicz (1935). Ajdukiewicz recognized two basic categories, called *s* and *n* (standing for 'sentence' and 'noun' or 'name'). From the two basic categories, an infinite number of derived categories can be constructed: if X and Y are any two categories, then X/Y is the category of expressions that combine with expressions of category Y to yield expressions of category X.[16] Thus, for Ajdukiewicz, *s/s* was the category of things that combine with sentences to yield sentences (thus, 'sentence adverbs' such as *necessarily* and *supposedly*), *s/n* was the category of things that combined with names to yield sentences (thus, intransitive verbs, or more generally, VP's of any internal structure), and *(s/n)/(s/n)* was the category of things that combined with VP's to yield VP's, thus VP-adverbs such as *quickly* or *with an axe*.

Montague also recognized two basic categories, though not exactly the same two that Ajdukiewicz did. Montague's category *t* (standing for 'truth value'—Montague named his categories after the types of their denotations) does in fact amount to Ajdukiewicz's category s. However, his other category, e (standing for 'entity'), differed from Ajdukiewicz's category n in that no expressions, whether basic or derived, belong to it: in Montague's syntax, e figures only as a constituent of more complex category names, and it owes its existence to the role that it plays in the translation of syntactic analyses into formulas of intensional logic. For Montague, an intransitive verb (or, more generally, a VP of any internal structure) is of category t/e, that is, it is of the category of things that combine semantically with entities to yield truth values. The things that VP's combine with SYNTACTIC-ALLY, however, that is, NP's, are not of category e but of category $t/(t/e)$. This choice of category for NP's is due in part to Montague's desire to have proper names and quantified NP's be of the same category (which would be impossible if proper names were of the category e).

In a number of instances, Montague set up two or more distinct categories that both combine with items of some category B to yield results of some category A. For example, he treated both intransitive verbs and common nouns as combining with an entity to yield a truth value. However, these categories must still be distinguished, since they are not interchangeable in all syntactic rules; for example, the rule for forming quantified NP's allows a quantifier to be combined with a common noun but not with an intransitive verb. Montague arbitrarily distinguished such categories by the number of slashes; for example, he represented intransitive verbs as t/e and common nouns as $t//e$.

One must distinguish between syntactic categories such as t/e and types in intensional logic such as $\langle e, t \rangle$. The only relation between categories and types is that the category of a given expression determines the type of its translation into intensional logic. Specifically, Montague maintained that syntactic category and logical type are related by a function f defined as follows:

13.3.4	Syntactic category a	Corresponding semantic type $f(a)$
	t	t
	e	e
	a_1/a_2	$\langle\langle s, f(a_2)\rangle, f(a_1)\rangle$

Thus the expressions of any syntactic category a/b denote functions whose arguments are intensions of the type of object that expressions of category b denote and whose values are objects of the type that expressions of category a denote. For example, t/e corresponds to the semantic type $\langle\langle s, e\rangle, t\rangle$, that is, VP's denote functions from intensions of entities to truth values. In the correspondence 13.3.4, multiple slashes are ignored; that is, $t//e$ corresponds to the same semantic type as does t/e.

Montague took predicates to be predicated of intensions because it is impossible to do semantics that is both completely extensional and completely 'compositional', in the sense that the translation of an item depends only on the extensions of its immediate constituents. For example, since the extension (= truth value) of *John believes that the world is round* depends on the content and not just the truth value of *the world is round* (e.g., he may believe that true proposition without believing many other true propositions), the extension of *John believes that the world is round* is not predictable from the extensions of *John, believe,* and *the world is round.* As a matter of fact, it is not clear that it can be predicated from the intensions of those constituents either. Thus, one might argue that two propositions can have the same intension and yet not make the same contribution to the intensions of propositions of which they are constituents, since any two self-contradictory propositions have the same intension (they are false in all possible worlds) and yet a person can believe one self-contradictory proposition without believing another one. There is an alternative to intensions and extensions as the items of which predicates are predicated in a translation scheme such as Montague's, namely, expressions of a formal language themselves. There is likewise the alternative (considered in Cresswell 1973 and Hintikka 1976) of generalizing the notion of 'world' so as to admit 'impossible worlds' and thus allow the possibility that two propositions are true in the same POSSIBLE worlds without being true in the same worlds. However, rather than exploring these possibilities here, I will confine myself to the specific framework within which Montague was operating, in which the intension of a proposition is a function specifying what possible worlds it is true in, and items with the same intensions are assumed to make the same contribution to the intensions of items of which they are constituents.

Montague generalized his treatment of sentential objects to a policy about VP's involving ANY kind of object. Thus, for Montague, the translation of *John loves Mary* involves not simply an individual constant m but rather a constant function ${}^{in}m$ (i.e., if m denotes the same individual c in every world, then ${}^{in}m$ will be the function f such that $f(i) = c$ for every world i). It might be conjectured that Montague did this in order to allow for proper names that have unusual referential properties, for example, proper names that do not have denotations in all worlds, as in 13.3.5a and a', or that have different denotations in different worlds, as in 13.3.5b, which involves a name that has been assigned to different dogs, as each holder of the name has retired or died and been replaced by a new one:

13.3.5   a. John worships Zeus.
           a'. John worships Zoroaster.
           b. John petted Lassie.

For example, one might want to say that 13.3.5a could be true and 13.3.5a' false in a given world in which neither *Zeus* nor *Zoroaster* denotes anything and treat *worship* as denoting a relation between persons and intensional objects, with *Zeus* and *Zoroaster* having different intensions (say, there is an alternative world in which Zeus exists but Zoroaster does not). Montague in fact did not give any account of such proper names. The partial grammars that figure in Montague 1970a, 1970b, and 1973 involve only proper names that are RIGID DESIGNATORS (i.e., they denote the same entity in every world)[17] and contain meaning postulates to the effect that those names are rigid designators; yet he did not exclude the possibility that other proper names might not be rigid designators. For the moment, let us not take a position on how best to analyze examples like 13.3.5 within Montague's framework, a question that I would like to postpone until I have discussed verbs such as *seek*, which it will be important to contrast with *worship*.

Montague generalized his treatment of sentential objects into an even more general policy than requiring that every object NP contribute an intension to the translation of the VP. Indeed, he adopted an exactly analogous policy for all combinations of something of category A/B (or A//B, etc.) with something of category B. Using Tr(X) to stand for the translation of X into intensional logic, Montague's policy can be summarized in the schema:

13.3.6   If β is of category B, γ is of category A/B (or A//B, etc.), and α is an expression of category A constructed from β and γ by some syntactic rule, then $\mathrm{Tr}(\alpha) = \mathrm{Tr}(\gamma)(^{\mathrm{in}}\mathrm{Tr}(\beta))$

For example, if $\alpha = Probably\ John\ is\ sick$, $\beta = John\ is\ sick$, and $\gamma = probably$, then $\mathrm{Tr}(\alpha) = \mathrm{probably}'(^{\mathrm{in}}\mathrm{Tr}(John\ is\ sick))$; probably' is a function which in any world maps intensions of sentences onto truth values, and the translation of *Probably John is sick* is the image under that function of the intension of the translation of *John is sick*. There is of course more to Montague's translation scheme than 13.3.6, since an expression need not be put together out of items of categories A and A/B; for example, a sentence (member of category t) may be constructed not only out of items of categories t/e and $t/(t/e)$ (by rule 4) but also out of items of categories $t/(t/e)$ and t, that is, out of a NP and a S, by rule 3. Thus there are additional translation rules to cover cases not included in 13.3.6.

The scheme 13.3.6 has a peculiar consequence which plays a central role in Montague's treatment of NP's. Recall that NP's are of the category $t/(t/e)$. Taking A $= t$ and B $= t/e$, we can derive from 13.3.6 that if α is a S consisting of a NP γ and a VP β, say, $\gamma = John$ and $\beta = sleep$, then

13.3.7 $\mathrm{Tr}(John\ sleeps) = \mathrm{John}'(^{\mathrm{in}}\mathrm{Tr}(sleep))$

Note that John′ is here the function and $^{in}\text{Tr}(sleep)$ its argument, rather than vice versa. The only way to make this coherent is to take John′ to be a function that maps one-place predicates into truth values. The way that Montague accomplished that was to take John′ to denote not an individual but the property of being a property of that individual; the translation of *John sleeps* would then amount to: sleeping is one of John's properties.

As a first try at formalizing this proposal, we might write

13.3.8   John′ $= (\lambda P)P(j)$

where j is an appropriately chosen individual constant. Equation 13.3.8 conflicts with two of Montague's policies. First, Montague wanted the variable P to be of the same type as the translations of ordinary intransitive verbs such as *walk*. However, in accordance with 13.3.6, such verbs must be translated as one-place predicates whose arguments are of type $\langle s, e \rangle$ rather than e; that is, they are predicated not of ordinary entities but of 'intensional entities'. We can remedy this first conflict by replacing j with ^{in}j in 13.3.8; ^{in}j is a function from worlds to individuals, and if *John* is an ordinary proper name, we can take ^{in}j to be a constant function: it has the same value in all possible worlds. Second, Montague wanted P to range over 'properties in intension': the values of P are not to be of type $\langle e, t \rangle$, that is, functions associating a truth value to each individual, but rather of type $\langle s, \langle e, t \rangle \rangle$, that is, functions associating to each world a function of the latter type. This second discrepancy can be corrected by replacing P by its extension. Thus, we arrive at 13.3.9a, which allows the translation of *John sleeps* to proceed as in 13.3.9b:[18]

13.3.9   a. John $\Rightarrow (\lambda P)([^{ex}P](^{in}j))$
            b. John sleeps $\Rightarrow (\lambda P)([^{ex}P](^{in}j))(^{in}(\lambda x)(\text{sleep}'(x)))$
               $\rightarrow$ $^{ex\,in}(\lambda x)(\text{sleep}'(x))(^{in}j)$
               $\rightarrow$ $^{ex\,in}(\text{sleep}'(^{in}j))$
               $\rightarrow \text{sleep}'(^{in}j)$

Montague took not only proper names but all NP's to have translations of this type: $\langle \langle s, \langle e, t \rangle \rangle, t \rangle$. This is the case even when the NP corresponds to a variable. Thus, for Montague, the translation of 13.3.10a is not 13.3.10b but 13.3.10c, though 13.3.10b is obtainable by λ-conversion, as indicated:

13.3.10   a. he$_0$walks.
            b. $\text{walk}'(x_0)$
            c. $[(\lambda P)(^{ex}P)(x_0)](^{in}(\lambda x)\text{walk}'(x))$
               $\rightarrow (^{ex\,in}((\lambda x)\text{walk}'(x))(x_0)$
               $\rightarrow (\lambda x)\text{walk}'(x)(x_0)$
               $\rightarrow \text{walk}'(x_0)$

Since for Montague, transitive verbs are of the category $(t/e)/(t/(t/e))$, that is, they combine with NP's to yield VP's, and since Montague followed the policy given in 13.3.6, the translations of transitive verbs into intensional logic must have type $\langle\langle s, a\rangle, b\rangle$, where a is the type of the translation of NP's and b is the type of the translation of VP's. Since $a = \langle\langle s, \langle\langle s, e\rangle, t\rangle\rangle, t\rangle$, and $b = \langle\langle s, e\rangle, t\rangle$, transitive verbs have translations of the type $\langle\langle s, \langle\langle s, \langle\langle s, e\rangle, t\rangle\rangle, t\rangle\rangle, \langle\langle s, e\rangle, t\rangle\rangle$. This means that the translation of a transitive verb will not be an expression of the form $(\lambda y)(\lambda x)f(x, y)$ involving a function f whose arguments are both of the same type (here, $\langle s, e\rangle$): rather, it will be of the form $(\lambda\mathscr{P})(\lambda x)g(x, \mathscr{P})$, involving a function whose first argument is of the type $\langle s, e\rangle$ but whose second argument is of a 'higher' type, namely, $\langle s, \langle s, \langle\langle s, e\rangle, t\rangle\rangle, t\rangle\rangle$.

The translation of *John kicked Bill* thus can proceed as follows:

13.3.11   kick $\Rightarrow (\lambda\mathscr{P})(\lambda x)\text{kick}'(x, \mathscr{P})$
Bill $\Rightarrow (\lambda P)[^{\text{ex}}P](^{\text{in}}b)$
kick Bill $\Rightarrow (\lambda\mathscr{P})(\lambda x)\text{kick}'(x, \mathscr{P})[^{\text{in}}(\lambda P)[^{\text{ex}}P](^{\text{in}}b)]$
$\qquad \rightarrow (\lambda x)\text{kick}'(x, {}^{\text{in}}(\lambda P)[^{\text{ex}}P](^{\text{in}}b))$
John $\Rightarrow (\lambda Q)[^{\text{ex}}Q](^{\text{in}}j)$
John kicked Bill $\Rightarrow (\lambda Q)[^{\text{ex}}Q](^{\text{in}}j) \; {}^{\text{in}}(\lambda x)\text{kick}'(x, {}^{\text{in}}(\lambda P)[^{\text{ex}}P](^{\text{in}}b))$
$\qquad\qquad \rightarrow {}^{\text{ex}\,\text{in}}(\lambda x)\text{kick}'(x, {}^{\text{in}}(\lambda P)[^{\text{ex}}P](^{\text{in}}b))(^{\text{in}}j)$
$\qquad\qquad \rightarrow \text{kick}'(^{\text{in}}j, {}^{\text{in}}(\lambda P)[^{\text{ex}}P](^{\text{in}}b))$

The final line of 13.3.11 is disconcerting. Can't we arrive at something that is closer to the usual formalization of *John kicked Bill* as something on the order of kick(j, b)? We in fact can, but only by invoking a meaning postulate that Montague provides for verbs (such as *kick*) whose objects are 'extensional', that is, verbs such that the truth value of 'a V-ed b' in any given world depends on only the extension of b in that world, not on b's intension (its extension in other worlds).

To lead up to the meaning postulate, let us first note that there is a natural correspondence between things of the type we would like for the second argument of the predicate and a subset of the set of functions over which the second argument of kick$'$ ranges. To see this, note that for any object m of type a, there is a closely related function of type $\langle\langle a, b\rangle, b\rangle$, namely, $(\lambda F)F(m)$, where F is a variable of type $\langle a, b\rangle$. This function maps any function F into the value of that function at m. Thus, if we take P to be a variable of type $\langle s, \langle\langle s, e\rangle, t\rangle\rangle$ (i.e., a function that associates to each world a one-place predicate of 'intensional entities') and m to be of type $\langle s, e\rangle$, then $(\lambda P)(^{\text{ex}}P)(m)$ will be a function of type $\langle\langle s, \langle s, e\rangle, t\rangle\rangle, t\rangle$. Let us denote that function by m^*:

13.3.12 $m^* = (\lambda P)(^{\text{ex}}P)(m)$

Note that the second argument of kick′ is of the same type as $^{\text{in}}(m^*)$. Accordingly, we can derive from kick′ a function kick″ whose arguments are both of type $\langle s, e \rangle$:

13.3.13 $\text{kick}''(x, y) = \text{kick}'(x, {}^{\text{in}}(y^*))$.

Definition 13.3.13 allows us to construct kick″ from kick′ but not to go in the reverse direction: the behavior of a function $f(x, \mathscr{P})$ need not be predictable from its behavior for those values of $\mathscr{P}$ that are of the special form $^{\text{in}}(y^*)$. Montague provided a meaning postulate to the effect that kick′ is predictable from kick″. Specifically, the postulate given by Montague says that when a predicate is the translation of an 'extensional' verb such as *kick* or *find*, the function that is in its second argument position may be 'exported' from that position and the predicate replaced by a predicate taking extensions as its arguments:[19]

13.3.14   For each δ in the list *kick, find, kiss,* ... (NB: the list does not include *seek* or *imagine*), there is a function S_δ such that
$$(\forall x)(\forall \mathscr{P}) \square\, [\delta'(x, \mathscr{P}) \leftrightarrow {}^{\text{ex}}\mathscr{P}(^{\text{in}}(\lambda y)^{\text{ex}}S_\delta(^{\text{ex}}x, {}^{\text{ex}}y))]$$

On the basis of 13.3.14, one can easily establish the following correspondence between δ′ and δ″ for each verb δ in the above list:

13.3.15   For δ = *kick, find, kiss,* ... (but not *seek, imagine,*...),
$$(\forall x)(\forall \mathscr{P}) \square\, (\delta'(x, \mathscr{P}) \leftrightarrow {}^{\text{ex}}\mathscr{P}(^{\text{in}}(\lambda y)\delta''(x, y)))$$

To prove 13.3.15, consider first what 13.3.14 says about the special case where $\mathscr{P}$ is $^{\text{in}}(m^*)$. In any world and for any m and n of type $\langle s, e \rangle$, by 13.3.14 we will have

13.3.16 $\delta'(n, {}^{\text{in}}(m^*)) \leftrightarrow {}^{\text{ex in}}(m^*)(^{\text{in}}(\lambda y)^{\text{ex}}S_\delta(^{\text{ex}}n, {}^{\text{ex}}y))$

Using 13.3.12, the right-hand side of 13.3.16 can be converted into

13.3.17 $(^{\text{ex in}}(\lambda y)^{\text{ex}}S_\delta(^{\text{ex}}n, {}^{\text{ex}}y))(m)$
$\rightarrow {}^{\text{ex}}S_\delta(^{\text{ex}}n, {}^{\text{ex}}m)$.

But the left-hand side of 13.3.16 is $\delta''(n, m)$; thus, in any world and for any n and m, $\delta''(n, m)$ has the same truth value as $^{\text{ex}}S_\delta(^{\text{ex}}n, {}^{\text{ex}}m)$. Substituting $\delta''(x, y)$ for $^{\text{ex}}S_\delta(^{\text{ex}}x, {}^{\text{ex}}y)$ in 13.3.14, we obtain 13.3.15.

We are now in a position to continue the translation of *John kicked Bill* (13.3.11.) as follows:

13.3.18 $\text{kick}'(^{\text{in}}j, {}^{\text{in}}(\lambda P)[^{\text{ex}}P](^{\text{in}}b))$
$\rightarrow {}^{\text{ex in}}(\lambda P)[^{\text{ex}}P](^{\text{in}}b)[^{\text{in}}(\lambda y)\text{kick}''(^{\text{in}}j, y)]$
$\rightarrow {}^{\text{ex in}}(\lambda y)\text{kick}''(^{\text{in}}j, y)(^{\text{in}}b)$
$\rightarrow \text{kick}''(^{\text{in}}j, {}^{\text{in}}b)$

We thus end up with the formula that we might have expected as the translation of *John kicked Bill*, given that argument positions are to be filled by intensions, though we are only able to arrive at it by employing a meaning postulate that expresses the 'extensionality' of the object of *kick*.

The translation of *John kicked Bill* given in 13.3.11 and 13.3.18 corresponds to the analysis tree 13.3.19a; the sentence of course allows other analyses, such as 13.3.19b and 13.3.19c:

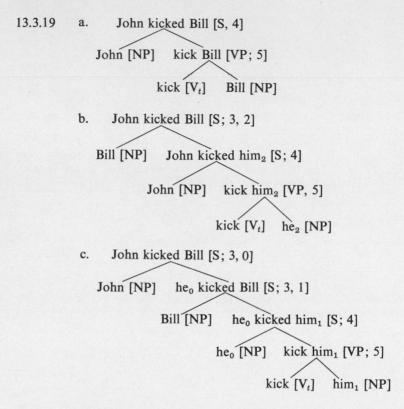

13.3.19   a.   John kicked Bill [S, 4]

John [NP]   kick Bill [VP; 5]

kick [V_t]   Bill [NP]

b.   John kicked Bill [S; 3, 2]

Bill [NP]   John kicked him$_2$ [S; 4]

John [NP]   kick him$_2$ [VP, 5]

kick [V_t]   he$_2$ [NP]

c.   John kicked Bill [S; 3, 0]

John [NP]   he$_0$ kicked Bill [S; 3, 1]

Bill [NP]   he$_0$ kicked him$_1$ [S; 4]

he$_0$ [NP]   kick him$_1$ [VP; 5]

kick [V_t]   him$_1$ [NP]

The translations corresponding to 13.3.19b and 13.3.19c yield the same formula as appears in the last line of 13.3.18, via a slightly different route, for example, for 13.3.19b:

13.3.20   John $\Rightarrow (\lambda P)(^{\text{ex}}P)(^{\text{in}}j)$;   Bill $\Rightarrow (\lambda Q)(^{\text{ex}}Q)(^{\text{in}}b)$;
he$_2 \Rightarrow (\lambda R)(^{\text{ex}}R)(x_2)$
kick him$_2 \Rightarrow (\lambda \mathscr{P})(\lambda x)\text{kick}'(x, \mathscr{P})^{\text{in}}(\lambda R)(^{\text{ex}}R)(x_2)$
$\rightarrow (\lambda x)\text{kick}'(x, {}^{\text{in}}(\lambda R)(^{\text{ex}}R)(x_2))$
$\rightarrow (\lambda x)^{\text{ex in}}(\lambda R)(^{\text{ex}}R)(x_2)[^{\text{in}}(\lambda y)\text{kick}''(x, y)]$(by 13.3.15)
$\rightarrow (\lambda x)(\lambda R)(^{\text{ex}}R)(x_2)^{\text{in}}(\lambda y)\text{kick}''(x, y)$
$\rightarrow (\lambda x)^{\text{ex in}}(\lambda y)\text{kick}''(x, y)(x_2)$
$\rightarrow (\lambda x)\text{kick}''(x, x_2)$

John kicked $him_2 \Rightarrow (\lambda P)(^{ex}P)(^{in}j)^{in}(\lambda x)kick''(x, x_2)$
$\rightarrow^{ex\,in}(\lambda x)kick''(x, x_2)(^{in}j)$
$\rightarrow(\lambda x)kick''(x, x_2)(^{in}j)$
$\rightarrow kick''(^{in}j, x_2)$

To continue the translation in an acceptable fashion, we will have to make a change in the translation rule for quantified sentences that is forced on us by the policy on NP's developed in the last few pages. Specifically, we must introduce 'in' into the translation rule corresponding to the rule that forms a S from a (quantified, in general) NP and a S:[20]

13.3.21   If α is a NP translated as A, β is a S translated as B, and γ is the S formed from β by substituting α for an occurrence of $he_n/$ him_n and pronominalizing all other occurrences of he_n/him_n, then
$$Tr(\gamma) = A(^{in}(\lambda x_n)B)$$

We can then proceed as follows:

13.3.22   John kicked Bill $\Rightarrow (\lambda Q)(^{ex}Q)(^{in}b)^{in}(\lambda x_2)kick''(^{in}j, x_2)$
$\rightarrow^{ex\,in}(\lambda x_2)kick''(^{in}j, x_2)(^{in}b)$
$\rightarrow(\lambda x_2)kick''(^{in}j, x_2)(^{in}b)$
$\rightarrow kick''(^{in}j, {}^{in}b)$

The derivation of $kick''(^{in}j, {}^{in}b)$ for the analysis corresponding to 13.3.19c works essentially the same way.

Let us now consider a sentence with a 'nonextensional verb', with an object that is genuinely ambiguous with regard to an 'extensional' or 'non-existensional' interpretation:

13.3.23   a. John sought a unicorn.

    b.

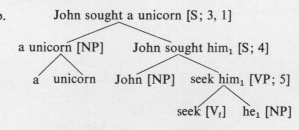

    c.

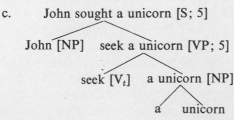

Example 13.3.23*b* ought by all rights to correspond to the interpretation of 13.3.23*a*, in which there is a unicorn such that John is looking for *it*; 13.3.23*c* is a reasonable candidate for an analysis corresponding to the sense of 13.3.23*c* in which John's search is for any unicorn at all, not for some specific unicorn, and Montague so interpreted it. Let us see if we can make the translations corresponding to these two analyses correspond to these two understandings of 13.3.23*a*. The translation corresponding to 13.3.23*b* is as follows:

13.3.24   seek him$_1$ $\Rightarrow$ (λx)seek$'(x,$ $^{in}(\lambda R)(^{ex}R)(x_1))$
            John sought him$_1$ $\Rightarrow$ seek$'(^{in}j,$ $^{in}(\lambda R)(^{ex}R)(x_1))$

While we cannot employ the meaning postulate 13.3.14 to 'export' $^{in}(\lambda R)(^{ex}R)$ from the second argument, we can still replace the last formula by one involving seek$''$, since the definition of $''$ depended only on the type of the second argument, not on whether that position was 'extensional'. Thus we can replace the last formula in 13.3.24 by seek$''(^{in}j, x_1)$ and continue as follows:

13.3.25   John sought a unicorn
            $\Rightarrow$ $(\lambda P)(\exists x) \wedge (\text{unicorn}'(x),$ $^{ex}P(x))^{in}(\lambda x_1)$seek$''(^{in}j, x_1)$
            $\rightarrow (\exists x) \wedge (\text{unicorn}'(x),$ $^{ex\,in}(\lambda x_1)$seek$''(^{in}j, x_1)(x))$
            $\rightarrow (\exists x) \wedge (\text{unicorn}'(x),$ seek$''(^{in}j, x))$

Consider now the translation corresponding to the analysis 13.3.23*c*:

13.3.26   seek a unicorn $\Rightarrow (\lambda x)$seek$'(x,$ $^{in}(\lambda P)(\exists y) \wedge (\text{unicorn}'(y),$ $^{ex}P(y))$
            John sought a unicorn $\Rightarrow$
                        seek$'(^{in}j,$ $^{in}(\lambda P)(\exists y) \wedge (\text{unicorn}'(y),$ $^{ex}P(y))$

Note that we cannot replace the last formula in 13.3.26 by anything involving seek$''$: the second argument of seek$'$ is not of the special form that figures in the definition of seek$''$, and the meaning postulate that might lead to something of that form is inapplicable because *seek* is not among the verbs to which it applies.

We thus end up with two distinct formulas corresponding to the two analyses of *John sought a unicorn*. The formula that we obtained for the analysis 13.3.23*b* fits perfectly the interpretation that it is supposed to represent: the last line of 13.3.25 corresponds directly to 'there is a unicorn that John seeks'. It is less obvious that the last formula in 13.3.26 adequately represents the other interpretation of 13.3.23*a*, since we as yet have no policy regarding when seek$'(x, \mathscr{P})$ should be assigned the value T for those $\mathscr{P}$ that are not of the special form $^{in}(y^*)$. Montague gave a meaning postulate that amounts to the popular proposal (suggested by Quine 1960:154) that *seek* is analyzable as *try to find*:

13.3.27 $\Box(\text{seek}'(x, \mathscr{P}) \leftrightarrow \text{try}'(x, {}^{\text{in}}\text{find}'(x, \mathscr{P})))$

Since *find* is one of the verbs for which the meaning postulate 13.3.14 is applicable, 13.3.27 amounts to 13.3.28, which would yield 13.3.29 as an equivalent of the last formula of 13.3.26:

13.3.28 $\Box(\text{seek}'(x, \mathscr{P}) \leftrightarrow \text{try}'(x, {}^{\text{in}\,\text{ex}}\mathscr{P}({}^{\text{in}}(\lambda y)\text{find}''(x, y))))$

13.3.29 $\text{try}'({}^{\text{in}}j, {}^{\text{in}\,\text{ex}\,\text{in}}(\lambda P)(\exists y) \wedge (\text{unicorn}'(y), {}^{\text{ex}}P(y))\ {}^{\text{in}}(\lambda z)\text{find}''({}^{\text{in}}j, z))$
$\rightarrow \text{try}'({}^{\text{in}}j, {}^{\text{in}}(\exists y) \wedge (\text{unicorn}'(y), {}^{\text{ex}\,\text{in}}(\lambda z)\text{find}''({}^{\text{in}}j, z)(y)))$
$\rightarrow \text{try}'({}^{\text{in}}j, {}^{\text{in}}(\exists y) \wedge (\text{unicorn}'(y), \text{find}''({}^{\text{in}}j, y)))$

If the second argument of try' is to be filled by a proposition indicating the condition for the attempt to be successful, then 13.3.29 fits the intended interpretation of 13.3.23a very well: John's attempt is successful if there is a unicorn which he finds.

It should be remarked, though, that Montague rejected the idea that ALL nonreferential objects could be explained away in terms of meaning postulates such as 13.3.28: 'Such a proposal, however, would not be naturally applicable, for want of a paraphrase, to such intensional verbs as *conceive* and such intensional prepositions as *about*; and I regard it as one of the principal virtues of the present treatment... that it enables us to deal directly with intensional locutions' (1973:267). Montague was thus willing to regard 13.3.30a as having a translation such as 13.3.30b that irreducibly involved a 'higher-order' function as an argument:

13.3.30 a. John conceived of a unicorn.
          b. conceive$'({}^{\text{in}}j, {}^{\text{in}}(\lambda P)(\exists y) \wedge (\text{unicorn}'(y), {}^{\text{ex}}P(y)))$

Let us now turn to the question of how another type of 'nonreferential' NP might be accommodated in Montague grammar, namely, proper names such as *Zeus* and *Santa Claus* that do not denote objects that exist in the real world. Montague dealt in detail only with the more garden variety of proper names whose designation both exists and is always the same. In the fragmentary grammar given in Montague 1973, this characteristic of the relevant proper names was embodied in the following meaning postulate (1973:263):

13.3.31 $(\exists u)\Box(u = \alpha)$, where α is $j, m, b,$ or n.

The grammar contained no proper names other than *John, Mary, Bill*, and *ninety*, and the individual constants $j, m, b,$ and n denote the entities to which those names refer; u is a variable of type e. The postulate 13.3.31

thus asserts for each of the four names that there is an entity that is the denotation of that name in all worlds, that is, that the name is a rigid designator. Montague set up the semantics of his system in such a way that the variables of type e range over exactly the same domain in every world. One fairly plausible way in which Montague's system could be modified so as to accommodate proper names such as *Zeus* would be to relax this last condition as follows: (i) to each world i there corresponds a set A_i of objects that 'exist in that world', and the truth in that world of a quantified formula $(\exists u)\varphi(u)$ depends on whether there is a member a of A_i for which $\varphi(a)$ is true; (ii) 'intensional objects' (i.e., objects of type $\langle s, e \rangle$) can have nonexistent extensions: an 'intensional object' is a function associating to each world a 'possible object' (i.e., a member of the union of the A_i's), and the object that it makes correspond to a given world need not exist in that world. Thus, under this policy, *Santa Claus* could be translated by a constant sc of type $\langle s, e \rangle$ having the same extension in every world, but with the object that serves as its extension existing in only some worlds, the real world not among them.

Consider now the sentences 13.3.32*a* and 13.3.32*b*; by the same steps as in 13.3.20, we will be able to obtain the translations:

13.3.32   a. John sought Santa Claus
          a'. seek"(^{in}j, sc)

          b. John worships Zeus
          b'. worship"(^{in}j, zs)

There is a sense in which $\exists$-introduction can be applied to the second argument position of these formulas and a sense in which it cannot be. We can derive the following consequences, which involve a variable ranging over intensional entities:

13.3.33   a. $(\exists x)$seek"(^{in}j, x)
          b. $(\exists x)$worship"(^{in}j, x)

However, we cannot derive corresponding formulas in which an existential quantifier binds a variable that ranges over entities:[21]

13.3.34   a. $(\exists u)$seek"(^{in}j, ^{in}u)
          b. $(\exists u)$worship"(^{in}j, ^{in}u)

This follows from the fact that while 13.3.32*a* and 13.3.32*b* involve constants of type $\langle s, e \rangle$ and thus of the type over which x ranges, there is no way to insure the existence of a corresponding object of the form ^{in}a (where *a* is an existing object of type *e*), since seek′ and worship′ are not subject to the meaning postulate 13.3.14. According to this treatment, the 'referential' interpretation of *John is looking for a unicorn* ought not, strictly speaking, to imply that a unicorn exists. I think that in fact it does not. In support of this judgment, I offer the fact that 13.3.35 has a non-contradictory interpretation:

13.3.35   John is looking for someone who does not exist, namely, Santa Claus.

This is noncontradictory as long as *someone who does not exist* is taken as having the whole sentence for its scope, its variable is taken as ranging over intensional objects, and *exist* is taken to mean 'exist as a real world entity'. Note also the possibility of saying 13.3.36 even if one believes that no such things as gods exist:

13.3.36   Oscar worships the same god that Lucille does.

This fact is consistent with the treatment suggested in the last paragraph provided that gods are intensional objects that need not have a real world extension.

Another problematic type of proper name that Montague did not provide an analysis for is a proper name that does not always denote the same individual, for example, the name *Lassie*, which has denoted different dogs as the various Lassies have died or retired and new dogs have assumed the role. Montague gave a meaning postulate that would prevent such a proper name from functioning as the subject of the more ordinary common nouns:

13.3.37 $\square[\supset(\delta(x), (\exists u)(x = {}^{in}u))]$, where δ is any basic (as opposed to derived) member of the category $t//e$ (i.e., common noun) other than price′, temperature′, ...

This postulate would force *Lassie is a dog* to be assigned the value 'false': if *l* is the intensional individual whose denotation at each moment is the Lassie of that moment, then *l* is not of the form ${}^{in}u$ (i.e., it is not a constant function, mapping each world onto the same individual), and thus dog′(*l*) must be false if 13.3.37 is to be maintained.

While Montague's analysis did not allow for such an individual as 'Lassie', it did allow for intensional individuals whose denotations changed through time, and indeed, the provision for such individuals is essential if Montague's treatment of such sentences as *The temperature is rising* is to work. Since Montague's discussion of that example rests heavily on his treatment of the verb *be*, it will be necessary first to digress into that matter. Montague treated *be* as a transitive verb (thus, of the same syntactic category as *kick*), with the translation:

13.3.38   be $\Rightarrow (\lambda \mathscr{P})(\lambda x)^{\text{ex}}\mathscr{P}^{\text{in}}((\lambda y)(^{\text{ex}}x = {}^{\text{ex}}y))$

As an illustration of 13.3.38 in action, consider the following translation:

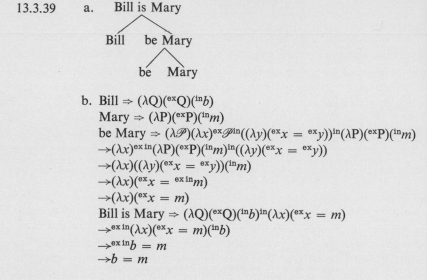

13.3.39   a.   Bill is Mary

          Bill   be Mary

              be   Mary

       b. Bill $\Rightarrow (\lambda Q)(^{\text{ex}}Q)(^{\text{in}}b)$
          Mary $\Rightarrow (\lambda P)(^{\text{ex}}P)(^{\text{in}}m)$
          be Mary $\Rightarrow (\lambda \mathscr{P})(\lambda x)^{\text{ex}}\mathscr{P}^{\text{in}}((\lambda y)(^{\text{ex}}x = {}^{\text{ex}}y))^{\text{in}}(\lambda P)(^{\text{ex}}P)(^{\text{in}}m)$
          $\rightarrow (\lambda x)^{\text{ex in}}(\lambda P)(^{\text{ex}}P)(^{\text{in}}m)^{\text{in}}((\lambda y)(^{\text{ex}}x = {}^{\text{ex}}y))$
          $\rightarrow (\lambda x)((\lambda y)(^{\text{ex}}x = {}^{\text{ex}}y))(^{\text{in}}m)$
          $\rightarrow (\lambda x)(^{\text{ex}}x = {}^{\text{ex in}}m)$
          $\rightarrow (\lambda x)(^{\text{ex}}x = m)$
          Bill is Mary $\Rightarrow (\lambda Q)(^{\text{ex}}Q)(^{\text{in}}b)^{\text{in}}(\lambda x)(^{\text{ex}}x = m)$
          $\rightarrow {}^{\text{ex in}}(\lambda x)(^{\text{ex}}x = m)(^{\text{in}}b)$
          $\rightarrow {}^{\text{ex in}}b = m$
          $\rightarrow b = m$

It can also be shown that *Bill is a man* leads to the translation man$'(^{\text{in}}b)$. I will not go through the derivation here; the interested reader is referred to Partee (1975:290–91) for details. Note thus that in Montague's treatment, *be* plays a role in the translation of *Bill is a man* into intensional logic, but the translation of *be* is set up in such a way that it will 'cancel out'; that is, it will yield the same result as if there were no *be* and the predicate noun were treated as an intransitive verb.

Or at least that is the case when the predicate noun is an 'ordinary' noun such as *man*. The derivation of man$'(^{\text{in}}b)$ from *Bill is a man* depends on the meaning postulate 13.3.37 and thus cannot be carried out if the predicate noun is *price* or *temperature*. Let us now look at an example involving one of those nouns and see if, in the process, we can solve the puzzle of why the following argument is invalid:

13.3.40   The temperature is rising.
          The temperature is 90.
          Therefore, 90 is rising.

The translation of *The temperature is 90* is as follows:

13.3.41   be 90 $\Rightarrow [(\lambda\mathscr{P})(\lambda x)^{\text{ex}}\mathscr{P}^{\text{in}}(\lambda y)(^{\text{ex}}x = {}^{\text{ex}}y)]^{\text{in}}(\lambda P)(^{\text{ex}}P)(^{\text{in}}90)$

$\rightarrow(\lambda x)^{\text{ex in}}[(\lambda P)(^{\text{ex}}P)(^{\text{in}}90)]^{\text{in}}(\lambda y)[^{\text{ex}}x = {}^{\text{ex}}y]$

(conversion of $\lambda\mathscr{P}$)

$\rightarrow(\lambda x)[(\lambda P)(^{\text{ex}}P)(^{\text{in}}90)]^{\text{in}}(\lambda y)[^{\text{ex}}x = {}^{\text{ex}}y]$ ($^{\text{ex in}}$ cancellation)

$\rightarrow(\lambda x)^{\text{ex}}(^{\text{in}}(\lambda y)[^{\text{ex}}x = {}^{\text{ex}}y](^{\text{in}}90))$ (conversion of λP)

$\rightarrow(\lambda x)((\lambda y)[^{\text{ex}}x = {}^{\text{ex}}y](^{\text{in}}90))$ ($^{\text{ex in}}$ cancellation)

$\rightarrow(\lambda x)[^{\text{ex}}x = {}^{\text{ex in}}90]$ (conversion of λy)

$\rightarrow(\lambda x)[^{\text{ex}}x = 90]$

the temperature $\Rightarrow (\lambda P)(\exists y)[\wedge((\forall z)(\text{temp}'(z)\leftrightarrow z = y), (^{\text{ex}}P)(y))]$

the temperature is 90

$\Rightarrow (\lambda P)(\exists y)[\wedge((\forall z)(\text{temp}'(z) \leftrightarrow z = y), (^{\text{ex}}P)(y))]$

$^{\text{in}}(\lambda x)[^{\text{ex}}x = 90]$

$\rightarrow(\exists y)[\wedge((\forall z)(\text{temp}'(z) \leftrightarrow z = y), {}^{\text{ex in}}(\lambda x)[^{\text{ex}}x = 90](y))]$

$\rightarrow(\exists y)[\wedge((\forall z)(\text{temp}'(z) \leftrightarrow z = y), (\lambda x)[^{\text{ex}}x = 90](y))]$

$\rightarrow(\exists y)[\wedge((\forall z)(\text{temp}'(z) \leftrightarrow z = y), [^{\text{ex}}y = 90])]$

The translation of *The temperature is rising* can easily be shown to be

13.3.42   The temperature is rising

$\Rightarrow (\exists y)[\wedge((\forall z)(\text{temp}'(z) \leftrightarrow z = y), \text{rise}'(y))]$

No conversion of 13.3.42 to anything involving $^{\text{ex}}y$ is possible, since the meaning postulate that Montague gives for intransitive verbs specifically excludes rise′ and that for nouns excludes temperature′. The translations of the two premises of 13.3.40 thus do not share anything that would justify the inference in 13.3.40: while the same (intensional) object is picked out as 'the temperature' in 13.3.42 as in 13.3.41, example 13.3.42 predicates something of that object but 13.3.41 only predicates something of the extension of that object. Thus, according to Montague's treatment, 13.3.40 is invalid in exactly the same way as is the inference:

13.3.43   The janitor is sleeping.
The janitor's brother is the archbishop.
Therefore the archbishop is sleeping.

The meaning postulate 13.3.37 provides the difference between the invalid 13.3.40 and the valid 13.3.44:

13.3.44   The balloon is rising.
The balloon is a manufactured object.
Therefore, a manufactured object is rising.

13.4. Exercises

1. For each of the following formulas, (i) simplify it by λ-conversion, and (ii) provide plausible English translations for both the original formula and the simplified formula.

a. $[(\lambda x)\text{love}'(x, x)](a)$

b. $[(\lambda P)(\exists x) \wedge (\text{linguist}'(x), P(x))]\ (\lambda y)(\forall z) \supset (\text{relative}'(z, y), \text{love}'(y, z))$

c. $[(\lambda P)(\forall x)(\forall y) \supset (Pxy, Pyx)]\ (\lambda(z_1, z_2))(\exists w) \wedge (\text{love}'(w, z_1), \text{love}'(w, z_2))$

2. Suppose the following symbols are variables of the indicated type:

$u \quad e$

$x \quad \langle s, e \rangle$

$P \quad \langle \langle s, e \rangle, t \rangle$

What is the type of

a. $^{\text{in}}u$

b. $(\lambda P)P(x)$

c. $(\lambda u)P(^{\text{in}}u)$

3. In Montague's system of syntactic categories, what would be the category of

a. The *almost* in *almost all*.

b. The *'s* in *This hat is Bill's*.

4. Discuss informally what problems would be involved in formulating a Montague syntactic rule that had the effect of a passive transformation and getting it to interact properly with the other syntactic rules and with semantic rules.

5. The following analyis tree is consistent with the syntactic rules alluded to in this chapter. Determine whether the translation based on this analysis has the same truth conditions as that corresponding to the more obvious analysis, in which each quantifier has a single conjunct as scope:

Every dog barks and every bird sings

every dog He_0 barks and every bird sings

every bird He_0 barks and he_1 sings

He_0 barks He_1 sings

14. Further Topics in Quantification

14.1. Other Quantifiers

The only quantifier words that we have discussed in any detail so far are those that correspond roughly to the ∀ and ∃ of standard logic. In this section I wish to take up other words that appear in the same syntactic positions as do *all, each, some*, and the like and which play a role in the binding of a variable: the numerals *one, two, three*, . . ., vague numerals such as *several, a couple, a few*, and perhaps *many*, approximate numerals such as *roughly one hundred* and *over fifty*, near-universal quantifiers such as *almost all* and *all but one/two/* . . ., negative quantifiers such as *no* (= *not any*), *few*, and *not many*, and the unclassifiable *most*.

There is a syntactic test that allows one to identify some of these items as 'existential', namely, the possibility of using existential *there* when the subject NP has the given quantifier:

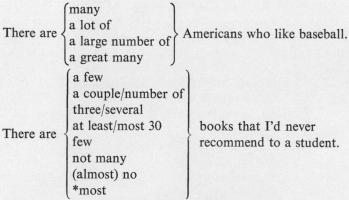

14.1.1   There are some people who think Daley was a saint.

There are {many / a lot of / a large number of / a great many} Americans who like baseball.

There are {a few / a couple/number of / three/several / at least/most 30 / few / not many / (almost) no / *most} books that I'd never recommend to a student.

There aren't any hangers in the closet.
*There are (almost) all of the books on the table.

425

*There is every book by Chomsky in our library.
*There is each person in his own room.
*There is any two-year-old capable of assembling this cabinet.

These facts pose the problem of how to analyze the various expressions in such a way that something can be identified that is shared by quantifiers that according to this test are 'existential' but is absent from the other quantifiers.

It is easy to come up with an analysis in which the various 'existential' quantifiers all correspond to logical structures in which an existential quantifier binds a set variable; for example, one might analyze 14.1.2a as 14.1.2b:

14.1.2   a. Many Americans like baseball.
          b. $(\exists M: \wedge (M$ is large, $(\forall x: x \in M)(x$ is an American$))[(\forall x: x \in M)$ $(x$ likes baseball$)]$

That is, there is a large set consisting of Americans such that the members of that set all like baseball. What is not so easy is to exclude similar analyses of the other quantifiers. For example, the existentially quantified set variable in 14.1.2b will not serve to identify *many* as 'existential' if the *most* of 14.1.3a can be analyzed as in 14.1.3b:

14.1.3   a. Most Americans like baseball.
          b. $(\exists M: M$ is more than half of $\{x: x$ is an American$\})$ $[(\forall x: x \in M)(x$ likes baseball$)]$

It will be worthwhile to consider seriously whether 14.1.3b really adequately represents the meaning of *most*, in view of the fact that some apparent paraphrases of *most* (including one that directly matches 14.1.3b) do allow existential *there* and thus, unlike *most*, are existential quantifiers by our test:

14.1.4   There are more than half/50 percent of all Americans who distrust politicians.
          There are over half/50 percent of all Americans who distrust politicians.
          There are a/*the majority of (all) Americans who distrust politicians.
          *There are most Americans who distrust politicians.

If the possibility of using existential *there* is to depend on the logical structure of the sentence, as I conjecture it ought to, there must be some difference in meaning between *most* and *more than half of*. There are, in fact, contexts in which the two expressions convey different things:

14.1.5   Most of the ladies and more than half of the gentlemen wore evening clothes. (Sinclair Lewis, *It can't happen here*)

14.1.6   a. Most positive integers are greater than 10^{80}.
              a'. More than half of all positive integers are greater than 10^{80}.
              b. Most positive integers are composite.
              b'. More than half of all positive integers are composite.

Example 14.1.5 strongly suggests that a greater proportion of ladies than of gentlemen were dressed in evening clothes. Of the four sentences in 14.1.6, only 14.1.6*b* is a fairly normal use of English. Example 14.1.6*b* can reasonably be held to express a true proposition, but 14.1.6*b'* is clearly false, whereas 14.1.6*a'* is more clearly true than 14.1.6*a* is.

These differences in what is conveyed by *most* and *more than half* could be accounted for in a fanciful way by describing their meanings in terms of procedures for verifying the sentence, where the procedure for *most* begins with the instruction 'Look' and the procedure for *more than half* begins with the instruction 'Count'. The reason that 14.1.5 conveys what it does about the numbers of ladies and gentlemen wearing evening clothes is that it suggests that you can tell 'by inspection' that ladies in evening clothes outnumber other ladies (i.e., just about everywhere you look, there are more ladies in evening clothes than ladies in other garb), whereas you have to count to tell that the gentlemen in evening clothes outnumber the gentlemen in less formal clothing. Since both prime numbers and composities are infinite in number, neither set constitutes 'more than half of' the positive integers, and thus 14.1.6*b'* comes out false; but since all primes greater than three are locally outnumbered by composites (i.e., they are surrounded by composites) but composites are only occasionally surrounded by primes, 'inspection' tells you (albeit wrongly) that composites outnumber primes. Example 14.1.6*a* is true for the trivial reason that the infinitely many integers greater than 10^{80} outnumber the 10^{80} positive integers not exceeding 10^{80}; however, integers less than 10^{80} are not surrounded by integers greater than 10^{80} and thus the procedure for verifying 14.1.6*a'* fails.

In the proposal of the last paragraph, the procedure for *most* involved comparing a set directly with its complement, whereas with *more than half* a set was counted and its cardinal number was compared with that of the larger domain. This can be reinterpreted as an analysis in which 'Most A's are B' is analyzed not along the lines of 14.1.3*b* but as something like 'the set of A's which are not B is smaller than the set of A's which are B' or even 'the set of A's which are not B is small'. The latter version is essentially what is proposed by Peterson (1979), who analyzes *most* as *few not*, that is, as *not many not*. Peterson's proposal in fact solves the problems with which I am grappling. First, it explains the impossibility of *there*-insertion with *most*: *there*-insertion requires that the existential quantifier be immediately above the clause into which *there* is to be inserted, as illustrated by the fact that while the existential quantifier of 14.1.7*a* is ambiguous with regard to whether it has the main or the complement clause as scope, 14.1.7*b* allows only an interpretation in which the complement clause is the scope of the quantifier:

14.1.7   a. Bill thinks that some drugs are in short supply.
              b. Bill thinks that there are some drugs in short supply.

Under Peterson's proposal a negation intervenes between the existential quantifier *many* and the clause in which the *there* would be inserted, and that negation can be taken as blocking *there*-insertion.[1] Second, this proposal allows the vagueness of *large* to be built into an analysis of *many* and thus also into an analysis of *most* and hence can allow for the subjective factors that may affect whether a particular subset is interpreted as constituting most of the whole. The dividing line between large and not large can be below, at, or conceivably above 50 percent,[2] and the difference between large and not large can depend on the distribution of the subset in the larger set rather than just on the proportion it makes up of the larger set. It is only because 50 percent is such a natural dividing line between large and not large that *most* often conveys the same thing as *more than half*.

The remaining nonexistential quantifiers are the universal and near-universal quantifiers. The only problem in maintaining the proposed generalization about existential and nonexistential quantifiers is in insuring that near-universals are not analyzed in a way that would make them 'existential'. The most obvious analyses of near-universals in fact do involve an existential quantifier in a structure similar to that of 14.1.2*b*. For example, using the makeshift 'No(M, 3)' to indicate that M has three members, one might analyze 14.1.8*a* as 14.1.8*b*:[3]

14.1.8   a. All but three presidents were crooks.
              b. $(\exists M: \wedge ((\forall x: x \in M)(x$ is a president), No(M, 3)))
                 $(\forall y: \wedge (y$ is a president, $\sim (y \in M)))(y$ was a crook)

In order to identify a detail of logical structure on which to pin the blame for the difference in behavior between existentials like *many* and near-universals like *all but three*, let us get into some detail about the derivations of sentences with existential quantifiers.

Let us begin with the simplest case, that of numerals. According to what we have said so far, 14.1.9*a* should be analyzed along the lines of 14.1.9*b*:

14.1.9   a. Three linguists were drunk.
           b. $(\exists M: \wedge ((\forall x: x{\in}M)(x$ is a linguist), No(M, 3))
               $(\forall y: y{\in}M)(y$ was drunk)

I wish to propose that the derivation of 14.1.9*a* goes through steps in which $(\forall y: y{\in}M)(y$ be drunk) is collapsed into (M be drunk) and $(\exists M: \wedge ((\forall x: x{\in}M)(x$ be a linguist), No(M, 3))) is collapsed into $(\exists M:$ M is three linguists). The rule, here called AGGREGATION, that converts[4] $(\forall y: y{\in}M)(y$ be drunk) into (M be drunk) is required anyway so as to provide derivations for sentences as in 14.1.10, in which NP's referring to to members of a set individually count as identical to NP's referring to that set as a whole (note the application of conjunction reduction):

14.1.10   a. The persons in the next room are linguists and are three in
               number.
           b. The persons in the next room are linguists and met at a
               conference on bilingualism.

The conversion of $\wedge ((\forall x: x{\in}M)(x$ be a linguist), No(M, 3)) into (M be 3 linguists) can be accomplished by aggregation in conjunction with existing transformations. Let us assume that No(M, 3) can be realized as 'M is 3' or 'M is 3 in number', just as 'x is blue' and 'x is blue in color' would be alternative realizations of a proposition Color(x, blue) expressing a relation between objects and colors.[5] The result of applying aggregation to 14.1.11*a* is 14.1.11*b*, which is converted into 14.1.11*c* and 14.1.11*d* by the rules for forming restrictive relative clauses and reducing restrictive clauses to prenominal modifiers:

14.1.11   a. $\wedge ((\forall x: x{\in}M)(x$ be linguist), No(M, 3))
           b. $\rightarrow \wedge$ (M be linguist, M be 3)   (by aggregation)
           c. $\rightarrow$ M be linguist(who be 3)   (by restrictive-relative forma-
                                                 tion)
           d. $\rightarrow$ M be (3 linguist)   (by relative clause reduction and
                                          adjective preposing)

The familiar transformation of quantifier-lowering will then have 14.1.12*a* as its input and 14.1.12*b* as its output, which will in turn be converted into

14.1.12*c* by the usual rules for reducing the domain expression to its predicate noun:

14.1.12   a. ($\exists$M: M be 3 linguist)(M be drunk)$\rightarrow$
          b.

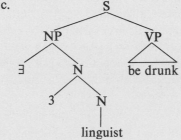

The appropriate surface structure is derived from 14.1.12*c* by agreement rules (making *linguist* and *be* plural) and a rule giving $\exists$ zero realization when it introduces a NP that has a numeral.

One noteworthy feature of this derivation is that it makes the numeral not, strictly speaking, a quantifier but rather an adjective. As a consequence of this detail, it is possible for NP's with numerals to differ in constituent structure from NP's having universal quantifiers, and I have in fact argued (McCawley 1978*a*) that while articles and universal quantifiers combine with nouns and restrictive relative clauses in structures of the shape 14.1.13*a*, numerals appear in structures of both of the shapes 14.1.13*b* and 14.1.13*b'*:

14.1.13   a.   b.

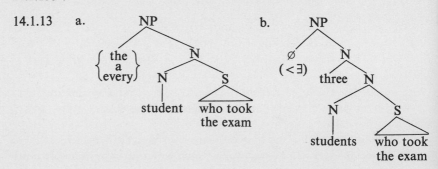

b′.

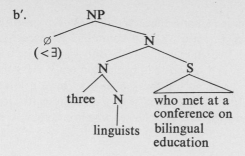

The restrictive relative clause in each case is derived from a conjoined clause containing an index that appears in the other conjunct as the subject of a predicate noun. It is the possibility of (derived) structures in which *three linguists* is a predicate noun that makes relative clause structures such as appear in 14.1.13b′ possible. Note that relative clauses in which the relativized NP refers to a set rather than an individual are possible with numerals but not with universal quantifiers (14.1.14a), and in such structures two or more numeral + noun combinations may be conjoined with one another (14.1.14b):

14.1.14   a. Three/several/*all/*any linguists who met at a conference on bilingual education were drinking and carousing.
           b. Three linguists, two anthropologists, and one sociologist who had met at a conference on bilingual education were among those arrested.

Moreover, while *the* can appear in quantifier position in sentences parallel to 14.1.14a, the conjuncts in sentences parallel to 14.1.14b must be all indefinite or (perhaps marginally) all definite, but combinations mixing conjuncts with *the* and conjuncts with only a numeral are excluded:[6]

14.1.15   a. The linguists who met at the conference were arrested.
           b. The linguists and (?the) anthropologists who met at the conference were among those arrested.
           b′. *Two linguists and the anthropologists who met at the conference were among those arrested.
           b″. The two linguists and (the) three anthropologists who met at the conference were among those arrested.

These restrictions are consequences of the approach suggested here: the structure introduced by ∃M can involve any description of M (e.g., that M consists of three linguists and two anthropologists) and the clause specifying what M consists of can be conjoined with another clause that would underlie a restrictive relative clause, say, a clause specifying that all members of M were among those arrested. A true quantifier (including a definite description operator) must command all occurrences of the variable that it binds, which means that the only way in which a true quantifier could be involved in a structure in which conjoined NP's share a restrictive relative clause would be for the sentence to have a logical structure in which the quantifier is combined with a domain expression that provides all the nouns and the relative clause, which is to say, a structure of the shape 14.1.16:

14.1.16

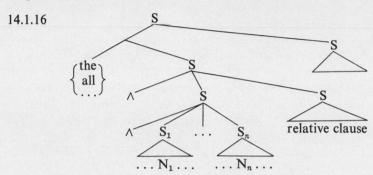

This can give rise to 14.1.15*b* or 14.1.15*b″* if *the* is allowed to distribute itself over the conjuncts (i.e., logically there is only one *the*, but it is manifested in all conjuncts); any of the S_i can itself be a coordinate structure with a conjunct that provides a source for a numeral. Example 14.1.15*b′* could not be derived from anything of this form, since if the *the* originates in the position indicated in 14.1.16, it must either be manifested on all the conjuncts or appear at the very beginning of the NP, applying to all conjuncts jointly.

In the derivation proposed in 14.1.11 and 14.1.12, the logical structure is of the general shape 14.1.17*a*, and applications of aggregation and the relative clause rules convert it into 14.1.17*b–c*:

14.1.17   a. $(\exists M: \wedge ((\forall x: x \in M)(x f), M\, g))\, (\forall x: x \in M)(x\, h)$
       b. $(\exists M: \wedge (Mf, Mg))(M\, h)$
       c. $(\exists M: M\, gf)(M\, h)$

Since *there*-insertion is contingent upon the existential quantifier being immediately above the clause into which *there* is to be inserted, the principle of the transformational cycle imples that 14.1.17*c* will be the stage of the derivation to which *there*-insertion applies if it is to apply at all. The problem of analyzing quantifiers so that the right ones allow *there*-insertion thus resolves into the problem of analyzing the various quantifiers in such a way that intermediate stages like 14.1.17*c* can be derived precisely in the case of those quantifiers that allow *there*-insertion.

One can no doubt construct reasonably plausible analyses of the form 14.1.17a for all of the quantifiers in question, the universal and near-universal ones as well as the existential ones ((M g) could be an expression specifying that M consists of all but three presidents or of almost all presidents). However, it is possible to distinguish the existential from the nonexistential quantifiers on the basis of the form of g: the analyzed quantifier is existential if and only if (M g) gives the size of M, whether (M g) is of the form No(M, n), giving a specific cardinal number for M, or is of the form $(\exists n) \wedge (No(M,n), k(n))$, giving a less specific description of the cardinal number of M (e.g., $k(n)$ might be 'n is large' or 'n is close to 100'). Note that all quantifiers of the form *a Adj number of*, which is the canonical form for expressing $(\exists n) \wedge (No(M,n), k(n))$, are existential:

14.1.18

$$\text{There are a(n)} \begin{cases} \text{large} \\ \text{huge} \\ \text{small} \\ \text{significant} \\ \text{insignificant} \\ \text{paltry} \\ \text{astonishingly large/small/}\ldots \\ \text{unbelievable} \end{cases} \begin{array}{l} \text{number of} \\ \text{books in} \\ \text{John's study.} \end{array}$$

The only way that one could analyze universal or near-universal quantifiers with a formula of that shape would be to bring in a superfluous reference to the number of elements in the domain, for example, to analyze *All linguists are insane* with a formula that corresponded literally to 'A number of linguists such that there are that many linguists are insane'—more idiomatically, 'As many linguists as there are are insane'. Such an analysis yields correct truth conditions only when the domain is finite: it is not the case that all integers are even, though it is the case that $\aleph_0$ integers are even and there are $\aleph_0$ integers. Even where it does yield correct truth conditions, such a formula can be rejected as a candidate for THE logical structure of the sentence, on the grounds that it violates Grice's maxim of manner, which I take as requiring not only the avoidance of unnecessarily complex surface structures as expressions of a given thought but also the avoidance of unnecessarily complex logical analyses of given surface structures. Thus, universally quantified subject NP's could meet the conditions for *there*-insertion only if given an analysis that could be ruled out as uncooperative.

14.2. Mass Expressions

The nouns that appear in examples in logic texts are in virtually all cases COUNT nouns: they denote properties that are predicated of individuals and they serve to define sets of individuals such as the set of all kangaroos or the set of all books on astrophysics. Natural languages contain not only count nouns but also MASS nouns such as *water, sand, furniture,* or *prose,* which refer without regard to individuation and serve to define not sets but 'masses' that need not have any minimal parts in the way that a single kangaroo (perhaps better, a set consisting of a single kangaroo) is a minimal part of the set of all kangaroos. While there are in many cases minimal quantities of what a mass noun refers to (e.g., water is composed of H_2O molecules and one such molecule is the minimum quantity in which water can exist; furniture comes in 'pieces', and part of a piece of furniture is not furniture, for example, an arm of a chair or a nail in a bookcase is not furniture), that fact is irrelevant to the use of mass nouns. The development of the molecular conception of the structure of matter did not change the way in which the word *water* is used. Moreover, indeterminacy of individuation causes no difficulty in the application of mass nouns; for example, a crateful of modules that can be put together in different ways to make up anything from two to ten pieces of furniture is a crateful of furniture even though it is not any determinate number of pieces of furniture. In addition, mass terms can refer to substances that are not infinitely divisible but which do not have any clear minimal quantities. For example, there is no such thing as a molecule of dirty water—a single molecule of water cannot in itself be dirty—and there is no clear minimum number of H_2O molecules and molecules of impurities that can constitute dirty water. Succotash[7] usually consists of discrete grains of corn and lima beans, and no number of lima beans and grains of corn constitutes a minimum quantity of succotash, for example, one grain of corn and one lima bean cannot be described as succotash (except when viewed as the remains of a larger quantity of succotash, though note that the remains of a bowl of succotash can be called succotash even if one of the essential ingredients is missing—one can say *Johnny left some succotash in his bowl* even if what is left is three lima beans and no corn).[8]

Mass nouns (more generally, MASS EXPRESSIONS, such as *dirty water* or *footwear that has been inspected by the county clerk*) can combine with quantifiers, indeed with many of the same quantifiers that combine with count nouns:

14.2.1   a. All human blood is red.
               b. Most succotash is high in protein.
               c. Some sand is black.
               d. A lot of whiskey is under 90 proof.

Moreover, the quantifier words in 14.2.1 appear to have the same meanings as when they are combined with count nouns. In English, the quantifier words that cannot combine with mass nouns are *each*, *every*, numerals (including vague numerals such as *several*), and *many*.

14.2.2   a. Each poem/*poetry was discussed by the poet.
            b. Every chair/*furniture was in poor condition.
            c. Fred bought several vases/*pottery.
            d. Susan performed several compositions/*music.

The only quantifiers that do not combine with count nouns appear to be *much* and *little*:

14.2.3   Much poetry/*poem(s) is rarely read.

In view of the fact that most languages have the same word for 'much' as for 'many' (German *viel*, French *beaucoup*, Japanese *takusan*) and that there is no obstacle to treating *much* and *many* as meaning the same thing (at least, no more of an obstacle than there is to identifying the meaning of *most* in *most water* with that of *most* in *most kangaroos*), I will henceforth treat *many* and *much* as being two forms of the same word (like *this* and *these*) rather than two different words. Accordingly, I recognize quantifiers (including *much/many* and *few/little*) that combine both with count and with mass expressions, and quantifiers that combine only with count expressions, but no quantifiers that combine only with mass expressions. I will attempt below to find a semantic explanation for this gap.

The rules of inference for universal and existential quantifiers seem to carry over without change to the mass noun case:

14.2.4   a. All water is wet.
             This puddle is water.
             Therefore, this puddle is wet.

          b. This puddle is water.
             This puddle is dirty.
             Therefore, some water is dirty.

It is not so easy, however, to formalize the rules of inference so that they will apply to the mass noun case and to state truth conditions for quantified propositions that will cover the mass noun case as well as the count noun case. These problems manifest themselves with the greatest vengeance if one attempts to give an account of mass terms within the framework of unrestricted quantification. Suppose that we were to symbolize 14.2.4*a* as 14.2.5:

14.2.5 $(\forall x) \supset (\text{water } x, \text{wet } x)$
          water(p)
          wet(p)

The problem with this formalization is that it is far from clear what must be allowed as values of the bound variable for it to make sense. The values must include things of which 'is water' can be predicated,[9] and while there are many entities of which 'is water' can innocuously be predicated (puddles, pools, drops), it is not clear that any set of such entities would provide enough values for the bound variable, since the first premise of 14.2.4a implies not merely that the various discrete bodies of water are wet but also that all parts of those bodies are wet. Example 14.2.4a is valid not only for a believer in the modern atomic and molecular conception of matter but also for someone of A.D. 1700 who believed that matter is continuous and infinitely divisible, and an adequate account of mass terms must be as consistent with the latter view as with the former, since the logic of quantifiers cannot by itself establish or refute any theory of matter. Thus in any state of affairs, the 'universe of discourse' would have to include all 'parts' of all objects, according to whatever notion of part corresponds to the theory of matter that is true in that state of affairs; this makes for a whopping big universe of discourse, especially for states of affairs in which a preatomic conception of matter holds and all physical objects will have uncountably many parts.

There have also been analyses that attempt to do without such predicates as 'is water', though, as far as I can determine, they leave quite unclear what the 'universe of discourse' is to be. For example, Parsons (1970) treats mass nouns as proper names and treats quantified mass expressions as involving a relationship Q 'is a quantity of'; for example, he analyzes *All water is wet* as $(\forall x) \supset (Qxw, \text{wet } x)$, where w is the denotation of *water*. For Parsons, in effect, quantifiers only combine with count nouns, and apparent instances of a quantifier combining with a mass noun m really involve the count expression 'quantity of m'. I find Parsons's approach unappealing in view of two prejudices that I hold: (i) I believe that mass nouns are semantically more basic than count nouns—that the meaning of a count noun involves something over and above what goes into the meaning of a mass noun, namely, the specification of an individuation; and (ii) I think that any adequate account of the semantics of mass expressions must explain the oddity of sentences such as 14.2.2, whereas Parsons's approach provides no reason why there should be any difference in the acceptability of the various combinations of quantifier and mass noun—if you can supply an understood 'quantity of' in interpreting the examples in 14.2.1, why shouldn't you be able to do the same in interpreting those in 14.2.2? In addition, Parsons's approach has no chance of coping with the semantics of *most* and *much*: to the extent that any sense can be made of a notion of 'most quantities of gold', that notion has no bearing on the truth conditions of such sentences as *Most gold is still under ground*. Parsons in fact makes this very point himself and adopts a quite different analysis for *most* than he has for *all* and *some*.

I will be concerned in most of the remainder of this section with a proposal by Harry Bunt (1976) in which the syntax and semantics of count nouns is a special case of that of mass nouns and the semantics is done in terms of a notion of which 'set' is a special case. Specifically, Bunt introduces a notion of 'ensemble' as an entity structured in terms of a relationship of 'is a part of', where that relationship amounts to the relationship of 'is a subset of' in the case where the ensemble is a set.

Bunt's notion of ensemble leans heavily on an important distinction in set theory, that between an element a and the set $\{a\}$ that has that element as its sole member. The semantics of mass terms must be developed in such a way as to allow something to be gold without being a ring even in a state of affairs where all gold is in the form of rings and all rings are gold, since, for example, in that state of affairs half a ring would be gold but would not be a ring.[10] Bunt set up his notion of ensemble in such a way that 'gold' and 'ring' have two different ensembles G and R as their denotations in this state of affairs. A given ring r will be a part of G but not a part of R, though $\{r\}$ will be a part of R:

14.2.6 $r \subseteq G$
               $\{r\} \subseteq R$

In ensemble theory, $\{r\}$ denotes an ensemble whose only parts are 'improper parts', that is, $\{r\}$ itself and the empty ensemble. Bunt uses the symbol $\underline{\varepsilon}$ to denote the relationship between r and $\{r\}$ and generalizes ε to a relation that holds between an element a and an ensemble containing $\{a\}$ as a part:

14.2.7 $a\underline{\varepsilon}b$ if and only if $b = \{a\}$
               $a\varepsilon b$ if and only if $\{a\} \subseteq b$

An ensemble can thus have 'members'. However, an ensemble can perfectly well have no members and still be nonempty, as will be the case if none of its nonempty parts is minimal. It is easy to construct an object having parts none of which is minimal. For example, suppose we take the 'parts' of a line to be half-open intervals (that is, sets $[a, b)$ consisting of all real numbers x such that $a \leq x < b$: the left end point is included but the right end point is not) and unions of finitely many half-open intervals. Clearly, none of these parts is minimal, since every half-open interval contains still smaller half-open intervals; note in particular that a one-member set $\{a\}$ is not a half-open interval and is thus not part of the ensemble under discussion.

In Bunt's notion of ensemble, not only does every member of an ensemble correspond to a minimal part of the ensemble, but every minimal part corresponds to a member; that is, according to one of his postulates, if b is a minimal part of an ensemble E, then there is an a such that $b = \{a\}$, and thus $a\varepsilon E$. One can speak of a as the 'content' of b. Members of an ensemble can themselves be ensembles. Thus, if one considers a ring to be an ensemble whose parts are the 'quantities of matter' contained in it, then any part of a ring is a part of G though of course it is neither a part of R nor a member of R. In the states of affairs in which all gold is in rings and all rings are made of gold, G is the UNION of R: the ensemble whose parts are parts of members of R or are 'sums' of parts of members of R.[12]

Bunt's approach allows one to take the denotation of any noun, count or mass, to be an ensemble. In the case of a count noun, the ensemble will be a set; in the case of a mass noun, it need not be (but could be) a set. Simple propositions with predicate nouns will be true if and only if the denotation of the subject is a part of the ensemble denoted by the predicate noun. Whether the predicate noun is singular or plural (*Tom is a lawyer* vs. *Tom and Dick are lawyers*) is taken here to be semantically irrelevant: its denotation is the same in either case (here, the ensemble of lawyers, that is, the ensemble having all sets of lawyers as its parts). To make this consistent it will be necessary to change one detail of the analyses accepted in the earlier chapters, namely, that singular count NP's that apparently refer to an individual must now be taken as referring to the set having that individual as its sole member; for example, if a is the individual that *Tom* refers to, then the subject of *Tom is a lawyer* must be taken to denote $\{a\}$ rather than a. Note that this gives equivalent truth conditions to what we had earlier: a is a member of the set of all lawyers if and only if $\{a\}$ is a part of the ensemble of lawyers. Predicate mass nouns will work in exactly parallel fashion: *This puddle is water* will be true only if the denotation of the subject is part of the ensemble that is the denotation of *water*.

Variables bound by quantifiers that combine with both count and mass nouns will take as values parts of the ensemble denoted by the noun, for example, the truth of *All water is wet* depends on the truth of 'x is wet' for values of x which are parts of the ensemble denoted by *water*: if 'x is wet' is true of all such x, then the sentence expresses a true proposition. This analysis can be carried over to a treatment of combinations of *all* with a count noun only if two changes are made in the proposals of chapter 6. First, the noun to which the quantifier is attached must be taken as defining an ensemble, and second, the values of the bound variable must be taken to be parts of that ensemble (here, subsets of a set) rather than individuals. Otherwise preserving the analysis of chapters 4 and 6, we would then analyze 14.2.8*a* as 14.2.8*b*:

14.2.8　　a. All politicians are crooks.
　　　　　　b. (All M: politician″(M))crook″(M).

I have used double primes to indicate typographically that the predicates in the formula are different from those that we have hitherto used as translations of *politician* and *crook*; they are related to the earlier predicates as follows:

14.2.9   politician″(M) if and only if $(\forall x\colon x\varepsilon M)$politician′$(x)$.

That is, politician″ holds of a set if and only if politician′ holds of all the members of that set. The truth conditions for 14.2.8*b* suggested here agree with those of chapter 6: every set of politicians is a set of crooks if and only if every politician is a crook.

Bunt notes that a distinction parallel to that between count nouns and mass nouns can be made in predicate adjectives:

14.2.10   a. Count adjectives
                     This blanket is warm. (in the sense: 'keeps one warm')
                     This apple is red.
                     The ladder is long.

             b. Mass adjectives
                     This soup is warm.
                     This ink is red.
                     The ladder is wooden.

Mass predicates, whether nouns or adjectives, have the property of being DISTRIBUTIVE: a proposition with a mass predicate implies corresponding propositions about nonempty parts of what is denoted by the subject; for example, if this soup is warm, then any spoonful of it is warm, and if this ink is red, then any drop of it is red.[13] By contrast, count predicates are generally not distributive; for example, if this blanket is warm, it need not be the case that every 6-inch square of it is warm, and if this apple is red, it need not be the case that its core is red. Mass predicates are also CUMULATIVE: if an entity is the union of parts, each of which the predicate is true of, then the predicate is true of that entity; for example, if every spoonful of the soup is warm, then the soup is warm. By contrast, count predicates are normally not cumulative; for example, this stack of books may be heavy even though every book in it is light. Count predicates express properties of entities as wholes; mass predicates express properties that are distributed homogeneously over an entity. I note here one important property of mass predicates that will prove of some importance later in this section, namely, that the negation of a mass predicate generally is not a mass predicate. Let yellow$_m(x)$ correspond to the mass sense of *yellow*, that is, yellow$_m(x)$ is true if and only if every part of x (not just the surface) is yellow. Let a be an object that has both red parts and yellow parts and let b be a yellow part of a. Then $\sim\text{yellow}_m(a)$ is true but $\sim\text{yellow}_m(b)$ is false. Thus $\sim\text{yellow}_m(x)$ is not distributive: it can apply to an object without applying to all parts (even to all 'sufficiently large' parts) of that object.

In the above discussion, I have spoken informally of the 'union' of two or more ensembles. Let us at this point be more specific about the operations that can be applied to construct ensembles out of ensembles. The union of two ensembles is the smallest ensemble of which both are parts:

14.2.11 $E_1 \subseteq E_1 \cup E_2,\ E_2 \subseteq E_1 \cup E_2$
$(\forall z) \supset (\wedge(E_1 \subseteq z,\ E_2 \subseteq z),\ E_1 \cup E_2 \subseteq z).$

More generally, if E is a set whose members are ensembles, $\cup E$ is the smallest ensemble containing each of the members of E as parts; that is, the parts of $\cup E$ are entities composed of parts of one or more members of E. (In the case treated in 14.2.11, E is $\{E_1, E_2\}$.) Similarly, for any set of ensembles there is an ensemble (the INTERSECTION) whose parts are those entities that are parts of all members of the set. Bunt's postulates for ensemble theory imply that every nonempty set of ensembles has a union and an intersection.

Let us now consider how we can extend to ensembles the device that we have for using a predicate to define a subset of a given set, that is, analogues to $\{x \in M : P(x)\}$, which defines the set of all members of M that have the property P. There are two distinct and nonequivalent ways in which we could do this: we might take the ensemble-theoretic analogue to the union to be the minimal ensemble containing all parts of the given ensemble that have the given property 14.2.12a, or we might take it to be the maximal part of the given ensemble such that all of its parts have the given property 14.2.12b:

14.2.12   a. If $y \subseteq E$ and $P(y)$, then $y \subseteq \{x \subseteq E : P(x)\}$;
$\{x \subseteq E : P(x)\}$ is minimal: if $(\forall x : \wedge(x \subseteq E, P(x))(x \subseteq z)$, then $\{x \subseteq E : P(x)\} \subseteq z$.
b. if $y \subseteq /x \subseteq E : P(x)/$, then $P(y)$;
$/x \subseteq E : P(x)/$ is maximal: if $(\forall x : x \subseteq z)P(x)$, then $z \subseteq /x \subseteq E : P(x)/$.

Note that we cannot simply form an entity having as parts all parts of E that have the property P, since such an entity need not be an ensemble (for example, the union of two parts having P might not have P, as would be the case if P is 'weighs 1 gram', whereas the union of two parts of an ensemble must itself be part of the ensemble). For every E and P there is a unique $\{x \subseteq E : P(x)\}$, but not all parts of that ensemble need have the property P. There need not be a unique $/x \subseteq E : P(x)/$: if P is not cumulative, there may be many equally maximal parts of E that have P. Bunt's axioms for ensemble theory imply that any two ensembles E_1 and E_2 have a unique 'difference' $E_1 - E_2$: a maximal part of E_1 whose intersection with E_2 is empty. If P is not distributive, then an entity whose parts are those parts of E having P may fail to be an ensemble, since E_1 and E_2 could have P without $E_1 - E_2$ having it (e.g., E_1 and E_2 might weigh 1 gram and $E_1 - E_2$ weigh only 0.2 grams). However, if P is a mass predicate, that is, is both distributive and cumulative, then $\{x \subseteq E: P(x)\}$ and $/x \subseteq E: P(x)/$ coincide and have as parts precisely those parts of E that have the property P.

To provide an analysis in which *many* and *much* come out semantically identical, as it was proposed earlier in this section that they are, it will be necessary to revise slightly the analysis of *many* sketched in 14.1. If 14.2.13*a* and 14.2.13*b* are to have fully parallel analyses and if *black* in 14.2.13*a* is to correspond to a predicate that is predicated of ensembles, then *insane* in 14.2.13*b* will have to be predicated not of individuals but of ensembles, that is, in this case the relevant values will be not linguists but subsets of the set of all linguists:

14.2.13   a. Much coal is black.
            b. Many linguists are insane.

Thus, using the notation introduced in 14.2.9, *insane* will be rendered not as insane$'(x)$ but as insane$''(M)$, where insane$''(M)$ is true if and only if insane$'(x)$ is true for all x that are members of M. Thus we can tentatively represent the logical structures of 14.2.13*a*–*b* as

14.2.14   a. $(\exists M: \wedge (coal(M), large(M)))black(M)$
            b. $(\exists M: \wedge (linguist''(M), large(M)))insane''(M)$

('Large' here is the count predicate that attributes great size to an ensemble; thus 14.2.14*b* must be interpreted 'There is a large set of linguists ...', not as 'There is a set of large linguists ...'.)

Let us now see whether the analysis of *most* as 'not many not' that was sketched in 14.1 can be revised so as to be applicable to combinations of *most* with a mass term. The most direct analogue to that proposal would be an analysis in which 14.2.15*a* is rendered as 14.2.15*b*:

14.2.15   a. Most gold is yellow.
            b. $\sim(\exists E: \wedge (gold(E), large(E)))\sim yellow(E)$.

Under the most obvious interpretation of the predicates (in particular, the interpretation of 'yellow' as a mass predicate—an ensemble will have the property 'yellow' if and only if all its parts are yellow), 14.2.15*b* can be false for irrelevant reasons. If there is a large ensemble E_1 of gold that is yellow and a nonempty ensemble E_2 of gold that is not yellow, then $\sim yellow(E_1 \cup E_2)$ will be true, $E_1 \cup E_2$ will be large (I assume that an ensemble having a large ensemble as a part must itself be large), and hence 14.2.15*b* will be false by virtue of the existence of a large ensemble of gold (namely, $E_1 \cup E_2$) that has the property $\sim$yellow(E). This would have the catastrophic consequence that *Most gold is yellow* would have the same truth conditions as *All gold is yellow*: both would be false as long as there is any nonyellow gold. The closest variant of 14.2.15*b* that would be free of this defect would be a formula that involved not the negation of yellow(E) but a mass predicate corresponding to 'not yellow', that is, a predicate that was true of an ensemble if and only if no part of the ensemble was yellow. Let us introduce an operator N, referred to as 'mass negation', defined by

14.2.16   (NF)(E) if and only if $(\forall E': \wedge (E'$ nonempty, $E' \subseteq E)) \sim F(E')$.

That is, (NF)(E) if and only if no nonempty part of E has the property F. It can be proven that if F is distributive, then NF is distributive and cumulative. The analyses of sentences with *most* would then have to be as follows if *most* is to combine in the same way with count terms as with mass terms:

14.2.17   a. Most gold is yellow.
            a'. $\sim(\exists E: \wedge(gold(E), large(E)))$ (Nyellow)(E)
            b. Most linguists are insane.
            b'. $\sim(\exists E: \wedge(linguist''(E), large(E)))$ (Ninsane'')(E)

The truth conditions for 14.2.17*a'* seem to fit 14.2.17*a*, for 14.2.17*a'* will be true if and only if there is no large ensemble of gold, all of whose parts are nonyellow, that is, there is no large uniformly nonyellow ensemble of gold. The truth conditions for 14.2.17*b'* also fit 14.2.17*b* and agree with those of the analysis of 14.1: (Ninsane'')(E) is true if and only if no member of E is insane, that is, all members of E are sane, and thus 14.2.17*b'* is true if and only if there is no large set of linguists who are all sane.

14.3. Generic Sentences

The term 'generic' is often applied to sentences such as the following:

14.3.1   a. Bears hibernate in caves.
            b. A dog has four legs.
            c. The dodo is extinct.
            c'. Cockroaches are widespread.
            d. Fido chases cars.

In each example there are one or more NP's (*bears, caves, a dog, the dodo, cockroaches, cars*) that can be said to be 'used generically', and it is common to see analyses in which generic sentences are analyzed as having logical structures in which one of those NP's has a universal or near-universal quantifier or the 'sort of universal' quantifier *most*.

It should be noted at the outset that the different kinds of 'generic NP' differ semantically from one another and that none of them is adequately represented as involving universal, near-universal, or 'sort of universal' quantification. First, *caves* in 14.3.1*a* and *cars* in 14.3.1*d* cannot be analyzed as involving such quantifiers, since 14.3.1*a* does not imply that all or most or even very many caves ever have bears hibernating in them: 14.3.1*a* could express a true proposition even if only one cave in every thousand has ever been used as a hibernation site by a bear; and 14.3.1*d* can be true even if Fido has only chased a hundred or so of the hundreds of millions of existing cars.[14]

Second, 'counterexamples' falsify universal propositions but not generic propositions: if there is a bear, Waldo, who does not hibernate in caves, then *All bears hibernate in caves* is false even though 14.3.1*a* may be true. Similarly, a freak dog that had a fifth leg or only three legs would make *All dogs have four legs* false but would not show that 14.3.1*b* was false. Even near-universal and 'sort of universal' propositions have different truth conditions from generics. For example, Carlson notes that sentences such as 14.3.2 can be true even if the corresponding sentences with *most* or *almost all* are false:

14.3.2   a. Sea turtles lay approximately two hundred eggs at a time.
            b. Dutchmen are good sailors.[15]
            c. Horses were first ridden by the Egyptians.

Only female sea turtles lay eggs, and if male sea turtles outnumber females, *Most sea turtles lay approximately two hundred eggs at a time* is false even though 14.3.2*a* is true. Most Dutchmen are not sailors at all and thus are not good sailors, but that fact does not prevent 14.3.2*b* from being true. Most horses have never been ridden by Egyptians, and yet 14.3.2*c* may well be true.

Third, the universal or near-universal analogue to a generic sentence may not even be semantically coherent, let alone logically equivalent to it. For example, *All dodos are extinct* makes no sense: only a species can be extinct, not an individual member of that species. Likewise, *All cockroaches are widespread* makes no sense: the species is widespread, but Archie, an individual member of the species, is not widespread, even if he gets around a lot.

The plural generic and the definite generic can be used, as in 14.3.1*c–c'*, to refer to properties of a species as whole, whereas the indefinite singular generic can be used only with reference to properties that characterize members of the species:

14.3.3   a. *A dodo is extinct.
           b. *A cockroach is widespread.

The indefinite plural generic and the indefinite singular generic can be used for kinds that are defined by pretty much any combinations of properties, whereas the definite generic requires that the referent be a 'natural' kind:

14.3.4   a. A bed that was slept in by George Washington is easy to find.
           b. Beds that were slept in by George Washington are easy to find.
           c. *The bed that was slept in by George Washington is easy to find. (OK only if it refers to a specific bed and is thus nongeneric).

Carlson lavishes attention on the indefinite plural generic, the most frequent of the three constructions and also the one that appears to be the least uniform in its semantic interpretation. He argues that indefinite plural generics are basically references to KINDS rather than to objects or sets of objects and that they often appear to make reference to objects only because many properties of kinds are derivatives of properties of the members of the kind. The central idea of Carlson's approach is to distinguish predicates with regard to whether they are basically predicated of kinds, of individuals, or of 'stages' (this term will be explained below) and to provide rules whereby under certain circumstances derived predicates can be formed that are predicated of a different type of things. For example, *run* is basically predicated of 'stages', but there is also a derived usage in which it is predicated of individuals, as in the habitual present *Fido runs* (not the 'narrative present' that appears in an on-the-spot report by a radio announcer, in which *run* is predicated of a 'stage'), as well as a derived usage in which it is predicated of kinds, as in *Rabbits run* or *The rabbit runs*.

A 'stage' for Carlson is an instantiation of a kind or of an individual. For example, two hours worth of Fido (say, the two hours beginning at 4:37 P.M. Eastern Daylight time on 12 July 1971) is an instantiation of both the individual Fido and the kind 'dogs'. While there are predicates that are basically predicated of stages, there are no NP's that basically refer to stages. Thus predicates referring basically to stages must be combined with other semantic material that bridges the gap between kind and stage or between individual and stage. Carlson does this by having an individual subject not combine directly with a stage predicate like $\text{run}'(y)$ but rather combine with an expression like $(\exists y) \wedge (\text{R}(y, x), \text{run}'(y))$, where $\text{R}(y, x)$ means 'y is an instantiation of x'. I will adopt Carlson's practise of superscripting the first occurrence of a variable or a constant with s, i, or k to indicate whether it refers to a stage, an individual, or a kind; for example, the last formula would be written $(\exists y^s) \wedge (\text{R}(y, x^i), \text{run}'(y))$. (Note that y and y^s are thus 'the same symbol': the superscript is merely a reminder that the values of y are stages, and the reminder need not be repeated every time y recurs.) Omitting the intension signs that the Montague framework employed by Carlson, strictly speaking, calls for, we have the following translation:

14.3.5 $\text{barked}_{\text{event}} \Rightarrow (\lambda y^s)\text{bark}'(y)$
            $\text{Fido} \Rightarrow f^i$
            $\text{Fido barked} \Rightarrow (\lambda x^i)(\exists y^s) \wedge (\text{R}yx, \text{bark}'(y))\,(f)$
            $\quad \rightarrow (\exists y^s) \wedge (\text{R}yf, \text{bark}'(y))$

That is, there is a stage of Fido which barked. Carlson's approach has the happy consequence of providing an explanation of why indefinite plural NP's in certain sentences have an existential interpretation rather than the truly generic interpretation that is often mistaken for universal quantification, for example, *Dogs barked* can be interpreted as 'There was barking by (some) dogs'. For Carlson the translation is exactly parallel to that for *Fido barked*:

14.3.6 $\text{dogs} \Rightarrow d^k$
            $\text{Dogs barked} \Rightarrow (\lambda x^i)(\exists y^s) \wedge (\text{R}yx, \text{bark}'(y))\,(d)$
            $\quad \rightarrow (\exists y^s) \wedge (\text{R}yd, \text{bark}'(y))$

The application of λ-conversion in 14.3.6 is legitimate provided one allows d to serve as a value for x, which Carlson does, in accordance with his policy of of interpreting 'individual' in the broad sense in which kinds are a special case of individuals (and names of kinds are in effect proper names). The result in 14.3.6 implies that there were dogs barking, since stages of a kind are also stages of members (or of sets of members) of that kind.

The 'habitual' sense of *Fido barked* (likewise of *Dogs barked*) refers not to an event of barking but to a property of Fido (or of the kind 'dogs'), roughly, the property of (occasionally or normally) barking. Carlson treats the habitual VP as derived from the homophonous VP that is predicated of stages, via a rule that does nothing syntactically to the VP but has an appropriate semantic effect on it. If f is the translation of an event VP, then the translation of the corresponding habitual VP is $\text{G}(f)$, with G being of type $(t/e^i)/(t/e^s)$; that is, G converts predicates of stages into predicates of individuals. More specifically, since G is to be a function of a variable corresponding to the subject NP, the translation of *Fido barks* will have to be taken to be something like 14.3.7:

14.3.7 $\text{bark}_{\text{habit}} \Rightarrow (\lambda x^i)G(x, (\lambda y^s)\text{bark}'(y))$
Fido $\Rightarrow a$
Fido barks $\Rightarrow (\lambda x^i)G(x, (\lambda y^s)\text{bark}'(y))$ (a)
    $\rightarrow G(a, (\lambda y^s)\text{bark}'(y))$

In a full account of G, G will have to be analyzed as itself binding a variable that ranges over stages of the first argument, with the second argument evaluated at values of that variable (i.e., the relevant values of y are stages of Fido). For present purposes, however, let us take the analysis of G no further than in 14.3.7.

Carlson's approach provides an explanation of the fact that in sentences like *Foxes eat chickens*, *foxes* receives a true generic interpretation, whereas *chickens* has rather an 'existential' interpretation. *Eat*, being basically a predicate of stages will combine with $\exists$ and R as in 14.3.5 and 14.3.6:

14.3.8 $\text{eat}_{\text{event}}$ chickens $\Rightarrow (\lambda x^s)(\exists z^s) \wedge (Rzc, \text{eat}'(x, z))$

The habitual sense of *Foxes eat chickens* involves a VP that is predicated of individuals, derived from the VP of 14.3.8, which is predicated of stages:

14.3.9 $\text{eat}_{\text{habit}}$ chickens $\Rightarrow (\lambda w^i)G(w, (\lambda x^s)(\exists z^s) \wedge (Rzc, \text{eat}'(x, z)))$
Foxes eat chickens $\Rightarrow (\lambda w^i)G(w, (\lambda x^s)(\exists z^s) \wedge (Rzc, \text{eat}'(x, z)))$ (f)
    $\rightarrow G(f, (\lambda x^s)(\exists z^s) \wedge (Rzc, \text{eat}'(x, z)))$

Since the translation of the habitual VP is of the form (λw^i) . . . rather than (λw^s) . . ., we do not add $(\exists u^i) \wedge (Ruw, \ldots)$ in the translation of the sentence, and thus *foxes* is not given an 'existential' interpretation the way *dogs* was in 14.3.6. However, *chickens* receives an existential interpretation since the part of the translation that it figures in directly is the translation of the embedded event VP.

Generic clauses can involve either or both of two 'dimensions of generalization': one may be generalizing over time (as in *Fido barks*, which refers to barking by a single individual over a potentially long period of time) and/or individuals (as in *Dogs bark*, which refers to barking by what may be a huge set of dogs). Carlson's approach does not distinguish these two dimensions of generalization, with G binding a stage variable whose values may differ in their temporal location and/or. in the individual involved. For example, Carlson employs G in providing an explanation of why *Dogs are male or female* does not imply *Dogs are male or dogs are female*. For Carlson, *Dogs are male or female* involves G, and ∨ does not 'distribute over' G; that is, 14.3.10*a* does not imply 14.3.10*b*:

14.3.10   a. $G(d, (\lambda x) \vee (\text{male}'(x), \text{female}'(x)))$
         b. $\vee (G(d, (\lambda x)\text{male}'(x)), G(d, (\lambda y)\text{female}'(y)))$

The generalization in 14.3.10 is over individuals rather than (or besides) times.

Carlson leaves somewhat unclear how his treatment of generics will relate to questions of tense and time reference. The 'habitual' properties of an individual may change through time:

14.3.11   a. When I was in high school, I went to baseball games, but I don't go to baseball games nowadays.
         b. When he started practising surgery, Dr. Novotny performed lobotomies, but he doesn't perform them anymore.

Two possibilities suggest themselves as ways of accommodating this fact in Carlson's general approach: (i) we might continue to treat generic VP's as predicated of individuals, though allowing the clauses in question to take different truth values at different times; or (ii) we might take generic VP's to be predicated of entities intermediate in temporal extent between 'stages' and full-length individuals, that is, entities sufficiently extended to provide a domain for a stage variable to range over though not necessarily taking in the entire temporal compass of an individual. Either way, G would still bind a stage variable.

The evidence for the truth of a generic proposition, say, the proposition that Fido barks, would normally be instances of Fido barking during the period in question, in whatever number and under whatever circumstances it takes to establish that a property of Fido is being manifested in those events (for example, it takes far fewer instances of Dr. Novotny performing a lobotomy to establish that Dr. Novotny performs lobotomies than it takes instances of Dr. Novotny voting for Democrats to establish that Dr. Novotny votes for Democrats). The relationship of the habitual proposition to the instances is the epistemological relationship of a proposition to the evidence for it rather than any logical relationship such as that of a proposition to its logical consequences.

14.4. Branching Quantifiers

Certain bound variables are 'dependent on' others. For example, when 14.4.1*a* has the meaning that is representable as 14.4.1*b*, *y* depends on *x* in the sense that the value of *y* that makes '*x* have *y*' true will generally vary with *x*—14.4.1*b* tells you that for each person there is a fault *y* such that x has y, but it does not tell you that different persons have the same fault.

14.4.1   a. Every person has a fault.
          b. $(\forall: \text{person } x)_x(\exists: \text{fault } y)_y(x \text{ have } y)$

This dependency could be made explicit in the notation by, say, writing a subscript x on the variable y: .

14.4.2 $(\forall: \text{person } x)_x(\exists: \text{fault } y_x)_{y_x}(x \text{ have } y_x)$

If one enlarges one's formal language so as to countenance 'second-order' bound variables, that is, variables that range not over individuals but over functions or sets or predicates of individuals, one can propose something on the order of 14.4.3a, which I will informally abbreviate as 14.4.3b, as an alternative to 14.4.1b and 14.4.2:

14.4.3   a. $(\exists: (\forall: \text{person } z)_z(\text{fault } fz))_f (\forall: \text{person } x)_x(x \text{ have } fx)$
          b. $(\exists f: \text{person} \rightarrow \text{fault})(\forall: \text{person } x)(x \text{ have } fx)$

(The notation adopted here is a makeshift device to indicate that the values of f are functions that associate to every person a fault.)

    Note that this sort of dependency is possible only when an existential quantifier is in the scope of another quantifier. With a universal quantifier immediately below an existential quantifier, as in 14.4.4b, which expresses the meaning of 14.4.4a, there is no longer any dependency between variables:[16]

14.4.4   a. There is a fault that every person has.
          b. $(\exists: \text{fault } y)_y(\forall: \text{person } x)_x(x \text{ have } y)$

Example 14.4.4b corresponds to a very special instance of 14.4.3, namely, that in which the value of f that makes $(\forall: \text{person } x)(x \text{ have } fx)$ true is a constant function: a function that has the same value no matter what x is. Thus, 14.4.4b clearly implies 14.4.3 but 14.4.3 does not imply 14.4.4b; for example, if 1/3 of all people are miserly and stupid but neat, 1/3 are stupid and untidy but generous, and 1/3 are untidy and miserly but smart, and we treat only miserliness, stupidity, and untidiness as faults, then 14.4.3 is true but 14.4.4b is false.

    More complex dependencies are possible in logical structures that involve more complicated sequences of quantifiers. Consider, for example, 14.4.5a in the interpretation that is representable as 14.4.5b:

14.4.5   a. Every day a senator told every newspaper about a crooked judge.
          b. $(\forall: \text{day } x)_x(\exists: \text{senator } y)_y(\forall: \text{newspaper } z)_z(\exists: \text{crooked judge } u)_u(y \text{ told } z \text{ about } u \text{ on } x)$

Here u depends on both z and x: on each day a different senator may well have been talking to the press, and on any given day a talkative senator may have told each newspaper about a different judge, with each paper learning about a different judge from the one it has been told about the day before by another senator.[17] The result of recasting 14.4.5b in a form comparable to 14.4.3b would be 14.4.6:

14.4.6   ($\exists f$: day $\rightarrow$ senator)($\exists g$: (day, newspaper) $\rightarrow$ crooked judge)
        ($\forall$: day x)($\forall$: newspaper z)(fx tell z about $g(x,z)$ on x).

Suppose, however, that we wanted to set up a logical structure with different dependencies from those in 14.4.5b, say, a logical structure in which the value of the judge u that exemplifies 'y told z about u on x' for given x and z depended only on z and not on x (i.e., for each newspaper there would be a judge that it would be hearing about every day, though not always from the same senator, and without necessarily only that judge being denounced on any day). Using the expressive framework of 14.4.6, this is no problem: the second existential quantifier would simply bind a function of one variable rather than of two, and the 'matrix' would be 'fx tell z about gz on x'.

Can this dependency among the variables be expressed using only first-order predicate logic, as in 14.4.5b? In important but largely neglected work by Henkin, Ehrenfeucht, and Walkoe, the significance of which is pointed out in Hintikka 1974, it is shown that the general question of which this is an instance has negative answer: there is no formula of first-order predicate logic that is systematically equivalent to 14.4.7:

14.4.7   ($\exists f$)($\exists g$)($\forall x$)($\forall z$)F(x, fx, z, gz)

Hintikka argues that there are natural language sentences involving bound variables whose dependencies are of a type not expressible in first-order logic. He points out that 14.4.8a (the simplest such example that he has been able to construct) cannot be adequately analyzed with a formula such as 14.4.8b, since in the situation in which the only hatred in the population is that the eldest relative of each villager$_i$ and the relative$_j$ of each townsman who$_j$ knows the villager$_i$ best hate each other, 14.4.8b will be true and 14.4.8a false:

14.4.8   a. Some relative of each villager and some relative of each
                townsman hate each other.
        b. ($\forall$: villager x)$_x$($\exists$: relative y x)$_y$($\forall$: townsman z)$_z$($\exists$: relative
                u z)$_u$ (y and u hate each other)

In 14.4.8b, u is allowed to be dependent on x, as in the state of affairs just described, where each villager could perfectly well have different relatives

450   14. Further Topics in Quantification

who stood in a relationship of mutual hatred with different relatives of each
townsman. Hintikka claims (correctly, I think, though my judgment
wavers) that in that state of affairs, 14.4.8a is false in its most natural
interpretation. Note the difference between the second-order formulas
corresponding to 14.4.8a and to 14.4.8b:

14.4.9   a. $(\exists f: \text{villager}_x \to \text{relative of } x)(\exists g: \text{townsman}_y \to \text{relative of } y)$
                  $(\forall: \text{villager } x)(\forall: \text{townsman } y)(fx \text{ and } gy \text{ hate each other})$
              b. $(\exists f: \text{villager}_x \to \text{relative of } x)(\exists g: (\text{villager}_x, \text{townsman}_y) \to$
                  $\text{relative of } y) (\forall: \text{villager } x)(\forall: \text{townsman } y)(fx \text{ and } gxy$
                  hate each other)

Hintikka (1974) elaborates on a proposal by Henkin (1950) that
extends the combinatory possibilities of first-order quantifiers in such a
way as to match the expressive power of second-order quantifiers.
Specifically, Henkin proposed an enlarged conception of logical structure
in which logical structures need not be trees—he allowed distinct chains of
quantifiers to be combined with a single 'matrix', in structures representable by formulas such as 14.4.10a or 'convergent' graphs such as 14.4.10b:

14.4.10   a.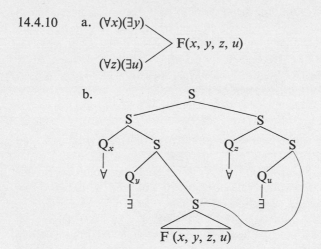

The command relations among the quantifiers in the graph indicate the
potential dependencies among the variables, for example, from inspection
of 14.4.10b one can tell that y is dependent on x but not on z or u and that
u is dependent on z but not on x or y.

The semantics that Hintikka provides for expressions like those in
14.4.10 is a version of the 'game semantics' that he has developed in
various publications (e.g., Hintikka 1973). He defines truth and validity in

terms of strategies in a game in which the goal of one player (referred to by Hintikka as 'me') is to make the game end with a true atomic proposition and the goal of his opponent (whom Hintikka calls 'Nature') is to make it end with a false atomic proposition. The game can be illustrated with the rules for $\wedge$ and $\vee$:

14.4.11   a. If the formula on which the game is being played is $\vee AB$, then it is my move and I must pick either A or B as the formula on which play will continue.
            b. If the formula on which the game is being played is $\wedge AB$, then it is Nature's move and Nature must pick either A or B as the formula on which play will continue.

Suppose that p and q are true and r is false and that Nature and I are given $\wedge(p, \vee qr)$ to play with. Since the formula is an *and*-conjunction, it is Nature's move and Nature picks $\vee qr$ (if Nature had picked p, the game would be over and I would have won, since p is true). It is now my move and I pick q, which makes me the winner, since q is true. The proposition is true in the given state of affairs if there is a set of moves by me that insures that I will win regardless of what moves Nature makes.

Hintikka's rules for quantifiers are as follows:

14.4.12   a. If the formula on which the game is being played is $(\exists x)Fx$, it is my move and I must pick an individual a; the game continues with Fa as the formula.
            b. If the formula on which the game is being played is $(\forall x)Fx$, it is Nature's move and Nature must pick an individual a; the game continues with Fa as the formula.

Regardless of who (me or Nature) is to do something with a quantified formula, his move is to replace it by a formula with a constant in place of the bound variable. What constant he picks will depend on what his goal is: I will attempt to pick one that makes the matrix true and Nature will attempt to pick one that makes it false. The reason that 14.4.12*a* and 14.4.12*b* provide the basis for a reasonable semantic analysis of quantifiers is that both the truth of an existential proposition and the falsehood of a universal proposition can be established by giving an example. The additional rules of the game are such that if we are given a formula $(\exists x)Fx$ and I am able to find a constant a such that Fa is true, given complete knowledge of what atomic propositions are true, then I am guaranteed to win the game regardless of what Nature does; and if we are given a formula $(\forall x)Fx$ and Nature is able to find a constant a such that Fa is false, then I am guaranteed to lose the game to Nature regardless of what I do subsequently.

Hintikka's treatment of quantification is in terms of unrestricted quantification. In a trivial fashion one can replace the rules 14.4.12 by corresponding rules for restricted quantifiers:

14.4.13   a. If the formula on which the game is being played is ($\exists$: Fx)Gx, it is my move and I must pick an individual a; the game continues with $\land$ (Fa, Ga) as the formula.
            b. If the formula on which the game is being played is ($\forall$: Fx)Gx, it is Nature's move and Nature must pick an individual a; the game continues with $\supset$ (Fa, Ga) as the formula.

These rules are of course modeled on the standard ploy for avoiding restricted quantification. No doubt a more satisfactory alternative to 14.4.13 could be found in which the rules for quantified propositions involve first setting up a subgame played on Fa and a subsequent game played on Ga; however, I will not work out such a revision here, since my only concern at this point is to establish that Hintikka's treatment can be carried out in terms of restricted as well as unrestricted quantifiers.

In the case of an ordinary formula such as 14.4.9, the sequence of moves in the game is unproblematic: Nature picks a villager to substitute for x, then I pick a relative of that villager to substitute for y, then Nature picks a townsman to substitute for z (NB: in picking the townsman, Nature has full knowledge of what relative of the villager I have picked and can use that knowledge in making his choice of the townsman), and then I pick a relative of that townsman (with full knowledge of the preceding three choices). In the case of formulas with branching quantifiers such as 14.4.10a, Hintikka takes the moves as given by 14.4.12, but with each move made without any knowledge of moves involving the other branch. Thus, in 14.4.10a Nature has to pick values for x and z and I have to pick values for y and u; in picking my value for u I know what value Nature has picked for z but not what he has picked for x, and in picking my value for y I know what value Nature has picked for x but not what he has picked for z. (Here the metaphor has become a bit muddled—it sounds as if I acquire knowledge about both of Nature's moves but forget one piece of information before I make each of my moves; it might be better to speak of me and Nature as teams: I have one player on the upper branch and one on the lower branch, and each of them knows what the Nature player on his own branch has done but not what the Nature player on the other branch has done). To win playing on 14.4.10a, I have to pick a value of y

that will make $F(x, y, z, u)$ true regardless of what value Nature has picked for z, and a value of u that will make $F(x, y, z, u)$ true regardless of what value Nature has picked for x. This fits quite well what Hintikka claims to be the normal interpretation of 14.4.8. The 'second-order' version of 14.4.10a can be taken as providing the basis of a strategy for me to win the game:

14.4.14 $(\exists f)(\exists g)(\forall x)(\forall z)F(x, fx, z, gz)$

If I know the functions f and g, then whatever value a that Nature picks for x, I can pick fa as the value for y, and whatever value b that Nature picks for z, I can pick gb as the value for u. Since these choices of y and u make $F(x, y, z, u)$ true if anything does, if I can win the game at all I can win it by making those moves.

   Hintikka points out that the number of branches in structures like 14.4.10a can be arbitrarily large. For example, 14.4.15a would have a three-branch logical structure 14.4.15b, and the addition of extra conjuncts could increase the number of branches without limit:

14.4.15   a. Each player on every baseball team has a fan, each actress
                in every musical has an admirer, and each aide of every
                senator has a friend who are cousins.

            b.

$(\forall: \text{ballteam } x_1)_{x_1}$ $(\forall: \text{player } x_2\, x_1)_{x_2}$ $(\exists: \text{fan } x_3\, x_2)_{x_3}$

$(\forall: \text{musical } y_1)_{y_1}$ $(\forall: y_2 \text{ actress in } y_1)_{y_2}$ $(\exists: \text{admirer } y_3\, y_2)_{y_3}$ $(x_3, y_3, z_3$ are cousins)

$(\forall: \text{senator } z_1)_{z_1}$ $(\forall: z_2 \text{ aide of } z_1)_{z_2}$ $(\exists: \text{friend } z_3\, z_2)_{z_3}$

Noting that Walkoe has shown that every formula of predicate logic with branching quantifiers is equivalent to one of the form 14.4.16, Hintikka remarks that the existence of the class of sentences illustrated by 14.4.15a shows that English provides the full expressive power of predicate logic with branching quantifiers:

14.4.16 $(\forall x_1)(\forall x_2)(\exists x_3)$
           $(\forall y_1)(\forall y_2)(\exists y_3)$ $\quad F(x_1, x_2, x_3, y_1, y_2, y_3, \ldots, u_1, u_2, u_3)$
           $\cdots$
           $(\forall u_1)(\forall u_2)(\exists u_3)$

   In certain cases a formula with branching quantifiers is equivalent to a formula with nonbranching quantifiers. For example, any formula of the form 14.4.17a has an equivalent nonbranching formula 14.4.17b, in view of the fact that when the existential quantifiers precede the universal quantifiers, the variables bound by the latter are not dependent on those bound by the former:[18]

14.4.17   a. $(\exists x_1)(\exists x_2) \ldots (\exists x_m)$
              $(\forall y_1)(\forall y_2) \ldots (\forall y_n)$ $\Big\rangle F(x_1, x_2, \ldots, x_m, y_1, y_2, \ldots, y_n)$

           b. $(\exists x_1)(\exists x_2) \ldots (\exists x_m)(\forall y_1)(\forall y_2) \ldots (\forall y_n)$
              $F(x_1, x_2, \ldots, x_m, y_1, y_2, \ldots, y_n)$

In addition, whether a sentence demands an analysis involving branching quantifiers can depend on details of the analysis of things other than overtly quantified NP's. For example, whether a sentence such as 14.4.18a demands an analysis with branching quantifiers as in 14.4.18b depends on how one analyzes the comparative construction, since an analysis in terms of an 'extent' variable allows 14.4.18a to be analyzed as in 14.4.18c:

14.4.18   a. Every writer likes some book he has written almost as much as every actress dislikes some director she has worked with.

           b.
           $(\forall: \text{writer } x)_x(\exists: \wedge (\text{book } y, x \text{ wrote } y))_y$
           $(\forall: \text{actress } z)_z(\exists: \wedge (\text{director } u,$
              $z \text{ worked worked with } u))_u$ $\Big\rangle$ $(x \text{ dislikes } y \text{ almost as much as } z \text{ dislikes } u)$

           c. $(\exists: \text{extent } e) \wedge [(\forall: \text{writer } x)(\exists: \wedge (\text{book } y, x \text{ wrote } y))(x \text{ likes } y \text{ almost to extent } e), (\forall: \text{actress } z)(\exists: \wedge (\text{director } u, z \text{ worked with } u)(z \text{ dislikes } u \text{ to extent } e)]$

The analysis in 14.4.18c allows the two pairs of quantified variables to be in separate conjuncts of a coordinate structure and thus independent of each other.

Hintikka has suggested that a logical structure in terms of branching quantifiers may be appropriate even in cases where an equivalent structure without branching is available. While his discussion (1974: 169–70) does not contain any explicit generalization, Hintikka appears to take the position that bound variables (perhaps just those bound by certain quantifiers) will be independent of other variables whenever possible, for example, the reason why the most normal interpretation of 14.4.19a appears to be 14.4.19b is that the most normal interpretation is really the one in which the variables are maximally independent, that is, 14.4.19*c*, and 14.4.19*c* happens to be equivalent to 14.4.19*b*:

14.4.19   a. John has shown all of his paintings to some of his friends.
          b. $(\exists\colon \text{friend } x\, j)_x(\forall\colon y \text{ painting by } j)_y(j \text{ has shown } y \text{ to } x)$
          c. $(\exists\colon \text{friend } x\, j)_x$ ⟶
             $(\forall\colon y \text{ painting by } j)_y$ ⟶ $(j \text{ has shown } y \text{ to } x)$

Hintikka also suggests that sentences with multiple 'nonstandard' quantifiers (i.e., quantifiers such as *many* or *five*, which are not translatable simply as $\forall$ or as $\exists$) have extra interpretations that are representable as branching quantifier structures but not as structures with one of the quantifiers in the scope of the other(s). For example, recall the extra interpretation of 14.4.20 that we simply ignored in 4.2. the one in which there was dancing involving most of the boys and most of the girls, without any boy necessarily having danced with most of the girls or any girl having danced with most of the boys:

14.4.20   Most of the boys danced with most of the girls.

Hintikka's discussion of similar examples suggests that he would analyze that reading of 14.4.20 as having a branching quantifier structure in which the two bound variables are independent. To say exactly what that structure is, one would have to say something about the semantics of plural NP's, since the propositional function in this case would presumably have to correspond not to 'he danced with her' but to 'they danced with them' (i.e., the sentence does not say that there is a set consisting of most of the boys and a set consisting of most of the girls, such that each boy in the former set danced with each girl in the latter set—only that the boys in the former set all danced with girls in the latter set and that the girls in the latter set all danced with boys in the former set). Until a specific analysis of plural NP's is settled on, it will not be clear that a branching quantifier analysis has any advantage over a nonbranching analysis of the extra reading of 14.4.20. But it is clear that the bound variables in that reading are independent and thus that a branching structure will work if any nonbranching structure does.

Hintikka and Saarinen (1975) apply game semantics and branching quantifiers to Bach-Peters sentences. They maintain that Bach-Peters sentences have a reading other than the two with which Karttunen was concerned[19] and that that reading is naturally representable as a branching quantifier structure in which the variables bound by the two complex definite description operators are independent. The structure that they propose for 14.4.21*a* has the interesting property that it is not expressible as a coherent combination (branching or not) of restricted quantifiers (i.e., of expressions in terms of ι), namely, 14.4.21b, in which the quantifiers of Russell's formulas have been separated out and applied to a matrix made up of the residues of two Russellian formulas:[20]

14.4.21   a. The boy who was fooling her kissed the girl who loved him.

b.

$(\exists x)(\forall y)$
$\wedge [\wedge (x$ boy who was fooling $z, \supset (\sim = yx, \sim (y$ boy who was fooling
$(\exists z)(\forall u)$ $\wedge (z$ girl who loved $x, \supset (\sim = uz, \sim (u$ girl who loved $x)), (x$ kissed y

Playing Hintikka's game on this expression, I will be sure of winning if and only if I can find two individuals a and b such that a is a boy, a was fooling b, no other boy was fooling b, b is a girl, b loved a, no other girl loved a, and a kissed b. Note that since here (by contrast with 14.4.10, 14.4.15, and 14.4.18), the outermost quantifiers in both branches are existential, I get to make both of my moves before Nature makes either of his. If I have picked a and b so as to meet the conditions just listed, then I will win regardless of what values of y and u Nature picks. This means that the states of affairs in which I can be sure of winning are those containing one or more pairs of a boy and a girl such that he and no other boy was fooling her, she and no other girl loved him, and he kissed her. Interestingly, as Hintikka and Saarinen point out, there need not be only one such pair: as long as there is at least one pair, regardless of whether there are any others, I can pick that boy and girl as my values for x and z and be sure of winning, and thus the formula 14.4.21b will be true in that state of affairs. The question now arises, does 14.4.21a in fact have an interpretation in which it is true if there are one OR MORE such boy-girl pairs? This question is difficult to answer, in view of the fact that cooperativity would normally demand that one use the sentence to pick out one specific boy-girl pair. The best domain in which to look for evidence regarding whether the definite descriptions allow that interpretation is probably sentences in which 14.4.21a is embedded in a negative or conditional superstructure, for example,

14.4.22   a. If the boy who is fooling her kisses the girl who loves him, I'll scream.
        b. I doubt that the boy who was fooling her kissed the girl who loved him.

In a state of affairs in which there are several boy-fooling-loving-girl pairs, can one use 14.4.22a to state that one will scream if the boy of ANY of these pairs kisses the girl? At the moment of writing this, I think I would answer affirmatively, but my judgment here is very shaky.

14.5. Quantifiers with Multiple Variables

Logicians and mathematicians occasionally use, at least as an informal device, formulas in which a single quantifier binds two or more variables, for example,

14.5.1 $(\exists x, y)f(x, y)$

In a system of unrestricted quantification, such formulas can always be interpreted as abbreviations of formulas having multiple occurrences of the quantifier; for example, 14.5.1 would be an informal abbreviation of 14.5.2:

14.5.2 $(\exists x)(\exists y)f(x, y)$

However, in a system of restricted quantification, there are formulas in which a 'double quantifier' expression cannot be regarded as standing for a sequence of single quantifier expressions. Moreover, there are English sentences for which a formula involving a double quantifier appears to be the most plausible analysis, for example, Perlmutter and Ross's (1970) sentence 14.5.3a, to which I assign the logical structure 14.5.3b:

14.5.3   a. A man entered and a woman left who had met in Vienna.
            b. $(\exists: \wedge(\wedge(\text{man } x, \text{ woman } y), x \text{ and } y \text{ met in Vienna}))_{x,y}$
               $\wedge(x \text{ entered}, y \text{ left})$

The problem presented by 14.5.3a is that of accommodating the relative clause, which involves both bound variables. I know of only one alternative to an analysis with a double quantifier, namely, an analysis that arbitrarily combines the relative clause with one of the two nouns, as in 14.5.4a, a formula which, however, corresponds more directly to 14.5.4b than to 14.5.3a:

14.5.4   a. $(\exists: \text{man } x)_x(\exists: \wedge(\text{woman } y, x \text{ and } y \text{ met in Vienna}))_y$
               $\wedge(x \text{ entered}, y \text{ left})$
            b. A man entered and a woman such that he and she had met in Vienna left.

I regard 14.5.4a as unacceptable as the logical structure of 14.5.3a, since the relative clause in 14.5.3a clearly modifies *a man* and *a woman* jointly rather than just one of them.

Sentences like 14.5.4b can also be given an analysis with a quantifier that binds more than one variable:[21]

14.5.5   a. Two linguists and three sociologists who had met at a conference on graffiti were among those arrested.
            b. $(\exists: \wedge(\wedge(\text{M is two linguists, N is three sociologists}), \text{M}\cup\text{N}$
               $\text{met at a conference on graffiti})_{M, N} (\forall: x{\in}\text{M}\cup\text{N})(x \text{ was}$
               among those arrested)

A slightly different analysis of these sentences was suggested in 14.1, namely, one in which there was an extra bound variable: the analysis in 14.1 corresponded to 'there is a set having a subset of two linguists and a subset of three sociologists such that that set met at a conference on graffiti . . .', whereas 14.5.5*b* corresponds to 'there are a set of two linguists and a set of three sociologists such that the union (of the two sets) met at a conference on graffiti . . .'. I consider the latter analysis superior to the former since it is the only one of the two that can be adapted to sentences such as 14.5.3*a* and 14.5.6*a*–*b*:[22]

14.5.6   a. Two linguists were chanting and three sociologists were shouting the same slogan.

a'. ($\exists$: slogan x)($\exists$: $\land$ (M is two linguists, N is three sociologists))$_{\text{M, N}}$ $\land$ (M was chanting x, N was shouting x)

b. Tom bought and Dick sold securities totalling over a million dollars in value.

b'. ($\exists$: $\land$ ($\land$ (securities x, securities y), x and y total over a million dollars in value))$_{x, y}$ $\land$ (Tom bought x, Dick sold y)

The examples given so far of double quantifiers have all involved double existential quantifiers. Examples that require a double universal quantifier are much harder to construct. The best examples that I have been able to devise are fairly marginal sentences such as 14.5.7*a*, which, according to the analysis sketched above, ought to express the logical form 14.5.7*b*:

14.5.7   a. ?Every man wore a gaudy shirt and every woman wore a matching blouse who were partners in the dance marathon.

b. ($\forall$: $\land$ ($\land$ (man x, woman y), x and y were partners in the dance marathon)) $\land$ (x wore a gaudy shirt, y wore a matching blouse)

It is much easier to construct examples where a definite description operator binds multiple variables:

14.5.8   a. The man entered and the woman left who had met in Vienna.

b. (ι x, y: $\land$ ($\land$ (man x, woman y), x and y met in Vienna)) $\land$ (x entered, y left)

A particularly interesting type of sentence whose logical structure involves a definite description operator binding several variables is discussed by Lakoff (1972*a*: 644–45), who notes that 14.5.9*a* has multiple occurrences not only of *the* but also of *usual*, corresponding to a logical structure in which those items are represented only once each:[23]

14.5.9   a. The usual men were talking to the usual women about the usual subjects.

          b. $(\iota\, x, y, z: \wedge(\wedge(\text{man } x, \text{woman } y, \text{subject } z), \text{usual}(x \text{ talk to } y \text{ about } z))$ $(x$ was talking to y about $z)$

14.6. Exercises

1. Can *all presidents but Washington, Cleveland, and Ford* be analyzed along lines close to the analysis of *all but three presidents* given in this chapter? If so, show how; if not, show why not. Discuss not only the logical form of the relevant examples but also their derivations.

2. Show that the different readings of *Two linguists reviewed three books* (one reading where *two linguists* has higher scope than *three books*, one where it has lower scope) have different truth conditions.

3. The examples of near-universal quantifiers given in this chapter have all involved the word *all* (*all but two, almost all*, etc.). To what extent can near-universal quantifiers be formed from *every, any,* and *each*? Are the facts predictable from what was said in chapter 4 about the differences among *each, every, any,* and *all*?

4. Find examples of predicates that are distributive but not cumulative and of predicates that are cumulative but not distributive.

5. Give logical structures for the following sentences according to the proposals of 14.5:

    a. A linguist and an anthropologist that had met in Salzburg were respectively whistling and humming "Dixie".
    b. Two friends and three relatives of each senator were on the senate payroll.

Treat *meet* as taking a set subject (thus, *a* should involve a constituent 'M met in Salzburg'), and treat *respectively* constructions as derived by a generalized form of conjunction reduction, as in

Tom was whistling 'Dixie' and Dick was humming 'Dixie' →
Tom and Dick were respectively whistling and humming 'Dixie'.

6. Sketch how the rules of inference of chapter 4 might be restated so that they would cover quantifiers that bind two or more variables.

Notes

Chapter One

1. According to its etymology, *ambiguous* should mean 'having two interpretations'. However, I will follow the general practise among linguists of using it in the sense 'having more than one interpretation', since it is the latter sense that a word is needed for. There are few occasions when it is of any importance whether the number of interpretations is exactly two but many when it is important whether it is more than one.

2. Zwicky and Sadock 1975 give an excellent and thorough survey of tests for ambiguity.

3. When there is no auxiliary verb in the clause affected by VP-deletion, a semantically empty *do* is inserted to serve as bearer of the tense marker (here the -s of *believes* and *does*). Insertion of *do* is a general concomitant to grammatical phenomena that would otherwise leave an unattached tense marker (Chomsky 1957).

4. It should be noted, however, that in many cases a conjoined structure will be unambiguously one or the other. There are heavy restrictions on the occurrence of the 'consecutive' interpretation. For example, the use of *respectively* forces a 'symmetric' interpretation on the coordinate structure:

    a. Rocky fired at the guard and Creepy fired at the detective.
    b. Rocky and Creepy fired at the guard and the detective respectively.

While *a* can be given either a 'symmetric' or a 'consecutive' interpretation, *b* is open only to the 'symmetric' interpretation, which is noncommittal on the temporal order of the two shots.

Chapter Two

1. The use of the terms 'syntax' and 'semantics' by logicians deviates considerably from linguists' use of the terms. For a linguist, 'semantics' has to do with meaning rather than with truth conditions and includes at least the study of what meanings are possible (which corresponds roughly to the

logicians' formation rules, which are part of the logicians' 'syntax' rather than their 'semantics'). The study of the relationship between sentences and their meanings is often referred to by linguists as 'semantics', though it could equally well be called syntax; the stratificational grammarians' term 'semolexemics' has the advantage of avoiding an arbitrary extension of the terms 'syntax' and 'semantics', though it has no currency except among stratificational grammarians.

2. I am begging one important question here by assuming that all the ways of constructing complex propositions out of the three atomic propositions yield results that should be regarded as different from one another. It is not at all obvious, though, that 'p and q' is a different proposition from 'q and p' or that 'p and (q and p)' is a different proposition from 'p and q'.

The role of parentheses in the notation employed here will be clarified later in this section. I regard parentheses, like spaces between words, as not, strictly speaking, being parts of the expressions in which they appear but as a typographical convenience for conveying details of the structures of these expressions.

3. The following formulas illustrate some alternative notations that have some currency:

Notation used here	Alternative notations
$\sim p$	$-p$, $\neg p$, $\bar{p}$, Np
$\vee pq$	$p+q$, Apq
$\wedge pq$	$p\&q$, $p\cdot q$, Kpq
$\supset pq$	$p \to q$, Cpq

4. In saying this, I am taking the examples 2.1.3 to be pronounced with 'neutral stress'. *John dóes love his wife*, with contrastive stress on the auxiliary verb, is perfectly normal but is a different sentence from 2.1.3*b*. Its negation (if it can really be said to have one) is not 2.1.3*a* but *John dóesn't love his wife*.

5. The word 'conjoin' is used in a broader sense by linguists than by logicians: logicians use 'conjunction' to refer to the combining of two (or more) propositions with *and* and 'disjunction' to refer to the combining of two (or more) propositions with *or*; linguists (and traditional grammarians) have generally used 'conjunction' to take in both combination with *and* and combination with *or*. For convenience' sake, I will adopt the linguist's terminology here and will use '*and*-conjunction' and '*or*-conjunction' where logicians speak of 'conjunction' and 'disjunction'.

6. I assume throughout this book a conception of transformations as rules that associate sentences with the corresponding semantic structures by converting the semantic structures via intermediate stages into the corresponding sentences. This conception of transformation is elaborated and argued for in such works as McCawley 1973*a* and G. Lakoff 1971. It differs from the various notions of 'transformation' found in the works of Chomsky, for whom transformations relate sentences to their 'deep structures' and deep structures

need not stand in any systematic relation to the meanings of sentences. (Chomsky briefly held, but has since repudiated, a conception of deep structure in which the deep structure of a sentence determined its meaning [e.g., Chomsky 1965, 1966]; for a presentation of his later views, see Chomsky 1976.) For discussion of different conceptions of transformation and their relation to meaning, see McCawley 1975.

7. See McCawley 1973c and Ross 1967 for evidence that sentences such as *Richie wants a Mustang* are derived from underlying structures with a sentence as direct object of *want*.

8. Strictly speaking, the diagram is not a tree itself but only a representation of a tree. A diagram is a typographical object, whereas a tree may be an object of any nature (e.g., a linguistic structure) that consists of parts structured in the fashion sketched here. For a more detailed exposition of the notion of tree, see McCawley 1968 and Wall 1972:144-52.

9. The initial letter of 'proposition' is of course 'P', 'S' being the initial of 'sentence'. My choice of symbols accords with terminology to be introduced in 4.1, in which 'sentence' will cover both 'proposition' (to be called 'closed sentence') and 'propositional function' (to be called 'open sentence'). Though this terminology undermines my efforts to distinguish between 'sentence' and 'proposition', it makes sense from the point of view of a conception of syntactic category in which corresponding items in the different levels of analysis of a linguistic object are assigned to the same category: the objects in logical structure that here are assigned to the category S are expressible most directly by expressions that belong to the syntactic category 'S', i.e., 'sentences' and 'clauses' in more traditional terminology.

10. For reasons that have never been clear to me, authors employing 'Polish notation' have generally avoided the more widely used symbols for the connectives and have instead substituted K for $\wedge$, A for $\vee$, N for $\sim$, and C for $\supset$.

11. The idea of organizing rules of inference into introduction rules and exploitation rules was devised by Frederic Fitch (1952), who developed an approach first worked out by Gerhard Gentzen (1969). A system of rules organized in this fashion is referred to as a system of NATURAL DEDUCTION. Where Fitch used the term 'elimination', I here use the term 'exploitation' instead: the term 'elimination' might misleadingly suggest to some that a premise can be used only once (i.e., that a connective in that premise is gone forever once it is 'eliminated'), whereas a given premise can in fact be 'exploited' any number of times.

12. See, however, 11.1, where an analysis of conditionals is presented in which the same *if* figures in both indicative and counterfactual conditionals.

13. See Rescher 1969:148-54 for discussion of several senses of the term 'law of the excluded middle' which have to be distinguished.

14. One can regard the first use of $\vdash$ as a special case of the second: $\vdash A$ can be identified with $\varnothing \vdash A$, where $\varnothing$ is the empty set of premises. On the notion 'empty set', see 5.3.

15. I have replaced Thomason's notation by that of this chapter.

16. For discussion and application of the linguistic notion of command, see Langacker 1969 and Ross 1969.

17. A line in a proof is an immediate constituent of the 'deepest' subproof that contains it. In terms of the diagrams that we have been using, it is an immediate constituent of the subproof corresponding to the vertical line immediately to its left. For example, in 2.5.3, line 3 is an immediate constituent of the subproof that runs from line 3 to line 5 (subproof 3–5, for short), line 9 is an immediate constituent of subproof 2–9, and line 10 is an immediate constituent of the entire proof.

18. To say that a subproof commands something is not to say that the individual lines of that subproof command it. For example, in 2.5.3, subproofs 3–5 and 6–8 both command line 9, but none of lines 3 through 8 commands line 9.

19. As I have set up the definition, a line commands itself, a detail that is not of any apparent significance.

20. In constructing these examples, I have conformed to the alternation between future tense (*will* or *'ll*) in an *if*-clause and present tense in a main clause. Note that under the most normal interpretation of *If the White Sox win the World Series, I'll buy drinks for everyone*, what is at issue is not the proposition expressed by *The White Sox win the World Series* (which is in fact not a normal English sentence) but rather that expressed by *The White Sox will win the World Series*. It is necessary, however, to distinguish between the future sense of *will* and the 'consent' sense of *will*. As Palmer (1965:110) has noted, only the future *will* is deleted:

> If he comes tomorrow, I'll give him these books.
> If he'll come tomorrow, I'll give him these books.

Chapter Three

1. Logicians commonly cite examples like *If Kathmandu is in Denmark, then I'm a monkey's uncle* as evidence for the correctness of the last line of the standard table. However, what makes such examples reasonable things to say is not just that both clauses are false but that the consequent is *blatantly* false. When the consequent is false, though not blatantly so, as in 3.1.3c, the sentence sounds quite odd. [Note: Lima is in fact slightly farther east than Miami; the *west* coast of South America is due south of the *east* coast of North America.]

2. This argument is taken from Geach (1972:196).

3. Combinations of these three possibilities also come into the picture. For example, one might maintain that 3.2.4 is ambiguous between a sense that is true and a sense that has no truth value.

4. Keep in mind that we are talking about what *can* be proven, not about what *has* been proven. The fact that no one has yet proven a certain proposition does not make it false in this assignment of truth values: if a proposition has neither been proven nor shown not to be provable, it is still either true or false, but you don't yet know which.

5. Or at least, you can't prove anything in the specific system adopted here. In versions of propositional logic in which there are *axioms*, i.e., formulas, instances of which are allowed to appear anywhere in a proof, there are of course formulas that can be proved without the use of suppositions, namely, those that are instances of the axioms.

6. The rules, of course, might be redundant—perhaps the work of one of them could be done by some combination of applications of the others. However, for our specific choice of rules, that seems pretty unlikely.

7. Since 'expressive completeness' could not reasonably be demanded of a system in which the connectives were not truth-functional, the term is generally used only with reference to systems whose connectives are taken to be truth-functional.

8. For discussion of the possibility that all *or*'s in English are really inclusive and that supposed instances of exclusive *or* can be explained as determined by the context, see 8.3, Pelletier 1977, and Gazdar 1979:79–83.

9. This point is made in Reichenbach 1947, but not, to my knowledge, in any other existing textbook of logic.

10. Jacobs and Rosenbaum (1967) present 3.5.4 not as an example of bizarre conjoining but as their stock example of conjoining. Until such recent works as Wierzbicka 1972 and R. Lakoff 1971, logicians and linguists have remained oblivious to the oddity of conjoining many of the things that they have merrily conjoined.

11. I say 'a' rather than 'the' since there is nothing to prevent one from using more than one metalanguage in a single discussion.

12. Using the notions of set theory developed in 5.2, one can show that those formulas can in fact be arranged into a complete enumeration, i.e., they can be arranged in a sequence in such a way that each formula turns up after a finite number of steps.

Chapter Four

1. I hope that no confusion will be created by the use of 'argument' in the two distinct senses 'justification offered for a conclusion' and 'item of which a predicate is predicated'.

2. I assume here the analysis of restrictive relative clauses that I argue for in McCawley 1978*a*, 1978*b*, in which the combination of noun and relative clause is a complex predicate derived from conjoined (open) sentences: '*y* is a woman and *y* hates *x*'→'*y* is a [woman who hates *x*]'. This analysis should not be confused with another proposal (e.g., Thompson 1971) in which restrictive relative clauses are derived from a different type of coordinate structure; the analysis assumed here is basically an analysis of relative clauses on predicate nouns and can provide an analysis for restrictive relative clauses on non-predicate nouns when it is combined (as it is here) with an analysis in which all nouns correspond to predicates in logical structure.

3. Logicians have generally chosen to assign an interpretation by hook or crook to structures such as 4.1.7 rather than to rule them out as incoherent. The contrary approach taken here will pay a dividend when we get to formulating rules of inference for quantifiers: if structures such as 4.1.7*c*–*d* were not excluded outright, it would be necessary to complicate the formulation of the rules of inference by adding clauses that have the effect of excluding them, since otherwise the rules of inference would yield illegitimate conclusions (namely, the interpretations that logicians have chosen to impose on the structures that we here choose to exclude as incoherent).

4. For clarity's sake, I have replaced the 'unrestricted quantifiers' (see 4.3) of Quine's formulas by 'restricted quantifiers' such as figure in this section.

5. Interestingly, *each* does not allow *almost*: **Almost each student took a different examination.*

6. For further remarks on the analysis of *any*, see Horn 1972 and LeGrand 1975.

7. Not all uses of *a/an* correspond to an existential quantifier. While *a* can be analyzed as indicated, *b* allows no plausible analysis involving an existential quantifier; *b* is a type of generic construction, expressing the proposition that it is typical of beavers to build dams, not that there is a beaver who builds dams:

> a. John insulted a policeman. ($\exists$: Policeman x)(John insulted x)
> b. A beaver builds dams.

A less clear case is presented by predicate NP's, as in *John is a policeman*, which I will argue should be analyzed with the noun as a predicate and the article making no contribution to logical structure *c*, rather than as in the frequently encountered proposal (e.g., Montague 1974:267) in which the indefinite article of a predicate noun is treated as an existential quantifier (*c'*):

> c. policeman(j)
> c'. ($\exists x$: policeman x) $=jx$.

I reject *c'* in favor of *c* principally on the grounds that predicate NP's normally do not participate in linguistic phenomena to which identity of reference is relevant. Thus, in *d* the antecedent of *him* can only be *Sam*, not *a policeman*, as contrasted with *d'*, in which *a policeman* is the antecedent of a pronoun whose use depends on identity of sense rather than of reference, and *d"*, in which a nonpredicate occurrence of *a policeman* may be the antecedent of an 'identity of reference' pronoun:

> d. *Sam* is a policeman. I'm glad I'm not *him*.
> d'. Sam is *a policeman*. I'm glad I'm not *that*.
> d". Sue insulted *a policeman*. I'm glad I'm not *him*.

Similarly, sentences such as *e* cannot be analyzed as identity propositions, since the negation is not the negation of an identity proposition. Example *e'* does not mean that Jack and Ruth's husband are not the same person but rather that Jack does not stand in the husband relation to Ruth; it does not presuppose that Ruth has a husband:

e. Jack is Ruth's husband.
e′. Jack isn't Ruth's husband. (They're only living together.)

8. Or at least, the result is deductively equivalent to the original if it is coherent, which it is if (as in 4.2.10) each of the Q's involves only one variable. However, the result of interchanging the Q's in the formula $(\forall: Fx)_x(\forall: Kxy)_y Lxy$ (e.g. *All voters are disappointed in everyone that they vote for*) would be incoherent and thus not deductively equivalent to the original.

9. It is not clear what this would mean, if anything, if infinitely many things have the property F. The problem does not arise in the instance to be discussed, in which only finitely many things have the relevant properties. See 14.1 for a more thorough treatment of *most*, including discussion of cases where it binds a variable with an infinite domain.

10. This argument is plagiarized from a lecture by Peter T. Geach at the University of Chicago in 1967.

11. Unrestricted quantification was first employed in Frege 1879. Its prevalence in twentieth-century logic is probably due to Bertrand Russell, who was profoundly influenced by Frege's logic and philosophy of mathematics. Frege did not give any serious consideration to any alternative to unrestricted quantification, despite the fact that predicate logic had been done in terms of restricted quantification by everyone from Aristotle to Frege's contemporaries.

12. There is a still more common notation, that in which (x) is written rather than $(\forall x)$. I have adhered to using an explicit symbol $\forall$ for the universal quantifier so as to make clear that $(\forall x)$ and $(\exists x)$ differ with regard to WHAT quantifier occurs and not with regard to WHETHER one occurs.

13. 'Over 50 percent' is an oversimplification, for reasons that will be made clear in 14.1.

14. As usual, subscripts indicate the intended pronoun-antecedent relationships. Thus, what is at issue in 4.7.1b is an interpretation in which *himself* refers to John. The approximate statement of the distribution of reflexives that I have just given is an oversimplification; see Jackendoff 1972 and Cantrall 1974 for detailed treatments of this question.

15. There will also have to be a transformation that reduces the S of the Q to its predicate noun, here converting (every: American x) into *every American*.

16. Subscripts on rule names indicate 'application of reflexivization to S_2', and so forth.

17. The statement that the NP x and the NP y are distinct should not be taken as implying that x and y must take on distinct values. All combinations of a value for x and a value for y play a role in determining the truth value of a proposition containing 'admire x y', even combinations in which they have the same value.

18. Not all infinitives are involved in such a parallelism. For example, there

is no counterpart to 4.7.7*b* in which the embedded clause surfaces with a subject of its own:

> *The court forced Nixon for Kalmbach to turn over the tapes.
> *The court forced Nixon that Kalmbach would turn over the tapes.

Force is analyzed as having both an object and a sentential complement, rather than just a sentential complement, for a number of reasons. *Force* can only be followed by a NP denoting the person on whom the force was exerted, rather than just any NP that could be subject of a clause describing what the force brought about:

> *The court forced the tapes to be turned over.
> *The court forced there to be separate trials for the defendants.

Contrast this with the behavior of *require*, which would be analyzed as having only a sentential complement:

> The court required the tapes to be turned over.
> The court required there to be separate trials for the defendants.

By the same token, as pointed out by Chomsky (1965), the following sentences differ only with regard to whether the complement clause is passivized (i.e., they differ by as little as active/passive pairs otherwise do):

> John wants the Yankees to beat the Orioles.
> John wants the Orioles to be beaten by the Yankees.

but corresponding sentences with *force* differ as regards who the force is imposed on:

> John forced Dr. Krankheit to examine Fred.
> John forced Fred to be examined by Dr. Krankheit.

19. Example 4.7.8*b* is actually three ways ambiguous, having not only an interpretation corresponding to 4.7.9*b* but also interpretations corresponding to the formulas

> b'. (every: American x)(every: American y)(x want (y get rich))
> b″. (every: American y)(every: American x)(x want (y get rich))

Examples *b'* and *b″* are deductively equivalent, though they count as distinct logical structures. Each is true when for each pair of Americans, each wants the other to get rich. Example 4.7.9*b* means that each American has a desire that all Americans get rich. Note that *b'* and *b″* could be true and 4.7.9*b* false in a given situation: if I have benevolent feelings toward each and every American (and if having benevolent feelings toward someone implies wanting him to get rich) though I do not have a blanket desire that all Americans be rich, I would 'want every American to get rich' in a sense that appears in *b'* but not in the sense that appears in 4.7.9*b*.

20. Example 4.7.13*b* is ambiguous: it can be interpreted not only like 4.7.13*a* but also with the meaning '... and Bill loves John's wife too'.

21. My brief remarks here do not do justice to the remarkable complexity of the behavior of negative polarity items. See Horn 1972, 1975, 1978 for detailed discussion, including a demonstration that negative polarity items differ from one another with regard to where they can be located relative to the negative items that 'trigger' them and how strongly negative the 'trigger' of each negative polarity item must be. Note, for example, such differences as:

I'll be amazed if Phil gives Lucy a red cent.
*I'll be amazed if Sam finishes the report until Friday.

Chapter Five

1. If $M \subseteq N$ and $M \neq N$, then M is called a PROPER subset of N. The symbol $\subseteq$ is formed on the analogy of the symbol $\leq$ 'less than or equal to': if $\subset$ were used to mean 'is a proper subset of', then $\subseteq$ would stand for 'is a proper subset of or is equal to' in the same way that $\leq$ stands for 'is less than or equal to'.

2. This disconcerting property of a 'set of all sets' was discovered by Bertrand Russell and is generally referred to as 'Russell's paradox'.

3. In this informal presentation, I have been very cavalier about some important mathematical points. I have been assuming that 'can be put into a one-to-one correspondence with a subset of' is a good analogue to the relationship 'is less than or equal to' among finite numbers. To establish that, I would have to establish analogues to the propositions (i) for all x, y, if $x \leq y$ and $y \leq x$, then $x = y$; (ii) for all x, y, either $x \leq y$ or $y \leq x$. While analogues to these propositions can in fact be proven (e.g., it can be proven that if there is a one-to-one correspondence between A and a subset of B and there is a one-to-one correspondence between B and a subset of A, then there is a one-to-one correspondence between A and B), the proofs are quite involved and rest on assumptions that, though widely accepted, are far from self-evident. One of those assumptions, the so-called AXIOM OF CHOICE, played a role in the informal argument that the positive integers are the smallest infinite set: the axiom of choice says that for any set of nonempty sets there is a function that picks one element of each of those sets, and that axiom is the basis of the claim that the sequence x_1, x_2, x_3, ... can be formed.

4. The terms 'countable' and 'denumerable' are sometimes used in a broader sense that includes finite sets. Under that terminological practise, what we are calling a 'countable set' would be called a 'countably infinite set'.

5. Strictly speaking, '$f(1)$ is true' is superfluous here: showing that if f is true of all natural numbers less than 1, $f(1)$ is also true, is equivalent to showing that $f(1)$ is true, since there aren't any natural numbers less than 1. I have included the superfluous clause, since in actual practise one would generally have to treat the case of $n = 1$ separately in proving that 'if f is true of all natural numbers less than n, then it is true of n'.

6. It is possible for either *a* or *b* to be a degenerate case of the second type, i.e., for $i = 1$ or $j = 1$. However, that case obviously also results in a representation of *n* as a product of primes.

7. The expression 'either case' is somewhat misleading, since it suggests that there is a difference in meaning between 'predicate' and 'relation'. Aside from one minor point, namely, that it is normal to speak of a 'one-place predicate' but not to speak of a 'one-place relation', there is in fact no difference between 'predicates' and 'relations'.

Chapter Six

1. The term 'proposition' is most often used by modern logicians in a way that is quite at odds with that in which it is used here. Specifically, in such works as Montague 1974 and Cresswell 1975, a 'proposition' is taken to be a function associating to every world a truth value, that is, the proposition is identified with the function specifying what its truth value in each world is. This is in some respects a narrower and in some respects a broader conception of 'proposition' than that adopted here: it is broader in that it allows as propositions functions from worlds to truth values that need not correspond to a propositional function of the given system applied to objects that figure in the domains of the given worlds; it is narrower in that it implies that there is only one contradictory proposition (namely, the function whose value in all worlds is F) and only one tautological proposition (namely, the function whose value in all worlds is T), whereas I adopt here a conception of proposition in which there are distinct contradictory propositions (for example, the proposition that Carter has teeth and does not have teeth is different from the proposition that all linguists are insane and some linguists are not insane) and different tautological propositions.

2. One very special sort is propositions; 7.5 is devoted to a discussion of predicates that require arguments of that sort. However, this sort has a special status in that states of affairs cannot differ arbitrarily from one another with regard to what objects of this sort there are (the way that, for example, they can differ arbitrarily from one another with regard to what persons there are): the logical system and the domain determine what propositions there are.

Chapter Seven

1. In anticipation of a point that will be discussed shortly, I have made one small change in Russell's analysis, namely, that of replacing $\supset(KFy, =yx)$ by $\supset(\sim =yx, \sim KFy)$. For the specific cases that Russell discussed, this difference is immaterial; however, the form that I have adopted is more suggestive of a generalization of Russell's analysis, in addition to conforming more closely to idiomatic paraphrases ('no one but him is king of France').

2. It is often held that examples like 7.1.2 (or such sentences as *The postman brought three letters today* or *The dog has fleas*) conform to the Russell analysis

but can be used properly only if one assumes a restricted universe of discourse that contains only one restaurant on Clark Street (postman, dog, and so on). But that suggestion is inadequate, since it rules out any plausible analysis of such sentences as:

> The restaurant on Clark Street is better than all other restaurants on Clark Street.
> The postman likes all postmen.

Their normal use will be with reference to a universe of discourse containing other restaurants on Clark Street, and so forth. See 9.6 for further discussion of this point.

3. I have adopted this notation in preference to the more popular notational practises that involve formulas such as

> a. $B(\iota x: KFx)$
> b. $(\iota x: KFx)B(\iota x: KFx)$

Both are objectionable: *a* does not indicate explicitly the scope of the definite description operator, and *b* is redundant (the repetition of the iota and the predicate contributes nothing). More importantly, *b* makes false claims about the logical constituent structure of various sentences. For example, consider the ambiguous sentence *The teacher of Alexander was necessarily a teacher*. Using 'Nec' to stand for 'necessary', 'T' for 'be the teacher of', and 'A' for Alexander, and analyzing 'be a teacher' as 'be the teacher of someone', the two interpretations of the sentence could be symbolized as

> c. $Nec(\iota x: TxA)(\exists y)Txy$
> d. $(\iota x: TxA)Nec(\exists y)Txy$

This makes it clear that one of the two interpretations of the sentence is true (the one which says that 'The teacher of Alexander was a teacher' is a necessary proposition) and the other one false (the one which says of the teacher of Alexander, that is, of Aristotle, that it is necessary that he was a teacher). However, if the notation employed in *b* were used, the formula corresponding to the latter interpretation would not be obviously false in the way that *d* is:

> e. $(\iota x: TxA)Nec(\exists y)T(\iota x: TxA)y$

Note that *e* suggests that the complement of Nec (in the false interpretation of the example) is 'the teacher of Alexander was a teacher', whereas *d* makes clear that the complement of Nec is '*x* was a teacher'.

4. The now voluminous literature on the Bach-Peters sentence includes Bach 1970, Dik 1973, Hausser 1978, Hintikka and Saarinen 1975, Karttunen 1971*a*, Kuroda 1971, McCawley 1973*b*, and Wasow 1973.

5. In this section, I treat ι as a quantifier rather than as an abbreviation for the combination of quantifiers, conjunctions, and negation into which Russell analyzes is. The point made here would remain equally true, however, if that expression were used in place of ι: the quantifier binding *y* (namely, the

existential quantifier of Russell's formula) would still not command the y of 'hit $x\ y$'.

6. See Klooster 1972 for a demonstration that *weigh 210 pounds* is exactly parallel in underlying syntax to *be 6 feet tall*.

7. See Bierwisch 1967 and Teller 1969 for discussion of what dimensions adjectives such as *long* and *wide* refer to, a question that turns out to be far harder to answer than is generally recognized.

8. Exclusive *or*, if there is such a thing (see 8.3 for arguments that English really has only an inclusive *or*), could be identified with the quantifier *one*: *one*/ $\lor_e$ would be predicated of a set of propositions, and the whole proposition would be true if and only if exactly one member of that set was true.

9. For consistency, we should write '$\in xM$' rather than '$x \in M$'. I have nevertheless retained the more familiar order of symbols.

10. As it stands, SF-intro$_2$ is perniciously overgeneral. Unless something is done to restrict the bound variable introduced by it to a specific 'type' (in the sense of Russell and Whitehead 1912), it can be used to introduce the sorts of spurious 'sets' that give rise to Russell's paradox; for example, we must rule out inferences like the following, in which the bound variable M is supposed to range over 'all sets':

$$\sim(\varnothing \in \varnothing)$$
$$\varnothing \in \{M : \sim(M \in M)\}$$

I will tacitly assume that the appropriate restrictions on this rule are in effect.

11. In Lakoff and Peters 1969 and McCawley 1970, it has been held that there IS such a constraint in natural language, in view of the oddity of structures with repeated conjuncts:

*John is Irish, Bill is Italian, and John is Irish.
*My mother and my mother are short and fat, respectively.

However, this oddity can be ascribed to the pointlessness of the extra conjuncts: one could be just as informative by omitting the supernumerary conjuncts. Derived coordinate constituents with repeated constituents are normal when not pointless:

Tom, Dick, and Harry voted for Nixon, Nixon, and Humphrey/
*Nixon, respectively.

12. The *other* of *each other* and *one another* can reasonably be identified with the clause '$\sim = yx$', which would also serve as an analysis of *other* in such sentences as *Roberta loves no one other than Otto* or *You must be referring to some other poem of Heine's*. For more extensive comments on the analysis of reciprocals, see Fiengo and Lasnik 1973.

13. The conclusion that only these three 'syntactic categories' play a role in logical structure does not imply (contrary to the erroneous arguments given in such works as McCawley 1972, 1973*b*) that only those categories play a role in syntax in general. See McCawley 1980 for a sketch of an approach to syntax in

which syntactic category names such as 'VP' are regarded as merely informal abbreviations for combinations of factors that play a role in syntax, with logical category being merely one of several such factors. Logical structures such as are envisioned here, which are built up from conceptual units rather than morphemes of a particular language, are unspecified for at least one factor that plays a role in syntax, namely, the 'lexical category' (noun versus verb versus adjective, etc.) of the head of each constituent; it is only with the substitution of lexical items for combinations of conceptual units that a distinction between, for example, VP and AP emerges.

Chapter Eight

1. In some circumstances, a verb can be used performatively with *must* or *will*:

> In view of the gravity of your offence, I will/must hereby sentence you to 20 years of hard labor.

See McCawley 1977 and Fraser 1974*b* for discussions of the conditions under which this is possible.

2. An exception must be made for certain types of sentences that do not allow reasonable paraphrases that have an explicit performative verb, for example, exclamatory sentences (such as *Boy, was I ever embarrassed!* or *The nerve of the bastard, asking me to patch his underwear!*) and 'echo questions' (such as *You order me to clean the latrine with what?*).

3. At the end of a passage that begins with the question 'What then is left of the distinction of the performative and constative utterance?' Austin says, 'But the real conclusion must surely be that we need (*a*) to distinguish between locutionary and illocutionary acts, and (*b*) specially and critically to establish with respect to each kind of illocutionary act—warnings, estimates, verdicts, statements, and descriptions—what if any is the specific way in which they are intended, first to be in order or not in order, and second, to be "right" or "wrong"; what terms of appraisal and disappraisal are used for each and what they mean. This is a wide field and certainly will not lead to a simple distinction of "true" and "false"; nor will it lead to a distinction of statements from the rest, for stating is only one among very numerous speech acts of the illocutionary class' (Austin 1962:144–46).

4. An illustration of the way in which cooperativity influences the interpretation of things other than speech is provided by the difference between how one interprets a painting and how one interprets a photograph. Everything in the painting is of significance, since the artist took the trouble to put it there; but the very same details in a photograph are often of no significance, since the photographer controls only a limited range of features of the things that he photographs.

5. Of course, even that utterance could be interpreted in such a way as to exploit 'relevance': *B*'s utterance might convey that *A* should get his groceries

at the nearby store rather than at the store on the other side of town that he had been planning to go to, or even that A should give up the trip that he was about to embark on and should buy the groceries that he will need to hold him over until morning. Of course, for it to convey any of these things, it is necessary that A and B share appropriate assumptions: in the one case, that A's trip is to buy groceries and that 14th Street is nearby, in the other case, that if A does not make his planned trip, he will need groceries.

6. Another type of implicature, namely, 'conventional implicature', is discussed later in this section.

7. This will have to be qualified if its coverage is to be extended to 'negative questions'; see Pope 1973 for a detailed account of question-answering devices. My statement about *yes* is actually more correct as a general description of how *Uh-huh* (with rising intonation) is used.

8. I am concerned here with the 'neutral' pronunciation of 8.3.11a, in which *some* is not heavily stressed. If *some* is heavily stressed, the normalness of the answers is reversed. This is because *some* is then being contrasted with other items that could be used in its place, and 8.3.11b' is then an appropriate answer because *some* is not the 'most correct' member of the set of contrasted items; however, in 8.3.11a with 'neutral' pronunciation, the proposition that some men are mortal is being contrasted with its negation (the proposition that no men are mortal).

9. In the 'fuzzy logic' treated in chap. 11, $\sim \supset AB$ implies $\sim B$, but it doesn't imply A. If one broadens the scope of this discussion by making that logic the 'base logic', what we will be concerned with is not whether for ordinary speakers 8.3.15 implies that God is dead but whether it implies that not everything is permitted. Ex. 8.3.15 might be felt to imply that, but that is probably just a reflection of the fact that a person who utters 8.3.15 can be expected to both believe in God and believe that not everything is permitted. A more useful example might be *It is not the case that if $2 + 3 = 4$, then $4 + 3 = 7$.* A person could agree to that sentence without being held to believe that $4 + 3 \neq 7$.

10. See Hall 1959 for an interesting study of words like *fake* and *imitation*.

11. See also Gruber 1967 for a statement of essentially the same principle and many instances of its application.

12. There is, however, a difference between the two cases that arises when they are used in yes-no questions:

> (i) Did only Southerners vote for Hubert?
> Yes, indeed, only Lyndon did.
> (ii) Did only Muriel vote for Hubert?
> ?Yes, indeed, no one did.
> (?)No, indeed, no one did.
> (iii) Did only Muriel, Ed, and Lyndon vote for Hubert?
> ?Yes, indeed, only Muriel and Ed did.

I am not yet clear as to what the significance of these facts is.

13. This is incorrect as it stands, in view of Postal and Grinder's (1971) discussion of such examples as *Bill doesn't have a car, but Susan does, and it's*

parked in front of her house. Note that the *it* refers to the understood *a car* of *Susan does (have a car).* The correct form of the generalization is probably that an existential quantifier creates a constant only if it occurs overtly or is anaphorically connected to something that occurs overtly. The zero VP of the second clause is an anaphoric device referring to the VP *(have a car)* of the first clause.

14. Note also that in a narration each clause reflects the narrator's knowledge at that point in the events being narrated. A narrator inside the lunchroom sees the door opening before he sees the two men come in, and thus his knowledge that the opening of the door was an act of the two men does not come about until later in the events being narrated.

15. The discussion of 8.3.27 here is based on Kamp's (1975) analysis of permission.

16. I have replaced Grice's 'A; therefore, B' by a structure in which the A and B are syntactically coordinate and in which conjunction reduction has taken place. Sentences of the form 'It is not the case that [A; therefore B]' are not possible, since a clause introduced by *that* must be syntactically a sentence, whereas 'A; therefore, B' is syntactically a sequence of sentences; while the sentences of that sequence are grouped together into a larger unit, that unit is a sentence only typographically, not syntactically.

17. Sentences with *even* convey a third thing, namely, that the individual in question is less likely than the 'others' to have the property in question, for example, that Carter is less likely than 'the others' to favor deregulation. This part of what *even* conveys can be treated as a conversational implicature.

18. For an interesting and detailed proposal of a way to extend classical logic so as to encompass conventional implicature, see Karttunen and Peters 1979, and for a detailed treatment of *even* according to that proposal, Karttunen and Karttunen 1977. In the Karttunen-Peters proposal, a proposition is treated as an ordered triple of logical formulas, the first formula being the logical form in the narrow sense, the second being the conventional implicature, and the third specifying how the given sentence contributes to the conventional implicatures of sentences in which it is embedded. Leaving aside this third component, a proposition will then allow four possible truth values, namely the four possible combinations of values of T or F for the two component formulas.

Chapter Nine

1. I have used a 'pseudo-cleft' construction rather than a 'cleft' construction, since a cleft version of 9.2.10 would be very awkward by virtue of its having a clause in the middle of a clause (as noted in Ross 1967):

?*It's that he is a member of the SLA that Nixon regrets.

A pseudo-cleft example is equally relevant here, since cleft and pseudo-cleft constructions appear to have the same logical content, though there are different restrictions on their use.

2. See van Fraassen 1969:76–77 and 1971:157–59 for a precise statement of what a conservative presuppositional system is.

3. We have $\#$ rather than $T/\#$ since the conditions under which $\supset(mA, A)$ might be T are not met here. Let v_X be a supervaluation for which $v_X(A) = v_X(mA) = \#$. For $v_X(\supset(mA, A))$ to be T, it must be the case that all classical valuations which make all of X T and make mA T also make A T. But there are classical valuations which make all of X T and make A F (that's what it means to say that $v_X(A) \neq T$), and among those there must be classical valuations which make mA T, since in classical logic, A and mA are independent of each other. Thus, if $v_X(A) = v_X(mA) = \#$, then $v_X(\supset(mA, A)) = \#$.

4. According to 9.4.8, (i) should be $\sim A \gg C$. However, since a proposition and its negation have the same presuppositions, it can be given in the form $A \gg C$.

5. Example 9.4.15 should be distinguished from such sentences as

> Nixon regrets that he doesn't belong to the Elks, and, by the way, he doesn't belong to the Elks.

which are quite normal but which do not affect the point being made here, since they involve afterthought. The function of the afterthought is, in effect, to replace the sentence that the speaker was originally going to utter (the first conjunct) by another sentence in which the material of the afterthought appears earlier.

6. This statement of the conditions under which a proposition A belongs to the 'context' is somewhat misleading, in that what is at issue is not whether each participant in the discourse individually takes A for granted but whether the participants treat A as 'common property' of the group that they form in conducting the conversation. In certain situations, propositions that none of the parties to the conversation believes may be 'taken for granted' by them. For example, the proposition that there is a Santa Claus may belong to the context of a Christmastime conversation between a parent and his child, neither of whom believes that there is a Santa Claus or even believes that the other believes that there is a Santa Claus. The parties to the conversation may, of course, have conflicting conceptions of what their 'common property' is; however, when such discrepancies become apparent, some sort of 'repair' procedure is initiated (e.g., one might delete a proposition from the set that he had assumed to belong to the context or might challenge or query the other party so as to lead *him* to stop regarding a certain proposition as belonging to the context).

7. We actually used the letters T and F at that point, but since we are now using capital letters for truth values based on a narrow conception of falsehood and small letters for truth values based on a broad conception of falsehood, it is small letters that are appropriate here.

8. Given the analysis presented so far, it makes no sense to speak of the logical structure of a VP. See, however, 13.1 for a proposal in which sentences are taken to be more highly structured than we have hitherto taken them to be and in which it does make sense to speak of the logical structure of a VP.

9. The full range of existential NP's may be found in the *if*-clause of conditional sentences that have a pronoun in the consequent clause that refers back to the quantified NP:

    i. If Dave finds several copies of *Fanny Hill*, he'll give them all to the Wichita Public Library.
    ii. If a lot of people come to Janet's party, they'll drink lots of beer.
    iii. If at least 10 people sign a petition to the chairman, they're entitled to present their grievance at a board meeting.
    iv. If Sam buys two cars, he'll let me drive one of them.

These do not present an insuperable problem for the Quine analysis but do at least force its adherents to adopt an analysis in which a set variable is bound by a zero universal quantifier, for example ii would have to be analyzed as 'For every set of a lot of people, if the members of that set come to Janet's party, they will drink lots of beer'; note that *a lot* cannot simply be taken itself to have wide scope—ii does not mean 'There are a lot of people such that, if they come to Janet's party, they'll drink a lot of beer'. A more serious problem that ii presents for Quine's analysis is that of getting *a lot* to pick out sets that are large by appropriate standards (e.g., *a lot* in ii might be around 30; but 30 fans attending a Vikings football game isn't a lot); for the Klima and Horn analysis, this is no problem: the antecedent of ii will be *A lot of people come to Janet's party*, and the standards relative to which *a lot* is interpreted will be the same as if the antecedent were an independent sentence.

10. Actually, it is available in a slightly more general slice of the discourse, namely, those parts referring to states of affairs in which the antecedent is supposed true. In a sentence such as

> If a war breaks out in Uganda, it will spread to Tanzania, but I strongly doubt that it will spread to Mozambique.

the second *it* refers to the war mentioned in the antecedent. But the clause containing that second *it* is not part of the consequent of that conditional: the sentence cannot have the logical form 'If *p*, then (*q* but *r*)', since your doubts, mentioned in the putative *r*, are real doubts that you have now, not something contingent on war breaking out in Uganda.

11. Real world events may fail to conform to the relevant scripts. However, the hearer takes the events mentioned as conforming to the script unless the speaker gives him reason to believe that they may not conform to it.

Chapter Ten

1. In saying this, I am claiming that a moral theory need concern itself only with logically possible states of affairs. If there are any moral philosophers who do not accept that restriction, I would probably have difficulty communicating with them about why they do not accept it.

2. To say that the R for epistemic possibility is reflexive is to say that *know* is a factive verb: that only what is true in a given state of affairs can be known in that state of affairs.

3. See Hughes and Cresswell (1968:58) for comments on the 'somewhat tenuous' relationship of this formula to Brouwer and intuitionist mathematics.

4. As before, I include 'axioms' under 'rules of inference'.

5. The Lewis systems S1, S2, and S3 do not have this property (Hughes and Cresswell 1968:236).

6. The numbering of some of the additions to the Lewis hierarchy is misleading in that not all systems of the hierarchy are comparable. For example, S7, S8, and S9 are special cases of S3 but are not comparable with S4 or S5 (some theorems of S7 are not theorems of S4 and some theorems of S4 are not theorems of S7, etc.).

7. The introduction to Linsky 1971 provides a highly insightful survey of this entire controversy.

8. I say 'generally', since there are instances in which the terms 'morning star' and 'evening star' refer to other planets. When Mercury is visible in the early evening and Venus is not, Mercury is referred to as the evening star; there is a passage in Isaac Asimov's story "Heredity", which is set on the planet Mars, in which a character uses the expression *the morning star* to refer to the manifestation of Earth in the Martian sky.

9. I owe this point to Roman Jakobson (lecture in Tokyo, July 1967).

10. This was pointed out by David Lewis (1968).

11. Cross-world identification must take in not only persons and physical objects but also more abstract entities such as events. For example, when one says *That car could have run me over* after being narrowly missed by a recklessly driven car, one is not saying merely that there is an alternative world in which that car ran him over (say, a world in which the same near-miss occurred, whereupon the driver turned around and took a second shot at running the speaker over) but rather that there is an alternative world in which the same events that occurred in the real world (including the driver driving the way he did) had a different outcome.

12. Lewis does not make clear whether individuals such as numbers are to be subject to this policy; he does not state whether the 87 of the real world is identical to or only a counterpart of the 87 of w_{149}. A qualification calling for identity rather than counterparthood in such cases would not change things greatly.

13. Note that the same is not true of ESSENTIAL properties: an essential property is a property that an object has to have in order to retain its identity, which leaves completely open the question of whether the object exists in all worlds. Note, thus, that under policies i and ii, f could be an essential property of a and yet $\Box fa$ not true.

The reason that I speak in the text of necessary ATOMIC properties is that one can construct complex properties that an object can have even in worlds in which it does not exist, for example, the property 'x is mortal if x exists'. Even under policies i and ii, this would be a necessary property of all existing men.

14. The formula of which 10.3.17 is the converse, namely,

$$\supset ((\forall x) \Box fx, \; \Box (\forall x) fx))$$

is called the BARCAN FORMULA, after Ruth Barcan (Marcus), who included it in her 1946 axioms for a system of modal predicate logic. The Barcan formula is valid only in modal systems in which the situation discussed in connection with 10.3.2a' cannot arise. It will be invalid in any modal system in which there are worlds w and w' such that Rww' and the domain of w' includes elements not in the domain of w, since fx then could be true in both w and w' of all elements that are in the domain of w but false in w' of some element in the domain of w' that is not in the domain of w. It will be valid in modal systems in which all worlds have the same domain.

15. Hughes and Cresswell (1968) point out that the symbol $\dashv$ first appeared in print in Lewis 1912, $\Diamond$ in Lewis and Langford 1932, and $\Box$ in Barcan 1946. Lewis of course wrote $\dashv$ between the items that it connected, for example, A $\dashv$ B. I will continue my policy of writing connectives at the left and write instead $\dashv$ AB.

16. Anderson and Belnap actually call this system FE$\rightarrow$, reserving the name E$\rightarrow$ for an equivalent system involving axioms that do the work of $\rightarrow$-introduction. I will likewise write E$\approx$ below for the system that they actually call FE$\approx$.

17. While this rule is not one of the rules of inference for propositional logic given in chapter 2, it is available as a 'derived' rule of inference: its effect can be simulated by a combination of other rules of inference.

18. All that the distinguishability assumption tells us directly is that there is a proposition that is true in one of the two worlds and false in the other. However, if we had a proposition that was false in w_1 and true in w, we could take its negation as A_1. Thus the distinguishability assumption insures that for any worlds w' and w'', there will be a proposition true in w' and false in w''.

Chapter Eleven

1. George Lakoff has pointed out that while standard rules of inference allow one to derive $\supset (\land AC, B)$ from $\supset AB$, many apparent instances of that inference, even where the conditionals are indicative, are dubious, for example,

> If they went to Jamaica last Christmas, they had a relaxing holiday.
> Therefore, if they went to Jamaica and to Hawaii last Christmas, they had a relaxing holiday.

As most easily interpreted, the premise of this argument would not guarantee the truth of the conclusion: it would be taken as referring to holidays to Jamaica that did not involve extraneous diversions like a side trip to Hawaii. While it is possible to regard the premise of this argument as involving a sloppy use of the indicative conditional and thus not really to be a counterexample to the principle of 'strengthening the antecedent', it is not clear that that principle holds up any better for indicative conditionals than for counterfactuals.

2. See McCawley 1976*a* for remarks suggesting that this condition should perhaps not be imposed if certain puzzles involving causation are to be avoided.

3. Throughout this section I will assume that R is reflexive.

4. This proposal amounts to a special case of what is proposed by Lycan 1977.

5. Within Rescher's approach, the most promising treatment of *might* counterfactuals is to take them to be true when $M' \cup \{A\}$ is consistent with B.

6. The asterisks here relate only to nonreferential interpretations of the NP's in question; throughout this section, referential interpretations will be ignored.

7. For perceptive remarks about the nature of pictorial representation, presented within a framework radically different from that of this chapter, see Jackendoff 1975.

8. I am speaking of blanks being filled by individuals, real or fictitious, not by names of individuals. The individual need not be one to whom anyone has ever given a name, for example, the woman in Grant Wood's *American Gothic*.

9. Goffman (1974) provides much insightful discussion of the status of actions (including speech) carried out in theatrical performances, rehearsals, games, deceptions and other 'frames'.

10. The most comprehensive surveys of research in tense logic are to be found in Prior 1967 and Rescher and Urquhart 1971.

11. I will cite only English data in treating the various linguistic considerations that I take up. I hope eventually to determine on the basis of a cross-linguistic survey what features of the linguistic treatment of time have the universality and intralinguistic importance that would justify my using them as constraints on the construction of a hopefully not too language-particular tense logic. In view of this goal and the fact that many languages, strictly speaking, do not have tense systems, I am not fully happy with the term 'tense logic'. It should be clear from what follows that much of the 'tense logic' that I discuss in relation to English examples has relatively little to do with tense per se, though temporal notions are at the center of everything discussed here.

12. In 11.3.19*b* I have employed the makeshift of writing '∃3I' for 'there are three values of I such that . . .'; see 14.1 for an explicit proposal for the logical structure of sentences in which numerals appear to be used as quantifiers. As in the case of 11.3.11, the formulas are deficient by virtue of having no indication that the event (John's marrying Sue) is in the past.

13. One could object that the T and D of 11.3.20 do not provide adequate expressive possibilities, since they involve no symbol for the time being referred to whereas it can be necessary to refer to that time elsewhere in the sentence or discourse. For example, in 11.3.18*a* the time adverbial clause in the first sentence also provides the time reference of the second sentence. However, if we accept the treatment of pronouns and definite descriptions given in 9.6, the problem embodied in this objection vanishes: whether or not the logical structures of the sentences in which the various times are introduced involve symbols for those times, the fact that one has referred to those times is enough

to insure that the times will become members of the contextual domain and thus will be available as constants (say, as the *a* of $C_p(a)$) in the subsequent discourse.

14. While the relation between E and S never affects the choice of a tense and an auxiliary verb in the given clause (that is, in the clause expressing E), it may give rise to a conflict that renders a sentence unsayable. For example, if John arrived one week ago and will leave one week from now, the following sentences ought to be possible ways of expressing the relation between his arrival and his departure, but they sound quite odd because they violate a constraint requiring time adverbial clauses to agree in tense with the clauses that they modify:

> ??John will leave two weeks after he arrived.
> ??John arrived two weeks before he leaves.

This restriction has to do with tense and not with time reference, since corresponding sentences in which one of the tense markers is absent are acceptable:

> John will leave two weeks after his arrival.

15. English is unusual in using a present perfect in such sentences as 11.3.26. A simple present is much more common (e.g., German, French, Russian).

16. However, the stative present perfect excludes *already* and *by now*.

Chapter Twelve

1. It would never be F, since if the antecedent is future contingent, the antecedent might turn out to be false, and the conditional would then turn out to be true. Thus, an instance of $\supset$ II could at worst be future contingent.

2. This truth table figures in an alternative version of many-valued logic proposed by Kurt Gödel (summarized in Rescher 1969:44–45). However, Gödel's system involved a different truth table for negation than Łukasiewicz had: in Gödel's system, $\sim$ A is F whenever A is not T, that is, the negation of an I proposition is I for Łukasiewicz but F for Gödel.

3. There are several distinct ways that one might replace Łukasiewicz's original truth table by formulas for the two classes of cases. For example: $/\supset AB/ = 1$ if $/A/ \le /B/$, $/\supset AB/ = 1 - /A/ + /B/$ if $/A/ > /B/$. These two parts could be combined into the single formula $/\supset AB/ = \min(1, 1 - /A/ + /B/)$, since '$/A/ \le /B/$' is equivalent to '$1 - /A/ + /B/ \ge 1$'.

4. Strictly speaking, we should say 'least upper bound' rather than 'maximum', and 'greatest lower bound' rather than 'minimum', since it might be that there is no element of the domain which makes $/fx/$ a maximum (or a minimum). For example, suppose that we took the truth value of 'x is colossal' to be always less than 1 but allow it to get as close to 1 as one might like (say, if x ranges over numbers, $/x$ is colossal$/$ might be taken to be $1 - 1/x$). In that case 1 is the 'least upper bound' of the set of truth values that x can assume, but it is not the 'maximum' value of $/fx/$, since $/fx/$ never takes that value.

However, to simplify the exposition, I will say 'minimum' where I should say 'greatest lower bound', and 'maximum' where I should say 'least upper bound'.

5. I ignore here the contribution of *person* to the content of 12.2.1.

6. One oddity about this measure is that it comes out negative some of the time, namely, when $|ga| > |fa| > 0$. If one wishes, one can amend the proposal so as to make the degree of counterexamplehood be zero rather than negative in such cases.

7. The notion of a fuzzy alternativeness relation has some similarity to Lewis's notion of different worlds differing in how 'close' they are to one another (see 11.1) but has the important difference that for a fuzzy alternativeness relation, $|Rww'|$ may be 1 even if $w' \neq w$, whereas for Lewis any two distinct worlds are always 'some distance apart'.

8. To prove this properly, it would be necessary to refrain from assuming that $|fx|/(|fx| - |gx|)$ ever attains its least upper bound. The interested reader is invited to redo these proofs with that modification.

9. For a fuller treatment of the matters sketched in this section, see Zadeh 1965, 1971.

10. The effect of these arbitrary decisions remains attenuated in combinations put together with $\wedge$, $\vee$, and $\sim$, but can have a more profound effect on the truth values of conditional propositions, according to the truth conditions proposed in 12.1.

11. *Not quite* is not simply a negation of *quite*, in view of its different combinatoric properties:

> The watchman was not quite dead when the policeman arrived.

12. Lakoff (1972*b*, §3) has stated that 12.5.4*b* 'presupposes that Esther Williams is not literally a fish'. However, *regular* in fact does not carry with it a presupposition that the predicate is literally inapplicable, since it is easy to imagine a situation in which both of the following would be correct things to say:

> Peoria is a regular disaster area.
> Technically, Peoria is a disaster area.

and thus the applicability of *a regular disaster area* does not require that the place under discussion fail to be literally a disaster area.

13. The use of connotational properties is often highly conventionalized. For example, when we speak of Esther Williams as being 'a regular fish' or 'at home in the water', we refer only to the skill and effortlessness of her swimming: we know that she sleeps on a mattress and not under the water and that she eats off of a plate and with a knife and fork rather than ingesting plankton and smaller fish (even smaller regular fish) while she swims.

14. Of course, if we broaden the notion of tautology to mean a formula that can assume only the values T and *t*, that is, if we take *t* as well as T to be a 'designated' truth value, then exactly the same formulas will be tautologies here as in classical propositional logic.

Chapter Thirteen

1. The equality sign here means 'has the same denotation as'; the expressions on either side of this equation are different expressions that denote the same proposition.

2. The deletion in question actually applies not only to VP's as usually understood but also to 'adjective phrases', such as *easy to talk to* in 13.1.4c, and predicate NP's, as in *Schwartz is a director of this corporation, and McGonigle is ∅ too.*

3. There is a further ambiguity, namely, that of which persons the two occurrences of *he* refer to. I will only consider here interpretations in which the *he* of the first conjunct refers to Sam and that of the second conjunct to Bill.

4. Again, I am ignoring additional readings that 13.1.7b and 13.1.7b′ might have, for example, readings in which the first *him* refers to someone other than Alan.

5. These terms were introduced by Ross (1967).

6. Since every VP contributes its own λ, many examples that might at first sight be thought to involve occurrences of the same variable in two different VP's really do not. For example, Sag's proposal does not imply that VP-deletion is possible in i, since the logical structure for Sag is not ii but iii:

> i. *Many linguists are neither easy to please nor hard to.
> ii. (Many linguist u) ∧ (not([Δ please u] be easy), not([Δ please u] be hard))
> iii. (Many linguist u) ∧ (not(u, (λx)([Δ please x] be easy), not(u, (λy)([Δ please y] be hard))

The Δ here and in 13.1.10b is the 'unspecified subject' that has been postulated by various linguists in analyses of subjectless infinitives and reduced passives (such as *Bill was attacked*). The discussion here is neutral as to what contribution the Δ makes to the logical structure of the sentence.

7. Sag sidesteps the issue of how to represent coreference and indicates it informally by subscripts. The difference between *Betsy$_i$* and *she$_i$* will have to be ignored for the two VP's to count as identical, as Sag wants them to. This observation suggests that in logical structure the name *Betsy* should not appear in the position of subject of *say* but rather the corresponding referential index.

8. The notion of intension could be generalized by formulating it in terms of an accessibility relation among worlds: the intension of X in a world i would be the function that associates to each world j accessible from i the extension of X in j. This generalized notion of intension does not appear to have figured in any of the literature on intensional logic.

9. A × B is called the CARTESIAN PRODUCT of A and B. This term honors René Descartes' work in analytic geometry, which rests on the representation of points in plane geometry as ordered pairs of real numbers.

10. This notion of 'type' is essentially the same as that of Bertrand Russell except for the incorporation of the notion 'possible world' into it. Montague

may have chosen s as the symbol for 'world' by virtue of its being the initial of Latin *saeculum*, though I know of no statement by him to that effect.

11. I have substituted ^{in}X and ^{ex}Y for the more standard $^{\wedge}X$ and $^{\vee}Y$, since it is easier to remember what ^{in} and ^{ex} stand for than what $^{\wedge}$ and $^{\vee}$ stand for, to say nothing of its being cheaper to print them.

12. Montague's principal works in this area are conveniently collected in Montague 1974. For more recent representatives of this approach, see Cresswell 1973, Dowty 1979, Karttunen and Peters 1977, 1979, and Partee 1975, 1976.

13. The second number in [S; 3, 0] indicates the value of i; the expression at the top of 13.3.1 is thus formed by substituting *every man* for he_0 in he_0 *loves some woman*.

14. I will follow Montague's informal practise of using primes to indicate the predicates of the system of intensional logic that correspond to English words that (in the given exposition) are not further analyzed, for example, $love'(x, y)$ is the two-place predicate that figures in the translation of *love*. This practise is a direct analog to the capitalization (e.g., LOVE) employed by many linguists for the same purpose. Many steps in this translation are greatly oversimplified. The oversimplification will be corrected below.

15. The symbols x and P that appear here are used purely as illustrations. The actual choice of variables is made in such a way as to avoid incoherent combinations, as in 13.1.3, where y rather than x appears as the variable bound by the universal quantifier.

Montague's treatment of the syntax of quantifiers was not exactly as in 13.3.1, in that he treated the quantifiers not as 'basic expressions' but as inserted by syntactic rule: his rule actually formed *every man* from *man* rather than from *every* and *man*. This illustrates the point that in Montague grammar there is the same kind of nonuniqueness of analysis that there was in early transformational grammar, where elements such as negation could be either present in base structures or inserted by transformations; Montague grammar is in fact more unconstrained in this respect than was early transformational grammar: in transformational grammar, transformations have sentences as input, whereas in Montague grammar, the operations analogous to transformations differ among themselves in terms of the syntactic category of the expressions to which they apply.

16. For Ajdukiewicz, any number of category symbols could appear after the slash, for example, $(s/n\ n)$ is the category of items that combine with two names to yield a sentence. Montague generally confined his categories to those in which only one item appears after the slash, that is, to categories which yield 'binary branching' analysis trees.

17. Kripke's definition of rigid designator (1972:269–70) is different from this in a small but important respect: Kripke only required that a rigid designator have the same denotation in all worlds in which it has a denotation and left it open whether it has a denotation in every world. However, this difference can be ignored here, since Montague did not require that the denotation of an individual constant in a given world be an object that exists in that world (i.e., the denotations of individual constants are possible entities, not necessarily

actual entities), and thus he could take a constant as denoting the same entity in all worlds even if the entity that it denotes does not exist in all worlds.

18. Following Partee 1975, a double-shafted arrow is used to indicate 'is translated into' and a single-shafted arrow for 'is converted into' (by λ-conversion, meaning postulates, or other principles of equivalence). The end result in such 'derivations' as 13.3.9 is, loosely speaking, a translation of the original expression into a formula of intensional logic, in that it is 'equivalent to' a translation in the narrow sense.

19. The formula in 13.3.14 involves Montague's symbol $\leftrightarrow$, standing for 'if and only if'.

20. This change will force us to introduce ^{ex} into the translations given earlier for *every* and *a*:

$$every\ man \Rightarrow (\lambda Q)(\forall x) \supset (man'(x), (^{ex}Q)(x))$$
$$a\ man \Rightarrow (\lambda Q)(\exists x) \wedge (man'(x), (^{ex}Q)(x))$$

21. The formulas given here involve ^{in}u, which is the only plausible expression based on u that is of the right type to serve as the second argument of seek" or worship".

Chapter Fourteen

1. Under the specific analysis of *many* suggested above, the statement that nothing may intervene in logical structure between an $\exists$ and the clause in which *there* is to be inserted will have to be weakened so as to allow the universal quantifier expression to intervene; see, however, p. 432.

2. A case where something greater than 50 percent could conceivably count as 'not large' and thus something below 50 percent count as 'most' is that in which more than 50 percent of something is spread out over time in such a way as to be of relative insignificance. It is not outlandish to say *You have to pay most of the money in advance* with reference to an arrangement in which you pay 40 percent down and the remainder over the next ten years.

3. The proposition that three presidents were not crooks is a conversational implicature rather than a logical implication of 14.1.8*a*; accordingly, 14.1.8*b* is formulated in such a way as to be neutral about whether the members of M were crooks.

4. It should be emphasized that the conversions referred to here are grammatical transformations, not rules of inference, i.e., the output is not the logical form of a consequence of the given proposition but is an intermediate stage in the grammatical derivation of a sentence expressing the given proposition.

5. This treatment of color words provides an immediate solution to the problem discussed by Fodor (1975:148–49) of identifying what justifies the inference from 'x is blue' to 'x is colored': 'x is blue' is Color(x, blue), 'x is colored' is $(\exists y)$Color(x, y), and the inference from the former to the latter is by an application of $\exists$-introduction.

6. The interpretations at issue in 14.1.15*b–b"* are those in which the relative

clause jointly modifies both nouns. Example 14.1.15b' is, of course, acceptable if the relative clause modifies only *the anthropologists*.

7. The significance of succotash for the philosophy of language was first pointed out in Sharvy 1979.

8. The word *water* is indeed most commonly used in such a way that one molecule of H_2O is not a quantity of water: *water* normally refers to a liquid, and one molecule of anything is far too little to be liquid. Indeed, there is no clear minimum amount of H_2O that will be determinately liquid. Thus there is the same sort of indeterminacy with water as with dirty water or even succotash as to what quantities can count as instances of the substance in question.

9. 'Is water' must not be confused with 'is *a* water', which means 'is a kind of water', as in *Perrier is a water that has recently become very popular in the United States*.

10. Similarly (this example is based on one by Bunt), it may be that all poetry is contained in poems and all peoms are poetry, but while the final couplet of Milton's sonnet on his blindness is poetry, it is not a poem. And a volume that contains 2/3 of Milton's poems but not *Paradise Lost* and *Samson Agonistes* contains most of Milton's poems but not most of his poetry.

11. I follow here the standard convention of using a square bracket to indicate that the end point is included in the interval and a round bracket to indicate that it is not. Thus [0, 1) is the set of all real numbers x for which $0 \le x < 1$, [0, 1] is the set of all real numbers x for which $0 \le x \le 1$, and so on.

12. The notion of 'sum' invoked here is that of Goodman and Leonard (1940), according to which any two (or more) individuals (e.g. the lower half of my ring and the inner third of your ring) have a sum that is itself an 'individual'. The principles governing the relations among such individuals constitute what is called the 'calculus of individuals'.

13. This statement will have to be qualified, in that there is sometimes a lower limit on how small the part may be if the inference is still to be valid. For example, given that this stew is spicy or smelly, it is probably the case that every spoonful of it is spicy or smelly but not that every cubic millimeter of it is.

14. The bulk of this section leans heavily on the insightful discussion of generics in Carlson 1977.

A defender of an analysis of generics as (near-)universals might argue that 14.3.1d is not very different from *Fido chases all cars*, which is normally understood not as implying that Fido chases cars that are in Guatemala or Nepal or are on display in the Smithsonian Institution but only that he chases all cars that he has an opportunity to chase: whenever a car drives down the street that Fido happens to be on at the moment, Fido chases that car. (Note that since one cannot chase an object that is not moving, stationary cars don't come into the picture.) Even with this understanding of *all*, *Fido chases cars* and *Fido chases all cars* still don't mean the same thing: failure by Fido to chase a car that drove past him would falsify the second sentence but not the first.

15. Carlson quotes this example from the Port-Royal logic (Arnauld 1662).

16. In view of what was said in 11.3, it is apparent that this statement must be weakened: if an existential quantifier binds a time variable, any variables

bound by variables in its scope will depend on it, since their domains will reflect differences in what objects exist at what times.

17. It is not clear whether one should speak of u as depending on x and z, or on y and z, or on x, y, and z, in view of the fact that y depends on x. I will follow the practise of speaking in terms of the 'most independent' variables and thus speak of u as depending on x and z.

18. This result applies with full generality to the case of unrestricted quantifiers. In the case of restricted quantifiers, the qualification made in note 16 is applicable.

19. Karttunen in fact recognized a third reading beyond the two discussed in 7.2, and Hintikka and Saarinen suggest that their interpretation may be identifiable with Karttunen's third reading, though Karttunen's description of the third reading is too obscure for them to be able to say for sure. Hintikka and Saarinen indeed claim that the Bach-Peters sentence is unambiguous, having ONLY the interpretation that they discuss. As far as I can see, nothing in their argument depends on the Bach-Peters sentence NOT having the two interpretations discussed in 7.2. I will continue to assume that it has those two readings and simply comment here on the reading that Hintikka and Saarinen wish to assign to it.

20. In the interests of clarity I have regrouped the conjuncts in 14.4.21b and given 'x boy who was fooling z' as a unit rather than as a coordinate structure.

21. In the interests of simplicity, I have written 'M is two linguists' and 'N is three sociologists' instead of the more complicated expressions that underlie them, according to the arguments of 14.1.

22. Examples like 14.5.6 were brought to my attention by Jackendoff (1977:190–94). The intended interpretation is that in which *the same slogan* is the object of both *chant* and *shout*. As a makeshift, I have treated *the same* in 14.5.6a' as if it were simply a wide scope existential quantifier. That treatment loses the structural parallelism between *the same* and *similar* and *different*:

    a. A linguist was shouting and a philosopher was chanting two
       similar slogans.
    b. Several students were humming and a few professors were
       singing at least ten different tunes.

Second-order logic offers a means of treating these three words alike. Specifically, suppose that each of c, d, e has a logical structure involving a function from students to slogans, with *same*, *similar*, and *different* expressing characteristics of the values of that function, as in c', d', e', where M is the set of students that is referred to and 'M $\rightarrow$ slogan' is an informal way of indicating that f associates a slogan to each member of M:

    c. All the students were chanting the same slogan.
    c'. $(\exists: \wedge (f: \text{M}\rightarrow\text{slogan}, \text{same } \{fx: x\in\text{M}\}))$ $(\forall: x\in\text{M})(x \text{ chant } fx)$
    d. All the students were chanting similar slogans.
    d'. $(\exists: \wedge (f: \text{M}\rightarrow\text{slogan}, \text{similar}\{fx: x\in\text{M}\}))(\forall: x\in\text{M})(x \text{ chant } fx)$
    e. All the students were chanting different slogans.
    e'. $(\exists: \wedge (f: \text{M}\rightarrow\text{slogan}, \text{different}\{fx: x\in\text{M}\}))$ $(\forall: x\in\text{M})(x \text{ chant } fx)$

Two difficulties must be resolved before these formulas can be accepted as logical structures of the given sentences. First, as the notion of set was developed in chap. 5, *different* cannot be taken as predicated of sets: if twelve students were chanting two slogans, e should be false, but e' would presumably be true because the two members of the set of slogans would be different from each other. A possible solution to this problem would be to replace the notion of set in these formulas by a notion that is referred to in computer science as a BAG. A bag is an entity that is like a set except that elements can have multiple memberships in it, e.g., the bag having three instances of 1 and four instances of 2 as members is different from the bag having five instances of 1 and two instances of 2, and neither bag is the same as the set {1, 2}. A more serious problem with the formulas $c'-e'$ is that it is not obvious that they can be integrated with otherwise valid rules for the relationship of logical form to surface syntactic structure. Whether this problem can be solved satisfactorily will depend on what principles can be given for the syntactic realization of functions such as appear in the formulas.

23. Lakoff notes that complex sentences may be ambiguous as to the scope of *usual*. For example, *The usual men want to meet in the usual places* may imply either that it is usual for those men to meet in those places or that it is usual for those men to want to meet in those places.

References

Ajdukiewicz, Kazimierz. 1935. Über die syntaktische Konnexität. *Studia Philosophica* 1:1–27.

Anderson, Alan Ross, and Belnap, Nuel D., Jr. 1975. *Entailment.* Vol. 1. Princeton, N.J.: Princeton University Press.

Anderson, Stephen R. 1970. On the linguistic status of the performative/ constative distinction. Harvard University Computation Laboratory Report NSF-26.

Arnauld, Antoine. 1662. *The art of thinking.* Reprinted 1962. New York: Bobbs-Merrill.

Austin, J. L. 1957. A plea for excuses. *Proceedings of the Aristotelian Society* 57:1–30. Reprinted in Austin 1961:123–52.

———. 1961. *Philosophical papers.* Oxford: Oxford University Press.

———. 1962. *How to do things with words.* Oxford: Oxford University Press.

———. 1963. Performative-constative. In Caton 1963:22–54.

Bach, Emmon. 1970. Problominalization. *Linguistic Inquiry* 1:121–22.

Bakunin, Mikhail. 1871. *God and the state.* Translated 1916; reprinted 1970. New York: Dover.

Barcan [Marcus], Ruth. 1946. A functional calculus of first order based on strict implication. *Journal of Symbolic Logic* 11:1–16.

Bastiat, Frederic. 1850. What is seen and what is not seen. In F. Bastiat, *Selected essays on political economy.* Princeton: Van Nostrand, 1962.

Belnap, Nuel D. Jr. 1977. A useful four-valued logic. In M. Dunn and G. Epstein, eds., *Modern uses of multiple-valued logic,* pp. 5–37. Dordrecht: Reidel.

Bennett, David. 1975. *Spatial and temporal uses of English prepositions.* London: Longmans.

Bierwisch, Manfred. 1967. Some semantic universals of German adjectivals. *Foundations of Language* 3:1–36.

488

Bouton, Lawrence R. 1970. Antecedent-contained pro-forms. *Papers from the sixth regional meeting, Chicago Linguistic Society*, pp. 154–67.

Braine, Martin D. S. 1978. On the relation between the natural logic of reasoning and standard logic. *Psychological Review* 85:1–30.

Bunt, Harry. 1976. The formal semantics of mass terms. In F. Karlsson, ed., *Papers from the third Scandinavian conference of linguistics*, pp. 81–94. Turku: Academy of Finland.

———. 1979. Ensembles and the formal properties of mass terms. In Pelletier 1979:249–77.

Cantrall, William. 1974. *Viewpoint, reflexives, and the nature of noun phrases*. The Hague: Mouton.

Carden, Guy. 1973. *English quantifiers: logical structure and linguistic variation*. Tokyo: Taishukan; New York: Academic Press.

Carlson, Gregory. 1977. Reference to kinds in English. Ph.D. diss., University of Massachusetts at Amherst.

Carnap, Rudolph. 1947. *Meaning and necessity*. Chicago: University of Chicago Press.

Caton, Charles E. 1963. *Philosophy and ordinary language*. Urbana and Chicago: University of Illinois Press.

Chomsky, Noam A. 1957. *Syntactic structures*. The Hague: Mouton.

———. 1965. *Aspects of the theory of syntax*. Cambridge, Mass.: MIT Press.

———. 1966. *Topics in the theory of generative grammar*. The Hague: Mouton.

———. 1972. *Studies on semantics in generative grammar*. The Hague: Mouton.

———. 1976. *Essays on form and interpretation*. Amsterdam: North Holland.

Cohen, L. Jonathan. 1972. Remarks on Grice's analysis of logical particles in natural language. In Y. Bar-Hillel, ed., *Pragmatics of natural language*, pp. 50–68. Dordrecht: Reidel.

Cresswell, M. J. 1973. *Logics and languages*. London: Methuen.

Davidson, Donald, and Harman, Gilbert. 1972. *Semantics of natural language*. Dordrecht: Reidel.

Davison, Alice. 1973. Performative verbs, adverbs, and felicity conditions. Ph.D. diss., University of Chicago.

Dik, Simon. 1973. Crossing coreference again. *Foundations of Language* 9:306–26.

Donnellan, Keith. 1966. Reference and definite descriptions. *Philosophical Review* 75:281–304. Reprinted in Steinberg and Jakobovits 1971:100–14.

Dowty, David. 1979. *Word meaning and Montague grammar*. Dordrecht: Reidel.

Dummett, Michael. 1958. Truth. *Proceedings of the Aristotelian Society* 59:141–62. Reprinted in Strawson 1967:49–68.

Fiengo, Robert, and Lasnik, Howard. 1973. The logical structure of reciprocal sentences in English. *Foundations of Language* 9:447–68.

Fillmore, Charles J. 1975. Pragmatics and the description of discourse. *Berkeley studies in syntax and semantics* 1.

Fillmore, Charles J., and Langendoen, D. T. 1971. *Studies in linguistic semantics*. New York: Holt, Rinehart and Winston.

Fitch, Frederic B. 1952. *Symbolic logic: an introduction*. New York: Ronald.

Fodor, Jerry A. 1975. *The language of thought*. New York: Crowell.

Fodor, Jerry A. and Katz, Jerrold J. 1964. *The structure of language*. Englewood Cliffs: Prentice-Hall.

Fraser, Bruce. 1974a. An examination of the performative analysis. *Papers in Linguistics* 7:1–40.

————. 1974b. An analysis of vernacular performative verbs. In R. W. Shuy and C.-J. Bailey, eds., *Towards tomorrow's linguistics*, pp. 139–58. Washington, D.C.: Georgetown University Press.

Frege, Gottlob. 1879. *Begriffsschrift*. English translation in J. van Heijenoort, ed., *From Frege to Gödel: a source book in mathematical logic, 1879–1931*. Cambridge, Mass.: Harvard University Press.

Gazdar, Gerald. 1979. *Pragmatics*. New York: Academic Press.

Geach, P. T. 1967. Intentional identity. *Journal of Philosophy* 64:627–32. Reprinted in Geach 1972:146–53.

————. 1972. *Logic matters*. Oxford: Blackwell.

Geis, Michael. 1973. *If* and *unless*. In B. J. Kachru, et al. eds., *Issues in linguistics: papers in honor of Henry and Renee Kahane*, pp. 231–53. Urbana and Chicago: University of Illinois Press.

Gentzen, Gerhard. 1969. *Collected papers of Gerhard Gentzen*. Amsterdam: North-Holland.

Gleitman, Lila. 1965. Coordinating conjunctions in English. *Language* 41:260–93. Reprinted in Reibel and Schane 1969:80–112.

Goffman, Erving. 1974. *Frame analysis*. New York: Harper.

Goodman, Nelson. 1947. The problem of counterfactual conditionals. *Journal of Philosophy* 44:113–28.

————. 1951. *The structure of appearance*. Cambridge, Mass.: Harvard University Press.

Goodman, Nelson, and Henry Leonard. 1940. The calculus of individuals and its uses. *Journal of Symbolic Logic* 5:45–55.

Grice, H. P. 1967. Logic and conversation. Unpublished lectures, Harvard University.

————. 1975. Logic and conversation [extract from Grice 1967]. In P. Cole and J. L. Morgan, *Speech acts*, pp. 45–58. Syntax and semantics 3. New York: Academic Press.

Grinder, John. 1976. *On deletion phenomena in English*. The Hague: Mouton.

Gruber, Jeffrey. 1967. Functions of the lexicon in formal descriptive grammars. System Development Corporation report. Reprinted in Jeffrey Gruber, *Lexical structures in syntax and semantics*, pp. 213–367. Amsterdam: North Holland, 1976.

Hall, Roland. 1959. Excluders. *Analysis* 20:1–7. Reprinted in Caton 1963:67–73.

Hausser, Roland. 1978. How do pronouns denote? In F. Heny and H. Schnelle, eds., *Selections from the third Groningen Round Table*, pp. 93–139. Syntax and semantics 10. New York: Academic Press.

Henkin, Leon. 1950. Completeness in the theory of types. *Journal of Symbolic Logic* 15:81–91.

———. 1961. Some remarks on infinitely long formulas. In *Infinitistic methods*, pp. 167–83. New York: Pergamon.

Herzberger, Hans. 1975a. Dimensions of truth. In D. Hockney, et al., eds., *Contemporary research in philosophical logic and linguistic semantics*, pp. 71–92. Dordrecht: Reidel.

———. 1975b. Supervaluations in two dimensions. *Proceedings of the 1975 international symposium on multiple-valued logic*, pp. 429–35. Long Beach, Calif.: IEEE Computer Society.

Hintikka, Jaakko. 1969a. Semantics for propositional attitudes. In J. W. Davis, et al., eds., *Philosophical logic*, pp. 21–45. Dordrecht: Reidel. Reprinted in Hintikka 1969b:87–111 and in Linsky 1971:145–67.

———. 1969b. *Models for modalities*. Dordrecht: Reidel.

———. 1973. *Logic, language-games, and information*. Oxford: Clarendon.

———. 1974. Quantifiers vs. quantification theory. *Linguistic Inquiry* 5:153–77.

Hintikka, Jaakko, and Rantala, Veikko. 1976. A new approach to infinitary languages. *Annals of Mathematical Logic* 10:95–115.

Hintikka, Jaakko, and Saarinen, Esa. 1975. Semantical games and the Bach-Peters paradox. *Theoretical Linguistics* 2:1–20.

Hockney, Donald, et al. 1975. *Contemporary research in philosophical logic and linguistic semantics*. Dordrecht: Reidel.

Horn, Laurence R. 1969. A presuppositional analysis of *only* and *even*. *Papers from the fifth regional meeting, Chicago Linguistic Society*, pp. 318–27.

———. 1972. *On the semantic properties of logical operators in English*. Bloomington: Indiana University Linguistics Club.

————. 1975. Neg-raising predicates: toward an explanation. *Papers from the eleventh regional meeting, Chicago Linguistic Society*, pp. 279–94.

————. 1978. Remarks on neg-raising. In P. Cole, ed., *Pragmatics*, pp. 129–220. Syntax and Semantics 9. New York: Academic Press.

Householder, Fred. 1971. *Linguistic speculations*. London and New York: Cambridge University Press.

Hughes, G., and Cresswell, M. J. 1968. *Introduction to modal logic*. London: Methuen.

Humberstone, Lloyd. 1975. Review of Davidson and Harman 1972. *York Papers in Linguistics* 5:195–224.

Jackendoff, Ray S. 1972. *Semantic interpretation in generative grammar*. Cambridge, Mass.: MIT Press.

————. 1975. Belief contexts. *Linguistic Inquiry* 6:53–93.

————. 1977. *X̄ syntax: a study of phrase structure*. Cambridge, Mass.: M.I.T. Press.

Jacobs, Roderick, and Rosenbaum, P. S. 1967. *English transformational grammar*. Boston: Ginn.

Kamp, Hans. 1974. Free choice permission. *Proceedings of the Aristotelian Society* 74:57–74.

Karttunen, Frances, and Karttunen, Lauri. 1977. *Even* questions. *Proceedings of the seventh annual meeting, Northeastern Linguistic Society*, pp. 115–34.

Karttunen, Lauri. 1971*a*. Definite descriptions with crossing coreference: a study of the Bach-Peters paradox. *Foundations of Language* 7:157–87.

————. 1971*b*. Implicative verbs. *Language* 47:340–58.

————. 1971*c*. *The logic of English predicate complement constructions*. Bloomington: Indiana University Linguistics Club.

————. 1973. Presuppositions of compound sentences. *Linguistic Inquiry* 4:169–93.

————. 1974. Presupposition and linguistic context. *Theoretical Linguistics* 1:182–94. Also in Rogers, Wall, and Murphy 1977:149–60.

————. 1976. Discourse referents. In McCawley 1976*b*:363–85.

Karttunen, Lauri, and Peters, P. S. 1977. Requiem for presupposition. *Proceedings of the third annual meeting, Berkeley Linguistics Society*, pp. 360–71.

————. 1979. Conventional implicature. In Oh and Dinneen 1979:1–56.

Kiparsky, Paul, and Kiparsky, Carol. 1970. Fact. In M. Bierwisch and K. Heidolph, eds., *Progress in linguistics*, pp. 143–73. The Hague: Mouton. Reprinted in Steinberg and Jakobovits 1971:345–69.

Klima, E. S. 1964. Negation in English. In Fodor and Katz 1964:246–323.

Klooster, W. G. 1972. *The structure underlying measure phrase sentences*. Dordrecht: Reidel.

Kripke, Saul. 1959. A completeness theorem in modal logic. *Journal of Symbolic Logic* 24:1–14.

———. 1972. Naming and necessity. In Davidson and Harman 1972:253–355.

Kuroda, S.-Y. 1971. Two remarks on pronominalization. *Foundations of Language* 7:183–98.

Lakoff, George. 1971. Generative semantics. In Steinberg and Jakobovits 1971:232–96.

———. 1972*a*. Linguistics and natural logic. In Davidson and Harman 1972:545–665.

———. 1972*b*. Hedges: a study in meaning criteria and the logic of fuzzy concepts. *Papers from the eighth regional meeting, Chicago Linguistic Society*, pp. 183–228. Corrected version in Hockney, et al. 1975:221–71.

Lakoff, George, and Peters, P. S. 1969. Phrasal conjunction and symmetric predicates. In Reibel and Schane 1969:113–42.

Lakoff, Robin. 1971. If's, and's, and but's about conjunction. In Fillmore and Langendoen 1971:214–49.

Langacker, Ronald. 1969. Pronominalization and the chain of command. In Reibel and Schane 1969:160–86.

Langendoen, D. T., and Savin, Harris. 1971. The projection problem for presuppositions. In Fillmore and Langendoen 1971:54–60.

Laudan, Larry. 1976. *Progress and its problems*. Berkeley and Los Angeles: University of California Press.

Leech, Geoffrey. 1969. *Towards a semantic description of English*. London: Longmans.

LeGrand, Jean Ehrenkrantz. 1975. *Or* and *any*: the semantics and syntax of two logical operators. Ph.D. diss., University of Chicago.

Lewis, C. I. 1912. Implication and the algebra of logic. *Mind* NS 21:522–31.

———. 1918. *A survey of symbolic logic*. Berkeley: University of California Press.

Lewis, C. I., and Langford, C. H. 1932. *Symbolic logic*. New York: Dover.

Lewis, David. 1968. Counterpart theory and quantified modal logic. *Journal of Philosophy* 65:113–26.

———. 1973. *Counterfactuals*. Cambridge, Mass.: Harvard University Press.

———. 1979. Score-keeping in a language game. *Journal of Philosophical Logic* 8:339–59.

Linsky, Leonard. 1971. *Reference and modality*. Oxford: Clarendon.

Lycan, William. 1977. A syntactically motivated semantics for conditionals. Unpublished paper.

McCawley, James D. 1968. Concerning the base component of a transformational grammar. *Foundations of Language* 4:243–69. Reprinted in
McCawley 1973*a*:35–58.

———. 1970. Semantic representation. In P. Garvin, ed., *Cognition: a
multiple view*, pp. 227–47. New York: Spartan. Reprinted in McCawley
1973*a*:240–56.

———. 1971. Tense and time reference in English. In Fillmore and
Langendoen 1971:96–113. Reprinted in McCawley 1973*a*:257–73.

———. 1972. A program for logic. In Davidson and Harman 1972:157–
212. Reprinted in McCawley 1973*a*:285–319.

———. 1973*a*. *Grammar and Meaning*. Tokyo: Taishukan; New York:
Academic Press.

———. 1973*b*. Where do noun phrases come from? [revised version].
In McCawley 1973*a*:133–54.

———. 1974. On identifying the remains of deceased clauses. *Language
Research* (Seoul, Korea) 9/2:73–85. Reprinted in McCawley 1979:84–95.

———. 1975. Review of Chomsky 1972. *Studies in English Linguistics*
3:209–311.

———. 1976*a*. Remarks on what can cause what. In M. Shibatani, ed.,
The grammar of causative constructions, pp. 117–29. Syntax and Semantics 6. New York: Academic Press. Reprinted in McCawley 1979:101–12.

———. 1976*b*. *Notes from the linguistic underground*. Syntax and semantics
7. New York: Academic Press.

———. 1977. Remarks on the lexicography of performative verbs. In
Rogers Wall, and Murphy 1977:13–25. Reprinted in McCawley
1979:151–64.

———. 1978*a*. Restrictive relatives and surface constituent structure.
*Proceedings of the eighth regional conference, Northeastern Linguistic
Society*, pp. 154–66.

———. 1978*b*. Relative and relative-like clauses. *Grammarij* (Nijmegen)
9:149–88.

———. 1979. *Adverbs, vowels, and other objects of wonder*. Chicago:
University of Chicago Press.

———. 1980. An un-syntax. In E. Moravcsik, ed., *Current approaches to
syntax*. Syntax and Semantics 13. New York: Academic Press.

Massey, Gerald. 1970. *Understanding symbolic logic*. New York: Harper
and Row.

Miller, George, and Johnson-Laird, Philip. 1976. *Language and perception*.
Cambridge, Mass.: Belknap Press.

Montague, Richard. 1970*a*. English as a formal language. In B. Visentini,
et al., eds., *Linguaggi nella Società e nella Tecnica*, pp. 189–224. Milan:
Edizioni di Communità. Reprinted in Montague 1974:188–221.

————. 1970*b*. Universal grammar. *Theoria* 36:373–98. Reprinted in Montague 1974:222–46.

————. 1973. The proper treatment of quantification in ordinary English. In J. Hintikka, J. Moravcsik, and P. Suppes, eds., *Approaches to natural language*. Dordrecht: Reidel. Reprinted in Montague 1974:247–70.

————. 1974. *Formal philosophy*. New Haven: Yale University Press.

Morgan, J. L. 1973. Presupposition and the representation of meaning: prolegomena. Ph.D. thesis, University of Chicago.

Nute, Donald. 1975*a*. Counterfactuals. *Notre Dame Journal of Formal Logic* 16:476–82.

————. 1975*b*. Conterfactuals and the similarity of worlds. *Journal of Philosophy* 72:773–78.

Oh, Choon-Kyu, and Dinneen, David A. 1979. *Presupposition*. Syntax and Semantics 12. New York: Academic Press.

Palmer, Frank. 1965. *The English verb*. London: Longmans.

Parsons, Terry. 1970. An analysis of mass terms and amount terms. *Foundations of Language* 6:362–88.

Partee, Barbara Hall. 1970. Negation, conjunction, and quantifiers: Syntax vs. semantics. *Foundations of Language* 6:153–65.

————. 1975. Montague grammar and transformational grammar. *Linguistic Inquiry* 6:203–300.

————. 1976. *Montague grammar*. New York: Academic Press.

Pelletier, F. J. 1977. Or. *Theoretical linguistics* 4:61–74.

————. 1979. *Mass terms*. Dordrecht: Reidel.

Perlmutter, David M., and Ross, John Robert. 1970. Relative clauses with split antecedents. *Linguistic Inquiry* 1:350.

Peterson, Philip. 1979. On the logic of *few, many*, and *most. Notre Dame Journal of Formal Logic* 20:155–79.

Pope, Emily. 1973. Question-answering systems. *Papers from the ninth regional meeting, Chicago Linguistic Society*, pp. 482–92.

Popper, Karl. 1962. What is dialectic? In K. Popper, *Conjectures and refutations*, pp. 312–35. London: Routledge and Kegan Paul. Reprinted from *Mind* NS 49(1940):403–26.

Postal, Paul M., and Grinder, John T. 1971. Missing antecedents. *Linguistic Inquiry* 2:269–312.

Prior, A. N. 1960. The runabout inference-ticket. *Analysis* 21:38–39. Reprinted in Strawson 1967:129–31.

————. 1967. *Past, present, and future*. Oxford: Oxford University Press.

Quine, Willard van Orman. 1943. Notes on existence and necessity. *Journal of Philosophy* 40:113–27.

————. 1953. Reference and modality. In Quine, *From a logical point of view*, pp. 139–57. Cambridge, Mass.: Harvard University Press. Reprinted in Linsky 1971:17–34.

——. 1956. Quantifiers and propositional attitudes. *Journal of Philosophy* 53:177–87. Reprinted in Linsky 1971:100–111.

——. 1960. *Word and object*. Cambridge, Mass.: MIT Press.

——. 1962. *Methods of logic*. 2d ed. London: Routledge and Kegan Paul.

——. 1969. *Ontological relativity and other essays*. New York: Columbia University Press.

Reibel, David, and Schane, Sanford. 1969. *Modern studies in English*. Englewood Cliffs: Prentice-Hall.

Reichenbach, Hans. 1947. *Elements of symbolic logic*. New York: Macmillan.

Reinhart, Tanya. 1975. On certain ambiguities and uncertain scope. *Papers from the eleventh regional meeting, Chicago Linguistic Society*, pp. 451–66.

Rescher, Nicholas. 1964. *Hypothetical reasoning*. Amsterdam: North Holland.

——. 1969. *Many-valued logic*. New York: McGraw-Hill.

Rescher, Nicholas, and Urquhart, A. 1971. *Temporal logic*. New York: Springer.

Rogers, Andy; Wall, Robert; and Murphy, John, eds. 1977. *Proceedings of the Texas Conference on performatives, presuppositions, and implicatures*. Arlington, Va.: Center for Applied Linguistics.

Ross, John Robert. 1967. Constraints on variables in syntax. Ph.D. thesis, Massachusetts Institute of Technology.

——. 1969. The cyclic nature of English pronominalization. In Reibel and Schane 1969:187–200.

——. 1970. On declarative sentences. In Roderick Jacobs and P. S. Rosenbaum, *Readings in English transformational grammar*, pp. 222–72. Boston: Ginn.

——. 1976. To have have and not to have have. In E. Polome, et al., eds., *Linguistic and literary studies in honor of Archibald A. Hill*. Vol. 1, pp. 263–70. Lisse: de Ridder.

Russell, Bertrand. 1905. On denoting. *Mind* NS 14:479–93. Reprinted in I. Copi. and J. Gould, *Contemporary readings in logical theory*. New York: Macmillan, 1967.

Russell, Bertrand, and Whitehead, A. N. 1910–13. *Principia mathematica*. London: Cambridge University Press.

Rutherford, William. 1970. Some observations concerning subordinate clauses in English. *Language* 46:97–115.

Sadock, Jerrold. 1974. *Toward a linguistic theory of speech acts*. New York: Academic Press.

————. 1977. Truth and approximations. *Proceedings of the third annual meeting, Berkeley Linguistics Society*, pp. 430–39.

Sag, Ivan. 1976. Deletion and logical form. Ph.D. thesis, Massachusetts Institute of Technology.

Schank, Roger, and Abelson, Robert. 1977. *Scripts, plans, goals, and understanding*. Hillsdale, N.J.: Lawrence Erlbaum.

Searle, John. 1969. *Speech acts*. London and New York: Cambridge University Press.

Seuren, Pieter. 1973. The comparative. In F. Kiefer and N. Ruwet, eds., *Generative grammar in Europe*, pp. 528–64. Dordrecht: Reidel.

Sharvy, Richard. 1979. The indeterminacy of mass predication. In Pelletier 1979:47–54.

Smullyan, A. F. 1948. Modality and description. *Journal of Symbolic Logic* 13:31–37. Reprinted in Linsky 1971:35–43.

Stalnaker, Robert. 1969. A theory of conditionals. In N. Rescher, ed., *Studies in logical theory*, pp. 98–112. Oxford: Blackwell

Steinberg, D., and Jakobovits, L. 1971. *Semantics: an interdisciplinary reader*. Cambridge: Cambridge University Press.

Strawson, P. F. 1950. On referring. *Mind* NS 59:320–44. Reprinted in Strawson 1971:1–27.

————. 1964. Identifying reference and truth values. *Theoria* 30:96–118. Reprinted in Strawson 1971:75–95.

————. 1967. *Philosophical logic*. Oxford: Clarendon.

————. 1971. *Logico-linguistic papers*. London: Methuen.

Teller, Paul. 1969. Some discussion and extension of Manfred Bierwisch's work on German adjectivals. *Foundations of Language* 5:185–217.

Thomason, Richmond. 1970. *Symbolic Logic*. New York: Macmillan.

Thompson, Sandra A. 1971. The deep structure of relative clauses. In Fillmore and Langendoen 1971:78–94.

van Fraassen, Bas. 1969. Presuppositions, supervaluations, and free logic. In K. Lambert, ed., *The logical way of doing things*, pp. 67–91. New Haven: Yale University Press.

————. 1971. *Formal logic and semantics*. New York: Macmillan.

Vendler, Zeno. 1967a. *Linguistics in philosophy*. Ithaca: Cornell University Press.

————. 1967b. Each and every, any and all. In Vendler 1967a:70–96.

Wall, Robert. 1972. *Introduction to mathematical linguistics*. Englewood Cliffs: Prentice-Hall.

Wason, P. C., and Johnson-Laird, P. N. 1972. *Psychology of reasoning: structure and content*. London: Batsford.

Wasow, Tom. 1973. More MIGs and pilots. *Foundations of Language* 9:297–305.

Wierzbicka, Anna. 1972. "And" and plurality. In A. Wierzbicka, *Semantic primitives*, pp. 166–90. Frankfurt: Athenäum.

Wundt, Wilhelm. 1900. *Völkerpsychologie*. Vol. 1, part 2. Leipzig: Engelmann.

Zadeh, Lotfi A. 1965. Fuzzy sets. *Information and control* 8:338–53.

———. 1971. Similarity relations and fuzzy orderings. *Information sciences* 3:177–200.

———. 1972. A fuzzy-set-theoretic interpretation of linguistic hedges. *Journal of cybernetics* 2:4–34.

Zwicky, Arnold M., and Sadock, Jerrold M. 1975. Ambiguity tests and how to fail them. In J. Kimball, ed., Syntax and semantics 4. New York: Academic Press. 1–36.

List of Symbols

499

SET THEORY

$\in a\mathrm{A}$; $a \in \mathrm{A}$ (p. 140)	$a\ \varepsilon\ \mathrm{A}$	a is a member of A
$\subseteq \mathrm{AB}$: $\mathrm{A} \subseteq \mathrm{B}$ (p. 141)		A is a subset of B
$\mathrm{A} \cup \mathrm{B}$ (p. 143)		union of A and B
$\mathrm{A} \cap \mathrm{B}$ (p. 143)		intersection of A and B
$\mathrm{A} - \mathrm{B}$ (p. 143)		the members of A not in B
none	$\bar{\mathrm{A}}$; CA	complement of A
$\varnothing$ (p. 145)		empty set
$\{a_1, a_2, \ldots, a_n\}$ (p. 142)		set having $a_1, a_2, \ldots$ and a_n as its members
$\{fx|gx\}$; $\{fx: gx\}$ (p. 142)		set having as members all items fx for which x meets the condition gx
$\aleph_0$ (p. 148)		smallest infinite cardinal number
$\mathrm{A} \times \mathrm{B}$ (p. 402)		Cartesian product of A and B: set of all ordered pairs of a member of A and a member of B
A^B (p. 402)		set of all functions from B into A

METALINGUISTIC SYMBOLS

$\vdash \mathrm{A}$ (p. 39)	A is provable (by the given rules of inference)
$\mathrm{A}_1, \ldots, \mathrm{A}_n \vdash \mathrm{A}$ (p. 39)	A is provable from the set of premises $\{\mathrm{A}_1, \ldots, \mathrm{A}_n\}$
$\mathrm{A} \dashv\vdash \mathrm{B}$ (p. 41)	A is deductively equivalent to B
$\Vdash \mathrm{A}$ (p. 73)	A is valid, i.e., true in all states of affairs
$\mathrm{A}_1, \ldots, \mathrm{A}_n \Vdash \mathrm{A}$ (p. 73)	$\mathrm{A}_1, \ldots, \mathrm{A}_n$ entail A, i.e. A is true in all states of affairs in which $\mathrm{A}_1, \ldots, \mathrm{A}_n$ are all true
$\mathrm{A} \gg \mathrm{B}$ (p. 236)	A semantically presupposes B
A/X (p. 257)	A is acceptable relative to context X

v_X (p. 243)   supervaluation defined by the set of propositions X

$(a/x, b/y, \ldots)$ (p. 165)   assignment of a as value of x, b as value of y, ...

A^α (p. 163)   denotation of A in interpretation α

$A^{Q,i}$ (p. 405)   denotation of A in world i of interpretation Q

MODAL LOGIC

$\square A$ (p. 275)   NA; LA   Necessarily, A

$\Diamond A$ (p. 279)   MA   Possibly, A

$\square\!\!\rightarrow AB$ (p. 313) $A \;\square\!\!\rightarrow B$ If A were the case, B would be the case

$\Diamond\!\!\rightarrow AB$ (p. 322) $A \;\Diamond\!\!\rightarrow B$ If A were the case, B might be the case

$\rightarrow AB$ (p. 299) $A \rightarrow B; A \rightarrow\!\!\!\!| B$ A implies B

Rw_1w_2 (p. 276) w_2 is possible relative to w_1

TENSE LOGIC

$R_t(A)$ (p. 341)   A is true at time t

$P\,t_1 t_2$ (p. 342) t_1 is prior to t_2

MONTAGUE GRAMMAR

$(\lambda x)A$ (p. 395)   A, treated as a function of x

$\langle a, b \rangle$ (p. 403)   logical type of functions from entities of type a to entities of type b

A/B (p. 409)   syntactic category of expressions that combine with expressions of category B to yield expressions of category A

^{in}X (p. 405) $^\frown X$ intension of X

^{ex}X (p. 405) $^\smile X$ extension of X

$Tr(X)$ (p. 412)   translation of X into intensional logic

$A \Rightarrow \alpha$ (p. 413)   expression A translates into logical formula α

$\alpha \rightarrow \beta$ (p. 413)

α is convertible into β by λ-conversion and/or meaning postulates

LINGUISTIC SYMBOLS

*Me Tarzan.

Me Tarzan is abnormal as a sentence of the given language.

?Give him and me one.

Give him and me one is somewhat odd as a sentence of the given language.

S: NP VP (p. 21)

A S may consist of a NP followed by a VP

/NP ___ PP (p. 91)

In the context immediately preceded by NP and immediately followed by PP

Index